劳伦斯论文艺

◎黑马译

图书在版编目(CIP)数据

劳伦斯论文艺:英汉对照/(英)劳伦斯(Laurance,D. H.)著;黑马译.—北京:团结出版社,2006,4

(励志与启蒙丛书)

ISBN 978-7-80130-766-8

Ⅰ.劳… Ⅱ.①劳…②黑… Ⅲ.①英语-汉语-对照读物②劳伦斯,D. H.(1885~1930)-文艺理论 Ⅳ.H319.4:I

中国版本图书馆 CIP 数据核字(2006)第 014999 号

出　版:团结出版社

(北京市东城区东皇城根南街 84 号　邮编:100006)

电　话:(010)65228880　65244790(总编室)

(010)87755968　87394600(发　行)

网　址:http://www.tjpress.com

E-mail:65244790@163.com

经　销:全国新华书店

印　刷:北京中印联印务有限公司

开　本:1/16 开

字　数:491 千字

印　张:33

印　次:2009 年 10 月第 2 次印刷

书　号:ISBN 978-7-80130-766-8/H·25

定　价:58.00 元

(如有印装差错,请与本社联系)

目录

INTRODUCTION

文艺批评

美国经典文学研究

文艺批评

Dostoevsky

Art is the evidence of the conscious and of the unconscious self in the artist, and nearly all drama, nearly all tragedy, consists in the conflict between this conscious and this unconscious self. In his consciousness, the great artist is, or has been, nearly always conservative, aristocratic. In his unconsciousness he is subversive to the old order.

This is evident in all the great tragedians: Aeschylus, Shakespeare, Corneille. In Shakespeare, the conscious, or the immediate man adheres to the established order; he reveres kingship and fatherhood as the supreme dignity and significance of man. God is King of the world, and Father of mankind. Manhood in the King and the father is likest, nearest to Godhood. This is the old belief on which the mediaeval world was established. It is also the root and blossoming of Shakspere's early plays, such as *Henry V*. And for this reason, *Henry V* and its equivalent plays are not tragedies: they are written entirely from the ready, immediate self of the artist.

David Herbert Lawrence

陀思妥耶夫斯基

艺术是艺术家之意识与潜意识自我的见证。几乎所有的戏剧和悲剧都存在于意识与潜意识自我的冲突之中。在意识中，伟大的艺术家几乎总是保守的、贵族气的。但在他的潜意识中，他则要颠覆旧的秩序。

伟大的悲剧家都可以证实这一点：埃斯库罗斯、莎士比亚和高乃依。至于莎士比亚，在他的意识层面他拥护已建立起来的秩序，推崇王位和父道，视之为人的最高尊严和意义。上帝就是世界的王，是人类之父。国王的人性和父亲的人性是最接近神性的。中世纪的世界就建立在这种信仰之上。它是莎士比亚的早期剧作如《亨利五世》(Henry V)的根，其戏剧之花也绽开在这种信仰之树上。但也正因此，《亨利五世》及其同类剧作绝算不上悲剧，它们不过是全然出自艺术家固有的和表层的自我。

但在他的后期剧作中，如《哈姆雷特》(Hamlet)，《李尔王》(Lear)和《麦克白斯》(Macbeth)，潜意识之人开始挺起身与意识，与已被认可的规则、固

In the later plays, however, *Hamlet*, *Lear*, *Macbeth*, the unconscious man has risen against the conscious, against the accepted formula, against the established order. It is the unconscious self of Shaksepeare—characterised as a woman—who really murders this king and father who represents almost all that is divine in man. It is Gertrude, Lady Macbeth, Goneril and Regan who destroy the supreme image of man, the image of God in man. The punishment is meted out to them severally, afterwards. But nevertheless, the king, the father is dead, killed, cast down from supremacy.

This is the dramatic portrayal of the whole change that took place at the Renaissance, and it is the presentiment of the execution of Charles I in actual life, just as *Le Cid** is the presentiment of the French Revolution.

The order in this case was, first the philosophic and religious departure from the old position, in the Humanists, in Erasmus, Savonarola, and Luther.* Then came the personal and artistic departure, in the dramatists, Shakespeare, Milton, then the political and social departure, of the Commonwealth.

It is these great philosophical and religious revolutions, the revolution in thought, the change in conception of the spiritual world, which divide and which

有的秩序作对了。此时莎士比亚的潜意识自我具体表现为女人,它真正杀死了几乎代表了全部男性之神圣的国王和父亲。是葛特鲁德 [哈姆雷特的母亲],麦克白斯夫人,高纳莉尔和里甘[李尔王的两个女儿]这些女人毁灭了男人的最高神圣形象。尽管她们后来分别受到了惩治,可是国王和父亲却死了,被从崇高的神位上拉了下来。

这是文艺复兴(Renaissance)时期全部变革的戏剧性描写,它预示着后来真实生活中查理一世的被处决 [查理一世(Charles I,1600—1649),斯图亚特王朝的英国国王,英国资产阶级革命中被推上断头台,英国宣布成为共和国],正像《熙德》(Le Cid) [高乃依的著名诗剧]预示着法国大革命的到来一样。

在这方面,先是人文主义者(Humanists)伊拉斯谟斯[Erasmus,1466—1536,荷兰学者,文艺复兴运动的领导者]、萨文纳罗拉 [Savonarola,1452—1498,意大利僧侣,宗教改革者及殉道者]和路德 [Luther,1483—1546,德国神学家,宗教改革领袖]从哲学和宗教上脱离了旧的位置。然后是个人的和艺术上的脱离,代表人物是戏剧家莎士比亚和弥尔顿,再其后是政治和社会上的脱离,产生了共和国 (the Commonwealth) [指 1649 年克伦威尔处死英王查理一世到 1660 年封建王朝复辟这段时间的英伦三岛共和国]。

make the great periods in history.

The mediaeval world believed in an Almighty and Everlasting God, Maker of Heaven and Earth, Lord of all life, in Whom was absolute power, Whose law was eternal, Who had however a Son, Jesus, who would intercede with the Almighty God, and obtain mercy for repentant sinners. This on earth was carried out in the imperial state, an absolute monarch, invested with all power, yet open to clemency.

At the Renaissance all this collapsed, philosophically, even religiously. God was no longer the Almighty, the Wielder of Power, the Creator and the Destroyer. The medieval saints had modified this conception.

Christ was God. Christ, the Lamb, the Dove, Christ, who was all love, all mercy, all humility. The symbol now was the Shepherd carrying the lamb and leading the sheep to the fold. The people of the world were the sheep. And God was Love* for his people. For the sake of the sheep the shepherd sought the green pastures, for the sake of the sheep, always for the sake of the sheep.

This was the very reverse of the old idea of Almighty God Who held the thunderbolt in His right hand, and balanced the firmament in His left. The fulfilling of this new conception meant the subversion of the established order, entirely.

是这些哲学和宗教革命——思想革命，精神世界观念上的变革划分出、创造出一些伟大的历史阶段来。

中世纪的世界相信全能和永恒的上帝是天地的造物主，是众生的主宰，他有着绝对权力，其法律是永恒的。他有个儿子叫基督，基督可以向上帝说情，为忏悔的罪人求得同情与怜悯。这种东西在皇权国家中施行起来，这种绝对君主制被赋予全部的权力，但还能开恩。

可在文艺复兴时期，这东西在哲学上和宗教上全然崩溃了。上帝不再是全能的，不再是权力的掌握者，不再是创造者和毁灭者。中世纪的圣人们大大淡化了这种观念。

基督曾是上帝，基督，羔羊，鸽子，基督，他是全部的爱、怜悯和谦逊。这形象现在变成了牧羊人赶着羊把它们关进羊圈中。世上的人就是羊群，上帝是爱，爱他的子民。为了羊的缘故，牧羊人寻找着草色青青的牧场，为了羊的缘故，总是为了羊的缘故。

这就从根本上改变了旧的观念即全能的上帝右手握着雷电霹雳，左手擎着天穹。这种新观念就是要彻底推翻旧的固有秩序。

但是戏剧家莎士比亚头脑中绝无这等新秩序。他不是什么思想家。

In the dramatist, in Shakspere, there is no conception of the new order. Shakespeare was not a thinker. His conscious self was slow and reluctant, he found it difficult, as every artist must, to attend to abstract propositions, or to think in generalisations. He could only *feel* supremely the things which reformers could settle in the mind.

And he could only feel that his old self, his great, immediate, conscious and subconscious self, that which he conceived himself wholly to be, the whole establishment of his soul, was impeached, arraigned, condemned. His whole being was condemned to nullification.

"It is a tale told by an idiot—"

"How weary, stale, flat and unprofitable
*Seem to me all the uses of this world."**

What was it but tragedy and annihilation, madness and horror? Shakespeare is, in his dual self, Gertrude and Hamlet, Duncan and Banquo on the one hand, and Lady Macbeth and Macbeth on the other, Lear and Lear's fool and Cordelia, and then Goneril and Regan. He is the murdered and the murderer, the King and the regicide, the father and the patricide. And as such he ends in a convulsion of horror

他的意识自我是迟钝迟疑的，他像任何一个艺术家一样发现自己难以把握抽象的命题、无法概括地思想。他只能高度地感受那些改革家们头脑中的东西。

他只会感觉到他的意识和潜意识自我和他原先要成为的那个人及他整个固有的灵魂都被弹劾了，被审讯了，被谴责了。他整个的生命都被谴责为虚无。

这是一个白痴讲的故事——[见《麦克白斯》]

无聊，陈腐，无益
我眼中的世界毫无用处[见《哈姆雷特》]。

这难道不是悲剧、虚无、疯狂和恐怖吗？莎士比亚有着一个双重的自我，他既是葛特鲁德又是哈姆雷特，既是邓肯[《麦克白斯》中的苏格兰王]又是班果[邓肯的军事统帅]，既是麦克白斯夫人又是麦克白斯，既是李尔王又是李尔王身边的傻子，又是他女儿科第莉亚，还是高纳莉尔和里甘。他既是被谋

and self-annihilation, self-obliteration.

This is the whole condition of tragedy, when the formed soul of the artist is to be destroyed by the unconscious, unformed will. This will, being unconscious, as yet is purely destructive. It must destroy the old consciousness before itself can rise to occupy the field.

The condition of tragedy occurs naturally half way between the change in the philosophical and spiritual conception of life and the world, and the change in the actual living frame of life to fit this new conception. The first change is made in the minds and in the spirit of the few. It is a purely personal thing, and not necessarily in its first form at all subversive to the existing order, because it has no immediate relation to it. It is only when the new light, the new spirit, the new conception soaks through into the blood, and the actual feelings of the simple, not-intellectual people are changed, set in a new order, a new category, that a new system is created on the face of the earth: is created, or takes place.

But this process, of the gradual infusing and informing of the very blood of a people, by a new light, a new spiritual conception, is very slow. It is the artist who is first submitted to the change. Just as the philosopher's is the first mind into which

杀者又是杀人者,是国王也是弑君者,是父亲也是弑父者。正因此,他才最终因了恐怖、自我毁灭和自我泯灭而抽搐。

这是悲剧的全部条件——当艺术家固有的灵魂被潜在的、未成形的意志所毁灭。这潜意识的意志纯粹是一种毁灭。它非得毁灭旧的意识才能挺起身去占据它的地盘。

这种悲剧的条件是自然生成的,它生成于生命与世界之哲学与精神观念上发生的变化和实际生活框架为适应这新观念而发生的变化之间。这前一种变化发生在少数人的头脑与精神中,它纯属个人的东西,并非是要颠覆固有的秩序,因为它们之间毫无直接关系。只是当这新启示、新精神和观念浸入到血液中,当那些普通无知的人的感情发生变化,顺应了新的秩序和新的范畴,世上才创造出一个新的制度——或称之创造或称之为发生。

不过,这种新启迪新精神观念渐渐浸透人之血液的过程是十分缓慢的。艺术家是首先服从这种变化的人。正如哲学家的头脑是最先被新观念穿透,艺术家的灵魂也是最先受到影响的。它首先感到的是死,是自身的颠覆和毁灭。现存的灵魂形式必须打破,新的灵魂才能形成。

the new idea penetrates, so the artist's is the first soul to be affected. And it is affected first, necessarily, with a sense of death, of its own subversion, destruction. For the form of the existing soul must be broken before the new soul can have being.

The Greek tragedians came between the real philosophic revolution, of Heraclitus and the Pythagoreans. and Parmenides and Anaxagoras,* and the later social and political revolution, when the spirit of democracy supplanted the spirit of kingship. Aeschylus, who leaned back to the conservative form, ended in confidence of the conservative order: but Agamemnon was murdered, nevertheless. Euripides, who leaned to the advanced thought, ended in a spirit of pure death, pure not-being, of complete passing-away.

Turgenev, Tolstoi, and Dostoevsky occupy somewhat the position in the crisis of late European history that Shakspere and Corneille and Cervantes occupied with relation to the Renaissance, the crisis of middle European history, and that Aeschylus and Sophocles and Euripides occupied in the Grecian era.

[end of manuscript]

1916.

希腊悲剧家们就诞生在真正的哲学革命(以赫拉克立特[Heraclitus,540—480B.C.,古希腊哲学家和数学家]、毕达哥拉斯 [Pythagoreans,? 一 497B.C.,希腊哲学家、数学家]的信奉者们,巴曼尼狄斯 [Parmenides,纪元前 5 世纪希腊哲学家]和亚那萨格拉斯[Anaxagoras,500? —428B.C.,希腊哲学家]为标志)和以后的社会与政治革命之间,这期间,民主精神取代了王权。埃斯库罗斯倾向于保守,因此最终相信了保守的秩序。不过,阿伽门农 [阿伽门农是埃斯库罗斯同名戏剧中出征特洛亚的统帅。他杀死女儿祭神,妻子为女儿复仇而杀夫。后其子奥烈斯特为父报仇而杀母。劳伦斯在此似乎是表明埃斯库罗斯潜意识与主观意识的对立]还是被谋杀了。至于欧里彼德斯,他倾向于先进的思想,可最终却以死的精神而告结束,成为纯粹的非存在(not—being),全然一个过客而已。

屠格涅夫、托尔斯泰和陀思妥耶夫斯基在后来的欧洲历史危机中占据的位置同莎士比亚、高乃依和塞万提斯在文艺复兴时中世纪欧洲历史的危机中占据的位置大致相似,也同埃斯库罗斯、索福克勒斯和欧里彼德斯在希腊时期占据的位置大致相似。

1916 年

Foreword to Women in Love

This novel was written in its first form in the Tyrol, in 1913. It was altogether re-written and finished in Cornwall in 1917. So that it is a novel which took its final shape in the midst of the period of war, though it does not concern the war itself. I should wish the time to remain unfixed, so that the bitterness of the war may be taken for granted in the characters.

The book has been offered to various London publishers. Their almost inevitable reply has been "We should like very much to publish, but feel we cannot risk a prosecution." They remember the fate of *The Rainbow*, and are cautious. This book is a potential sequel to *The Rainbow*.

In England, I would never try to justify myself against any accusation. But to the Americans, perhaps I may speak for myself. I am accused, in England, of uncleanness and pornography. I deny the charge, and take no further notice. In Ameri-

David Herbert Lawrence

《恋爱中的女人》自序

[本前言是应美国出版商 Thomas Seltzer 1919 年 11 月 7 日来信的建议所写。曾于 1920 年印在本书的广告上,后曾三次收入小说中。不知出于何故,以后未再收入。]

这部小说草拟于梯罗尔,1913 年。1917 年在康沃尔重写后杀青 [1913 年 3 月,劳伦斯夫妇住在意大利北部嘎达湖畔的威拉村,草就了《姐妹》一书。其上半部于 1915 年以《虹》的书名出版。1916 年劳氏夫妇移居赞诺的特拉嘎森,在《姐妹》的基础上写作《恋爱中的女人》并于 1917 年杀青。1919 年对原稿再次进行了改动]。因此可以说,这是一部在第一次世界大战期间成形但与大战本身无甚关系的小说。不过,我希望不要把小说置于一个特定的时间段中。这样一来就可以把小说人物的痛苦看做是战争所致。

这本书稿曾投给一些伦敦的出版社[这部书稿曾被几家英国出版社退稿,包括麦

ca the chief accusation seems to be one of "Eroticism." This is odd, rather puzzling to my mind. Which Eros? Eros of the jaunty "amours," or Eros of the sacred mysteries? And if the latter, why accuse, why not respect, even venerate?

Let us hesitate no longer to announce that the sensual passions and mysteries are equally sacred with the spiritual mysteries and passions. Who would deny it any more? The only thing unbearable is the degradation, the prostitution of the living mysteries in us. Let man only approach his own self with a deep respect, even reverence for all that the creative soul, the God-mystery within us, puts forth. Then we shall all be sound and free. Lewdness is hateful because it impairs our integrity and our proud being.

The creative, spontaneous soul sends forth its promptings of desire and aspiration in us. These promptings are our true fate, which it is our business to fulfil. A fate dictated from outside, from theory or from circumstances, is a false fate.

This novel pretends only to be a record of the writer's own desire, aspirations, struggles: in a word, a record of the profoundest experiences in the self. Nothing that comes from the deep, passional soul is bad, or can be bad. So there is no apol-

修恩与达克华斯等著名出版社]，他们最终的回答几乎都是："我们对出版这本书甚有诚意。但若因此被起诉，则不敢冒此风险。"《虹》的厄运仍叫他们记忆犹新[1915年11月13日，伦敦法院以"淫秽"罪名命令麦修恩销毁未售出的和可以收回的《虹》]，不得不慎之又慎。而这本书潜意上又是《虹》的续篇。

在英国，我从不企图在任何指控面前替自己辩解。但对美国人，我似乎可以自辩一二。在美国，我被指控为"不洁"和色情(pornography)。我不认错，也不理会它。对我最主要的指责是"情欲狂"(Eroticism)。这就奇了，实在叫我困惑。它指的是哪种情欲？是那种逍遥自得的情欲还是圣洁的情爱女神爱洛斯(Eros)[请注意，Eros与Eroticism词根相同]？如果是后者，为什么要责难，为什么不敬重，甚至崇拜之？

让我们毫不犹豫地宣称：肉欲的激情与神秘同神的神秘与激情同样神圣。谁还会对此加以否定？惟一不可容忍的是糟贱我们身上活生生的神秘之物，这纯属堕落。

让男人深怀敬重地认识自己吧，对我们体内那富有创造性的灵魂所张扬的一切甚至要报以敬重，因为它是上帝的神话。这样一来我们才能

ogy to tender, unless to the soul itself, if it should have been belied.

Man struggles with his unborn needs and fulfilment. New unfoldings struggle up in torment in him, as buds struggle forth the midst of a plant. Any man of real individuality tries to know and to understand what is happening, even in himself, as he goes along. This struggle for verbal consciousness should not be left out in art. It is a very great part of life. It is not the superimposition of a theory. It is the passionate struggle into conscious being.

We are now in a period of crisis. Every man who is acutely alive is acutely wrestling with his own soul. The people that can bring forth the new passion, the new idea, this people will endure. Those others, that fix themselves in the old idea, will perish with the new life strangled unborn within them. Men must speak out to one another.

In point of style, fault is often found with the continual, slightly modified repetition. The only answer is that it is natural to the author, and that every natural crisis in emotion or passion or understanding comes from this pulsing, frictional to-

身心健康,自由自在。淫猥是可恨之物,它戕害了我们的正直与高尚。

富有创造性的自然冲动之魂激荡起我们体内的欲望与渴求,这是我们真正的命运,有待于我们去满足并实现之。而来自外界的指令如来自理念和环境,是虚幻的命运。

这部小说自诩为作者自身欲望之渴求与抗争的纪录。一言以蔽之,是自我至深经验的纪录。举凡来自灵魂深处的东西均无不良可言。所以,本作者毫无歉意可表,除非这小说背叛了自家灵魂。

男人为其即将生出的欲求而挣扎并寻求满足。如同蓓蕾在树木中挣扎而出,新的欲求之花在磨难中生自人的体内。任何一个真正有个性的男人都会试图认识并了解他身心中正在发生什么,他要挣扎,以得出语言上的表达。这种挣扎绝不应该在艺术中被忽略,因为它是生命之重大部分;这绝非理念强加于人,而是为获得意识生命而进行的激情抗争。

我们正处在一个危机的时期。任何一个敏感的活生生的男人都在激烈地与自己的灵魂抗争。能够生出新的激情和新的理念,这样的人才能坚忍下去。而那些禁锢在旧理念中的人,会因着新生命扼死在体内不能

and-fro, which works up to culmination.

D.H. Lawrence
Hermitage, 12 September 1919.

出生而灭亡。男人们必须相互吐露心声。

论及文体,书中常有稍作变动的重复之处,往往被视作败笔。惟一的解释是,对本作者来说这纯属自然。因为,情绪、激情或领悟上的每一个危机都来自这种搏动着摩擦中的往复,只有这样才能导致其高潮。

D.H.劳伦斯
1919 年 9 月 12 日于 Hermitage

[Hermitage 位于伯克郡。劳氏夫妇于 1918 和 1919 年断断续续在此地村舍居住。]

GIOVANNI VERGA

It seems curious that modern Italian literature has made so little impression on the European consciousness. A hundred years ago, when Manzoni's *I Promessi Sposi* came out, it met with European applause. Along with Sir Walter Scott and Byron, Manzoni stood for 'Romance' to all Europe. Yet where is Manzoni now, even compared to Scott and Byron? Actually, I mean. Nominally, *I Promessi Sposi* is a classic, in fact, it is usually considered *the* classic Italian novel. It is set in all 'literature courses'. But who reads it? Even in Italy, who reads it? And yet, to my thinking, it is one of the best and most interesting novels ever written: surely a greater book than *Ivanhoe* or *Paul et Virginie* or *Werther*. Why then does nobody read it? Why is it found boring? When I gave a good English translation to the late Katherine Mansfield, she said, to my astonishment: I couldn't read it. Too long and bor-

David Herbert Lawrence

乔万尼·维尔迦

[Giovanni Verga(1840—1922),意大利小说家。]

现代意大利文学对欧洲的思想影响之小令人纳闷儿。一百年前曼佐尼(**Manzoni**)之《婚约夫妇》(**I Promessi Sposi**)的出版赢得了欧洲的赞赏欢呼。曼佐尼因此而与斯各特(**Sir Walter Scott**)和拜伦(**Byron**)一起在欧洲人心中成为"罗曼司"的代表人物。可是现在,与斯各特和拜伦相比,谁还记得他曼佐尼？这是事实。名义上《婚约夫妇》是一部经典,可事实上,它是意大利的过时小说罢了。"文学教程"中都提到它,可谁读它？甚至在意大利,谁读？但我认为它是有史以来最优秀最有趣的小说之一,当然比斯各特之《艾凡赫》(**Ivanhoe**),《保罗与薇吉妮》(**Paul et Virginie**)[法国小说家 Bernardin de Saint-Fierre(1737—1814)的著名小说]和歌德的《少年维特之烦恼》要强得

ing.

It is the same with Giovanni Verga. After Manzoni, he is Italy's accepted greatest novelist. Yet nobody takes any notice of him. He is, as far as anybody knows his name, just the man who wrote the libretto to *Cavalleria Rusticana*. Whereas, as a matter of fact, Verga's story *Cavalleria Rusticana* is as much superior to Mascagni's rather cheap music as wine is superior to sugar-water. Verga is one of the greatest masters of the short story. In the volume *Novelle Rusticane* and in the volume entitled *Cavalleria Rusticana* are some of the best short stories ever written. They are sometimes as short and as poignant as Chekhov. I prefer them to Chekhov. Yet nobody reads them. They are 'too depressing'. They don't depress me half as much as Chekhov does. I don't understand the popular taste.

Verga wrote a number of novels, of different sorts: very different. He was born about 1850, and died, I believe, at the beginning of 1921. So he is a modern. At the same time, he is a classic. And at the same time, again, he is old-fashioned.

The earlier novels are rather of the French type of the seventies-Octave Feuillet, with a touch of Gyp. There is the depressing story of the Sicilian young man who made a Neapolitan marriage, and on the last page gives his wife a much-belat-

多。可为什么没人读它呢？为什么人们觉得它无聊呢？我曾把一部优秀的英译本给已故的凯瑟琳·曼斯菲尔德(**Katherine Mansfield**)看，令我吃惊的是，她说她读不下去，嫌它太冗长太烦人。

乔万尼·维尔迦的下场也一样。他是曼佐尼之后公认的意大利最优秀的小说家了。可没人拿他当回事。听这个名字，人们只知道他写了歌剧《乡村骑士》(**Cavalleria Rusticana**)。事实上，维尔迦的《乡村骑士》故事本身比马斯卡尼(**Mascagni**)的廉价音乐可强多了，两相比较，一个是酒，一个是糖水[这故事改编成歌剧后由马斯卡尼(著名作曲家)谱曲]。维尔迦算得上是短篇小说大师了。他的小说集《乡村故事》(**Novelle Rusticane**)和《乡村骑士》中有一些世上顶优秀的故事。有时就像契诃夫(**Chekhov**)的小说那样短小精悍又尖刻。相比之下我更喜欢维尔迦的。可就是没人读它们。因为这些故事“太让人压抑”。不过它们并不比契诃夫的故事更令人压抑。我实在不懂大众的口味。

维尔迦还写过不少长篇小说，题材不同，大不相同。他大概生于 **1850** 年，我相信他是在 **1921** 年初殁的。所以说他是现代人。同时他也算经典，

ed slap across the face. There is the gruesome book, *Tigre Reale*, of the Russian countess–or princess, whatever it is–who comes to Florence and gets fallen in love with by the young sicilian, with all the subsequent horrid affair: the weird woman dying of consumption, the man weirdly infatuated, in the suicidal South–Italian fashion. It is a bit in the manner of Matilda Serao. And though unpleasant, it is impressive.

Verga himself was a Sicilian, from one of the lonely agricultural villages in the south of the island. He was a gentleman–but not a rich one, presumably with some means. As a young man, he went to Naples, then he worked at journalism in Milan and Florence. And finally he retired to Catania, to an exclusive, aristocratic old age. He was a shortish, broad man with a big red moustache. He never married.

His fame rests on his two long Sicilian novels, *I Malavoglia* and *Mastro–don Gesualdo*, also on the books of short pieces, *Cavalleria Rusticana*, *Novelle Rusticane*, and *Vagabondaggio*. These are all placed in Sicily, as is the short novel, *Storia di una Capinera*. Of this last little book, one of the leading literary young Italians in Rome said to me the other day: Ah, yes, Verga! Some of his things! But a thing like *Storia di una Capinera*, now, is ridiculous.

并且是个老派作家。

他的早期小说很有点七十年代的法国味儿，如奥斯塔夫·福莱特(**Octave Feuillet**)，带点吉卜赛色彩。小说写一个西西里小伙子娶了个拿波里妻子，而在最后一页上我们看到他终于扇了她一个耳光。也有像《金虎》(**Tigre Reale**)这样令人讨厌的小说，讲俄国女伯爵或公主来到佛罗伦萨，被西西里小伙子爱上，接下来就是挺烦人的爱情故事。那古怪的女人死于肺病，那恋情怪诞的男人以意大利南部的方式殉了情。这很有点玛蒂苔·塞拉奥(**Matilda Serao**)的风格。尽管让人不舒服，但印象很深。

维尔迦本人是西西里人，出生于岛上南部最孤独的一个小村子。他是个绅士，似乎有点钱财但不富，年轻时他就去了那不勒斯(**Naples**)，然后在米兰和佛罗伦萨干新闻。最终退休回他的卡塔尼亚，度过了一个孤傲贵族的晚年。他个子不高，身材宽大，长着红色的大胡子。他终生未娶。

使他名声大噪的是他的两部写西西里的长篇小说《马拉沃里亚一家》(**I Malavoglia**)和《堂杰苏阿多师傅》(**Mastro–don Gesualdo**)，还有短篇小说集《乡村骑士》、《乡村故事》及《流浪者》(**Vagabondaggio**)。这些故事都发

But why? It is rather sentimental, maybe. But it is no more sentimental than *Tess*. And the sentimentality seems to me to belong to the Sicilian characters in the book, it is true to type, quite as much so as the sentimentality of a book like Dickens' *Christmas Carol*, or George Eliot's *Silas Marner*, both of which works are 'ridiculous', if you like, without thereby being wiped out of existence.

The trouble with Verga, as with all Italians, is that he never seems quite to know where he is. When one reads Manzoni, one wonders if he is not more 'Gothic' or Germanic, than Italian. And Verga, in the same way, seems to have a borrowed outlook on life: but this time, borrowed from the French. With d'Annunzio the same, it is hard to believe he is really being himself, He gives one the impression of 'acting up'. Pirandello goes on with the game to-day. The Italians are always that way: always acting up to somebody else's vision of life. Men like Hardy, Meredith, Dickens, they are just as sentimental and false as the Italians, in their own way. It only happens to be our own brand of falseness and sentimentality.

And yet, perhaps, one can't help feeling that Hardy, Meredith, Dickens. and Maupassant and even people like the Goncourts and Paul Bourget, false in part though they be, are still looking on life with their own eyes. Whereas the Italians

生在西西里，正像中篇小说《莺之死》(Storia di una Capinera)一样。关于这后一部作品，罗马的一位意大利著名青年作家有一天对我说：哦，对了。维尔迦！他的东西嘛！像《莺之死》，现在看起来很可笑。

可为什么呢？可能太伤感了吧？可它绝不比《苔丝》(Tess)更伤感。而且在我看来，这种伤感是书中西西里人特有的，真实的，正像狄更斯(Dickens)的《圣诞欢歌》(Christmas Carol)和乔治·艾略特的《织工马南传》(Silas Marner)，这后两部作品你也可以说是“可笑的”，可它们并未消逝。

维尔迦的麻烦在于，像所有的意大利作家一样，他似乎永远弄不大清自己的所在。人们读曼佐尼时，人们会以为他是不是更有“哥特”气或德国味而非意大利味。同样，维尔迦看上去也是从别处借来的生命观，这次是从法国借来的。邓南遮(Gabriele D'Annunzio)也是一样，他很难让人相信他就是他自己。他给人一种“仿造”的印象。今日的皮兰德娄(Pirandello)也一样。意大利作家总那样，总在追着别人的生命观。像哈代(Hardy)、梅瑞迪斯(Meredith)和狄更斯(Dickens)这一类人吧，他们也像这些意大利人一样伤感做作，不同的是，他们的那种做作与伤感是我们英国式的。

give one the impression that they are always borrowing of emotion into a borrowed vision.

This is the trouble with Verga. But on the other hand, everything he does has a weird quality of Verga in it, quite distinct and like nothing else. And yet, perhaps the gross vision of the man is not quite his own. All his movements are his own. But his main motive is borrowed.

This is the unsatisfactory part about all Italian literature, as far as I know it.

The main motive, the gross vision of all the nineteenth century literature, is what we may call the emotional-democratic vision or motive. It seems to me that since 1860 or even 1830, the Italians have always borrowed their ideals of democracy from the northern nations, and poured great emotion into them without ever being really grafted by them. Some of the most wonderful martyrs for democracy have been Neapolitan men of birth and breeding. But none the less, it seems a mistake: an attempt to live by somebody else's lights.

Verga's first Sicilian novel, *I Malavoglia*, is of this sort. It was considered his greatest work. It is a great book. But it is *parti pris*. It is one-sided. And therefore it dates. There is too much, too much of the tragic fate of the poor, in it. There is a

尽管他们有些做作，可你仍然无法不感到，哈代、梅瑞迪斯、狄更斯，还有莫泊桑(**Maupassant**)，甚至龚古尔兄弟(**the Goncourts**)和保罗·布尔热(**Paul Bourget**)，这些人仍然是在用自己的眼睛观察生活。而这几个意大利人则让人觉得总在借别人的眼观察，然后将自己大量的情绪释放进这借来的眼光中去。

这就是维尔迦的麻烦。不过在另一方面，他每做一件事都有着维尔迦的古怪特点，很独特，不像别的什么人。但是，或许他的总体眼光不是他自己的，只是他的行动是他自己的。他的主题也是借来的。

就我所知，这是所有意大利文学不尽人意的地方。

19 世纪文学的主题或眼光就是我们所谓的情感-民主的眼光或着说主题。我觉得，从 **1860** 年开始，甚至更早，从 **1830** 年始，意大利人总是从北方民族那里采借民主思想，并且未经真正消化就向其投入巨大的感情。一些为民主而牺牲的英烈要么是拿波里生人要么是拿波里祖籍。可这似乎是个错误：他们是试图在别人的光耀下生活。

维尔迦的第一部西西里长篇小说《马拉沃里亚一家》就是这类作品。

sort of wallowing in tragedy: the tragedy of the humble. It belongs to a date when the 'humble' were almost the most fashionable thing. And the Malavoglia family are most humbly humble. Sicilians of the sea-coast, fishers, small traders-their humble tragedy is so piled on, it becomes almost disastrous. The book was published in America under the title of *The House by the Medlar Tree*, and can still be obtained. It is a great book, a great picture of poor life in Sicily, on the coast just north of Catania. But it is rather overdone on the pitiful side. Like the woebegone pictures by Bastien Lepage. Nevertheless, it is essentially a true picture, and different from anything else in literature. In most books of the period-even in *Madame Bovary*, to say nothing of Balzac's earlier *Lys dans la Vallée*-one has to take off about twenty per cent of the tragedy. One does it in Dickens, one does it in Hawthorne, one does it all the time, with all the great writers. Then why not with Verga? Just knock off about twenty per cent of the tragedy in *I Malavoglia*, and see what a great book remains. Most books that live, live in spite of the author's laying it on thick. Think of *Wuthering Heights*. It is quite as impossible to an Italian as even *I Malavoglia* is to us. But it is a great book.

The trouble with realism-and Verga was a realist-is that the writer, when he is

它被认为是他最伟大的作品。这是一本好书,可它片面。所以说它过时了。这书里有着太多太多穷人的悲剧命运,似乎像在穷人的悲剧中沉溺打滚儿。它属于一个"寒酸"几乎最时髦的时代。而马拉沃里亚一家人正好是十分十分寒酸的。于是沿海一带的西西里人——渔民们和小贩儿们的悲剧便铺天盖地而至,几乎弄得悲剧成灾。这本书在美国出版时书名改为《欧楂树旁的房子》(**The House by the Medlar Tree**),现仍可以买到。这是一部大书,是一幅描绘西西里穷苦生命的宏大图卷,这种图景就在卡塔尼亚北部的海边上。可它过分描述那可怜的一面了,正如同巴斯蒂安·拉培格(**Bastien Lepage**)那凄凄惨惨的绘画。但无论如何它基本上是一幅逼真的图画,与文学中别的东西不同。而同一时期的多数小说——甚至《包法利夫人》(**Madame Bovary**),更不用提巴尔扎克早期的《幽谷百合》(**Lys dans la Vall´ee**),都可以删掉其中百分之二十的悲剧篇幅。狄更斯的、霍桑的,对所有大作家的作品都可以这样做。对维尔迦为什么不能?砍掉《马拉沃里亚一家》中百分之二十的悲剧,再看看剩下的是怎样一部大书吧。大多数作品之所以能立住,绝不是靠作者给书增加厚度。想想《呼啸

a truly exceptional man like Flaubert or like Verga, tries to read his own sense of tragedy into people much smaller than himself. I think it is a final criticism against *Madame Bovary* that people such as Emma Bovary and her husband Charles simply are too insignificant to carry the full weight of Gustave Flaubert's sense of tragedy. Emma and Charles Bovary are a couple of little people. Gustave Flaubert is not a little person. But, because he is a realist and does not believe in 'heroes', Flaubert insists on pouring his own deep and bitter tragic consciousness into the little skins of the country doctor and his uneasy wife. The result is a discrepancy. *Madame Bovary* is a great book and a very wonderful picture of life. But we cannot help resenting the fact that the great tragic soul of Gustave Flaubert is, so to speak, given only the rather commonplace bodies of Emma and Charles Bovary. There's a misfit. And to get over the misfit you have to let in all sorts of seams of pity. Seams of pity, which won't be hidden.

The great tragic soul of Shakespeare borrows the bodies of kings and princes–not out of snobbism, but out of natural affinity. You can't put a great soul into a commonplace person. Commonplace persons have commonplace souls. Not all the noble sympathy of Flaubert or Verga for Bovarys and Malavoglias can prevent the

山庄》(**Wuthering Heights**)吧，它对意大利人来说简直不可思议正如《马拉沃里亚一家》在我们看来不可思议一样，可它是一部伟大的著作。

现实主义的毛病在于(维尔迦是个现实主义作家了)，当一个作家真的是福楼拜(**Flaubert**)或维尔迦这样的不凡者，他会试图把自己的悲剧观塞给比他渺小得多的人物。我想这就是对《包法利夫人》的彻底批评——像爱玛·包法利包法利和她丈夫查理斯这样的人实在太渺小了，他们可承受不住作者居斯塔夫·福楼拜之悲剧观的重荷。爱玛和查理斯·包法利是一对儿小人物，而居斯塔夫·福楼拜可一点不小。正因为他是个现实主义者，不相信什么“英雄”，所以福楼拜才要强行把他自己深刻苦涩的悲剧意识灌入那乡村郎中和他那焦虑的太太那浅薄的皮肤中去。其结果是不协调。《包法利夫人》是一部佳构，是一幅绝妙的生活图卷。可让我们无法不抵触的是，与居斯塔夫·福楼拜之伟大的悲剧灵魂相匹配的却是爱玛和查理斯·包法利的凡俗肉身。这怕有点不合身。要让它们成龙配套，你就得留下一身的针脚儿--遗憾的针脚儿，这针脚儿是掖藏不住的，全暴露无遗。

said Bovarys and Malavoglias from being commonplace persons. They were deliberately chosen because they were commonplace, and not heroic. The authors insisted on the treasure of the humble. But they had to lend the humble by far the best part of their own treasure, before the said humble could show any treasure at all.

So, if *I Malavoglia* dates, so does *Madame Bovary*. They belong to the emotional-democratic, treasure-of-the-humble period of the nineteenth century. The period is just now rather out of fashion. We still feel the impact of the treasure-of-the-humble too much. When the emotion will have quite gone out of us, we can accept *Madame Bovary* and *I Malavoglia* in the same free spirit with the same detachment as that in which we accept Dickens or Richardson.

Mastro-don Gesualdo, however, is not nearly so much treasure-of-the-humble as *I Malavoglia*. Here, Verga is not dealing with the disaster of poverty, and calling it tragedy. On the contrary, he is a little bored by poverty. He must have a hero who wins out, and makes his pile, and then succumbs under the pile.

Mastro-don Gesualdo started life as a barefoot peasant brat, not a don at all. He becomes very rich. But all he gets out of it is a great tumour of bitterness inside, which kills him.

莎士比亚那伟大的悲剧灵魂借的是国王和王子之类的身体，倒不是出于势利，而是出于它们自然的相匹配。你万万不可把一个伟大的灵魂镶嵌入一个凡人的体内。因为凡人自有平凡的灵魂。并不是因为福楼拜或维尔迦对包法利们或马拉沃里亚们怀有高尚的同情心就能使他们成为不凡之人。他们之所以被有意写进书中，是因为他们是凡人而非英雄。作者坚持卑贱者是宝贵的观点。可是作者们必须先把自己最宝贵的东西借给这些人，这些人才能展示一下他们宝贵在何处。

因此上，如果说《马拉沃里亚一家》过时了，《包法利夫人》也一样过时。它们同属那个情感-民主和卑贱者宝贵的**19**世纪。那一段日子早不时兴了。我们现在仍能感到太多的"卑贱者宝贵"之影响。当情感离我们而去时，我们会以一种自由精神和超然态度接受《包法利夫人》和《马拉沃里亚一家》的，正像我们用这种超然的精神和态度接受狄更斯和理查森(**Rechardson**)一样。

《堂杰苏阿多师傅》则没有《马拉沃里亚一家》中那么多的"卑贱者宝贵"。在此，维尔迦面对的不是贫穷的灾难并称之为悲剧。相反，他已经让

Verga must have known, in actual life, the prototype of Gesualdo. We see him in the marvellous realistic story in *Cavalleria Rusticana*, of a fat little peasant, who has become enormously rich, grinding his labourers, and now is diseased and must die. This little fellow is quite unheroic. He has the indomitable greedy will, but nothing else of Gesualdo's rather attractive character.

Gesualdo is attractive, and, in a sense, heroic. But still he is not allowed to emerge in the old heroic sense, with swagger and nobility and head-and-shoulders taller than anything else. He is allowed to have exceptional qualities, and above all, exceptional force. But these things do not make a hero of a man. A hero must be a hero by grace of God, and must have an inkling of the same. Even the old Paladin heroes had a great idea of themselves as exemplars. And Hamlet had the same. 'O cursed spite that ever I was born to set it right.' Hamlet didn't succeed in setting anything right, but he felt that way. And so all heroes must feel.

But Gesualdo, and Jude, and Emma Bovary are not allowed to feel any of these feelings. As far as destiny goes, they felt no more than anybody else. And this is because they belong to the realistic world.

Gesualdo is just an ordinary man with extraordinary energy. That, of course, is

贫穷弄烦了。他必须写一个发迹的英雄，先让他发达了，然后让他毁于财富。

堂杰苏阿多师傅起初可不是个堂(don 即绅士)，不过是个光脚丫子的农家小子。后来他富了，可他得到的只是内心巨大的伤痛，这创伤终于毁了他。

维尔迦一定了解现实生活中杰苏阿多的原型。我们在他绝妙的现实主义作品《乡村骑士》中见过这样的人，一个矬胖子农夫，暴富后又压榨他的劳工，再后来就病了，非死不可。这个小人物十分的不英雄。他是个贪心不足欲壑难填的主儿，却没有半点杰苏阿多那种迷人的性格。

杰苏阿多迷人，而且有点英雄气。可是他却不准以旧观念中的英雄形象出现，既没有狂劲儿也没有贵族气，比谁也不高大。他只被许可有非凡的特点，首要的是有一把子非凡的力气。可光凭这个，男人是成不了英雄的。一个英雄一定要是天赐的，且要有点神之气。甚至古老的骑士英雄们就已自视不凡，以楷模自居了。哈姆雷特就是这样的——"哦，可咒的恶意，我生来就是校正你的。"尽管哈姆雷特从未成功地校正任何东西，

the intention. But he is a Sicilian. And here lies the difficulty. Because the realisitic-democratic age has dodged the dilemma of having no heroes by making every man his own hero. This is reached by what we call subjective intensity, and in this subjectively-intense every-man-his-own-hero business the Russians have carried us to the greatest lengths. The merest scrub of a pick-pocket is so phenomenally aware of his own soul, that we are made to bow down before the imaginary coruscations that go on inside him. That is almost the whole of Russian literature: the phenomenal coruscations of the souls of quite commonplace people.

Of course your soul will coruscate, if you think it does. That´s why the Russians are so popular. No matter how much of a shabby animal you may be, you can learn from Dostoevsky and Chekhov, etc., how to have the most tender, unique, coruscating soul on earth. And so you may be most vastly important to yourself. Which is the private aim of all men. The hero had it openly. The commonplace person has it inside himself, though outwardly he says: Of course I´m no better than anybody else! His very asserting it shows he doesn´t think it for a second. Every character in Dostoevsky or Chekhov thinks himself *inwardly* a nonesuch, absolutely unique.

可人家有那种感觉。是英雄就得有这等感觉才行。

可是,杰苏阿多、裘德(Jude)和爱玛·包法利是不许有这种感觉的。由于命中注定,他们并不比别人感觉多一个点儿。因为他们属于现实主义世界。

杰苏阿多只是一个有把子超凡力气的凡人，当然这是有意安排的。可他是个西西里人,于是困难出现了。现实主义-民主时代躲避的是不要英雄但又要让每个人成为自己的英雄这样一个窘境。靠主观努力,这个目的算达到了。俄国人在主观努力使每个人成为自己的英雄方面达到了登峰造极的地步。最下等的小偷却十分不凡地注意自己的灵魂,于是我们不得不冲想像出来的他内心的闪光鞠躬。那似乎就是俄国文学的全部了:十足的凡人灵魂中不凡的闪光。

当然,如果你愿意这么想,你的灵魂也会闪光的。正因此,俄国人才颇有知名度。无论你是个怎样寒伧的动物,你都可以从陀思妥耶夫斯基和契诃夫之类的人那儿学会如何获得世上最温柔、最独特的闪光灵魂。于是你对你自己就变得十二分重要了。人们私下里都把这当成自己的目

And here you get the blank opposite, in the Sicilians. The Sicilians simply don't have any subjective idea of themselves, or any souls. Except, of course, that funny little *alter ego* of a soul which can be prayed out of purgatory into paradise, and is just as objective as possible.

The Sicilian, in our sense of the word, doesn't have any soul. He just hasn't got our sort of subjective consciousness. the soulful idea of himself. Souls, to him, are little naked people uncomfortably hopping on hot bricks, and being allowed at last to go up to a garden where there is music and flowers and sanctimonious society, Paradise. Jesus is a man who was crucified by a lot of foreigners and villains, and who can help you against the villainous lot nowadays: as well as against witches and the rest.

The self-tortured Jesus, the self-tortured Hamlet, simply does not exist. Why should a man torture himself? Gesualdo would ask in amazement. Aren't there scoundrels enough in the world to torture him?

Of course, I am speaking of the Sicilians of Verga's day, fifty and sixty years ago, before the great emigration to America, and the great return, with dollars and bits of self-aware souls: at least politically self-aware.

标。英雄们公开这个目标,普通人则暗地里怀着这目标,表面上却说:我比别人一点不强!这样说表明他这话根本就没过脑子。陀思妥耶夫斯基或契诃夫笔下的每个人物都在内心里把自己看成无可匹敌的人,绝对与众不同。

而西西里人则截然相反。西西里人干脆就没有什么主观自我观念或什么灵魂之类。当然了,他们还是有另一个小小怪怪的另一个灵魂自我,它通过祈祷可以走出炼狱进入天堂。

用我们的话说,西西里人是没什么灵魂的。他们没有我们这种主观意念,这种自我灵魂的观念。对他们来说,灵魂是一个在热砖头上蹦跳的裸体小人儿,他终于被允许进入一个有音乐和鲜花的花园,一个伪善的社会,人们称之为天堂。在他们眼中,耶稣是让一群外国人和恶棍钉死在十字架上的,他可以帮助你对付噩运,还可以对付巫婆什么的。

自我折磨的耶稣和自我折磨的哈姆雷特干脆就不存在。一个人干吗要折磨自个儿?杰苏阿多会惊讶地自问。世上不是有那么些个坏蛋折磨他吗?

So that in *Mastro-don Gesualdo* you have the very antithesis of what you get in *The Brothers Karamazov*. Anything more un-Russian than Verga it would be hard to imagine: save Homer. Yet Verga has the same sort of pity as the Russians. and, like the Russians, he is a realist. He won't have heroes, nor appeals to gods above nor below.

The Sicilians of to-day are supposed to be the nearest thing to the classic Greeks that is left to us: that is, they are the nearest descendants on earth. In Greece to-day there are no Greeks. The nearest thing is the Sicilian, the eastern and south-eastern Sicilian.

And if you come to think of it, Gesualdo Motta might really be a Greek in modern setting, except that he is not intellectual. But this many Greeks were not. And he has the energy, the quickness, the vividness of the Greek, the same vivid passion for wealth, the same ambition, the same lack of scruples, the same queer openness, without ever really openly committing himself. He is not a bit furtive, like an Italian. He is astute instead, far too astute and Greek to let himself be led by the nose. Yet he has a certain frankness, far more than an Italian. And far less fear than an Italian. His boldness and his queer sort of daring are Sicilian rather

当然我指的是维尔迦时代的西西里人，那是五六十年前人们尚未大举移民美国又大举返乡，不仅带回美元还带回点儿灵魂的自我意识，至少在政治方面。

所以在《堂杰苏阿多师傅》中你看到了在《卡拉马佐夫兄弟》(**the Brothers Karamazov**)中看到的同样的东西。你无法想像维尔迦哪点不像俄国人。维尔迦有着与俄国人同样的怜悯心肠。所以他同俄国人一样是现实主义作家。他不要英雄，也不祈求天上地下的上帝。

今天的西西里人据说是顶接近古希腊人了，就是说他们是世上最接近希腊遗风的人。今日希腊，找不到一个古希腊那样的人。最像的在西西里，在西西里东部和东北部。

说到此，杰苏阿多·莫塔可真算得上现代背景下的古希腊人，只是他没古希腊人那点智慧。其实不少古希腊人也并不很智慧。他精力充沛，反应机敏，生动活泼，这方面像古希腊人。他像古希腊人一样对财富颇有激情，有抱负，毫无顾忌，心胸开阔(尽管从不真正公开地承担什么义务)。他可不像意大利人那么叫人难以捉摸。他诡计多端，太狡猾太希腊气，绝不

than Italian, so is his independent manliness.

He is Greek above all in not having any soul or any lofty ideals. The Greeks were far more bent on making an audacious splendid impression than on fulfilling some noble purpose. They loved the splendid look of a thing, the splendid ring of words. Even tragedy was to them a grand gesture, rather than something to mope over. Peak and pine they would not, and unless some Fury pursued them to punish them for their sins, they cared not a straw for sins: their own or anyone else's.

As for being burdened with souls, they were not such fools.

But alas, ours is the day of souls, when soul pays, and when having a soul is as important to the young as solitaire to a valetudinarian. If you don't have feelings about your soul, what sort of person can you be?

And Gesualdo didn't have feelings about his soul. He was remorselessly and relentlessly objective, like all people that belong to the sun. In the sun men are objective, in the mist and snow, subjective. Subjectivity is largely a question of the thickness of your overcoat.

When you get to Ceylon, you realize that, to the swarthy Cingalese, even Buddhism is a purely objective affair. And we have managed to spiritualize it to such a

会让人牵着鼻子走。可他又很直率,比意大利人直爽多了,也不像意大利人那么胆小怕事。他的冒失和奇特的勇气是属于西西里的,而不属于意大利,他独立的男子气也一样。

说他是希腊人,首先是因为他没什么灵魂或什么崇高理想。古希腊人更注重制造鲜明绝妙的印象而非达到什么高尚的目的。他们喜爱辉煌的外表,喜爱妙语连珠。甚至悲剧在他们来说也是一种辉煌夺目的姿态而非令人忧伤的东西。他们不做高山青松,他们毫不在意自己的或别人的罪恶,至于惩罚他们的罪过,那是复仇女神的事,随她去。

让什么灵魂拖累自己,他们才没那么傻。

可是啊,咱们处在一个灵魂的时代,灵魂值钱,灵魂对年轻人来说像单人纸牌戏对一个体弱多病的人一样重要。如果你对你的灵魂毫无感觉,那么你到底想当个什么样的人?

杰苏阿多对他的灵魂压根儿没感觉。他是一个纯粹的客体,就像所有属于太阳的人那样。在太阳下,人是客体;而在雾霭和飞雪中人是主体。这种主体性主要取决于你外衣的厚度。

subjective pitch.

Then you have the setting to the hero. The south-Sicilian setting to *Mastro-don Gesualdo* is perhaps nearer to the true medieval than anything else in modern literature, even barring the Sardinian medievalism of Grazia Deledda*. You have the Sicily of the Bourbons, the Sicily of the kingdom of Naples. The island is incredibly poor and incredibly backward. There are practically no roads for wheeled vehicles, and consequently no wheeled vehicles, neither carts nor carriages, outside the towns. Everything is packed on asses or mules, man travels on horseback or on foot, or, if sick, in a mule litter. The land is held by the great landowners, the peasants are almost serfs. It is as wild, as poor, and in the ducal houses of Palermo even as splendid and ostentatious as Russia.

Yet how different from Russia! Instead of the wild openness of the north, you have the shut-in, guarded watchfulness of the old Mediterranean. For centuries, the people of the Mediterranean have lived on their guard, intensely on their guard, on the watch, wary, always wary, and holding aloof. So it is even to-day, in the villages: aloof, holding aloof, each individual inwardly holding aloof from the others; and this in spite of the returned 'Americans'.

当你来到锡兰，你会意识到，对那些皮肤黝黑的僧伽罗人(Cingalese)来说，甚至佛教(Buddhism)也是一种纯粹客体的东西。而我们却把它高度精神化了，化成主体。

于是你看到了，这就是本书男主人公的背景。《堂杰苏阿多师傅》之西西里南部的背景或许是现代文学中最接近真正中世纪的，甚至格拉齐娅·黛莱达(Grazia Deledda)[意大利著名女作家(1871—1936),1926年诺贝尔文学奖得主]作品中撒丁岛(Sardinia)的中世纪景象也无法与之相比。你看到的是波旁王朝(Bourbon)时的西西里，是那不勒斯王国的西西里。这座岛贫穷落后得出奇，几乎没有公路供有轮子的东西行驶，因此也没有有轮子的东西，城外没马车也没双轮马车。东西都是靠驴和骡子驮，人要么骑马要么步行，病了就坐骡子轿。土地全让大地主占了，农民几乎沦为奴隶。它与俄国一样野蛮穷困，而巴勒莫(Palermo)那地方的公爵府第也像俄国的公爵府一样流光溢彩，铺张奢华。

可这里与俄国又是多么不同！这里没有北方的粗犷开阔，你看到的是古老的地中海人那种封闭和警觉。几个世纪以来，地中海人一直在警

How utterly different it is from Russia, where the people are always-in the books-expanding to one another, and pouring out tea and their souls to one another all night long. In Sicily, by nightfall, nearly every man is barricaded inside his own house. Save in the hot summer, when the night is more or less turned into day.

It all seems, to some people, dark and squalid and brutal and boring. There is no soul, no enlightenment at all. There is not one single enlightened person. If there had been, he would have departed long ago. He could not have stayed.

And for people who seek enlightenment, oh, how boring! But if you have any physical feeling for life, apart from nervous feelings such as the Russians have, nerves, nerves-if you have any appreciation for the southern way of life, then what a strange, deep fascination there is in *Mastro-don Gesualdo*! Perhaps the deepest nostalgia I have ever felt has been for Sicily, reading Verga. Not for England or anywhere else-for Sicily, the beautiful, that which goes deepest into the blood. It is so clear, so beautiful, so like the physical beauty of the Greek.

Yet the lives of the people all seem so squalid, so pottering, so despicable: like a crawling of beetles. And then, the moment you get outside the grey and squalid walls of the village, how wonderful in the sun, with the land lying apart.

觉、紧张地生活着，总是审慎，审慎，与人保持着距离。所以，甚至在今日，在村子里，人们仍与他人保持距离，每个人都在心中提防着别的人，连那些还乡的“美国人”也不例外。

这与俄国又是多么地不同。俄国人总是——书中的俄国人总是相互坦诚以待，整个晚上都可以为你倒着茶水，掏着心窝子说心里话。而在西西里，天一擦黑儿，几乎每个人都把自己严严实实地关在自家屋里——炎热的夏天除外，因为夏天天长，天黑得晚。

对一些人来说，这里的一切都看似黑暗、肮脏、野蛮而乏味。没有灵魂，无知无识。连个有知识的人都找不到。如果有过，那也是早就走了的，因为他在这儿呆不住。

对寻求知识的人来说，这地方太讨厌了！不过，如果你对生活有肉体的感受的话(不是俄国人那种神经质的感受，神经，神经)，如果你欣赏南方的这种生活方式，你会发现，《堂杰苏阿多师傅》是多么奇妙、迷人。可能我有生以来顶浓郁的乡愁是为西西里而怀的，因为我读了维尔迦。对英国或别处都不曾怀有这样的乡愁，却单单对西西里有，那儿的美浸透

And isolated, the people too have some of the old Greek singleness, carelessness, dauntlessness. It is only when they bunch together as citizens that they are squalid. In the countryside, they are portentous and subtle, like the wanderers in the Odyssey. And their relations are all curious and immediate, objective. They are so little aware of themselves, and so much aware of their own effects.

It all depends what you are looking for. Gesualdo′s lifelong love-affair with Diodata is, according to our ideas, quite impossible. He puts no value on sentiment at all, or almost none: again a real Greek, Yet there is a strange forlorn beauty in it, impersonal, a bit like Rachel or Rebecca. It is of the old, old world, when man was aware of his own belongings, acutely, but only very dimly aware of his own feelings. And feelings you are not aware of, you don′t have.

Gesualdo seems so potent, so full of potency. Yet nothing emerges, and he never says anything. It is the very reverse of the Russian, who talks and talks, out of impotence.

And you have a wretched, realistic kind of tragedy for the end. And you feel, perhaps the book was all about nothing, and Gesualdo wasn′t worth the labour of Verga.

了血液。它太明朗,太美了,就像希腊人肉体的美。

可这儿人的生活看上去是那么悲惨,吊儿郎当,那么让人看不起:就像一只爬行的甲壳虫。可是一走出村子那灰暗肮脏的大墙,你会发现阳光下的田野是那么美妙。单个儿看,这里的人有着古希腊人的那种孤独、无忧无虑、英勇无畏。只是当他们凑在一块儿成了城里人时他们才显得悲惨。在乡间,他们自命不凡而又内心纤敏,恰似《奥德赛》(Odyssey)中的流浪汉。而且,他们之间的关系十分奇特,直截了当,很客观——他们很少意识到自己,而是意识到自己行为的效果。

这全看你寻找什么了。杰苏阿多与迪奥达塔(Diodata)之间长达一生的爱情在我们看来是不可能的。他几乎一点不看中感情,这一点又像个真正的希腊人了。可是它里面有一种奇特的凄凉美,非个人的美,有点像拉切尔(Rachel)或里蓓佳(Rebecca)[这两个人可能指的是《圣经》中的两个女人。Rebecca是以萨(Issac)的妻子,雅可(Jacob)的母亲;Rachel是雅可的两妻之年轻的一位]。它是关于久远久远的世界,那时人对他的所有物抱有十分敏感的意识,而对自己的感情却没什么意识。你不在意感情,那说明你压根儿没有。

But that is because we are spiritual snobs, and think, because a man can fume with 'To be or not to be', therefore he is a person to be taken account of. Poor Gesualdo had never heard of it: To be or not to be, and he wouldn't have taken any notice if he had. He lived blindly, with the impetuosity of blood and muscles, sagacity and will, and he never woke up to himself. Whether he would have been any the better for waking up to himself, who knows!

杰苏阿多看上去十分强悍,一身的精力。可没出什么彩儿,他什么也没说。而俄国人正相反,没完没了地说,全是因了无能。

结尾处是一个悲惨而现实的悲剧。你或许会感到这书等于什么都没说,杰苏阿多并不值得维尔迦去写。

那是因为我们是一群精神上的势利眼。我们以为一个人只有为着"活下去还是死"[此句是莎士比亚名剧《哈姆雷特》中的名句,原文为:To be or not to be,译法颇多,有"活着还是死去"及"生存还是死亡"等,无法统一。似应按上下文灵活理解]而焦虑他才算得上是个人物,才值得人们重视。可怜的杰苏阿多从没听到过这个"活下去还是死",就算他听到过,他也不会拿它当一回事儿。他活得混混沌沌,由着他的血液和肌肉去躁动,任他的灵性和冲动去盲动,他从未清醒过来意识到他自己。是不是他醒过来会好些? 天知道!

1922 年

BOOKS

Are books just toys? the toys of consciousness?

Then what is man? The everlasting brainy child?

Is man nothing but a brainy child, amusing himself for ever with the printed toys called books?

That also. Even the greatest men spend most of their time making marvellous fine toys. Like *Pickwick* or *Two on a Tower*.

But there is more to it.

Man is a thought-adventurer.

Man is a great venture in consciousness.

Where the venture started, and where it will end, nobody knows. Yet here we are-a long way gone already, and no glimpse of any end in sight. Here we are,

书 话

书只是玩具，思想的玩具吗？

那，人是什么呢？是永远聪明的孩童吗？

难道人只是个聪明的孩童，永远用一种印刷的玩具自娱自乐？那玩具叫书。

还有，甚至那些大伟人也花去他们的大部分时间制造精美绝伦的玩具，如《匹克威克》(**Pickwick**)[狄更斯的小说。劳伦斯认为这书“不怎么样”]或《一塔双人》(**Two ona Tower**) [哈代的小说。劳伦斯对此书评价不高]。

但不仅如此。

人是思想中的一大赌注。

miserable Israel of the human consciousness, having lost our way in the wilderness of the world's chaos, giggling and babbling and pitching camp. We needn't go any further.

All right, let us pitch camp, and see what happens. When the worst comes to the worst, there is sure to be a Moses to set up a serpent of brass. And then we can start off again.

Man is a thought-adventurer. He has thought his way down the far ages. He used to think in little images of wood or stone. Then in hieroglyphs on obelisks and clay rolls and papyrus. Now he thinks in books, between two covers.

The worst of a book is the way it shuts up between covers. When man had to write on rocks and obelisks, it was rather difficult to lie. The daylight was too strong. But soon he took his venture into caves and secret holes and temples, where he could create his own environment and tell lies to himself. And a book is an underground hole with two lids to it. A perfect place to tell lies in.

Which brings us to the real dilemma of man in his long adventure with consciousness. He is a liar. Man is a liar unto himself. And once he has told himself a lie, round and round he goes after that lie, as if it was a bit of phosphorus on his

人是意识中的一大赌注。

这赌注从何开始又将止于何处,没人知道。不过我们已经走了很远,还是看不到终点。我们现在正是人类意识之痛苦的犹太人(Israel),在世界的混乱荒野中迷了路,嘻嘻傻笑着安营扎寨。就此打住,不必再往前走。

好吧,就让我们扎寨,看看会怎么样吧。当事情变得不能再坏的时候,肯定会出现一个摩西,他会竖起一个铜做的蛇[离开埃及后,以色列人“在荒野中度过了四十年”。见《旧约·申命记》第八章,第二节和《旧约·民数记》第二十一章,第九节]。于是我们便可以重新出发了。

人是思想的冒险家,他多少个世纪以来一直在思想。他曾借助小木头人和小石头人思想。再后来是借助象形文字(写在方尖碑上、黏土上和纸莎草上)来思想。现在他在书中、在封面和封底之间思想。

书之最害人处在于它用封面和封底把东西封闭起来。当人不得不在石头上和方尖碑上写字时,他是很难撒谎的。白天的光线太亮了。后来他就钻进山洞里,秘密的洞里和庙宇中,在那里他可以创造自己的环境去撒谎。书正是一个地下的洞,还带有两个盖子,是个绝好的撒谎地点。

nose-end. The pillar of cloud and the pillar of fire wait for him to have done. They stand silently aside, waiting for him to rub the *ignis fatuus* off the end of his nose. But man, the longer he follows a lie, becomes all the surer he sees a light.

The life of man is an endless venture into consciousness. Ahead goes the pillar of cloud by day, the pillar of fire by night, through the wilderness of time. Till man tells himself a lie, another lie. Then the lie goes ahead of him, like the carrot before the ass.

There are, in the consciousness of man, two bodies of knowledge: the things he tells himself, and the things he finds out. The things he tells himself are nearly always pleasant, and they are lies. The things he finds out are usually rather bitter to begin with.

Man is a thought-adventurer. But by thought we mean, of course, discovery. We don't mean this telling himself stale facts and drawing false deductions, which usually passes as thought. Thought is an adventure, not a trick.

And of course it is an adventure of the whole man, not merely of his wits. That is why one cannot quite believe in Kant, or Spinoza. Kant thought with his head and his spirit, but he never thought with his blood. The blood also thinks, inside a

让我们回过头来说说人之长久的思想探险中陷入的真正两难之境。人是个撒谎者，是个自欺欺人的骗子。他对自己说个谎言，然后围着谎言打转转，似乎那谎言是他鼻子上的一点磷光。云柱和火柱[见《圣经·出埃及记》第十三章，第二十一节："日间，耶和华在云柱中为他们领路；夜间，在火柱中光照他们。"]等待着他结束谎言，它们默默地等在一边，等他抹掉鼻尖上的那点鬼火。可是人，他追随谎言时间越久，他越相信他看到了光芒。

人的一生就是一场在意识中无休止的探险。他的前方，白天是云柱，夜间是火柱，穿越过时光的荒野。他对自己撒一个又一个的谎，从而这谎言就先行引路，就像一只胡萝卜摆在一头驴面前一样。

在人的意识中有两种知识：一种是他自己告知自己的，另一种是他所发现的。他告知自己的东西几乎永远令人愉快，这就是谎言。而他们发现的东西则一般来说是很痛苦的。

人是思想的冒险家。所谓思想，我们当然指的是发现，而不是指对自己讲些发了霉的事实并做些虚假的演绎——后者常常被当成是思想。思想是一种探险而非耍花招儿。

man, darkly and ponderously. It thinks in desires and revulsions, and it makes strange conclusions. The conclusion of my head and my spirit is that it would be perfect, this world of men, if men all loved one another. The conclusion of my blood says nonsense, and finds the stunt a bit disgusting. My blood tells me there is no such thing as perfection There is the long endless venture into consciousness down an ever dangerous valley of days.

Man finds his head and his spirit have led him wrong. We are at present terribly off the track, following our spirit, which says how nice it would be if everything was perfect, and listening to our head, which says we might have everything perfect if we would only eliminate the tiresome reality of our obstinate blood-being.

We are sadly off the track, and we're in a bad temper, like a man who has lost his way. And we say: I'm not going to bother. Fate must work it out.

Fate doesn't work things out. Man is a thought-adventurer, and only his adventuring in thought rediscovers a way.

Take our civilization. We are in a tantrum because we don't really like it now we've got it. There we've been building it for a thousand years, and built it so big we can't shift it. And we hate it, after all.

当然这是一个人全身心投入的探险，并非仅仅是智慧的探险。正因此，人们无法十分信服康德或斯宾诺莎[作为理性主义和理想主义哲学家，斯宾诺莎(Spinoza，1632—1677)或康德(Kant，1724—1804)都不受劳伦斯的推崇。劳伦斯认为："我们的头脑可以出毛病，可我们的血液之所感、所信和所言却总是真切的。"]。康德只用头脑和精神思想，但从不用血液思想。其实人的血液也在冥冥中沉重地思想着，它在欲望和情感剧变中思想着，会得出奇特的结论来。我的头脑和我的精神得出的结论是，这个人的世界，如果人们相爱着[见《新约·约翰福音》第十五章，第二节]，就会变得完美。可我的血液却认为这想法是胡说八道，并指出这一招很有点叫人恶心。我的血液告诉我，就没有完美这回事。有的只是在意识中无休止的探险，走过的是永远危险的时光峡谷。

人会发现他的头脑和精神给他领错了路。眼下我们就十分可怕地偏离了轨道，只顾追着精神走了——精神说如果每件事物都完美那该多好；只顾倾听头脑的——头脑说只要我们摒弃我们血的存在这顽固而又讨厌的真实，我们就可以让任何事物都完美起来。

我们十分沮丧地偏离了轨道，还在大发脾气，正像一个迷途的人那

Too bad! What's to be done?

Why, there's nothing to be done! Here we are, like sulky children, sulking because we don't like the game we're playing, feeling that we've been made to play it against our will. So play it we do, badly, in the sulks.

We play the game badly, so of course it goes from bad to worse. Things go from bad to worse.

All right, let'em! Let'em go from bad to worse. *Aprés moi le déluge*.

By all means! But a *deluge* presupposes a Noah and an Ark. The old adventurer on the old adventure.

When you come to think of it, Noah matters more than the *deluge*, and the ark is more than all the world washed out.

Now we've got the sulks, and are waiting for the flood to come and wash out our world and our civilization. All right, let it come. But somebody's got to be ready with Noah's Ark.

We imagine, for example, that if there came a terrible crash and terrible bloodshed over Europe, then out of the crash and bloodshed a remnant of regenerated souls would inevitably arise.

样。我们在说:我才不找那麻烦,命运会解决问题的。

命运并不会解决问题。人是思想的冒险家,而且只有在思想中的探险能替自己找到出路。

就说我们的文明吧。我们在发脾气,是因为我们虽得到了它却并不真的喜欢它。我们为它营造了几千年,把它建设得如此庞大以至于我们都挪不动它了。总之我们恨它。

太糟糕了!怎么办?

怎么办?没辙!我们像恼怒的孩童,恼怒,是因为我们不喜欢正玩着的游戏,深感那是被迫玩的。于是我们玩得了无情趣,满心的恼火。

我们玩不好这游戏,越玩越坏。事情也就越变越糟。

好吧,由它们去!让它们每况愈下吧!我死后发洪水,与我何干?

没错!不过,有洪水必有挪亚方舟(**Noah and an Ark**)。这是旧式探险中的探险家。

想到此,你会认为挪亚比洪水重要,方舟比冲走的整个世界都重要。

我们现在怒了,在等待洪水的到来,冲走我们的世界和我们的文明。

We are mistaken; if you look at the people who escaped the terrible times of Russia, you don't see many regenerated souls. They are more scared and senseless than ever. Instead of the great catastrophe having restored them to manhood, they are finally unmanned.

What's to be done? If a huge catastrophe is going only to unman us more than we are already unmanned, then there's no good in a huge catastrophe. Then there's no good in anything, for us poor souls who are trapped in the huge trap of our civilization.

Catastrophe alone never helped man. The only thing that ever avails is the living adventurous spark in the souls of men. If there is no living adventurous spark, then death and disaster are as meaningless as tomorrow's newspaper.

Take the fall of Rome. During the Dark Ages of the fifth, sixth, seventh centuries A.D., the catastrophes that befell the Roman Empire didn't alter the Romans a bit. They went on just the same, rather as we go on to-day, having a good time when they could get it, and not caring. Meanwhile Huns, Goths, Vandals, Visigoths, and all the rest wiped them out.

With what result? The flood of barbarism rose and covered Europe from end to

好吧，让它来。不过，总有人要准备上挪亚方舟。

比如，我们想像，如果来一场可怕的冲突并血洗欧洲，冲突与血洗之后注定会有残存的人再生。

我们错了。看看那些可怕的俄国时代的幸存者吧，你从中很难发现再生的人。他们比以往更恐惧、更失魂落魄。大灾大难非但没有让他们还原成人，反而最终让他们失去了人之勇气。

怎么办？如果说一场大灾难只会使我们比现在更懦弱，这大灾难还有什么好？于是，就再也没有什么算得上好了。因为我们这些可怜的人正被困在我们文明的巨大笼子中。

仅仅灾难本身从没对人有所帮助。对人惟一有所帮助的是人之灵魂中冒险的火花。假如没有这活生生的冒险火花，那么死亡与灾难就都如同明日的报纸一样毫无意义。

就说罗马的灭亡吧。公元后五、六、七世纪那段“蒙昧时代”(**Dark Ages**)里使罗马帝国(**the Roman Empire**)灭顶的灾难并未动摇罗马人一根毫毛。他们仍像我们今天一样今朝有酒今朝醉，一派满不在乎的样子。而

end.

But, bless your life, there was Noah in his Ark with the animals. There was young Christianity. There were the lonely fortified monasteries, like little arks floating and keeping the adventure afloat. There is no break in the great adventure in consciousness. Throughout the howlingest deluge, some few brave souls are steering the ark under the rainbow.

The monks and bishops of the Early Church carried the soul and spirit of man unbroken, unabated, undiminished over the howling flood of the Dark Ages. Then this spirit of undying courage was fused into the barbarians, in Gaul, in Italy, and the new Europe began. But the germ had never been allowed to die.

Once all men in the world lost their courage and their newness, the world would come to an end. The old Jews said the same: unless in the world there was at least one Jew passionately praying, the race was lost.

So we begin to see where we are. It's no good leaving everything to fate. Man is an adventurer, and he must never give up the adventure. The venture is the venture: fate is the circumstance around the adventurer. The adventurer at the quick of the venture is the living germ inside the chaos of circumstance. But for the living

灭了他们的是匈奴人(Huns),哥特人(Goths),汪达尔人(Vandals)和西哥特人(Visigoths)等等。

其结果呢? 野蛮之洪水涨潮,彻底淹没了欧洲。

不过幸运的是,还有挪亚带着他的动物躲入了方舟。有年轻的基督教,还有孤独但固若金汤的修道院像一艘艘小小的方舟在洪水上漂泊从而继续着思想的探险。思想的探险没有中断。就在那场惨绝人寰的大洪水中,有几个勇敢的人硬是在虹[《圣经》上说,虹是上帝与尘世订下永约的标记,保佑尘世不被洪水灭顶]之下驾着方舟与洪水搏斗。

早期教会的僧侣和主教们在蒙昧时代的大洪水中支撑着人之灵魂与精神,教它不折不屈不灭。以后这不死的勇气精神融入了野蛮人,同化了高卢人(Gaul)和意大利人,随之出现了新的欧洲。但这精神的萌芽却一直生生不死。

一旦世人失去了其勇气和创新,这世界就算走到头了。古犹太人也说过同样的话:只要这世上还有哪怕一个犹太人(Jew)激情地祈祷,这个种族就不会灭亡。

germ of Noah in his Ark, chaos would have redescended on the world in the waters of the flood. But chaos couldn't redescend, because Noah was afloat with all the animals.

The same with the Christians when Rome fell. In their little fortified monasteries they defended themselves against howling invasions, being too poor to excite much covetousness. When wolves and bears prowled through the streets of Lyons, and a wild boar was grunting and turning up the pavement of Augustus's temple, the Christian bishops also roved intently and determinedly, like poor forerunners, along the ruined streets, seeking a congregation. It was the great adventure, and they did not give it up.

But Noah, of course, is always in an unpopular minority. So, of course, were the Christians, when Rome began to fall. The Christians now are in a hopelessly popular majority, so it is their turn to fall.

I know the greatness of Christianity: it is a past greatness. I know that, but for those early Christians, we should never have emerged from the chaos and hopeless disaster of the Dark Ages. If I had lived in the year 400, pray God, I should have been a true and passionate Christian. The adventurer.

由此我们知道自己的所在了。不能把一切都交给命运。人是冒险者，他永远也不应放弃探险。冒险就是冒险，命运不过是冒险周围的环境。冒险中心的冒险家就是混乱环境中的一棵萌芽。若不是因了方舟中挪亚那活生生的萌芽，混乱还会让大洪水重降世上。但混乱无法重降，因为挪亚同所有的生灵一起漂浮着。

罗马陷落时，基督教徒们也遇上过同样的情境。面对野蛮人的入侵，他们躲入坚固的小修道院中自卫，已经可怜到没有占有欲的地步。当狼和熊横扫里昂的大街，当一只野猪呼哧着掀翻奥古斯都大帝庙宇里铺砖的路面，基督教主教们仍然专心致志、毫不动摇地在被践踏过的街上漫游，寻找着教友。这是一大冒险，但他们没有放弃。

当然，挪亚总是少数派。同样，当罗马帝国开始陷落时，基督教徒也是少数派。现在，基督教徒不可救药地成了多数，是该他们灭顶的时候了。

我了解基督教的伟大，那是过去的伟大。我懂这个。若不是因为有了那些早期的基督教徒们，我们永远也不会逃脱蒙昧时代的混乱与灾难。

But now I live in 1924, and the Christian venture is done. The adventure is gone out of Christianity. We must start on a new venture towards God.

假如我生活在公元 400 年，上帝保佑，我会是个真正热情的基督教徒，一个冒险家。

可我现在是在 1924 年，基督教的探险已经完成。这探险已经与基督教无干。我们必须踏上新的探险之路，向着上帝。

1924 年

Art and Morality

It is part of the common clap-trap, that "art is immoral." Behold everywhere artists running to put on jazz underwear, to demoralise themselves: or at least, to *débourgeoiser* themselves.*

For the bourgeois is supposed to be the fount of morality. Myself, I have found artists far more morally finicky.

Anyhow, what has a water-pitcher and six insecure apples on a crumpled tablecloth got to do with bourgeois morality? Yet I notice that most people, who have not learnt the trick of being arty, feel a real moral repugnance for a Cézanne* still-life. They think it is not right.

For them, it isn't.

Yet how can they feel, as they do, that it is subtly immoral?

The very same design, if it was humanised, and the tablecloth was a draped

艺术与道德

人们爱哗众取宠说"艺术无行"。你看看吧,这世上的艺术家们,争先恐后地穿上爵士乐手短打,一副很无行的样子。这至少是要把他们自己与中产阶级区分开来[20世纪20年代,艺术家们往往着装鲜艳夺目,以反传统和耸人听闻著称,以求有别于中产阶级的市俗气]。

中产阶级据说是道德的神圣守护者。而我个人则发现艺术家们过于道德了。

说到底,一块皱皱巴巴的桌布上摆一只水罐子和六只摇摇欲坠的苹果,这与中产阶级的道德有何干系?但我注意到了,大多数不谙艺术之道的人面对这类塞尚[Paul Cézanne,1839—1906,法国后期印象主义绘画大师]的静物写生

nude and the water-pitcher a nude semi-draped, weeping over the draped one, would instantly become highly moral. Why?

Perhaps from painting better than from any other art we can realise the subtlety of the distinction between what is dumbly felt to be moral, and what is felt to be immoral. The moral instinct of the man in the street.

But instinct is largely habit. The moral instinct of the man in the street is largely an emotional defence of an old habit.

Yet what can there be, in a Cézanne still-life, to rouse the aggressive moral instinct of the man in the street? What ancient habit in man do these six apples and a water-pitcher succeed in hindering?

A water-pitcher that isn't so very much like a water-pitcher, apples that aren't very appley, and a tablecloth that's not particularly much of a tablecloth. I could do better myself!

Probably! But then, why not dismiss the picture as a poor attempt? Whence this anger, this hostility? The derisive resentment?

Six apples, a pitcher, and a tablecloth can't suggest improper behaviour. They don't—not even to a Freudian. If they did, the man in the street would feel much

确会生出道德上的反感。他们认为他画得不对。

对他们来说,这不是画。

可凭什么就要说这画有点不道德呢?

同样的设计,如果把它弄成人的模样,把垂落的桌布变成裸体人像,把水罐子也设计成一个哭泣着的裸体人,那就十分道德了。为什么?

可能绘画比其他艺术形式更能让我们意识到什么让人感到是道德的或不道德的,这种感觉的区别是很微妙的。这是普通人的道德本能。

但是,本能主要是一种习惯。普通人的道德主要是对一种旧习惯的情绪化护卫。

可是,塞尚的静物写生中哪一点激怒了普通人的道德本能?那六只苹果和水罐子怎么妨碍人们的古旧习惯了?

那画上的水罐子不怎么像水罐子,苹果也不像苹果,桌布更不像桌布。我可以画得比塞尚像!

可能!可你为什么不拿塞尚的画当成一个败笔看?哪儿来的这股怒气和敌视?哪儿来的这种可笑的反感情绪?

more at home with them.

Where, then, does the immorality come in? Because come in it does.

Because of a very curious habit that civilised man has been forming down the whole course of civilisation, and in which he is now hardboiled. The slowly-formed habit of seeing just as the photographic camera sees.

You may say, the object reflected on the retina is always photographic. It may be. I doubt it. But whatever the image on the retina may be, it is rarely, even now, the photographic image of the object which is actually taken in by the man who sees the object. He does not, even now, see for himself. He sees what the kodak* has taught him to see. And man, try as he may, is not a kodak.

When a child sees a man, what does the child take in, as an impression? Two eyes, a nose, a mouth of teeth, two straight legs, two straight arms: a sort of hieroglyph, which the human child has used through all the ages, to represent man. At least, the old hieroglyph was still in use when I was a child.

Is this what the child actually *sees*?

If you mean by seeing, consciously registering, then this is what the child actually sees. The photographic image may be there all right, upon the retina. But

六只苹果,一只罐子和一张桌布是无法让人联想到不合时宜的行为的,甚至无法让一个弗洛伊德主义者产生这种联想。反之,如果它们有这等启发力,倒会使普通俗众们更心安理得地对待它们。

是否是在这节骨眼儿上闹出"不道德"来了?没错,是这样。

文明人在整个文明过程中形成了一种十分奇特的习惯,他已经让这习惯禁锢住了,这渐渐形成的习惯就是看什么都要像照相机一样准确无误。

你尽可以说,反射在视网膜上的东西总是像照片一样的呀。可能是吧。但我表示怀疑。不管视网膜上反射的是什么,它极难说就准是人所看到的那个东西。因为他并没有亲眼看见它,他看见的是"柯达"产品叫他看的东西。而人,无论怎样努力,也不会成为一件"柯达"产品[Kodak,柯达公司的照相机,这里泛指快照机]。

当一个孩子看见一个人,这个人给他的是什么印象?两只眼,一个鼻子,一张包着牙的嘴巴,两条腿和两只胳膊,像一幅象形文字画儿一般。小孩子们惯于用这形象来表示什么是人,至少我小时候是这么做的。

there the child leaves it: outside the door, as it were.

Through many ages, mankind has been striving to register the image on the retina as it is: no more glyphs and hieroglyphs. We'll have the real objective reality.

And we have succeeded. As soon as we succeed, the kodak is invented, to prove our success. Could lies come out of a black box, into which nothing but light had entered? Impossible! It takes life to tell a lie.

Colour also, which primitive man cannot really see, is now seen by us, and fitted to the spectrum.

Eureka! We have seen it, with our own eyes.

When we see a red cow, we see a red cow. We are quite sure of it, because the unimpeachable kodak sees exactly the same.

But suppose we had all of us been born blind, and had to get our image of a red cow by touching her, and smelling her, hearing her moo, and "feeling" her. Whatever should we think of her? Whatever sort of image should we have of her, in our dark minds? Something very different, surely!

As vision developed towards the kodak, man's idea of himself developed towards the snapshot. Primitive man simply didn't know what he was: he was always

难道这就是孩子确实看到的吗?

如果你把看当做是意识的记录,可以说,这是孩子的所见。照相式的印象可能准确地反射在视网膜上了,可孩子却置视网膜于不顾。

多少年代以来,人类努力要记录下视网膜上的准确印象,不要什么雕刻文字和象形文字,以为这样就能得到客观的真实了。

我们成功了。一经成功,就有"柯达"的诞生来证明我们的成功。谎言能从一只暗盒中出来吗?只需让光线进去就行吗?不可能!讲个谎言是需要付出生命的。

原始人看不见色彩,而我们现在看见了,还能把它们弄进光谱中去呢。

尤里卡!我们亲眼看到了。

见到一头红色的母牛,那就是红色。我们确信这一点,因为无懈可击的"柯达"看到的正是这种颜色。

可是,假如我们生来都是瞎子呢?我们不得不通过触摸、嗅觉、听觉和感觉来获得一头红牛的印象,那我们怎样认识这头牛呢?在我们那黑

half in the dark. But we have learned to see, and each of us has a complete kodak-idea of himself.

You take a snap of your sweetheart, in the field among the buttercups, smiling tenderly at the red cow with a calf, and dauntlessly offering a cabbage-leaf.

Awfully nice, and absolutely "real." There is your sweetheart, complete in herself, enjoying a sort of absolute objective reality: complete, perfect, all her surroundings contributing to her, incontestable. She is really "a picture."

This is the habit we have formed: of visualising *everything*. Each man to himself is a picture. That is, he is a complete little objective reality, complete in himself, existing by himself, absolutely, in the middle of the picture. All the rest is just setting, background. To every man, to every woman, the universe is just a setting to the absolute little picture of himself, herself.

This has been the development of the conscious ego in man, through several thousand years: since Greece first broke the spell of "darkness." Man has learnt to see himself. So now, he is what he sees. He makes himself in his own image.

Previously, even in Egypt, men had not learned to see straight. They fumbled in the dark, and didn't quite know where they were, or what they were. Like men

暗的头脑中它是什么样子？截然不同，的的确确不同！

视觉在向“柯达”发展，人对自己的认识也向快照发展了。原始人简直不知道他是什么样子，因为他总是一半在黑暗之中的。但我们学会了看自己，对自己有了一个全面的“柯达”式概念。

在花草丛中你给你的甜妞儿拍一张快照，照下她温柔地微笑着给红母牛和小牛犊递上一片白菜叶子。

这十分漂亮，而且绝对“真实”。照片上，你的情人很完整，正欣赏着一种绝对客观的真实。完整完美的环境让她看上去更为完美，她真的变成了“一幅画”。

这就是我们养成的习惯：让任何事物都变成可视的图像。每个人对自己来说都是一帧照片，这就是说他是一个小小的完整的客观真实，那个真实完全自立存在着，就存在于那帧照片中，其余的只是背景。对每个男人和女人来说，宇宙不过是他/她自己那帧小照的背景。

这是几千年来人之理性自我发展的结果。是希腊人最早冲破“黑暗”之魔力的，从那以后，人就学会了如此看自己。现在嘛，他就是他看到的

in a dark room, they only *felt* their own existence surging in the darkness of other existences.

We, however, have learned to see ourselves for what we are, as the sun sees us. The kodak bears witness. We see as the All-seeing Eye sees, with the universal vision. And we *are* what is seen: each man to himself an identity, an isolated absolute, corresponding with a universe of isolated absolutes. A picture! A kodak snap, in a universal film of snaps.

We have achieved universal vision. Even God could not see differently from what we see: only more extensively, like a telescope, or more intensively, like a microscope. But the same vision. A vision of images which are real, and each one limited to itself.

We behave as if we had got to the bottom of the sack, and seen the Platonic Idea with our own eyes, in all its photographically-developed perfection, lying in the bottom of the sack of the universe. Our own ego!

The identifying of ourselves with the visual image of ourselves has become an instinct; the habit is already old. The picture of me, the me that is seen, is me.

As soon as we are supremely satisfied about it, somebody starts to upset us.

自己那个样子,他是在他自己的图像中造就着自己。

以前,甚至在古埃及,人们也没学会如此直观地看。他们在黑暗中摸索,仍搞不清他们身处何方,他们是谁。正像人在黑暗的屋子里那样,他们只能在别人的黑暗存在中随之涌动,从而感觉到自己的存在。

可我们现在学会了看自己的模样,正像太阳看我们那样。"柯达"是一个见证。我们像万能之眼一样看自己,用的是全世界通用的眼光,从而我们是我们看到的自己。每个人在自己眼中都是一个与自己相同的人,一个孤独的整体,与一个孤独整体们的世界相呼应。一张照片!一张"柯达"快照,用的是通用的快照相纸。

我们终于获得了通用的眼光, 甚至上帝的眼光都与我们的无所区别,我们的只能更广远,像望远镜,或更专注,像显微镜。但这目光是一样的,是图像的目光,是有限的。

我们似乎探到了口袋的底部,亲眼看到了柏拉图式的理想被照片完美地表达出来,躺在宇宙这条大麻袋的最下面,这就是我们的自我!

把我们自己与我们的照片相等同已经变成了一种本能,这种习惯已

Comes Cézanne with his pitcher and his apples, which not only are not life-like, but are a living lie. The kodak will prove it.

The kodak will take all sorts of snaps, misty, atmospheric, sundazed, dancing—all quite different. Yet the image is the image. There is only more or less sun, more or less vapor, more or less light and shade.

The All-seeing Eye sees with every degree of intensity and in every possible kind of mood; Giotto, Titian, El Greco, Turner, all so different, yet all the true image in the All-seeing Eye.

This Cézanne still-life, however, is contrary to the All-seeing Eye. Apples, to the eye of God, could not look like that, nor could a tablecloth, nor could a pitcher. So, it is *wrong*.

Because man, since he grew out of a personal God, has taken over to himself all the attributes of the Personal godhead. it is the all-seeing human eye which is now the Eternal Eye.

And if apples don't look like that, in any light or circumstance, or under any mood, then they shouldn't be painted like that.

Oh la-la-la! The apples are just like that, to me! cries Cézanne. They are

变得十分古老而成为本能。我的照片，被自己看到的我就是我。

就在我们对此十分满意的时候，偏偏有个人出来招人嫌，这就是塞尚。他画的什么水罐子和苹果，岂止是不像？简直就是活脱脱的谎言。“柯达”可以证明这一点。

“柯达”能拍各种快照，雾状的，气状的，强光的，跳跃状的，样样俱全。但是，照片毕竟只是照片而已，上面只是或强或弱的光，或轻或重的雾，或深或浅的影子。

所谓全能的眼能看出各种强度来，能看出各种情绪来。乔托 [Giotto di Bondone, 1267—1337, 意大利画家，以壁画著名]，提香[Titian, 1490—1576, 意大利画家，以宗教绘画著名]，埃尔·格里科[Greco, El, 1544—1614, 西班牙画家，以戏剧化用色而著名]和透纳[Turner, 1775—1851, 英国风景画家，绘画以奇特的光线而著名]，虽然各有千秋，但在“全能眼”看来都是真实的。

但塞尚的静物写生则与“全能眼”相反。在全知全能的上帝眼中，苹果不是塞尚画的那个模样，桌布和水罐子亦非如此，所以说塞尚画得不对。

like that, no matter what they look like.

Apples are always apples! says *Vox Populi*, *Vox Dei*.*

Sometimes they're a sin, sometimes they're a knock on the head, sometimes they're a bellyache, sometimes they're part of a pie, sometimes they're sauce for the goose—

And you can't see a bellyache, neither can you see a sin, neither can you see a knock on the head. Do paint the apple in these aspects, and you get—probably, or approximately—a Cézanne still-life.

What an apple looks like to an urchin, to a thrush, to a browsing cow, to Sir Isaac Newton, to a caterpillar, to a hornet, to a mackerel who finds one bobbing on the sea, I leave you to conjecture. But the All-seeing must have mackerel's eyes, as well as man's.

And this is the immorality in Cézanne: he begins to see more than the All-seeing Eye of humanity can possibly see, kodak-wise. If you can see in the apple a bellyache and a knock on the head, and paint these in the image, among the prettyness, then it is the death of the kodak and the movies, and must be immoral.

It's all very well talking about decoration and illustration, significant form, or

因为,人是由人化的上帝创造出来的,他继承了人化上帝的头脑,所谓"永恒的眼睛"与"全能眼"是一回事。

因此,如果在任何光线和情境中或在任何情绪下看它们都不像苹果,那就不该那么画。

哦——哦——哦!塞尚发话了,他喊着说在我眼中苹果就是那个模样儿!那就是苹果,管它看着像什么!

苹果就是苹果!大众的声音这样说。大众的声音就是上帝的声音[此处用的是拉丁语成语 Vox Populi, Vox Dei:大众的声音即上帝的声音。劳伦斯惯用这句话来表示对从众心理的反讽]。

有时苹果是一种罪孽,有时是冲脑袋上的一击,有时是肚子痛,有时像一只饼的一角,有时是鹅食的调料——

可你看不见肚子痛,看不见罪孽,看不见往头上的一击。如果你把苹果照这个路子画,你可能——大约就会画出塞尚的静物写生来。

在刺猬眼中苹果是什么样?在画眉鸟眼里呢?在吃草的牛眼里?在牛顿先生眼里?在毛毛虫、大黄蜂和鲭鱼眼中呢?你们自己猜吧。但是,那

tactile values, or plastique, or movement or space-compostiton or colour-mass relations, afterwards. You might as well force your guest to eat the menu card, at the end of the dinner.

What art has got to do, and will go on doing, is to reveal things in their different relationships. That is to say, you've got to see in the apple the bellyache, Sir Isaac's knock on the cranium, the vast moist wall through which the insect bores to lay her eggs in the middle, and the untasted unknown quality which Eve saw hanging on a tree. Add to this the glaucous glimpse that the mackerel gets as he comes to the surface, and Fantin Latour's apples* are no more to you than enamelled rissoles.

The true artist doesn't substitute immorality for morality. On the contrary, he always substitutes a finer morality for a grosser. And as soon as you see a finer morality, the grosser becomes relatively immoral.

The universe is like Father Ocean, a stream of all things slowly moving. We move, and the rock of ages moves. And since we move and move forever, in no discernible direction, there is no centre to the movement, as far as we can see. To us, the centre shifts at every moment. Even the pole-star ceases to sit on the pole. Al-

种“全能眼”则应该既有人的眼光也有鲭鱼的眼光才行。

塞尚的不道德即在于此——他比人的“全能眼”看到的还多，比“柯达”还聪明。若是你能在苹果身上看出肚子痛和脑袋受到的一击并把这些画得惟妙惟肖，那等于宣布了“柯达”和电影的死亡。因此你必属“无行”类无疑。

你尽可以大谈什么装饰、图解、意蕴形式、深厚质感、可塑性、动感、空间构成及杂色关系等术语，你甚至还可以在吃完一顿饭后迫使你的客人吃下菜单呢。

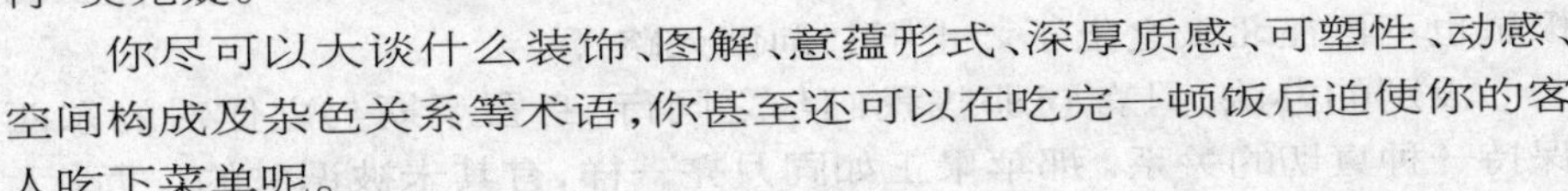

但艺术要做的并且要继续做的，是在不同的关系中揭示事物。这就是说，你应该在苹果中看出腹痛来，看出牛顿敲脑壳的感觉来，看到昆虫产卵时要冲破的巨大而湿润的屏障，看出夏娃未曾尝过的禁果的味道。如果再加上鲭鱼浮出水面时看到的灰蓝色，那么，方汀·拉多 [Ingnace Henri Jean Theodore Fantin-Latour，1836—1904，法国画家，以画静物和花卉著称]笔下的苹果相形之下可就跟炸肉卷儿差不多了。

真正的艺术家是不会用不道德取代道德的。相反，他们总是用更美

lons! there is no road before us!

There is nothing to do, but to maintain a true relationship to the things we move with and amongst and against. The apple, like the moon, has still an unseen side. The movement of Ocean will turn it round to us, or us to it.

There is nothing man can do, but maintain himself in true relationship to his contiguous universe. An ancient Rameses can sit in stone absolute, absolved from visual contact, deep in the silent ocean of sensual contact. Michael Angelo's Adam* can open his eyes for the first time, and see the old man in the skies, objectively. Turner can tumble into the open mouth of the objective universe of light, till we see nothing but his disappearing heels. As the stream carries him, each in his own relatedness, each one differently, so a man must go through life.

Each thing, living or unliving, streams in its own odd, intertwining flux, and nothing, not even man nor the God of man, nor anything that man has thought or felt or known, is fixed or abiding. All moves. And nothing is true, or good, or right, except in its own living relatedness to its own circumambient universe; to the things that are in the stream with it.

Design, in art, is a recognition of the relation between various things, various

好的取代粗糙的。一旦你看到更美好的道德，那原先粗糙一些的就相对成为不道德的了。

宇宙就如大海，百川终归大海。我们在动，岁月之石也在动。既然我们永不停息地在运动，向着某个并不明确的方向运动着，那也就没有什么运动中心这一说了。对我们来说，每动一下，中心就变动一次。甚至北极星也不再在北极之上了。走吧！前面无路了。

没别的办法，只有同那些我们与之同行、身置于斯与之作对的东西保持一种真切的关系。那苹果正如同月亮一样，有其未被识破的一面。大海的运动会教它转向我们或把我们甩到它的那一面去。

人没别的办法，只有与他周遭的世界保持真切的联系。一个古埃及的国王完全可坐着对一切视而不见，只在内心深处感受一切。米开朗基罗的亚当[此处指米开朗基罗(Michael Angelo)所作壁画，讲的是上帝创造人的故事。此画作于西斯廷教堂]能够首次睁开眼，客观地审视天上的这位老人。透纳可以跌跌撞撞冲出光的客观世界之口，我们只能看到他的脚后根儿。川流裹挟着每个关系各不相同的人，教人走过生命。

elements in the creative flux. You can't invent a design. You recognise it, in the fourth dimension. That is, with your blood and your bones, even more than with your eyes.

Egypt had a wonderful relation to a vast living universe, only dimly visual in its reality. The dim eye-vision and the powerful blood-feeling of the negro African, even today, gives us strange images, which our eyes can hardly see, but which we know are surpassing. The big, silent statue of Rameses is like a drop of water, hanging through the centuries in dark suspense, and never static. The African fetish-statues have no movement, visually represented. Yet one little motionless wooden figure stirs more than all the Parthenon frieze.* It sits in the place where no kodak can snap it.

As for us, we have our kodak-vision, all in bits that group or jig. Like the movies, that jerk but never move.* An endless shifting and rattling together of isolated images, "snaps," miles of them, all of them jigging, but each one utterly incapable of movement or change, in itself. A kaleidoscope of inert images, mechanically shaken.

And this is our vaunted "consciousness," made up, really, of inert visual im-

任何事物，有生命的还是没生命的，都随奇特混杂的川流而动，没有哪个人(甚至人的上帝)或哪个人自以为懂得的或有感触的事物是一成不变的。一切都在动。没什么是真、是善、是正确的，它们只是与周围世界及同流者活生生相连时才真、才善、才正确。

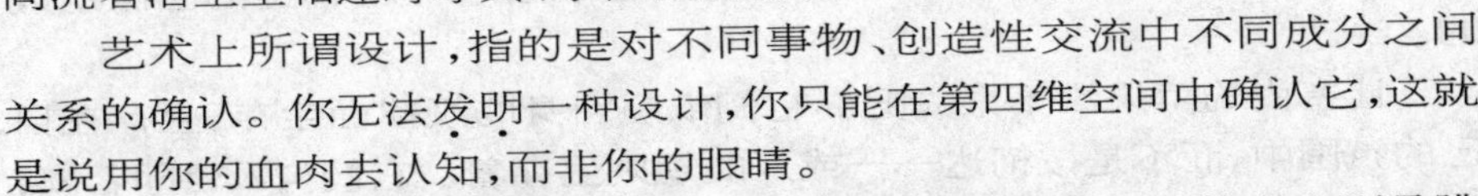

艺术上所谓设计，指的是对不同事物、创造性交流中不同成分之间关系的确认。你无法发明一种设计，你只能在第四维空间中确认它，这就是说用你的血肉去认知，而非你的眼睛。

埃及就与一种广大的活生生宇宙神奇地连在了一起，其真实则是朦胧的。非洲黑人的视觉模糊，可血的感知却强烈。甚至在今天，这种感知和眼光给予我们的都是奇异的形象，而我们的目光却看不出这些奇景，我们深知那是我们无法企及的。古埃及国王那沉默的巨大塑像就像穿越世纪的一滴水珠，从来不是静止的。那些非洲拜物神像并不会动，可这静止的小木头雕像却比巴台农神庙(**Parthenon**)的中楣更令人浮想联翩。它静处一方，任何柯达产品都无法用照片来表现它。

至于我们，我们有着柯达式的眼光，星星点点地聚合或闪动着，就如

ages and little else: like the cinematograph.

Let Cézanne´s apples go rolling off the table for ever. They live by their own laws, in their own ambiente, and not by the law of the kodak—or of man. They are casually related to man. But to those apples, man is by no means the absolute.

A new relationship between ourselves and the universe means a new morality. Taste the unsteady apples of Cézanne, and the nailed-down apples of Fantin Latour are apples of Sodom.* If the *status quo* were paradise, it would indeed be a sin to taste the new apples. But since the *status quo* is much more prison than paradise, we can go ahead.

同电影,它颤动但并非在真动[在此指早期电影的特征]。独立的图像在没完没了地变动晃悠,但其本身并不能运动和变化,这纯属惰性图像的万花筒,在机械地晃动。

这就是我们自以为是的“思想”,像摄影机那样是由惰性的图像组成的。

让塞尚的苹果滚下桌去吧。它们依照自身的规律而生存,生存在自己的氛围中,而不是按柯达——或人的规则生存着。它们与人若即若离,而人对它们来说远非一成不变。

我们与宇宙间崭新的关系意味着一种崭新的道德。去尝尝塞尚那远非稳定的苹果吧。方汀·拉多的稳定的苹果则是所多玛之果 [据古代传说,这是一种外表美丽,摘下便成灰烬的果子]。如果现状是个天堂,那么食禁果就是罪过了。可是,现状比监狱还坏,那我们只好去食塞尚之果了。

1925 年

The Novel

Somebody says the novel is doomed. Somebody else says it is the green bay tree getting greener. Everybody says something, so why shouldn't I!

Mr Santayana* sees the modern novel expiring because it is getting so thin; ——which means, Mr Santayana is bored.

I am rather bored myself. It becomes harder and harder to read the whole of any modern novel. One reads a bit, and knowe the rest; or else one doesn't want to know any more.

This is sad. But again, I don't think it's the novel's fault. Rather the novelists'.

You can put anything you like in a novel. So why do people always go on putting the same thing? Why is the *vol au vent* always chicken! Chicken *vol au vents* may be the rage. But who sickens first shouts first for somenthing else.

The novel is a great discovery: far greater than Galileo's telescope or somebody

David Herbert Lawrence

关于小说

有人说小说被判了死刑。又有人说小说本是一棵绿树,现在更青翠了。别人都在说三道四,我为什么不说上几句?!

在桑塔亚纳先生[George Santayana,1863—1952,美国哲学家,诗人,批评家。著有《美感》等多部名著]看来,小说之寿数已尽,因为小说越来越瘦弱了。这就是说桑塔亚纳先生对此厌烦了。

我自己也一样厌烦小说了。卒读一本现代小说越来越让人吃力了。只读一点儿就知道其他部分了;或者,根本就不想去知道。

这是件伤心的事。不过我再说一遍,这不怨小说,要怨的是小说家。

你喜欢什么都可以往小说里塞。难怪人们写得千篇一律了。怪不得一写馅饼就是鸡肉馅的!鸡肉馅儿饼可能是流行口味,可是总会吃腻的,第一个感到腻的人会第一个要求换口味。

小说是一大发现,比之伽利略的望远镜或别人的无线电都伟大。小

else's wireless. The novel is the highest form of human expression so far attained. Why? Because it is so incapable of the absolute.

In a novel, everything is relative to everything else, if that novel is art at all. There may be didactic bits, but they aren't the novel. And the author may have a didactic "purpose" up his sleeve. Indeed most great novelists have, as Tolstoi had his Christian-socialism, and Hardy his pessimism, and Flaubert his intellectual desperation. But even a didactic purpose so wicked as Tolstoi's or Flaubert's cannot put to death the novel.

You can tell me, Flaubert had a "philosophy," not a "purpose." But what is a novelist's philosophy but a purpose on a rather higher level? And since every novelist who amounts to anything has a philosophy—even Balzac—any novel of importance has a purpose. If only the "purpose" be large enough, and not at outs with the passional inspiration.

Vronsky* sinned, did he? But also the sinning was a consummation devoutly to be wished. The novel makes that obvious: in spite of old Leo Tolstoi. And the would-be-pious Prince in *Resurrection* is a muff,* with his piety that nobody wants or believes in.

说是迄今为止人类拥有的最高表现形式。为什么？因为它太无力表现绝对的东西了。

在小说中，一物与他物间的关系是相对的，这才叫艺术。里面或许有点儿说教，但它们绝算不得小说。作者很可能怀揣某种说教"企图"，不错，大多数大作家都这样，如托尔斯泰的基督教社会主义，哈代的悲观主义和福楼拜的精神绝望。但是，说教的企图再坏如托尔斯泰和福楼拜，它也不会毁灭小说的。

你可以对我说，福楼拜的说教不是企图而是一种"哲学"。但是，难道一个小说家的哲学不正是较高水准上的企图吗？如果说任何一位够格的小说家都心怀一种哲学(甚至巴尔扎克)，那么任何像样的小说都有一种企图，只要这"企图"十分巨大且与激情的灵感不冲突就行。

渥伦斯基[托尔斯泰名著《安娜·卡列尼娜》中安娜的情人]有罪，不是吗？但这种罪过也正是某种虔诚企求的完美实现。尽管老托尔斯泰不承认，可小说使之昭然。而《复活》中那个后来变得虔诚的公爵则是个大傻瓜，没人需要或相信他的虔诚[这里指的是聂赫留朵夫公爵。他曾在年轻时诱奸了玛丝洛娃，后来又面对犯了罪的玛丝洛娃起了忏悔之心]。

There you have the greatness of the novel itself. It won't let you tell didactic lies, and put them over. Nobody in the world is anything but delighted when Vronsky gets Anna Karenin. Then what about the sin?—Why, when you look at it, all the tragedy comes from Vronsky's and Anna's fear of society. The monster was social, not phallic at all. They couldn't live in the pride of their sincere passion, and spit in Mother Grundy's eye.* And that, that cowardice, was the real "sin." The novel makes it obvious, and knocks all old Leo's teeth out. "As an officer, I am still useful. But as a man, I am a ruin," says Vronsky—or words to that effect. Well what a skunk, collapsing as a man and a male, and remaining merely as a social instrument; an "officer," God love us! —merely because people at the opera turn their backs on him! *—As if people's backs weren't preferable to their faces, anyhow!

And old Leo tries to make out, it was all because of the phallic sin. Old liar! Because where would any of Leo's books be, without the phallic splendour? And then to blame the column of blood, which really gave him all his life riches! The Judas! Cringe to a mingy, bloodless Society, and try to dress up that dirty old Mother Grundy in a new bonnet and face-powder of Christian-Socialism. Brothers

小说自身的伟大正在于此--它不许你说教撒谎,说教与谎言无法在小说中自圆其说。看到渥伦斯基把安娜·卡列尼娜追到了手,没人不为此高兴。可对待他们的罪过呢？整个悲剧是因为渥伦斯基和安娜害怕社交圈造成的。这魔鬼是社会魔鬼而绝非阳物(phallic)。他们无法为自己真诚的激情感到骄傲，不敢公然唾弃格隆迪大妈 [这个人物出自托马斯·莫顿(Thomas Morton,1764-1838)的小说,代表着假正经]们的清规戒律。正是这种懦弱才算得上真正的"罪过"——小说本身使之昭然若揭,让老托尔斯泰无话可说。"作为一个军官,我尚有用处。可作为一个人,我算废了。"渥伦斯基这样说。真是个卑鄙小人。作为一个人,一个男人他算完了,只剩下当一个社会工具的份儿了。"军官",上帝呀！他落到这步田地,仅仅是因为剧院里的人们冷落了他！ [这段话似乎是劳伦斯记错了而误写的。事实上是安娜在剧院里受到了上流社会的讥讽和冷落]似乎人们的肩背不如人们的脸让他觉得顺眼[这里是个双关语。背——back与turn back连用表示"冷落"]！

而老托尔斯泰试图说明这罪过是阳物之罪 [阳物即phallic,劳伦斯用这个词表达生命活力即男性力量]。老骗子！托尔斯泰的书哪一本没有这种阳物的辉煌？他倒咒骂起这血性的支柱来了,正是这东西赋予了他全部生命的财富！纯

indeed! Sons of a castrated Father!

The novel itself gives Vronsky a kick in the behind, and knocks old Leo's teeth out, and leaves us to learn.

It is such a bore that nearly all great novelists have a didactic purpose, otherwise a philosophy, directly opposite to their passional inspiration. In their passional inspiration, they are all phallic worshippers. From Balzac to Hardy, it is so. Nay, from Apuleius to E. M. Forster. Yet all of them, when it comes to their philosophy, or what they think they are, they are all crucified Jesuses. What a bore! And what a burden for the novel to carry!

But the novel has carried it. Several thousands of thousands of lamentable crucifixions of self-heroes and self-heroines. Even the silly duplicity of *Resurrection*, and the wickeder duplicity of *Salammbô*, with that flayed phallic Matho, tortured upon the Cross of a gilt Princess.*

You can't fool the novel. Even with man crucified upon a woman: his "dear cross." The novel will show you how dear she was: dear at any price. And it will leave you with a bad taste of disgust against these heroes who turn their women into a "dear cross," and ask for their own crucifixion.

粹是个犹大[Judas,《圣经》中背叛耶稣的门徒,通指叛徒]! 委身于一个卑贱又无血性的社会,还要用基督教社会主义的新帽子和脂粉来装扮那个肮脏的老大妈格隆迪。这些人真是一丘之貉! 同是一个阉父的儿子!

这部小说在渥伦斯基背后踹了一脚，从而敲掉了老托尔斯泰的牙，也给我们留下了反思的余地。

令人大为烦恼的是,几乎所有大作家的某种说教企图或哲学都与他们的激情灵感大相径庭。他们的激情灵感让他们成为阳物崇拜者,从巴尔扎克到哈代莫不如此。不,从艾普利乌斯[Apuleius,纪元二世纪罗马哲学家与讽刺家]到 E.M.福斯特[E.M.Forster, 1879—1970,英国作家,著有《印度之旅》等名著]都是。可是,一到他们的哲学或一想到他们自己，他们就全变成了十字架上的耶稣了。真讨厌! 小说竟然背负着如此的大包袱!

小说就这样背着包袱,背着可悲的十字架上成千上万自我英雄的男男女女。《复活》就是一部傻乎乎的复制品而已,更恶毒的复制品则属《萨朗波》[福楼拜的历史小说。小说把起义军首领马托写成一个正义阳刚的男性,与萨朗波真诚相爱],那里头被挖了心的马托(Matho)是个阳刚之人,他在珠光宝气的公主的十字架上大受刑罚。

You can fool pretty nearly every other medium. You can make a poem pietistic, and still it will be a poem. You can write Hamlet in drama: if you wrote him in a novel, he'd be half comic, or a trifle suspicious: a suspicious character, like Dostoevsky's Idiot.* Somehow, you sweep the ground a bit too clear in the poem or the drama, and you let the human Word fly a bit too freely. Now in a novel there's always a tom-cat, a black tom-cat that pounces on the white dove of the Word, if the dove doesn't watch it; and there is a banana-skin to trip on; and you know there is a water-closet on the premises. All these things help to keep the balance.

If, in Plato's *Dialogues*, somebody had suddenly stood on his head and given smooth Plato a kick in the wind, and set the whole school in an uproar, then Plato would have been put into a much truer relation to the universe. Or if, in the midst of the *Timaeus*, Plato had only paused to say: "And now, my dear Cleon*—(or whoever it was)—I have a belly-ache, and must retreat to the privy: this too is part of the Eternal Idea of man," then we never need have fallen so low as Freud.

And if, when Jesus told the rich man to take all he had and give it to the poor,* the rich man had replied: "All right, old sport! You are poor, aren't you? Come on, I'll give you a fortune. Come on! "—Then a great deal of snivelling and

你无法欺骗小说，就是让一个男人死在一个女人——他"亲爱的十字架"身上也骗不了小说。小说会教你看清她如何亲爱：付出任何代价。读后你会感到恶心，讨厌那种把女人变成他们的"亲爱十字架"并自愿钉死在十字架上的英雄好汉们。

你尽可以欺骗几乎任何一种别的文学形式。比如，你可以把一首诗写得很虔诚，它仍是一首诗。你可以用戏剧来写《哈姆雷特》，但如果你用小说来写哈姆雷特，他就有点喜剧色彩了，或许会把他写成陀思妥耶夫斯基笔下的"白痴"那样可疑的人物[陀氏小说《白痴》中的人物]。诗和戏剧，人们可以写得风扫残云般干净利落，尽可以让人类的字词无拘无束地飞翔。可在小说中总有一只雄猫，一只捕食字词这只白鸽的黑雄猫。白鸽稍不注意，猫就来扑食它。还有一块让人踩上去滑倒的香蕉皮。在这房基之上建有一个盥洗室。这些东西有助于保持平衡。

如果在柏拉图的《对话录》中有个什么人突然站在他头上偷偷地狠踢他一脚，并把他的学堂搅乱，那就会让柏拉图处在一个与宇宙较为真实的关系中。或者说，如果柏拉图在《蒂美厄斯》(Timaeus)中停下来说上一句："哦，我亲爱的克里昂(或随便什么人)，我肚子痛，得上厕所——这也

mistakenness would have been spared us all, and we might never have produced a Marx and a Lenin. If only Jesus had accepted the fortune!

Yes, it's a pity of pities that Matthew, Mark, Luke, and John didn't write straight novels. They did write novels; but a bit crooked. The Evangels are wonderful novels, by authors "with a purpose." Pity there's so much Sermon-on-the-Mounting.

"Matthew, Mark, Luke, and John

Went to bed with their breeches on! "—*

as every child knows. Ah, if only they'd taken them off!

Greater novels, to my mind, are the books of the Old Testament, Genesis, Exodus, Samuel, Kings, by authors whose purpose was so big, it didn't quarrel with their passional inspiration.* The purpose and the inspiration were almost one. Why, in the name of everything bad, the two ever should have got separated, is a mystery! But in the modern novel they are hopelessly divorced. When there is any inspiration there: to be divorced from.

This, then, is what is the matter with the modern novel. The modern novelist is possessed, hag-ridden, by such a stale old "purpose," or idea-of-himself, that his

是人之永恒理念的一部分啊。"[这里指柏拉图(Plato)《对话录》中的一段,出场人有四位]那样的话,我们就用不着像弗洛伊德[即心理学家弗洛伊德(Freud)。劳伦斯一直反对弗洛伊德的精神分析法,认为他代表理性主义]一样低下了。

如果,当耶稣要求那富人变卖他的所有并把它分给穷人[见《马太福音》第十九章,第二十一节。耶稣建议富人变卖财产救济穷人]时那富人说:"好吧,老兄!你不是穷吗?来,我把财产给你,来吧!"那我们就会省去多少悲啼少犯多少错误,我们也就用不着产生马克思和列宁这两位人物。如果耶稣接受了那笔财富该多好啊!

十足可惜的是,马太,马可,路加和约翰[马太(Mattew),耶稣十二门徒之一,著有《马太福音》。马可(Mark),《马可福音》的作者。路加(Luke),《路加福音》的作者。约翰(John),耶稣十二门徒之一,著有《约翰福音》]这四位不曾直抒胸臆来写小说。他们写过,但写得走了样。福音书是精妙的小说,但是一些"有目的"的作者写的,太可惜了,里头的布道太多。

马太,马可,路加和约翰,

穿着裤子上床![源自《马太福音》第五章。此为著名的顺口溜]

inspiration succumbs. Of course he denies having any didactic purpose at all: because a purpose is supposed to be like catarrh, something to be ashamed of. But he's got it. —They've all got it: the same snivelling purpose.

They're all little Jesuses in their own eyes, and their "purpose" is to prove it. Oh Lord! —Lord Jim! Sylvestre Bonnard! If Winter Comes! Main Street! Ulysses! Pan! *—They are all pathetic or sympathetic or antipathetic little Jesuses *accomplis or manqués*.* And there is a heroine who is always "pure," usually, nowadays, on the muck-heap! Like the Green Hatted Woman.* She is all the time at the feet of Jesus, though her behaviour there may be misleading. Heaven knows what the Saviour really makes of it: whether she's a Green Hat or a Constant Nymph* (eighteen months of constancy, and her heart failed), or any of the rest of'em. They are all, heroes and heroines, novelists and she-novelists, little Jesuses or Jesusesses. They may be wallowing in the mire: but then didn't Jesus harrow Hell! *A la bonne heure*! *

Oh, they are all novelists with an idea of themselves! Which is a "purpose," with a vengeance! For what a weary, false, sickening idea it is nowadays! The novel gives them away. They can't fool the novel.

每个孩子都会唱这几句。哦,他们脱了裤子该多好!

在我看来,更伟大的小说是《旧约》中的那些章节,《创世记》(Genesis),《出埃及记》(Exodus),《撒姆尔记》(Samuel)和《列王记》(Kings)等。那些作者们志向远大,其企图绝不与其激情的灵感相悖。两者几乎是一体,居然没有分开,这真叫奇怪!而在当代小说中它们则是分离的,毫无希望成为一体。

这就是现代小说的毛病。现代小说家被陈腐的"目的"或自我观念所约束,从而让灵感屈就了目的和观念。当然他会否认他有任何说教企图,因为企图像一种黏膜炎,令人难堪。可他就是患了这病,他们都患了这病,同样的病。

他们全以小耶稣自居,他们的企图就是证实这一点。天啊,《吉姆爷》(Lord Jim)[英国作家康拉德(1857—1924)的名著],《西尔维斯特·伯纳德》(Sylvestre Bonnard)[法国作家法郎士(1844—1924)的小说],《如果冬天将至》(If Winter Comes)[美国通俗小说家哈钦森(1879—1971)的小说],《大街》(Main Street)[美国作家刘易斯(1885—1951)的小说],《尤利西斯》(Ulysses)[英国作家乔伊斯的名作]和《潘》(Pan)[哈姆森(Knut Hamsun,1859—1952)的小说],全是些个悲悯的、同情的或恶毒的耶稣,或完美或

Now really, it´s time we left off insulting the novel any further. If your purpose is to prove your own Jesus qualifications, and the thin stream of your inspiration is "sin," then dry up, for the interest is dead. Life as it is! What´s the good of pretending that the lives of a set of tuppenny Green Hats and Constant Nymphs is Life-as-it-is, when the novel itself proves that all it amounts to is life as it is isn´t life, but a sort of everlasting and intricate and boring habit: of Jesus peccant and Jesusa peccante.

These wearisome sickening little personal novels! After all, they aren´t novels at all. In every great novel, who is the hero all the time? Not any of the characters, but some unnamed and nameless flame behind them all. Just as God is the pivotal interest in the books of the Old Testament. But just a trifle too intimate, too *frère et cochon*, there. In the great novel, the felt but unknown flame stands behind all the characters, and in their words and gestures there is a flicker of the presence. If you are too personal, too human, the flicker fades out, leaving you with something awfully lifelike, and as lifeless as most people are.

We have to choose between the quick and the dead. The quick is God-flame, in everything. And the dead is dead. In this room where I write, there is a little

尚有缺憾。小说中总有那么一个永远纯洁的女主角,却是一朵花插到了牛粪上!正像《绿帽女人》(Green Hatted Woman)[阿伦(Michael Arlen,1895—1956)的小说]一样,纯洁的女主角总是拜倒在耶稣脚下,尽管她的行为可能是误人歧途的。天知道救世主怎么看她们,不管她是谁。不管她们是绿帽女人还是永恒的仙女[见 1924 年出版的同名通俗小说,作者是 Magaret Kennedy (1896-1967)],还是别的谁。他们是一群男女主人公,男女小说家,男女基督。他们正在污泥中打着滚。基督不是在地狱中捞过东西吗?很好[据说耶稣复活时从地狱中救出了封藏的早期财富]!

他们都是有自我观念的小说家!他们的"目的"未免太过分了!这种观念是那么令人厌倦,那么虚假,那么令人作呕!小说抛弃了它们,它们骗不了小说。

现在是我们停止玷污小说的时候了。如果你的目的只是想证明你有资格做基督,而你灵感的细小溪流正在流向罪恶,那就让这小溪流干涸算了,因为它已经死了。还生活以本来面目!为什么要把廉价的"绿帽女人"和"永恒的仙女"之类的生活假作生活的真实?其实小说证实她们的生活绝非生活的本来面目,不过是没完没了的、复杂的、令人生厌的习

table that is dead: it doesn't even weakly exist. And there is a ridiculous little iron stove, which for some unknown reason is quick. And there is an iron wardrobe trunk, which for some still more mysterious reason is quick. And there are several books, whose mere corpus is dead, utterly dead and non-existent. And there is a sleeping cat, very quick. And a glass lamp, that, alas, is dead.

What makes the difference? *Quien sabe*! But difference there is. And I know it.

And the sum and source of all quickness, we will call God. And the sum and total of all deadness we may call human.

And if one tries to find out, wherein the quickness of the quick lies, it is in a certain weird relationship between that which is quick and—I don't know; perhaps all the rest of things. It seems to consist in an odd sort of fluid, changing, grotesque or beautiful relatedness. That silly iron stove somehow belongs. Whereas this thin-shanked table doesn't belong. It is a mere disconnected lump, like a cut-off finger.

And now we see the great, great merits of the novel. It can't exist without being "quick." The ordinary unquick novel, even if it be a best seller, disappears into absolute nothingness, the dead burying their dead with surprising speed. For even the dead like to be tickled. But the next minute, they've forgotten both the tickling

惯——病态的男基督或女基督。

这些个令人生厌、令人作呕的小说！它们根本不叫小说。在每部大作品中，有哪个人从头到尾都是英雄的？没有哪个人物是，从头到尾的英雄是人物背后无名的火焰，正如《旧约》中上帝是兴趣的中心一样，只是那里面的亲昵程度有点过火了。在大作品中，所有人物的背后是虽不可知但可感受到的火焰，在人物的语言和举止中闪烁着这火焰的一星星火花。如果你过于个性了，过于人情味了，这火花就会熄灭，你获得的就是某种类似生活实则毫无生气的东西，正如同大多数人一样。

我们必须在生死之间做出选择。生，就是上帝之火，存在于一切之中。死，即死物儿。在我写作的屋中，一张小桌子，它是死物，它甚至生气全无。还有一只可笑的小铁炉，但不知为什么，却是个活物；还有一只铁抽屉，天知道为什么它也是活物。另有几册书，全然已死。可那只睡着的猫却十二分有生气。那只玻璃灯则是个死物件了。如何区别生死？谁知道呢！可区别是有的，我知道。

如何区别生死？天知道！可区别是有的，我知道。

我们不妨称上帝是一切的生和生之源泉。人是一切的死。

and the tickler.

Secondly, the novel contains no didactive absolute. All that is quick, and all that is said and done by the quick, is, in some way, godly. So that Vronsky's taking Anna Karenin we must count godly, since it is quick. And that Prince in *Resurrection*, following the convict girl, we must count dead. The convict train is quick and alive. But that would-be-expiatory Prince is as dead as lumber.

The novel itself lays down these laws for us, and we spend our time evading them. The man in the novel must be "quick." And this means one thing, among a host of unknown meaning: it means he must have a quick relatedness to all the other things in the novel: snow, bed-bugs, sunshine, the phallus, trains, silk-hats, cats, sorrow, people, food, diphtheria, fuchsias, stars, ideas, God, tooth-paste, lightning, and toilet-paper. He must be in quick relation to all these things. What he says and does must be relative to them all.

And this is why Pierre, for example, in *War and Peace*,* is more dull and less quick than Prince André. Pierre is quite nicely related to ideas, tooth-paste, God, people, food, trains, silk-hats, sorrow, diphtheria, stars. But his relation to snow and sunshine, cats, lightning and the phallus, fuchsias and toilet-paper, is

如果你想发现生之精髓所在,它存在于生与未知物之间的超然关系中。它似乎存在于某种奇特的关系中,这是一种流动的、变化的、美好的关联。那可笑的铁炉子就说不清为什么属于生,可那细腿桌子就不算,它不过是一块孤零零的东西,像一只切掉的手指头。

现在我们明白小说的最大长处了。它没有"生气"就无法存在。普通无生气的小说,即便是畅销小说,照样沦为虚无。死物埋葬死物,速度之快,令人吃惊。死物也喜欢逗逗乐,可很快逗的和被逗的都会被忘却。

第二点,小说是不容什么说教和绝对的。任何有生命的东西及其所说和所做的,都有那么点儿神圣。所以,渥伦斯基占有安娜必定算得上神圣,因为这做法是富有生命力的。而《复活》中的那位女犯和那位公爵则该算死物儿了。那囚车是生气勃勃的,可那个要赎罪的公爵却像一截死木头桩子一样。

是小说自己为我们设下了这些个法规,可我们却花着时间去躲避它们。小说中的人物必须"有生气"。这句话的意思是:他必得与小说中别的东西之间有生命的联系——雪啦,臭虫啦,阳光啦,阴茎啦,火车啦,丝帽,猫,悲伤,人,吃喝,白喉,倒挂的金钟花,星星,观念,上帝,牙膏,闪电,

sluggish and mussy. He's not quick enough.

The really quick, Tolstoi loved to kill them off or muss them over. Like a true Bolshevist. One can't help feeling Natasha is rather mussy and unfresh, married to that Pierre.

Pierre was what we call, "so human." Which means, "so limited." Men clotting together into social masses in order to limit their individual liabilities: this is humanity. And this is Pierre. And this is Tolstoi, the philosopher with a very nauseating Christian-brotherhood idea of himself. Why limit man to a Christian-brotherhood? I myself, I could belong to the sweetest Christian-brotherhood one day, and ride after Attila with a raw beefsteak for my saddle-cloth,* to see the red cock crow in flame over all Christendom, next day.

And that is man! That, really, was Tolstoi. That, even, was Lenin, God in the machine of Christian-brotherhood, that hashes men up into social sausage-meat.

Damn all absolutes. Oh damn, damn, damn all absolutes! I tell you, no absolute is going to make the lion lie down with the lamb: unless, like the limerick, * the lamb is inside.

还有手纸什么的。人物与这些东西之间定要有一种活生生的关系,他所说所做的必得与它们有关才行。

正因此,像《战争与和平》[托尔斯泰的长篇小说]中的彼埃尔就比安德烈公爵缺少生气。彼埃尔与之保持细微关系的是观念,牙膏,上帝,人,食品,火车,丝帽,悲伤,白喉和星星这类东西。而他对别的东西就不敏感,如雪,阳光,猫,闪电,阴茎,倒挂的金钟花和手纸。总之他缺少生气。

托尔斯泰要扼杀的或混淆的正是那最有生命力的东西。这倒像个真正的布尔什维克。当我们看到娜塔莎嫁给了那个彼埃尔时,我们不禁会认为这女人糊涂,没新鲜味儿。

彼埃尔是那种我们称之为"太像人"的人。就是说他局限性太强。人们黏成社会的一群,就是为了限定每个人的责任,这就是人类。彼埃尔就是这种人。这也是托尔斯泰,一个鼓吹基督教博爱观念的哲学家。干吗要把人局限在基督教博爱上面? 至于我自己,某一天我会变成一个最可爱的基督教博爱者,学着阿蒂拉 [Attila,匈奴人的首领。劳伦斯在《欧洲历史演变》中曾把他们描绘成把肉当成马鞍,在人的胯下压熟]那样把一块生牛排铺在马背上当马鞍子,骑上去奔向基督的王国,第二天就能看到遍地是火红的公鸡,一个个在

"*They returned from the ride*
With lamb Leo inside
And a smile on the face of the tiger!
Sing fol-di-lol-lol!
Fol-di-lol-lol!
Fol-di-lol-ol-di-lol-olly! "

For man, there is neither absolute nor absolution. Such things should be left to monsters like the right-angled triangle, which does only exist in the ideal consciousness. A man can't have a square on his hypotenuse, let him try as he may.

Ay! Ay! Ay! —Man handing out absolutes to man, as if we were all books of geometry with axioms, postulates and definitions in front. God with a pair of compasses! Moses with a set-square! Man a geometric bifurcation, not even a radish!

Holy Moses!

"Honour thy father and thy mother! "—That's awfully cute! But supposing they are not honorable? How then, Moses?

Voice of thunder from Sinai:—"Pretend to honour them! "

"Love thy neighbour as thyself."*

打着鸣儿。

这就是人！真真的托尔斯泰。那甚至是列宁，是基督教博爱机器中的神，把人们都绞成肉去做社会香肠。

去他的绝对吧！我诅咒一切绝对，诅咒！告诉你吧，没有什么绝对之物可以让狮子与羊并卧在一起[见《圣经·以赛亚书》(Isaiah)第十一章，第六节]，除非像那首五行打油诗说的那样，那羊在狮子的肚子里[此诗是劳伦斯对一首通俗打油诗的模仿之作]。

他们骑马回到家，
列奥小羊肚中藏，
老虎脸上笑哈哈！
嘻嘻嘻，哈哈哈！
嘻嘻嘻嘻哈哈哈！

对人来说没有什么绝对或绝对物。这种事对有三个直角的三角形魔鬼说去吧，它只存在于理念之中。如果谁认为可以在三角形斜边上找出

Alas, my neighbour happens to be mean and detestable.

Voice of the lambent Dove, cooing: "Put it over him, that you love him."

Talk about the cunning of serpents! * I never saw even a serpent kissing his instinctive enemy.

Pfui! I wouldn't blacken my mouth, kissing my neighbour, who, I repeat, to me is mean and detestable.

Dove, go home!

Everything is relative. Every Commandment that ever issued out of the mouth of God or man, is strictly relative: adhering to the particular time, place and circumstance.

And this is the beauty of the novel; everything is true in its own relationship, and no further.

For the relatedness and interrelatedness of all things flows and changes and trembles like a stream, and like a fish in the stream the characters in the novel swim and drift and float and turn belly-up when they're dead.

So, if a character in a novel wants two wives—or three—or thirty: well, that is true of that man, at that time, in that circumstance. It may be true of other men,

个直角来,那就让他试试吧。

嘿!嘿!嘿!人把绝对的东西传给别人,似乎我们都是几何书,前面写着原理、规则和定义。上帝的圆规!摩西的三角板!人不过是几何图上的一个交叉点,连一只小萝卜都算不上!

神圣的摩西!

"孝敬汝父汝母!"[见《出埃及记》第二十章,第十二节]那当然不错,可假如他们并不体面呢?摩西,那又会怎么样?

西奈(Sinai)山上传来一声雷:"假装孝敬!"

"爱邻如爱己。"[见《马太福音》第十九章,第十九节]

完了,我的邻居碰巧是令人生厌的卑鄙小人。

那闪光的圣灵(Dove)低声说:"假装你爱他嘛。"

这是蛇的狡猾![见《马太福音》第十章,第十六节:"像蛇一样狡猾,像鸽子一样无害。"]可我从未见过蛇亲吻他的天敌。

呸!我才不亲吻我的邻居,他是个讨厌的卑鄙小人,亲他会脏了我的嘴。

圣灵,回家去吧。

elsewhere and elsewhen. But to infer that all men at all times want two, three, or thirty wives; or that the novelist himself is advocating furious polygamy;* is just imbecility.

It has been just as imbecile to infer that, because Dante worshipped a remote Beatrice,* every man, all men, should go worshipping remote Beatrices.

And that wouldn't have been so bad, if Dante had put the thing in its true light. Why do we slur over the actual fact that Dante had a cosy bifurcated wife in his bed, and a family of lusty little Dantinos? Petrarch, with his Laura in the distance,* had twelve little legitimate Petrarchs of his own, between his knees. Yet all we hear is Laura! Laura! Beatrice! Beatrice!

What bunk! Why didn't Dante and Petrarch chant in chorus:

"Oh be my spiritual concubine
Beatrice!
Laura!
My old girl's got several babies that are mine,
But thou be my spiritual concubine,
Beatrice!

的确是山羊与圆规[The Goat and Compasses 是 God encompasses(神的规矩)的委婉说法,见前面"上帝的圆规一说]!

任何事物都是相对的。上帝嘴中或人的嘴中发出的每一条戒律都是严格地相对的,与其特定的时间、地点和环境相关联。

这才是小说之美:每件事只在其自身的关系中才是真的,除此之外便不是真。

一切事物的关联和内在联系就如同溪水一样流淌,变化和震颤。就像溪水中的鱼儿一样,小说中的人物游水、随波逐流,死的时候也会肚皮朝上漂起来的。

因此,如果小说中的某个人物想娶个二三房老婆,甚至三十房,在他所处的时间和环境中那都算真切。别的男人在别处或别的时间里做这般想法那也可能是真情。可如果由此得出结论,说所有的男人在所有的时候都想要二三房或三十房老婆,或者说写这书的小说家本人就提倡疯狂的一夫多妻[当时正有人指责劳伦斯在小说《丛林少年》中宣扬了一夫多妻制],那可就愚不可及了。

若因但丁崇拜着远方的比阿特丽丝 [但丁的一系列诗中都表达了对比阿特丽丝

Laura! ”

Then there would have been an honest relation between all the bunch. Nobody grudges the gents their spiritual concubines. But keeping a wife and family—twelve children—up one's sleeve, has always been recognised as a dirty trick.

Which reveals how immoral the absolute is! Invariably keeping some vital fact dark! Dishonorable!

Here we come upon the third essential quality of the novel. Unlike the essay, the poem, the drama, the book of philosophy, or the scientific treatise: all of which may beg the question, when they don't downright filch it; the novel inherently is and must be:

1. Quick.
2. Interrelated in all its parts, vitally, organically.
3. Honorable.

I call Dante's *Commedia** slightly dishonorable, with never a mention of the cosy bifurcated wife, and the kids. And *War and Peace* I call downright dishonorable,

的爱。他九岁时见过她，十八岁时又见她一面]就推论说每个男人都该崇拜远方的比阿特丽丝，那同样是愚不可及。

如果但丁把这事说个明白，没什么不好。凭什么我们要含糊其辞掩盖事实呢？其实但丁床上有个姣好的老婆，养了一窝子健壮的小但丁。还有那个彼德拉克[Petrach，1265—1321，意大利著名诗人。他的一系列爱情诗都是给劳拉的]，怀念着远方的劳拉，可他膝下至少有十二个合法的小彼德拉克了。可我们听到的却只是他们在叫：“劳拉！”“劳拉！”“比阿特丽丝！”“比阿特丽丝！”

胡说八道，为什么但丁和彼德拉克不来一首这样的合唱。

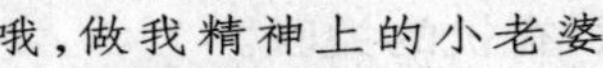

哦，做我精神上的小老婆
　比阿特丽丝！
　劳拉！
我那老伴儿给我生了一窝崽，
可你才是我精神上的小老婆，
　比阿特丽丝！
　劳拉！

with that fat, diluted Pierre for a hero, stuck up as preferable and desirable, when everybody knows that he wasn't attractive, even to Tolstoi.

Of course Tolstoi, being a great creative artist, was true to his characters. But being a man with a philosophy, he wasn't true to his own character.*

Character is a curious thing. It is the flame of a man, which burns brighter or dimmer, bluer or yellower or redder, rising or sinking or flaring according to the draughts of circumstance and the changing air of life, changing itself continually, yet remaining one single, separate flame, flickering in a strange world: unless it be blown out at last by too much adversity.

If Tolstoi had looked into the flame of his own belly, he would have seen that he didn't really like the fat, fuzzy Pierre, who was a poor tool, after all. But Tolstoi was a personality even more than a character. And a personality is a self-conscious I am: being all that is left in us of a once-almighty Personal God. So being a personality and an almighty I am, Leo proceeded delibeately to lionise that Pierre, who was a domestic sort of house-dog.

Doesn't anybody call that dishonorable on Leo's part? He might just as well have been true to himself! But no! His self-conscious personality was superior to

这些东西之间应该有一种诚实的关系。没人妒忌这些家伙有精神上的小老婆。但另一方面养着一个太太和一窝十二个孩子，这就让人觉着是一种肮脏的把戏了。

这说明"绝对"是多么不道德，它总是掩盖某种重要的事实，使其不见天日！欺骗！

由此，我们该谈到小说的第三种特性了。小说与散文、诗歌、戏剧、哲学著作和科学论文不同之处是：这些东西都可以用不切实的假定来辩论，而小说则是而且必须是：

①有生命。

②各部分有内在关联，是生命的关联、有机的关联。

③诚实的。

我称但丁的《神曲》有点不诚实，它从不提及但丁那娇妻及其儿女。而《战争与和平》则彻头彻尾地不诚实，书中那个肥胖而无聊的彼埃尔成了主角，把他树立成一个令人赞叹向往的形象，可事实上谁都知道他没有魅力，连托尔斯泰都吸引不了。

当然了，作为一个有创造力的大艺术家，托尔斯泰对他笔下的人物

his own belly and knees, so he thought he´d improve on himself, by creeping inside the skin of a lamb: the doddering old lion that he was! Leo! León! *

Secretly, Leo worshipped the human male, man as a column of rapacious and living blood. He could hardly meet three lusty, roisterous young guardsmen in the street, without crying with envy: and ten minutes later, fulminating on them black oblivion and annihilation, utmost moral thunder-bolts.*

How boring, in a great man! And how boring, in a great nation like Russia, to let its old-Adam manhood be so improved upon by these reformers, who all feel themselves short of something, and therefore live by spite, that at last there´s nothing left but a lot of shells of men, improving themselves steadily emptier and emptier, till they rattle with words and formulae, as if they´d swallowed the whole encyclopædia of socialism.

But wait! There is life in the Russians.

Count Tolstoi had that last weakness of a great man: he wanted the absolute: the absolute of love, if you like to call it that. Talk about the "last infirmity of noble minds"! It´s a perfect epidemic of senility. He wanted to be absolute: a universal brother. Leo was too tight for Tolstoi. He wanted to puff, and puff, and puff, till he

是真诚的。可作为一个有着自己哲学观点的人,他对自己的脾性是不忠诚的[在此人物与脾性英文都是 Character]。

脾性是个怪东西。它是人之火,或燃得明亮或燃得黯淡,或蓝或黄或红,升腾或泯灭或恍惚,全依照情境之风势和生命之气不断变幻。但它永远是一束独特的火光,在一个奇特的世界里闪烁——除非它被太厉害的蹇运所扑灭。

如果托尔斯泰曾细看一眼他体内这束火焰,他就会看到,他并不喜欢那个肥胖、面相模糊的彼埃尔,这人不过是个可怜的工具罢了。可是,托尔斯泰更是个存在。所谓存在就是有自我意识"我是"的人,即万能的上帝在我们身上的遗迹。作为这样的人,他有意美化了彼埃尔,一只看家狗而已。

会不会有人称列奥(托尔斯泰的名字)不诚? 他可能会很忠实于他自己! 可他不! 他作为有自我意识的人比他自身的腹和膝更重要。他要使自己变完美些,于是他披上了羊皮,蹒跚的老狮子,他就是列奥! 列奥! 列奥 [此处列奥的名字与狮子(lion)拼写和发音都相似]!

列奥偷偷地崇拜着男性,视其为一根强取豪夺、血运旺盛的支柱。在

became Universal Brotherhood itself, the great gooseberry* of our globe.

Then pop went Leo! And from the bits sprang up Bolshevists.

It's all bunk. No man can be absolute. No man can be absolutely good or absolutely right, nor absolutely lovable, nor absolutely beloved nor absolutely loving. Even Jesus, the paragon, was only relatively good and relatively right. Judas could take him by the nose.

No god, that men can conceive of, could possibly be absolute or absolutely right. All the gods that men ever discovered are still God: and they contradict one another and fly down one another's throats, marvellously. Yet they are all God: the incalculable Pan.*

It is rather nice, to know what a lot of gods there are, and have been, and will be, and that they are all of them God all the while. Each of them utters an absolute: which, in the ears of all the rest of them, falls flat. This makes even eternity lively.

But man, poor man, bobbing like a cork in the stream of time, must hitch himself to some absolute star of righteousness overhead. So he throws out his line, and hooks on. Only to find, after a while, that his star is slowly falling: till it drops

街上若遇上三个健壮、大摇大摆的卫兵他非妒忌得大叫不可。十分钟后就大骂着说要把他们忘个一干二净，真正算道德的霹雷了[这段描述转述自高尔基所著《回忆列奥·尼古拉耶维奇·托尔斯泰》一书。此书于1920年由伦纳多·伍尔夫等人译成英文出版]！

这样的伟大真叫讨厌！俄罗斯这样的伟大民族竟让这样的改革者来改进他们的固有人性。这类改革者都感到自己缺少点什么，便靠仇恨活着，最终剩下的不是别的，而是人的空壳，渐渐把自己改进得空空如也，只会说一些套话，似乎他们吞下了一整套社会主义的百科全书。

不过，请等待！俄国人是有生命力的，那是他们奇怪地转变为布尔什维克的过程中呈现出的某种新奇的东西。

托尔斯泰伯爵有着伟人那个最后的缺点：他想要绝对，你可以称之为爱之绝对。这是“高尚思想家的最虚弱之点”！这是衰老的传染病。他想变得绝对——全世界皆兄弟。托尔斯泰嫌列奥这个名字太狭隘了。他想膨胀，膨胀，直到变成世界博爱，成为我们地球上巨大的醋栗[醋栗(gooseberry)的词根goose有傻瓜的意思]。

随之列奥“砰”地爆了，其碎片变成了布尔什维克分子。

into the stream of time with a fizzle, and there's another absolute star gone out.

Then we scan the heavens afresh.

As for the babe of love, we're simply tired of changing its napkins. Put the brat down, and let it learn to run about, and manage its own little breeches.

But it's nice to think that all the gods are God all the while. And if a god only genuinely feels to you like God, then it is God. But if it doesn't feel quite, quite altogether like God to you, then wait awhile, and you'll hear him fizzle.

The novel knows all this, irrevocably. "My dear," it kindly says, "one God is relative to another god, until he gets into a machine; and then it's a case for the traffic cop!"

"But what am I to do!" cries the despairing novelist. "From Amon and Ra to Mrs Eddy, from Ashtaroth and Jupiter to Annie Besant,* I don't know where I am."

"Oh yes you do, my dear!" replies the novel. "You are where you are, so you needn't hitch yourself on to the skirts either of Ashtaroth or Eddy. If you meet them, say how-do-you-do! to them quite courteously. But don't hook on, or I shall turn you down."

Refrain from hooking on! says the novel.

全是胡说。没哪个人是绝对的。没谁是绝对好或绝对正确或绝对可爱。甚至基督这样的完美典范也只是相对好、相对正确,犹大就能牵着他的鼻子走。

人能想像出的神没有哪个是绝对好或绝对正确的。人们迄今发现的神竟相互矛盾,还相互攻击。可他们都是神,是神奇莫测的潘神(Pan)[希腊丰饶之神,但受了惊吓也会做错事。英文里惊恐 panic 一词可能源于此]。

了解一下都有什么神,他们的过去和未来是个什么样子,这很有趣。他们一贯是神,每个神都讲着绝对,可在别的神听来这话却毫无意义。这,甚至令永恒显得可爱。

但是,可怜的人却像时间之河中的一只随波逐流的软木塞儿,一定要把自己拴在某颗所谓"正确"的星星上不可。于是他抛出自己的绳子,去钩那星星。他只能发现,那星星在缓缓坠落,直到"嘶"的一声坠入时间之河,又一颗绝对之星从此消失。

于是我们又重新在天上寻找。

至于说到爱情婴儿,我们已经懒得为它换擦嘴布了。放下这孩子,让它自己去学跑,自己系自己的裤腰带吧。

But be honorable among the host! he adds.

Honour! Why, the gods are like the rainbow, all colours and shades. Since light itself is invisible, a manifestation has got to be pink or black or blue or white or yellow or vermilion, or "tinted."

You may be a theosophist, and then you will cry: *Avaunt*! Thou dark-red aura! Away!!! —Oh come! Thou pale-blue or thou primrose aura, come!

This you may cry if you are a theosophist. And if you put a theosophist in a novel, he or she may cry *avaunt*! to the heart´s content.

But a theosophist cannot be a novelist. as a trumpet cannot be a regimental band. A theosophist, or a Christian, or a Holy Roller,* may be contained in a novelist. But a novelist may not put up a fence. The wind bloweth where it listeth, and auras will be red when they want to.

As a matter of fact, only the Holy Ghost knows truly what righteousness is. And heaven only knows what the Holy Ghost is! But it sounds all right. So the Holy Ghost hovers among the flames. from the red to the blue and the black to the yellow, putting brand to brand and flame to flame, as the wind changes, and life travels in flame from the unseen to the unseen, men will never know how or why.

不过应该想到所有的神都是神。如果你觉得哪个神是神,那它就是神了。如果你觉得它不怎么像神,那就稍候,你会听到他"嘶"的一声消失。

小说对此十分明白。"亲爱的,"它友善地说,"一个神是相对别的神而言的,除非它钻入汽车,那就变成交通警的一个案子了!"

"可我该怎么办?"失望的小说家说,"从埃蒙(**Ammon**)[埃及神]、拉(**Ra**)[埃及太阳神]到埃迪夫人 [Mary Baker Eddy,1821-1910,美国基督教科学的创始人],从阿什塔罗斯(**Ashtaroth**) [古闪米特丰饶之神]到朱庇特(**Jupiter**)[奥林匹亚众神之父]到安妮·比森特[安妮·比森特(Annie Besant),通神论学会主席(1907)],我弄不清我在哪儿。"

"不,你清楚亲爱的!"小说说道,"你知道你在哪儿。所以你用不着把自己拴在什么阿什塔罗斯或埃迪的裙裾上。如果你遇上她们,只需客客气气地问声好,但不必往上拴,否则我会不理睬你的。"

别往上拴自个儿!小说这样说。

要诚实,小说又补充说。

诚实!神像虹一样,有各种颜色和形状。光是看不见的,其表现形式必须是各种色彩如粉、黑、蓝、白、黄、朱红或杂色。

Only travel it must, and not die down in nasty fumes.

And the honour, which the novel demands of you, is only that you shall be true to the flame that leaps in you. When that Prince in *Resurrection* so cruelly betrayed and abandoned the girl, at the beginning of her life, he betrayed and wetted on the flame of his own manhood. When later, he bullied her with his repentant benevolence, he again betrayed and slobbered upon the flame of his waning manhood, till in the end his manhood is extinct, and he´s just a lump of half-alive elderly meat.

It´s the oldest Pan-mystery. God is the flame-life in all the universe. Multifarious, multifarious flames, all colours and beauties and pains and sombrenesses. Whichever flame flames in your manhood, that is you, for the time being. It is your manhood, don´t make water on it, says the novel. A man´s manhood is to honour the flames in him, and to know that none of them is absolute. Even a flame is only relative.

But see old Leo Tolstoi wetting on the flame. As if even his wet were absolute!

Sex is flame, too, the novel announces. Flame burning against every absolute, even against the phallic. For sex is so much more than phallic, and so much deeper

如果您是一位通神论者,你就会大叫:走开吧,你这黑红色!走开!来吧,淡蓝色或淡黄!来吧!

你可以这样喊,如果你是个通神论者。如果你在小说中弄一位通神论者,他可以这样尽情大叫“滚开”!

可一位通神论者是不能当小说家的。这正如同一只喇叭是不能充当军号一样。一个通神论者、基督教徒或“圣滚者”(**Holy Roller**)[一派宗教信徒用在地上打滚表达宗教狂喜]可以是一个小说家的一部分,但一个小说家却不能把自己局限于此。风刮起来是随心所欲的(见《约翰福音》3:8),色彩也一样,它想是红就是红。

事实上只有圣灵(**Holy Ghost**)才懂什么叫正确。而天只知道圣灵是怎么回事!可听起来满像回事的。于是圣灵就在火焰中徘徊,从红到蓝到黑到黄,给一个标记打上另一个标记,给一团火加另一团火,做这些完全随风向而动,生命在火中穿行,从幽冥到幽冥,人永远不知怎么和为什么。它只需旅行,别死在恶臭气中。

小说所要求你忠实去做的,只是忠实你心中跳动的火焰。《复活》中那位公爵在那少女的花季就残酷地背叛和抛弃了她,他其实也是泯灭了

than functional desire. The flame of sex singes your absolute, and cruelly scorches your ego. What, will you assert your ego in the universe? Wait till the flames of sex leap at you like striped tigers.

"They returned from the ride
With the lady inside,
And a smile on the face of the tiger."

You will play with sex, will you! You will tickle yourself with sex as with an ice-cold drink from a soda-fountain! You will pet your best girl, will you, and spoon with her, and titillate yourself and her, and do as you like with your sex?

Wait! Only wait till the flame you have dribbled on flies back at you, later! Only wait!

Sex is a life-flame, a dark one, reserved and mostly invisible. It is a deep reserve in a man, one of the core-flames of his manhood.

What, would you play with it? Would you make it cheap and nasty!

Buy a king-cobra, and try playing with that.

Sex is even a majestic reserve in the sun.

Oh, give me the novel! Let me hear what the novel says.

他的人性之火。后来,他又用忏悔和慈悲来折磨她,于是他等于再次背叛并往他苍白的人性上吐口水,最终他的人性全然灭绝,他本人只成了一块半死不活的老肉。

潘神时代的神话说上帝是宇宙的生命之火,五花八门的火焰,颜色不同,情绪不一,美丽的,痛苦的或忧郁的。不管哪种火在你的人性中燃烧,它在那一刻就是你了。那是你的人性,别往上头撒尿啊,小说这样说。一个人的人性就是尊重他心中的火焰并且懂得没有哪种火是绝对的。甚至一团火本身也只是个相对物。

再看看老列奥·托尔斯泰吧,他竟往火上泼水,似乎他泼上去的水是绝对的。

性也是一束火焰,小说说。这火燃烧任何绝对物,甚至燃烧阳物。因为性远非阳物可及,比功能性的欲望要深刻得多。性之火焰烧焦你的绝对并残酷地炙烫你的自我。你打算在宇宙中表现一种怎样的自我呢?那就等待,直到性之火像一只花条纹的老虎烧燎你。

他们骑马回家,

As for the novelist, he is usually a dribbling liar.

1925.

带回个女人，
老虎笑容满面。

你尽可以玩性游戏，玩吧！你可以逗引你的性，就像搅拌一杯冰镇苏打水。你可以拍拍你最爱的姑娘，对她动手动脚，逗引你自己也逗引她，怎么摆弄你的性都可以。

可要等待！直到你曾对之吐过口水的火焰又回到你身上再这样做！只需等待！

性是一束生命之火，黑暗，冥冥难察。它是一个人体内最深厚的积淀，是他人性的中心之火。

你打算拿它怎么玩耍？那样，你只能让它变贱，变恶心。

去买一条大毒蛇来玩玩吧。

性甚至是太阳里高贵的储备。

哦，把小说给我！让我听听小说怎么说。

至于小说家嘛，他常常口水四溅地扯谎。

1925 年

Morality and the Novel

The business of art is to reveal the relation between man and his circumambient universe, at the living moment. As mankind is always struggling in the toils of old relationships, art is always ahead of the "times," which themselves are always far in the rear of the living moment.

When Van Gogh paints sunflowers,* he reveals, or achieves, the vivid relation between himself, as man, and the sunflower, as sunflower, at that quick moment of time. His painting does not represent the sunflower itself. We shall never know what the sunflower itself is. And the camera will visualise the sunflower far more perfectly than Van Gogh can.

The vision on the canvas is a third thing, utterly intangible and inexplicable, the offspring of the sunflower itself and Van Gogh himself. The vision on the canvas is forever incommensurable with the canvas, or the paint, or Van Gogh as a human

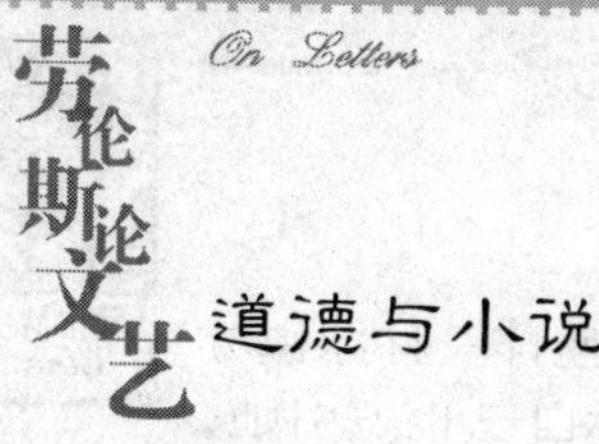

道德与小说

艺术的任务是展现人与其周围世界在活生生之时的关系。人类总在旧的恢恢关系网中挣扎,"时代"离活生生之时要久远得多,而艺术却总是超前于"时代"的。

当凡·高[1853—1890,荷兰后期印象派画家]绘向日葵时,他揭示的或获得的是一瞬间作为一个人的他与作为向日葵的向日葵之间的活的关系。他的绘画压根儿不是再现向日葵本身。我们永远也弄不清向日葵自身是个什么物件。而照相机可以比凡·高干得完美得多,它可以照下完美的视觉形象来,凡·高则差远了。

画布上的视觉现象是全然不可捉摸、难以言表的第三者——不是那

organism, or the sunflower as a botanical organism. You cannot weigh nor measure nor even describe the vision on the canvas. It exists, to tell the truth, only in the much-debated fourth dimension.* In dimensional space it has no existence.

It is a revelation of the perfected relation, at a certain moment, between a man and a sunflower. It is neither man-in-the-mirror nor flower-in-the-mirror, neither is it above or below or across anything. It is in-between everything, in the fourth dimension.

And this perfected relation between man and his circumambient universe is life itself, for mankind. It has the fourth-dimensional quality of eternity and perfection. Yet it is momentaneous.

Man and the sunflower both pass away from the moment, in the process of forming a new relationship. The relation between all things changes from day to day, in a subtle stealth of change. Hence art, which reveals or attains to another perfect relationship, will be forever new.

At the same time, that which exists in the non-dimensional space of pure relationship, is deathless, lifeless, and eternal. That is, it gives us the feeling of being beyond life or death. We say an Assyrian lion or an Egyptian hawk's-head* "lives."

向日葵,也不是凡·高,而是这两者结合的产物。画布上的视觉形象与画布、颜料、作为人的有机体的凡·高以及作为植物有机体的向日葵永远不可同日而语。你无法衡量甚至无法描述画布上的视觉形象。这视觉形象,说实在的,只存在于大有争议的所谓第四维空间[相对论中指长、宽、高以外的第四度空间,即"时间"]中。在可度量的空间中它是不存在的。

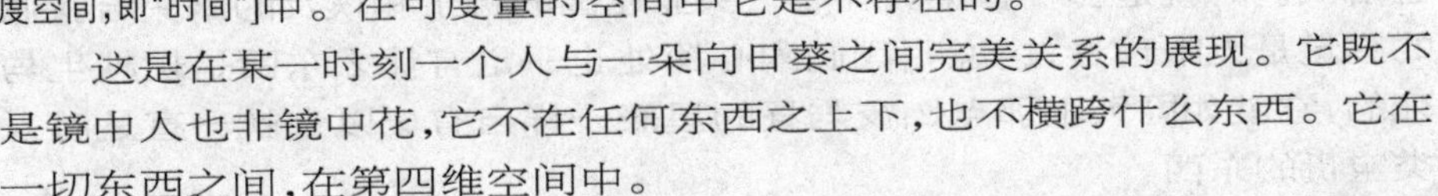

这是在某一时刻一个人与一朵向日葵之间完美关系的展现。它既不是镜中人也非镜中花,它不在任何东西之上下,也不横跨什么东西。它在一切东西之间,在第四维空间中。

对人类来说,这种人与其周围世界之间的完美关系就是人类的生命本身。它具有永恒与完美这种四维空间的性质。但是它是倏忽即逝的。

人与向日葵在形成新的关系的那一刻就双双失去了自身。一切事物之间的关系都在悄然变化中一天天地变化着。因此,那揭示或获得另一种完美关系的艺术将永远是崭新的。

同理,那些存在于纯关系的不可度量空间中的东西是无所谓死也无

What we really mean is that it is beyond life, and therefore beyond death. It gives us that feeling. And there is something inside us which must also be beyond life and beyond death, since that "feeling" which we get from an Assyrian lion or an Egyptian hawk´s-head is so infinitely precious to us. As the evening star, that spark of pure relation between night and day, has been precious to man since time began.

If we think about it, we find that our life consists in this achieving of a pure relationship between ourselves and the living universe about us. This is how I "save my soul," by accomplishing a pure relationship between me and another person, me and other people, me and a nation, me and a race of men, me and the animals, me and the trees or flowers, me and the earth, me and the skies and sun and stars, me and the moon; an infinity of pure relations, big and little, like the stars of the sky: that makes our eternity, for each one of us. Me and the timber I am sawing, the lines of force I follow, me and the dough I knead for bread, me and the very motion with which I write, me and the bit of gold I have got. This, if we knew it, is our life and our eternity: the subtle, perfected relation between me and my whole circumambient universe.

And morality is that delicate, forever trembling and changing balance between

所谓生的,是永恒的。这就是说,它给予我们一种超越生与死的感觉。我们说一头亚述国[西亚古国,盛于公元前750–612年。亚述国的巴比伦狮子塑像矗立在古巴比伦城的废墟上。埃及的鹰头可能指的是太阳神(又称鹰头神)]的狮子或一头埃及苍鹰的头还"活着",我们这话的真正意思是它超越了生命,因此也就超越了死亡。它给我们的就是那种感觉。既然一头亚述国的狮子和埃及的鹰头给我们的感觉是无限珍贵,这说明我们内心深处也一定有什么东西是超越生与死的,它就如同天上那点燃夜与昼的星辰一样自有史以来就一直是对人类宝贵的东西。

思量一下,我们会发现我们的生命就寓于我们自己和周围活生生世界的纯粹关系的形成之中。我就是通过如下途径"拯救我的灵魂"的:完善我与另一个人、别人、一个民族、一个种族、动物、盛开鲜花的树、土地、天空、太阳、星星和月亮之间纯粹的关系。这是无数纯粹的关系,或大或小,就像天上的星星一样数也数不清。就是这种关系使我们永恒——我们每一个人,我和我正锯着的木头,我所服从的力量,我和我手中揉着的

me and my circumambient universe, which precedes and accompanies a true relatedness.

Now here we see the beauty and the great value of the novel. Philosophy, religion, science, they are all of them busy nailing things down, to get a stable equilibrium. Religion, with its nailed down One God, who says Thou shalt, Thou shan't, and hammers home every time; philosophy, with its fixed ideas; science, with its "laws": they all of them, all the time, want to nail us on to some tree or other.

But the novel, no. The novel is the highest complex of subtle interrelatedness that man has discovered. Everything is true in its own time, place, circumstance, and untrue outside of its own place, time, circumstance. If you try to nail anything down, in the novel, either it kills the novel, or the novel gets up and walks away with the nail.

Morality in the novel is the trembling instability of the balance. When the novelist puts his thumb in the scale, to pull down the balance to his own predilection, that is immorality.

The modern novel tends to become more and more immoral, as the novelist

做面包的面团，我和我书写时的这个动作及我和我所有的这一点金子。这个，如果我们懂得它的话，就是我们的生命和我们的永恒——我与我周围全部世界之间微妙而完美的关系。

而道德就是我与周围世界之间永远微微颤动和变化着的天平，这天平先于一种真正的关系而存在，同时也伴随着这种关系。

现在我们看出小说之美及其伟大价值何在了吧。哲学、宗教和科学都忙于把事物固定住，以求获得一种稳定的平衡。宗教只有一个在说"你应该，你不应该"的上帝，每次他都斩钉截铁。哲学的概念是固定的；科学有自己的"定律"。这些东西总是想把我们钉在这棵或那棵树上才罢休。

可小说却不这样。小说是人类迄今发现的细微内在联系的集大成者。任何东西只要是在自身的时间、地点和环境中就是真实的，否则就是虚假的。如果你想在小说中把什么钉住，那么，不是你把小说给害了就是小说自己站起来带着这枚钉子一走了之。

小说中的道德是颤动不稳的天平。一旦小说家把手指按在天平盘上

tends to press his thumb heavier and heavier in the pan: either on the side of love, pure love: or on the side of licentious "freedom."

The novel is not, as a rule, immoral because the novelist has any dominant idea, or purpose. The immorality lies in the novelist's helpless, unconscious predilection. Love is a great emotion. But if you set out to write a novel, and you yourself are in the throes of the great predilection for love, love as the supreme, the only emotion worth living for, then you will write an immoral novel.

Because no emotion is supreme, or exclusively worth living for. All emotions go to the achieving of a living relationship between a human being and the other human being or creature or thing he becomes purely related to.

All emotions, including love and hate, and rage and tenderness, go to the adjusting of the oscillating, unestablished balance between two people who amount to anything. If the novelist puts his thumb in the pan, for love, tenderness, sweetness, peace, then he commits an immoral act: he prevents the possibility of a pure relationship, a pure relatedness, the only thing that matters: and he makes inevitable the horrible reaction, when he lets his thumb go, towards hate and brutality, cruelty and destruction.

按自己的偏向意愿改变其平衡，这就是不道德了。

现代小说似越变越不道德了，因为小说家正趋于把手指愈来愈有力地压在天平上：不是偏向纯粹的爱就是偏向于无法无天的“自由”。

当然，一般来说小说并不因小说家有任何明显的观点或目的而显得不道德。所谓不道德指的是小说家不能自持的、无意识的偏向。爱本来是一种很伟大的情绪，可当你写起小说来沉溺于对爱的偏向，把爱当成最高的、惟一值得为其而活的情感来写，那你就会写出一部不道德的小说来。

这是因为，没有哪种情感是至高无上、惟一值得让人视同生命的。全部的情感都用于获得一个人与他人、他物、他事之间的活生生关系上。

全部的情感，包括爱和恨、怒与柔，都用于调整两个颇有价值的人之间频频振荡不定的天平。如果小说家把手指压在天平上，偏向爱、柔情、甜蜜、淡雅，他于是就犯了一个道德错误——他阻碍了纯粹关系与联系这最重要事物的可能性。而一旦他抬起手，就不可避免地造成可怕的反

Life is so made, that opposites sway about a trembling centre of balance. The sins of the fathers are visited on the children.* If the fathers drag down the balance on the side of love, peace, and production, then in the third or fourth generation the balance will swing back violently to hate, rage, and destruction. We must balance as we go.

And of all the art forms, the novel most of all demands the trembling and oscillating of the balance. The "sweet" novel is more falsified, and therefore more immoral than the blood and thunder novel.

The same with the smart and smudgily cynical novel, which says it doesn't matter what you do, because one thing is as good as another, anyhow, and prostitution is just as much "life" as anything else.

This misses the point entirely. A thing isn't life, just because somebody does it. This the artist ought to know, perfectly well. The ordinary bank-clerk buying himself a new straw hat isn't "life" at all: it is just existence, quite all right, like everyday dinners: but not "life."

By life, we mean something that gleams, that has the fourth dimensional quality. If the bank-clerk feels really piquant about his hat, if he establishes a lively re-

作用——走向仇恨、野蛮、残酷和毁灭。

生活就是如此，相反的东西在一个震颤的天平中心上摇摆着。父亲犯下的罪会使儿子得到惩罚[见《旧约·出埃及记》第二十章，第五节]。如果父辈把天平压向爱、淡雅和创造，到了第三、四代人那里，天平会剧烈地倒向仇恨、愤怒和毁灭。我们必须随时调整自己才对。

在各种艺术形式中，数小说最需要天平的颤抖了。"甜蜜"的小说愈是作假就愈是不道德，相比之下，倒是那些刺激性情节的小说更道德些。

那些写得精明但又说不清道不明外加玩世不恭的小说也是一样，在这些小说中你尽可以为所欲为，怎么着都无甚关系，因为作者认为做什么都一样。照这说法，卖淫也同其他东西一样是"生命"。

这说法全然不着边际。一件事并不因为有人为之就成为生命。艺术家应该明白这一点才对。一个普通的银行职员买了一顶新草帽，这根本不是什么"生命"，只是一种存在罢了，就如同每日三餐，但并非是"生命"。

lation with it, and goes out of the shop with the new straw on his head, a changed man, be-aureoled, then that is life.

The same with the prostitute. If a man establishes a living relation to her, if only for one moment, then it is life. But if he doesn't: if it is just money and function, then it is no life, but sordidness, and a betrayal of living.

If a novel reveals true and vivid relationships, it is a moral work, no matter what the relationships may consist in. If the novelist honours the relationship in itself, it will be a great novel.

But there are so many relationships which are not real. When the man in *Crime and Punishment** murders the old woman for sixpence, although it is actual enough, it is never quite real. The balance between the murderer and the old woman is gone entirely, it is only a mess. It is actuality, but it is not "life," in the living sense.

The popular novel, on the other hand, dishes up a rechauffé of old relationships: *If Winter Comes.** And old relationships dished up are likewise immoral. Even a magnificent painter like Raphael does nothing more than dress up in gorgeous new dresses relationships which have already been experienced. And this

所谓生命指的是某种闪烁着的具有第四空间性质的东西,如果那银行职员确实为他的帽子感到高兴,与帽子之间建立起了一种活生生的关系,头戴草帽走出商店时跟换了个人似的神采奕奕,那么这就是生命。

妓女也是一样。如果一个男人与她之间建立起了活生生的关系,哪怕只是一瞬间,这也是生命。反之,如果他们之间只是金钱和行为的关系,那么这关系就算不得生命,只能称之为肮脏,是背叛生命。

如果一部小说揭示的是真实而生动的关系,不管是什么样的关系,这部小说就算得上一部道德作品。如果小说家尊重这种关系,他的小说就会成为一部伟大的小说。

有不少关系就不真实。比如《罪与罚》中那年轻小伙子[指小说中的人物拉斯科尔尼柯夫]为了六个便士而杀死了一位老妇人,尽管这事情很实在,可它永远也不会让人觉得真切。杀人者与老妇人之间的关系天平全无平衡可言,简直一团糟。它是实事儿,可它永远也算不上是"生命"。

在另一方面,通俗小说则不过是在炒剩饭,把旧的关系翻新花样儿,如《如果冬天将至》[1921 年出版的通俗小说,作者是美国作家 A.S.M.Hutchinson (1879—1971)]

gives a gluttonous kind of pleasure to the mass: a voluptuousness, a wallowing. For centuries, men say of their voluptuously ideal woman: "She is a Raphael Madonna." And women are only just learning to take it as an insult.

A new relation, a new relatedness hurts somewhat in the attaining: and will always hurt. So life will always hurt. Because real voluptuousness lies in re-acting old relationships, and at the best, getting an alcoholic sort of pleasure out of it, slightly depraving.

Each time we strive to a new relation, with anyone or anything, it is bound to hurt somewhat. Because it means the struggle with and the displacing of old connections, and this is never pleasant. And moreover, between living things at least, an adjustment means also a fight; for each party, inevitably, must "seek its own" in the other, and be denied. When, in the two parties, each of them seeks his own, her own, absolutely, then it is a fight to the death. And this is true of the thing called "passion." On the other hand, when, of the two parties, one yields utterly to the other, this is called sacrifice, and it also means death. So The Constant Nymph died of her eighteen-months of constancy.*

It isn't the nature of nymphs to be constant. She should have been constant in

那样。这种换汤不换药的做法也是不道德的。甚至大画家拉斐尔也不过是给旧的经验穿上新的美丽衣裳。这种做法只能让芸芸众生得到一种暴食暴饮的痛快感:纵情于声色。几个世纪以来男人们都把他们心目中理想的肉感女人称作:"她是拉斐尔笔下的圣母。"而女人们呢,她们只把这当成是对她们的一种污辱而已。

要获得一种新的关系是痛苦的,永远会是如此痛苦的。所以生命永远会使人痛苦,因为真正的肉欲放纵在于重演旧的关系,至多只能获得一种酗酒后的快感,这不免有点堕落之嫌。

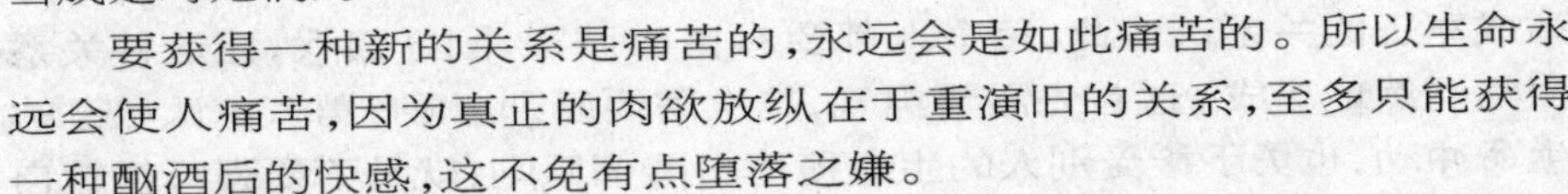

每次我们欲与某人某事结成一种新的关系时总是要痛苦的。因为这意味着与旧的联系作斗争,要取代旧的,这永远不会是件愉快的事。再说,在活生生的事物之中要做出调整亦意味着各自的斗争,这是不可避免的,因为斗争的双方都要在对方中"寻到自己的自我",通过寻找自我而否定自我从而达到协调。一旦双方要寻找绝对的自我,这种斗争将会导致死亡。所谓"激情"就是这东西。另一方面,当一方彻底屈从于另一方

her nymphhood. And it is unmanly to accept sacrifices. He should have abided by his own manhood.

There is, however, the third thing, which is neither sacrifice nor fight to the death: when each seeks only the true relatedness to the other. Each must be true to himself, herself, his own manhood, her own womanhood, and let the relationship work out of itself. This means courage above all things: and then discipline. Courage to accept the life-thrust from within oneself, and from the other person. Discipline, not to exceed oneself any more than one can help. Courage, when one has exceeded oneself, to accept the fact and not whine about it.

Obviously, to read a really new novel will always hurt, to some extent. There will always be resistance. The same with new pictures, new music. You may judge of their reality by the fact that they do arouse a certain resistance, and compel, at length, a certain acquiescence.

The great relationship, for humanity, will always be the relation between man and woman. The relation between man and man, woman and woman, parent and child, will always be subsidiary.

And the relation between man and woman will change forever, and will forever

时，这是一种牺牲，其实也是一种死亡。所以，那《永恒的仙女》[1924 年出版的通俗小说，作者是 Magaret Kennedy (1896—1967)]只永恒了 18 个月就死了。

这些仙女是水性杨花的，但她们本来应该是固守本分的。至于男人，接受她们的牺牲是不够男子气的做法，男人应该做一个男子汉。

还有第三种选择，这既不是牺牲也不是战死，而是各自寻求与对方结成真正的关系。为此，每个人都要对自己诚实，固守自我，让这种关系自然而然地形成。这首先需要勇气，其次需要原则。既有勇气承认自己的生命冲动，也勇于接受别人的生命喷薄。所谓原则，就是不要强行超越自我。而一旦超越了自己，就要勇于承认事实，而不要为此抱怨。

很明显，读一本全新的小说总是要令人感到创痛的——不同程度上的创痛。总会有抵抗力在作祟。这正如同看新绘画，听新音乐。你尽可以通过这些新东西所激起的阻抗力和最终被迫认可它们的程度来估量它们的真实。

对人类来讲，最伟大的关系不外乎就是男女间的关系了。至于男人与男人、女人与女人、父母与子女之间的关系则次之。

be the new central clue to human life. It is the relation itself which is the quick and the central clue to life, not the man, nor the woman, nor the children that result form the relationship, as a contingency.

It is no use thinking you can put a stamp on the relation between man and woman, to keep it in the *status quo*. You can't. You might as well try to put a stamp on the rainbow of the rain.

As for the bond of love, better put it off when it galls. It is an absurdity, to say that men and women must love. Men and women will be forever subtly and changingly related to one another, no need to yoke them with any "bond" at all. The only morality is to have man true to his manhood, woman to her womanhood, and let the relationship form of itself, in all honour. For it is, to each, life itself.

If we are going to be moral, let us refrain from driving pegs through anything, either through each other or through the third thing, the relationship, which is forever the Ghost of both of us. Every sacrificial crucifixion needs five pegs, four short ones and a long one, each one an abomination. But when you try to nail down the relationship itself, and write over it Love instead of This is the King of the Jews, then you can go on putting in nails forever. Even Jesus called it the Holy Ghost, to

而男女间的关系永远是变化着的，永远是通往人类生活的新的中心线索。这里的关键是关系本身，而非男人、女人及男女关系的偶然结果——孩子。

你若想给男女之间的关系贴上标签使其维持现状，这做法会是徒劳的，没门儿。你倒不如给彩虹或雨水贴上标签试试看。

说到爱的约束，最好是一感到它约束得发痛就弃之。如果说男女一定要相爱，真是荒谬之至。男人和女人永远是微妙而又在变化中联系在一起的，没必要用什么“契约”把他们约束在一起。最道德的事就是让男人忠于自己的男子汉之道，女人忠于自己的女人之道，从而让男女间的关系自然而然地形成。因为，对各自双方来说这都是生命。

如果我们讲道德，那么我们就不要给什么都钉上钉子，既不要把双方钉在一起也不要钉第三方，这种关系永远是我们各自的魔鬼。每个十字架上钉人都需要五枚钉子，四根短的，一根长的，每一根都很可怕。可是一旦你试图把这种关系钉住并在上面书写“爱”而不是“这是犹太人之王”，你就会没完没了地到处去钉钉子。甚至基督都称之为“圣灵”，那意

show you that you can't lay salt on its tail.

The novel is a perfect medium for revealing to us the changing rainbow of our living relationships. The novel can help us to live, as nothing else can: no didactic Scripture, anyhow. If the novelist keeps his thumb out of the pan.

But when the novelist has his thumb in the pan, the novel becomes an unparalleled perverter of men and women. To be compared only, perhaps, to that great mischief of sentimental hymns like *Lead Kindly Light*! * which have helped to rot the marrow in the bones of the present generation.

思是说你是无法诱惑它的，它是神圣的。

小说是揭示我们活生生关系变化之虹的最佳手段。小说可以帮助我们生活，而别的东西就做不到这一点，反正经文是做不到这一点的。当然，这要求小说家不要在天平上施加压力。

一旦小说家把手指按在天平盘上施加压力，他就篡改了男人与女人，只能与那伤感小曲如《善良之光引路》[1833 年间开始传唱的赞美诗]之类的恶作剧相媲美，这类东西只能帮倒忙，腐蚀这一代人的骨髓。

1925 年

Why the Novel Matters

We have curious ideas of ourselves. We think of ourselves as a body with a spirit in it, or a body with a soul in it, or a body with a mind in it. *Mens sana in corpore sano.** The years drink up the wine, and at last throw the bottle away: the body, of course, being the bottle.

It is a funny sort of superstition. Why should I look at my hand, as it so cleverly writes these words, and decide that it is a mere nothing compared to the mind that directs it? Is there really any huge difference between my hand and my brain? —or my mind? My hand is alive, it flickers with a life of its own. It meets all the strange universe, in touch, and learns a vast number of things, and knows a vast number of things. My hand, as it writes these words, slips gaily along, jumps like a grasshopper to dot an i, feels the table rather cold, gets a little bored if I write too

David Herbert Lawrence

小说[英文中“小说”通常指长篇小说,特注]何以重要

我们对自己的看法真是奇怪:我们自以为是一个装有精神、灵魂或心灵的肉体,正如古拉丁语所说:“健全的心智寓于健全的肉体中。”[见罗马讽刺诗人朱文诺尔(60?—140?)之《讽刺诗》]岁月喝干了瓶中酒,最终把酒瓶丢弃。看来,肉体就是瓶子了。

这是一种可笑的迷信。为何我看着这只能如此灵活地写出这些文字的手就断言它与指挥它的头脑相比是微不足道的呢?难道我的手和我的头脑或心智之间竟有如此巨大的差别吗?我的手是活生生的,它自身的生命在闪烁着火花。它通过触觉与整个奇妙的宇宙相识,学到了许多的东西,认识了许多东西。我的手在写这些字时欢快地滑动着,像一只蚱蜢蹦跳着,它能感到桌子的冷暖,如果我写得太久它就会感到有点儿厌烦,

long, has its own rudiments of thought, and is just as much me as is my brain, my mind, or my soul. Why should I imagine that there is a me which is more me than my hand is? Since my hand is absolutely alive, me alive.

Whereas, of course, as far as I am concerned, my pen isn´t alive at all. My pen isn´t me alive. Me alive ends at my finger-tips.

Whatever is me alive is me. Every tiny bit of my hands is alive, every little freckle and hair and fold of skin. And whatever is me alive is me. Only my finger-nails, those ten little weapons between me and an inanimate universe, they cross the mysterious Rubicon* between me alive and things like my pen, which are not alive, in my own sense.

So, seeing my hand is all alive, and me alive, wherein is it just a bottle, or a jug, or a tin can, or a vessel of clay, or any of the rest of that nonsense? True, if I cut it it will bleed, like a can of cherries. But then the skin that is cut, and the veins that bleed, and the bones that should never be seen, they are all just as alive as the blood that flows. So the tin can business, or vessel of clay, is just bunk.

And that´s what you learn, when you´re a novelist. And that´t what you are

它有它自己的思维方式。它跟我一样,就像我和我的头脑、心智或灵魂是一回事一样。为什么我非要设想有一个比我的手更是我自己的我呢?既然我的手是肯定活着的,我也是活着的。

当然,就我所言,我的笔绝不是活着的。我的笔绝非我的生命,我的生命到我的手指尖端就完了。

凡是我活着的部分都是我。我手上每一个微小的部分都是活着的——每个小斑点、每一根毛发、每丝皱纹都活着。凡是我活着的部分都是我。在我的感觉中,只有我的手指甲是死的。这十个介于活生生的我与无生命的宇宙之间的小武器就是跨越介于活生生的我和我的笔之类的东西之间神秘的卢比孔河[公元49年恺撒率军跨过卢比孔河去与庞培决战。这个词现用于比喻采取重大措施]上的桥梁。

所以,既然我的手整个都是活着的,那它怎么会只是一只酒瓶、一只罐子、一筒罐头或一只陶器或其他什么无聊的东西?不错,它会像一个樱桃罐头一样,如果我割它一刀,会流血。可这割破的皮肤、这流血的血管还有那看不见的骨头都像流淌的鲜血一样是活生生的。所以,把手比做罐头筒或陶器纯属废话。

very liable not to know, if you're a parson, or a philosopher, or a scientist, or a stupid person. If you're a parson, you talk about souls in heaven. If you're a novelist, you know that paradise is in the palm of your hand, and on the end of your nose: because both are alive; and alive, and man-alive, which is more than you can say, for certain, of paradise. Paradise is after life, and I for one am not keen on anything that is after life.—If you are a philosopher, you talk about infinity, and the pure spirit which knows all things. But if you pick up a novel, you realise immediately that infinity is just a handle to this self-same jug of a body of mine; while as for knowing, if I put my finger in the fire, I know that fire burns, with a knowledge so emphatic and vital, it leaves Nirvana merely a conjecture. Oh yes, my body, me alive, knows, and knows intensely. And as for the sum of all knowledge, it can't be anything more than an accumulation of all the things I know in the body, and you, dear reader, know in the body.

These damned philosophers, they talk as if they suddenly went off in steam, and were then much more important than they are when they're in their shirts. It is nonsense. Every man, philosopher included, ends in his own finger-tips. That's the

当你成为一个小说家,你就会懂得这个道理。可如果你是个牧师、一个哲学家、一个科学家或是一个蠢人,你就很可能不懂这个。如果你是个牧师,你会宣讲灵魂升天之说。而如果你是个小说家,你则知道天堂就在你手中,就在你鼻尖上,因为手和鼻子都是活生生的。活着的,活着的人,这些肯定比天堂更重要。天堂是人死以后的事,而我是个对死后之事毫无兴趣的人。如果你是个哲学家,你会大谈什么无穷和全知全能的纯粹精神。可如果你拿起一部小说,你马上会意识到所谓无穷不过是被称为罐子的我的肉体的一只把手罢了。说到全知全能,如果我把手指放入火中,我会强烈地感知到火在燃烧,这种活生生的感知会使涅槃的佛教教义成为泡影。哦,是的,我的肉体,活生生的我可以认知、深刻地认识一切。至于说全部的知识,那不过是我的肉体所认知的积累,也是你,亲爱的读者,是你的肉体知识的积累。

那些该死的哲学家们夸夸其谈,似乎云里雾里蒸发了一般,可比正襟危坐时还要有派头。他们简直是胡扯。每个人,包括哲学家,他的生命都终止在指尖上,那是活人的极限。至于他的语言、思想、叹息和欲望这些飞出他体外的东西不过是在以太[以太曾被认为是传导无线电波和电磁放射的媒质。

end of his man alive. As for the words and thoughts and sighs and aspirations that fly from him, they are so many tremulations in the ether,* and not alive at all. But if the tremulations reach another man alive, he may receive them into his life, and his life may take on a new colour, like a chameleon creeping from a brown rock on to a green leaf. All very well and good. It still doesn't alter the fact that the so-called spirit, the message or teaching of the philosopher or the saint, isn't alive at all, but just a tremulation upon the ether, like a radio message. All this spirit stuff is just tremulations upon the ether. If you, as man alive, quiver from the tremulation of the ether into new life, that is because you are man alive, and you take sustenance and stimulation into your alive man in a myriad ways. But to say that the message, or the spirit which is communicated to you, is more important than your living body, is nonsense. You might as well say that the potato at dinner was more important.

Nothing is important but life. And for myself, I can absolutely see life nowhere but in the living. Life with a capital L is only man alive. Even a cabbage in the rain is cabbage alive. All things that are alive are amazing. And all things that are dead

这一概念在19世纪被普遍接受。但随着相对论和场的发现,以太就成了陈旧的概念被抛弃。劳伦斯对当时最新的科学理论没有及时地把握,也说明了新理论的普及需要较长的过渡阶段]中的震颤而已,绝没有生气。可一旦这震动波被另一个活生生的人所接收并进入这个人的生命,这人的生命就会改变颜色,就如同一条变色虫从一块褐色的石头爬到一片绿叶上就变成绿色的一样。这话没错,一点不错,可这改变不了这种事实。所谓哲学家或圣人的精神、启示或教导是没有生气的,不过是像无线电讯号一样是在空中震颤着的某种波。所有这些称做精神的东西都只是以太中的震波。作为一个活生生的人,如果你因着这种震颤而变为新的生命的话,这是因为你是个活人,你以各种方式从这种震颤中汲取了营养和刺激物。但如果说传达给你的启示或精神比你活生生的肉体还重要那是胡说。你还不如说吃饭时土豆比吃土豆的人更重要。

什么也不如生命重要。至于我自己,我只能在活生生的东西中才能找到生命,而不是在别处。大写的生命只能是活生生的人。就是雨中的白菜也是活生生的白菜。所有活生生的东西都令人惊叹。所有死了的东西都比不上活着的。宁为活狗,勿为死狮。当然活狮还是比活狗强的。这就

are subsidiary to the living. Better a live dog than a dead lion. But better a live lion than a live dog. *C'est la vie*.*

It seems impossible to get a saint, or a philosopher, or a scientist, to stick to this simple truth. They are all, in a sense, renegades. The saint wishes to offer himself up as spiritual food for the multitude. Even Francis of Assisi* turns himself into a sort of angel cake, of which anyone may take a slice. But an angel cake is rather less than man alive. And poor St. Francis might well aoplogise to his body, when he was dying. "Oh pardon me, my body, the wrong I did you through the years! "—It was no wafer, for others to eat.

The philosopher on the other hand, because he can think, decides that nothing but thoughts matter. It is as if a rabbit, because he can make little pills, should decide that nothing but little pills matter. As for the scientist, he has absolutely no use for me so long as I am man alive. To the scientist, I am dead. He puts under the microscope a bit of dead me, and calls it me. He takes me to pieces, and says first one piece, and then another piece, is me. My heart, my liver, my stomach have all been scientifically me, according to the scientist; and nowadays I am either

是生命！

这个简单的真理是无法让那些圣人、哲学家或科学家相信的。在某种意义上说，他们全是些叛逆。圣人希望把自己当做精神食粮奉献给大众。就连阿西西的芳济[圣芳济(1181? —1226)，全名阿西西的芳济，芳济会的创始人，大圣徒]也把自己变做一块天使般的蛋糕，谁都可以切一块。可这样的一块蛋糕还是比不上一个活生生的人。当可怜的芳济临死时他真该对自己的肉体深表歉意："哦，宽恕我吧，我的肉体，这些年来我亏待你了！"他的肉体绝不是让他人割食的华夫饼。

而哲学家则相反，因为他可以思考，所以他就认为只有思想才重要。这似乎是说如果一只兔子能拉出小屎球来它就该认为小屎球是最重要的东西。至于科学家，只要我还是个活生生的人，我对他来说就一钱不值。在科学家眼里，我是个死物件。他弄一点我死尸上的东西放在显微镜下，竟把这东西看做是我了。他把我剁成碎片，先说这一片是我，又说那一片是我。在他们眼里，我的心，我的肝和我的胃都足以代表我本身。这年头科学发达了，名词更新了，看来我不是一只脑子，就是神经，什么腺或生理组织中有着更时髦名称的东西。

a brain, or nerves, or glands, or something more up-to-date in the tissue line.

Now I absolutely flatly deny that I am a soul, or a body, or a mind, or an intelligence, or a brain, or a nervous system, or a bunch of glands, or any of the rest of these bits of me. The whole is greater than the part. And therefore I, who am man alive, am greater than my soul, or spirit, or body, or mind, or consciousness, or anything, else that is merely a part of me. I am a man, and alive. I am man alive, and as long as I can, I intend to go on being man alive.

For this reason I am a novelist. And being a novelist, I consider myself superior to the saint, the scientist, the philosopher and the poet, who are all great masters of different bits of man-alive, but never get the whole hog.

The novel is the one bright book of life. Book are not life. They are only tremulations on the ether. But the novel as a tremulation can make the whole man-alive tremble. Which is more than poerty, philosophy, science or any other book-tremulation can do.

The novel is the book of life. In this sense, the Bible is a great confused novel. You may say, it is about God. But it is really about man-alive. Adam, Eve, Sarai,

我决然否认我是一个灵魂、一具肉体、一副头脑或是智力、脑子、一套神经系统、一组什么腺或任何别的诸如此类的东西。整体比部分要伟大。所以,作为一个活生生的我比我的灵魂、精神、肉体、思想、意识或任何只是部分的我都伟大。我是一个人,一个活生生的人。只要我能够,我会永远做一个活人。

正是为了永远做一个活人,我才成为一个小说家。作为一个小说家,我自认为比圣人、科学家、哲学家和诗人更优越。这些人能主宰活人的不同部分,可他们永远也无法获得人的整体。

长篇小说是闪光的生命之书。书当然并非生命,它们只是以太中的震颤。可是作为一种震颤的小说却可以让活人全身战抖,而诗、哲学、科学或任何别类的书却不能产生这种效果。

长篇小说是生命之书。依照这个观点,《圣经》算是一部杂乱的伟大小说了。你或许会说它写的是上帝,可其实它说的是活人的事。亚当,夏娃,萨拉[萨拉是希伯莱始祖亚伯拉罕的妻子,以撒的母亲],亚伯拉罕,以撒,雅各[雅各是以撒的次子,也叫以色列],撒母耳[希伯莱之士师兼先知],大卫[以色列第二任国王,约公元前1000年],巴什巴[大卫钟情的有夫之妇],路丝[《旧约》中的一位默阿布寡妇,陪婆母到伯利恒后

Abraham, Isaac, Jacob, Samuel, David, Bathsheba, Ruth, Esther, Solomon, Job, Isaiah, Jesus, Mark, Judas, Paul, Peter;* what is it but man-alive, from start to finish? Man-alive, not mere bits. Even the Lord is another man-alive, in a burning bush, throwing the tablets of stone at Moses' head.*

I do hope you begin to get my idea, why the novel is supremely important, as a tremulation on the ether. Plato makes the perfect ideal being tremble in me. But that's only a bit of me. Perfection is only a bit, in the strange make-up of man-alive. The Sermon on the Mount makes the selfless spirit of me quiver. But that too is only a bit of me. The Ten Commandments sets the old Adam shivering in me, warning me that I am a thief and a murderer, unless I watch it. But even the old Adam is only a bit of me.

I very much like all these bits of me to be set trembling with life and the wisdom of life. But I do ask that the whole of me shall tremble in its wholeness, some time or other.

And this, of course, must happen in my living.

But as far as it can happen from a communication, it can only happen when a

嫁给一个希伯莱人]，以斯特[波斯王赫谢斯的犹太妻子]，所罗门 [以色列的贤明国王]，约伯[希伯莱族长]，以赛亚[希伯莱人的大先知]，耶稣，马可[四部《福音》书的作者之一，著其中一部《马可福音》]，犹大，保罗[耶稣门徒之一，广泛传播基督教，终被害于罗马。新约中书信大多出自他手]，彼得[耶稣门徒之一]，他们哪一个不是活生生的人来着？他们是活人，不是碎片。甚至主也是另一个活着的人，他在燃烧的灌木丛中把刻有“十诫”的石碑[见《圣经·出埃及记》，碑文上刻着“至高无上的神对以色列人民的训诫”。上帝在森林中召唤摩西，这森林一直燃烧着，永烧不尽]推向摩西。

我真的希望你现在开始明白我的观点——为什么作为以太中一种震颤的小说实在重要。柏拉图令我完美而理想的生命颤动，不过那只是我生命的一丁点。完美在活生生人的奇怪构筑中只是一丁点。耶稣的登山训诫令我无私的精神震颤，可那也只是我生命的一丁点在震颤。十诫足以令我的犯罪天性震颤，警告自己：如果我不监视自己的本性，我就会成为一个贼或一个杀人犯。但即使是这种犯罪天性也只是我生命的一丁点。

我多么喜欢让这些“丁点儿”与我的生命和生命的智慧一起颤动啊。但是我更愿意在某个时候我的全部都颤动起来。

whole novel communicates itself to me. The Bible—but all the Bible—and Homer, and Shakespeare: these are the supreme old novels. These are all things to all men. Which means that in their wholeness they affect the whole man alive, which is the man himself, beyond any part of him. They set the whole tree trembling with a new access of life, they do not just stimulate growth in one direction.

I don't want to grow in any one direction any more. And if I can help it, I don't want to stimulate anybody else into some particular direction. A particular direction ends in a *cul de sac*. We're in a *cul de sac* at present.

I don't believe in any dazzling revelation, or in any supreme Word. "The grass withereth, the flower fadeth, but the Word of the Lord shall stand for ever."*—That's the kind of stuff we've drugged ourselves with. As a matter of fact, the grass withereth, but comes up all the greener for that reason, after the rains. The flower fadeth, and therefore the bud opens. But the Word of the Lord, being man-uttered and a mere vibration on the ether, becomes staler and staler, more and more boring, till at last we turn a deaf ear and it ceases to exist, far more finally than any withered grass. It is grass that renews its youth like the eagle,* not any Word.

当然这只能发生在活生生的我的身上。

既然这种颤动可以通过交流产生,它只能通过一部小说传达给我时我身上才会产生颤动。《圣经》——整部《圣经》,荷马史诗和莎士比亚的作品是卓越的古老小说。它们对所有的人来说就是一切。这就是说完整的小说感染整个活生生的人,即人本身,而不是人的某些部分。这些小说令整棵树获得新的生命并为之战抖,而不是刺激它朝某一个方向生长。

我可不想再朝某一个方向生长了。同时,只要我能够,我绝不鼓励任何别人向某一个特定方向成长。某一个特定的方向总要走向死胡同。现如今我们已经在死胡同里了。

我不相信任何闪烁其词的启示或任何至高无上的圣经。"芳草枯干,鲜花凋谢,但主的教诲永存。"[见《旧约·以赛亚书》第四十章,第八节]我们就是一直用这东西麻醉自己的。事实上,枯死的青草会在春雨滋润下变得更葱茏。鲜花凋落了,才会有新蕾绽开。可是主的话是靠人来传达的,只是空气中的震颤,它会变得愈来愈陈腐,愈来愈令人生厌,直到我们都闻而不知其声,它也就失去了存在的意义,比枯干的草还不如。芳草一岁一枯荣,像鹰一样可获新生[见《旧约·诗篇》第一百零三章,第五节],但主的话就不能这样。

If there is one thing more repulsive than the social being positive, it is the social being negative, the mere anti. In the great débâcle of decency, this gentleman is the most indecent. In a subtle way, Bosinney and Irene are more dishonest and more indecent than Soames and Winifred. But they are anti, so they are glorified. It is pretty sickening.

The introduction to *The Island Pharisees* explains the whole show. —"Each man born into the world is born to go a journey, and for the most part he is born on the high road —As soon as he can toddle, he moves, by the queer instinct we call the love of life, along this road: —his fathers went this way before him, they made this road for him to tread, and, when they bred him, passed into his fibre the love of doing things as they themselves had done them. So he walks on and on. —Suddenly one day, without intending to, he notices a path or opening in the hedge, leading to right or left, and he stands looking at the undiscovered. After that, he stops at all the openings in the hedge; one day, with a beating heart, he tries one. And this is where the fun begins." —Nine out of ten get back to the broad road again, and side-track no more. They snuggle down comfortably in the next inn, and think where they might have been. —"But the poor silly tenth is faring on. Nine

口,于是他便驻足寻找那未被发现的。从那以后,每遇到篱笆上的缺口,他都要驻足观望。有那么一天他的心怦怦跳着踏上了一条新径。从此有了乐趣。"——十个人里有九个人又折回原来的大路,不再另辟蹊径。他们会舒舒服服地蜷缩在下一个小旅店里想自己可能会去过的什么地方。"可是还有一个可怜的伙计接着朝前行呢。十次中有九次他会陷进沼泽地中,让那些未被发现的事物吞没他。"可是终于在第十次他却闯过去了,一条新的道路就此展开在人类面前。

把生命看成是两道篱墙中的公路是一种阶级局限意识的表现,至少是一种毫无希望的社会意识。惟一的出路就是寻到篱墙中的缝隙,跑出去顽童般地游戏一次!可这些反叛的人十次有九次会溜回原先稳定、舒服的生活中去;再有一次就是陷入沼泽中。只有百年不遇的某一次他们会闯过去开拓出一条新的道路。

在高尔斯华绥的小说中,我们看到人们九次、九十九次、一百九十九次地溜回稳定的幸福生活中去,我们只看到罕见的一个波西尼钻了汽车

times out of ten he goes down in a bog; the undiscovered has engulfed him." —But the tenth time, he gets across, and a new road is opened to mankind.

It is a class-bound consciousness, or at least a hopeless social consciousness which sees life as a high-road between two hedges. And the only way out is gaps in the hedge, and excursions into naughtiness! These little anti excursions. From which the wayfarer slinks back to solid comfort, nine times out of ten: an odd one goes down in a bog: and a very rare one finds a way across and opens out a new road.

In Mr Galsworthy's novels we see the nine, the ninety-nine, the nine hundred and ninety-nine slinking back to solid comfort; we see an odd Bosinney go under a bus, because he hadn't guts enough to do something else, the poor anti; but that rare figure sidetracking into the unknown we do not see.

Because as a matter of fact, the whole figure is faulty at that point. If life is a great high-way, then it must forge on ahead into the unknown. Sidetracking gets nowhere. That is mere anti. The tip of the road is always unfinished, in the wilderness. If it comes to a precipice and a canyon—well, then there is need for some exploring.

轮子，因为他没有勇气做点别的什么，可怜的反叛！不过我倒看不出他是另辟蹊径走向了未知世界。事实上，在这一点上，对这个人的塑造是虚假的。如果说生活是一条大路，那它就必须通向未知才对。另辟旁路是走不到那儿去的，只是反叛而已。路是没尽头的，总是断在荒野中。如果它是断在悬崖畔或峡谷上，那就需要一番探险了。可是从《乡间别墅》之后，我们则看到高尔斯华绥先生很安稳地停留在旧的公路上安富尊荣。他至少是没有陷入沼泽中，没有为寻找新的路而奋争。如今的篱墙上可是有不少缺口，谁都可以从此溜出去“反传统”一下子。可是福赛特家的路却没什么改观，只是因为有些人玩弄反叛的把戏，反传统把这条大路弄得乱糟糟、肮脏得很，在路上扔下了不少罐头瓶子。

在《法利赛人岛》、《有产业的人》和《友爱》三部早期小说中，高尔斯华绥先生似乎要用他的讽刺炸药炸破大路尽头的死障，以此帮助我们走上新的旅程。可是他使用的性炸药却是湿的，炸不响，只能“哗哗啦啦”变得很缠绵，于是情况比原先更糟糕。

But we see Mr Galsworthy, after *The Country House*, very safe on the old high-way, very secure in comfort, wealth, and renown. He at least has gone down in no bog, nor lost himself striking new paths. The hedges nowadays are ragged with gaps, anybody who likes strays out on the little trips of "unconvention." But the Forsyte road has not moved on at all. It has only become dishevelled and sordid with excursionists doing the anti tricks and being "unconventional," and leaving tin cans behind.

In the three early novels, *The Island Pharisees*, *The Man of Property*, *Fraternity*, it looked as if Mr Galsworthy might break through the blind end of the high-way, with the dynamite of satire, and help us out on to a new lap. But the sex ingredient of his dynamite was damp and muzzy, the explosions gradually fizzled off in sentimentality, and we are left in a worse state than before.

The later novels are purely commercial, and, if it had not been for the early novels,* of no importance. They are popular, they sell well, and there's the end of them. They contain the explosive powder of the first books, in minute quantities, fizzling as silly squibs. When you arrive at *To Let*, and the end, at least the *promised* end of the Forsytes, what have you? Just money! Money, money, mon-

后期的小说则一派商业气。如若不是因为有了前面几部，这后几部就无足轻重了。这几本流行，销得动，不过如此而已。这后几部中太缺少前几部的爆炸力了，只像几个小鞭炮罢了。你读《出让》时，那最美好的结局是什么？只是金钱！金钱，金钱，金钱和势利的傻气，再就是几个反叛的把戏和姿态。再没有别的什么。其故事虚弱得很，人物也没有血肉，情感假得很，十分地虚假。这是一个大虚假！这倒不见得是高尔斯华绥先生的责任，而是人物自身的毛病，他们尽制造假情绪。这对我们可没好处。如果你审视一下这些人物，你会发现他们身上那种卑琐和庸俗之气实在令人反感。你看到了福赛特家的所有卑琐处，却看不到他们身上的活力。朱利昂和伊琳妮在他们的儿子眼中显得比老福赛特们更卑琐。这些年轻的比他们的先辈如斯威辛或詹姆斯更狭隘、呆板、庸俗、利己。你会感到小说中有一种为富的庸俗，我们可以说他们毫无真正的情感，特别是女人如弗鲁尔、伊琳妮、安纳蒂和简。她们能言善辩，愚不可及，充满年少的冲动，这副样子实在粗鄙而缺少感情。总潜藏着一种庸俗的“占有”金钱感

ey, and a certain snobbish silliness, and many more anti tricks and poses. Nothing else. The story is feeble, the characters have no blood and bones, the emotions are faked, faked, faked. It is one great fake. Not necessarily of Mr Galsworthy's. The characters fake their own emotions. But that doesn't help us. And if you look closely at the characters, the meanness and low-level vulgarity are very distasteful. You have all the Forsyte meanness, with none of the energy. Jolyon and Irene are meaner and more treacherous to their son than the older Forsytes were to theirs. The young ones are of a limited, mechanical vulgar egoism far surpassing that of Swithin or James, their ancestors. There is in it all a vulgar sense of being rich, and therefore we do as we like: an utter incapacity for anything like true feeling, especialy in the women, Fleur, Irene, Annette, June: a glib crassness, a youthful spontaneity which is just impertinence and lack of feeling; and all the time, a creeping, "having" sort of vulgarity of money and self-will, money and self-will:—so that we wonder, sometimes, if Mr Galsworthy is not treating his public in real bad faith, and being cynical and rancorous under his rainbow sentimentalism.

Fleur he destroys in one word: she is "having." It is perfectly true. We don't blame the young Jon for clearing out.—Irene he destroys in a phrase out of Fleur's

和自我意志，所以我们怀疑高尔斯华绥先生是否有时在欺骗他的读者，是否在他那伤感的虹拱之下潜藏着愤世嫉俗和仇恨。

他一个字就把弗鲁尔给打发了：她是个"占有"式的人。太对了。我们绝不谴责年轻的乔恩清算他们。对伊琳妮，他则通过弗鲁尔对简的一句话予以打发："她是不是也毁了你的生活？"——伊琳妮的确做了这种事。她鬼鬼祟祟，卑鄙下作，害的简没有得到她的情人，还同样坏了弗鲁尔的事。她是个占着茅坑不拉屎的母狗，是个鬼鬼祟祟的反叛。伊琳妮，你这世上最美的女子！可高尔斯华绥先生却以一个成功的老伤感者的犬儒口吻通过简的口说："我亲爱的，没人能毁掉生活。这纯属胡扯。出了什么事也不怕，我们还会恢复元气的。"

这就是最终的哲学了。"出了什么事也不怕，我们还会恢复元气的。"很好，那就照着这个调子写书吧，这是一个坦诚的老玩世不恭者的基调。没必要把事情伤感化，没必要做一个鬼鬼祟祟的老玩世不恭者。为何要假装真诚地抛出一腔感情又用这么一句话打发感情呢？出了什么事也不

mouth to June: "Didn't she spoil your life too?" —And it is precisely what she did. Sneaking and mean, Irene prevented June from getting her lover. Sneaking and mean, she prevents Fleru. She is the bitch in the manger. She is the sneaking *anti*. Irene, the most beautiful woman on earth! —And Mr Galsworthy, with the cynicism of a successful old sentimentalist, turns it off by making June say: "Nobody can spoil a life, my dear. That's nonsense. Things happen, but we bob up."

This is the final philosophy of it all. "Things happen, but we bob up." Very well, then write the book in that key, the keynote of a frank old cynic. There's no point in sentimentalising it and being a sneaking old cynic. Why pour out masses of feelings that pretend to be genuine, and then turn it all off with: "Things happen, but we bob up."

It is quite true, things happen, and we bob up. If we are vulgar sentimentalists, we bob up just the same, so nothing has happened, and nothing can happen. All is vulgarity. But it pays. There is money in it.

Vulgarity pays, and cheap cynicism smothered in sentimentalism pays better than anything else. Because nothing can happen to the degraded social being. So let's pretend it does, and then bob up!

怕，我们还会恢复元气的。

很对。出了什么事也不怕，我们会东山再起的。如果我们是庸俗的感伤者，再生还是个感伤者，这等于什么都没发生，什么都不能发生，什么都庸俗之极。可这很值，庸俗里头有金钱。

庸俗值钱，窒息在伤感主义中的廉价玩世不恭比什么都值钱。因为什么都拿低下的社会生物奈何不得。让我们自以为会出点什么事然后让它恢复元气吧！

是时候了，该有人唾弃感伤主义，至少要唾弃那窒息了"恢复"哲学的感伤主义。是时候了，我们该让年轻的福赛特感伤主义者们曝曝光，这群老鼠。世上有成千上万福赛特式的感伤主义者。是感伤主义窒息着我们。只要这些社会生物有能力，就让他们再生吧。可我们该把水龙头照着他们这些感伤主义者直浇一通。他们把什么都污染了，这世界就是他们分泌的一团黏糊糊的东西，这群小福赛特的确在里面还阳了，可是真诚的感情却难以将息。

It is time somebody began to spit out the jam of sentimentalism, at least, which smothers the "bobbing-up" philosophy. It is time we turned a straight light on this horde of rats, these younger Forsyte sentimentalists whose name is legion. It is sentimentalism which is stifling us. Let the social beings keep on bobbing up while ever they can. But it is time an effort was made to turn a hose-pipe on the sentimentalism they ooze over everything. The world is one sticky mess, in which the little Forsytes indeed may keep on bobbing still, but in which an honest feeling can't breathe.

But if the sticky mess gets much deeper, even the little Forsytes won't be able to bob up any more. They'll be smothered in their own slime, along with everything else. Which is a comfort.

可如果这团黏糊糊的东西再深厚些，那些小福赛特们就无法在里面还阳了。他们就会与别的东西一道在他们自身的分泌液中窒息死。这还能让人感到些许安慰。

1927 年

INTRODUCTION TO THESE PAINTINGS

The reason the English produce so few painters is not that they are, as a nation, devoid of a genuine feeling for visual art: though to look at their productions, and to look at the mess which has been made of actual English landscape, one might really conclude that they were, and leave it at that. But it is not the fault of the God that made them. They are made with aesthetic sensibilities the same as anybody else. The fault lies in the English attitude to life.

The English, and the Americans following them, are paralysed by fear. That is what thwarts and distorts the Anglo-Saxon existence, this paralysis of fear. It thwarts life, it distorts vision, and it strangles impulse: this overmastering fear. And fear of what, in heaven's name? What is the Anlgo-Saxon stock so petrified with fear about? We have to answer that before we can understand the English failure in the visual arts: for, on the whole, it is a failure.

David Herbert Lawrence

直觉与绘画[此文是劳伦斯为自己的绘画集(曼德里克版)所写的序言。现在的标题为译者所加,副标题为原标题]

——《D.H.劳伦斯绘画集》自序

英国哺育出的画家为数如此之寥寥,这并非因为英国这个民族缺乏视觉艺术的真正感觉。诚然,看看英国的绘画,看看实实在在的英国风景被他们画得一塌糊涂,你会认为英国人是这样的民族。但这并不是创造英国人的上帝之错误使然。他们与任何别的民族一样天生具有审美情感,错就错在英国人对生命的态度上。

英国人,还有随后的美国人,全因着恐惧而瘫痪。就是这个恐惧造成的瘫痪,歪曲了盎格鲁-撒克逊的存在,令其受挫。它同样挫败了生命,歪曲了眼光,扼杀了冲动,这压倒了一切的恐惧。天知道,到底怕什么呢?盎

It is an old fear, which seemed to dig in to the English soul at the time of the Renaissance. Nothing could be more lovely and fearless than Chaucer. But already Shakespeare is morbid with fear, fear of consequences. That is the strange phenomenon of the English Renaissance: this mystic terror of the consequences, the consequences of action. Italy, too, had her reaction, at the end of the sixteenth century, and showed a similar fear. But not so profound, so overmastering. Aretino* was anything but timorous, he was bold as any Renaissance novelist, and went one better.

What appeared to take full grip on the northern consciousness at the end of the sixteenth century was a terror, almost a horror of sexual life. The Elizabethans, grand as we think them, started it. The real 'mortal coil' in Hamlet is all sexual; the young man's horror of his mother's incest, sex carrying with it a wild and nameless terror which, it seems to me, it had never carried before. Oedipus and Hamlet are very different in this respect. In Oedipus there is no recoil in horror from sex itself: Greek drama never shows us that. The horror, when it is present in Greek tragedy, is against *destiny*, man caught in the toils of destiny. But with the Renaissance itself, particularly in England, the horror is sexual. Orestes* is dogged by

格鲁-撒克逊这个种族到底被什么吓成这副呆板相？若要弄明白英国在视觉艺术上的失败，我们得先回答这个问题才行。是的，总的来说，英国视觉艺术是个败笔。

这是一股古已有之的恐惧，它浸入到了英国人的灵魂里，可以追溯到文艺复兴时期。没有谁比乔叟更可爱、更无畏的了。可到了莎士比亚就出现了可怕的恐惧，害怕后果。这是英国文艺复兴运动的奇特现象：对后果神秘的恐惧，害怕行动的后果。它在十六世纪末的意大利也有反应，出现了相似的恐惧，不过不像英国的恐惧来得这样大，这样不可收拾。阿里蒂诺[Pietro Aretino(1492—1556)，意大利讽刺家和戏剧家]就不胆小，他像所有文艺复兴时期的小说家一样勇敢，甚至还更高他们一筹。

而十六世纪末叶紧紧攫住北方[指意大利以北的欧洲地区]人的是一种恐惧，是对性生活的恐惧。这正是从我们认为很不可一世的伊丽莎白时期开端的。哈姆雷特真正“尘世的烦恼”全然来自性——这小伙子怕的是他母亲的乱伦。在我看来，性这东西带来了史无前例的混乱与无以言表的恐惧。

destiny and driven mad by the Eumenides. But Hamlet is over-powered by horrible revulsion from his physical connexion with his mother, which makes him recoil in similar revulsion from Ophelia and almost from his father, even as a ghost. He is horrified at the merest suggestion of physical connexion, as if it were an unspeakable taint.

This, no doubt, is all in the course of the growth of the 'spiritual-mental' consciousness, at the expense of the instinctive-intuitive consciousness. Man came to have his own body in horror, especially in its sexual implications: and so he began to suppress with all his might his instinctiveintuitive consciousness, which is so radical, so physical, so sexual. Cavalier poetry, love poetry, is already devoid of body. Donne, after the exacerbated revulsion-attraction excitement of his earlier poetry, becomes a divine. 'Drink to me only with thine eyes' sings the cavalier: an expression incredible in Chaucer's poetry. 'I could not love thee, dear, so much, loved I not honour more', sings the Cavalier lover. In Chaucer the 'dear' and the 'honour' would have been more or less identical.

But with the Elizabethans the grand rupture had started in the human consciousness, the mental consciousness recoiling in violence away from the physical,

在这方面,俄狄浦斯与哈姆雷特则全然不同。在于俄狄浦斯,他不惧怕性——希腊戏剧从没有向我们展示这一点。当希腊戏剧中出现恐惧时,那是对命运的恐惧,人被命运所束缚,因此感到恐惧。可是,文艺复兴,尤其是英国的文艺复兴却带来了对性的恐惧。奥列斯特[Orestes,希腊神话中阿伽门农之子,杀其母为父报仇]是为命运所驱使并被复仇女神逼疯的。可哈姆雷特却是害怕与母亲的肉体联系,这种恐惧也使他厌恶欧菲利娅,甚至厌恶已成鬼魂的亲生父亲。他一想到肉体联系就害怕,似乎那是什么见不得人的脏东西。

毫无疑问,这全是牺牲了本能-直觉意识去发展"精神-理智"意识的结果。人开始惧怕自己的肉体,谈性色变,于是开始死命压抑那激进、肉感和性感的本能-直觉意识。骑士诗和爱情诗已经开始脱离肉体了。堂恩早期狂热地写了一阵子亲亲爱爱的诗,后来就变神圣了。"只需你的双眸凝视我"已成了骑士的表达方式,这在乔叟的诗中是绝对没有的。"我爱你,亲爱的,就像我爱荣誉一样,"骑士情人这样唱着。在乔叟的诗里,这

instinctive-intuitive. To the Restoration dramatists sex is, on the whole, a dirty business, but they more or less glory in the dirt. Fielding tries in vain to defend the Old Adam. Richardson with his calico purity and his underclothing excitements sweeps all before him. Swift goes mad with sex and excrement revulsion. Sterne flings a bit of the same excrement humorously around. And physical consciousness gives a last song in Burns, then is dead. Wordsworth, Keats, Shelley, the Brontës, all are post-mortem poets. The essential instinctive-intuitive body is dead, and worshipped in death-all very unhealthy. Till Swinburne and Oscar Wilde try to start a revival from the mental field. Swinburne's 'white thighs' are purely mental.

Now, in England-and following, in America-the physical self was not just fig-leafed over or suppressed in public, as was the case in Italy and on most of the Continent. In England it excited a strange horror and terror. And this extra morbidity came, I believe, from the great shock of syphilis and the realization of the consequences of the disease. Wherever syphilis, or 'pox', came from, it was fairly new in England, at the end of the fifteenth century. But by the end of the sixteenth, its ravages were obvious, and the shock of them had just penetrated the thoughtful and the imaginative consciousness. The royal families of England and Scotland were

"亲爱的"与那"荣誉"大体上意思相似。

可到了伊丽莎白时期,人们的意识开始了大裂变。人的理智开始从肉体、本能和直觉那里退缩。对于王朝复辟时期的戏剧家们来说,性总的来说是件肮脏的事,可他们好歹还在肮脏中取点乐。费尔丁试图为人的犯罪本能辩护,却毫不奏效。理查德逊清心寡欲,即便是激动也是偷偷摸摸的,他把什么都一扫而光。斯威夫特则对性和排泄发疯地反感。斯泰恩对同样的排泄显出幽默的态度。肉体意识在彭斯那里成了绝唱,从此就死了。华兹华斯、济慈、雪莱和勃朗特三姐妹全是些个死气沉沉的诗人。最重要的本能-直觉的肉体已经死了,他们只崇拜死了的肉体,这种做法才太不健康。到了史文朋和奥斯卡·王尔德,他们试图把肉体从理智手中解救出来。可史文朋的"白色大腿"则纯属理智。

在英国,随后是在美国,肉体的自我不只是像在意大利或大多数欧洲大陆国家那样被蒙上遮羞布或在公共场合遭到禁忌。在英国,它引起了奇怪的恐怖。这种额外的恐怖,我想,是来自梅毒及其后果引起的震

syphilitic; Edward VI and Elizabeth born with the inherited consequences of the disease. Edward VI died of it, while still a boy. Mary* died childless and in utter depression. Elizabeth had no eyebrows, her teeth went rotten; she must have felt herself, somewhere, utterly unfit for marriage, poor thing. That was the grisly horror that lay behind the glory of Queen Bess. And so the Tudors died out: and another syphilitic-born unfortunate came to the throne, in the person of James I. Mary Queen of Scots had no more luck than the Tudors, apparently. Apparently Darnley was reeking with the pox, though probably at first she did not know it. But when the Archbishop of St Andrews was christening her baby James, afterwards James I of England, the old clergyman was so dripping with pox that she was terrified lest he should give it to the infant. And she need not have troubled, for the wretched infant had brought it into the world with him, from that fool Darnley. So James I of England slobbered and shambled, and was the wisest fool in Christendom, and the Stuarts likewise died out, the stock enfeebled by the disease.

With the royal families of England and Scotland in this condition, we can judge what the noble houses, the nobility of both nations, given to free living and promiscuous pleasure, must have been like. England traded with the East and with

惊。梅毒这东西弄不清源自何处,在十五世纪末的英国还算是件新鲜事。可到了十六世纪,其危害大大明显起来,它震惊了人们的思想和想像。英格兰和苏格兰的皇族们染上了梅毒,爱德华六世和伊丽莎白一生下来就受到这种家族遗传病的影响。爱德华六世还是个孩子时就因梅毒而死,玛丽[指玛丽·都铎,即玛丽一世,英格兰女王(1553-1558在位)]则死而无嗣,为此抱恨。伊丽莎白不长眉毛,牙齿溃烂。她一定认为自己全然不适合结婚,可怜的人儿。这就是伊丽莎白女王盛誉背后隐藏着的恐惧。都铎家族就这样灭绝了,继承王位的却是另一个不幸的梅毒患者詹姆斯一世。很明显,苏格兰的玛丽女王也并不比都铎家族的人幸运。很明显,她丈夫丹利染上了梅毒,不过也许一开始玛丽并不知道。可是当圣·安德鲁斯的大主教给她的儿子、未来英国的詹姆斯一世施洗礼时,那老牧师手上梅毒淋漓,玛丽吓得魂飞魄散,生怕他把梅毒传给婴儿。其实她的担心为时已晚,因为这可怜的孩子已经从丹利这个傻父亲那里继承了梅毒。这位英格兰的詹姆斯一世于是就淌着口水,步履蹒跚,是基督教世界中最聪明的傻瓜。斯图

America; England, unknowingly, had opened her doors to the disease. The English aristocracy travelled and had curious taste in loves. And pox entered the blood of the nation, particularly of the upper classes, who had more chance of infection. And after it had entered the blood, it entered the consciousness, and hit the vital imagination.

It is possible that the effects of syphilis and the conscious realization of its consequences gave a great blow to the Spanish psyche, precisely at this period. And it is possible that Italian society, which was on the whole so untravelled, had no connexion with America, and was so privately self-contained, suffered less from the disease. Someone ought to make a thorough study of the effects of 'pox' on the minds and the emotions and imaginations of the various nations of Europe, at about the time of our Elizabethans.

The apparent effect on the Elizabethans and the Restoration wits is curious. They appear to take the whole thing as a joke. The common oath, 'Pox on you' was almost funny. But how common the oath was! How the word 'pox' was in every mind and in every mouth. It is one of the words that haunt Elizabethan speech. Taken very manly, with a great deal of Falstaffian bluff, treated as a huge joke! Pox!

亚特王朝也同样毁灭了,整个家族全为这种病而衰竭。

英格兰和苏格兰的皇族们都是这种情形,我们据此可以判断这两个民族中生活放浪、纵情乱交的贵族们该是什么样的人。英格兰与东方和美洲都有贸易关系,于是它就不知不觉中为梅毒打开了大门。英国贵族四处旅行,品尝着爱的奇味儿,于是梅毒进入了这个民族的血液中,特别是进入贵族的血液中,他们更有传染的机遇。梅毒先是入血,随后进入思想,击毙了人们活生生的想像力。

很可能,梅毒的影响和人们对其后果的认识就在这个时期给西班牙人的心理带来了重大的打击。而意大利人的履历不太广,与美洲没什么联系,他们自成一家,因此受梅毒之苦就轻得多。真应该有人对伊丽莎白时期梅毒对各不同民族的心灵、感情和想像力所产生的影响做一番全面的研究。

对伊丽莎白时期的人和王朝复辟时期的智者们来说,这种影响是奇怪的。他们似乎只把这种事当玩笑,口头上用来咒人的话就是"让你得点

Why, he´s got the pox! Ha–ha! What´s he been after?

There is just the same attitude among the common run of men today with regard to the minor sexual diseases. Syphilis is no longer regarded as a joke, according to my experience. The very word itself frightens men. You could joke with the word 'pox'. You can´t joke with the word 'syphilis'. The change of word has killed the joke. But men still joke about clap! which is a minor sexual disease. They pretend to think it manly, even, to have the disease, or to have had it. 'What! never had a shot of clap! ' cries one gentleman to another. 'Why, where have you been all your life?' If we changed the word and insisted on 'gonorrhoea', or whatever it is, in place of 'clap', the joke would die. Anyhow I have had young men come to me green and quaking, afraid they´ve caught a 'shot of clap'.

Now, in spite of all the Elizabethan jokes about pox, pox was no joke to them. A joke may be a very brave way of meeting a calamity, or it may be a very cowardly way. Myself, I consider the Elizabethan pox joke a purely cowardly attitude. They didn´t think it funny, for by God it wasn´t funny. Even poor Elizabeth´s lack of eyebrows and her rotten teeth were not funny. And they knew it. They may not have known it was the direct result of pox: though probably they did. This fact remains,

梅”,听起来很好笑。这咒语也太司空见惯了!“梅”这个词在人们心中和嘴中竟如此平常,伊丽莎白时期的人张口闭口皆是“梅”,他们很有男子气地对待它,如同福斯塔夫似的哈哈一笑了之!梅!你染了点梅!哈哈,你干了些什么好事儿?

这正如今天的普通人对待微小的性病一样。可就我的经验而言,梅毒已不再被看成一种玩笑了。光这个词儿本身就够吓人的了。你可以拿“梅”开玩笑,可“梅毒”二字却玩笑不得。一字之差就让人笑不起来。人们仍然拿“淋”开玩笑,因为这是一种无关紧要的性病。人们装作男子汉对待“淋”,甚至装作得了这病或装作得过这东西。“什么!你连点儿淋都没染上过吗,真是的!”绅士们相互叫着。“怎么回事,你这辈子怎么活的?”可如果换成“淋病”,就玩笑不得了。不过的确有年轻人面色铁青瑟瑟发抖地来告诉我他们怕是“染上了点儿淋”。

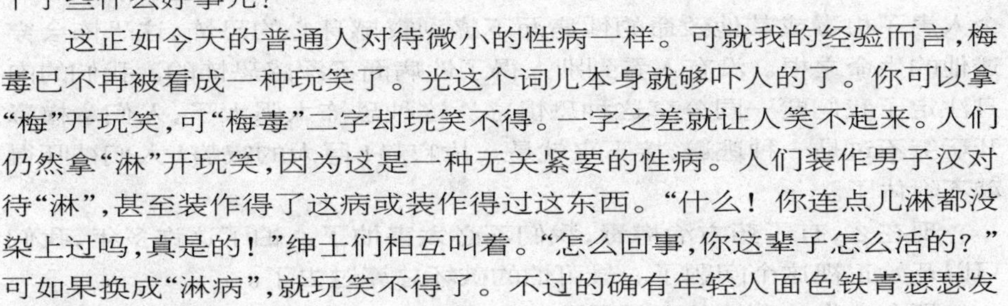

尽管伊丽莎白时期的人们都拿梅毒开玩笑,可对他们来说这并非儿戏。玩笑可以说是一种对付灾难的勇敢办法,但也可以说是一种胆小鬼

that no man can contract syphilis, or any deadly sexual disease, without feeling the most shattering and profound terror go through him, through the very roots of his being. And no man can look without a sort of horror on the effects of a sexual disease in another person. We are so constituted that we are all at once horrified and terrified. The fear and dread has been so great that the pox joke was invented as an evasion, and following that, the great hush! hush! was imposed. Man was *too* frightened: that's the top and bottom of it.

But now, with remedies discovered, we need no longer be *too* frightened. We can begin, after all these years, to face the matter. After the most fearful damage has been done.

For the overmastering fear is poison to the human psyche. And this overmastering fear, like some horrible secret tumour, has been poisoning our consciousness ever since the Elizabethans, who first woke up with dread to the entry of the original syphilitic poison into the blood.

I know nothing about medicine and very little about disease, and my facts are such as I have picked up in casual reading. Nevertheless I am convinced that the secret awareness of syphilis, and the utter secret terror and horror of it, has had an

的办法。反正我就觉得伊丽莎白时期的玩笑是一种纯粹懦弱的表现。他们并不以为这东西好玩。天晓得这一点都不好玩。甚至可怜的伊丽莎白没有眉毛、牙齿溃烂,这并不好玩。他们都懂这一点。他们可能还不知道这是梅毒造成的直接后果,尽管他们很可能知道。这个事实说明,没有哪个人患了梅毒或其他致命的性病而不感到震撼身心的恐怖,这恐怖会穿透他的生命之根。没有人看到别人得了性病而不深感恐怖的。我们的肉身注定了我们要一同分享这种恐惧感。这种恐怖太强大了,人们拿梅毒开玩笑不过是一种逃避,接下来就是一片寂静!巨大的寂静!人们被吓得魂不附体了。

现在么,有了药方治梅毒,我们不必太害怕了。怕了这许多年,我们可以开始正视这个问题了。最可怕的破坏总算过去了。

那令人失魂落魄的恐惧是人类心灵的一剂毒药,它就像一个可怕的神秘毒瘤,从伊丽莎白时期起就毒害着我们的意识。那个时期的人第一次发现梅毒之毒会进入人的血液,于是大惊失色,梅毒令人代代恐惧。

enormous and incalculable effect on the English consciousness and on the American. Even when the fear has never been formulated, there it has lain, potent and overmastering. I am convinced that some of Shakespeare's horror and despair, in his tragedies, arose from the shock of his consciousness of syphilis. I don't suggest for one moment Shakespeare ever contracted syphilis. I have never had syphilis myself. Yet I know and confess how profound is my fear of the disease, and more than fear, my horror. In fact, I don't think I am so very much afraid of it. I am more horrified, inwardly and deeply, at the idea of its existence.

All this sounds very far from the art of painting. But it is not so far as it sounds. The appearance of syphilis in our midst gave a fearful blow to our sexual life. The real natural innocence of Chaucer was impossible after that. The very sexual act of procreation might bring as one of its consequences a foul disease, and the unborn might be tainted from the moment of conception. Fearful thought! It is truly a fearful thought, and all the centuries of getting used to it won't help us. It remains a fearful thought, and to free ourselves from this fearful dread we should use all our wits and all our efforts, not stick our heads in the sand of some idiotic joke, or still more idiotic don't-mention-it. The fearful thought of the consequences of syphilis,

我对医学一窍不通，也不大懂病理，我举的几个例子都是读书中的偶然巧得。但是我相信，对于梅毒的悄然意识及其对梅毒全然神秘的恐怖对英国和美国人的思想产生了巨大、无法估量的影响。甚至当这种恐怖只显露端倪之时它就已经很厉害了。我相信，莎士比亚悲剧中的某些恐惧和失望就是因为他意识到了梅毒的危害、受了惊吓才有的。我从未猜测过莎翁是否也染上过梅毒，反正我自个儿是没得过这种病。但我承认我太怕这玩意儿了，不仅是怕，而且是恐惧。其实我倒不怎么怕它，只是一想到这东西的存在我内心深处就不寒而栗。

这些话听起来似乎与绘画离题十万八千里了。可其实离题并不远。我们内心深处所想像的梅毒对我们的性生活着实是一大打击。从此以后，乔叟的真正自然纯朴就不存在了。为了生殖的性行为可能会导致一种脏病，那未出生的孩子在怀上的那一刻就沾上了这东西。想想就吓死人！是太可怕了，几个世纪以来尽管我们对此司空见惯，可还是怕它。它一直让人想起就害怕，为了让我们得到解脱，我们应该苦思冥想，竭尽全力，而

or of any sexual disease, upon the unborn gives a shock to the impetus of fatherhood in any man, even the cleanest. Our consciousness is a strange thing, and the knowledge of a certain fact may wound it mortally, even if the fact does not touch us directly. And so I am certain that some of Shakespeare's father-murder complex, some of Hamlet's horror of his mother, of his uncle, of all old men came from the feeling that fathers may transmit syphilis, or syphilis-consequences, to children. I don't know even whether Shakespeare was actually aware of the consequences to a child born of a syphilitic father or mother. He may not have been, though most probably he was. But he certainly was aware of the effects of syphilis itself, especially on men. And this awareness struck at his deep sex imagination, at his instinct for fatherhood, and brought in an element of terror and abhorrence there where men should feel anything but terror and abhorrence, into the procreative act.

The terror-horror element which had entered the imagination with regard to the sexual and procreative act was at least partly responsible for the rise of Puritanism, the beheading of the king-father Charles, and the establishment of the New England colonies. If America really sent us syphilis, she got back the full recoil of the horror of it, in her puritanism.

不是像鸵鸟一样躲进沙丘中编几个傻乎乎的玩笑或更为愚蠢地置之不提。梅毒或任何别的性病会传染未出生的婴儿，这后果让人们害怕极了，它令任何做父亲的包括那些最干净的父亲深感震惊。我们的思想真是个奇怪的东西，意识到了什么东西思想就会受到致命伤，尽管这东西并未直接触动我们。所以，我相信莎士比亚笔下的某些弑父情结、哈姆雷特对母亲、对叔父及所有老年男人的惧怕，这些全是因为他觉得父亲会传染给孩子梅毒。我甚至不知道莎士比亚是否的确意识到对患梅毒的父母所生育的孩子来说梅毒意味着什么。他或许没意识到，但他极有可能意识到了。他肯定意识到了梅毒本身对人，特别是对男人的影响。这种意识撞击着他内心深处的性想像力，撞击着他做父亲的本能并给他的生殖行为增添了些许恐怖感。

恐怖感进入了人们对于性和生殖行为的想像中，这至少是清教主义兴起的部分原因，处决查理斯一世和建立新英格兰殖民地也与此有关。如果真是美国人带来了梅毒，那么他们就该得到清教主义，让梅毒彻底

But deeper even than this, the terror-horror element led to the crippling of the consciousness of man. Very elementary in man is his sexual and procreative being, and on his sexual and procreative being depend many of his deepest instincts and the flow of his intuition. A deep instinct of his kinship joins men together, and the kinship of flesh-and-blood keeps the warm flow of intuitional awareness streaming between human beings. Our true awareness of one another is intuitional, not mental. Attraction between people is really instinctive and intuitional, not an affair of judgement. And in mutual attraction lies perhaps the deepest pleasure in life, mutual attraction which may make us 'like' our travelling companion for the two or three hours we are together, then no more; or mutual attraction that may deepen to powerful love, and last a life-time.

The terror-horror element struck a blow at our feeling of physical communion. In fact, it almost killed it. We have become ideal beings, creatures that exist in idea, to one another, rather than flesh-and-blood kin. And with the collapse of the feeling of physical, flesh-and-blood kinship, and the substitution of our ideal, social or political oneness, came the failing of our intuitive awareness, and the great unease, the *nervousness* of mankind. We are *afraid* of the instincts. We are *afraid* of

吓破胆。

比这更严重的是,这种恐惧感会使人的思想瘫痪。人之最基本的东西就是他的性与生殖生命,他不少强壮的本能和流动的直觉所依赖的就是他的性和生殖生命。根深蒂固的亲缘本能使人们携起手来,这种血肉的亲和力促使本能意识的热流在人与人之间流淌。我们之所以能真正意识到对方,靠的是直觉而绝非理智。人与人之间相吸引,实在凭的是本能和直觉,绝不是靠判断。或许在人与人的相互吸引中存在着人生最大的愉悦。相互的吸引可以使我们在两三个小时之内喜欢我们的旅伴然后就此结束,也可以加深感情,使之变成强大的爱,持续一辈子。

可梅毒造成的恐怖感对我们肉体的交流感觉带来一大打击,事实上扼杀了它。我们从此变成了理智的人,我们只存在于各自的理念中而不是有血有肉的亲朋。肉体和血肉亲和感崩溃了,取而代之的是我们思想上、社会上和政治上的同一,于是我们的直觉就瘫痪了,人类那了不起的紧张躁动也随之失灵了。我们惧怕自己的本能,惧怕自身的直觉。我们压

the intuition within us. We suppress the instincts, and we cut off our intuitional awareness from one another and the world. The reason being some great shock to the procreative self. Now we know one another only as ideal or social or political entities, fleshless, bloodless, and cold, like Bernard Shaw's creatures. Intuitively we are dead to one another, we have all gone cold.

But by intuition alone can man really be aware of man, or of the living, substantial world. By intuition alone can man live and know either woman or world, and by intuition alone can he bring forth again images of magic awareness which we call art. In the past men brought forth images of magic awareness, and now it is the convention to admire these images. The convention says, for example, we must admire Botticelli or Giorgione, so Baedeker stars the pictures, and we admire them. But it is all a fake. Even those that get a thrill, even when they call it ecstasy, from these old pictures are only undergoing cerebral excitation. Their deeper responses, down in the intuitive and instinctive body, are not touched. They cannot be, because they are dead. A dead intuitive body stands there and gazes at the corpse of beauty: and usually it is completely and honestly bored. Sometimes it feels a mental coruscation which it calls an ecstasy or an aesthetic response.

抑本能，割断了我们与别人和这世界之间的直觉意识，这就是生殖自我受到了重大打击的原因。我们现在只把各自当成是思想、社会和政治实体，没血没肉，像萧伯纳笔下的人物一样冷酷。我们相互之间的直觉感应已经死了，我们全变冷了。

只凭着直觉，人就可以真正地意识到他人活生生的实体世界。仅凭着直觉男人就可以爱并懂得女人或世界，而且仅凭着直觉他就可以再现神奇意识的意象，我们称这东西叫艺术。过去的人再现了神奇意识的意象，现在我们按习惯仰慕这些东西。比如，习惯告诉我们要仰慕波提切利或乔尔乔尼[Giorgione(1478? —1511)，意大利文艺复兴时期威尼斯画家]，所以旅行指南上给他们的绘画标上星标让我们去瞻仰。可这全是虚假的。甚至那激动，甚至人们号称从这些旧画中获得的激情，也不过是理性的激动。其实他们的直觉和本能的肉体深处并没有产生回应，并没有受到触动。他们不能这样，因为他们已经死了。一具直觉上僵死的肉体站在那里凝视美丽的躯体时往往只会产生厌恶。有时他们会感到理性的闪耀，于是他们称

Modern people, but particularly English and Americans, cannot feel anything with the whole imagination. They can see the living body of imagery as little as a blind man can see colour. The imaginative vision, which includes physical, intuitional perception, they have not got. Poor things, it is dead in them. And they stand in front of a Botticelli Venus, which they know as conventionally 'beautiful', much as a blind man might stand in front of a bunch of roses and pinks and monkey-musk, saying: 'Oh, do tell me which is red; let me feel red! Now let me feel white! Oh, let me feel it! What is this I am feeling? Monkey-musk? Is it white? Oh, do you say it is yellow blotched with orange-brown? Oh, but I can't feel it! What can it be? Is white velvety, or just silky?'

So the poor blind man! Yet he may have an acute perception of alive beauty. Merely by touch and scent, his intuitions being alive, the blind man may have a genuine and soulsatisfying experience of imagery. But not pictorial images. These are forever beyond him.

So those poor English and Americans in front of the Botticelli Venus. They stare so hard; they do so want to see. And their eyesight is perfect. But all they can scc is a sort of nude woman on a sort of shell on a sort of pretty greenish water. As

之为狂喜或美的回应。

现代人,特别是英美人,是无法发挥自己全部的想像力去感受什么的。他们像瞎子看不到颜色一样地看待活生生的意象。想像力,包括肉体上直觉的感悟能力正是他们所没有的。可怜的人们,他们肉体上直觉的感悟力已死。他们站在波提切利所画的维纳斯前面,按习惯说这是一幅"美丽"的图画。这就如同一个瞎子站在一束玫瑰、石楠花和麝香前一样,他们会说:"请告诉我,哪个是红的,让我摸一下那红色吧!让我摸一下白色!哦,让我摸一下吧!我摸的这是什么?是麝香吗?是白的吗?你是说黄色上点缀着橙色吗?可是,我摸不出来啊!它到底是什么颜色啊?是白丝绒样的还是纯粹像绸缎?"

可怜的瞎子啊!可他也许对活生生的美有一种强烈的感悟。只凭着触摸和嗅觉,他的直觉就可以很活跃,因此他可以获得一种真正心灵上满足的想像经验。可这绝非图像,图像是他永远也不能企及的。

可怜的英美人在波提切利画的维纳斯面前就是这副瞎相,他们拼命

a rule they rather dislike the 'unnaturalness' or 'affectation' of it. If they are high-brows they may get a little self-conscious thrill of aesthetic excitement. But real imaginative awareness, which is so largely physical, is denied them. *Ils n´ont pas de quoi*, as the Frenchman said of the angels, when asked if they made love in heaven.

Ah, the dear high-brows who gaze in a sort of ecstasy and get a correct mental thrill! Their poor high-brow bodies stand there as dead as dust-bins, and can no more feel the sway of complete imagery upon them than they can feel any other real sway. *Ils n´ont pas de quoi.* The instincts and the intuitions are so nearly dead in them. and they fear even the feeble remains. Their fear of the instincts and intuitions is even greater than that of the English Tommy who calls: 'Eh, Jack! Come an´ look at this girl standin´ wi´ no clothes on, an´ two blokes spittin´ at´ er.' That is his vision of Botticelli´s Venus. It is, for him, complete, for he is void of the image-seeing imagination. But at least he doesn´t have to work up a cerebral excitation, as the high-brow does, who is really just as void.

All alike, cultured and uncultured, they are still dominated by that unnamed, yet overmastering dread and hate of the instincts deep in the body, dread of the

地睁大眼睛,多么想看看啊。要知道他们的视力是没毛病的,可他们看到的只是一个光身子的女人站在碧水托着的一只什么壳子中。按一般常规,他们着实不喜欢这幅画的"做作劲儿"。如果他们是些高雅之士,他们从中获得的是一点儿自作聪明的审美快感。可是那更属于肉体的真正想像意识却与他们无缘。"什么也没有啊,"正如人们问法国人天使们是否在天上做爱时他们所说的那样。

哦,这些情趣高雅之士,他们满怀狂喜地凝望着这幅画,从中获得一种毫无偏差的理智激动!这些高雅之士那可怜的肉体站在那儿就仿佛一座座呆板的垃圾箱,根本不能感受全部的想像在他们身上的震动。"什么也没有啊。"本能和直觉在他们身上几乎已经死了,他们甚至还害怕那仅剩的一丁点。他们对本能和直觉的惧怕比听到英国士兵的叫喊更甚——"喂,杰克!来看呀,这女孩儿一丝不挂,有两个醉鬼正朝她啐唾沫呢!"这就是那当兵的对波提切利的维纳斯的看法,对他来说这幅画就意味着这些,因为他不具备想像力,看不出这画的意境。不过,他至少不会像那些

strange intuitional awareness of the body, dread of anything but ideas, which can't contain bacteria. And the dread all works back to a dread of the procreative body, and is partly traceable to the shock of the awareness of syphilis.

The dread of the instincts included the dread of intuitional awareness. 'Beauty is a snare' –'Beauty is but skin-deep' –'Handsome is as handsome does' –'Looks don't count' –'Don't judge by appearances' –if we only realized it, there are thousands of these vile proverbs which have been dinned into us for over two hundred years. They are all of them false. Beauty is not a snare, nor is it skin-deep, since it always involves a certain loveliness of modelling, and handsome doers are often ugly and objectionable people, and if you ignore the look of the thing you plaster England with slums and produce at last a state of spiritual depression that is suicidal, and if you don't judge by appearances, that is, if you can't trust the impression which things make on you, you are a fool. But all these base-born proverbs born in the cash-box, hit direct against the intuitional consciousness. Naturally, man gets a great deal of his life's satisfaction from beauty, from a certain sensuous pleasure in the look of the thing. The old Englishman built his hut of a cottage with a childish joy in its appearance, purely intuitional and direct. The

高雅之士一样故作一阵子理智上的激动,这些人才真正是毫无眼光呢。

何其相似,有教养和没教养的,他们都受制于那种无可名状却压倒一切的对肉体深处本能的恐惧和仇恨,惧怕肉体上奇妙的直觉意识。怕,除了思想他们什么都怕,思想倒是不会染毒菌。可这种恐惧可以反过来变成对生殖肉体的惧怕,这部分地可以追溯到梅毒给人们带来的震惊。

对本能的恐惧包括对直觉意识的恐惧。“美是一个陷阱”——“美是肤浅的”——“行为美才是美”——“外表不算数”——“人不可貌相”——你如果注意的话,你会发现有成百上千个诸如此类不值钱的谚语喋喋不休地吵了我们二百多年了。全是假的。美不是陷阱,也不肤浅,因为它总是与造型美有关,而行为美的人往往是些丑陋、令人生厌的人。如果你不在乎事物的外表,你会让英国布满贫民窟,最终导致精神上的沮丧,那简直是自杀。如果你不是凭外表作判断,也就是说如果你不相信事物给你留下的印象,那么你就是个傻瓜。所有这些低俗的谚语都出自钱匣子,都是直接与直觉意识作对的。自然的是,人们从美、从事物外形的美感中得

modern Englishman has a few borrowed ideas, simply doesn't know what to feel, and makes a silly mess of it: though perhaps he is improving, hopefully, in this field of architecture and house-building. The intuitional faculty, which alone relates us in direct awareness to physical things and substantial presences, is atrophied and dead, and we don't know what to feel. We know we ought to feel something, but what?-Oh, tell us what! And this is true of all nations, the French and Italians as much as the English. Look at new French suburbs! Go through the crockery and furniture departments in the *Dames de France* or any big shop. The blood in the body stands still, before such *crétin* ugliness. One has to decide that the modern bourgeois is a *crétin*.

This movement against the instincts and the intuition took a moral tone in all countries. It started in hatred. Let us never forget that modern morality has its roots in hatred, a deep, evil hate of the instinctive, intuitional, procreative body. This hatred is made more virulent by fear, and an extra poison is added to the fear by unconscious horror of syphilis. And so we come to modern bourgeois consciousness, which turns upon the secret poles of fear and hate. That is the real pivot of all bourgeois consciousness in all countries: fear and hate of the instinctive, intuitional,

到不少生活的满足。老派的英国人满怀童趣建筑自己的房舍,这种乐趣纯粹是发自直觉的。而现代英国人有了几种舶来的思想,反倒不知该如何感受了,把建筑弄得一团糟,尽管他们也许是在建筑和造房子方面进行改良。那惟一把我们与肉体和实体直接相连的直觉已被窒息而死,我们已经不懂得去如何感受了。我们明知自己该去感触点什么,可,是什么呢?哦,告诉我们是什么吧!这是所有民族的现实,法国人和意大利人与英国人情况一样。看看法国的新式郊区吧!逛逛"太太商场"或其他法国的大商店,浏览一下那里的陶器和家具吧。在这些傻呆呆的丑恶东西跟前,你体内的热血都会冰冷了。在此你不得不承认现代中产阶级是大傻瓜。

在所有的国度里,反本能、反直觉的行为都会打出一副道德腔调,它起始于仇恨。我们永远不能忘记,现代的道德扎根于仇恨,那是对本能、直觉和生殖的肉体所抱有的深仇大恨。这股子仇恨因为人们的恐惧而加深,而无意识中对梅毒的恐惧又是新添的一服毒药。于是,我们明白当代

procreative body in man or woman. But of course this fear and hate had to take on a righteous appearance, so it became moral, said that the instincts, intuitions and all the activities of the procreative body were evil, and promised a reward for their suppression. That is the great clue to bourgeois psychology: the reward business. It is screamingly obvious in Maria Edgeworth´s tales, which must have done unspeakable damage to ordinary people. Be good, and you´ll have money. Be wicked, and you´ll be penniless at last, and the good ones will have to offer you a little charity. This is sound working morality in the world. And it makes one realize that, even to Milton, the true hero of *Paradise Lost* must be Satan. But by this baited morality the masses were caught and enslaved to industrialism before ever they knew it; the good got hold of the goods, and our modern 'civilization' of money, machines, and wage-slaves was inaugurated. The very pivot of it, let us never forget, being fear and hate, the most intimate fear and hate, fear and hate of one´s own instinctive, intuitive body, and fear and hate of every other man´s and every other woman´s warm, procreative body and imagination.

Now it is obvious what result this will have on the plastic arts, which depend entirely on the representation of substantial bodies, and on the intuitional perception

中产阶级的思想了，原来这思想是围绕着恐惧与仇恨之秘密支柱旋转的。这才是所有国家里中产阶级思想的轴心——惧怕和仇恨本能、直觉和生殖的男女肉体。当然了，这恐惧和仇恨要以某种正义的面目出现，于是有了道德。道德说，本能、直觉以及生殖肉体的一切行为都是罪恶的；同时它还许诺，如果人们压抑这一切，就可以得到回报。这是了解中产阶级心理的一条主要线索——回报。这种心理在玛丽亚·埃基渥斯[Maria Edgeworth(1767—1849)，爱尔兰作家]的故事中表现得最明显，她的故事肯定对普通人造成了难以言状的破坏：当好人，你就会得到金钱；恶毒，你最终会一文不名，那些好人会给你一点施舍。这是世上顶有说服力的道德箴言了。事实上人们发现，即使在弥尔顿心中，《失乐园》中的真正英雄也该是撒旦。可俗众们受这种道德的引诱，还未等到意识到这一点就做了工业主义的奴隶；那些好样的占有了财富，从而由金钱、机器和工资奴隶构成的我们的现代“文明”开始了。我们千万不要忘记，它的核心是恐惧和仇恨，极度地恐惧和仇恨自己的本能与直觉肉体，恐惧和仇恨别的男人和

of the reality of substantial bodies. The reality of substantial bodies can only be perceived by the imagination, and the imagination is a kindled state of consciousness in which intuitive awareness predominates. The plastic arts are all imagery, and imagery is the body of our imaginative life, and our imaginative life is a great joy and fulfilment to us, for the imagination is a more powerful and more comprehensive flow of consciousness than our ordinary flow. In the flow of true imagination we know in full, mentally and physically at once, in a greater, enkindled awareness. At the maximum of our imagination we are religious. And if we deny our imagination, and have no imaginative life, we are poor worms who have never lived.

In the seventeenth and eighteenth centuries we have the deliberate denial of intuitive awareness, and we see the results on the arts. Vision became more optical, less intuitive and painting began to flourish. But what painting! Watteau, Ingres, Poussin, Chardin* have some real imaginative glow still. They are still somewhat free. The puritan and the intellectual has not yet struck them down with his fear and hate obsession. But look at England! Hogarth, Reynolds, Gainsborough,* they are all already bourgeois. The coat is really more important than the man. It is amazing how important clothes suddenly become. how they cover the subject. An old

女人热烈的生殖肉体和想像力。

这种恐惧和仇恨将对造型艺术造成何种影响，现在变得明显了。造型艺术全然依赖对物质实体的描述和对物质实体之真实的直觉感悟。物质实体的真实只能通过想像来感知，而想像则是由直觉意识所主宰的激动状态中的意识。造型艺术都是形象，形象是我们想象生命的实体，而想像生命是我们的一大乐事和满足，因为想像是一种较之其他东西更有力、更完整的意识流动。在真正想像的流动中，我们完整地——肉与灵同时在更为激动的意识支配下感知。想像的极致是我们达到宗教境界之时。如果我们否认自己的想像，没有想像的生活，我们就是一群没有生活过的可怜虫。

十七和十八世纪有过对直觉意识的刻意否定，我们看到了这种否定对艺术产生的影响：意象变得更直观而缺少直觉，绘画竟开始繁荣。可那是什么样的绘画啊！华多[Jean-Antoine Watteau(1684—1721)，法国洛可可风格画家]、安格尔 [Jean-Auguste-Dominique Ingres (1780—1867)，法国著名新古典主义画家]、普桑 [Nicolas

Reynolds colonel in a red uniform is much more a uniform than an individual, and as for Gainsborough, all one can say is: What a lovely dress and hat! What really expensive Italian silk! This painting of garments continued in vogue, till pictures like Sargent's seem to be nothing but yards and yards of satin from the most expensive shops, having some pretty head popped on the top. The imagination is quite dead. The optical vision, a sort of flashy coloured photography of the eye, is rampant.

In Titian, in Velasquez, in Rembrandt* the people are there inside their clothes all right, and the clothes are imbued with the life of the individual, the gleam of the warm procreative body comes through all the time, even if it be an old, halfblind woman or a weird, ironic little Spanish princess. But modern people are nothing inside their garments, and a head sticks out at the top and hands stick out of the sleeves, and it is a bore. Or, as in Lawrence or Raeburn,* you have something very pretty but almost a mere cliché, with very little instinctive or intuitional perception to it.

After this, and apart from landscape and water-colour, there is strictly no English painting that exists. As far as I am concerned, the pre-Raphaelites don't

Poussin(1593—1665),法国古典主义画家]和夏尔丹[Jean-Baptiste-Simēon Chardin(1699-1799),法国著名静物画家]的作品还闪烁着一些真正的想像之光。在某种意义上说他们还是自由的。清教主义和理性主义还没有用恐惧和仇恨压垮他们。可是,请看看英国吧!霍迦斯[William Hogarth(1697-1764),英国风俗画家]、雷诺兹[Sir Joshua Reynolds(1723—1792),英国著名人像画家,皇家美术学院首任院长]和庚斯博罗[Thomas Gainsborough(1727—1788),英国人像画家、风景画家]这些人早已变成了中产阶级。对于他们,衣服已经比人更重要了。衣服突然令人吃惊地变得重要起来,他们是如何给主体穿上衣服的呀。老雷诺兹笔下着红色制服的上校更多是强调他的红制服而不是一个个人。至于庚斯博罗,我们可以用一句话打发他:多漂亮的衣服和帽子呀!真正昂贵的意大利绸缎!这类画着衣服的绘画一直很时髦,以至于到后来发展到萨金特[John Singer Sargent(1856—1925),旅居英国的美国著名肖像画家]的画画的全是最贵重的缎子,缎子上露着一个很标致的小脑袋。想像力已经快死了,那些画给人的视觉是一片耀眼的彩色照片,风靡一时。

exist; Watts* doesn't, Sargent doesn't, and none of the moderns.

There is the exception of Blake.* Blake is the only painter of imaginative pictures, apart from landscape, that England has produced. And unfortunately there is so little Blake, and even in that little the symbolism is often artificially imposed. Nevertheless, Blake paints with real intuitional awareness and solid instinctive feeling. He dares handle the human body, even if he sometimes makes it a mere ideograph. And no other Englishman has ever dared handle it with alive imagination. Painters of composition-pictures in England, of whom perhaps the best is Watts, never quite get beyond the level of cliché, sentimentalism, and funk. Even Watts is a failure, though he made some sort of try: even Etty's* nudes in York fail imaginatively, though they have some feeling for flesh. And the rest, the Leightons,* even the moderns don't really do anything. They never get beyond studio models and clichés of the nude. The image never gets across to us, to seize intuitively. It remains merely optical.

Landscape, however, is different. Here the English exist and hold their own. But, for me, personally, landscape is always waiting for something to occupy it. Landscape seems to be meant as a background to an intenser vision of life, so to my

提香、委拉斯凯支[Diego Velasquez(1599—1660),西班牙画家]和伦勃朗[Rambrandt Harmensz van Rijn(1606—1669),荷兰著名画家]的画中,人尽管也穿着衣服,可那衣服上充满了个性的生命,热烈的生殖肉体光芒透过衣服直射而出,即便是半瞎的老妪或是怪诞的西班牙小公主,都如此。可现代人呢,除了衣服再也不意味着别的什么了,只见头从衣服上露出,手臂从袖子中露出,真让人讨厌。或者在劳伦斯[Sir Thomas Lawrence(1769—1830),英国人像画家,曾任皇家美术学院院长]和雷本[Sir Henry Raeburn(1756—1823),苏格兰人像画家]的画笔下,你看到的是些可爱但千篇一律的小东西,画中极少透出本能和直觉的感悟力。

除了这些风景画及水彩画,严格地说,英国没有绘画。至少我认为,"拉斐尔前派"是没地位的,华兹[George Frederic Watts(1817--1904),英国画家、雕塑家,作品富于深奥的哲理]也不行,萨金特也不行,现代的这些个画家一个都不行。

布莱克[William Blake,英国十九世纪诗人、画家,神秘主义者。他的诗歌早已为我国读者熟知。劳伦斯很钦羡布莱克的才华。评论家们也常把布氏说成是劳氏的思想祖先之一]倒是个例外。除了风景画他不擅长以外,他是英国哺育的惟一一个富有想像力的

feeling painted landscape is background with the real subject left out.

Nevertheless, it can be very lovely, especially in watercolour, which is a more bodiless medium, and doesn't aspire to very substantial existence, and is so small that it doesn't try to make a very deep seizure on the consciousness. Watercolour will always be more of a statement than an experience.

And landscape, on the whole, is the same. It donesn't call up the more powerful responses of the human imagination, the sensual passional responses. Hence it is the favourite modern form of expression in painting. There is no deep conflict. The instinctive and intuitional consciousness is called into play, but lightly, superficially. It is not confronted with any living, procreative body.

Hence the English have delighted in landscape, and have succeeded in it well. It is a form of escape for them, from the actual human body they so hate and fear, and it is an outlet for their perishing aesthetic desires. For more than a century we have produced delicious water-colours, and Wilson, Crome, Constable, Turner* are all great landscape-painters. Some of Turner's landscape compostitons are, to my feelings, among the finest that exist. They still satisfy me more even than Van Gogh's or Cézanne's landscapes, which make a more violent assault on the emo-

画家。可惜的是,画坛上没他什么地位,即便有那么点地位,还被错划到象征派里去。但无论如何,布莱克是以真正的直觉意识和坚实的本能感觉做画的。他敢于摆弄人体,当然有时他只把人体当做一种表意符号。再没有第二个英国人敢于像布氏这样以活泼的想像处理人体。英国的创作型画家中也许就数华兹有成就了,可他都没有超越陈腐气、感伤主义和恐惧。甚至华兹也是个失败的画家,尽管他尽了力。约克美术馆收藏的埃蒂[William Etty(1787—1849),英国裸体画画家,其佳作被其故乡约克市美术馆收藏]的裸体画在想像力上一败涂地,尽管透出了些肉感。其余的画家如莱顿[Frederic, Baron Leighton(1830—1896),英国画家、雕刻家,是晚期维多利亚艺术的最后一位代表,曾任皇家学会主席]们甚至现代的画家们也没什么真正的作为。他们的画不过是些室内模特儿的临摹和一些个陈旧的裸像,都只是些视觉图像而已。

风景画则不同。英国的风景画倒还有其独特之处。可我觉得,风景似乎总在等待什么东西来充实它。对更富有张力的生命眼光来说,风景似乎意味着背景,所以我觉得画出的风景只是背景,而真正的主体却不在

tions, and repel a little for that reason. Somehow I don't want landscape to make a violent assault on my feelings. Landscape is background with the figures left out or reduced to minimum, so let it stay back. Van Gogh's surging earth and Cézanne's explosive or rattling planes worry me. Not being profoundly interested in landscape, I prefer it to be rather quiet and unexplosive.

But, of course, the English delight in landscape is a delight in escape. It is always the same. The northern races are so innerly afraid of their own bodily existence, which they believe fantastically to be an evil thing–you could never find them feel anything but uneasy shame, or an equally shameful gloating, over the fact that a man was having intercourse with his wife, in his house next door–that all they cry for is an escape. And, especially, art must provide that escape.

It is easy in literature. Shelley is pure escape: the body is sublimated into sublime gas. Keats is more difficult–the body can still be felt dissolving in waves of successive death–but the death–business is very satisfactory. The novelists have even a better time. You can get some of the lasciviousness of Hetty Sorrell's 'sin',* and you can enjoy condemning her to penal servitude for life. You can thrill to Mr Rochester's passion,* and you can enjoy having his eyes burnt out. So it is, all the

里边。

不过,风景画还是可以招人喜欢的,特别是水彩风景画更是这样,它是无实体的媒介,也不追求什么很实在的存在,它太渺小,无法攫取人的意识。水彩画永远只是一种说明而非一种体验。

总的来说,风景画大致如此这般,它无法唤起人类想像的强大回应,即肉欲激情的回应,因此,它成了现代绘画中的一种受宠的形式,毫无什么深刻的冲突;本能的和直觉的意识倒是有所动作,但很轻,很肤浅,因此无法与任何活生生的生殖肉身相撞击。

所以,英国人喜欢风景画,从而在这方面很有了点成就。这对英国人来说是一种逃避,既可以借此逃避他们万分痛恨的真实的人之肉身,又可以借此发泄他们那了无情趣的审美欲望。一个多世纪以来,我们英国出了很不错的水彩画,而威尔逊[Richard Wilson(1714—1782),英国第一个专工风景画的画家]、克罗姆[John Crome(1768—1821),英国风景画家]、康斯太勃和透纳[John Constable(1776—1837),Joseph Mallard William Turner(1775—1851),均为英国杰出的风景画家,劳伦斯对透

way: the novel of 'passion'!

But in paint it is more difficult. You cannot paint Hetty Sorrell's sin or Mr Rochester's passion without being really shocking. And you daren't be shocking. It was this fact that unsaddled Watts and Millais.* Both might have been painters if they hadn't been Victorians. As it is, each of them is a washout.

Which is the poor, feeble history of art in England, since we can lay no claim to the great Holbein.* And art on the continent, in the last century? It is more interesting, and has a fuller story. An artist can only create what he really religiously feels is truth, religious truth really felt, in the blood and the bones. The English could never think anything connected with the body religious–unless it were the eyes. So they painted the social appearance of human beings, and hoped to give them wonderful eyes. But they could think landscape religious, since it had no sensual reality. So they felt religious about it and painted it as well as it could be painted, maybe, from their point of view.

And in France? In France it was more or less the same, but with a difference. The French, being more rational, decided that the body had its place, but that it should be rationalized. The Frenchman of today has the most reasonable and ratio-

纳的作品尤为钦敬]就是几位了不起的风景画家。我觉得泰纳的一些风景画是有史以来最好的,它们甚至比凡·高和塞尚的风景画更让我满足,因为后两位的风景画对人的情绪撞击得更猛烈些,为此会让人产生抵触,反正我不喜欢风景画猛烈撞击我的感情。风景只是背景,里面不要有人物或该使人物缩到最小才好,凡·高笔下那澎湃般的土地和塞尚笔下那爆破性鼓噪着的平面让我觉得闹得慌。我不大对风景画感兴趣,因此,我喜欢它娴静些,别太闹了。

当然了,英国人喜欢风景画为的是逃避,到处都这样。北方民族太惧怕他们的肉体存在,他们认为肉体这东西是个魔鬼,真是不可思议。你发现他们谈起隔壁有个男人正同自己的女人做爱时他们是那样不安、难为情、羞耻。他们惟一渴求的就是逃避,所以,艺术应该特别提供这种逃避。

在文学中逃避是容易的。雪莱就是个纯粹的逃避者,肉体在于他早已升华为空气了。济慈则逃得不太容易——你还可以感到肉体在不断的

nalized body possible. His conception of sex is basically hygienic. A certain amount of copulation is good for you. *Ca fait du bien au corps*! sums up the physical side of a Frenchman's ideas of love, marriage, food, sport and all the rest. Well, it is more sane, anyhow, than the Anglo-Saxon terrors. The Frenchman is afraid of syphilis and afraid of the procreative body, but not quite so deeply. He has known for a long time that you can take precautions. And he is not profoundly imaginative.

Therefore he has been able to paint. But his tendency, just like that of all the modern world, had been to get away from the body, while still paying attention to its hygiene, and still not violently quarrelling with it. Puvis de Chavannes* is really as sloppy as all the other spiritual sentimentalizers. Renoir* is jolly: *ca fait du bien au corps*! is his attitude to the flesh. If a woman didn't have buttocks and breasts, she wouldn't be paintable, he said, and he was right. *Ca fait du bien au corps*! What do you paint with, Maitre?-With my penis, and be damned! Renoir didn't try to get away from the body. But he had to dodge it in some of its aspects, rob it of its natural terrors, its natural demonishness. He is delightful, but a trifle banal. *Ca fait du bien au corps*! Yet how infinitely much better he is than any English equivalent.

死亡中消融,可死亡是件十分令人满足的事。小说家们日子则更好过。你可以看到海蒂·索利尔[英国作家乔治·艾略特的小说《亚当·贝德》中的人物]犯的淫荡“罪”,你可以欣赏对她做出的终身苦役判决。你可以为罗切斯特先生[英国女作家夏洛蒂·勃朗特的小说《简·爱》中的人物]的激情感到惊讶,也可以看到他的眼睛烧瞎了而感到解气。就这些,“激情”小说都是这个路子!

可在绘画中就不那么容易处理这样的主题了,你如果没有真正受到震惊你就绘不出海蒂·索利尔的罪恶或罗切斯特先生的激情。可你又不敢受那份震惊。就是出于这个原因华兹和米莱斯 [John Everett Millais (1829—1896),英国拉斐尔前派画家]才洗手不干了。如果他们不是生在维多利亚时代,他们会成为好画家的。可他们生不逢时,没有成功。

英国艺术史就是这么可怜,既然我们不能强行把伟大的荷尔拜因[Hans Holbein(1497—1543),生于德国,1526 年移居英国,成为宫廷画家]纳入英国艺术家之列。那么,上个世纪欧洲大陆上的艺术又如何呢?它更有趣,更全面些。一位艺术家只能创作他真正虔诚地感受到的真实,是骨血里真正感到的宗

Courbet, Daumier,* Degas, they all painted the human body. But Daumier satirized it, Courbet saw it as a toiling thing, Degas saw it as a wonderful instrument. They all of them deny it its finest qualities, its deepest instincts, its purest intuitions. They prefer, as it were, to industrialize it. They deny it the best imaginative existence.

And the real grand glamour of modern French art, the real outburst of delight came when the body was at last dissolved of its substance, and made part and parcel of the sunlight-and-shadow scheme. Let us say what we will, but the real grand thrill of modern French art was the discovery of light, the discovery of light, and all the subsequent discoveries, of the impressionists, and of the post-impressionists, even Cézanne. No matter how Cézanne may have reacted from the impressionists, it was they, with their deliriously joyful discovery of light and 'free' colour, who really opened his eyes. Probably the most joyous moment in the whole history of painting was the moment when the incipient impressionists discovered light, and with it, colour. Ah, then they made the grand, grand escape into freedom, into infinity, into light and delight. They escaped from the tyranny of solidity and the menace of mass-form. They escaped, they escaped from the dark procreative body

教真理。英国人永远也不会认为与肉体有关的东西有宗教意义,除了人的眼睛。所以他们描绘人的社会面貌,希望给他们美好的眼睛。可他们认为风景是有宗教意义的,因为风景中没有肉体的真实,所以他们对风景大发宗教感想,尽自己最大的努力从各自的角度去描绘它。

在法国又如何呢?情况大致如此,但稍有区别。更为理性的法国人认为肉体应该占一席之地,但要使之理性化才行。或许今日法国人的肉体是世上顶顶理性化的了。法国人的性观念根本上是保健的。适度的性交对人是有好处的,有益于身体健康!这句话概括了法国人从身体角度对于爱、婚姻、饮食和运动所抱的观念。这当然比盎格鲁一撒克逊的恐惧要明智得多。法国人也恐惧梅毒和生殖的肉体,不过不像英国人那么过分。法国人早就懂得可以采取预防措施,他们不够有幻想力。

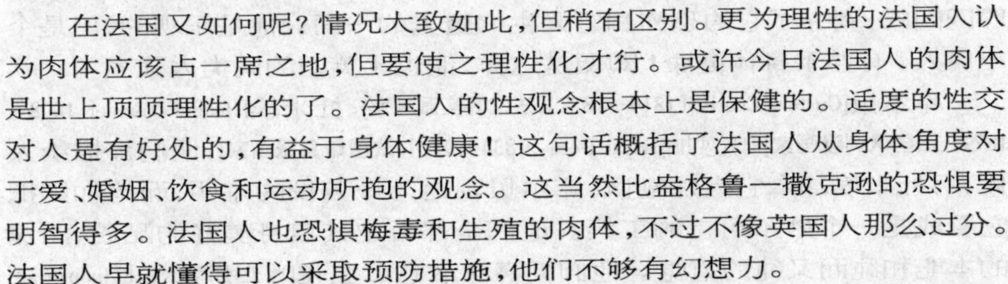

所以法国人可以搞油画。但他们像所有的现代画家一样要躲避肉体,很注意其保健作用,当然他们不那么太与肉体作对。甫维·德·沙旺[Pierre Puvis de Chavannes(1824—1898),法国重要壁画家]的确像所有的感伤主义者一样

which so haunts a man, they escaped into the open air, *plein air and plein soleil*: light and almost ecstasy.

Like every other human escape, it meant being hauled back later with the tail between the legs. Back comes the truant, back to the old doom of matter, of corporate existence, of the body sullen and stubborn and obstinately refusing to be transmuted into pure light, pure colour, or pure anything. It is not concerned with purity. Life isn't. Chemistry and mathematics and ideal religion are, but these are only small bits of life, which is itself bodily, and hence neither pure nor impure.

After the grand escape into impressionism and pure light, pure colour, pure bodilessness–for what is the body but a shimmer of lights and colours! –poor art came home truant and sulky, with its tail between its legs. And it is this return which now interests us. We know the escape was illusion, illusion, illusion. The cat had to come back. So now we despise the 'light' blighters too much. We haven't a good word for them. Which is nonsense, for they too are wonderful, even if their escape was into *le grand néant*, the great nowhere.

But the cat came back. And it is the home-coming tom that now has our sympathy: Renoir, to a certain extent, but mostly Cézanne, the sublime little gri-

多愁善感。雷诺阿[Pierre-Auguste Renoir(1841—1919),法国印象派画家。其名言"我用画笔做爱"被讹传为"用阳具"做画]就很乐观,他对肉欲的态度就是"有益于身体健康"。他说,如果一个女人没有丰乳肥臀,她就不值得画。太对了。大师,您用什么作画?用我的阳具,怎么样!雷诺阿并不曾试图远离人体,但他总是躲躲闪闪的,剥夺了它的恐怖和它天生的魔鬼的一面。他是乐观的,但是个小庸人。有益于身体健康!即便是这样,他也比英国的同类人强多了。

库尔贝[Gustave Courbet(1819—1877),法国写实派画家]、杜米埃[Honoré Daumier(1808—1879),法国讽刺漫画家]和德加[Edgar Degas(1834-1917),法国印象派画家],他们都描绘人体,可杜米埃却拿它大加嘲讽,库尔贝视之为做苦役的东西,而德加则把它看成是一个妙不可言的工具。他们全都否定其自身美好的品质、深邃的本能和纯而又纯的直觉。他们更喜欢拿它工业化[此处所谓工业化(industrialize)可能是指缺乏想像和创造性的"成批生产"],而否认它是最美好的想像存在。

现代法兰西艺术真正闪光之时、真正爆发出其欢愉之时是肉体的实体消融、成为阳光和阴影的一部分之时。不管我们怎么说,现代法兰西艺

malkin, who is followed by Matisse and Gauguin and Derain and Vlaminck and Braque* and all the host of other defiant and howling cats that have come back, perforce, to form and substance and thereness, instead of delicious nowhereness.

Without wishing to labour the point, one cannot help being amused at the dodge by which the impressionists made the grand escape from the body. They metamorphosed it into a pure assembly of shifting lights and shadows, all coloured. A web of woven, luminous colour was a man, or a woman–and so they painted her, or him: a web of woven shadows and gleams. Delicious! and quite true as far as it goes. A purely optical truth: which paint is supposed to be. And they painted delicious pictures: a little too delicious. They bore us, at the moment. They bore people like the very modern critics intensely. But very modern critics need not be so intensely bored. There is something very lovely about the good impressionist pictures. And ten years hence critics will be bored by the present run of post-impressionists, though not so passionately bored, for these post-impressionists don´t move us as the impressionists moved our fathers. We have to persuade ourselves, and we have to persuade one another to be impressed by the post-impressionists, on the whole. On the whole, they rather depress us. Which is perhaps good for us.

术的真正让人激动处在于印象派和后印象派(甚至包括塞尚在内)对于光的发现以及其后的一系列发现。不管塞尚怎么与印象派作对,是印象派画家们以其谵狂般的光和“自由”色彩的发现使他大开眼界。或许绘画史上顶兴奋的时刻就是早期印象派画家发现光和色彩之时。哦,就是从这以后,他们奔向了自由,奔向了无限,奔向光和狂喜。他们借此逃避了固体的强暴和群体的威胁。他们逃走了;逃离了纠缠人的黑暗生殖肉体,逃到了露天地里、光线中并因此变得几乎是欣喜若狂。

就像其他各种人的逃亡一样，这意味着以后还会夹着尾巴被拖回来。逃跑者回来了,回到这物质的、肉体的厄运,阴郁、固执的肉体拒绝变成纯粹的光、纯粹的色彩或任何纯粹的东西,它与纯粹毫无关系。生命不是纯粹。化学、数学和理念宗教是纯粹的,可它们只算得上一星半点的生命,而生命本身又是肉体的存在,所以,化学什么的既算不上纯也算不上不纯。

向印象主义和纯粹光线、纯粹色彩和无形体大逃亡之后(肉体变成

But modern art criticism is in a curious hole. Art has suddenly gone into rebellion, against all the canons of accepted religion, accepted good form, accepted everything. When the cat came back from the delicious impressionist excursion, it came back rather tattered, but bristling and with its claws out. The glorious escape was all an illusion. There was substance in the world, a thousand times be damned to it! There was the body, the great lumpy body. There it was. You had it shoved down your throat. What really existed was lumps, lumps. Then paint´em. Or else paint the thin 'spirit' with gaps in it and looking merely dishevelled and 'found out'. Paint had found the spirit out.

This is the sulky and rebellious mood of the post-impres-sionists. They still hate the body-hate it. But, in a rage, they admit its existence, and paint it as huge lumps, tubes, cubes, planes, volumes, spheres, cones, cylinders, all the 'pure' or mathematical forms of substance. As for landscape, it comes in for some of the same rage. It has also suddenly gone lumpy. Instead of being nice and ethereal and non-sensual, it was discovered by Van Gogh to be heavily, overwhelmingly substantial and sensual. Van Gogh took up landscape in heavy spadefuls. And Cézanne had to admit it. Landscapes, too, after being, since Claude Lorraine,* a thing of

了闪烁的光线和色彩),可怜的艺术逃亡者阴郁地夹着尾巴而归。就是这种回归令我们感起兴趣来。我们知道这种逃避是一种幻想,幻想,幻想。逃走的猫终于归来了,所以我们现在实在看不起那些"光线"的鼓吹者们。我们对他们不赞一词。这也是荒谬的,其实他们也是很了不起的,尽管他们曾逃向伟大的虚无。

但逃走的猫终归是回来了。回头的浪子令人同情,雷诺阿颇让人同情,但最让人同情的还是塞尚这位崇高的老猫,随后是马蒂斯[Henry Martisse(1869—1954),法国画家、雕塑家,野兽派领袖]、高更[Paul Gauguin(1848—1903),法国画家,与塞尚和凡·高等同属后印象派]、戴乐[Andre Derain(1880—1954),法国画家]、弗拉芒克[Maurice de Vlaminck(1876—1958),法国野兽派画家,提倡使用非自然色彩]、布拉克[Georges Braque(1882—1963),法国画家,与毕加索共创立体派]和其他挑战、嚎叫的猫们,他们必然要返归有形和实体,离弃那美好的虚无。

毋庸赘言,人们不禁为印象派画家逃离肉体感到有趣。他们使肉体变形,成为变幻着的光线和阴影,涂满了色彩。他们就用一团迷人的色彩

pure luminosity and floating shadow, suddenly exploded, and came tumbling back on to canvases of artists in lumps. With Cézanne, landscape 'crystallized', to use one of the favourits terms of the critics, and it has gone on crystallizing into cubes, cones, pyramids, and so forth ever since.

The impressionists brought the world at length, after centuries of effort, into the delicious oneness of light. At last, at last! Hail, holy Light! the great natural One, the universal, the universalizer! We are not divided, all one body we-one in Light, lovely light! No sooner had this paean gone up than the post-impressionists, like Judas, gave the show away. They exploded the illusion, which fell back to the canvas of art in a chaos of lumps.

This new chaos, of course, needed new apologists who therefore rose up in hordes to apologize, almost, for the new chaos. They felt a little gulity about it, so they took on new notes of effrontery, defiant as any Primitive Methodists, which, indeed, they are: the Primitive Methodists of art criticism. These evangelical gentlemen at once ran up their chapels, in a Romanesque or Byzantine shape, as was natural for a primitive and a methodist, and started to cry forth their doctrines in the decadent wilderness. They discovered once more that the aesthetic experience

涂抹出一个男人和女人来，那是一团乱糟糟交织着的阴影和光线。好极了！这不能不说也是真实，一种纯视觉的真实，是颜料要达到的效果。他们画得很有味道，不过有太有味道了一点。一时间他们令我们厌烦了。不过赶时髦的批评家可用不着太厌烦，要知道，优秀的印象派画家的作品还是有其十分美妙的作品的。十年以后，批评家们会对时下这批后印象派画家感到厌烦，尽管不会十分厌烦，因为这些后印象派们不像印象派感动我们的父辈那样感动我们。我们得说服自己，还要相互说服去对后印象派产生好感。总的来说，他们令我们失望。或许这对我们是件好事。

可是，现代艺术批评却是处在一种奇怪的困境中。艺术突然成为一种反叛，反叛所有约定俗成的宗教信条、良好形式和一切的训诫。当印象派之猫从惬意的远足中归来时，虽已是支离破碎却张牙舞爪，毛发耸立。他们光彩的逃离全变成了幻想。世上还有实体，这可真是岂有此理！有肉体，庞大笨重的肉体。为此你感到如鲠在喉。可这些的确是存在的，一堆堆的肉体。那就画它们吧。否则就只能画那苍白残缺的精神，这精神看上

was an ecstasy, an ecstasy granted only to the chosen few, the elect, among whom said critics were, of course, the arch-elect. This was outdoing Ruskin. It was almost Calvin* come to art. But let scoffers scoff, the aesthetic ecstasy was vouchsafed only to the few, the elect, and even then only when they had freed their minds of false doctrines. They had renounced the mammon of 'subject' in pictures, they went whoring no more after the Babylon of painted 'interest', nor did they hanker after the flesh-pots of artistic 'representation'. Oh, purify yourselves, ye who would know the aesthetic ecstasy, and be lifted up to the 'white peaks of artistic inspiration'. Purify yourselves of all base hankering for a tale that is told, and of all low lust for likenesses. Purify yourselves, and know the one supreme way, the way of Significant Form. I am the revelation and the way! I am Significant Form, and my unutterable name is Reality. Lo, I am Form and I am Pure, behold, I am Pure Form. I am the revelation of Spiritual Life, moving behind the veil. I come forth and make myself known, and I am Pure Form, behold, I am Significant Form.*

So the prophets of the new era in art cry aloud to the multitude, in exactly the jargon of the revivalists, for revivalists they are. They will revive the Primitive

去憔悴得很,算是受到了报应。绘画让精神得到了报应。

后印象派们就是如此愠怒而反叛。他们仍然仇视肉体,仇视。但他们却在仇恨中承认了它的存在,把它绘成块状、管子、方块、平面、圆柱、球体、锥体和圆筒,全是些"纯粹的"数学形式。至于风景画,也是在同样仇恨下绘出来的,也是突然间变成了色块。凡·高不觉得它美妙、缥缈和清白,他发现它很实在,很肉感。凡·高把风景画处理得很沉重,塞尚不得不承认这一点。从克劳德·洛朗[Claude Lorraine(1600—1682),法国风景画家,以理想化的田园风光著称]以后,风景不再是纯粹的流光溢彩及飘忽的阴影,它突然爆炸了,摇摇摆摆奔向艺术家的画布,变成了一堆堆色块。引用批评家们最喜欢的字眼儿说,从塞尚开始,风景画变得"具象化"了,是的,它一直具象着,成了立体、锥体和金字塔什么的。

经过几个世纪的努力,印象派们最终把世界带入光的美妙同一中。终于,终于!嘿,神圣的光!伟大的、自然的同一,同一,同一者!我们没有分开,我们在光、可爱的光线中是一体!这首赞美诗还未唱起来,后印象派

Method-brethren, the Byzantines, the Ravennese, the early Italian and French primitives (which ones, in particular, we aren't told); these were Right, these were Pure, these were Spiritual, these were Real! And the builders of early Romanesque churches, O my brethren! these were holy men, before the world went a-whoring after Gothic. Oh, return, my brethren, to the Primitive Method. Lift up your eyes to Significant Form, and be saved.

Now myself, brought up a Nonconformist as I was, I just was never able to understand the language of salvation. I never knew what they were talking about,* when they raved about being saved, and safe in the arms of Jesus, and Abraham's bosom, and seeing the great light, and entering into glory: I just was puzzled, for what did it mean? It seemed to work out as getting rather drunk on your own self-importance, and afterwards coming dismally sober again and being rather unpleasant. That was all I could see in actual experience of the entering-into-glory business. The term itself, like something which ought to mean something but somehow doesn't, stuck on my mind like an irritating burr, till I decided that it was just an artificial stimulant to the individual self-conceit. How could I enter into glory, when glory is just an abstraction of a human state, and not a separate reality at all? If

们便像一群犹大放弃了这场表演。他们的幻想爆炸了，破灭的幻想落在艺术的画布上成了一堆乱糟糟的块状物。

当然，这种新的混乱需要新的辩护士。他们于是群起为新的混乱进行辩护。他们对此感到有点儿内疚，于是又厚颜无耻地换了一副新的腔调，像原始卫理会的教徒那样提出挑衅。是的，他们的确是艺术批评上的原始卫理会教徒。这些传教士般的绅士们立即匆忙搭起他们的教堂，搭成古罗马和拜占庭式——似乎这对于原始卫理派艺术家是最自然的样式，然后开始在颓废的荒野中吼出他们的教义。他们再一次发现，审美的经验是一种狂喜，一种只有少数人才被赐予的狂喜，他们是上帝的选民，而前面提到的这些批评家们则是上帝选民中的选民。罗斯金 [John Ruskin (1819—1900)，维多利亚时期最重要的艺术与社会批评家，强调道德与艺术之间直接的关系]就是这号人，简直是艺术中的加尔文[John Calvin(1509—1564)，法国宗教改革者，建立了加尔文派，强调道德]。让这些饕餮者们贪婪地给自己争抢美名吧，审美的狂喜的确属于少数人，属于上帝的选民，但只是当他们放弃了他们虚假的教义之

glory means anything at all, it means the thrill a man gets when a great many people look up to him with mixed awe, reverence, delight. To-day,it means Rudolph Valentino.* So that the cant about entering into glory is just used fuzzily to enhance the individual sense of self-importance -one of the rather cheap cocaine-phrases.

And I´m afraid 'aesthetic ecstasy' sounds to me very much the same, especially when accompanied by exhortations. It so sounds like another great uplift into self-importance, another apotheosis of personal conceit; especially when accompanied by a lot of jargon about the pure world of reality existing behind the veil of this vulgar world of accepted appearances, and of the entry of the elect through the doorway of visual art. Too evangelical altogether, too much chapel and Primitive Methodist, too obvious a trick for advertising one´s own self-glorification. The ego, as an American says, shuts itself up and paints the inside of the walls sky-blue, and thinks it is in heaven.

And then the great symbols of this salvation. When the evangelical says: Behold the lamb of God:* -what on earth does he want one to behold? Are we invited to look at a lamb, with woolly, muttony appearance, frisking and making its little pills? Awfully nice, but what has it got to do with God or my soul? Or the cross?

时,才属于他们。他们在绘画中放弃了“主体”的巨大财富,他们不再追求其巨大的“利益”,也不再追求艺术“表现”的享受了。哦,净化你自己,然后你就会懂得审美的狂喜,到达“艺术灵感的雪峰 ”。净化你自己,莫再追求那讲滥了的故事,净化追求雷同的低下欲望。净化你自己吧,然后你就会懂得那惟一一种高尚的意蕴形式。我就是这种昭示和这种形式!我就是意蕴形式,毋庸置疑我的名字叫真实。哦,我是形式,是纯粹的形式。我是在幕后行动的精神生活的昭示。我现在走到幕前来让人们知道我是纯粹的形式,看吧,我是意蕴形式[这一段里多处从《圣经》中借典,一些祈使句式直接套用《圣经》。这种暗喻是劳伦斯散文写作的一大特色,说明劳伦斯对《圣经》稔熟于心,在此不一一注出。这一段引号中的术语均来自克莱夫·贝尔(Clive Bell,1881—1964)《艺术》一书。此人是英国艺术与艺术哲学批评家,名作家伍尔夫夫人的姐夫,布鲁姆斯伯里文化圈的重要成员。劳伦斯对贝尔的一系列占主导地位的艺术批评术语,特别是“意蕴形式”表现出极大的反感,几乎随时在对此大加讽刺鞭挞]。

艺术新时代的预言者们就是如此这般地向大众高叫着,其实他们喊的全是复兴宗教热忱的福音传教士们那一套陈词滥调,因为他们本身就

What do they expect us to see in the cross? A sort of gallows? Or the mark we use to cancel a mistake?–cross it out! That the cross by itself was supposed to mean something always mystified me. The same with the Blood of the Lamb. –Washed in the Blood of the Lamb! always seemed to me an extremely unpleasant suggestion. And when Jerome says: He who has once washed in the blood of Jesus need never wash again! * –I feel like taking a hot bath at once, to wash off even the suggestion.

And I find myself equally mystified by the cant phrases like Significant Form and Pure Form. They are as mysterious to me as the Cross and the Blood of the Lamb. They are just the magic jargon of invocation, nothing else. If you want to invoke an aesthetic ecstasy, stand in front of a Matisse and whisper fervently under your breath: 'Significant Form! Significant Form!' –and it will come. It sounds to me like a form of masturbation, an attempt to make the body react to some cerebral formula.

No, I am afraid modern criticism has done altogether too much for modern art. If painting survives this outburst of ecstatic evangelism, which it will, it is because people do come to their senses, even after the silliest vogue.

And so we can return to modern French painting, without having to quake be-

是这样的福音传教士。他们要复兴原始卫理教友派艺术、拜占庭、拉温那[拉温那是拜占庭时期意大利的首都]、早期意大利和法国原始艺术(到底更注重哪个,我们尚未了解),这些才是正确的、纯粹的、精神的、真实的艺术!早期罗马式教堂的建筑者们,哦,我的兄弟!他们在人们崇尚哥特式建筑前是些神圣的人。哦,回归吧,我的兄弟,回归原始卫理艺术吧。抬起你的双眼求助于意蕴形式你就会得救。

可我一直是个不信英国国教的新教教徒,压根儿不懂什么救世的语言。我从来不懂他们谈论的那一套是什么——他们大谈被拯救,在耶稣的怀抱里安全,在亚伯拉罕的怀抱里安全,看到了神光,获得天国的荣耀,我根本不明白他们说的是什么意思[这里出现的几处专有名词均出自《圣经》]。那似乎是在摆出一副自以为是的样子并让自己沉醉其中,然后再清醒过来难受一阵子。这就是我理解的如何获得天国的荣耀。这个词儿本身应该是意味着什么但却没有表达清楚。它令我的头脑发昏,我不得不认为这是在刺激虚假的自傲。当荣耀只是一种抽象的人类状态而非与人分离的

fore the bogy, or the Holy Ghost of Significant Form: a bogy which doesn't exist if we don't mind leaving aside our self-importance when we look at a picture.

The actual fact is that in Cézanne modern French art made its first step back to real substance, to objective substance, if we may call it so. Van Gogh's earth was still subjective earth, himself projected into the earth. But Cézanne's apples are a real attempt to let the apple exist in its own separate entity, without transfusing it with personal emotion. Cézanne's great effort was, as it were, to shove the apple away from him, and let it live of itself. It seems a small thing to do: yet it is the first real sign that man has made for several thousands of years that he is willing to admit that matter actually exists. Strange as it may seem, for thousands of years, in short, ever since the mythological 'Fall', man has been preoccupied with the constant preoccupation of the denial of the existence of matter, and the proof that matter is only a form of spirit. And then, the moment it is done, and we realize finally that matter is only a form of energy, whatever that may be, in the same instant matter rises up and hits us over the head and makes us realize that it exists absolutely, since it is compact energy itself.

Cézanne felt it in paint, when he felt for the apple. Suddenly he felt the tyran-

实体时我怎么能获得它？如果说荣耀真意味着什么的话，可以说它是当千万人怀着敬畏和喜悦的心情仰望一个人时这个人心中产生的狂喜。今天，荣耀就意味着是鲁道夫·瓦伦蒂诺[1875—1926，原籍意大利的美国男影星，二十年代的大众情人]。所以，所谓获得荣耀的无稽之谈只是用来虚晃一枪，激励人们的自傲感，是一种廉价的麻醉药般的词儿。

恐怕所谓“审美狂喜”这样的字眼在我听来也是如此这般地虚假。讲这话时你的口气中越带着规劝它越是虚假。它听起来就像把你硬拔上自傲的高度，像是造神般羽化登仙。讲这话时，如果还带点什么“为人普遍接受的庸俗世界之幕后的真实纯粹世界”和“通过视觉艺术进入上帝选民之列”之类的滥调，就更显得像自吹自擂。太多的福音，太多的礼拜堂和原始卫理派艺术家，标榜自己的计谋也过于明目张胆。正如美国人所说，自己把自己封闭起来，把墙涂成天蓝色，然后自以为是生活在天上。

再说说救世的巨大象征吧。当福音传播者说：看这上帝的羔羊[上帝的羔羊指耶稣]，他想让人看到什么？我们是被请去看一只毛茸茸的羊蹦蹦跳跳

ny of mind, the white, worn-out arrogance of the spirit, the mental consciousness, the enclosed ego in its sky-blue heaven self-painted. He felt the sky-blue prison. And a graet conflict started inside him. He was dominated by his old mental consciousness, but he wanted terribly to escape the domination. He wanted to express what he suddenly, convulsedly knew! the existence of matter. He terribly wanted to paint the real existence of the body, to make it artistically palpable. But he couldn't. He hadn't got there yet. And it was the torture of his life. He wanted to be himself in his own procreative body-and he couldn't. He was, like all the rest of us, so intensely and exclusively a mental creature, or a spiritual creature, or an egoist, that he could no longer identify himself with his intuitive body. He wanted to, terribly. At first he determined to do it by sheer bravado and braggadocio. But no good; it couldn't be done that way. He had, as one critic says, to become humble. But it wasn't a question of becoming humble. It was a question of abandoning his cerebral conceit and his 'willed ambition' and coming down to brass tacks. Poor Cézanne, there he is in his self-portraits, even the early showy ones, peeping out like a mouse and saying: I am a man of flesh, am I not? For he was not quite, as none of us are. The man of flesh has been slowly destroyed through centuries, to

地拉屎吗？那可太好了，可它与上帝或我的灵魂有何干系？与十字架又有何干系？他们想让我们从十字架上看到什么？是一种绞刑架么，还是我们用来涂抹错字的标记号？算了吧！十字架被赋予的含义总是令我困惑，羊之血也是如此。在羊的血液中沐浴！这种暗示总让我感到十分恶心。杰罗姆说：在耶稣的血中沐过的人永不需要再洗澡了[St Jerome(340—420)，此语并非出自杰罗姆，可能属于劳伦斯记忆错误]！听着这话，我就想赶紧洗个热水澡，甚至把那个暗示也一齐冲掉。

同样我也对诸如“意蕴形式”和“纯粹形式”之类的空洞词儿感到困惑，这些词就像“十字架”和“羊羔的血”一样让我困顿。它们纯粹是些个呼神唤鬼的咒符，不会是别的了。如果你想召唤审美的狂喜，那就请站在某个马蒂斯式的人面前喘息不住地狂呼：“意蕴形式！意蕴形式！”于是该来的就来了。这呼唤让我听起来像是在手淫，其目的是让自己的肉体按照理智的想法动作。

我怀疑，现代批评是否对现代艺术染指太多了些。如果说绘画能

give place to the man of spirit, the mental man, the ego, the self-conscious I. And in his artistic soul Cézanne knew it, and wanted to rise in the flesh. He couldn't do it, and it embittered him. Yet, with his apple, he did shove the stone from the door of the tomb.

He wanted to be a man of flesh, a real man: to get out of the sky-blue prison into real air. He wanted to live, really live in the body, to know the world through his instincts and his intuitions, and to be himself in his procreative blood, not in his mere mind and spirit. He wanted it, he wanted it terribly. And whenever he tried, his mental consciousness, like a cheap fiend, interfered. If he wanted to paint a woman, his mental consciousness simply overpowered him and wouldn't let him paint the woman of flesh, the first Eve who lived before any of the fig-leaf nonsense. He couldn't do it. If he wanted to paint people intuitively and instinctively, he couldn't do it. His mental concepts shoved in front, and these he wouldn't paint-mere representations of what the mind accepts, not what the intuitions gather-and they, his mental concepts, wouldn't let him paint from intuition; they shoved in between all the time, so he painted his conflict and his failure, and the result is almost ridiculous.

福音教义的喷薄中幸存下来(肯定会的),那是因为人们总会恢复自己的理智,甚至在追求过最愚蠢的时尚之后。

所以我们尽可以回过头来谈现代法国绘画而无须在所谓"圣灵般的意蕴形式"这一怪物面前颤抖:只要我们在看一幅画时忘却自己的自傲感,这怪物就不存在了。

事实是,在塞尚的绘画中,现代法国艺术迈出了向实体和客体回归的一小步。凡·高笔下的土地仍然是主观的,他将自我投射在了土地上。可塞尚笔下的苹果则表明他真的努力让苹果成为分离的实体,不再用个人的情绪使苹果变形。塞尚极力要让苹果离开画家自己,让它自成一体。这看来似乎是件小事,可这是几千年来人第一次真正表明自己愿意承认物实际上是存在的这一事实。说起来都有点奇怪,自从人吃了禁果而神秘地"堕落"后,几千年来人们一直否认物的存在,一直在试图证明物不过是精神的一种形式。可我们终于认识到物只是能量的一种形式,不管它是什么。与此同时,物站起来撞击我们的头颅让我们意识到它的绝对

Woman he was not allowed to know by intuition; his mental self, his ego, that bloodless fiend, forbade him. Man, other men, he was likewise not allowed to know-execpt by a few, few touches. The earth likewise he was not allowed to know: his landscapes are mostly acts of rebellion against the mental concept of landscape. After a fight tooth-and-nail for forty years, he did succeed in knowing an apple, fully; and, not quite as fully, a jug or two. That was all he achieved.

It seems little, and he died embittered. But it is the first step that counts, and Cézanne's apple is a great deal, more than Plato's Idea. Cézanne's apple rolled the stone from the mouth of the tomb, and if poor Cézanne couldn't unwind himself from his cerements and mental winding-sheet, but had to lie still in the tomb, till he died, still he gave us a chance.

The history of our era is the nauseating and repulsive history of the crucifixion of the procreative body for the glorification of the spirit, the mental consciousness. Plato was an arch-priest of this crucifixion. Art, that handmaid, humbly and honestly served the vile deed, through three thousand years at least. The Renaissance put the spear through the side of the already crucified body, and syphilis put poison into the wound made by the imaginativc spcar. It took still three hunderd years for

存在,因为它是坚实的能量。

塞尚在作画时通过感知苹果而悟出了这一点。他突然感到理智的霸道,精神既苍白又傲慢,理性意识是一个封闭在自己绘成的蓝天里的自我。他感到这是一座天蓝色的牢狱。于是他心中开始了巨大的冲突。一方面他被旧的理性意识所统治,另一方面他死活也要冲破这个桎梏。他想表达他突然抽搐着认识到的东西!这就是物的存在。他极想描绘肉体的真实存在,让它变得有艺术感。可他办不到,他没达到那个境界。这对他的生活是一种折磨。他想成为一个自我,一具富有生殖力的肉体,可他不能。他与我们大家一样,是一个十分理性的物件,或者说是一个精神的、利己主义的物件,他已经无法将自己与自己直觉的肉体相同一了。可他太想这样了啊。最初,他想通过虚张声势和大吹大擂来实现同一,可这办不到。后来他又像某批评家所说的那样,想变得谦逊些。可这根本不是一个谦逊与否的问题,这是一个放弃他的理性自傲和他的“意志野心”然后接触实质的问题。可怜的塞尚,在他最初炫耀般的自画像中,他像一只

the body to finish: but in the eighteenth century it became a corpse, a corpse with an abnormally active mind: and today it stinketh.

We, dear reader, you and I, we were born corpses, and we are corpses. I doubt if there is even one of us who has ever known so much as an apple, a whole apple. All we know is shadows, even of apples. Shadows of everything, of the whole world, shadows even of ourselves. We are inside the tomb, and the tomb is wide and shadowy like hell, even if sky-blue by optimistic paint, so we think it is all the world. But our world is a wide tomb full of ghosts, replicas. We are all spectres, we have not been able to touch even so much as an apple. Spectres we are to one another. Spectre you are to me, spectre I am to you. Shadow you are even to yourself. And by shadow I mean idea, concept, the abstracted reality, the ego. We are not solid. We don't live in the flesh. Our instincts and intuitions are dead, we live wound round with the windingsheet of abstraction. And the touch of anything solid hurts us. For our instincts and intuitions, which are our feelers of touch and knowing through touch, they are dead, amputated. We walk and talk and eat and copulate and laugh and evacuate wrapped in our winding-sheets, all the time wrapped in our winding-sheets.

老鼠那样探头探脑地说:“我是个肉身人,不是吗?”他与我们一样,不那么有血有肉。有血有肉的人在过去几个世纪里被毁灭了,取而代之的是精神,理性人,自我和自我意识的“我”。塞尚那艺术的灵魂明白这一点,他极想作为一个肉身人挺立起来,可他做不到这一点。这实在令他痛苦不已。不过,他画出了这样的苹果,他借此把石头从坟墓的门口搬开了。

他想成为一个有血有肉的人,一个真正的人,摆脱那天蓝的囹圄进入真正的天空。他要真正肉体的生命,以自己的本能和直觉去感悟这个世界。他想成为有生殖力的血肉之人而不仅仅是理智与精神的人。他想这样,他太想这样了。可每当他努力的时候,他的理智意识都会像一个卑鄙的魔鬼一样阻挠他。当他要画一个女人时,他的理智意识却掣肘,不让他绘出一个肉身的女人,不让他绘出人间第一个女人,那是没有遮羞布的夏娃。他办不到,他无法直觉地、本能地描绘人,他的理智念头总是先行,使他做不出直觉与本能的画来。他的画只是他的头脑接受物的再现,而不是他直觉的感悟。他的理性不允许他凭直觉作画。他的理性总在插

So that Cézanne's apple hurts. It made people shout with pain. And it was not till his followers had turned him again into an abstraction that he was ever accepted. Then the critics stepped forth and abstracted his good apple into Significant Form, and henceforth Cézanne was saved. Saved for democracy. Put safely in the tomb again, and the stone rolled back. The resurrection was postponed once more.

As the resurrection will be postponed *ad infinitum* by the good bourgeois corpses in their cultured winding-sheets. They will run up a chapel to the risen body, even if it is only an apple, and kill it on the spot. They are wide awake, are the corpses, on the alert. And a poor mouse of a Cézanne is alone in the years. Who else shows a spark of awakening life, in our marvellous civilized cemetery? All is dead, and dead breath teaching with phosphorescent effulgence about aesthetic ecstasy and Significant Form. If only the dead would bury their dead. But the dead are not dead for nothing. Who buries his own sort? The dead are cunning and alert to pounce on any spark of life and bury it, even as they have already buried Cézanne's apple and put up to it a white tombstone of Significant Form.

For who of Cézanne's followers does anything but follow at the triumphant funeral of Cézannc's achievements? They follow him in order to bury him, and they

足，于是他的画印证的恰恰是他的冲突和他的失败，其结果极其可笑。

他的理性不允许他凭直觉去认识女人，他理性的自我这个无血无肉的魔鬼禁止他这样做；同样，也禁止他认识别的男人（只认识一点一滴）；也禁止他认识土地。可他的风景画却是对理性认识的反拨。经过四十年卓绝的奋斗，他终于成功地全面认识了一个苹果，并非如此全面地认识了一二个坛子。这就是他的全部成就。

这成就是显得小了点，为此他死得很痛苦。可这是决定性的第一步。塞尚的苹果要比柏拉图的《理念》强多了。塞尚的苹果搬开了坟墓口的石头，这样一来，即便可怜的塞尚无法挣脱身上的寿衣和精神裹尸布，即便他还躺在坟墓中至死也没关系，他毕竟是给了我们一个生的机会。

我们这个历史阶段，正是人们将勃勃的肉体绑在十字架上以此去礼赞精神-理性意识的时候，真让人恶心反感。柏拉图正是这种将人缚上十字架的大传教士。艺术这个仆人谦卑而忠诚地为这种罪恶的行为效忠了至少三千年。文艺复兴的剑戟刺透了早已上了十字架的身体，而梅毒又

succeed. Cézanne is deeply buried under all the Matisses and Vlamincks of his following, while the critics read the funeral homily.

It is quite easy to accept Matisse and Vlaminck and Friesz* and all the rest. They are just Cézanne abstracted again. They are all just tricksters, even if clever ones. They are all mental, mental egoists, egoists, egoists. And therefore they are all acceptable now to the enlightened corpses of connoisseurs. You needn't be afraid of Matisse and Vlaminck and the rest. They will never give your corpse-anatomy a jar. They are just shadows, minds mountebanking and playing charades on canvas. They may be quite amusing charades, and I am all for the mountebank. But of course it is all games inside the cemetery, played by corpses and *hommes d'esprit*, even *femmes d'esprit*, like Mademoiselle Laurencin.* As for *l'esprit*, said Cézanne, I don't give a fart for it. Perhaps not! But the connoisseurs will give large sums of money. Trust the dead to pay for their amusement, when the amusement is deadly!

The most interesting figure in modern art, and the only really interesting figure, is Cézanne: and that, not so much because of his achievement as because of his struggle. Cézanne was born in Aix in Provence in 1839: small, timorous, yet sometimes bantam defiant, sensitive, full of grand ambition, yet ruled still deeper

在被那想像力十足的剑戳出的伤口里注入毒液。这以后肉体又勉强存在了三百来年。到了十九世纪它就变成了一具死尸，一具头脑异常活跃的死尸。如今这尸首都发臭了。

咱们，亲爱的读者，我说的是你和我，咱们是生就的死尸，我们是死尸。我怀疑，我们当中有哪个人能够认识一只苹果，一只完整的苹果。我们所认识的都只是影子，甚至我们认识的苹果只是苹果的影子。一切的影子，全世界的影子，甚至是我们自己的影子。我们身处在坟墓中，它宠大而阴暗如同地狱，尽管乐观主义者把它绘成天蓝色也无济于事。我们认为这才是世界，可它是个大坟墓，里头鬼影憧憧，塞满了复制品。我们都是鬼影，我们甚至不能触摸到一个苹果。我们对各自来说也是幽灵。我对你来说是幽灵，你对我也是。你甚至对你自己来说都是影子。我说的影子指的是观念、概念、抽象的真实和自我。我们都不实在。我们都不是活生生的肉身。我们的本能和直觉死了，我们活活地被抽象之布裹着。每触到任何实在的东西我们都深感刺痛，这是因为我们的感知所依赖的本能

by a naive, Mediterranean sense of truth or reality, imagination, call it what you will. He is not a big figure. Yet his struggle is truly heroic. He was a bourgeois, and one must never forget it. He had a moderate bourgeois income. But a bourgeois in Provence is much more real and human than a bourgeois in Normandy. He is much nearer the actual people, and the actual people are much less subdued by awe of his respectable bourgeois money.

Cézanne was naive to a degree, but not a fool. He was rather insignificant, and grandeur impressed him terribly. Yet still stronger in him was the little flame of life where he felt things to be true. He didn't betray himself in order to get success, because he couldn't: to his nature it was impossible: he was too pure to be able to betray his own small real flame for immediate rewards. Perhaps that is the best one can say of a man, and it puts Cézanne, small and insignificant as he is, among the heroes. He would not abandon his own vital imagination.

He was terribly impressed by physical splendour and flamboyancy, as people usually are in the lands of the sun. He admired terribly the splendid virtuosity of Paul Veronese and Tintoretto,* and even of later and less good baroque painters. He wanted to be like that—terribly he wanted it. And he tried very, very hard, with

和直觉死了，被割断了。我们行走、交谈、吃喝、性交、欢笑、排泄，可我们身上却一直缠着那一层又一层的裹尸布。

就是因了这个，塞尚笔下的苹果才刺痛了人们，刺得他们大叫。如果不是他的追随者们再一次把他说成个抽象派，他是不会被人们接受的。随之批判家们更向前跨了一步，把他那挺好的苹果抽象地说成意蕴形式，于是塞尚得救了，为人们普遍接受了。但他等于又被人们结结实实地塞进了坟墓，堵坟墓的石头又滚回去了，他的再生又被耽搁了。

人类的复活被这些裹在教养尸布中善良的中产阶级无限期地拖延了。为此，他们要为复活中的肉体修起礼拜堂，把这复活中的肉体就地扼杀，尽管它仅仅是一只苹果。他们可是警觉地睁大着眼睛呢。塞尚这些年来像一只可怜的耗子，极其孤独。在我们这精美的文明墓地中还有哪位能展现出一星清醒生命的火花？全都死了，死去的精神却在闪着灵光教人们审美什么是狂喜和意蕴形式。如果死了的能埋葬死了的就好了。可是死了的并不肯就此罢手，谁会埋葬自己的同类呢？于是他们狡诈警觉

bitter effort. And he always failed. It is a cant phrase with the critics to say 'he couldn't draw.' Mr Fry says: 'With all his rare endowments, he happened to lack the comparatively common gift of illustration, the gift that any draughtsman for the illustrated papers learns in a school of commercial art.'

Now this sentence gives away at once the hollowness of modern criticism. In the first place, can one learn a 'gift' in a school of commercial art, or anywhere else? A gift surely is given, we tacitly assume, by God or Nature or whatever higher power we hold responsible for the things we have no choice in.

Was, then, Cézanne devoid of this gift? Was he simply incapable of drawing a cat so that it would look like a cat? Nonsense! Cézanne's work is full of accurate drawing. His more trivial pictures, suggesting copies from other masters, are perfectly well drawn-that is, conventionally: so are some of the landscapes, so even is that portrait of M. Geffroy and his books, which is, or was, so famous. Why all these cant phrases about not being able to draw? Of course Cézanne could draw, as well as anybody else. And he had learned everything that was necessary in the art-schools.

He could draw. And yet, in his terrifically earnest compositions in the late Re-

地盯着任何一朵生命的火花，不失时机地埋葬它，甚至就像埋葬了塞尚的苹果还要给它压上一块白色的“意蕴形式”的墓石。

塞尚的追随者们除了凑热闹参加塞尚成就的葬礼外还能干些什么？他们追随他的目的就是为了埋葬他，且他们成功了。塞尚被追随他的马蒂斯们或弗拉芒克们给深深埋葬了，而那篇千篇一律的悼辞则由批评家们来念。

要认识马蒂斯、弗拉芒克和弗里叶兹[Othon Friesz(1879—1949)，法国野兽派画家]之类的人是很容易的事，他们不过是抽象化了的塞尚。他们全是些个骗子，尽管是聪明的骗子。他们全是理性化的利己主义者、利己主义者、利己主义者。正因此，他们才为聪明如死尸般的鉴赏家所接受。你不必害怕马蒂斯和弗拉芒克这号人。你吓死了他们也不会为你收尸的。他们不过是一些影子，是些江湖骗子，就会在画布上胡折腾。或许他们折腾得还很有趣儿，我也十二分地喜欢他们的骗术。可这都是坟墓中的游戏，玩这游戏的是些僵尸，是精神化的男人，甚至女人如劳伦辛小姐 [Marie Laurencin

naissance or baroque manner, he drew so badly. Why? Not because he couldn't. And not because he was sacrificing 'significant form' to 'insignificant form', or mere slick representation, which is apparently what artists themselves mean when they talk about drawing. Cézanne knew all about drawing: and he surely knew as much as his critics do about significant form. Yet he succeeded neither in drawing so that things looked right, nor combining his shapes so that he achieved real form. He just failed.

He failed, where one of his little slick successors would have succeeded with one eye shut. And why? Why did Cézanne fail in his early pictures? Answer that, and you'll know a little better what art is. He didn't fail because he understood nothing about drawing or significant form or aesthetic ecstasy. He knew about them all, and didn't give a spit for them.

Cézanne failed in his earlier pictures because he was trying with his mental consciousness to do something which his living Provencal body didn't want to do, or couldn't do. He terribly wanted to do something grand and voluptuous and sensuously satisfying, in the Tintoretto manner. Mr Fry calls that his 'willed ambition', which is a good phrase, and says he had to learn humility, which is a bad phrase.

(1885—1956),法国画家、服装设计师和图书插图画家]。至于精神,塞尚说他才不理会那劳什子呢。可别这么说呀！那些行家们却为此花大钱呢。这等于请死人为他们的娱乐付钱,可这种娱乐是毫无生气的！

现代艺术中最耐人寻味的也是惟一真正有趣的人物就是塞尚了。这与其说是因了他的成就倒不如说是因了他的奋斗。塞尚于1839年生于普罗旺斯艾克斯城。他矮小、腼腆,但时而又显得好斗,敏感,一肚子的野心。但他仍然深深地受着天真的地中海式的真理观念的影响,或许你可以称之为想像力吧。他不是个魁伟的人,可他的奋争却很富有英雄气概。他是个小布尔乔亚,我们不该忘记这一点。他的收入微薄。但是,说起来,普罗旺斯的小布尔乔亚比诺曼底的小布尔乔亚要真实得多,更有普通人的意味。他是更接近现实的人,可现实生活中的人对他那份可敬的中产阶级收入却不怎么感到敬佩。

塞尚算是天真到了极点,不过他可不傻。他一点都不大气,宏大令他深感压抑。但是,他心中燃着一团小而顽强的生命之火,那是他的是非

The 'willed ambition' was more than a mere willed ambition -it was a genuine desire. But it was a desire that thought it would be satisfied by ready-made baroque expressions, whereas it needed to achieve a whole new marriage of mind and matter. If we believed in reincarnation, then we should have to believe that after a certain number of new incarnations into the body of an artist, the soul of Cézanne *would* produce grand and voluptuous and sensually rich pictures -but not at all in the baroque manner. Because the pictures he actually did produce with undeniabe success are the first steps in that direction, sensual and rich, with not the slightest hint of baroque, but new, the man's new grasp of substantial reality.

There was, then, a certain discrepancy between Cézanne's notion of what he wanted to produce, and his other, intuitive knowledge of what he could produce. For whereas the mind works in possibilities, the intuitions work in actualities, and what you intuitively desire, that is possible to you. Whereas what you mentally or 'consciously' desire is nine times out of ten impossible: hitch your wagon to a star, and you'll just stay where you are.

So the conflict, as usual, was not between the artist and his medium, but between the artist's mind and the artist's intuition and instinct. And what Cézanne had

感。他并不为了成功而背叛自己,因为他不能背叛自己,他的本性不允许他背叛自己——他这人太纯真,他不会为了既得利益而去背叛那微小的真理火花。或许对于一个人这是最好的评价了。正因此,塞尚才得以跻身于英雄之列,尽管他矮小,他绝不放弃他那生机勃勃的想像力。

他像阳光之乡里大多数人一样,被形状的奇光异彩所深深吸引。他极其崇拜委洛奈塞[Paolo Veronese(1525—1588),意大利威尼斯画派画家]、丁托莱托[Tintoretto(1518—1594),意大利威尼斯画画家],甚至巴罗克派[巴罗克艺术是16—17世纪末欧洲的主要艺术流派,其特征是夸张、宏伟,富于动感]后期逊色的画家们。他想成为那样的画家。他太想了。而且他的确在这方面下了苦功夫,可他总是失败。用批评家们的行话说就是"他作不成画"。弗莱先生说:"尽管他禀赋非凡,可他却偏偏缺少描绘的一般才能,这种才能是任何绘图师在商业艺术学校中就应学会的。"

就凭这一句话就可断定现代批评是多么空虚。难道在一家商业艺术学校中就可以学到一种"才能"么?我们无法不承认,才能是上苍、自然或

to learn was not humility–cant word! –but honesty, honesty with himself. It was not a question of any gift or significant form or aesthetic ecstasy: it was a question of Cézanne being himself, just Cézanne. And when Cézanne is himself he is not Tintoretto, nor Veronese, nor anything baroque at all. Yet he is something *physical*, and even sensual: qualities which he had identified with the masters of virtuosity.

In passing, if we think of Henri Matisse, a real *virtuoso*, and imagine him possessed with a 'willed ambition' to paint grand and flamboyant baroque pictures, then we know at once that he would not have to 'humble' himself at all, but that he would start in and paint with great success grand and flamboyant modern – baroque pictures. He would succeed because he has the gift of virtuosity. And the gift of virtuosity simply means that you don't have to humble yourself, or even be honest with yourself, because you are a clever mental creature who is capable at will of making the intuitions and instincts subserve some mental concept: in short, you can prostitute your body to your mind, your instincts and intuitions you can prostitute to your 'willed ambition', in a sort of masturbation process, and you can produce the impotent glories of virtuosity. But Veronese and Tintoretto are real painters; they are not mere *virtuosi*, as some of the later men are.

任何高级力量所赋予的,我们无法选择才能。

那么,塞尚没有这种天赋才能吗?难道他连一只猫也画不像?一派胡言!塞尚的作品画得很准确。他那些效仿别的大师所作的小型作品画得很好——就是说画得很传统。他的不少风景画也是如此,甚至他画的那幅《M.杰夫罗伊与书》的画也是这样,而且这幅画还很有名呢。那为什么还有人说他不会作画呢?塞尚当然会作画,他跟别人一样画得好。他学到了艺术学校里所有必须学的东西。

他会作画。可当他十分认真地按照文艺复兴后期或巴罗克风格作画时,他却画得很差。为什么呢?并不是因为他不会画,也不是他牺牲了"意蕴形式"去追求"非意蕴形式"或熟练的再现,这是批评家所描述的绘画。塞尚太懂绘画了,他也像批评家们一样懂得意蕴形式为何物。可他无法把东西画得很正确,他也不能把他的造型组合起来变成真正的形式。反正他失败了。

他在这方面失败了,可他的画技熟练的继承者却闭着一只眼都可以

The point is very important. Any creative act occupies the whole consciousness of a man. This is true of the great discoveries of science as well as of art. The truly great discoveries of science and real works of art are made by the whole consciousness of man working together in unison and oneness: instinct, intuition, mind, intellect all fused into one complete consciousness, and grasping what we may call a complete truth, or a complete vision, a complete revelation in sound. A discovery, artistic or otherwise, may be more or less intuitional, more or less mental: but intuition will have entered into it, and mind will have entered too. The whole consciousness is concerned in every case. -And a painting requires the activity of the whole imagination, for it is made of imagery, and the imagination is that form of complete consciousness in which predominates the intuitive awareness of forms, images, the physical awareness.

And the same applies to the genuine appreciation of a work of art, or the grasp of a scientific law, as to the production of the same. The whole consciousness is occupied, not merely the mind alone, or merely the body. The mind and the spirit alone can never really grasp a work of art, though they may, in a masturbating fashion, provoke the body into an ecstasized response. The ecstasy will die out into

成功。这是为什么？为什么塞尚的早期绘画成了败笔？回答了这个问题，你就会更好地了解什么是艺术。他并不是因为不懂绘画、意蕴形式或审美狂喜才失败的，他对那一套全懂，但绝不拿它们当一回事。

塞尚的早期绘画失败了，那是因为他使唤自己的理性去做他的活生生的普罗旺斯人的肉体不想做或无法做的营生。他实在太想像丁托莱托那样画点庞大而能满足肉欲和美感的东西。弗莱先生称之为“意志的野心”，这词儿太精当了。他还说要他学会谦逊，这个词可不好。

所谓“意志的野心”并不仅仅是意志的野心，它是一种真正的欲望。这欲望自以为会通过现成的巴罗克表现形式得到满足，其实它需要的是精神和物质的新结合。如果我们相信再生的话，那么我们就该相信，既然塞尚的灵魂能在他艺术家的肉体中一次次获得再生，他就会做出庞大而极富肉感的绘画来，但绝不是以巴罗克的形式。他真正毫无疑问的成功之作正是他向那个方向迈出的第一步——肉感、浓郁，但毫无巴罗克的痕迹。其新颖表现着人对实体的全新把握。

ash and more ash. And the reason we have so many trivial scientists promulgating fantastic 'facts' is that so many modern scientists likewise work with the mind alone, and *force* the intuitions and instincts into a prostituted acquiescence. The very statement that water is H_2O is a mental *tour de force*. With our bodies we know that water is not H_2O, our intuitions and instincts both know it is not so. But they are bullied by the impudent mind. Whereas if we said that water, under certain circumstances, produces two volumes of hydrogen to one of oxygen, then the intuitions and instincts would agree entirely. But that water is composed of two volumes of hydrogen to one of oxygen we cannot physically believe. It needs something else. Something is missing. Of course, alert science does not ask us to believe the commonplace assertion of: water is H_2O, but school children have to believe it.

A parallel case is all this modern stuff about astronomy, stars, their distances and speeds and so on, talking of billions and trillions of miles and years and so forth: it is just occult.The mind is revelling in words, the intuitions and instincts are just left out, or prostituted into a sort of ecstasy. In fact, the sort of ecstasy that lies in absurd figures such as 2,000,000,000,000,000,000,000,000,000 miles or years or tons, figures which abound in modern scientific books on astronomy, is just

· 当然了,在塞尚想要描绘什么与他直感中能描绘什么之间是有分歧的。当理智产生可能性时,直觉却在现实中动作。而只有你直觉地渴望着的,那才是可能的。你在理智上"有意识"地渴望的十有八九达不到目的:你想把马车推上星球,可你却只能原地不动。

所以,按常理来说,这不是艺术家与媒介之间的冲突,而是艺术家的理性与他的直觉和本能之间的冲突。而塞尚要学会的绝不是谦逊(这是说教!)而是诚实,对自己诚实。这不是有没有意蕴形式或审美狂喜的天分的问题,而是塞尚能否成为自我而且仅仅是塞尚的问题。当塞尚是他自己时,他就不再是丁托莱托、委罗奈塞或任何巴罗克派画家。他是一个实体,甚至是性感的实体,这才是他和那些艺术大师们的共同之处。

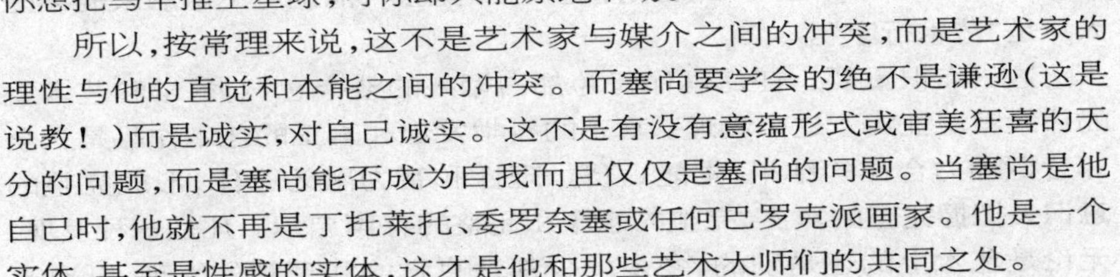

顺便说说, 如果我们想像一下亨利·马蒂斯这样的大师具有描绘宏大而色彩浓艳的巴罗克绘画的"意志的野心",我们会知道,他用不着谦逊就可以动笔而一举成功。他能成功,那是因为他有大师的天分。所谓大师的天分其实就是说你用不着谦卑,用不着对自己诚实,因为你是一个

the sort of aesthetic ecstasy that the over-mental critics of art assert they experience to-day from Matisse's pictures. It is all poppycock. The body is either stunned to a corpse, or prostituted to ridiculous thrills, or stands coldly apart.

When I read how far off the suns are, and what they are made of, and so on, and so on, I believe all I am able to believe, with the true imagination. But when my intuition and instinct can grasp no more, then I call my mind to a halt. I am not going to accept mere mental asseverations. The mind can assert anything, and pretend it has proved it. My beliefs I test on my body, on my intuitional consciousness, and when I get a response there, then I accept. The same is true of great scientific 'laws', like the law of evolution. After years of acceptance of the 'laws' of evolution -rather desultory or 'humble' acceptance -now I realize that my vital imagination makes great reservations. I find I can't, with the best will in the world, believe that the species have 'evolved' from one common life-form. I just can't feel it, I have to violate my intuitive and instinctive awareness of something else, to make myself believe it. But since I know that my intuitions and instincts may still be held back by prejudice, I seek in the world for someone to make me intuitively and instinctively feel the truth of the 'law' -and I don't find anybody. I find scientists,

聪明的理性动物，你有能力使你的直觉和本能服从你的理智。简言之，你可以使你的肉体向你的理智卖淫；你可以使你的本能和直觉向你的“意志的野心”卖淫；在短暂的近似手淫的过程中，你可以做出毫无生气的艺术品。当然，委罗奈塞和丁托莱托是真正的画家，他们可不像后来的某些人只是“艺术行家”。

这一点很重要。任何创作行为都占据人的整个意识，科学和艺术上的伟大发现证实了这个真理。真正的科学发现和真正的艺术作品是人全部意识通力合作的结果：本能、直觉、理性和智力融为一体，形成完整的意识去把握完整的真实、完整的想像和完整的有声启示。凡是一种发现，无论是艺术上的还是别的，多多少少都是直觉的和理智的发现，既有直觉也有理智在起作用。整体的意识时时都在介入。一幅绘画要求整体想像的运动，因为它是意象的产物。而想像正是整体意识的形式，它受制于直觉对形式和意象的意识，这就是肉体意识。

与创作一样，欣赏一件艺术品或掌握一个科学定律也需要这样。全

just like artists, asserting things they are mentally sure of, in fact cocksure, but about which they are much too egoistic and ranting to be intuitively, instinctively sure. When I find a man, or a woman, intuitively and instinctively sure of anything, I am all respect. But for scientific or artistic braggarts how can one have respect? The intrusion of the egoistic element is a sure proof of intuitive uncertainty. No man who is sure by instinct and intuition brags, though he may fight tooth and nail for his beliefs.

Which brings us back to Cézanne, why he couldn't draw, and why he couldn't paint baroque masterpieces. It is just because he was real, and could only believe in his own expression when it expressed a moment of wholeness or completeness of consciousness in himself. He could not prostitute one part of himself to the other. He could not masturbate, in paint or words. And that is saying a very great deal, to-day; the great day of the masturbating consciousness, when the mind prostitutes the sensitive responsive body, and just forces the reactions. The masturbating consciousness produces all kinds of novelties, which thrill for the moment, then go very dead. I cannot produce a single genuinely new utterance.

What we have to thank Cézanne for is not his humility, but for his proud high

部的意识都要投入,不仅仅是理性或肉体。单单理性和精神是无法把握一件艺术品的,尽管它们或许会用手淫的方式撩拨肉体产生激动的反应。可这种狂喜只会死亡并变成一堆灰烬。为什么有那么多的小科学家在散布一些莫名其妙的"事实"?这是因为不少的现代科学家只用理性工作,他们强迫直觉和本能卖淫般地承受理性。所谓水是氢二氧一(H_2O)之说就是理性的杰作。可我们的肉体,我们的直觉和本能却明白水不是氢二氧一(H_2O),这只是理性的蛮横所为。如果我们说在某些条件下水会分解为两个单位的氢和一个单位的氧,我们的直觉和本能会完全同意的。可硬要说水是由两个单位的氢和一个单位的氧组成的,我们的肉体却不能苟同。还缺点儿什么。当然,机警的科学并不要我们相信水是氢二氧一这一普通说法,可学校的学生却不得不相信。

同样的例子就是现代人对天文学、行星及其距离和速度的一通说法,大谈几十亿、几兆英里和几兆年等,实在玄妙至极。人的头脑在数字中陶然忘机,可直觉和本能却被忘却或向某种狂喜卖淫。其实,在诸如

spirit that refused to accept the glib utterances of his facile mental self. He wasn't poor-spirited enough to be facile-nor humble enough to be satisfied with visual and emotional clichés. Thrilling as the baroque masters were to him in themselves, he realized that as soon as he reproduced them he produced nothing but cliché. The mind is full of all sorts of memory, visual, tactile, emotional memory, memories, groups of memories, systems of memories. A cliché is just a worn-out memory that has no more emotional or intuitional root, and has become a habit. Whereas a novelty is just a new grouping of clichés, a new arrangement of accustomed memories. That is why a novelty is so easily accepted: it gives the little shock or thrill of surprise, but it does not disturb the emotional and intuitive self. It forces you to see nothing new. It is only a novel compound of clickés. The work of most of Cézanne's successors is just novel, just a new arrangement of clichés, soon growing stale. And the clichés are Cézanne's clichés, just as in Cézanne's own earlier pictures the clichés were all, or mostly, baroque clichés.

Cézanne's early history as a painter is a history of his fight with his own cliché. His consciousness wanted a new realization. And his ready-made mind offered him all the time a ready-made expression. And Cézanne, far too inwardly proud and

2,000,000,000,000,000,000,000,000,000 英里或年或吨这样荒唐的数字(这样的数字充斥着现代天文学著作)后隐藏着的狂喜与那些过分理性的艺术批评家们的狂喜没什么两样,他们号称自己从马蒂斯的绘画中获得了这样的审美狂喜。纯粹是胡言乱语。它要么让肉体吓成僵尸,要么让肉体向荒谬的狂喜卖淫或冷漠视之。

当我从书上看到恒星离我们有多远,是由什么组成的云云,我就尽最大的努力、尽量发挥自己的想象力去相信这些说法。可一旦我的直觉和本能再也无法把握这些数字,我就不再思想了,我不再接受纯粹理性的断言。人的理智可以对任何事物下断言并佯装这断言得到了证实。我要把我的信念在我的肉体上进行考验,用我的直觉意识去考验我的信念。一旦我从那里得到了反应,我才接受这种信念。对诸如进化的规律这样的伟大科学"定律"我亦持同样态度。多少年来人们平白无故地、"谦卑"地接受进化规律,可现在我那生机勃勃的想象力却要对此做出巨大保留了。我发现,我就是费尽心机也无法相信物种是从一种普通的生命

haughty to accept the ready-made clichés that came from his mental consciousness, stocked with memories, and which appeared mocking at him on his canvas, spent most of his time smashing his own forms to bits. To a true artist, and to the living imagination, the cliché is the deadly enemy. Cézanne had a bitter fight with it. He hammered it to pieces a thousand times. And still it reappeared.

Now again we can see why Cézanne´s drawing was so bad. It was bad becuse it represented a smashed, mauled cliché, terribly knocked about. If Cézanne had been willing to accept his own baroque cliché, his drawing would have been perfectly conventionally 'all right', and not a critic would have had a word to say about it. But when his drawing was conventionally all right, to Cézanne himself it was mockingly all wrong, it was cliché. So he flew at it and knocked all the shape and stuffing out of it, and when it was so mauled that it was all wrong, and he was exhausted with it, he let it go; bitterly, because it still was not what he wanted. And here comes in the comic element in Cézanne´s pictures. His rage with the cliché made him distort the cliché sometimes into parody, as we see in pictures like *The Pasha* and *La Femme*. 'You will be cliché, will you?' he gnashes. 'Then be it! ' And he shoves it in a frenzy of exasperation over into parody. And the sheer exas-

形式“进化”而来的。我实在无法感受到这一点。要让我相信它，我就不得不违背我的直觉意识和本能意识。因为我知道我的直觉和本能仍旧会受偏见的阻碍，于是我在这世上寻找一个能让我直觉、本能地感受这“规律”之真理的人，可我找不到任何一个这样的人。我发现科学家们像艺术家一样自以为直觉、本能地确信什么，其实那不过是他们的理性所为。一旦我发现一个直觉、本能地自信的男女，我就对他们肃然敬佩起来。可对科学上和艺术上的牛皮大王们你怎么能尊敬得起来？利己主义的介入是造成直觉上不自信的原因。本能和直觉上自信的人是不会吹牛皮的，尽管他会为自己的信仰进行殊死的斗争。

这又把我们的话题引回到塞尚身上：为什么他做不成画，为什么他绘不出巴罗克风格的杰作？这是因为他真诚，他只相信自我的表现，只相信它所表现的自身意识完整的一瞬。他不能让自己的某一部分向另一部分卖淫。无论是在绘画中还是语言上他都不会手淫。这很说明不少今日的问题。今日的世界，正是手淫意识泛滥之时，理智迫使反应敏感的肉体

peration makes the parody still funny; but the laugh is a little on the wrong side of the face.

This smashing of the cliché lasted a long way into Cézanne's life; indeed, it went with him to the end. The way he worked over and over his forms was his nervous manner of laying the ghost of his cliché, burying it. Then when it disappeared perhaps from his forms themselves, it lingered in his composition, and he had to fight with the edges of his forms and contours, to bury the ghost there. Only his colour he knew was not cliché. He left it to his disciples to make it so.

In his very best pictures, the best of the still-life compositions, which seem to me Cézanne's greatest achievement, the fight with the cliché is still going on. But it was in the still-life pictures he learned his final method of avoiding the cliché; just leaving gaps through which it fell into nothingness. So he makes his landscape succeed.

In his art, all his life long, Cézanne was tangled in a twofold activity. He wanted to express something, and before he could do it he had to fight the hydra-headed cliché, whose last head he could never lop off. The fight with the cliché is the most obvious thing in his pictures. The dust of battle rises thick and the splinters

卖淫，强迫肉体有所反应。这种手淫意识一时间可弄出各种耸人听闻的新鲜货色，但这东西来得快去得也快。它怎么也折腾不出任何真正新鲜的东西来。

我们要感谢的不是塞尚的谦卑，而是他那拒绝理性自我花言巧语的高傲精神。他不至于因精神贫乏而轻浮起来，也不会谦逊到满足于视觉与情绪的陈腐。尽管巴罗克风格的大师们令他震惊，可他还是意识到一旦自己模仿他们，他绘出的东西就一钱不值了，只能算旧货一堆。人的头脑里充斥着各式各样的记忆，视觉的，触觉的，情绪的，记忆群和记忆系列。一种陈货就是失去情绪和直觉之根的陈旧记忆，只能算一种习惯。而一种翻新的花样只是陈腐货色的再组装，是习惯性记忆的重新组合。这就是新花样易于为人接受的原因：它让你小有震惊，可它却不能搅动情绪和直觉的自我。它强迫你去看，却看不到什么新货色。它只是陈旧货色的翻新罢了。塞尚的追随者们当中，大多数人的作品都仅仅是花样翻新，是旧货的重新组装，所以很快就没滋味了。而他们笔下的货正是塞尚画

fly wildly. And it is this dust of battle and flying of splinters which his imitators still so fervently imitate. If you give a Chinese dressmaker a dress to copy, and the dress happens to have a darned rent in it, the dressmaker carefully tears a rent in the new dress, and darns it in exact replica. And this seems to be the chief occupation of Cézanne's disciples, in every land. They absorb themselves reproducing imitation mistakes. He let off various explosions in order to blow up the stronghold of the cliché, and his followers make grand firework imitations of the explosions, without the faintest inkling of the true attack. They do, indeed, make an onslaught on representation, true-to-life representation: because the explosion in Cézanne's pictures blew them up. But I am convinced that what Cézanne himself wanted was representation. He wanted true-to-life representation. Only he wanted it more true to life. And once you have got photography, it is a very, very difficult thing to get representation more true-to-life: which it has to be.

Cézanne was a realist, and he wanted to be true to life But he would not be content with the optical cliché. With the impressionists, purely optical vision perfected itself and fell at once into clichés, with a startling rapidity. Cézanne saw this. Artists like Courbet and Daumier were not purely optical, but the other element in

过的旧货,正如塞尚早期的绘画大都是巴罗克风格的旧货一样。

画家塞尚的早期历史就是他与自身的陈腐斗争的历史。他的意识要获得一种新的认知。可他那陈旧的头脑为他提供的总是一种陈旧不堪的表达方式。但是,塞尚的内心是太傲慢了,他绝不要接受那来自理性、充斥着记忆的头脑(理性似乎还不住地嘲弄他的绘画)的陈旧货色,于是他花大量的时间把他的表达方式砸得稀烂。对于一位真正的艺术家,对于生机勃勃的想像力来说,陈旧是一个不共戴天的敌人,塞尚与此进行了艰苦的搏斗。他千遍万遍地把它砸成齑粉,可它却仍旧重现。

现在我们总算明白为什么塞尚的画不好了。他画不好,是因为他的画再现了一种被击碎了的陈腐货色。如果塞尚乐意接受传统的巴罗克陈货,他的绘画就会是"毫无毛病"的传统画,也就没哪个批评家说个不字了。可是,偏偏他觉得这种传统上"毫无毛病"的画全走了样,是对他的一种讽刺。于是他对自己的画大光其火。他把画的形式全砸烂,让它干瘪无形。等他的画全走形了,他也为此疲惫不堪了,这才罢休。可他仍旧伤心,

these two painters, the intellectual element, was cliché. To the optical vision they added the concept of force-pressure, almost like an hydraulic brake, and this force-pressure concept is mechanical, a cliché, though still populat. And Daumier added mental satire, and Courbet added a touch of a sort of socialism: both cliché and unimaginative.

Cézanne wanted something that was neither optical nor mechanical nor intellectual. And to introduce into our world of vision something which is neither optical nor mechanical nor intellectual-psychological requires a real revolution. It was a revolution Cézanne began, but which nobody, apparently, has been able to carry on.

He wanted to touch the world of substance once more with the intuitive touch, to be aware of it with the intuitive awareness, and to express it in intuitive terms. That is, he wished to displace our present mode of mental-visual consciousness, the consciousness of mental concepts, and substitute a mode of consciousness that was predominantly intuitive, the awareness of touch. In the past the primitives painted intuitively, but in the direction of our presesnt mental-visual, conceptual form of consciousness. They were working away from their own intuition. Mankind

因为这还不是他所渴求的那种样子。从此,塞尚的绘画中注入了喜剧的因素。他由于仇视陈腐,所以对陈腐施以扭曲术,以至于成为对陈腐的滑稽模仿,如《帕莎》和《女人》。"你会成为陈词滥调,对吗?"他咬牙切齿地叫道。"那就随你便吧!"于是他在极度愤怒中把绘画做成一种滑稽模仿的货色,他的怒火使他的作品看上去有些让人发噱,可那笑容却把脸笑走了样儿。

塞尚的一生中久久地与陈腐作斗争,要砸烂它。是的,这斗争一直伴随他至死。他一遍又一遍地调整自己的形式,其实就是紧张地摆列陈腐的魔鬼并把它埋葬。可即便是当魔鬼从他的形式中消失了时,它还仍旧徘徊在他的画中,他仍旧得同形式的边沿与剪影作斗争,从而把魔鬼彻底消灭。他知道,只有他的色彩才不是陈腐。他把色彩留给了他的信徒们。

塞尚最优秀的绘画即最优秀的静物写生,在我看来是他最了不起的成就,可就在这些作品中,仍蕴藏着与陈腐的斗争。在静物写生中,他终

has never been able to trust the intuitive consciousness, and the decision to accept the trust marks a very great revolution in the course of human development.

Without knowing it, Cézanne, the timid little conventional man sheltering behind his wife and sister and the Jesuit father, was a pure revolutionary. When he said to his models: 'Be an apple! Be an apple! ' he was uttering the foreword to the fall not only of Jesuits and the Christian idealists together, but to the collapse of our whole way of consciousness, and the substitution of another way. If the human being is going to be primarily an apple, as for Cézanne it was, then you are going to have a new world of men: a world which has very little to say, men that can sit still and just be physically there, and be truly non-moral. That was what Cézanne meant with his: 'Be an apple! ' He knew perfectly well that the moment the model began to intrude her personality and her 'mind', it would be cliché and moral, and he would have to paint cliché. The only part of her that was not banal, known *ad nauseam*, living cliché, the only part of her that was not living cliché was her appleyness. Her body, even her very sex, was known, nauseously: *connu! connu!* the endless chance of known cause-and-effect, the infinite web of the hated cliché which nets us all down in utter boredom. He knew it all, he hated it all, he refused

得避免陈腐的真谛:只需留下鸿沟,让陈腐从中坠落,落入虚无。就这样,他使他的风景画成功了。

在他一生的艺术生涯中,塞尚都纠缠在一种双重的运动中。他要表达什么,可在这之前他必须与纷呈变幻的陈腐作斗争,他永远也无法取得最后的胜利。在他绘画中表现顶充分的就是与陈腐的斗争。战场上硝烟弥漫,血肉横飞,而他的模仿者们狂热地临摹的却正是这战尘和碎尸。如果你把一件衣服交给一个中国裁缝去仿造,碰巧衣服上有一块织补的绣片,你看吧,这位裁缝会把新衣服悉心地挖一个洞,然后仿照原来的样子丝毫不走样地补上一块绣片。塞尚的信徒们似乎就主要忙于干诸如此类的营生,各国的信徒皆如此。他们着迷于生产模仿的错误。塞尚引燃了许多炸药,为的是轰掉陈腐的堡垒。可他的信徒们却照此规模大放烟花,对于真正的攻击是怎么回事毫无所知。但他们的确对忠于生活的表现进行了攻击,只因为塞尚的绘画把这种表现全炸烂了。可我相信,塞尚自己渴望的却正是表现,他要的是忠于生活的表现,他就怕他的画不能忠诚

it all, this timid and 'humble' little man. He knew, as an artist, that the only bit of a woman which nowadays escapes being ready-made and ready-known cliché is the appley part of her. Oh, be an apple, and leave out all your thoughts, all your feelings, all your mind and all your personality, which we know all about and find boring beyond endurance. Leave it all out-and be an apple! It is the appleyness of the portrait of Cézanne's wife that makes it so permanently interesting: the appleyness, which carries with it also the feeling of knowing the other side as well, the side you don't see, the hidden side of the moon. For the intuitive apperception of the apple is so tangibly aware of the apple that it is aware of it all round, not only just of the front. The eye sees only fronts, and the mind, on the whole, is satisfied with fronts. But intuition needs all-roundedness, and instinct needs insideness. The true imagination is for ever curving round to the other side, to the back of presented appearance.

So to my feeling the portraits of Madame Cézanne, particularly the portrait in the red dress, are more interesting than the portrait of M. Geffroy, or the portraits of the housekeeper or the gardener. In the same way the *Card-Players* with two figures please me more than those with four.

地表现生活。而一旦你有了摄影,再想让绘画忠实于生活地表现什么怕是很难了,尽管它必须这样。

塞尚是个写实派,他要的是忠于生活,可他绝不容忍视觉上的俗套。印象派画家们使纯粹的视觉想像变得完美,随之落入了俗套,从完美到俗套的过程竟是令人吃惊地迅速,塞尚看出了这一点。像库尔贝和杜米埃这样的艺术家虽然并非纯视觉派,但他们画中的智力因素是一种陈腐。他们给这种视觉想像增添了一种力的强压概念,如同液压一般,这也是一种俗套式的机械概念,尽管它很流行。杜米埃为它增添了一种理性的嘲讽,而库尔贝则为它添上点社会主义味道。这两样全是毫无想像力的俗套子。

塞尚需要的既不是视觉也不是机械和理性。可若要把一种非视觉、非机械性、也非理性-心理性的东西介绍到我们的想像世界中来,这需要一场真正的革命。这是一场由塞尚发起的革命,可很明显,却无人将其继续进行下去。

But we have to remember, in his figure-paintings, that while he was painting the appleyness he was also deliberately painting out the so-called humanness, the personality, the 'likeness', the physical cliché. He had deliberatedly to paint it out, deliberately to make the hands and face rudimentary, and so on, because if he had painted them in fully they would have been cliché. He never got over the cliché denominator, the intrusion and interference of the ready-made concept, when it came to people, to men and women. Especially to women he could only give a cliché response-and that maddened him. Try as he might, women remained a known, ready-made cliché object to him, and he could not break through the concept obsession to get at the intuitive awareness of her. Except with his wife-and in his wife he did at least know the appleyness. But with his housekeeper he failed somewhat. She was a bit cliché, especially the face. So really is M. Geffroy.

With men Cézanne often dodged it by insisting on the clothes, those stiff cloth jackets bent into thick folds, those hats, those blouses, those curtains. Some of the *Card-Players*, the big ones with four figures, seem just a trifle banal, so much occupied with painted stuff, painted clothing, and the humanness a bit cliché. Not good colour, nor clever composition, nor 'planes' of colour, nor anything else will

他想要再次直觉地触摸实体的世界，直觉地意识它并用直觉的语汇表现它。这就是说，他要用直觉的意识形式即触觉取代我们目前的理性视觉意识也即理性观念意识。在过去的年月里，原始人是凭直觉做画的，但他们遵循的方向却正是我们现在的理性视觉方向，是观念意识。他们其实是渐渐远离了他们的直觉意识。人类从未信任过自己的直觉意识，而当有人要信任它时，这决断本身就标志着人类发展上一个极其伟大的革命。

塞尚这位躲在老婆、姐姐和身为耶稣会会士的父亲背后胆小而传统的人其实是个纯粹的革命者，对此他并不自知。当他冲他的模特儿说“做一只苹果！做一只苹果！”时，他喊出的是耶稣会和基督教理性主义者堕落的预言，不仅如此，还是我们整个理性方式崩溃的预言，还预言它会被取而代之。如果人类要从根本上做一只苹果，塞尚的意思是，那样就会有一个人的新世界：一个没什么思想要表达的世界，只需静坐一处，只做一个肉体，而没有精神。这就是塞尚“做一只苹果”的意思。他十分明白，一

save an emotional cliché from being an emotional cliché, though they may, of course, garnish it and make it more interesting.

Where Cézanne did sometimes escape the cliché altogether and really give a complete intuitive interpretation of actual objects is in some of the still-life compositions. To me these good still-life scenes are purely representative and quite true to life. Here Cézanne did what he wanted to do: he made the things quite real, he didn't deliberately leave anything out, and yet he gave us a triumphant and rich intuitive vision of a few apples and kitchen pots. For once his intuitive consciousness triumphed, and broke into utterance. And here he is inimitable. His imitators imitate his accessories of tablecloths folded like tins, etc. -the unreal parts of his pictures-but they don't imitate the pots and apples, because they can't, It's the real appleyness. and you can't imitate it. Every man must create it new and different out of himself: new and different. The moment it looks 'like' Cézanne, it is nothing.

But at the same time Cézanne was triumphing with the apple and appleyness he was still fighting with the cliché. When he makes Madame Cézanne most still, most appley, he starts making the universe slip uneasily about her. It was part of his desire: to make the human form, the life form, come to rest. Not static-on the con-

旦模特儿开始让人格与“理性”介入,那就又变成了俗套子和精神,他依此绘出的就只能是俗套。模特的不俗,惟一不俗之处就是这种“苹果”性质,这一点让她不再是活死人。她的肉体,甚至她的性本身被人了解了,这是件令人厌恶的事。了解!了解!没完没了的因果关系,可恶的陈腐之网纠缠得我们不得安生。他明白这一切,恨这一切,拒绝这一切,这个腼腆、“谦卑”的小个子。作为一个艺术家,他知道女人惟一能逃避陈腐气和稔熟之处就是她的“苹果”特质。哦,做一只苹果,什么思想,什么感情,什么理性和人格全都不要。我们对这些全了解,已经忍无可忍了。不要这些个东西,做一只苹果吧!倒是塞尚画他夫人的那幅画中透出的“苹果”性质令人永远回味:这种性质同时还蕴藏着一种了解人的另一面的感觉,那是你所看不见的月亮的另一面。直觉对苹果的意识是实感的,它意识到的是苹果的全部,而绝非一个侧面。人眼只能看到正面,头脑总的来说也只满足于看到正面。但直觉需要整体,本能需要内在物。真正的想像力总是要迂回到另一面,到正面的背后去。

所以,我觉得塞尚画他夫人的那些画像(尤其是着红装的那一幅)比

trary. Mobile but come to rest.And at the same time he set the unmoving material world into motion. Walls twitch and slide, chairs bend or rear up a little, cloths curl like burning paper. Cézanne did this partly to satisfy his intuitive feeling that nothing is really statically at rest –a feeling he seems to have had strongly –as when he watched the lemons shrivel or go mildewed, in his still–life group, which he left lying there so long so that he could see that gradual flux of change: and partly to fight the cliché, which says that the inanimate world is static, and that walls are still. In his fight with the cliché he denied that walls are still and chairs are static. In his intuitive self he felt for their changes.

And these two activities of his consciousness occupy his later landscapes. In the best landscapes we are fascinated by the mysterious shiftiness of the scene under our eyes; it shifts about as we watch it. And we realize, with a sort of transport, how intuitively true this is of landscape. It is not still. It has its own weird anima, and to our wide–eyed perception it changes like a living animal under our gaze. This is a quality that Cézanne got marvellously.

Then again, in other pictures he seems to be saying: Landscape is not like this and not like this and not like this and not…etc.–and every not is a little blank

画 M.杰夫罗伊、女管家和园丁的画更有趣。同样,《两个玩纸牌者》就比《四个玩纸牌者》更让我喜欢。

但我们要记住,他在人物画像中虽然画出了“苹果”性,但他也有意画出所谓的人性、人格和“肖像”这些陈腐的物性东西。他刻意把这些绘出来,刻意把手和脸画得普通,因为如果他画得太完美这些东西就又落俗套了。一涉及到人,男人和女人,他就无法超越陈腐的观念,不得不让它们介入、影响自己。特别是对女人,他只能做出俗套的反应,这一点真令他发疯至极。无论怎样努力,女人对他来说仍旧是一个已知的、陈旧的客体,他无法冲破理性概念用直觉去感知女人。对他妻子则是个例外,他至少了解到了她的“苹果”性。可对他的女管家他却做不到这一点,把她画得落俗套,特别是她的脸,他画的 M.杰夫罗伊亦是如此。

画男人时,塞尚时常为了避免陈腐而固执地画他们的衣服,画棉布外衣厚厚的褶子,帽子,袍子还有门帘子。《玩纸牌者》系列里那些大幅的、四个人的,看上去挺俗,那些充斥画面的东西、衣服和人太落俗套了。鲜亮的颜色、精巧的构图和色彩的“层次”等等都无法拯救陈腐的情感,

space in the canvas, defined by the remains of an assertion. Sometimes Cézanne builds up a landscape essentially out of omissions. He puts fringes on the complicated vacuum of the cliché, so to speak, and offers us that. It is interesting in a repudiative fashion, but it is not the new thing. The appleyness, the intuition has gone. We have only a mental repudiation. This occupies many of the later pictures: and ecstasizes the critics.

And Cézanne was bitter. He had never, as far as his life went, broken through the horrible glass screen of the mental concepts, to the actual touch of life. In his art he had touched the apple, and that was a great deal. He had intuitively known the apple and intuitively brought it forth on the tree of his life, in paint. But when it came to anything beyond the apple, to landscape, to people, and above all to nude woman, the cliché had triumphed over him. The cliché had triumphed over him, and he was bitter, misanthropic. How not to be misanthropic when men and women are just clichés to you, and you hate the cliché? Most people, of course, love the cliché -because most people are the cliché. Still, for all that, there is perhaps more appleyness in man, and even in nude woman, than Cézanne was able to get at. The cliché obturded, so he just abstracted away from it. Those last water-colour land-

最多不过是将陈旧的情感巧加伪装让它看上去有点意思罢了。

如果说塞尚有时能够避免陈腐并能对客观实体进行完全直觉的解释,那是在他的一些静物画中。我以为这些静物是纯粹的描述,很忠实生活。在此,塞尚做了他想做的事:他把东西画得很逼真,他没有故意舍弃什么,他成功地,极其直觉地给予我们的是几只苹果和几件炊具的视觉图像。一旦他的直觉意识占了上风并发出喊声,此时他是无法被人模仿的。他的模仿者们模仿的是他笔下的小物件如卷成筒状的台布,那是他绘画中不真实的部分,可他们却不去模仿他笔下的苹果和炊具,因为他们模仿不来。就是这种“苹果”气质让你无法模仿。每个人都该绘出新鲜的与众不同的作品才对,一旦你画得“像”塞尚画的,这画就毫无价值了。

与此同时,塞尚的苹果虽然成功了,他仍然在与俗套作斗争。当他把塞尚太太画得如此“静”,如此富有的“苹果”气时,他让世界不安了。他的希望之一就是让人类的形式和生命的形式停下来,但绝不是静止。他要的是动的静。同时,他把不动的物质开动了起来:墙壁扭曲塌落,椅子弯了、翘了,衣服卷得像燃烧的纸。塞尚这样做的目的之一是要满足他的直

scapes are just coloured sort of edges. The blank is vacuum, which was Cézanne's last word against the cliché. It is a vacuum and the edges are there to assert the vacuity.

And the very fact that we can reconstruct almost instantly a whole landscape from the few indications Cézanne gives, shows what a cliché the landscape is, how it exists already ready-made, in our minds, how it exists in a pigeon-hole of the consciousness, so to speak, and you need only be given its number to be abe to get it out, complete. Cézanne's last watercolour landscapes, made up of a few touches on blank paper, are a satire on landscape altogether. They leave so much to the imagination! -that immortal cant phrase, which means they give you to a cliché and the cliché comes. That's what the cliché exists for. And that sort of imagination is just a ragbag memory stored with thousands and thousands of old and really worthless sketches, images, etc., clichés.

We can see what a fight it means, the escape from the domination of the ready-made mental concept, the mental consciousness stuffed full of clichés that intervene like a complete screen between us and life. It means a long, long fight, that will probably last for ever. But Cézanne did get as far as the apple. I can think of

感:没什么是真正静止的。当他看着柠檬萎缩或腐烂时他似乎更强烈地产生了这样的感觉(他保留了一组静物,为的是观察它们的渐渐变化);目的之二是为了同这样的陈腐观念作斗争:无生物世界是静止的,墙壁是静止的。他否认墙和椅子是静止的,他的直觉感到了它们的变化。

他的这两种意识活动占据了他后期的风景画。优秀的风景画会以其景物神秘的动感迷住我们,它就在我们眼前动着。我们会凭直觉激动地意识到,风景画就是如此富有直觉的真。它绝不是静止的,它自有其超自然的灵魂,对我们拭目以待的感悟力来说,它就像一只活生生的动物在我们的视凝视中变幻。塞尚的绘画就具有这种了不起的特色。

可在别的画中,塞尚又似乎在说:风景画不像这样,不像这样,不像这样……每一个"不像"都在画布上留下一个小小的空白。有时塞尚基本上是靠"省略"来构筑起一幅风景画的。他给陈腐的复杂真空镶上边框,然后把它奉献给我们。其否定的风格是有趣的,可这并不新鲜。因为,"苹果"气和直觉从中消失了。我们所有的只是一种理性的否定,这类东西占据了不少后期的绘画,可它却令那些批评家们兴奋了起来。

nobody else who has done anything.

When we put it in personal terms, it is a fight in a man between his own ego, which is his ready-made mental self which inhabits either a sky-blue, self-tinted heaven or a black, self-tinted hell, and his other free intuitive self. Cézanne never freed himself from his ego, in his life. He haunted the fringes of experience. 'I who am so feeble in life' -but at least he knew it. At least he had the greatness to feel bitter about it. Not like the complacent bourgeois who now 'appreciate' him!

So now perhaps it is the English turn. Perhaps this is where the English will come in. They have certainly stayed out very completely. It is as if they had received the death-blow to their instinctive and intuitive bodies in the Elizabethan age, and since then they have steadily died, till now they are complete corpses. As a young English painter, an intelligent and really modest young man, said to me: 'But I do think we ought to begin to paint good pictures, now that we know pretty well all there is to know about how a picture should be made. You do agree, don't you, that technically we know almost all there is to know about painting?'

I looked at him in amazement. It was obvious that a newborn babe was as fit to paint pictures as he was. He knew technically all there was to know about pictures:

塞尚是痛苦的。他一生中从来都没有冲破可怕的理性玻璃墙去实际触摸生命。在他的艺术中,他触到了苹果,这已经很了不起了。他直觉地了解了苹果并直觉地把它送上了他绘画的生命之树。可一旦当主题超出了苹果变成风光、人,特别是裸体女人时,陈腐又战胜了塞尚。他被战胜了,他于是变得痛苦,愤世嫉俗。当男人和女人对你来说是旧货色而你又仇恨陈腐时,你怎么能不变得愤世嫉俗呢?大多数人是喜欢陈腐的,因为大多数人都是陈旧货色。尽管如此,男人,甚至是裸体女人身上或许会有塞尚所难能领会的"苹果"气。陈腐气干扰人们,所以他抽身而去。他最后的水彩风景画只是对陈腐的抽取。这些画是些空白,周围画着几根淡黄的边框之类的东西。空白即是真空,他以此作为与陈腐作斗争的最终誓言。陈腐是一个真空,那些边框是用来强调其空虚的。

我们可以根据塞尚提供的少许启示就几乎可以立即恢复一整幅风景画,这个事实说明风景画是何等陈腐的东西,它是我们头脑中存在了许久的现成旧货,它存在于方寸之间,你只需得到它的号码就可以把它彻底唤出来。塞尚最后的几幅水彩风景画是涂在白纸上的那么几刷子色

all about two-dimensional and three-dimensional composition, also the colour-dimension and the dimension of values in that view of the composition which exists apart from form: all about the value of planes, the value of the angle in planes, the different values of the same colour on different planes: all about edges, visible edges, tangible edges, intangible edges: all about the nodality of form-groups, the constellating of mass-centres: all about the relativity of mass, the gravitation and the centrifugal force of masses, the resultant of the complex impinging of masses, the isolation of a mass in the line of vision: all about pattern, line pattern, edge pattern, tone pattern, colour pattern, and the pattern of moving planes: all about texture, impasto, surface, and what happens at the edge of the canvas: also which is the aesthetic centre of the canvas, the dynamic centre, the effulgent centre, the kinetic centre, the mathematical centre, and the Chinese centre: also the points of departure in the foreground, and the points of disappearance in the background, together with the various routes between these points, namely, as the crow flies, as the cow walks, as the mind intoxicated with knowledge reels and gets there: all about spotting, what you spot, which spot, on the spot, how many spots, balance of spots, recedence of spots, spots on the explosive vision and spots on the co-or-

彩,那是对风景画的讽刺。“它们给人留下很大的想像余地!”这句不朽的套话让你知道什么是俗套子了。俗套就是为这个而存在的。那种想像力不过是一只杂货袋,里面装着成千上万陈旧而无用的素描和意象,全是俗套子。

我们可以明白,这是一场什么样的斗争,意味着逃离陈旧理性观念的主宰,理性意识里充斥着陈旧货,像一块幕布把我们和生命完全隔开。这意味着一场永不休止的战斗。不过塞尚总算弄懂了一只苹果。除他之外我再也不知道还有谁在这方面做出了什么成就。

当我们把它具体到某个人时,应该说这是一个人自我的斗争:一方是占据了自诩的蓝天或自诩的黑地狱的陈腐理性自我,另一方则是他的另一个自由的直觉自我。塞尚一辈子也未曾从自我中解脱出来,他一直在经验的边缘上彳亍。“我在生活中是个软弱至极的人。”他至少明白这一点,他至少为此感到痛苦,这已说明了他的伟大。这和那些个“欣赏”他的自负中产阶级可大不一样!

或许现在该轮到英国人了,或许这正是英国人的可乘之机。他们一

dinative vision: all about literary interest and how to hide it successfully from the policeman: all about photographic representation, and which heaven it belongs to, and which hell: all about the sexappeal of a picture, and when you can be arrested for solicitation, when for indecency: all about the psychology of a picture, which section of the mind it appeals to, which mental state it is intended to represent, how to exclude the representation of all other states of mind from the one intended, or how, on the contrary, to give a hint of complementary states of mind fringing the state of mind portrayed: all about the chemistry of colours, when to use Winsor & Newton and when not, and the relative depth of contempt to display for Lefranc* on the history of colour, past and future, whether cadmium will really stand the march of ages, whether viridian will go black, blue, or merely greasy, and the effect on our great-great-grandsons of the flake white and zinc white and white lead we have so lavishly used: on the merits and demerits of leaving patches of bare, prepared canvas, and which preparation will bleach, which blacken: on the mediums to be used, the vice of linseed oil, the treachery of turps, the meanness of gums, the innocence of the unspeakable crime of varnish: on allowing your picture to be shiny, on insisting that it should be shiny, on weeping over the merest suspicion of gloss

直与此无关,似乎在伊丽莎白时代他们的本能与直觉肉体就受到了致命的打击,从此他们就缓缓死去,至今他们已成了僵尸。正如一位聪明而又实在的谦逊的英国青年画家对我说的那样:"我真的认为我们该开始绘出像样的画来了,因为我们已经懂得该怎么画好一幅画了。你难道不同意说我们在技术上该懂的都懂了吗?"

我吃惊地看着他。很明显,一个新生婴儿都像他一样够格儿去做画了。在技术上他是懂得了绘画的一切:平面和立体的构图,色彩的维度以及从脱离形式的构图角度得出的明暗配合,各种平面的配合,平面角度的配合,同样的色彩在不同平面上的不同配合;边缘,可见的边缘,有形的边缘,无形的边缘;形式群结,色块中心的星座化;色块的相对性,色块的重心引力和离心力,色块的综合撞击,色块在想像视线中的孤立;形状,线状,边状,色状和动感平面的模式;肌理,颜料的厚涂,表层和画布边缘效应及画布上的审美中心,动力中心,辉煌中心,活动中心,数学中心和模仿中心以及前景的出发点、背景隐没点和介于这些点之间的各种各样的途径,就是直线距离,沉醉于知识的头脑如何曲线到达,等等;还

and rubbing it with a raw potato: on brushes, and the conflicting length of the stem, the best of the hog, the length of bristle most to be desired on the many varying occasions, and whether to slash in one direction only: on the atmosphere of London, on the atmosphere of Glasgow, on the atmosphere of Rome, on the atmosphere of Paris, and the peculiar action of them all upon vermilion, cinnabar, pale cadmium yellow, mid-chrome, emerald green, Veronese green, linseed oil, turps, and Lyall´s perfect medium: on quality, and its relation to light, and its ability to hold its own in so radical a change of light as that from Rome to London-all these things the young man knew-and out of it, God help us, he was going to made pictures.

Now, such innocence and such nai vete, coupled with true modesty, must make us believe that we English have indeed, at least as far as paint goes, become again as little children: very little children, tiny children: babes: nay, babes unborn. And if we have really got back to the state of the unborn babe, we are perhaps almost ready to be born. The English may be born again, pictorially. Or, to tell the truth, they may begin for the first time to be born: since as painters of compostiton pictures they don´t really exist. They have reached the stage where their

有如何点涂，点涂什么，点涂哪里，多少涂点，涂点间的平衡，涂点的消退，爆炸性视觉中的涂点和辅助想像中的涂点；文学的兴趣以及如何成功地对警察隐瞒之；摄影描述及其所属的天堂和地狱；一幅画的性感召力，你何时因为拉客而被逮捕，何时因为淫秽而遭逮捕；绘画的心理学：它感动心智的哪一部分？它决意去展示哪种理性状况？何以排除展示其他理性状况的可能或者正相反，何以与此同时暗示与主题有关的其他补充性理性状况；颜料的化学性质：何时用温沙和牛顿公司的，何时不用，对拉弗朗斯的颜料则予以适度的蔑视 [这三人均是现代水彩的完善者和生产者。William Windsor(1804—1865),Henry Charles Newton(1805—1883)。Lefranc 是法国艺术用品的主要生产者]；颜料史，过去和将来都要懂，镉是否可以经得住岁月的考验，青绿色是否会变黑、变蓝或变成一团油墨，它对我们数代子孙所常用的碳酸铅白和氧化锌会有什么影响；在调制好的画布上留出空白的优劣，怎么调会撕裂，怎么条会发黑；用什么溶剂，亚麻籽油的坏处，松节油的危害，树脂的低劣，清漆所犯的无辜但难以言表的罪孽；让画有光泽，一定要有光泽，清除任何可以的光斑，用生土豆摩擦；关于画笔，刷子把的长短，小

innocent egos are entirely and totally enclosed in pale-blue glass bottles of insulated inexperience. Perhaps now they must hatch out!

'Do you think we may be on the brink of a Golden Age again in England?' one of our most promising young writers asked me, with that same half-timorous innocence and naivete of the young painter. I looked at him-he ws a sad young man-and my eyes nearly fell out of my head. A golden age! He looked so ungolden and though he was twenty years my junior, he felt also like my grandfahter. A golden age! in England! a golden age! now, when even money is paper! when the enclosure in the ego is final, when they are hermetically sealed and insulated from all experience, from any touch, from anything solid.

'I suppose it´s up to you,' said I.

And he quietly accepted it.

But such innocence, such naivete must be a prelude to something. It´s a *ne plus ultra.* So why shouldn´t it be a prelude to a golden age? If the innocence and naivete ae regards artistic expression doesn´t become merely idiotic, why shouldn´t it become golden? The young might, out of sheer sort of mental blankness, strike the oil of their live intuition, and get a gusher. Why not? A golden gush of artistic

羊毛的最佳部位，在各种情况下刷子上鬃毛的最佳长度，刷子是否向一个方向抹；伦敦的大气环境，格拉斯哥的大气环境，罗马和巴黎的大气环境以及这些地方大气环境对朱红色、朱砂、浅黄、中度含铬颜料、祖母绿、维洛纳绿、亚麻籽油、松节油和完美绘画的影响；关于品质，与光的关系，还有从罗马到伦敦光线发生巨变时如何保持本色——这年轻人什么都懂，天啊，他就要凭这些去做画。

凡此种种天真与诚恳的谦逊让我们确实相信，至少在绘画上我们英国人又变成了小孩子，小小孩儿，特小孩儿，婴儿，不，是未出生的胎儿。如果我们真的回到了未出生的胎儿阶段，或许我们是亟待出生了。在绘画上，英国人可以得到再生。或许，说实话，他们是第一次出生，因为他们压根儿不是画家。他们达到了这样一个阶段：他们纯真的自我全然被懵懂的浅蓝瓶子所封住，现在该跳出来了！

“你以为我们临近英国的黄金时代了吗？”一位顶有希望的青年作家带着与那位青年画家一样的胆怯和天真问我。我看看他，这可真是个可悲的年轻人，我几乎要把眼珠子瞪出来。黄金时代！他看上去一点都不

expression! 'Now we know pretty well everything that can be known about the technical side of pictures.' A golden age!

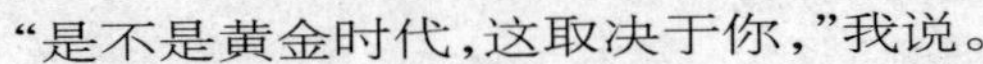

"黄金"。尽管他比我要小上二十岁,可让我觉得像我的祖父一样老气横秋。好一个英国的黄金时代哟!连货币都像废纸!自我被封得毫无希望,与人生经验全然隔绝,与触觉和任何实在物相隔绝了。

"是不是黄金时代,这取决于你,"我说。

他默认了。

不过,此种天真和幼稚一定是什么东西的前兆。这是最后的一步了,所以为什么不可以说它是一个黄金时代的前奏?如果这种天真和幼稚是艺术表现方面的,同时又不痴呆,它为何不能变得宝贵?年轻人很可以丢掉理性的茫然,发掘一下他们活生生的直觉油田,让它哗哗地淌出油来。为什么不呢?金子般的艺术井喷!"我们已经懂得了绘画的一切技巧。"好一个黄金时代!

1928 年

MAKING PICTURES

One has to eat one's own words. I remember I used to assert, perhaps I even wrote it: Everything that can possibly be painted has been painted, every brush-stroke that can possibly be laid on canvas has been laid on. The visual arts are at a dead end. Then suddenly, at the age of forty, I begin painting myself and am fascinated.

Still, going through the Paris picture shops this year of grace, and seeing the Dufys and Chiricos,* etc., and the Japanese Foujita with his wish-wash nudes with pearl-button eyes, the same weariness comes over one. They are all so would-be, they make such efforts. They at least have nothing to paint. In the midst of them a graceful Friesz* flower-piece, or a blotting-paper Laurencin,* seems a masterpiece. At least here is a bit of natural expression in paint. Trivial enough, when compared to the big painters, but still, as far as they go, real.

What about myself, then! What am I doing, bursting into paint? I am a writer,

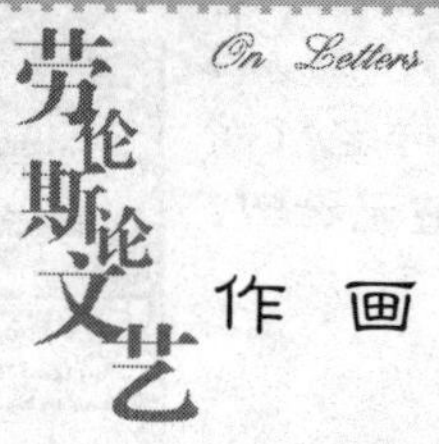

作　画

我得收回自己以前说的一些话了。记得我曾断言，或许还白纸黑字写下来过："能画的一切都画过了，所有能触到画布的画笔都触到了。视觉艺术走入了绝境。"可突然间在40岁上我自己却开始画起画来，而且让它迷住了。所以我得对自己的话道歉。

今年在巴黎的画店里徜徉，看杜飞[Raoul Duffy(1877—1953)，法国野兽派画家]和基里柯[Giorgio de Chirico(1888—1978)，意大利超现实主义画家和雕塑家]等人的画，还有日本伊藤[当时风行巴黎的一位日本画家，劳伦斯没有记住他的名字，如今也难以查找其下落]画的无聊的裸体画，那些裸体人都长着珍珠样的眼睛，这些都让人感到厌倦。他们都是些要成大气候的人，竭尽全力在做。他们至少没什么可画的了。在他们中间一二幅优雅的弗里叶兹[Othon Friesz (1879-1949)，法国野兽派画家]

I ought to stick to ink. I have found my medium of expression; why, at the age of forty, should I suddenly want to try another?

Things happen, and we have no choice. If Maria Huxley hadn't come rolling up to our house near Florence with four rather large canvases, one of which she had busted, and presented them to me because they had been abandoned in her house, I might never have started in on a real picture in my life. But those nice stretched canvases were too tempting. We had been painting doors and window-frames in the house, so there was a little stock of oil, turps, and colour in powder, such as one buys from an Italian drogheria. There were several brushes for house-painting. There was a canvas on which the unknown owner had made a start-mud-grey, with the beginnings of a red-haired man. It was a grimy and ugly beginning, and the young man who had made it had wisely gone no further. He certainly had had no inner compulsion: nothing in him, as far as paint was concerned, or if there was anything in him, it had stayed in, and only a bit of the mud-grey 'group' had come out.

So for the sheer fun of covering a surface and obliterating that mud-grey, I sat on the floor with the canvas propped against a chair-and with my house-paint brushes and colours in little casseroles. I disappeared into that canvas. It is to me

的花或劳伦辛[Marie Laurencin(1885—1956),法国画家、时装设计师和插图画家]画在吸墨纸上的画似乎还算上乘。至少这里有点什么绘画中的自然表现。与大画家比,他们微不足道,但仍然还算真实。

那我算怎么回事!我突然就画将起来,画的都是什么呀?我是个作家,我应该守着墨水过日子,我已经找到了表达的媒介,可为什么在40岁上我想要试试另一种呢?

事情已经如此,我奈何不得。如果不是玛利亚·赫胥黎坐车来到我在佛罗伦萨的房子,带来废弃在家里的四块很大的画布(其中一块她还弄破了)送给我,我这辈子也不会开始画一幅真正的画。那些绷得好好的画布是太诱人了。我们曾油过房子的门窗,所以攒下了些颜料、松节油和颜料粉,都是从一位意大利挑夫那里买来的,家里还有几把刷房子的刷子。有一块画布,上面有那位不知名的拥有者最先画上去的东西——一个灰乎乎的红发男人的雏形。那是个阴暗丑陋的开端,那个画画的小伙子很不明智,没再画下去。他肯定没有内心的冲动,就绘画而言,他心里空空荡荡。如果有什么并且停留在他心中,表现出来的也只是小小的一块"灰泥团"。

the most exciting moment–when you have a blank canvas and a big brush full of wet colour, and you plunge. It is just like diving into a pond–then you start frantically to swim. So far as I am concerned, it is like swimming in a baffling current and being rather frightened and very thrilled, gasping and striking out for all you´re worth. The knowing eye watches sharp as a needle; but the picture comes clean out of instinct, intuition and sheer physical action. Once the instinct and intuition gets into the brush–tip, the picture happens, if it is to be a picture at all.

At least, so my first picture happened –the one I have called 'A Holy Family'. In a couple of hours there it all was, man, woman, child, blue shirt, red shaw1, pale room–all in the rough, but, as far as I am concerned, a picture. The struggling comes later. But the picture itself comes in the first rush, or not at all. It is only when the picture has come into being that one can struggle and make it grow to completion.

Ours is an excessively conscious age. We know so much, we feel so little. I have lived enough among painters and around studios to have had all the theories – and how contradictory they are –rammed down my throat. A man has to have a gizzard like an ostrich to digest all the brass–tacks* and wire nails of modern art theo-

于是纯粹为了盖上画布上那块灰泥色，我把画布靠在椅子上，人坐在地上，颜料盛在焙盘里，用刷房的刷子就干了起来，一下子就沉溺在画布中了。那是我最激动的时刻——当你有了空白的画布，一把大刷子蘸满了颜料，你就会一头扎进画布中去。那情形就像一个猛子扎进水塘中，然后开始疯狂地游泳。对我来说，那就像在一条湍流中游泳，害怕、惊恐、喘着气挣扎着活命。理性的目光尖锐如针，但画就全然出自本能、直觉和纯粹的肉体动作。一旦本能和直觉进到了刷子尖里，那画就形成了，如果那能成为一幅画的话。

至少我的第一幅画就是这么画成的，就是我命名为《圣徒之家》的那一幅。在几个小时之内，一切都有了：男人，女人，孩子，蓝衫，红披肩，淡色的房间，一切都还粗糙，但对我来说那就是一幅画。以后会出现艰难的挣扎，但画却是在最初的冲动下要么成型要么一无所获。只有在那画有了雏形，才能挣扎，以令其成长直至完成。

我们所处的是一个过于理智的时代。我们知道得太多，可感知得太少。我在画家群中和画室里生活得很久，学得了全部的理论（这些理论之间相互过于矛盾），令我的喉咙发堵。人得像鸵鸟一样长一个砂囊来消化

ries. Perhaps all the theories, the utterly indigestible theories, like nails in an ostrich´s gizzard, do indeed help to grind small and make digestible all the emotional and aesthetic pabulum that lies in an artist´s soul. But they can serve no other purpose. Not even corrective. The modern theories of art make real pictures impossible. You only get these expositions, critical ventures in paint, and fantastic negations. And the bit of fantasy that may lie in the negation –as in a Dufy or a Chirico –is just the bit that has escaped theory and perhaps saves the picture. Theorize, theorize all you like–but when you start to paint, shut your theoretic eyes and go for it with instinct and intuition.

Myself, I have always loved pictures, the pictorial art. I never went to an art school, I have had only one real lesson in painting in all my life. But of course I was thoroughly drilled in ‘drawing’, the solid–geometry sort, and the plaster–cast sort, and the pin–wire sort. I think the solid–geometry sort, with all the elementary laws of perspective, was valuable. But the pin–wire sort and the plaster–cast light–and–shade sort was harmful. Plaster–casts and pin–wire outlines were always so repulsive to me, I quite early decided I ‘couldn´t draw’. I couldn´t draw, so I could never do anything on my own. When I did paint jugs of flowers or bread and potatoes, or cot-

现代艺术理论如铜丝铁钉般的细枝末节[细节(brass–tacks)的半个词是铜，劳伦斯在此把玩辞藻，意在批评现代艺术理论生硬庞杂难以消化]。或许所有的理论，最难以消化的理论就像鸵鸟砂囊里的铁钉，不过它倒是能帮助打磨和消化艺术家灵魂中情感和审美的平庸之处。但除此之外就没别的用处了。它们甚至没有矫正作用。现代艺术理论让人画不出真正的画来。你得到的只是那些阐释，是在绘画中进行的批判性冒险和幻想性否定。不过或许在否定中会有点幻想，如在杜飞或基里柯的画中那样，这点幻想恰恰就躲过了理论，也许就拯救了绘画也未可知。理论吧，你尽可以把什么都理论化，可一旦你开始作画，请闭上你的理论眼睛，用你的本能和直觉去画。

至于我自己，我一直喜欢绘画，喜欢画的艺术。我从未上过什么艺术学校，一辈子也只上过一堂真正的绘画课。不过我当然受到过完全的“图画”训练，如立体几何类、石膏模型类和线条类。我觉得立体几何类的透视基本原理是有价值的。可线条类和石膏模型的光与阴影类训练则是有害的。石膏模型和线条轮廓总让我反感。于是很小的时候我就断定我“不会画”。既然我不会画，我自己就什么也做不成。当我真正开始画栽花的坛子、面包、土豆或小街上的村舍，是从《自然》杂志上临摹下来的，其结

tages in a lane, copying from *Nature*, the result wasn't very thrilling. Nature was more or less of a plaster-cast to me-those plaster-cast heads of Minerva* or figures of *Dying Gladiators* which so unnerved me as a youth. The 'object', be it what it might, was always slightly repulsive to me once I sat down in front of it, to paint it. So, of course, I decided I couldn't really paint. Perhaps I can't. But I verily believe I can make pictures, which is to me all that matters in this respect. The art of painting consists in making pictures -and so many artists accomplish canvases without coming within miles of painting a picture.

I learnt to paint from copying other pictures -usually reproductions, sometimes even photographs. When I was a boy, how I concentrated over it! Copying some perfectly worthless scene reproduction in some magazine. I worked with almost dry water-colour, stroke by stroke, covering half a square-inch at a time, each square-inch perfect and completed, proceeding in a kind of mosaic advance, with no idea at all of laying on a broad wash. Hours and hours of intense concentration, inch by inch progress, in a method entirely wrong -and yet those copies of mine managed, when they were finished, to have a certain something that delighted me: a certain glow of life, which was beauty to me. A picture lives with the life you put into it. If

果并不怎么让我激动。《自然》对我来说多少像石膏模型，如密涅瓦[Minerva，罗马神话中的智慧与艺术女神，相当于希腊神话中的雅典娜女神]的石膏模型头颅或《濒死的角斗士》(Dying Gladiators) 简直让年轻的我失去了勇气。那些"对象"，无论是什么，只要我坐在其面前开始画它，总是让我觉得有点反感。于是我想当然断定我画不了真正的画。或许我是没那能耐。可我又确实相信我能作画，在这方面作画对我绝对重要。绘画的艺术就在做画中，无数的艺术家在画布上有了建树，但离画一张画还差的远着呢。

我学画是从临摹画开始的，临摹的一般都是复制品，有时甚至是照片。还是个孩子的我，在这上面花了多大的精力了啊！临摹的是杂志上一些完美但毫无价值的风景画复制品。我用的几乎是干水彩，一笔又一笔，一次画半英寸见方的一片，每一英寸都画得完美无缺，像马赛克一样一块一块地推进，对大面积的色彩毫无概念。几小时几小时地聚精会神，一英寸一英寸地推进，其手法全然是错的，可我那些临摹作品完成后还是挺让我愉快的：因为里面有生命在闪光，那对我来说就是美。一幅画是活的，是因为它与你投入的生命同在。如果你没有把生命注入——没有激动，没有视觉发现的欢欣或狂喜凝聚其中，那这画就是死的，就像很多画

you put no life into it –no thrill, no concentration of delight or exaltation of visual discovery–then the picture is dead, like so many canvases, no matter how much thorough and scienfific work is put into it. Even if you only copy a purely banal reproduction of an old bridge, some sort of keen, delighted awareness of the old bridge or of its atmosphere, or the image it has kindled inside you, can go over on to the paper and give a certain touch of life to a banal conception.

It needs a certain purity of spirit to be an artist, of any sort. The motto which should be written over every School of Art is: 'Blessed are the pure in spirit, for theirs is the kingdom of heaven'. But by 'pure in spirit' we mean pure in spirit. An artist may be a profligate and, from the social point of view, a scoundrel. But if he can paint a nude woman, or a couple of apples, so that they are a living image, then he was pure in spirit, and, for the time being, his was the kingdom of heaven. This is the beginning of all art, visual or literary or musical: be pure in spirit. It isn´t the same as goodness. It is much more difficult and nearer to the divine. The divine isn´t only good, it is all things.

One may see the divine in natural objects; I saw it today, in the frail, lovely little camellia flowers on long stems, here on the bushy and splendid flower–stalls of

布一样，不管在那上面进行了多么彻底与科学的劳作。即便是你临摹一座老桥的纯粹平庸的复制品，对这老桥或其氛围敏锐的意识和它引起的欢欣，或老桥的形象在你内心的反映，是可以传达到纸面上的，从而你的临摹会给原先平庸的构思增添些儿生命感。

无论要成为什么样的艺术家，某种精神上的纯净都是必须的。每家艺术学校的门上都应该写上这样的座右铭："保佑精神上纯净的人，因为他们身处天国。"所谓"精神纯净"，意思是精神上纯洁。一个艺术家可以是个品行不端的人，从社会的角度看，是个恶棍。可是如果他能画一个裸体女人或几只苹果，画得栩栩如生，那他就是精神上纯净的人，一时间他就是天国。这是所有艺术的开端，无论是视觉的、文学的还是音乐的：请在精神上纯净。这与善不可同日而语。做到这点更难，更接近神圣。神圣并非只是善，它是一切。

我们可以在自然物体中见神圣。我今天就看到了，在巴塞罗那大街上葱郁美丽的花摊上，我从长梗上柔弱可爱的小山茶花儿中看到了神圣。这些花与普通肥壮的山茶不同，这些小山茶更像栀子花，轻盈静谧，让我觉得像幻影。于是我就可以画它们了。可如果我买来一捧，然后开始

the Ramblas in Barcelona. They were different from the usual fat camellias, more like gardenias, poised delicately, and I saw them like a vision. So now, I could paint them. But if I had bought a handful, and started in to paint them 'from nature', then I should have lost them. By staring at them I should have lost them. I have learnt by experience. It is personal experience only. Some men can only get at a vision by staring themselves blind, as it were: like Cézanne; but staring kills my vision. That's why I could never 'draw' at school. One was supposed to draw what one stared at.

The only thing one can look into, stare into, and see only vision, is the vision itself: the visionary image. That is why I am glad I never had any training but the self-imposed training of copying other men's pictures. As I grew more ambitious, I copied Leader's* landscapes, and Frank Brangwyn's* cartoonlike pictures, then Peter de Wint and Girtin* water-colours. I can never be sufficiently grateful for the series of English water-colour painters, published by the *Studio* in eight parts, when I was a youth. I had only six of the eight parts, but they were invaluable to me. I copied them with the greatest joy, and found some of them extremely difficult. Surely I put as much labour into copying from those water-colour reproductions as most modern art students put into all their years of study. And I had enormous profit from

"照着自然"画，那我就画不出它们来。凝视它们，我反会失去它们。我是靠经验来学画画的。这只是个人经验而已。有些人只有凝视直到眼睛瞎了才能获得一种想像，就像塞尚。可凝视会毁了我的想像。因此我在学校里怎么也"画"不出来，因为学校要求人画那些他们凝视的物体。

人们惟一能深入观察、深入凝视并且只能看到想象的东西是想像本身：那就是想像的意象。因此我为自己从来没有受过训练而欣慰，我只是进行过自我训练，其手段是临摹别人的画。后来我野心大了些，就开始临摹里德[Benjamin Williams Leader(1831—1923)，英国自然主义画家]的风景画，弗兰克·布朗温[Frank Brangwyn(1867—1956)，英国画家]卡通似的画，然后是皮特·德·温特[Peter de Wint(1784—1849)，英国画家]和吉尔丁[Thomas Girtin(1775—1802)，英国浪漫派画家]的水彩画。在我青年时代，画室出版社出版过一套八册本的英国水彩画家的系列丛书，对此我怎样感激也不过分。我只有其中的六册，可那对我来说是无价之宝。我十分开心地临摹那些画，其中有些临摹起来十分困难。我花在临摹那些水彩画复制品上的精力与大多数现代艺术专业的学生们在几年学习中花的精力一样多，从而受益颇多。我不仅掌握了较高的处理水彩画的技巧——让任何人试着临摹英国水彩艺术家的作品，从保

it. I not only acquired a considerable technical skill in handling water-colour -let any man try copying the English water-colour artists, from Paul Sandby and Peter de Wint and Girtin, up to Frank Brangwyn and the impressionists like Brabazon,* and he will see how much skill he requires -but also I developed my visionary awareness. And I believe one can only develop one's visionary awareness by close contact with the vision itself: that is, by knowing pictures, real vision pictures, and by dwelling on them, and really dwelling in them. It is a great delight, to dwell in a picture. But it needs a purity of spirit, a sloughing of vulgar sensation and vulgar interest, and above all, vulgar contact that few people know how to perform. Oh, if art schools only taught that! If, instead of saying: This drawing is wrong, incorrect, badly drawn, etc., they would say: Isn't this in bad taste? isn't it insensitive? isn't that an insentient curve with none of the delicate awareness of life in it? -But art is treated all wrong. It is treated as if it were a science, which it is not. Art is a form of religion, minus the *Ten Commandment* business, which is sociological. Art is a form of supremely delicate awareness and atonement-meaning at-one-ness, the state of being at one with the object. But is the great atonement in delight? -for I can never look on art save as a form of delight.

罗·桑德比[Paul Sandby(1730—1809),英国书画刻印艺术家]、皮特·德·温特和吉尔丁,到弗兰克·布朗温和布拉巴赞[Hercules Brabazon(1821—1906),英国风格的印象主义画家]等印象派画家,他都会明白他获得了怎样的技巧,但我还培养了自己的眼光。而且我相信,一个人要培养自己的眼光,只能与眼光本身密切接触:那就是通过理解画,真正有眼光的画,寄寓其上并真正深入其中。深入到一幅画中去,那是一种十足的愉悦。但那需要一种精神上的纯净,屏弃庸俗的感知和庸俗的趣味,最首要的是屏弃庸俗的接触,这些,极少人能做得到。哦,如果艺术学校只教人们这个,那就够了!如果人们不说:这幅画不对劲,错了,画坏了之类的话,而是说:这画的品位是否很低?是否感觉迟钝?那道曲线是否毫无生命,对生命一点细腻的感觉都没有?可事实上艺术受到了完全错误的对待,人们把它当成了科学,其实不然。艺术是宗教的一种形式,《十诫》不在其列,那属于社会学之类。艺术是一种十分细腻的意识与“合一”的形式,所谓“合一”意思是一体,物我合一。但是在愉悦中合一吗?反正我从来都把艺术看成是一种愉悦的形式,而不是别的。

在我的一生中,我时常回头去画画,因为它给我一种难以言表的愉

All my life I have from time to time gone back to paint, because it gave me a form of delight that words can never give. Perhaps the joy in words goes deeper and is for that reason more unconscious. The conscious delight is certainly stronger in paint. I have gone back to paint for real pleasure–and by paint I mean copying, copying either in oils or waters. I think the greatest pleasure I ever got came from copying Fra Angelico's '*Flight into Egypt*' and Lorenzetti's big picture of the *Thebaid*,* in each case working from photographs and putting in my own colour; or perhaps even more a Carpaccio* picture in Venice. Then I really learned what life, what powerful life has been put into every curve, every motion of a great picture. Purity of spirit, sensitive awareness, intense eagerness to portray an inward vision, how it all comes. The English water–colours are frail in comparison –and the French and the Flemings are shallow. The great Rembrandt I never tried to copy, though I loved him intensely, even more than I do now; and Rubens I never tried, though I always liked him so much, only he seemed so spread out. But I have copied Peter de Hooch and Vandyck,* and others that I forget. Yet none of them gave me the deep thrill of the Italians, Carpaccio, or the lovely '*Death of Procris*'* in the National Gallery, or that '*Wedding*'* with the scarlet legs, in the Uffizi, or a Giotto*

悦。或许文字中的喜悦更深沉些，因此更存在于无意识中。而有意识的愉悦感当然在绘画时更为强烈些。我回头去画画是为了寻找真正的愉悦，我说的画是指临摹，临摹油画或水彩画。我觉得我最大的快乐来自临摹弗拉·安吉里柯[Fra Angelico（1400–1455）意大利早期文艺复兴时期画家]的《逃入埃及》(Flight into Egypt)和劳伦泽蒂[Pietro Lorenzetti（1280–1348）意大利拜占庭风格画家]的大幅《底拜得》(Thebaid)，都是临摹其绘画的照片，自己上的色。或许在威尼斯临摹卡帕西奥[Vittore Carpaccio(1450–1526)，威尼斯画派的主要画家]的一幅画时感觉更好些。至此，我真正明白了一幅伟大的绘画中注入了怎样的生命，每一根曲线、每一个动作里都注入了强大的生命。精神纯净，意识敏感，强烈渴求要画出内心里的景象，一切就这样水到渠成。而相比之下，英国的水彩画就弱多了，而法国和弗莱芒的则浅薄些。伟大的伦勃朗的作品我从未试图临摹，尽管我酷爱过，比现在还酷爱呢。鲁本斯我也从未试过，尽管我一直十分喜爱，但就是觉得他的画风太过张扬了。但我临摹过皮特·德·胡克 [Peter de Hooch (1629–1684)，荷兰画家] 和凡代克 [Sir Anthony van Dyck (1599–1641)弗莱芒画家，后成为查理一世的画师]，另外还临摹过一些人，但名字我忘记了。但他们谁也不像意大利画家那样让我感到深深的震撼：卡帕西奥，

from Padua. I must have made many copies in my day, and got endless joy out of them.

Then suddenly, by having a blank canvas, I discovered I could make a picture myself. That is the point, to make a picture on a blank canvas. And I was forty before I had the real courage to try. Then it became an orgy, making pictures.

I have learnt now not to work from objects, not to have models, not to have a technique. Sometimes, for a watercolour, I have worked direct from a model. But it always spoils the picture. I can only use a model when the picture is already made; then I can look at the model to get some detail which the vision failed me with, or to modify something which I feel is unsatisfactory and I don´t know why. Then a model may give a suggestion. But at the beginning, a model only spoils the picture. The picture must all come out of the artist´s inside, awareness of forms and figures. We can call it memory, but it is more than memory. It is the image as it lives in the consciousness, alive like a vision, but unknown. I believe many people have, in their consciousness, living images that would give them the greatest joy to bring out. But they don´t know how to go about it. And teaching only hinders them.

To me, a picture has delight in it, or it isn´t a picture. The saddest pictures of

或者是国家美术馆里的那幅可爱的《普罗克里斯之死》(**Death of Procris**)[这是弗罗伦萨画家 Piero di Cosimo 的一幅画，劳伦斯临摹时感到了“极大的喜悦”]，或那幅尤菲季博物馆(**Uffizi**)里绘有穿红裤子的人的《婚礼》[据考证，劳伦斯将弗罗伦萨尤菲季博物馆里的某幅画与米兰布列拉美术馆里拉斐尔著名的《少女的婚礼》混为一谈了，后者里女孩的追求者中有一位穿红紧身裤者]或乔托[Giotto di Bondone(1267—1337)，后人相信帕杜阿环型教堂里的环型壁画出自乔托之手]在帕杜阿(**Padua**)的壁画。我年轻的时候肯定临摹了无数幅这样的画，从中获得了无尽的欢乐。

后来我突然得到了一块空白的画布，便发现我可以自己画画。关键就在于此：在一块空白的画布上作画。我都四十岁了，才真正有勇气试一下。这一试，就变成了狂欢。

我现在学会了不画实物，不用模特，不讲技巧。有时画一幅水彩，我会直接画一个模特，但这么画总是画不好。我用模特都是在一幅画已经画完后，然后再找来模特，为的是从模特身上寻找我想像不出的一些细节，或者是为了修正我感到不满意但又不清楚为什么不满意的地方。这个时候模特能给我一点启发。可如果始初就用模特，那只能毁了那幅画。画一定要全部出自艺术家的内里，出自那里对形式和形状的感知。我们

Piero della Francesca or Sodoma or Goya* have still that indescribable delight that goes with the real picture. Modern critics talk a lot about ugliness, but I never saw a real picture that seemed to me ugly. The theme may be ugly, there may be a terrifying, distressing, almost repulsive quality, as in El Greco.* Yet it is all, in some strange way, swept up in the delight of a picture. No artist, even the gloomiest, ever painted a picture without the curious delight in image-making.

尽可以称之为记忆,可不仅是记忆二字能道清。那是意象,就如同活在意识中一般,活生生如同幻觉,但未知。我相信,很多人的意识中都有一些活生生的意象,将之付诸表现能带给他们最大的快乐。但他们不知道怎么做。而教育只能阻碍他们。

对我来说,一幅画本身得蕴涵着快乐,否则就不是画。最悲伤的绘画如皮埃罗·德拉·弗兰西斯卡[Piero della Francesca(1410/20—1492),意大利文艺复兴早期著名画家]、索德玛[Giovanni Antonio Bazzi Sodoma, 意大利画家]或戈雅[Francisco de Goya(1746—1828),西班牙画家]的画,仍然还是有真正的绘画中所具有的那种难以言表的快乐。现代批评家大谈丑陋,可我见过的真正的绘画,从来就没有哪幅让我觉得丑。主题可能是丑恶的,其质量或许可怕、令人丧气甚至令人厌恶,如埃尔·格列柯[El Greco(1541—1614),埃尔生于克里特岛,但主要在西班牙作画,以宗教绘画著名]的作品。但它就是充满了莫名的快乐。没有哪个艺术家,即使是最阴郁的艺术家也不会在画一幅画时不曾感到那种莫名的作画的快乐。

1929 年

PICTURES ON THE WALLS

Whether wall pictures are or are not an essential part of interior decoration in the home seems to be considered debatable. Yet since there is scarcely one house in a thousand which doesn´t have them, we may easily conclude that they are, in spite of the snobbism which pretends to prefer blank walls. The human race loves pictures. Barbarians or civilized, we are all alike, we straightway go to look at a picture if there is a picture to look at. And there are very few of us who wouldn´t love to have a perfectly fascinationg work hanging in our room, that we could go on looking at, if we could afford it. Instead, unfortunately, as a rule we have only some mediocre thing left over from the past, that hangs on the wall just because we´ve got it, and it must go somewhere. If only people would be firm about it, and rigorously burn all insignificant pictures, frames as well, how much more freely we should breathe in-doors. If only people would go round their walls every ten years and say, Now, what

David Herbert Lawrence

墙上的画

墙上挂画儿，这是不是家庭室内装饰的基本组成部分似乎还有争议。可既然不挂画的家连千里挑一都说不上，我们便很容易下结论说是，尽管有些势利眼的人佯装喜欢空白的墙。人类喜爱画儿，无论是野蛮人还是文明人，我们都一样，只要有画可看，我们就会直奔过去看。只要我们花得起钱，我们当中没几个人不愿意在屋里挂上一件完美而迷人的作品，从而可以不断地观赏。可不幸的是，过去留给我们的往往只是一些平庸的画作，它们挂在墙上，仅仅是因为我们得到了它们，而它们总得有地方可去才行。如果人们对此持坚决的态度，把所有意义微小的绘画都付之一炬，还有画框，我们就能在室内多么自由酣畅地呼吸啊。如果人们能

about that oil-painting, what about that reproduction, what about that photograph? What do they mean? What do we get from them? Have they any point? Are they worth keeping?-The answer would almost invariably be: No. And then what? Shall we say, Oh, let them stay! They´ve been there ten years, we might as well leave them! -But that is sheer inertia and death to any freshness in the home. A woman might as well say: I´ve worn this hat for a year, so I may as well go on wearing it for a few more years. -A house, home, is only a grearer garment, and just as we feel we must renew our clothes and have fresh ones, so we should renew our homes and make them in keeping. Spring cleaning isn´t enough. Why do fashions in clothes change? Because, really, we ourselves change, in the slow metamorphosis of time. If we imagine ourselves now in the clothes we wore six years ago, we shall see that it is impossible. We are, in some way, different persons now, and our clothes express our different personality.

And so should the home. It should change with us, as we change. Not so quickly as our clothes change, because it is not so close in contact. More slowly, but just as inevitably, the home should change around us. And the change should be more rapid in the more decorative scheme of the room: pictures, curtains, cushions;

每十年在屋里巡视一番并发问:那幅油画怎么样?那幅复制品如何?那幅照片行吗?我们从中获得了什么?它们有什么可取之处?值得保存吗?那回答几乎总会是不。然后呢?我们会说:哦,留着它们吧!都在那里呆了十年了,就留着吧!可对于家里的任何新鲜事物来说,这纯粹是惰性和死亡。一个女人也会说:这顶帽子我都戴了一年了,我还不如再戴它几年。一座房子,一个家,则是一件更大的衣服,就像我们要更新自己的衣服,我们也应该刷新自己的房子,将房子保护好。仅春天打扫一遍是不够的。服装的时尚为什么在变?那是因为我们自己在随着时间缓慢的变化而变,这一点不假。我们想像一下我们穿着六年前的衣服吧,那简直不可能。在某种意义上说,我们变成了另一个人,而我们的衣着则表明了我们在性格上与以前不同了。

家也如此。它应该随着我们的改变而改变,但不像我们的衣着变化那样快,因为它与我们的接触并不那么紧密。虽然过程更加缓慢,但我们家的环境应该改变。而变化应该更快地发生在房间装饰上:绘画,窗帘,靠垫等等;在硬性的家具上变化应该缓慢些。有些家具能让我们终生满

and slower in the solid furniture. Some furniture may satisfy us for a lifetime. Some may be quite unsuitable aftet ten years. But certain it is that the cushions and curtains and pictures will begin to be stale after a couple of years. And staleness in the home is stifling and oppressive to the spirit. It is a woman´s business to see to it. In England especially we live so much indoors that our interiors must live, must change, must have their seasons of fading and renewing, must come alive to fit the new moods, the new sensations, the new selves that come to pass in us with the changing years. Dead and dull permanency in the home, dreary sameness, is a form of inertia, is very harmful to the modern nature, which is in a state of flux, sensitive to its surroundings far more than we really know.

And, do as we may, the pictures in a room are in some way the key to the atmosphere of a room. Put up grey photogravures, and a certain greyness will dominate in the air, no matter if your cushions be daffodils. Put up Baxter* prines, and for a time you will have charm; after that, a certain stuffiness will ensue. Pictures are strange things. Most of them die as sure as flowers die, and, once dead, they hang on the wall as stale as brown withered bouquets. The reason lies in ourselves. When we buy a picture because we like it, then the picture responds fresh to some

意，有些则过十年就不合适了。但靠垫、窗帘和绘画过几年就变陈旧了。家里的陈旧感会令精神窒息压抑。关心这些是女人的天职。特别是在英国，我们大部分时间都在室内生活，所以我们的室内装饰一定要有生气，一定要变化，一定要吐故纳新，一定要活泼以适应新的情绪、新感触和随着年月的变化而变化的我们新的自己。家中一成不变的死气沉沉是一种惰性，对现代人的天性十分有害，现代人的天性是与其周围的环境共处于交互流动之中的，其敏感性是我们远不能了解的。

我们在房间里挂什么样的画决定了房间里的气氛。挂一幅灰色的凹版金属照片，屋里的气氛就被某种灰色调所主宰，即便你的靠垫上绘着水仙花也无法中和那灰色氛围。挂上巴克斯特[George Baxter(1804—1867)，英国版画复制家，1835年注册了彩色插图的专利]复制版画，一时间你将拥有美。可过后屋里肯定会令人觉得窒息。绘画是奇怪的东西，它们大多数都会像花一样死去，一旦死了，它们挂在墙上就如同干枯的花束一样陈腐。这里的原因在于我们自己。我们买一幅画是因为我们喜欢它，于是这绘画与我们内在的活生生的感觉发生清新的呼应。可感觉是会变的，或快或慢。如果你

living feeling in us. But feelings change: quicker or slower. If our feeling for the picture was superficial, it wears away quickly -and quickly the picture is nothing but a dead rag hanging on the wall. On the other hand, if we can see a little deeper, we shall buy a picture that will at least last us a year or two, and give a certain fresh joy all the time, like a living flower. We may even find something that will last us a lifetime. If we found a masterpiece, it would last many lifetimes. But there are not many masterpieces of any sort in this world.

The fact remains there are pictures of every sort, and people of every sort to be pleased by them; and there is, perhaps, a limit to the length of time that even a masterpiece will please mankind. Raphael now occasionally bores us, after several centuries, and Michael Angelo begins to.

But we needn't bother about Raphael or Michael Angelo, who keep up their fresh interest for centuries. Our concern is rather with pictures that may be dead rags in six months, all the fresh feeling for them gone. If we think of Landseer, or Alma Tadema,* we see how even traditional connoisseurs like Dukes of Devonshire* paid large sums for momentary masterpieces that now hang on the ducal walls as dead and ridiculous rags. Only a very uneducated person nowadays would want to

对画的感觉是表面的，那它去的也快，于是那绘画很快就变得微不足道，只是挂在墙上的一块破布而已。从另一方面说，假设我们能看得更深刻一点，我们就会买一幅至少能一两年都让我们不腻烦的画，在这期间它能一直给予我们清新与快乐，就如同一朵活生生的花朵一样。我们甚至能发现某种与我们相伴一生的东西呢。如果我们发现了一幅杰作，它则能让几代人受益。不过这世界上任何一种杰作都不多见。

其实，什么样的画都有人喜欢。还有，讨人喜欢的杰作总归会有人们不喜欢的那一天。拉斐尔的作品过了几百年现在就时不时令我们腻烦了，米开朗基罗的作品也开始不招人喜欢 了。

但我们不用为拉斐尔和米开朗基罗担心，他们的作品已经连续几百年常看常新了。我们现在关心的是那些挂在墙上不到半年就变成破布的那些画怎么办的问题，所有的新鲜感全都消失了。如果我们想想兰德西尔[Sir Edwin Landseer(1802—1873)，英国动物画画家，他的画以赋予动物人性感情而著名]或阿尔玛·塔德玛[Sir Lawrence Alma-Tadema(1836—1912)，居住在伦敦的荷兰画家，以画希腊和罗马生活著名]，我们就会明白，连久负盛名的鉴赏家如几代德汶郡公爵[William

put those two Landseer dogs, '*Dignity and Impudence*,' on the drawing-room wall. Yet they pleased immensely in their day. And the interest was sustained, perhaps, for twenty years. But after twenty years it has become a humiliation to keep them hanging on the walls of Chatsworth or wherever they hang. They should be burnt, of course. They only make an intolerable stuffiness wherever they are, and remind us of the shallowness of our taste.

And if this is true of '*Dignity and Impudence*' or Millais '*Bubbles*,'* which have a great deal of technical skill in them, how much more true is it of cheap photogravures, which have none. Familiarity wears a picture out. Since Whistler´s* portrait of his mother was used for advertisement, it has lost most of its appeal, and become for most people a worn-out picture, a dead rag. And once a picture has been really popular, and then died into staleness, it never revives again. It is dead for ever. The only thing is to burn it.

Which applies very forcibly to photograph and other such machine pictures. They may have fascinated the young bride twenty years ago. They may even have gone on fascinating her for six months or two years. But at the end of that time they are almost certainly dead, and the bride´s pleasure in them can only be a reminis-

Cavendish(1640–1707),于1694年成为第一代德汶郡公爵并开始在达比郡建设其宫殿般的查沃斯庄园,其后几代公爵不断扩大庄园。德汶郡公爵们热中于收藏绘画,庄园里到处陈列着这些价值各异的绘画。此地离劳伦斯的家乡很近,估计劳伦斯对词耳熟能详并曾亲眼见识过]花了大笔的金钱,买的不过是昙花一现的杰作,挂在公爵府的墙上就像破布一样死气沉沉、滑稽可笑。现如今只有教育水平极低的人才会把兰德西尔画的两条狗挂在家中客厅墙上,那画名为《尊严和无礼》。可他们那时却十分满意,对这画的兴趣保持了或许有足足二十年。可过了二十年,还把这种画挂在查沃斯庄园或别的什么地方的墙上就成了一种羞辱。那就该把这种画付之一炬才是。不管这些画挂在什么地方,只会让人感到一种无法忍受的沉闷,而且提醒我们自己的品位是怎样低下。

如果说《尊严和无礼》或米莱斯的《泡沫》[Sir John Everett Millais(1829—1896),是拉斐尔前派兄弟会的成员,其绘画以精细见长,后期绘画则流于肤浅和感伤。其画作《泡沫》曾被用作肥皂广告]这些颇含技能的作品都如此,那些连技能都没有的廉价复制版画就更是如此了。稔熟令绘画折价。自从惠斯勒为他母亲的画像为广告所用[Janmes McNeill Whistler(1834—1903),出生于美国但在伦敦定居的画家。他为母亲绘制的画

cent sentimental pleasure, or that rather vulgar satisfaction in them as pieces of property. It is fatal to look on pictures as pieces of property. Pictures are like flowers, that fade away sooner or later, and die, and must be thrown in the dustbin and burnt. It is true of all pictures. Even the beloved Giorgione* will one day die to human interest –but he is still very lovely, after almost five centuries, still a fresh flower. But when at last he is dead, as so many pictures are that hang on honoured walls, let us hope he will be burnt. Let us hope he won't still be regarded as a piece of valuable property, worth huge sums, like lots of dead–as–doornails canvases today.

If only we could get rid of the idea of 'property' in the arts! The arts exist to give us pleasure or joy. A yellow cushion gives us pleasure. The moment it ceases to do so, take it away, have done with it, give us another. –Which we do, and so cushions remain fresh and interesting, and the manufacturers manufacture continually new, fresh, fascinating fabrics. The natural demand causes a healthy supply.

In pictures it is just the opposite. A picture, instead of being regarded, like a flower or a cushion, as something that must be fresh and fragrant with attraction, is looked on as solid property. We may spend ten shillings on a bunch of roses, and

像长期被用在贺卡上]就大失魅力，在大多数人眼里就成了一块陈旧僵死的破布。一旦一幅绘画真正流行起来，就陈腐死亡，从此再也无法复活，它永远地死了。惟一要做的就是付之一炬了事。

复制版画和其他类似的机器制作的画儿就该受这种待遇。或许二十年前年轻的新娘让这种画迷住过，甚至一迷就是半年到二年。可时间一到，这些画基本上就死了，新娘子对它们的喜爱就变成了甜蜜的回忆，或变成拥有财产的庸俗满足感。把画当成财产是致命的错误。画就如同花儿，早晚要凋谢、要消亡，总要扔进垃圾箱并付之一炬。所有的画都如此。即使是广为人爱的乔尔乔尼[Giorgione(1477—1510)，意大利文艺复兴鼎盛时期威尼斯的重要画家]的画，早晚有一天也会没人对它感兴趣，不过现在他的画还是挺可爱的，几乎让人喜爱了近五百年了，还像一朵鲜花呢。不过当最终他的画死了，如同挂在许多声名显赫之家的墙上的画那样，让我们希望，烧了它算了。让我们希望，他的画别再被人们当成价值连城的财产了，就像如今许多僵死的画布一样。

我们真该摒弃艺术上的"财产"观念！艺术的存在本是给人以享受和

throw away the dead stalks without thinking we have thrown away ten shillings. We may spend two guineas on the cover of a lovely cushion, and strip it off and ascerd it the moment it is stale, without for a moment lamenting the two guineas. We know where we are. We paid for aesthetic pleasure, and we have had it. Lucky for us that money can buy roses or lovely embroidery. –Yet if we pay two pounds for some picture, and are tired of it after a year, we can no more burn that picture than we can set the house on fire. It is uneducated folly on our part. We ought to burn the picture, so that we can have real fresh pleasure in a different one, in fresh flowers and fresh cushions. In every school it is taught: Never leave stale flowers in a vase. Throw them away! –So it should be taught: Never leave stale pictures on the wall. Burn them! The value of a picture lies in the aesthetic emotion it brings, exactly as if it were a flower. The aesthetic emotion dead, the picture is a piece of ugly litter.

Which belies the tedious dictum that a picture should be part of the architectural whole, built into the room, as it were. This is fallacy. A picture is decoration, not architecture. The room exists to shelter and house us, the picture exists to please us, to give us certain emotions. Of course, there can be harmony or disharmony between the pictures and the whole ensemble of a room. But in any room in the world

愉悦的。一只黄色的靠垫令我们愉快。一旦没了这种愉悦，就撤下，放弃，换一只。我们这么做了，所以靠垫总是保持着新鲜感、招人喜欢，生产厂家不断地生产出花样翻新、迷人的布料。自然的需求导致了健康的供应。

可在绘画上则背道而驰。一幅画不仅没有被看成必须保持新鲜和芬芳的花或靠垫，而是被当成了实在的财产。我们或许会花上十先令买一束玫瑰，但扔掉那死花儿时我们不会觉得是扔了十先令。我们可以花上两个畿尼买一个靠垫套，一旦变旧就扯下来丢弃，一点也不心疼那两个畿尼。我们知道自己是怎么回事。我们花钱买美感，而且得到了。我们幸运，因为我们可以用钱买玫瑰和刺绣品。可如果我们花了两英镑买了一幅画，一年后对此厌倦了，我们绝不会烧了那画，就像我们绝不会烧自家的房子一样。这是我们缺少教育的愚蠢表现。我们就该烧了那画儿，从而我们可以在另一幅画中获得真正新鲜的感受，同样这种感受也可以在鲜花和新靠垫中获得。每家学校都这样教育学生：绝不要把腐败的花留在花瓶里。丢弃它们！既然如此，就也应该这样教育学生：绝不要把陈旧的绘画留在墙上。烧了它们！绘画的价值在于其带给人们美的情愫，恰如一

you could carry out dozens of difficult schemes of decoration, at different times, and to harmonize with each scheme of decoration there are hundreds of different pictures. The built-in theory is all wrong. A picture in a room is the gardenia in my buttonhole. If the tailor 'built' a permanent and irremovable gardenia in my morning-coat buttonhole, I should be done in.

Then there is the young school which thinks pictures should be kept in stacks like books in a library, and looked at for half an hour or so at a time, as we turn over the leaves of a book of reproductions. But this again entirely disregards the real psychology of pictures. It is true the great trashy mass of pictures are exhausted in half an hour. But then why keep them in a stack, why keep them at all? On the other hand, if I had a Renoir* nude, or a good Friesz* flower-study, or even a Brabazon* watercolour, I should want to keep it at least a year or two, and hang it up in a chosen place, to live with it and get all the fragrance out of it. And if I had the Titian '*Adam and Eve*,'* from the Prado, I should want to have it hanging in my room all my life, to look at:because I know it would give me a subtle rejoicing all my life, and would make my life delightful. And if I had Picassos* I should want to keep them about six months, and Braques* I should like to have for about a year:

朵鲜花。美的情愫死了,那幅画就成了一件丑陋的垃圾。

如此看来,所谓绘画应是融入整个建筑整体的一部分的格言既无聊又虚假。一幅画只是装饰,不是建筑的一部分。房屋的存在是为我们遮风挡雨的,绘画是用来让我们赏心悦目的,给我们带来某种情绪的。当然,在绘画和整个房屋组合上是会有和谐或不和谐。可世界上任何一间房在不同的时间里都可以有成打的颇具难度的装饰方案,为了与每个装饰方案相匹配,可以摆放上成百幅不同的绘画。那所谓融入的理论全然是谬论。房间里的一幅画就是我扣眼儿里的一朵栀子花。如果裁缝把一朵栀子花永久不动地"融入"我晨服中的扣眼儿里,那我就完了。

还有年轻一族认为绘画应该存放在书库里,就像图书馆保存图书一样。每次看上半个多小时,就像翻看书中的复制品。这也是对真正的绘画心理全然不敬。不错,大量的垃圾绘画看上半个钟头就够了。那为什么还把它们存在书库里呢,为什么还要留着它们?从另一方面说,如果我有一幅雷诺阿[Pierre-Auguste Renoir(1841—1919),法国印象派大师,以画美女著称]的裸体画,或一幅好看的弗里叶兹[Othon Friesz (1879—1949),法国野兽派画家]画的花,或者甚

then, probably, I should be through with them. But I would not want a Romney* even for a day.

And so it varies, with the individual and with the picture, and so it should be allowed to vary. But at present it is not allowed to vary. We all have to stare at the dead rags our fathers and mothers hung on the walls, just because they are property.

But let us change it. Let us refuse to have our vision filled with dust and nullity of dead pictures in the home. Let there be a grand conflagration of dead 'art,' immolation of canvas and paper, oil-colours, water-colours, photographs and all, a grand clearance.

Then what? Then ask Harrods about it. Don't for heaven's sake go and spend twenty guineas on another picture that will have to hang on the wall till the end of time just because it cost twenty guineas. Go to Harrods and ask them what about their Circulating Picture scheme. They have a circulating library -or other people have -huge circulating libraries. People hire books till they have assimilated their content. Why not the same with pictures?

Why should not Harrods have a great 'library' of pictures? Why not have a great 'pictuary,' where we can go and choose a picture? There would be men in

至是布拉巴赞[Hercules Brabazon(1821—1906),英国风格的印象主义画家]的水彩画,我还愿意将它们留上一二年,选个地方挂起来,与之共处,享尽其芬芳。如果我得到了存放在马德里普拉多美术馆的提香画的《亚当与夏娃》[提香的画题为《人的堕落》(1570),存放在马德里普拉多美术馆],我愿意把它挂在我房间了挂上一辈子,一辈子都看它,因为我知道它能给我一生的不可言说的愉悦感,让我生活快乐。如果我有一幅毕加索[Pablo Picasso(1881—1973),西班牙艺术家,影响二十世纪视觉艺术发展的领军人物] 的画,我想保留半年,而勃拉克 [Georges Braque(1882—1963),法国画家,与毕加索一同创立了立体派]的画我愿意保留上一年左右,然后我估计就厌烦它们了。可如果是罗姆尼[George Romney(1734—1802),英国人像画家,其作品在1914-1939年间受到过高评价,售价奇高]的画,我一天也不想留。

所以说,情况因人而异,因画不同,也本该如此。可现在的情况是不允许这样。我们都得看那些我们的父母挂在墙上的僵死破布,原因很简单,那是财产。

不过还是让我们改变这种情况吧。让我们拒绝家中那些死画的灰尘和卑微充斥我们的视觉。来一场大火,烧掉那些死了的"艺术",让画布和

charge who knew about pictures, just as librarians know about books. We subscribe, we pay a certain deposit, and our pictures ate sent home to us, to keep for one year, for two, for ten, as we wish: at any rate, till we have got all the joy out of them, and want a change.

In the pictuary you can have everything except machine-made rubbish that is not worth having. You can have big supplies of modern art, fresh from the artists, etchings, engravings, drawings, paintings, you can have the lovely new colour reproductions that most of us can't afford to buy; you can have frames to suit. And here you can choose, choose what will give you real joy and will suit your home for the time being.

There are few, very few great artists in any age. But there are hundreds and hundreds of men and women with genuine artistic talent and beautiful artistic feeling, who produce quite lovely works that are never seen. They are lovely works-not immortal, not masterpieces, not 'great', yet they are lovely, and will keep their loveliness a certain number of years; after which they will die, and the time will have come to destroy them.

Now it is a tragedy that all these pictures with their temporary loveliness should

纸张、油彩和水彩、还有照片什么的都成为祭品，彻底清理一下吧。

然后呢？去问问哈罗兹百货商店吧。花上二十畿尼再买一幅画回来挂在墙上，到头来发现挂的原因仅仅是因为它花了你二十畿尼，千万别再干这种事了。去哈罗兹商店，问问他们有什么租画的办法。他们或者是别的谁有外借图书馆，很大的外借图书馆。人们租书来看，不要书，只要吸收书的内容。画为什么不能也这么出租？

为什么哈罗兹不办个巨大的绘画“馆”？为什么不办个巨大的“画馆”，让我们去选绘画？那里的负责人应该懂画，就像图书馆员懂书一样。我们预订，交些租金，然后我们要的绘画就给送到家里来了，按照我们的意愿在家里挂上一二年或十来年，等我们欣赏够了，再去换一幅来挂上。

在这座画馆里，什么画都应有尽有，就是没有机器制造的垃圾画，那不值得要。你可以有大量的现代艺术品，是艺术家刚刚脱手的，蚀刻、雕刻、素描、油画，你可以得到我们大多数人买不起的漂亮的新彩色复制品。你可以得到合适的画框。在这里，你可以挑选，挑选那些真正给你愉悦并且适合你房间一时需要的画。

be condemned to a premature dust–heap. For that is what they are. Contemporary art belongs to contemporary society. Society at large needs the pictures of its contemporaries, just as it needs the books. Modern people read modern books. But they hang up pictures that belong to no age whatever, and have no life, and have no meaning, are mere blotches of deadness on the walls.

The living moment is everything. And in pictures we never experience it. It is useless asking the public to 'see' Matisee or Picasso or Brque. They will never see more than an odd horrific canvas, anyhow. But does the modern public read James Joyce or Marcel Proust?* It does not. It reads the great host of more congenial and more intelligible contemporary writers. And so the modern public is more or less up–to–date and on the spot about the general run of modern books. It is conscious of the literature of its day, moderately awake and intelligent in that respect.

But of the pictures and drawings of its day it is blankly unaware. The genral public feels itself a hopeless ignoramus when confronted with modern works of art. It has no clue to the whole unnatural business of modern art, and is just hostile. Even those who are tentatively attracted are uneasy, and they dare never buy. Prices are comparatively high, and you may so easily be let in for a dud. So the whole thing is

在任何时代，伟大的艺术家都是少而鲜见的。但却有成百上千的男人和女人有着真正的艺术天分和美好的艺术感觉，他们能做出少见漂亮的艺术品来。那是些美好的作品，并非不朽，也非杰作，更谈不上“伟大”，可它们就是美，而且能在很多年内不失其美。但过了些年就得死，就该毁了它们。

可现在所有这些一时招人喜爱的绘画却要被匆忙地蒙上灰尘，这是可悲的事。这是事实。当代艺术属于当代社会。社会总体上需要的是同时代人的艺术，就如同需要同时代人写的书一样。现代人读的是现代的书，可他们挂的却是没有时代归属的画儿，而且这些画儿没有生命，没有意义，不过是墙上死气沉沉的斑点而已。

活生生的那一刻最要紧。可在绘画中我们从来也不曾体验那一刻。因此，你要让大众去“看”马蒂斯、毕加索或勃拉克，此举纯属徒劳，他们看到的不过是一块奇怪吓人的画布。那么现代的读众们可曾读詹姆斯·乔伊斯[James Joyce(1882—1941)，英国作家，其作品被劳伦斯认为既不流畅也不清晰]或马赛·普鲁斯特[Marcel Proust(1871—1922)，法国作家，其作品被劳伦斯认为“黏糊”，评价甚低]呢？ 不

a deadlock.

Now the only way to keep the public in touch with art is to let it get hold of wourks of art. It was just the same with books. In the old fiveguinea and two-guinea days there was no public for literature, except the squire class. The great reading public came into being with the lending library. And the great picture-loving public would come into being with the lending pictuary. The public wants pictures hard enough. But it simply can't get them.

And this will continue so long as a picture is regarded as a piece of property, and not as a source of aesthetic emotion, of sheèr pleasure, as a flower is. The great public was utterly deprived of books till books ceased to be looked on as lumps of real estate, and came to be regarded as something belongine to the mind and consciousness, a spiritual instead of a gross material property. Today, if I say: "Doughty's 'Arabia Deserta'* is a favourite book of mine," then the man I say it to won't reply: 'Yes, I own a copy,' he will say: 'Yes, I have read it.' In the eighteenth century he would probably have replied: 'I have a fine example *in folio* in my library,' and the sense of 'property' would have overwhelmed any sense of literary delight.

读。他们读的是大量的更与之意气相投和更为明白易懂的当代作家作品。所以说现代读者对现代图书总的走向的了解或多或少算是同步的并且是与之相伴随的。他们懂得自己身边的文学，多少算是警醒的，在那方面是有辨别能力的。

可对身边的绘画和素描他们则毫无感知。在现代艺术作品面前，大众自觉是不可救药无知的一群。他们对整个不自然的现代艺术毫不摸门，干脆对此报以敌视。即便是那些浅尝并被此吸引者，也感到不自在，绝不敢买一件回家。价格相对来说有点高，而且很容易就买一件赝品。一切就此罢休。

要说有个惟一的办法让大众保持与艺术的接触，那就是让他们能得到艺术品。这和书是一样的。在一本书就要五个畿尼或二个畿尼的旧时代，文学就没有读众，只有乡绅阶层才读文学。阅读大众的出现是因为有了外借图书馆。而爱画的大众则要随着外借画馆的出现才会有。大众太需要绘画了，可就是买不起。

这种景况还会继续下去，只要绘画还被看做是财产而非像花朵一样

The cheapening of books freed them from the gross property valuation and released their true spiritual value. Something of the same must happen for pictures. The public wants and needs badly all the real aesthetic stimulus it can get. And it knows it. When books were made available, the vast reading public sprang into being almost at once. And a vast picture-loving public would arise, once the public could get at the pictures, personally.

There are thousands of quite lovely pictures, not masterpieces, of course, but with real beauty, which belong to today, and which remain stacked dustily and hopelessly in corners of artists´ studios, going stale. It is a great shame. The public wants them, but it never sees them; and if it does see an occasional few, it daren´t buy, especially as 'art' is high-priced, for it feels incompetent to judge. At the same time, the unhappy, work-glutted artists of today want above all things to let the public have their works. And these works are, we insist, and essential part of the education and emotional experience of the modern mind. It is necessary that adults should know them, as they know modern books. It is necessary that children be familiar with them, in the constant stream of creation. Our aesthetic education has become immensely important, since it is so immensely neglected.

是审美情愫和单纯愉悦的源泉。大众曾经被完全剥夺了读书的权利，直到图书不再被看作是巨大的房产，这种情况才有所改观，从此图书开始被看作是某种属于精神和思想的东西，而非完全是物质财富。今天如果我对谁说："多蒂的《阿拉伯沙漠》[Charles Montagu Doughty(1843—1926)，其1888年的游记《阿拉伯沙漠之旅》于1921年再版，劳伦斯读后认为属于无聊之作]是我最喜欢的书，"那人绝不会回答说："是的，我拥有一本，"而是说："对，我读过。"可在十八世纪，他很可能回答说："我书房里有一本精美的印制品，"于是乎一种"财产感"立即压倒了任何文学愉悦感。

图书价格下降后，人们不再用纯粹的财产价值衡量书了，从而使图书的精神价值显现了出来。绘画也必须这样才行。公众非常想而且非常需要得到所有能够得到的真正审美的刺激。他们懂得这一点。当图书唾手可得时，马上就出现了广大的阅读大众。而广大的爱画大众也会涌现出来，只要公众个人能获得绘画。

有成千上万的好画儿，虽然说不上是杰作，但确实真美，那是属于今天的画，可却毫无希望地堆在艺术家画室的角落里蒙尘、变旧。这委实可

And there we are, the pictures going to dust, for they don´t keep their freshness, any more than books or flowers or silks, beyond a certain time; yet their freshness now is the breath of life to us, since it means hours and days of delight. And the public is pining for the pictures, but daren´t buy, because of the money-property complex. And the artist is pining to let the public have them, but daren´t make himself cheap. And so the thing is an *impasse*, simple state of frustration.

Now for Messrs. Harrods and their lending library-or picturary-of modern works of art. Or, better still, and Artists´ Co-operative Society to supply pictures on loan or purchase, to the great public. Today nobody buys pictures, except as speculation. If a man pays a hundred pounds for a canvas, he does it in the secret belief that the canvas will be worth a thousand pounds in a few years´ time.

The whole attitude is disgusting. The reading public only asks of a book that it shall be entertaining, it doesn´t give a hang as to whether the book will be considered a great book five years hence. The great public wants to be entertained and, sometimes, delighted, and literature exists to supply the demand. Now there is a great deal of delight in even a very minor picture, produced by an artist who has delicate artistic feeling and some skill, even if he be not wildly original. There are

惜。公众想看到它们,可却看不到。偶尔看到了几幅,也不敢买这种高价的"艺术品",因为他们没有鉴别能力。与此同时,现在那些画了很多画的郁闷画家们最想的就是让公众得到他们的作品。而这些作品,我们坚持认为,是现代人的心灵教育和情感体验的基本部分。成年人应该了解这些,就如同他们了解现代图书一样。少年儿童应该熟悉它们,因为他们要不断地进行创造活动。我们的审美教育变得万分重要,因为它遭到了万分的忽视。

于是我们看到,绘画越来越陈旧,因为它们无法像书、花和丝绸一样超过一定时间后还能保鲜。可绘画的新鲜对我们来说就如同生命的呼吸,因为它意味着几小时和几天的愉悦。公众渴望绘画却不敢买,那全是所谓的金钱-财产的心理在作祟。艺术家渴望着让公众得到绘画,可他们不敢廉价出售。于是这事就此僵住,无可奈何。

现在就说说哈罗兹先生们和他们的外借图书馆——或者说是现代艺术的外借绘画馆。更好的名称应该是艺术家合作社,它为大众提供绘画,以租借的方式或购买的方式均可。现在没有人购买绘画,除非是为了

hundreds and hundreds of perfectly obscure pictures stuck away in corners of studios, which would, I know, give me a real delight if they were hung in my room for a year. After a while they would go stale; but not neatrly as quickly as a bunch of lilac, which yet I love and set with pleasure on the table. As a tree puts beauty into a flower that will fade, so all the hosts of minor artists one way and another, put beauty and delight into their pictures, that likewise will not last beyond their rhythmic season. But it is a wicked shame and waste that nearly all these pictures, with their modicum of beauty and their power of giving delight, should just be taken from the easel to be laid on the dust-heap, while a beauty-starved public doesn't even get a look at them. It is all very well saying the public should buy. A picture is cheap at twenty pounds, and very cheap at ten pounds, and 'given away' at five pounds. And the public is not only shy, it has a complex about buying any picture that hasn't at least the chance of turning out a masterpiece of ultimate extraordinary value.

It is all nonsensical and futile. The only way now is for the hosts of small artists to club together and form an Artists' Co-operative Society, with proper business intelligence and business energy, to supply the public with pictures on the public's

投机赚钱。如果一个人为一幅画花上一百英镑，其实他心里暗自盘算的是在几年之内这画升值到一千镑。

这样的态度全然令人生厌。读众对一本书的要求仅仅是有趣，根本不在乎五年后这书是否被看做是伟大的书。大众得到娱乐，有时是愉悦，文学于是就来满足这个要求。现在，甚至一幅渺小的绘画都会引起人们很大的乐趣，那位画家有细腻的艺术感，也有些技艺，即使并不怎么富有独创性也行。还有成百上千的完美绘画被埋没了，藏在画室的角落里，我知道这些画会给我真正的快乐，如果它们能在我屋里挂上一年。一年后不久它们就陈旧了，但不会像我喜欢并摆在桌上的一束丁香花凋谢得那么快。树木把自己的美投入花中，但花终归是要凋谢。同样，那些渺小的画家以不同的方式把美和愉悦投入他们的画中，他们的画同样无法超越自己鲜活的时节。几乎所有的绘画，虽然具备了美和给人带来美感的力量，竟然下了画架就蒙上了灰尘，而对美如饥似渴的公众却连看它一眼都看不上，这委实可惜，是可怕的浪费。说公众应该买自然不错，一幅画卖二十英镑算便宜，卖十镑算很便宜，而卖到五镑就算"甩卖"了。而公众

own terms. Or for the shrewd business men of the world to take the matter up and make a profitable concern of it, as publishers made a profitable concern of publishing books.

August 1929.

不仅是胆怯，他们还怕买的画最终不能成为价值连城的杰作。

说这些纯属胡扯无聊。惟一的办法就是让那些小艺术家们组成一个颇具商业头脑和活力的艺术家合作社，为公众提供他们买的起的绘画。否则就让世界上那些精明的商人来管这事，让画的买卖成为一个赚钱的营生，就像出版商们把出书变成了一个赚钱的营生一样。

1929 年

美国经典文学研究

CHAPTER I
The Spirit of Place

We like to think of the old-fashioned American classics as children's books. Just childishness, on our part. The old American art-speech contains an alien quality, which belongs to the American continent and to nowhere else. But, of course, so long as we insist on reading the books as children's tales, we miss all that.

One wonders what the proper high-brow Romans of the third and fourth or later centuries read into the strange utterances of Lucretius or Apuleius of Tertullian, Augustine or Athanasius.* The uncanny voice of Iberian Spain, the weirdness of old Carthage, the passion of Libya and North Africa; you may bet the proper old Romans never heard these at all. They read old Latin inference over the top of it, as we read old European inference over the top of Poe or Hawthorne.

It is hard to hear a new voice, as hard as it is to listen to an unknown lan-

地之灵

我们喜欢把旧式的美国经典著作看成是儿童读物，这反倒说明我们过于幼稚。这些文学作品具有某种非美洲大陆莫属的异域风情。可是，如果我们坚持把它们当做儿童故事来读的话，就无法领略这一切了。

我们无法想像三四世纪前后的那些性情高雅的罗马人是如何阅读卢克莱修 **[96? —?55B.C.，罗马哲学家、诗人]**、艾普利亚斯**[公元二世纪罗马哲学家、讽刺作家]**、塔图里安**[160? —220?，最早的基督教神学家]**、奥古斯丁 **[354—430，早期基督教会领袖]**或阿桑那希阿斯 **[296? —373，亚历山大城大主教]**奇特的著述的。伊比利亚半岛上西班牙人奇妙的声音，古老的迦太基人神奇莫测的语言，利比亚和北非的激情，我敢说，那些一本正经的古罗马人从来没听说过这一切。他们是通过读古拉丁文的结论来了解这些的，正如我们是通过阅读老欧洲人

guage. We just don't listen. There is a new voice in the old American classics. The world has declined to heat it, and has babbled about children's stories.

Why? –Out of fear. The would fears a new experience more than it fears anything. Because a new experience displaces so many old experiences. And it is like trying to use muscles that have perhaps never been used, or that have been going stiff for ages. It hurts horribly.

The world doesn't fear a new idea. It can pigeon-hole any idea. But it can't pigeon-hole a real new experience. It can only dodge. The world is a great dodger, and the Americans the greatest. Because they dodge their own very selves.

There is a new feeling in the old American books, far more than there is in the modern American books, which are pretty empty of any feeling, and proud of it. There is a 'different' feeling in the old American classics. It is the shifting over from the old psyche to something new, a displacement. And displacements hurt. This hurts. So we try to tie it up, like a cut fingrt. Put a rag round it.

It is a cut too. Cutting away the old emotions and consciousness. Don't ask what is left.

Art-speech is the only truth. An artist is usually a damned liar, but his art, if it

的陈旧结论来了解爱伦·坡和霍桑一样。

倾听一个新的声音是困难的，这就如同倾听一种未知的语言一样。我们呢，干脆不去听。而在旧的美国经典著作中是有一个新声音的。整个世界都拒绝倾听这个新声音，却一直把它们当成儿童故事叨念着。

为什么?是出自恐惧。这个世界比怕任何事都更怕一种新的体验。因为一种新的体验要取代许许多多旧的体验。这就如同启用从未使用过或僵硬了多年的肌肉一样，这样做会带来巨大的疼痛。

这个世界并不惧怕新的观念。它可以将一切观念束之高阁。但是它无法把一个真正清新的经验束之高阁，它只能躲避。这个世界是一个大逃避者，而美国人则是最大的逃避者，他们甚至躲避自己。

旧的美国书籍让人产生一种新颖的感觉，比现代书籍要强得多。现代书籍空洞麻木还自鸣得意。而美国的旧经典著作则令人产生一种"截然不同"的感知。让人觉出从旧灵魂向新灵魂的过渡，新的取代旧的。这种取代是令人痛苦的。它割破了什么，于是我们像粘合割破的手指头一样用一块布来包扎伤口。

这同时也是一种割裂。把旧的情绪与意识割掉。不要问剩下了些什

be art, will tell you the truth of his day. And that is all that matters. Away with eternal truth. Truth lives from day to day, and the marvellous Plato of yesterday is chiefly bosh today.

The old American artists were hopeless liars. But they were artists, in spite of themselves. Which is more than you can say of most living practitioners.

And you can please yourself, when you read *The Scarlet Letter*, whether you accept what that sugary, blue-eyed little darling of a Hawthorne has to say for himself, false as all darlings are, or whether you read the impeccable truth of his art-speech.

The curious thing about art-speech is that it prevaricates so terribly, I mean it tells such lies. I suppose because we always all the time tell ourselves lies. And out of a pattern of lies art weaves the truth. Like Dostoevsky posing as a sort of Jesus, but most truthfully revealing himself all the while as a little horror.

Truly art is a sort of subterfuge. But thank God for it, we can see through the subterfuge if we choose. Art has two great functions. First, it provides an emotional experience. And then, if we have the courage of our own feelings, it becomes a mine of practical truth. We have had the feelings *ad nauseam*. But we've never dared dig

么。

艺术化的语言是惟一的真实。一位艺术家往往是一个十足的说谎骗子，可是他的艺术——如果算得上艺术的话，会告诉你他所处时期的真相。这是至关紧要的东西。没有什么永恒的真理。真理是随着时光变迁的，昨日优秀的柏拉图今日就是一个满口胡言者。

旧日的美国艺术家是一批不可救药的说谎骗子。可是他们无论如何算得上是艺术家，这一点连他们自己都没意识到。眼下健在的大多数从艺者们更是如此。

当你读《红字》，不管你是否接受霍桑这位如此美好、蓝眼睛的宝贝为自己伸张的一切（他同一切可爱的人一样是在撒谎），还是读出了其艺术语言无懈可击的真实，为此你感到赏心悦目。

艺术化语言之奇特在于它谎话连篇却能自圆其说。我想这是因为我们一直在自欺欺人的缘故。而艺术正是用谎言模式来编织真理的。这正如陀斯妥耶夫斯基自诩为基督，可他真正露出的则是一副吓人的面孔[劳伦斯认为陀氏小说虽属伟大寓言，但是虚假的艺术，错在赋予普通人以神性]。

真正的艺术是一种遁词。感谢上苍，如果我们想看破这遁词的话我

the actual truth out of them, the truth that concerns us, whether it concerns our grandchildren or not.

The artist usually sets out—or used to—to point a moral and adorn a tale. The tale, however, points the other way, as a rule. Two blankly opposing morals, the artist's and the tale's. Never trust the artist. Trust the tale. The proper function of a critic is to save the tale from the artist who created it.

Now we know our business in these studies;* saving the American tale from the American artist.

Let us look at this American artist first. How did he ever get to America, to start with? Why isn't he a European still, like his father before him?

Now listen to me, don't listen to him. He'll tell you the lie you expect. Which is partly your fault for expecting it.

He didn't come in search of freedom of worship. England had more freedom of worship in the year 1700 than America had. Won by Englishmen who wanted freedom, and so stopped at home and fought for it.* And got it. Freedom of worship? Read the history of New England during the first century of its existence.

Freedom anyhow? The land of the free! * This the land of the free! Why, if I

们还是能做得到这一点的。艺术有两大作用。首先，它提供一种情感体验。其次，如果我们敢于承认自己的感情，我们可以说它可以成为真理的源泉。我们有过令人作呕的感觉，可我们从来不敢从中挖掘出切实的真理来，其实这真理与我们息息相关，是否与我们的子孙相关也未可知。

艺术家通常要（或者说惯于）挑明某种寓意并以此来使某个故事生辉。但往往这故事却另择他径。艺术家的寓意与故事的寓意竟是如此截然相反。永远不要相信艺术家，而要相信他笔下的故事。批评家的作用在于从创作故事的艺术家手中拯救这故事。

说到这里，我们明白了这本书[本篇以下12篇曾以《美国经典文学研究》为名结集出版英文版]研究的任务，这就是把美国故事从美国艺术家手中拯救出来。

还是让我们先来看看美国的艺术家吧。他最初是如何来到美国起家的？为什么他不像他的父辈一样仍然是欧洲人？

听我说，不要听他说。他会像你预料的那样说谎。从某种意义上说他说谎你也有责任，因为你预期他会这样。

他来美国并非出于追求信仰自由的缘故。在1700年，英国的信仰自由要比美国大得多。要自由的英国人取得胜利后，就在自己的国家里为

say anything that displeases them, the free mob will lynch me, and that´s my freedom. Free? Why, I have never been in any country where the individual has such an abject fear of his fellow countrymen. Because, as I say, they are free to lynch the moment he shows he is not one of them.

No, no, if you´re so fond of the truth about Queen Victoria, try a little about yourself.

Those Pilgrim Fathers and their successors never came here for freedom of worship. What did they set up when they goe here? Freedom, would you call it?

They didn´t come for freedom. Or if they did, they sadly went back on themselves.

All right then, what did they come for? For lots of reasons. Perhaps least of all in search of freedom of any sort: positive freedom, that is.

They came largely to get away –that most simple of motives. To get away. Away from what? In the long run, away from themselves. Away from everything. That´s why most people have come to America, and still do come. To get away from everything they are and have been.

'Henceforth be masterless.'

信仰自由而奋斗了[指17世纪英国人推翻詹姆斯二世的内战。但战后控制了议会的基督教长老会却完全压制宗教宽容]。他们终于获得了自由。信仰自由吗?请读一读新英格兰最初的历史记载吧。

是自由吗?自由人的国土[引自《星条旗之歌》]!这里是自由的土地!哦,如果我说句什么让他们不中听的话，这些自由的人群就会用私刑来折磨我的。这就是我的自由。自由吗?哦,我从未到过这样一个国家,在那儿人们如此惧怕自己的同胞。正如我前面所说,因为一旦有谁表示出他不是他们的同党,人们就可以自由地对他施以私刑。

不,不,如果你喜欢维多利亚女王的真理,那你就试试吧。

那些远游的父辈和他们的后代到美洲来压根儿不是为了寻求信仰自由。那他们在这儿落脚后建立起来的是什么呢?你认为是自由吗?

他们不是为自由而来。哦,如果是这样的话,他们会沮丧而归的。

那么他们是为何出走呢?原因很多。或许根本不是来寻求自由的——不是真正的自由。

他们的出走更多地是为了逃跑,这是最简单的动机。逃跑。逃离什么呢?最终,是为了脱离自我,脱离一切。人们就是为这个才来美国的,人们

Which is all very well, but it isn't freedom. Rather the reverse. A hopeless sort of constraint. It is never freedom till you find something you really positively want to be. And people in America have always been shouting about the things they are not. Unless, of course, they are millionaires, made or in the making.

And after all there is a positive side to the movement. All that vast flood of human life that has flowed over the Atlantic in ships from Europe to America has not flowed over simply on a tide of revulsion from Europe and from the confinements of the European ways of life. This revulsion was, and still is, I believe, the prime motive in emigration. But there was some cause, even for the revulsion.

It seems as if at times man had a frenzy for getting away from any control of any sort. In Europe the old Christianity was the real master. The Church and the true aristocracy bore the responsibility for the working out of the Christian ideals: a little irregularly, maybe, but responsible nevertheless.

Mastery, kingship, fatherhood had their power destroyed at the time of the Renaissance.

And it was precisely at this moment that the great drift over the Atlantic started. What were men drifting away from? The old authority of Europe? Were they

仍在继续这样。他们要与他们的现在和过去决断。

"从而摆脱主子。"

不错，是这样的。可这不是自由。恰恰相反，这是一种绝望的限制。除非你找到了某种你真正向往的东西，那才算得上自由。而美国人总呼喊他们不是自己向往成为的那种人。当然，百万富翁或即将成为百万富翁的人是不会这样吼叫的。

但无论如何，他们的运动是有其积极的一面的。那洪水一样乘船从欧洲跨过大西洋流向美洲的人们并非简单地是随大流要摆脱欧洲或欧洲生活方式的限制。当然，我相信这仍然是这种大规模移民的主要动机。但除此之外，还有别的原因。

似乎人时而会产生某种要摆脱一切控制的疯狂力量。在欧洲，古老的基督教是真正的霸主。教会和贵族创造了基督教教义，这似乎有点反常，但事实的确如此。

霸权、王权和父权力量在文艺复兴时就被摧毁了。

就是在这个时期人们开始漂洋过海奔向美洲。人们摆脱掉的是什么呢？是欧洲的旧权威吗？他们是否从此逃脱了权威的限制并获得了一种新

breaking the bonds of authority, and escaping to a new more absolute unrestrainedness? Maybe. But there was more to it.

Liberty is all very well, but men cannot live without masters. There is always a master. And men either live in glad obedience to the master they believe in, or they live in a frictional opposition to the master they wish to undermine. In America this frictional opposition has been the vital factor. It has given the Yankee his kick. Only the continual influx of more servile Europeans has provided America with an obedient labouring class. The true obedience never outlasting the first generation.

But there sits the old master, over in Europe. Like a parent. Somewhere deep in every American heart lies a rebellion against the old parenthood of Europe. Yet no American feels he has completely escaped its mastery. Hence the slow, smouldering patience of American opposition. The slow, smouldering corrosive obedience to the old master Europe, the unwilling subject, the unremitting opposition.

Whatever else you are, be masterless.

Ca Ca Caliban

*Get a new master, be a new man.**

Escaped slaves, we might say, people the republics of Liberia or Haiti.* Liberia

的绝对自由呢?或许是吧。但还有更重要的因素。

自由固然好,但人是不能没有主子的,总有一个主人。人要么心悦诚服地信任一个主人,要么与主人发生冲突,要毁灭这主人。在美国,与主人的冲突一直是一个重要现象,它成为美国人的一大动力。可是奴性十足的欧洲人蜂拥而至,为美洲提供了顺从的劳动阶级。当然这种驯服不过是第一代人的问题。

可是,在欧洲却端坐着他们的老主人,他像一位家长一样。在美洲人的心灵深处蕴藏着一种反欧洲家长的力量,但是没有任何美洲人感到自己彻底摆脱了欧洲的统治。于是美洲人就这样压抑着自己的反抗情绪,很有耐心地忍受着,与欧洲若即若离。他们在忍耐中服从着旧的欧洲主人,很不情愿,反抗情绪毫不减弱。

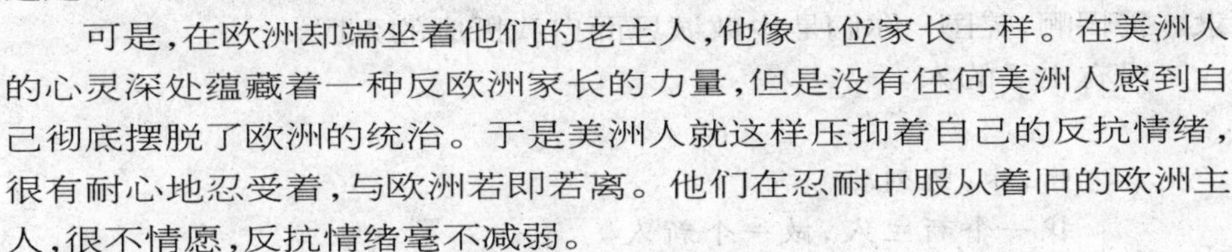

你无论如何都不要主子。

咔,咔,凯列班

找一个新主人,做一个新人。[此句摹仿莎士比亚《暴风雨》中凯列班的歌词]

enough! Are we to look at America in the same way? A vast republic of escaped slaves. When you consider the hordes from eastern Europe, you might well say it: a vast republic of escaped slaves. But one dare not say this of the Pilgrim Fathers, and the great old body of idealist Americans, the modern Americans tortured with thought. A vast republic of escaped slaves. Look out, America! And a minority of earnest, self-tortured people.

The masterless.

Ca Ca Caliban

Get a new master, be a new man.

What did the Pilgrim Fathers come for, then, when they came so gruesomely over the black sea? Oh, it was in a black spirit. A black revulsion from Europe, from the old authority of Europe, from kings and bishops and popes. And more. When you look into it, more. They were black, masterful men, they wanted something else. No kings, no bishops maybe. Even no God Almighty. But also, no more of this new 'humanity' which followed the Renaissance. None of this new liberty which was to be so pretty in Europe. Something grimmer, by no means free-amd-easy.

America has never been easy, and is not easy today. Americans have always

我们可以说利比里亚共和国和海地共和国的人是逃跑了的奴隶。仅利比里亚就够了![利比里亚于1847年成为一个独立的国家是为了收容返回非洲的奴隶。海地则于19世纪初独立]我们是否也用同样的眼光看美国人呢?说他们整整一大国的人都是逃亡的奴隶吗?当你想到东欧的游牧部落时,你可以说他们是一大批逃亡奴隶。可是谁也不敢这样称呼闯美洲的先驱们,不敢这么称呼理想主义十足的老美国人和受着思考折磨的现代美国人。一群逃亡奴隶。警惕啊,美国!你们是少数诚恳而自我折磨的人民。

没有主子的人。

咔,咔,凯列班

找一个新主人,做一个新人。

那些祖先们为何要漂过可怕的绝望海洋来到这里呢?啊,那是一种绝望的精神。他们绝望地要摆脱欧洲,摆脱古老的欧洲权威,摆脱那些国王、主教和教皇们。当然,还有更多更多的东西,这需要你细细研究。他们是一些阴郁而优秀的人物,他们需要别的什么。不要什么国王,不要什么

been at a certain tension. Their liberty is a thing of sheer will, sheer tension: a liberty of THOU SHALT NOT. And it has been so from the first. The land of THOU SHALT NOT. Only the first commandment is: THOU SHALT NOT PRESUME TO BE A MASTER. Hence democracy.

'We are the masterless.' That is what the American Eagle* shrieks. It's a Hen-Eagle.

The Spaniards refused the post-Renaissance liberty of Europe. And the Spaniards filled most of America.* The Yankees, too, refused, refused the post-Renaissance humanism of Europe. First and foremost, they hated masters. But under that, they hated the flowing ease of humour in Europe. At the bottom of the American soul was always a dark suspense, at the bottom of the Spanish-American soul the same. And this dark suspense hated and hates the old European spontaneity, watches it collapse with satisfaction.

Every continent has its own great spirit of place. Every people is polarized in some particular locality, which is home, the homeland. Different places on the face of the earth have different vital effluence, different vibration, different chemical exhalation, different polarity with different stars: call it what you like. But the spirit of

主教，甚至连上帝都不要。同时，也不要文艺复兴后的新"人类"。在欧洲的这种美好的自由解放全要不得。这东西令人郁闷，远非轻而易举。

美国从未顺利过，今天仍不那么轻松。美国人总是处在某种紧张状态中。他们的自由解放纯属一种意志紧张：这是一种"你不许如何如何"的自由。从一开始就如此。这是一片"你不许如何如何"的国土。他们的第一条训诫就是："你不许称王称霸。"于是就有了民主。

"我们是没有主子的人。"美洲之鹰[美元硬币和后来的纸币上都有白头鹫的图像，它是美国的国鸟]这样喊到。这是一只雌鹰。

西班牙人拒绝接受文艺复兴后欧洲的自由解放。于是美洲大部分地区都充斥着西班牙人[西班牙人曾征服南北美洲，在19世纪初在北美还很有势力，占领着美国的中西部]。美国人同样拒绝接受文艺复兴后欧洲的人道主义。他们最忌恨的就是主子。再就是忌恨欧洲人中流行的那种轻松的幽默。在美国人的灵魂深处凝聚着阴郁的紧张，美洲的西班牙人也莫不如此。就是这种阴郁的紧张仇恨古老的欧洲本能，它目睹着这种欧洲本能的幻灭而为此幸灾乐祸。

每一个大陆都有其伟大的地域之灵。每一国人都被某一特定的地域

place is a great reality. The Nile valley produced not only the corn, but the terrific religions of Egypt. China produces the Chinese, and will go on doing so. The Chinese in San Francisco will in time cease to be Chinese, for America is a great melting pot.

There was a tremendous polarity in Italy, in the city of Rome. And this seems to have died. For even places die. The Island of Great Britain had a wonderful terrestrial magnetism or polarity of its own, which made the British people. For the moment, this polarity seems to be breaking. Can England die? And what if England dies?

Men are less free than they imagine; ah, far less free. The freest are perhaps least free.

Men are free when they are in a living homeland, not when they are straying and breaking away. Men are free when they are obeying some deep, inward voice of religious belief. Obeying from within. Men are free when they belong to a living, organic, believing community, active in fulfilling some unfulfilled, perhaps unrealized purpose. Not when they are escaping to some wild west. The most unfree souls go west, and shout of freedom. Men are freest when they are most unconscious of free-

所吸引,这就是家乡和祖国。地球上的不同地点放射着不同的生命力,不同的生命振幅,不同的化学气体,不同的星座放射着不同的磁力——你可以任意称呼它。但是地域之灵确是一种伟大的真实。尼罗河峡谷不仅出产谷物还造就了埃及国土那了不起的宗教。中国造就了中国人,将来也还是这样。但旧金山的中国人将在某一天不成其为中国人,因为美国是一个大熔炉,会熔化他们。

在意大利,在罗马城就有一股强大的磁力。可如今这磁力似乎逝去了。地域也是可以死的。英伦曾产生过妙不可言的地磁力,这是它自身的吸引力,这力量造就了英国的民众。眼下,这力量似乎垮了。英国会死吗?如果英国死了,其后果如何呢?

人不像自己所想像的那么自由,哦,差远了。最自由的人或许是最不自由的。

人自由的时候是当他生活在充满生机的祖国之时,而不是他漂泊浪游之时。人在服从于某种宗教信仰的深刻内在的声音时才是自由的。服从要出自内心。人从属于一个充满生机、健全的、有信仰的群体,这个群体为某种未完成甚至未实现的目标而积极奋斗,只有这样他才是自由的

dom. The shout is a rattling of chains, always was.

Men are not free when they are doing just what they like. The moment you can do just what you like, there is nothing you care about doing. Men are only free when they are doing what the deepest self likes.

And there is getting down to the deepest self! It takes some diving.

Because the deepest self is way down, and the conscious self is an obstinate monkey. But of one thing we may be sure. If one wants to be free, one has to give up the illusion of doing what one likes, and seek what IT wishes done.

But before you can do what IT likes, you must first break the spell of the old mastery, the old IT.

perhaps at the Renaissance, when kingship and fatherhood fell, Europe drifted into a very dangerous half-truth: of liberty and equality. Perhaps the men who went to America felt this, and so repudiated the old world together. Went one better than Europe. Liberty in America has meant so far the breaking away from *all* dominion. The true liberty will only begin when Americans discover IT, and proceed possibly to fulfil IT. IT being the deepest whole self of man, the self in its wholeness, not idealistic halfness.

人。逃向荒蛮的西部时并非自由。那些最不自由的人们奔向西部去呼唤自由了。人只有在对自由毫无感知的情况下才是最自由的人。对于自由的呼唤其实是镣铐在哗哗作响,永远是这样。

当人做他喜爱做的事时他并非是自由人。一旦他能够做自己愿意做的事,他就不挑剔了。人只有做自我心灵深处想做的事时他才是自由人。

那就寻找灵魂深处的自我吧!这需要走向纵深地带。

最深秘处的自我距人很远,而清醒的自我则是一个固执的顽童。但我们可以相信一件事,如果你想获得自由,你就得放弃你喜欢做什么事的幻想,而要寻觅"它"希望做的事。

可是你要做"它"喜欢做的事,你首先要击破旧的"它"的统治。

或许,文艺复兴时,当王权和父权破灭后,欧洲获得了某种似是而非而有害的真理:自由和平等。可能奔向美洲的人都有所感,于是他们全盘否定旧的世界。他们去了一个比欧洲优越的地方。在美国,自由意味着与所有旧的统治决裂。而要获得真正的自由还需待美国人发现了"它"并实现"它"才行。"它"就是最隐秘处人完整的自我,是完整的自我而不是理想化的似是而非的自我。

That's why the Pilgrim Fathers came to America, then; and that's why we come. Driven by IT. We cannot see that invisible winds carry us, as they carry swarms of locusts, that invisible magnetism brings us as it brings the migrating birds to their unforeknown goal. But it is so. We are not the marvellous choosers and deciders we think we are. IT chooses for us, and decides for us. Unless, of course, we are just escaped slaves, vulgarly cocksure of our ready-made destiny. But if we are living people, in touch with the source, IT drives us and decides us. We are free only so long as we obey. When we run counter, and think we will do as we like, we just flee around like Orestes pursued by the Eumenides.*

And still, when the great day begins, when Americans have at last discovered America and their own wholeness, stilll there will be the vast number of escaped slaves to reckon with, those who have no cocksure, ready-made destinits.

Which will win in America, the escaped slaves, or the new whole men?

The real American day hasn't begun yet. Or at least, not yet sunrise. So far it has been the false dawn. That is, in the progressive American consciousness there has been the one dominant desire, to do away with the old thing. Do away with masters, exalt the will of the people. The will of the people being nothing but a figment,

当年的先驱就是为此才来美国的；这也是我们来美国的缘由。全受着"它"的驱使。我们无法看清那载我们而来的风，这风同样也载来了成群的蝗虫。这股看不见的磁力把我们吸引来，如同它把无数候鸟吸引到未知的目的地一样。这是真的。我们并非像自己想像的那样可以自行选择并做出决定。是"它"替我们做出选择和决定。当然，如果我们只是逃亡的奴隶，对注定的命运颇为自信到庸俗的地步，那又另当别论。可是，如果我们是生机勃勃的人，与生命源泉息息相关，就得听从"它"的驱使和决定。我们只有服从才能自由。一旦我们反其道而行之，自以为在自行其是，我们就成了被复仇女神追逐着的奥列斯特[迈锡尼王阿迦门农之子，杀其母替父报仇。——见埃斯库罗斯戏剧]了。

当美国人最终发现了美国，发现了他们完整的自我时，他们还要对付大批的对注定命运毫无信心的逃亡奴隶。

谁将在美国取胜呢?是逃亡的奴隶还是那些完整的新人?

真正的美国之日还未开始。至少可以说还不是朝阳初升之时，这黎明仍然是虚幻的。在美国人进步的意识中有着这样的重要欲望，那就是与旧事物决裂。与霸主决裂，让人民振奋精神。人民的意志不过是虚幻的

the exalthing doesn't count for much. So, in the name of the will of the people, get rid of masters. When you have got rid of masters, you are left with this mere phrase of the will of the people. Then you pause and bethink yourself, and try to recover your own wholeness.

So much for the conscious American motive, and for democracy over here. Democracy in America is just the tool with which the old master of Europe, the European spirit, is undermined. Europe destroyed, potentially, American democracy will evaporate. Americal will begin.

American consciousness has so far been a false dawn. The negative ideal of democracy. But underneath, and contrary to this open ideal, the first hints and revelations of IT. IT, the American whole soul.

You have got to pull the democratic and idealistic clothes off American utterance, and see what you can of the dusky body of IT underneath.

'Henceforth be masterless.'

Henceforth be mastered.

东西罢了，说不上振奋。那就以人民意志的名义，摆脱主子吧。一旦你摆脱了霸主，你所拥有的就仅仅是人民的意志这个词儿了。然后你就可以停下来自省，试图恢复你的完整性。

够了，不说美国人清醒的动机和民主了。美国的民主不过是摧毁旧的欧洲霸主和欧洲精神的武器。欧洲摧毁了，美国的民主就烟消云散了，美国得从头开始。

迄今为止的美国意识还是虚幻的。民主的理想尚属消极。可这其中已孕育着"它"的一线启示之光。"它"就是美国完整的灵魂。

你应该剥掉美国人言论中的民主与理想的外衣，去观察内在的"它"的混沌躯体。

"就这样不要主子。"

就这样被主宰。

CHAPTER 2
Benjamin Franklin

The Perfectibility of Man! Ah heaven, what a dreary theme! The perfectibility of the Ford car! The perfectibility of which man? I am many men. Which of them are you going to perfect? I am not a mechanical contrivance.

Education! Which of the various me´s do you propose to educate, and which do you propose to suppress?

Anyhow, I defy you. I defy you, oh society, to educate me or to supress me, according to your dummy standards.

The ideal man! And which is he, if you please? Benjamin Franklin or Abraham Lincoln? The ideal man! Roosevelt or Porfirio Diaz?*

There are other men in me, besides this patient ass who sits here in a tweed jacket. What am I doing, playing the patient ass in a tweed jacket? Who am I talk-

本杰明·富兰克林

人的完美！天啊，这是一个多么折磨人的主题！福特汽车是完美无缺的了！可哪个人是完美无瑕的？我是所有的人。你想让哪一个变得完美？我可不是一件机器制品。

教育！你要教育这芸芸众生中的哪一个？你又想压抑哪一个呢？

无论如何，我向你挑战。我不信，社会，你能教育我或压抑我，你要按照你那虚伪的模式来如此待我，我就不信。

理想的人！你认为哪一位是理想的人呢？本杰明·富兰克林还是亚伯拉罕·林肯？理想的人！是罗斯福还是波费里奥·迪厄兹[1830–1915，墨西哥将领和政治家，总统(1877–1880，1884–1911)，独裁者]？

ing to? Who are you, at the other end of this patience?

Who are you? How many selves have you? And which of these selves do you want to be?

Is Yale College going to educate the self that is in the dark of you, or Harvard College?

The ideal self! Oh, but I have a strange and fugitive self shut out and howling like a wolf or a coyote under the ideal windows. See his red eyes in the dark? This is the self who is coming into his own.

The perfectibility of man, dear God! When every man as long as he remains alive is in himself a multitude of conflicting men. Which of these do you choose to perfect, at the expense of every other?

Old Daddy Franklin will tell you. He'll rig him up for you, the pattern American. Oh, Franklin was the first downright American. He knew what he was about, the sharp little man. He set up the first dummy American.

At the beginning of his career this cunning little Benjamin drew up for himself a creed that should 'satisfy the professors of every religion, but shock none'.

Now wasn't that a real American thing to do?

David Herbert Lawrence

我身着花呢上衣，斜卧病榻。可我还是许多个别人。我在干什么，扮演病人吗？我在和谁说话？失去耐心的你又是什么人？

你是谁？你有多少个自我？你想成为这些个自我中的哪一个？

是耶鲁还是哈佛将要教化你黑暗中的自我？

理想的自我！哦，我有一个陌生、鬼鬼祟祟的自我，他像一头被关在理想之窗外的狼在嚎叫。你看到黑暗中的那双红赤赤的眼睛了吗？这就是将要成形的自我。

人的完美，亲爱的上帝！一个活生生的人自身就是一个多人的冲突体。你打算牺牲哪一个去使哪一个完善呢？

我们的老父亲富兰克林会告诉你的。他会为你树立一个美国人的样板。哦，富兰克林就是第一个十足的美国人。他知道自己是怎么回事，这个伶牙俐齿的小个子。他成了第一个样板美国人。

他刚刚开始他的职业之时，这个狡猾的小个子本杰明就给自己定下了训诫："让各种信仰的人都满意，而不伤害任何人。"

这是一个真正的美国人要做的事吗？

'That there is One God, who made all things.'

(But Benjamin made Him.)

'That He governs the world by His Providence.'

(Benjamin knowing all about Providence.)

'That He ought to be worsbipped with ador ation, prayer, and thanksgiving.'

(Which cost nothing.)

'But–' But me no buts, Benjamin, saith the Lord.

'But that the most acceptable service of God is doing good to men.

(God having no choice in the matter.)

'That the soul is immortal.'

(you'll see why, in the next clause.)

'And that God will certainly reward virtue and punisb vice, eitber here or bereafter.'

Now if Mr Andrew Carnegie, or any other millonaire, had wished to invent a God to suit his ends, he could not have done better. Benjamin did it for him in the eighteenth century. God is the supreme servant of men who want to get on, to produce. Providence. The provider. The heavenly storekeeper. The everlasting Wana-

"有一个无所不能的上帝。"

(但这是本杰明造的上帝。)

"是他用天理统治世界。"

(本杰明知道一切天理。)

"人们应该崇拜他、敬仰他、向他祈祷、向他表示感恩。"

(这些用不着付出代价。)

"但是——"

(没什么但是,主这么说,本杰明。)

"但是上帝为人类服务,为人类做善事。"

(上帝对此毫无选择。)

"灵魂不朽。"

(看看下一段你就明白这是为什么了。)

"上帝自然会奖励善行,惩罚罪恶,无论今生来世。"

如今,如果安德鲁·卡内基先生[1835–1919,美国富翁和慈善家]或别的百万富翁想制造一个上帝为自己服务的话,他不会比富兰克林做得更好。富兰

maker.

And this is all the God the grandsons of the Pilgrim Fathers had left. Aloft on a pillar of dollars.

'*That the soul is immortal.*'

The trite way Benjamin says it!

But man has a soul, though you can't locate it either in his purse or his pocket-book or his heart or his stomach or his head. The wholeness of a man is his soul. Not merely that nice little comfortable bit which Benjamin marks out.

It's a queer thing is a man's soul. It is the whole of him. Which means it is the unknown him, as well as the known. It seems to me just funny, professors and Benjamins fixing the functions of the soul. Why,the soul of man is a vast forest, and all Benjamin intended was a neat back garden. And we've all got to fit into his kitchen garden scheme of things. Hail Columbia!

The soul of man is a dark forest. The Hercynian Wood that scared the Romans so, and out of which came the white-skinned hordes of the next civilization.

Who knows what will come out of the soul of man? The soul of man is a dark vast forest, with wild life in it. Think of Benjamin fencing it off!

克林早在十八世纪就创造了上帝。上帝是那些要发达和生产的人创造出来为之服务的杰出仆人。上帝。供给人。天堂里看仓库的人。

这就是闯美洲的祖先们后代们留给人们的上帝。他高踞美元堆成的巨柱上。

"灵魂不朽。"

本杰明总用这种陈词滥调!

可人的确有灵魂，尽管你说不清它的位置，不知是在钱包中、手册中、心中、腹中还是在头脑中。人的完整就是人的灵魂，并非本杰明所描绘的那美好、令人愉悦的一点点东西。

人的灵魂是个奇妙的物件。灵魂是他的全部。它既是已知的他又是未知的他。那些教授和本杰明们试图让灵魂有固定的作用，这在我看来很可笑。为什么呢?因为人的灵魂是一座巨大的森林，而本杰明试图指出的不过是一处整洁的后花园。他还让我们都循规蹈矩。多好的美国!

人的灵魂是一座幽深的森林。古生代出现的赫西尼亚森林曾令罗马人惊恐，但就是从这座森林中诞生了下一个文明的白种人群。

Oh, but Benjamin fenced a little tract that he called the soul of man, and proceeded to get it into cultivation. Providence, forsooth! And they think that bit of barbed wire is going to keep us in pound for ever? More fools they.

This is Benjamin's barbed wire fence. He made himself a list of virtues, which he trotted inside like a grey nag in a paddock.

1. TEMPERANCE

Eat not to fulness; drink not to elevation.

2. SILENCE

Speak not but what may benefit others or yourself; avoid trifling conversation.

3. ORDER

Let all your things have their places; let each part of your business have its time.

4. RESOLUTION

Resolve to perform what you ought; perform without fail what you resolve.

5. FRUGALITY

Make no expense but to do good to others or yourself –i.e., waste nothing.

6. INDUSTRY

谁知道从人的灵魂中会生出些什么来？人的灵魂是一座浩瀚的黑森林，林中满是野性的生命。可是本杰明却要用樊篱把这野性的生命封锁起来！

哦，本杰明封锁的是一条他称之为“人的灵魂”的小径，还要继续修缮它。天啊，这可是真的！他们还以为那带刺的铁丝网会把我们永远限制住，他们可是太愚蠢了。

这就是本杰明筑起的带刺的铁丝网。他给自己编了一道美德樊篱，他自己则像一只小灰马在围场中蹦跳。

1.节制

饮食勿饱；饮酒勿醉。

2.沉默

不说与人与自己不利的话；避免闲言碎语。

3.秩序

你的一切应井然有序；一时一事都要计划周全。

Lose no time, be always employed in something useful; cut off all unnecessary action.

7. SINCERITY

Use no hurtful deceit; think innocently and justly, and, if you speak, speak accordingly.

8. JUSTICE

Wrong none by doing injuries, or oimitting the benefits that are your duty.

9. MODERATION

Avoid extremes, forbear resenting injuries as much as you think they deserve.

10. CLEANLINESS

Tolerate no uncleanliness in body, clothes, or babitation.

11. TRANQUILLITY

Be not disturbed at trifles, or at accidents common or unavoidable.

12. CHASTITY

Rarely use venery but for health and offspring, never to dulness, weakness, or the injury of your own or another´s peace or reputation.

13. HUMILITY

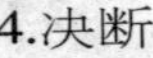
4.决断

应做之事要决然去做;定做之事就必然做成。

5.勤俭

为己为人切勿铺张浪费。

6.勤奋

时不我待,勤于做有益之事;不做任何无益的事。

7.诚恳

勿欺骗害人;欲念要纯正,言谈亦如此。

8.正义

勿以非义冤人,勿玩忽职守。

9.中庸

避免极端,忍为上策。

10.清洁

身体、服饰与居所之不洁均不可忍受。

11.宁静

Imitate Jesus and Socrates.

A Quaker friend told Franklin that he, Benjamin, was generally considered proud, so Benjamin put in the Humility touch as an afterthought. The amusing part is the sort of humility it displays. 'Imitate Jesus and Socrates,' and mind you don't outshine either of these two. One can just imagine Socrates and Alcibiades* roaring in their cups over Philadelphian Benjamin, and Jesus looking at him a little puzzled, and murmuring: 'Aren't you wise in your own conceit, Ben?'

'Henceforth be masterless,' retorts Ben. 'Be ye each one his own master unto himself, and don't let even the Lord put His spoke in.' 'Each man his own master' is but a puffing up of masterlessness.

Well, the first of Americans practised this enticing list with assiduity, setting a national example. He had the virtues in columns, and gave himself good and bad marks according as he thought his behaviour deserved. Pity these condusct charts are lost to us. He only remarks that Order was his stumbling block. He could not learn to be neat and tidy.

Isn't it nice to have nothing worse to confess?

He was a little model, was Benjamin. Doctor Franklin. Snuff-coloured little

勿为琐事或难免事故所烦恼。

12.贞节

性交偶尔为之,只为健康与生育,勿勉强,勿损健康,勿伤自己或他人的宁静或名誉。

13.谦卑

言行师从耶稣和苏格拉底。

一位教友派的教徒对富兰克林说,人们普遍认为他本杰明自傲,于是本杰明又在他的训诫后补上了"谦卑"这一条。最令人发噱的是他所谓的谦卑。"言行师从耶稣和苏格拉底",请注意,不许超越这两位。你可以想像得出苏格拉底和阿西比亚德[前450-前404,雅典政治家和将军,此人出现在柏拉图的《会饮》中,与苏格拉底争论爱情]醉酒以后冲费城的本杰明狂吼的情景,可以想像耶稣迷惑不解地看着本杰明叨念:"本,你这样自负可算明智?"

"所以,不要主人,"本杰明反驳说,"做你自己的主人,连主都不能干涉你的计划。""做自己的主人"不过是拒绝主人的一种更为厉害的说法。

man! Immortal soul and all!

The immortal soul part was a sort of cheap insurance policy.

Benjamin had no concern, really, with the immortal soul. He was too busy with social man.

(1) He swept and lighted the streets of young Philadelphia.

(2) He invented electrical appliances.

(3) He was the centre of a moralizing club in Philadelphia, and he wrote the moral humorisms of Poor Richard.

(4) He was a member of all the important councils of Philadelphia, and then of the American colonies.

(5) He won the cause of American Independence at the French Court, and was the economic father of the United States.

Now what more can you want of a man? And yet he is *infra dig.* Even in Philadelphia.

I admire him. I admire his sturdy courage first of all, then his sagacity, then his glimpsing into the thunders of electricity, then his common-sense humour. All the qualities of a great man, and never more than a great citizen. Middle-sized, sturdy,

美国人中的第一人努力按照这套迷人的训诫行事，为整个民族树立了榜样。他把美德分门别类一一开列，自我评判一番，给自己打了或好或坏的得分。可惜那些操行示范表早已不复存在了。他倒是说过“秩序”成了他的绊脚石。他从未学会整洁。

最好别再坦白出什么更糟的事来。

他，本杰明·富兰克林博士是一个小小的榜样。这黄褐脸膛的小个子！不朽的灵魂！

这“不朽的灵魂”之说是某种廉价的保险手段。

本杰明的确不在乎什么灵魂不朽。他太忙于对付尘世中的人了。

① 他为刚刚诞生的费城扫清街道，装上路灯。

② 他发明了电器。

③ 他是费城道德俱乐部的中心人物，他还写了《格言历书》这部道德幽默集。

④ 他是费城所有重要理事会的成员，后来又成为统治美国殖民地的政府成员。

snuff-coloured Doctor Franklin, one of the soundest citizens that ever trod or 'used venery'.

I do not like him.

And, by the way, I always thought books of Venery* were about hunting deer.

There is a certain earnest naiveté about him. Like a child. And like a little old man. He has again become as a little child, always as wise as his grandfather, or wiser.

Perhaps, as I say, the most complete citizen that ever 'used venery'.

Printer, philosopher, scientist, author and patriot ,impeccable husband and citizen, why isn't he an archetype?

Pioneer, Oh Pioneers! Benjamin was one of the greatest pioneers of the United States. Yet we just can't do with him.

What's wrong with him then? Or what's wrong with us?

I can remember, when I was a little boy, my father used to buy a scrubby yearly almanac with the sun and moon and stars on the cover. And it used to prophesy bloodshed and famine. But also crammed in corners it had little anecdotes and humorisms, with a moral tag. And I used to have my little priggish laugh at the woman

⑤ 他在法国朝廷上为美国争得了独立。他还是美利坚合众国的经济之父。

对于一个人你还能有什么更多的要求呢?可是他是个有失尊严的人,即使是在费城亦是如此。

我钦佩他,首先钦佩他顽强的勇气,然后是他的洞察力,他对雷电的发现以及他那令人易于接受的幽默情调。他有一个伟人的全部特质,同时他又是一位伟大的公民。中等身材,健壮,黄褐色的脸膛儿,富兰克林博士是一位身体极健壮的人,他也性交,或者说"使用性"。

我不喜欢他。

随便提一下,我总以为"Venery"[英文中"性欲"和"狩猎"都是"Venery"。富兰克林的原文是"use venery"]方面的书是有关狩猎的。

他有点孩子气。他像个孩子,是个老小孩。他像个孩子,像他的祖父一样聪明,甚至比祖父更聪明。

我或许可以说他是最会"使用性"的公民。

出版家,哲学家,科学家,作家和监护人,毫无瑕疵的丈夫和公民,可

who counted her chickens before they were hatched and so forth, and I was convinced that honesty was the best policy, also a little priggishly. The author of these bits was Poor Richard, and Poor Richard was Benjamin Franklin, writing in Philadelphia well over a hundred years before.

And probably I haven't got over those Poor Richard tags yet. I rankle still with them. They are thorns in young flesh.

Because, although I still believe that honesty is the best policy, I dislike policy altogether; though it is just as well not to count your chickens before they are hatched, it's still more hateful to count them with gloating when they are hatched. It has taken me many years and countless smarts to get out of that barbed wire moral enclosure that Poor Richard rigged up. Here am I now in tatters and scratched to ribbons, sitting in the middle of Benjamin's America looking at the barbed wire, and the fat sheep crawling under the fence to get fat outside, and the watch-dogs yelling at the gate lest by chance anyone should get out by the proper exit. Oh America! Oh Benjamin! And I just utter a long loud curse against Benjamin and the American corral.

Moral America! Most moral Benjamin. Sound, satisfied Ben!

是他为什么不能成为一个模范呢?

开拓者,啊,开拓者!本杰明是美利坚合众国最伟大的开拓者之一。可我们就是不待见他。

他有什么错?或者说我们有什么错?

我还记得,我小时候我父亲年年给我买一本小历书,封皮上画着太阳、月亮和星星。这历书可以预告天灾人祸。在书角上也写满了小故事和幽默词句,还有一条道德语录。我曾一本正经地讥笑过那些"蛋未孵就数鸡"的女人,我正儿八经地相信"诚实是上策"。我知道这些格言是《格言历书》上来的,而《格言历书》的作者就是本杰明·富兰克林,他是一百多年前在费城写的这本书。

或许我仍然无法超越那些格言语录。我仍然停留在那个水平上。它们像嫩肉中的刺儿。

尽管我仍然相信"诚实是上策",但我不喜欢任何策略;"蛋未孵就数鸡"固然不好,可孵出之后洋洋自得地数来数去更可恶。为了逃出《格言历书》这条带刺的道德铁丝网,我奋斗了好多年,绞尽了脑汁。如今我衣

He had to go to the frontiers of his State to settle some disturbance among the Indians. On this occasion he writes:

We found that they had made a great bonfire in the middle of the square; they were all drunk, men and women quarrelling and fighting. Their dark-coloured bodies, half-naked, seen only by the gloomy light of the bonfire, running after and beating one another with fire-brands, accompanied by their horrid yellings, formed a scene the most resembling our ideas of hell that could be well imagined. There was no appeasing the tumult, and we retired to our lodging. At midnight a number of them came thundering at our door, demanding more rum, of which we took no noitce.

The next day, sensible they had misbehaved in giving us that disturbance, they sent three of their counsellors to make their apology. The orator acknowledged the fault, but laid it upon the rum, and then endeavoured to excuse the rum by saying: 'The Great Spirit, who made all things, made everything for some use; and whatever he designed anything for, that use it should always be put to. Now, when he had made the rum, he said: "Let this be for the Indians to get drunk with." And it must be so.'

衫褴褛坐在本杰明的美国，看着那带刺的铁丝网，看着铁丝网下肥硕的羊在爬行，看门狗正冲着门口狂吠，防止任何人从这里逃出去。哦，美国！啊，本杰明！我对本杰明和美国的阵线发出大声的诅咒。

道德的美国！极讲道德的本杰明。健康心满意足的本！

他到过边界线去调解印第安人的纠纷，并写下了下面的话：

我们发现他们在广场中央燃起了巨大的篝火；他们都喝醉了，男男女女在吵骂、在打斗。透过昏暗的火光可见到他们半裸的黑色躯体，他们手举火棍追逐、厮打，不时发出可怕的吼叫，那情景极像我们想像中的地狱。这种混乱场面无法平息，我们就回到了自己的住处。半夜里他们一帮人来使劲擂我们的门要酒喝，对此我们不予理睬。

翌日，他们觉出自己做了错事，就派了几位律师来道歉。那雄辩家认了错，但把这一切责任都归咎于酒。他试图为酒开脱责任说：上帝创造了一切，物尽其才；不管他设计出什么，都应该使用才是。他制造了酒，他说："让它去醉倒印第安人吧。"就该如此。

And, indeed, if it be the design of Providence to extirpate these savages in order to make room for the cultivators of the earth, it seems not improbable that rum may be the appointed means. It has already annihilated all the tribes who formerly inhabited all the seacoast...

This, from the good doctor with such suave complacency, is a little disenchanting. Almost too good to be true.

But there you are! The barbed wire fence. 'Extirpate these savages in order to make room for the cultivators of the earth.' Oh, Benjamin Franklin! He even 'used venery' as a cultivator of seed.

Cultivate the earth, ye gods! The Indians did that, as much as they needed. And they left off there. Who built Chicago? Who cultivated the earth until it spawned Pittsburgh, Pa?

The moral issue! Just look at it! Cultivation included. If it's a mere choice of Kultur or cultivation, I give it up.

Which brings us right back to our question, what's wrong with Benjamin, that we can't stand him? Or else, what's wrong with us, that we find fault with such a paragon?

的确，如果上帝为了给垦荒者腾地方而根除野蛮人的话，似乎酒就是最切实际的办法。酒已经毁灭了从前居住在沿海的部落……

这位温和而自傲的优秀博士讲的这番话可有点让人清醒了。

可这带刺的樊篱仍存在！“为了给垦荒者腾地方而根除野蛮人。”啊，本杰明·富兰克林！他这位播种者还“使用性”呢。

垦荒，上帝啊！印第安人根据自己的需要这样做过。然后他们离开了那里。谁建成了芝加哥？是谁开垦了直到匹兹堡的土地？

道德问题！看看吧！开垦问题包括其中。如果这只是对文明或耕作的选择，就算了。

又回到我们的话题上了，本杰明哪一点错误令我们无法忍受？或者说，我们出了什么毛病要挑这位楷模的毛病？

人是有道德的动物。那好。我是一个道德的动物，我仍会是这样的人。我不会像本杰明期望的那样变成一个善良的小机器。“这样好。那样不好。转动一下这把小手柄，让这善良的龙头流溢，”本杰明这样说，所有

Man is a moral animal. All right. I am a moral animal. And I´m going to remain such. I´m not going to be turned into a virtuous little automaton as Benjamin would have me. 'This is good, that is bad. Turn the little handle and let the good tap flow.' saith Benjamin, and all America with him. 'But first of all extirpate those savages who are always turning on the bad tap.'

I am a moral animal. But I am not a moral machinte. I don´t work with a little set of handles or levers. The Temperance-silence-order-resolution-frugality-industry-sincerity-justice-moderation-cleanliness-tranquillity-chastity-humility keyboard is not going to get me going. I´m really not just an automatic piano with a moral Benjamin getting tunes out of me.

Here´s my creed, against Benjamin´s. This is what I believe:

'That I am I.'

'That my soul is a dark forest.'

'That my known self will never be more than a little clearing in the forest.'

'That gods, strange gods, come forth from the forest into the clearing of my known self, and then go back.'

'That I must have the courage to let them come and go.'

的美国人都站在他的一边，"但是首先要根除那些转动丑恶龙头的野蛮人。"

我是一个道德的动物。可我不是一台道德的机器。我并非靠一套手柄或杠杆工作。这套节制—沉默—秩序—决断—勤俭—勤奋—诚恳—正义—中庸—清洁—宁静—贞节—谦卑的键盘无法指挥我。我不是一台自动钢琴，让道德的本杰明弹出曲子来。

这是我反对本杰明的纲领。这是我的信仰：

"我就是我。"

"我的灵魂是一座幽深的森林。"

"我的已知自我不过是森林中的一小块空地。"

"神，陌生的神从森林中出来，来到林中空地上——我的已知自我中，然后又踱回去。"

"我必须有勇气任他们来去。"

"我绝不让人类将任何东西强加于我，但我永远会承认并服从我心中和其他男女心中的神。"

'That I will never let mankind put anything over me, but that I will try always to recognize, and submit to the gods in me and the gods in other men and women.'

There is my creed. He who runs may read. He who prefers to crawl, or to go by gasoline, can call it rot.

Then for a 'list'. It is rather fun to play at Benjamin.

1. TEMPERANCE

Eat and carouse with Bacchus, or munch dry bread with Jesus, but don't sit down without one of the gods.

2. SILENCE

Be still when you have nothing to say; when genuine passion moves you, say what you've got to say, and say it hot.

3. ORDER

Know that you are responsible to the gods inside you and to the men in whom the gods are manifest. Recognize your superiors and your inferiors, according to the gods. This is the root of all order.

4. RESOLUTION

Resolve to abide by your own deepest promptings, and to sacrifice the smaller

这是我的信条。会跑的人都能读懂[此句是对《旧约·哈巴谷书》的错引。人们经常以讹传讹。原文是"that he may run that readeth"]。那些愿意爬行或靠机车行走的人可以称它是废话。

我列出一个单子，与本杰明开开玩笑。

1.节制

与酒神巴克斯一起痛饮欢宴，与耶稣一起大吃干面包，与神同座。

2.沉默

无话可说时保持缄默；一旦真正的激情使你冲动，就不失时机地发表你的看法。

3.秩序

你对你心中的神或那些体现出神的灵气的人负有责任。按照神的标准分辨比你优越或低劣的人。这是一切秩序的根本。

4.决断

应该遵从你内心深处的冲动，敢于为伟大牺牲渺小。当你必须杀戮

thing to the greater. Kill when you must, andbe killed the same: the must coming from the gods inside you, or from the men in whom you recognize the Holy Ghost.

5. FRUGALITY

Demand nothing; accept what you see fit. Don't waste your pride or squander your emotion.

6. INDUSTRY

Lose no time with ideals; serve the Holy Ghost; never serve mankind.

7. SINCERITY

To be sincers is to remember that I am I, and that the other man is not me.

8. JUSTICE

The only justice is to follow the sincere intuition of the soul, angry or gentle. Anger is just, and pity is just, but judgement is never just.

9. MODERATION

Beware of absolutes. There are many gods.

10.CLEANLINESS

Don't be too clean. It impoverishes the blood.

11. TRANQUILLITY

或自戕时应敢作敢为：这个“必须”来自你内心深处的神或来自那些人——你在他们身上发现了神圣的天公。

5.勤俭

无所求；但接受应该得的东西。莫浪费你的骄傲，莫使感情蹉跎。

6.勤奋

莫想入非非；为上帝服务而不是服务于人类。

7.诚恳

诚恳即是记住“我就是我，他人非我”。

8.正义

惟一的正义就是遵从灵魂的真切直觉，无论愤懑还是温柔。愤懑是合理的，怜悯是合理的，但审判永远是不合理的。

9.中庸

意识到神的存在。有许多神存在。

10.清洁

勿过分清洁，它反会使血液枯竭。

The soul has many motions, many gods come and go. Try and find your deepest issue, in every confusion, and abide by that. Obey the man in whom you recognize the Holy Ghost; command when you honour comes to command.

12. CHASTITY

Never 'use' venery at all. Follow your passional impulse, if it be answered in the other being, but never have any motive in mind, neither offspring nor health nor even pleasure, nor even service. Only know that 'venery' is of the great gods. An offering-up of yourself to the very great gods, the dark ones, and nothing else.

13. HUMILITY

See all men and women according to the Holy Ghost that is within them. Never yield before the barren.

There's my list. I have been trying dimly to realize it for a long time, and only America and old Benjamin have at last goaded me into trying to formulate it.

And now I, at least, know why I can't stand Benjamin. He tries to take away my wholeness and my dark forest, my freedom. For how can any man be free, without an illimitable background? And Benjamin tries to shove me into a barbed wire paddock and make me grow potatoes or Chicagoes.

11.宁静

灵魂在不停地运动，众多的神在这里穿梭。试图在混乱中发现你最深刻的结论并固守它。要服从那些人——你在他们身上发现了神圣的天公；一旦有幸做统帅就应当去做。

12.贞节

切勿"使用"性。要依从你的激情冲动，看它是否得到另一个生命的回应；但切勿意淫，勿思虑什么子孙、健康，甚至快感或雌雄交合。只应知道，"性交"是伟大的神，是把你自己献给伟大的神——那黑暗的东西，除此之外别无他物。

13.谦卑

看待所有的男女，要根据他们心中的神灵来断定。对心中荒芜者不可屈服。

这就是我的信条。我长久以来一直试图将其付诸实施，是美国和老本杰明迫使我系统地阐明这些。

And how can I be free, without gods that come and go? But Benjamin won't let anything exist except my useful fellow men, and I'm sick of them; as for his Godhead, his Providence, He is Head of nothing except a vast heavenly store that keeps every imaginable line of goods, from victrolas to cat-o'-nine tails.

And how can any man be free without a soul of his own, that he believes in and won't sell at any price? But Benjamin doesn't let me have a soul of my own. He says I am nothing but a servant of mankind-galley -slave I call it -and if I don't get my wages here below -that is,if Mr Pierpont Morgan or Mr Nosey Hebrew or the grand United States Government, the great us, us or SOMEOFUS, manages to scoop in my bit, along with their lump-why, never mind, I shall get my wages HEREAFTER.

Oh Benjamin! Oh Binjum! You do not suck me in any longer.

And why, oh why should the snuff-coloured little trap have wanted to take us all in? Why did he do it?

Out of sheer human cussedness, in the first place. We do all like to get things inside a barbed wire corral. Especially our fellow men. We love to round them up inside the barbed wire enclosure of FREEDOM, and make'em work, '*Work, you free*

至少现在我知道我为何不能忍受本杰明了。他试图夺去我的完整性、我那黑色的森林和我的自由。谁能无条件地获得自由呢?本杰明试图把我推进带刺的铁丝围场中,让我种土豆或建设芝加哥这样的城市。

可是没有神的出入我何以自由呢? 可是本杰明除了我那些可利用的同胞们以外不让任何他人存在,而对这些人我厌烦透了。至于说他的上帝,他的天公,他掌管的只是一座巨大的天堂店铺,那里什么物件都有,从手摇留声机到九尾鞭。

一个人如果没有他相信的无价的灵魂,他怎么能自由呢?可本杰明不让我有我自己的灵魂。他说我不过是人类的仆人——我称之为苦役。如果我得不到我的工资——就是说,如果皮阿旁特·摩尔根[约翰·皮阿旁特·摩尔根(1837—1913)及其子小摩尔根(1867—1943)都是美国银行家]先生或大鼻子希伯莱[这个词是对富有的犹太人的讽刺语]先生或大美国政府、巨大的美国或我们当中的一些人侵吞了我的那一份,我并不在乎,我以后还会得到我的工资。

哦,本杰明! 本杰明! 你不会控制我太久的。

可是为什么,哦,为什么那黄褐色的小圈套欲把我们全部套进去?他

jewel, WORK! 'shouts the liberator, cracking his whip. Benjamin, I will not work. I do not choose to be a free democrat. I am absolutely a servant of my own Holy Ghost.

Sheer cussedness! But there was as well the salt of a subtler purpose. Benjamin was just in his eyeholes–to use an English vulgarism, meaning he was just delighted–when he was at Paris judiciously milking money out of the French monarchy for the overthrow of all monarchy. If you want to ride your horse to somewhere you must put a bit in his mouth. And Benjamin wanted to ride his horse so that it would upset the whole apple–cart of the old masters. He wanted the whole European apple–cart upset. So he had to put a strong bit in the mouth of his ass.

'Henceforth be masterless.'

That is, he had to break–in the human ass completely, so that much more might be broken, in the long run. For the moment it was the British Government that had to have a hole knocked in it. The first real hole it ever had: the breach of the American rebellion.

Benjamin, in his sagacity, knew that the breaking of the old world was a long process. In the depths of his own underconsciousness he hated England, he hated

为什么要这样?

首先,这纯粹出于人的劣根性。我们都喜欢把东西圈在一个带刺的网中。我们的同胞更是如此。我们喜欢用自由这带刺的网把他们封锁起来并迫使他们在围场中工作。“干吧,你这自由的宝贝儿,干!”那救世主挥着鞭子说。本杰明,我不干。我不乐意做自由的民主之人。我是我自己上帝的仆人。

纯粹的劣根性!当然还有细小的原因。当本杰明在巴黎以合法的手段从法国君主制朝廷那里谋到金钱去推翻一切君主制时，他的确太高兴了[《独立宣言》发表后,富兰克林以第一个美国的特使身份被派到法国路易十六的朝廷游说。法国政府支持十三个独立的州反对英国。1778 法国和西班牙签署协议,向美国派军队和军舰,给予经济援助]。如果你要骑马到什么地方,你就得在它嘴上勒嚼子。本杰明要骑他的马,于是他就破坏了旧主子的计划。他要让整个欧洲乱营。因此他必须给他的毛驴勒上一个结实的嚼子才行。

“从此不再被统治。”

这就是说,他得彻底驯服人类这头驴子,从而从长远的观点看,更多

Europe, he hated the whole corpus of the European being. He wanted to be American. But you can't change your nature and mode of consciousness like changing your shoes. It is a gradual shedding. Years must go by, and centuries must elapse before you have finished. Like a son escaping from the domination of his parents. The escape is not just one rupture. It is a long and half-secret process.

So with the American. He was a European when he first went over the Atlantic. He is in the main a recreant European still. From Benjamin Franklin to Woodrow Wilson may be a long stride, but it is a stride along the same road. There is no new road. The same old road, become dreary and futile. Theoretic and materialistic.

Why then did Benjamin set up this dummy of a perfect citizen as a pattern to America? Of course, he did it in perfect good faith, as far as he knew. He thought it simply was the true ideal. But what we think we do is not very important. We never really know what we are doing. Either we are materialistic instruments, like Benjamin, or we move in the gesture of creation, from our deepest self, usually unconscious. We are only the actors, we are never wholly the authors of our own deeds or works. It is the author, the unknown inside us or outside us. The best we can do is to try to hold ourselves in unison with the deeps which are inside us. And the worst

的东西将会被破坏掉。英国政府需要被砸破一个洞,它真被砸开了一个洞:这就是美国造反,分离了出去。

精明的本杰明知道,打破旧的世界是一个长久的过程。他的潜意识是仇视英国和欧洲的,他仇视欧洲这具僵尸。他想成为一个美国人。可改变你的本性和思维方式并不像换一双鞋那么简单。这是一个渐进的过程,需要好多年、好几个世纪才能完成。这就如同一个儿子要摆脱父母的管制一样。它并非一个断裂就能了事。它是一个长久而又有点秘密的过程。

美国的情况正是如此。他刚漂洋过海时是一个欧洲人,他仍是一个怯懦的欧洲人。从本杰明·富兰克林到伍德罗·威尔逊可能是很长的一步,可这么长的路程并未脱离旧的轨道。没有新的道路。那久也未变的路变得乏味而无望,是一条虚虚实实的路。

为什么本杰明·富兰克林成了标准的美国公民模式?当然就他自己而言,他自以为自己表现十分真诚。他认为这不过是一个真正的理想。可是,我们怎么看自己的所作所为非至关紧要。我们从不真正知道我们在

we can do is to try to have things our own way, when we run counter to IT, and in the long run get our knuckles rapped for our presumption.

So Benjamin contriving money out of the Court of France. He was contriving the first steps of the overthrow of all Europe, France included. You can never have a new thing without breaking an old. Europe happens to be the old thing. America, unless the people in America assert themselves too much in opposition to the inner gods, should be the new thing. The new thing is the death of the old. But you can′t cut the throat of an epoch. You′ve got to steal the life from it throught several centuries.

And Benjamin worked for this both directly and indirectly. Directly, at the Court of France, making a small but very dangerous hole in the side of England, through which hole Europe has by now almost bled to death. And indirectly in Philadelphia, setting up this unlovely, snuff-coloured little ideal, or automaton, of a pattern American. The pattern American, this dry, moral, utilitarian little democrat, has done more to ruin the old Europe than any Russian nihilist. He has done it by slow attrition, like a son who has stayed at home and obeyed his parents, all the while silently hating their authority, and silently, in his soul, destroying not only

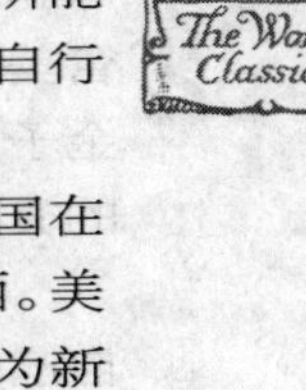

做什么。我们要么当本杰明那样的物质工具，要么按照上帝的旨意听从无意识深处自我的召唤而行动。我们只是执行者，永远不会是自己行动的主人。那未知的主人要么来自我们灵魂深处要么来自外界。我们所能做的就是试图使自己与内心深处的海洋保持一致。否则我们只能是自行其是，走向反面，最终因自以为是而碰得头破血流。

本杰明终于从法兰西朝廷那里谋到了钱，于是他向推翻包括法国在内的整个欧洲迈出了第一步。不破旧就不能立新。欧洲就是旧的东西。美国，如果她的人民不强烈地与自己内心中的神作对的话，她就会成为新生事物。新的诞生宣告着旧的死亡。但是你又无法把时代一刀斩断。因此，你得花几个世纪从旧的那里偷取生命。

本杰明为了这个目的从直接和间接两方面努力过。所谓直接，就是他在法兰西朝廷上狠狠地挖了英国一个墙角，为此欧洲大失血几乎致死。所谓间接，就是他在费城树起了美国式理想和模式，尽管这模式不那么招人喜欢，是那么微不足道。这个模式的美国——冷酷、道德化、功利性十足的民主国家比任何俄国虚无主义都更能毁灭旧欧洲。美国是缓慢

their authority but their whole existence. For the American spiritually stayed at home in Europe. The spiritual home of America was, and still is, Europe. This is the galling bondage, in spite of several billions of heaped-up gold. Tour heaps of gold are only so many muck-heaps, America, and will remain so till you become a reality to yourselves.

All this Americanizing and mechanizing has been for the purpose of overthrowing the past. And now look at America, tangled in her own barbed wire, and mastered by her own machines. Absolutely got down by her own barbed wire of shalt-nots, and shut up fast in her own 'productive' machines like millions of squirrels running in millions of cages. It is just a farce.

Now is your chance, Europe. Now let Hell loose and get your own back, and paddle your own canoe on a new sea, while clever America lies on her muck-heaps of gold, strangled in her own barbed wire of shalt-not ideals and shalt-not moralisms. While she goes out to work like millions of squirrels in millions of cages. Production!

Let Hell loose, and get your own back, Europe!

地做这件事的，就像一个呆在家中服从家长的儿子，默默地仇视着家长的权威，心目中不仅毁灭着家长的权威也毁灭着他们的存在。要知道美国和欧洲在精神上是一家。美国精神上的家过去是现在依然是欧洲。尽管美国有成堆成堆的金子，这令人恼火的枷锁仍摆脱不掉。你那成堆的金子，美国，如果你不能成为你自己的话，你那成堆的金子就只能是成堆的粪土。

一切美国化和机械化一直是为了甩掉过去。现在看看美国吧，她被自己带刺的网缠住，让她自己的机器统治着。她被多个"不许"的刺网缠住，被"生产"机器封锁住，就像成千上万的松鼠关在笼子中奔跑。这纯粹是一个笑话。

现在，欧洲，你的机会到来了。让地狱松弛，从而你找回曾属于你的，把你的独木舟划到新的海洋中——趁聪明的美国正躺在她粪土堆样的金山上，被"不许"的意识和道德刺网死死地缠着；趁她的人民像成千上万的松鼠在成千上万的笼子中干着活儿。生产！

让地狱松弛一下，从而找回曾属于你的吧，欧洲!

CHAPTER 3
Hector St John de Crèvecœur

Crèvecœur was born in France, at Caen, in the year 1735. As a boy he was sent over to England and received part of his education there. He went to Canada as a young man, served for a time with Montcalm in the war against the English, and later passed over into the United States, to become an exuberant American. He married a New England girl, and settled on the frontier. During the period of his 'cultivating the earth' he wrote the *Letters from an American Farmer*, which enjoyed great vogue in their day, in England especially, among the new reformers like Godwin and Tom Paine.

But Crèvecœur was not a mere cultivator of the earth. That was his best stunt, shall we say. He himself was more concerned with a perfect society and his own manipulation thereof, than with growing carrots. Behold him, then, trotthing off impor-

海克特·圣约翰·德·克里夫库尔

[海克特·圣约翰·德·克里夫库尔 (1735—1813) 原名米歇尔·基约姆·让·德·克里夫库尔。法国人，1754—1780年，1783—1790年生活在美国。散文家，农业家。1765年归化美国时用现名，但终老于法国。]

克里夫库尔1735年生于法国的卡城。小时候被送往英国受教育。年轻时去加拿大，在蒙特卡姆将军领导下抗击英军，后移居美国，成为一个非凡的美国人。他娶了一位新英格兰姑娘，在边疆定居下来。他"开垦疆域"期间写下了脍炙人口的《美国农夫信札》。此书风靡一时，特别是在英国，受到了诸如葛德汶和托马斯·潘恩这样的新型改革者的欢迎。

克里夫库尔并非仅仅是一位"垦荒者"。垦荒是他沽名钓誉的一招。其实他更关心一个完美的社会和他自己在这之中所起的作用，而不是种胡萝卜。他竟满怀理想煞有介事地一路风尘赶回法国，把他的农田荒掉、让印第安人点火烧掉，他的妻子流离失所。这事发生在美国独立战争期

tantly and idealistically to France, leaving his farm in the wilds to be burnt by the Indians, and his wife to shift as best she might. This was during the American War of Independence, when the Noble Red Man took to behaving like his own old self. On his return to America, the American Farmer entered into public affairs and into commerce. Again tripping to France, he enjoyed himself as a *littèrateur* Child-of-Nature-sweet-and-pure, was a friend of old Benjamin Franklin in Paris, and quite a favourite with Jean Jacques Rousseau's Madame d'Houdetot,* that literary soul.

Hazlitt, Godwin, Shelley, Coleridge, the English romanticists, were, of course, thrilled by the *Letters from an American Farmer*. A new world, a world of the Noble Savage and Pristine Nature and Paradisal Simplicity and all that gorgeousness that flows out of the unsullied fount of the ink-bottle. Lucky Coleridge, who got no farther than Bristol.* Some of us have gone all the way.

I think this wild and noble America is the thing that I have pined for most ever since I read Fenimore Cooper, as a boy. Now I've got it.

Franklin is the real practical prototype of the American. Crèvecœur is the emotional. To the European, the American is first and foremost a dollar-fiend. We tend to forget the emotional heritage of Hector St John de Crèvecœur. We tend to disbe-

间，那时，高贵的印第安人像他自己以前那样战斗。待他重返美国时，美国的农民已开始参与公共事务和商务。他再次回法国，以一个“美好而纯洁的自然之子”文人身分出现，在巴黎与本杰明·富兰克林交上了朋友并受到让·雅克·卢梭的女人德黄德特伯爵夫人［卢梭钟情于伯爵夫人并向她求爱，但伯爵夫人却青睐他人。伯爵夫人的全名是 Elizabeth de La Live de Bellegarde.］的赏识，伯爵夫人是文学界的灵魂。

哈兹里特、葛德汶、雪莱和柯勒律治这些英国浪漫主义者实在为《美国农夫信札》感到激动。这是一个新世界，这里有高贵的野蛮人，原始的自然和天堂般的纯真，如此美妙的景致都从那未被玷污的笔墨之泉中流溢而出。柯勒律治最远仅到过布里斯托尔港［浪漫诗人柯勒律治曾是布里斯托尔乌托邦运动的中心人物，不少成员都迁居美国，但他却最终退却了］，而我们不少人却一路走了下来。

我想，自从小时候读了费尼莫·库柏的书以后我就十分向往这个野性而崇高的美国了。现在我终于到了美国。

富兰克林的确是美国人的实际样板，而克里夫库尔则是一个感情冲动的样板。在欧洲人看来，美国人首先是个金钱魔鬼。可我们似乎忘了由

lieve, for example, in Woodrow Wilson´s wrung heart and wet hanky. Yet surely these are real enough. Aren´t they?

It wasn´t to be expected that the dry little snuff-coloured Doctor should have it all his own way. The new Americans might use venery for health or offspring, and their time for cultivating potatoes and Chicagoes, but they had got some sap in their veins after all. They had got to get a bit of luscious emotion somewhere.

NATURE.

I wish I could write it larger than that.

NATURE.

Benjamin overlooked NATURE. But the French Crèvecœur spotted it long before Thoreau and Emerson worked it up.* Absolutely the safest thing to get your emotional reactions over is NATURE.

Crèvecœur´s *Letters* are written in a spirit of touching simplicity, almost better than Chateaubriand. You´d think neither of them would ever know how many beans make five. This American Farmer tells of the joys of creating a home in the wilderness, and of cultivating the virgin soil. Poor virgin, prostituted from the very start.

The Farmer had an Amiable Spouse and an Infant Son, his progeny. He took

海克特·圣约翰·德·克里夫库尔所代表的感情传统。比如，我们都爱怀疑伍德罗·威尔逊总统痛苦的心和他哭湿的手帕。可事实上这是千真万确的，不是吗？

人们并非期望那冷酷矮小褐黄色脸膛儿的富兰克林博士用他的方式统治一切。新一代美国人可以将性欲用于促进身体健康也可以用于繁殖，可以把他们的时间用来种土豆也可以用来建设芝加哥之类的城市。他们的血液中充满了活力。他们还应该从某个地方获得丰富的情感才是。

自然。

我希望我把它写得更大一些。

自然。

本杰明忽视了自然。可是法国人克里夫库尔却先于梭罗和爱默森更早地找到了它的位置[梭罗与爱默森同是超验主义者，亦是莫逆。梭罗曾住在瓦尔登湖畔爱默森的领地达两年之久，写出了著名的随笔《瓦尔登湖或林中生活》(1854)。爱默森则写出了《自然》(1836)和《随笔》(1-2，1841—1844)]。能绝对准确战胜你情绪反应的东西就是自然。

the Infant Son–who enjoys no other name than this–

What is thy name?

I have no name.

I am the Infant Son–

to the fields with him, and seated the same I. S. on the shafts of the plough whilst he, the American Farmer, ploughed the potato patch. He also, the A.F., helped his Neighbours, whom no doubt he loved as himself, to build a barn, and they laboured together in the Innocent Simplicity of one of Nature's Communities. Meanwhile the Amiable Spouse, who likewise in Blakean simplicity has No Name, cooked the dough–nuts or the pie, though these are not mentioned. No doubt she was a deep–breasted daughter of America, though she may equally well have been a flat–bosomed Methodist. She would have been an Amiable Spouse in either case, and the American Farmer asked no more. I don't know whether her name was Lizzie or A-hoolibah, and probably Crèvecœur didn't. Spouse was enough for him. 'Spouse, hand me the carving knife.'

The Infant Son developed into Healthy Offspring as more appeared: no doubt Crèvecœur had used venery as directed. And so these Children of Nature toiled in

克里夫库尔的《信札》写得简洁而生动，几乎胜过夏多布里昂。你会以为他们二人谁也不知道精明为何物。这位美国农夫在书中讲述着在旷野中成家立业的乐趣，讲着开垦处女地的欢乐。可怜的处女地，从此就当上了娼妓。

这位农夫有一位温柔的妻子和儿子。他的儿子享有了这样的称呼：

你叫什么名字？

我没有姓名。

我是婴儿……

他把儿子带到田野中，把他放在犁扶手上，然后他拉着犁耕耘土豆垄。这位和蔼的父亲还乐于助人，像爱自己一样爱邻居。他帮他们建谷仓，大家共同在一个纯真的自然群体中劳动生息。与此同时，那温柔的妻子(她同样也没有名字) 肯定在家炸面饼圈或做馅饼——当然这些并未在书中提到。毫无疑问，她是个胸怀宽阔的美国的女儿。但是她也许会是一位心胸狭窄墨守成规的卫理会成员。无论她是哪一种人，她都会成为一个温柔

the Wilds at Simple Toil with a little Honest Sweat now and then. You have the complete picture, dear reader. The American Farmer made his own Family Picture, and it is still on view. Of course the Amiable Spouse put on her best apron to be *Im Bild*, for all the world to see and admire.

I used to admire my head off:before I tiptoed into the Wilds and saw the shacks of the Homesteaders. Particularly the Amiable Spouse, poor thing. No wonder she never sang the song of Simple Toil in the Innocent Wilds. Poor haggard drudge, like a ghost wailing in the wilderness, nine times out of ten.

Hector St John, you have lied to me. You lied even more scurrilously to yourself. Hector St John, you are an emotional liar.

Jean Jacques, Bernardin de St Pierre, Chateaubriand, exquisite Francois Le Vaillant,* you lying little lot, with your Nature-Sweet-and-Pure! Marie Antoinette got her head off for playing dairy-maid, and nobody even dusted the seats of your pants, till now, for all the lies you put over us.

But Crèvecœur was an artist as well as a liar, otherwise we would not have bothered with him. He wanted to put NATURE in his pocket, as Benjamin put the Human Being. Between them, they wanted the whole scheme of things in their pock-

的妻子，而这位美国农夫是不会有更多的要求的。我不知道，也许她的名字是莉兹或者阿赫利巴赫，很可能克里夫库尔也不知道。伴侣，对他来说就够了。“老伴儿，把刀子递给我。”

那婴孩长得愈来愈健康，看来毫无疑问克里夫库尔是正确地利用了性欲。这些自然之子从此辛苦地流着诚实的汗水在这块荒原上耕耘。亲爱的读者，你可以看到一幅完整的图景。这位美国农夫绘出了他自己的家庭图画，现在它依旧历历在目。当然了，他那温顺的伴侣也穿上了最漂亮的围裙，装扮成画中人，让全世界的人看，让大家都艳羡。

我曾对此仰慕已极。我曾走进荒野中，看到过那里的简陋小木屋。他那温柔的妻子真够可怜的。怪不得她在那纯洁的荒原中从未唱起过耕耘的歌谣。这可怜憔悴的苦人儿，几乎总像一个幽灵一样在荒野中嚎叫。

海克特·圣约翰，你对我撒了谎。你甚至很下作地向你自己撒谎。海克特·圣约翰，你是一个感情冲动的骗子。

让·雅克·卢梭、波拿丁·德·圣皮埃尔、夏多布里昂和高雅的弗兰索瓦·勒·瓦扬[F. le Vaillant(1753—1824)旅行家、鸟类学家，在非洲和美洲自然研究方面著述颇丰]，你们这些骗子，侈谈什么美好而纯洁的自然！路易十六的王后玛丽·安

ets, and the things themselves as well. Once you've got the scheme of things in your pocket, you can do as you like with it, even make money out of it, if you can't find in your heart to destroy it, as was your first intention. So H. St J. de C. tried to put Nature-Sweet-and-Pure in his pocket. But nature wasn't having any, she poked her head out and baa-ed.

This Nature-sweet-and-pure business is only another effort at intellectualizing. Just an attempt to make all nature succumb to a few laws of the human mind. The sweet-and-pure sort of laws. Nature seemed to be behaving quite nicely, for a while. She has left off.

That's why you get the purest intellectuals in a Garden Suburb or a Brook Farm experiment.* You bet, Robinson Grusoe was a high-brow of high-brows.

You can idealize or intellectualize. Or, on the contrary, you can let the dark soul in you see for itself. An artist usually intellectualizes on top, and his dark under-consciousness goes on contradicting him beneath. This is almost laughably the case with most American artists. Crèvecœur is the first example. He is something of an artist, Franklin isn't anything.

Crèvecœur the idealist puts over us a lot of stuff about nature and the noble

托奈蒂因装扮挤奶女工而丧了命[这位王后于1793年被国王断头。她曾在自己宫里开辟了一片农场，盖起茅草屋、马厩和谷仓，时而亲自喂鸡、挤牛奶]，现在，没有人为你掸去裤子上的灰尘，因为你对我们撒了谎。

但是克里夫库尔不仅是个骗子，他还是个艺术家，否则我们就不必找他的麻烦了。他想把自然装入他的衣袋，就像本杰明·富兰克林要把人类装入他的衣袋一样。这两个人要把一切从内容到形式装入他们的口袋。一旦你把什么装入了你的口袋，你就可以对它为所欲为，甚至可以用它来赚钱。海克特·圣约翰·德·克里夫库尔试图把美好而纯洁的自然装入自己的腰包。可自然却一无所得，于是它大叫着钻出来。

这所谓美好而纯洁的自然之说不过是一种把自然智识化的努力。就是要让自然屈服于人的几条法律。真是美好而纯洁的法律。大自然似乎一时间表现得美好起来，可不久就不辞而别了。

你就是这样在一处花园城郊或布鲁克农场的试验中看到了最纯洁的知识分子 [英国国会秘书霍华德爵士提出了建设绿色城郊的设想，1902年出版了《明日花园城》一书具体阐述其理念。随后英国开始花园城市的建设，开"花园城镇"、"城市规划"、"卫星城"和"城市绿化带"之先河。美国作家霍桑等人于1841—1847年间在麻省的布鲁克农场进行过类似的实

savage and the innocence of toil, etc., etc. Blarney! But Crèvecœur the artist gives us glimpses of actual nature, not writ large.

Curious that his vision sees only the lowest forms of natural life. Insects, snakes and birds he glimpses in their own mystery, their own pristine being. And straightway gives the lie to Innocent Nature.

'I am astonished to see,' he writes quite early in the *Letters*, 'that nothing exists but what has its enemy, one species pursue and live upon the other: unfortunately our king-birds are the destroyers of those industrious insects [the bees]; but on the other hand, these birds preserve our fields from the depredation of crows, which they pursue on the wing with great vigilance and astonishing dexterity.'

This is a sad blow to the sweet-and-pureness of Nature. But it is the voice of the artist in contrast to the voice of the ideal turtle. It is the rudimentary American vision. The glimpsing of the king-birds in winged hostility and pride is no doubt the aboriginal Indian vision carrying over. The Eagle symbol in human consciousness. Dark, swinging wings of hawkbeaked destiny, that one cannot help but feel, beating here above the wild centre of America. You look round in vain for the 'One being Who made all things, and governs the world by His Providence'.

验。这个实验被认为是与梭罗在瓦尔登湖的生活同样重要的实验，且这项实验的参加者众多，均为文人，实验目的是开创一种绿色和谐的社区生活]。你敢打赌，鲁滨孙这人是上等人中的上等人。

你可以使一切理想化、智识化。否则你就让你那黑暗的灵魂自行其是吧。一位艺术家，往往是他的头脑智识化了，可他黑暗的潜意识却截然相反，与他作对。这显得可笑，可这却是大多数美国艺术家的境况。克里夫库尔即是第一个例子。他还算得上是位艺术家，而富兰克林却微不足道。

克里夫库尔这个理想主义者对我们大谈自然、高贵的野蛮人和辛勤、纯洁云云，全是花言巧语！但是作为一个艺术家，他却为我们提供了对自然的真实窥视，毫无夸张之嫌。

令人感到奇怪的是，他只看到了自然生活的低级形式。昆虫、蛇和鸟儿在他看来富有其自己的神秘性，具有它们自己的原生态。随之他坦率地赋予自然以“纯洁”的假象。

他在《信札》中写道：“我惊奇地发现，什么都有自己的敌手。只有有敌手的东西才能生存。一个物种靠追逐和依赖另一个物种才能生存：不

'One species pursue and live upon another.'

Reconcile the two statements if you like. But, in America, act on Crèvecœur's observation.

The horse, however, says Hector, is the friend of man, and man is the friend of the horse. But then we leave the horse no choice. And I don't see much *friend*, exactly, in my sly old Indian pony, though he is quite a decent old bird.

Man, too,says Hector, is the friend of man. Whereupon the Indians burnt his farm; so he refrains from mentioning it in the *Letters*, for fear of invalidating his premises.

Some great hornets have fixed their nest on the ceiling of the living-room of the American Farmer, and these tigerstriped animals fly round the heads of the Healthy Offspring and the Amiable Spouse, to the gratification of the American Farmer. He liked their buzz and their tiger waspishness. Also, on the utilitarian plane, they kept the house free of flies. So Hector says. Therefore Benjamin would have approved. But of the feelings, of the Amiable S., on this matter, we are not told, and after all, it was she who had to make the jam.

Another anecdote. Swallows built their nest on the veranda of the American

幸的是,我们的食虫鸟是那些勤劳的昆虫(如蜂)的毁灭者;但从另一方面看,这些鸟又在保护我们的田野不受乌鸦的侵犯,它们追逐起乌鸦来显得十分机敏。"

这段描写可算是对"美好而纯洁的大自然"的一个不幸的打击。这也是一个艺术家与一个理想主义者在唱反调。这是美国人的基本看法。而把食虫鸟看成是虎视眈眈傲慢的敌人,这无疑是受了印第安土著人的影响。那是人心目中鹰的象征:黑暗、钩子嘴、展翅飞翔,人无法不感知到它的命运。这鹰就在美洲的荒原上盘旋。在此,你要环顾四周寻找"那创造一切并以神力统治世界的人"只能是枉然。

"一个物种靠追逐并依赖另一个物种才能生存。"

你尽可以将这两个论点进行调和。但是在美国,须以克里夫库尔的观察为准。

不过,海克特说马是人的朋友,人亦是马的朋友。可这样的话,我们就让马别无选择了。我的确无法从我那匹狡猾的印第安小红马身上看出多少朋友的影子来,别看他是个体面的老马。

人,海克特还说,也是人的朋友。可印第安人却烧了他的农场。于是

Farm. Wrens took a fancy to the nest of the swallows. They pugnaciously (I like the word pugnaciously, it is so American) attacked the harbingers of spring, and drove them away from their nice adobe nest. The swallows returned upon opportunity. But the wrens, coming home, violently drove them forth again. Which continued until the gentle swallows patiently set about to build another nest, while the wrens sat in triumph in the usurped home. The American Farmer watched this contest with delight, and no doubt loudly applauded those little rascals of wrens. For in the Land of the Freen, the greatest delight of every man is in getting the better of the other man.

Crèvecœur says he shot a king-bird that had been devouring his bees. He opened the craw and took out a vast number of bees, which little democrats, after they had lain a minute or two stunned, in the sun roused, revived, preened their wings and walked off debonair, like Jonah up the seashore; or like true Yanks escaped from the craw of the king-bird of Europe.

I don´t care whether it´s true or not. I like the picture, and see in it a parable of the American resurrection.

The humming-bird.

Its bill is as long and as sharp as a coarse sewing-needle; like the bee, nature

他在《信札》中不提这档子事了，深怕他以前的论点不攻自破。

一些大黄蜂在这位美国农夫客厅的天花板上筑巢，这些生着虎斑的东西在他健康的孩子和温柔的妻子头上飞旋令他感到满足。他喜欢它们的嗡嗡叫声和它们的刻毒。从实用的角度说，这些大黄蜂保护着这里不受苍蝇侵犯。海克特就是这么说的。本杰明会同意他的观点的。可是我们不知道那温柔的妻子做何感想，不管怎么说，做果酱的是她而不是别人。

还有一件趣事。燕子也在这位美国农夫的房檐下做窝。鹪鹩极喜欢这些燕窝。它们极好战(我喜欢"好战"这个词，这是个极美国化的词语)，他们捣毁了报春燕子的窝，把它们从舒适的窝中赶了出去。待燕子返回时，又被鹪鹩凶狠地赶出了家。这种情况一直持续到温顺的燕子耐心地重新搭窝为止。鹪鹩就这样大模大样地住在侵犯得来的家中。这位美国农夫看着这场争斗，心里自是欢喜并为那些卑鄙的鹪鹩大声欢呼。在那个自由之国，人最大的乐趣来自于征服别人。

克里夫库尔说他曾枪杀了一只正在吞噬他的蜜蜂的食虫鸟。他打开鸟的嗉囊，掏出不少蜜蜂来。它们在阳光下昏死了几分钟，随后振翅飞起

has taught it to find out in the calyx of flowers and blossoms those mellifluous particles that can serve it for sufficient food; and yet it seems to leave them untouched, undeprived of anything that our eyes can possibly distinguish. Where it feeds it appears as if immovable, though continually on the wing: and sometimes, from what motives I know not, it will tear and lacerate flowers into a hundred pieces; for, strange to tell, they are the most irascible of the feathered tribe. Where do passions find room in so diminutive a body? They often fight with the fury of lions, until one of the combatants falls a sacrifice and dies. When fatigued, it has often perched within a few feet of me, and on such favourable opportunities I have surveyed it with the most minute attention. Its little eyes appear like diamonds, reflecting light on every side; most elegantly finished in all parts, it is a miniature work of our great parent, who seems to have formed it smallest, and at the same time the most beautiful, of the winged species.

A regular little Tartar, too. Lions no bigger than inkspots! I have read about humming-birds elsewhere, in Bates and W. H. Hudson, for example. But it is left to the American Farmer to show me the real little raging lion. Birds are evidently no angels in America, or to the true American. He sees how they start and flash their

来，显得很轻松，就像约拿在海边上。这幅图景恰似美国人从欧洲的嗉囊中挣脱出来一样。

我不在乎这是否属实。反正我喜爱他描绘的这幅图景，觉得这正是美国复活的比喻。

关于蜂雀。

它的嘴巴又长又尖，恰似一根钝针；自然教会了它从花萼中找到蜜一样的东西充作自己的食物。它把这些东西吸走，又让花朵显得未被触动过，它对花朵的抢劫是我们的肉眼难以辨认出的。它吃东西时似乎全身都静了下来，只有翅膀在抖动。有时，不知为什么它也会把花朵捣得粉碎。令人奇怪的是，这东西是鸟类中性情最暴躁的。这样微小的躯体何以积蕴这样强烈的激情？它们经常像狮子一样殴斗，直至其中一个斗士战死。当它们疲惫时，常常趴在离我不远的地方，因此我就有难得的机会观察它们，细细地观察。那小眼睛像钻石一样反光。它的每一部分都制作得那么精美，它是我们祖先的精制品，虽然小，但它是翅膀物种中最美丽的。

wings like little devils, and stab each other with egoistic sharp bills. But he sees also the reserved, tender shyness of the wild creature, upon occasion. Quails in winter, for instance.

Often, in the angles of the fences, where the motion of the wind prevents the snow from settling, I carry them both chaff and grain the one to feed them, the other to prevent their tender feet from freezing fast to the earth, as I have frequently observed them to do.

This is beautiful, and blood-knowledge. Crèvecœur knows the touch of birds' feet, as if they had stood with their vibrating,sharp, cold-cleaving balance, naked footed on his naked hand. It is a beautiful, barbaric tenderness of the blood. He doesn't after all turn them into 'little sisters of the air', like St Francis.* or start preaching to them. He knows them as strange, shy, hot-blooded concentrations of bird-presence.

The *Letter* about snakes and humming-birds is a fine essay, in its primal, dark veracity. The description of the fight between two snakes, a great water-snake and a large black serpent, follows the description of the humming-bird:

Strange was this to behold; two great snakes strongly adhering to the ground,

这也是一个小小的剽悍鞑靼人，是墨水点大小的狮子！我曾读过贝茨和 **W.H.**哈德逊对蜂雀的描述。可是，只有这位美国农夫才向我展示出其小小的怒狮面貌。很明显在美国，或者说对真正的美国人来说，鸟并非什么天使。而是被看做会飞的魔鬼，专门用自私的尖嘴相互啄咬。同时美国人偶尔也发现这东西有其腼腆、温柔的一面，比如冬天鸟儿就显得胆怯。

在篱笆角落上，风时常把积雪吹净。我就拿些谷壳和谷粒儿来放在这里喂它们。谷粒儿是让它们吃的。谷壳是用来为它们垫脚的，免得它们的脚冻在地上。我就时常这样看着它们吃食。

这一段写得真美，这种体验是来自血液的。克里夫库尔知道鸟儿的足触，似乎那鸟儿的赤足就蹬在他赤裸的手掌上，冰凉的尖爪在剧烈地颤抖。这是来自血液的温柔之情，美好而原始。他并没有像圣芳济那样把它们比作"空中的姐妹"[圣芳济，全名是阿西西的圣芳济（1181？—1226），意大利僧侣，创立圣芳济修会。他以爱动物和鸟类著名。传说他对鸟儿布道时称它们为"我的鸟儿姐妹"]，也没有对

mutually fastened together by means of the writhings which lashed them to each other, and stretched at their full length, they pulled, but pulled in vain; and in the moments of greatest exertions that part of their bodies which was entwined seemed extremely small, while the rest appeared inflated, and now and then convulsed with strong undulations, rapidly following each other. Their eyes seemed on fire, and ready to start out of their heads; at one time the conflict seemed decided; the water-snake bent itself into two great folds, and by that operation rendered the other more than commonly outstretched. The next minute the new struggles of the black one gained an unexpected superiority; it acquired two great folds likewise, which necessarily extended the body of its adversary in proportion as it had contracted its own.

This fight, which Crèvecœur describes to a finish, he calls a sight 'uncommon and beautiful'. He forgets the sweet-and-pureness of Nature, and is for the time a sheer ophiolater, and his chapter is as handsome a piece of ophiolatry, perhaps, as that coiled Aztec rattlesnake carved in stone.

And yet the real Crèvecœur is, in the issue, neither farmer, nor child of Nature, nor ophiolater. He goes back to France, and figures in the literary salons, and is a friend of Rousseau's Madame d'Houdetot. Also he is a good business man, and ar-

鸟儿布道。他只是把它们看做是有血有肉、奇异而腼腆的鸟神。

《信札》中有关蛇和蜜蜂的段落可说是优美的散文，真切而纯朴。写完蜜蜂以后，接下来就是一段关于两条蛇搏斗的描写。一条是水蛇，一条是黑色的大毒蛇。

这场景看上去实在奇特：两条巨蛇紧紧贴在地上，扭缠在一起，浑身绷住了劲，它们在厮挣着，但无法扯开各自的躯体。在最紧张的时刻，它们那缠在一起的部位看上去缩紧了、变小了，而其他部位却胀大了，不时在抽搐在蠕动，互不相让。它们的眼睛似乎在喷火，随时都会从头上迸出来。有一刻，似乎这场争斗要有结局了，那水蛇的身体叠了起来，把另一条蛇挤扁，身子拉得老长。可下一刻那黑蛇又发起进攻并取得了优势，它也把身体折起来缠在对手身上，同样把敌手的身子挤压得又扁又长。

克里夫库尔称他描述的这场搏斗为“不同凡响、漂亮”。在此，他忘记了所谓的“美好而纯洁的大自然”之说，一时间变成了蛇的崇拜者。他的文章是蛇的赞歌，可以说如同阿兹台克人刻在石头上的那条响尾蛇一

ranges a line of shipping between France and America. It all ends in materialism, really. But the *Letters* tell us nothing about this.

We are left to imagine him retiring in grief to dwell with his Red Brothers under the wigwams. For the War of Independence has broken out, and the Indians are armed by the adversaries; they do dreadful work on the frontiers. While Crèvecœur is away in France his farm is destroyed, his family rendered homeless. So that the last letter laments bitterly over the war, and man´s folly and inhumanity to man.

But Crèvecœur ends his lament on a note of resolution. With his amiable spouse, and his healthy offspring, now rising in stature, he will leave the civilized coasts, where man is sophisticated, and therefore inclined to be vile, and he will go to live with the Children of Nature, the Red Men, under the wigwam. No doubt, in actual life, Crèvecœur made some distinction between the Indians who drank rum *à la* Franklin, and who burnt homesteads and massacred families, and those Indians, the noble Children of Nature, who peopled his own predetermined fancy. Whatever he did in actual life, in his innermost self he would not give up this self-made world, where the natural man was an object of undefiled brotherliness. Touchingly and vividly he describes his tented home near the Indian village, how he breaks the

样。

可真正的克里夫库尔既不是农夫，也不是自然之子，也不是蛇的崇拜者。他又回到法国，出现在文学沙龙中，成为卢梭的女人德黄德特伯爵夫人的朋友。他还是一位优秀的商人，负责法国到美国的船运航线。一切都以物质主义结束，真的。但《信札》对此只字未提。

我们难以想像他如何回到美国，沮丧地同印第安人同居于简陋的木屋中。独立战争爆发后，印第安人为敌军所武装，在边境上干了不少令人恐怖的事。克里夫库尔远在法国时，他的农场被毁了，他的家人流离失所。为此，《信札》中的最后一封信对这场战争和人对人的蠢行和残暴发出悲叹。

悲叹终以一个决议而告结束。他决定携带自己温柔的妻子和渐渐长大的健康的孩子离开文明化了的海岸——这里的人变得复杂了，可恶了，为此他决定与印第安人这些自然之子一起同住简陋的木棚。毫无疑问，在现实生活中，克里夫库尔对不同的印第安人是有区别的：有的印第安人像富兰克林所说的那样酗酒，还烧杀抢掠；而还有些印第安人则是高贵的自然之子，这些人构成了克里夫库尔的神话。不管在现实世界中

aboriginal earth to produce a little maize, while his wife weaves within the wigwam. And his imaginary efforts to save his tender offspring from the brutishness of unchristian darkness are touching and puzzling, for how can Nature, so sweet and pure under the greenwood tree, how can it have any contaminating effect?

But it is all a swindle. Crèvecœur was off to France in highheeled shoes and embroidered waistcoat, to pose as a literary man, and to prosper in the world. We, however, must perforce follow him into the backwoods, where the simple natural life shall be perfected, near the tented village of the Red Man.

He wanted, of course, to imagine the dark, savage way of life, to get it all off pat in his head. He wanted to know as the Indians and savages know, darkly, and in terms of otherness. He was simply crazy, as the Americans say, for this. Crazy enough! For at the same time he was absolutely determined that Nature is sweet and pure, that all men atre brothers, and equal, and that they love one another like so many cooing doves. He was determined to have life according to his own prescription. Therefore, he wisely kept away from any too close contact with Nature, and took refuge in commerce and the material world. But yet, he was determined to know the savage way of life, to his own mind´s satisfaction. So he just faked us the

他做什么，他内心深处绝不放弃他那个自己构想的世界，那里“自然人”被看成是未被玷污的兄弟情谊的象征。他生动感人地描述了他那个靠近印第安村落的家，他破开处女地种玉米，他的妻子在小木棚中织布。他写他如何历尽艰辛从野蛮的黑暗环境中救出柔弱的孩子，那颇富想像力的描写既动人又令人困惑。浓阴覆盖下美好而纯洁的自然何以有任何污染？

这些都是谎话。克里夫库尔脚蹬高跟鞋、身穿刺绣马甲回到法国，摆出一副文人的架式，混得不错。可是我们应该追随他到林子中去，那儿，在靠近印第安人帐篷村的地方，纯朴的自然生活是美好的。

当然，他要想像那黑暗野性的生活方式，为此殚精竭虑。他意欲像印第安人和野蛮人那样在黑暗中感知。正如美国人所说，他为之发疯了。太发疯了！与此同时，他绝对相信，自然是美好而纯洁的，所有的人都是兄弟，都平等，人们就像喁喁细语的鸽子一样相亲相爱。他决定按自己的设想去生活。于是，他明智地与自然保持一定距离，到商业和物质世界中去躲避。可他又决心要感知野性的生活方式，使自己的心智得到满足。为此他虚伪地写下了这本《信札》。这是一种意念的满足。

last *Letters*. A sort of wish-fulfilment.

For the animals and savages are isolate, each one in its own pristine self. The animal lifts its head, sniffs, and knows within the dark, passionate belly. It knows at once, in dark mindlessness. And at once it flees in immediate recoil; or it crouches predatory, in the mysterious storm of exultant anticipation of seizing a victim; or it lowers its head in blank indifference again; or it advances in the insatiable wild curiosity, insatiable passion to approach that which is unspeakably strange and incalculable; or it draws near in the slow trust of wild, sensual love.

Crèvecœur wanted this kind of knowledge. But comfortably, in his head, along with his other ideas and ideals. He didn't go too near the wigwam. Because he must have suspected that the moment he saw as the savages saw, all his fraternity and equality would go up in smoke, and his ideal world of pure sweet goodness along with it. And still worse than this, he would have to give up his own will, which insists that the world is so, because it would be nicest if it were so. Therefore he trotted back to France in high-heeled shoes, and imagined America in Paris.

He wanted his ideal state. At the same time he wanted to know the other state, the dark, savage mind. He wanted both.

动物和野蛮人是孤独的，各自有着自己原始的自我。动物抬起头，嗅一嗅，靠黑暗充满激情的腹腔感知。它尽可以靠黑暗的无意识在一瞬间感知事物。于是它立即逃逝，躲起来；或者它缩起来等待猎物，它以一种神秘的狂喜期待着牺牲品，随后又若无其事地低下头；或者它怀着极度的好奇和不满足的激情靠近那说不清道不明的怪物；或许它怀着一种野性的信任和肉欲缓缓靠近它的目标。

克里夫库尔要的恰是这种感知，但只想让它其他观念和理想在自己头脑中和谐并存。他并不过分接近那简陋木棚。他怀疑一旦他像野蛮人一样看世界，他全部的博爱和平等都会云消雾散，他理想中的美好纯洁善良世界亦会随风飘去。更有甚之，他还得放弃他的意志，那意志坚持认为这个世界本该如此。为此，他足蹬高靴回到法国，在巴黎幻想着美国的样子。

他要的是他的理想境界，同时他又要感知另外一个黑暗野性思维的境界。两者他都要。

这可不行，海克特。一个的存在就意味着另一个的死亡。

最好投入商务中去，从而你可以自行其是。

Can't be done, Hector. The one is the death of the other.

Best turn to commerce, where you may get things your own way.

He hates the dark, pre-mental life, really. He hates the true sensual mystery. But he wants to 'know'. To KNOW. Oh, insatiable American curiosity!

He's a liar.

But if he won't risk knowing in flesh and blood, he'll risk all the imagination you like.

It is amusing to see him staying away and calculating the dangers of the step which he takes so luxuriously, in his fancy, alone. He tickles his palate with a taste of true wildness, as men are so fond nowadays of tickling their palates with a taste of imaginary wickedness -just self-provoked.

'I must tell you,' he says, 'that there is something in the proximity of the woods which is very singular. It is with men as it is with the plants and animals that grow and live in the forests; they are entirely different from those that live in the plains. I will candidly tell you all my thoughts, but you are not to expect that I shall advance any reasons. By living in or near the woods, their actions are regulated by the wildness of the neighbourhood. The deer ofter come to eat their grain, the wolves

他仇恨那黑暗、前意识的生活，真的。他仇恨肉欲的神秘。可他又要"了解"。了解。哦，难以满足的美国人的好奇心!

他是个骗子。

可是如果他不愿以血和肉来"了解"，他就得牺牲他全部的幻想。

看到他远离美国，独自在幻想中算计他所采取步骤的危险，实在令人好笑。他品尝着真正的野性，就像如今人们喜欢品味想像中的恶毒一样——全是自己作弄自己。

我要告诉你，在林子中有一种十分奇特的东西。这东西与人、与植物和动物同在，生长在林子中，与生长在平原上的东西截然不同。我会把我的想法全告诉你的，但你不要期望我会讲出什么道理。他们居住在森林中或森林附近，因此他们的行动受到周围野物的制约。鹿时常来吃他们的粮食，狼时常来叼羊，熊来吃猪，狐狸时常来捕家禽。这充满敌意的环境令他们立即操起枪。他们监视着野兽，捕杀野兽，为了保护自己的财产而成为猎人。就是这样一个过程。一旦成为猎人，他们就告别了耕耘，追捕野兽使他们变得暴躁、阴郁、不合群。一个猎人不需要邻居，相反他仇

to destroy their sheep, the bears to kill their hogs, the foxes to catch their poultry. This surrounding hostility immediately puts the gun into their hands; they watch these animals, they kill some; and thus by defending their property they soon become professed hunters; this is the progress; once hunters, farewell to the plough. The chase renders them ferocious, gloomy, and unsociable; a hunter wants no neighbour, he rather hates them, because he dreads the competition. ...Eating of wild meat, whatever you may think, tends to alter their temper...'

Crèvecœur, of course, had never intended to return as a hunter to the bosom of Nature, only as a husbandman. The hunter is a killer. The husbandman, on the other hand, brings about the birth and increase. But even the husbandman strains in dark mastery over the unwilling earth and beast; he struggles to win forth substance, he must master the soil and the strong cattle, he must have the heavy blood-knowledge, and the slow, but deep, mastery. There is no equality or selfless humility. The toiling blood swamps the idea, inevitably. For this reason the most idealist nations invent most machines. America simply teems with mechanical inventions, because nobody in America ever wants to do anything. They are idealists. Let a machine do the doing.

恨邻居，因为他恐怕竞争……食吃野味渐渐地改变了他们的脾气禀性……

不错，克里夫库尔从未试图成为一个在自然界冲杀的猎人，他只想成为一个农民。猎人是杀手，农民则带来了人口的生殖和增长。即便是这样的农民也因为土地和野兽的不驯而感到一种冥冥的紧张。他为收获而奋斗，因此他必须控制土地和强壮的牛群，他必须靠着血性的感知力，渐渐地牢牢地把这一切掌控。不要平等，不要无私和谦逊。最终劳作的艰辛淹没了这一切理想。为此，最理想的国家发明了最多的机器。美国几乎为机器发明所充斥，因为没有哪个美国人想做点什么。他们是理想主义者。让机器去干活吧。

可克里夫库尔又说："我怕我的儿女被那种独特的魅力迷住，他们还很年轻，这样很危险。"——其所指是野性的生活。他还说："是什么力量使得那些从小被印第安人收养的孩子再也难以回归欧洲人的举止？那次大战后，我见到不少焦虑的父母在和平以后到印第安人的村落去寻找他们被俘的孩子。可令他们不安的是他们的孩子已完全印第安化了，不少

Again, Crèvecœur dwells on the 'apprehension lest my younger children should be caught by that singular charm, so dangerous at their tender years' –meaning the charm of savage life. So he goes on: 'By what power does it come to pass that children who have been adopted when young among these people [the Indians] can never be prevailed upon to readopt European manners? Many an anxious parent I have seen last war who, at the return of the peace, went to the Indian villages where they knew their children had been carried in captivity, when to their inexpressible sorrow they found them so perfectly Indianized that many knew them no longer, and those whose more advanced ages permitted them to recollect their fathers and mothers, absolutely refused to follow them, and ran to their adopted parents to protect them against the effusions of love their unhappy real parents lavished on them! Incredible as this may appear, I have heard it asserted in a thousand instances, among persons of credit.'

There must be in their (the Indians') social bond something singularly captivating, and far superior to anything to be boasted of among us; for thousands of Europeans are Indians, and we have no examples of even one of those Aborigines having from choice become Europeans...

人已不认识他们的父母；而那些年龄稍大还记得父母的人则拒绝追从自己的生身父母，反之他们投向养父母的怀抱以此抗拒他们真正不幸的父母所流露出的爱！或许这有些不可思议，可我听到不少很有名望的人这样说过：

他们(印第安人)的社会中一定有什么特殊迷人之处，比我们所吹嘘的自己的那一套优越得多；成百上千的欧洲人做了印第安人，可我们却没找到一例事件证明有土著人选择做欧洲人……

不唠叨了，海克特。

我喜爱这样的图卷：成千上万我们的子孙不再理会他们的白人父母，决然找印第安人做养父母。

我见过一些印第安人，你简直无法把他们与白人区分开来。可我却从未见过酷似印第安人的白人。因此，我说，海克特是个骗子。

可是克里夫库尔想成为一个有知识的野蛮人，就像我们见过的不少人那样。美好的自然之子。野蛮而嗜血的自然之儿女。

Our cat and another, Hector.

I like the picture of thousands of obdurate offspring, with faces averted from their natural white father and mother, turning resolurely to the Indians of their adoption.

I have seen some Indians whom you really couldn't tell from white men. And I have never seen a white man who looked really like an Indian. So Hector is again a liar.

But Crèvecœur wanted to be an intellectual savage, like a great many more we have met. Sweet children of Nature. Savage and bloodthirsty children of Nature.

White Americans do try hard to intellectualize themselves. Especially white women Americans. And the latest stunt is this 'savage' stunt again.

White savages, with motor-cars, telephones, incomes and ideals! Savages fast inside the machine; yet savage enough, ye gods!

美国白人确实竭力要使自己知识化。美国白人妇女尤其如此。这就是他们的最新花招,所谓"野性"。

白种野人,有汽车、电话、薪水和理想!这野性全在机器里!可算野得够味儿,哦,天啊!

CHAPTER 4
Fenimore Cooper's White Novels

Benjamin Franklin had a specious little equation in providential mathematics:

Rum+Savage=0.

Awfully nice! You might add up the universe to nought, if you kept on.

Rum plus Savage may equal a dead savage. But is a dead savage nought? Can you make a land virgin by killing off its aborigines?

The Aztec is gone, and the Incas. The Red Indian, the Esquimo, the Patagonian ate reduced to negligible numbers.

*Où sont les neiges d'antan?**

My dear, wherever they are, they will come down again next winter, sure as houses.

Not that the Red Indian will ever possess the broad lands of America. At least I

菲尼莫·库柏的白人小说

[James Fenimore Cooper(1789—1851),出身富家,在父亲的湖畔庄园长大。其父在纽约北部美加边界附近的河畔(不是劳伦斯所说的詹普伦湖)建起了库柏镇。这里是他很多小说的背景地。他就学于耶鲁,但遭到驱逐。婚后过着绅士农场主和作家的生活。1826—1833 在英国和法国度过,当过一段时间美国领事,彻底变成了一个"有教养的绅士"。1835 年回到库柏镇,终老于此。了解其身世对理解劳伦斯的叙述很有裨益。]

本杰明·富兰克林用神的数学方法推导出这样一个等式:

酒+野蛮人=0

妙不可言! 接下去你还可以在零后面加上世界。

酒加野蛮人可以等于一个死野人。可是一个死野人等于零吗?杀掉土著人就可使这土地成为处女地吗?

阿兹台克人灭种了,印加人没了,印第安人、爱斯基摩人和巴塔哥尼

presume not. But his ghost will.

The Red Man died hating the white man. What remnant of him lives, lives hating the white man. Go near the Indians, and you just feel it. As far as we are concerned, the Red Man is subtly and unremittingly diabolic. Even when he doesn't know it. He is dispossessed in life, and unforgiving. He doesn't believe in us and our civillization, and so is our mystic enemy, for we push him off the face of the earth.

Belief is a mysterious thing. It is the only healer of the soul's wounds. There is no belief in the world.

The Red Man is dead, disbelieving in us. He is dead and unappeased. Do not imagine him happy in his Happy Hunting Ground.* No. Only those that die in belief die happy. Those that are pushed out of life in chagrin come back unappeased, for revenge.

A curious thing about the Spirit of Place is the fact that no place exerts its full influence upon a ne-comer until the old inhabitant is dead or absorbed. So America. While the Red Indian existed in fairly large numbers, the new colonials, were in a great measure immune from the daimon, or demon, of America. The moment the last

亚人也所剩无几了。

从前的雪在哪里?[见法国诗人 F·Villon 的诗歌]

亲爱的,不管去了哪儿,他们下个冬季会回来的,真的。

这并非说印第安人将统治广大的美洲。至少我不这样认为。可他们的阴魂将会这样。

印第安人含恨而死,他们的后代仍仇恨白人。一接近印第安人你就会产生这种感觉。在我们看来,印第安人身上有一种魔鬼气息,这气息尽管微妙却持久。甚至他们自己对此也并无知觉。他们被剥夺了生的权利,因此他们没有宽容之心。他们不相信我们和我们的文明,因此他们成了我们神秘的敌人,是我们把他们推出了地球表面。

信仰是个神秘的东西。它是心灵创伤的惟一愈合剂。尘世间没有信仰。

印第安人死了,至死不相信我们。他至死也不服。不要以为他在他的幸福猎场[这是美国当地人对猎人来世之地的称谓]上感到幸福。不。只有那些怀着信仰而死的人才死得幸福。那些被剥夺了生活权利屈死的人不服气,会回

nuclei of Red life break up in America, then the white men will have to reckon with the full force of the demon of the continent. At present the demon of the place and the unappeased ghosts of the dead Indians act within the unconscious or under-conscious soul of the white American, causing the great American grouch, the Orestes-like frenzy of restlessness in the Yankee soul, the inner malaise which amounts almost to madness, sometimes. The Mexican is macabre and disintegrated in his own way. Up till now, the unexpressed spirit of America has worked covertly in the American, the white American soul. But within the present generation the surviving Red Indians are due to merge in the great white swamp. Then the Daimon of America will work overtly, and we shall see real changes.

There has been all the time, in the white American soul, a dual feeling about the Indian. First was Franklin's feeling, that a wise Providence no doubt intended the extirpation of these savages. Then came Crèvecœur's contradictory feeling about the noble Red Man and the innocent life of the wigwam. Now we hate to subscribe to Benjamin's belief in a Providence that wisely extirpates the Indian to make room for 'cultivators of the soil.' In Crèvecœur we meet a sentimental desire for the glorification of the savages. Absolutely sentimental. Hector pops over to Paris to en-

来报复的。

所谓“地之灵”的奇特在于，一个地方的老居民不死去或不被同化，这个地方就无法对新来者施加全部的影响。美洲即是如此。当印第安人人数蔚为可观时，新的殖民者丝毫不受美洲之魔的影响。一旦印第安人的生活核心被破坏，白人就得对付这大陆上魔鬼的力量了。目前，这地域之魔和死去的印第安人的阴魂在美洲白人的无意识和潜意识中跃动，造就了美洲人的脾气——他们的灵魂深处有着奥列斯特般的疯狂，有时到了歇斯底里的程度。墨西哥人则受着死亡的恐吓，精神陷入分裂。直至今日，未经表白的美洲精神一直隐藏在美洲白人的灵魂深处。而在这一代人中，残存下来的印第安人将会被白人的沼泽所吞噬。随后美洲之魔将会显露端倪，从而我们会看到真正的转机。

在美国白人心中，一直对印第安人怀有双重感情。首先是富兰克林，相信聪明的上帝无疑是要根除野蛮人的。还有就是克里夫库尔对高贵的印第安人和小木棚中纯洁生活所怀的那种有争议的感情。我们不赞同本杰明的信仰，认为上帝会机智地根除印第安人从而为“垦荒者”腾地方。

thuse about the wigwam.

The desire to extirpate the Indian. And the contradictory desire to glorify him. Both are rampant still, today.

The bulk of the white people who live in contact with the Indian today would like to see this Red brother exterminated; not only for the sake of grabbing his land, but because of the silent, invisible, but deadly hostility between the spirit of the two races. The minority of whites intellectualize the Red Man and laud him to the skies. But this minority of whites is mostly a high-brow minority with a big grouch against its own whiteness. So there you are.

I doubr if there is possible any real reconciliation, in the flesh, between the white and the red. For instance, a Red Indian girl who is servant in the white man's home, if she is treated with natural consideration, will probably serve well, even happily. She is happy with the new power over the white woman's kitchen. The white world makes her feel prouder, so long as she is free to go back to her own people at the given times. But she is happy because she is playing at being a white woman. There are other Indian women who would never serve the white people, and who would rather die than have a white man for a lover.

而在克里夫库尔身上我们发现了某种多情的意愿，他要赞美野蛮人。绝对的多情！海克特跑到巴黎去关心起美国的小木棚来了。

根除印第安人的欲望和赞美他们的欲望时下都很强烈。

今日大多数与印第安人在生存上有密切联系的白人希望看到他们的印第安兄弟被根除。这并非单是为了夺取土地，还因为这两个种族间默默存在着令人难以察觉却是极致命的敌意。少数白人则把印第安人讲得很有智慧，把他们捧上了天。这一小批白人大多数是一些雅士，对自己身为白种人深感不满。就是这样。

我怀疑白人同印第安人会在肉体上有什么真正的调和。比如，一个在白人家当使唤丫头的印第安姑娘，如果她的待遇是公平自然的，她就可以干得很好，甚至工作得很幸福。她管着白种女人的厨房，这让她开心。白人世界令她感到骄傲，只要让她在特定的时间自由回到自己人中去就行。她幸福，这是因为她扮演着白人的角色。有些印第安女人绝不要伺候白人，宁死也不找白人做情人。

在这两种情况下都不会有什么调和。这两个种族在精神上毫无神秘

In either case, there is no reconciliation. There is no mystic conjunction between the spirit of the two races. The Indian girl who happily serves white people leaves out her own raceconsideration, for the time being.

Supposing a white man goes out hunting in the mountains with an Indian. The two will probably get on like brothers. But let the same white man go alone with two Indians, and there will start a most subtle persecution of the unsuspecting white. If they, the Indians, discover that he has a natural fear of steep places, then over every precipice in the country will the trail lead. And so on. Malice! That is the basic feeling in the Indian heart, towards the white. It may even be purely unconscious.

Supposing an Indian loves a white woman, and lives with her. He will probably be very proud of it, for he will be a big man among his own people, especially if the white mistress has money. He will never get over the feeling of pride at dining in a white dining-room and smoking in a white drawing-room. But at the same time he will subtly jeer at his white mistress, try to destroy her white pride. He will submit to her ,if he is forced to, with a kind of false, unwilling childishness, and even love her with the same childlike gentleness, sometimes beautiful. But at the bottom of his heart he is gibing, gibing, gibing at her. not only is it the sex resistance, but the

联系可言。只不过那伺候白人的姑娘一时间把自己是哪个种族的人忘到脑后了。

假如一个白人同一个印第安人一起上山打猎,这两人很可能似兄弟相处。可是如果这同一个白人与两个印第安人同行的话,这无辜的白人就会受到某种微妙的迫害。如果印第安人发现这白人害怕陡峭之地,他们就专挑险峻的乡间路来走。如此等等。可恶!印第安人心里就是这样对待白人的。这或许完全是无意识行为。

假如一个印第安人爱上了一个白人妇女并与之共同生活,他很可能为此感到十分骄傲,这样的话他在自己的同胞中就变得高大起来,如果这白人妇女很有钱的话,那他的形象就更不一般。在白人家吃饭或吸烟会令他产生无法自制的骄傲感。可同时他又不免有点嘲笑他的白人情妇,企图毁灭她的自傲。在迫不得已的情况下,他会像个孩子一样不情愿但又不得不假惺惺地依从她, 甚至爱她的时候也显出孩子般的温顺,有时这样子很美。可他内心深处却看不起她,嘲笑她。这不仅是一种性抵抗,亦是一种种族抵抗。

race resistance as well.

There seems to be no reconciliation in the flesh.

That leaves us only expiation, and then reconciliation in the soul. Some strange atonement: expiation and oneing.

Fenimore Cooper has probably done more than any writer to present the Red Man to the white man. But Cooper´s presentment is indeed a wish-fulfilment. That is why Fenimore is such a success still.

Modern critics begrudge Cooper his success.* I think I resent it a little myself. This popular wish-fulfilment stuff makes it so hard for the real thing to come through, later.

Cooper was a rich American of good family. His father founded Cooperstown, by Lake Champlain. And Fenimore was a gentleman of culture. No denying it.

It is amazing how cultured these Americans of the first half of the eighteenth century were. Most intensely so. Austin Dobson and Andrew Lang are flea-bites in comparison. Volumes of very *raffiné* light verse and finely drawn familiar literature will prove it to anyone who cares to commit himself to these elderly books. The English and French writers of the same period were clumsy and hoydenish, judged

在肉体上,似乎没有调和的可能。

我们只有先赎罪,心灵上才能得以与印第安人和平共处。这是一种奇特的调和:赎罪与融合。

菲尼莫·库柏或许在向白人介绍印第安人方面比任何别的作家做得都多。可是库柏的作品实际上是一种愿望的满足。因此他现在依然走红。

现代批评家对库柏的成功[库柏当年与华盛顿·欧文齐名,整个19世纪在欧美都是最畅销的美国作家。仅《最后一个莫希干人》一本书就风靡欧美五十年,多次再版]显得很苛刻。我也有点这样。这种愿望的满足尽管受人欢迎却难以让人了解事实真相。

库柏出身于良家,是个富裕的美国人:他的父亲在詹普伦湖畔创建了库柏镇。菲尼莫是个有教养的绅士,这毫无疑问。

十八世纪上半叶的这些美国人有着令人吃惊的教养。真是这样的。与他们相比,奥斯丁·多布森[Henry Austin Dobson(1840—1921),美国诗人]和安德鲁·朗[Andrew Lang(1844-1921),美国诗人]就黯然失色了。极高雅的一首首精美小诗和语言精巧的文学作品都可以向酷爱这些旧书的人证实这一点。用这同一

by the same standards.

Truly, European decadence was anticipated in America; and American influence passed over to Europe, was assimilated there, and then returned to this land of innocence as something purplish in its modernity and a little wicked. So absurd things are.

Cooper quotes a Frenchman, who says, '*L'Amérique est purrie avant d'être mûre*.' And there is a great deal in it. America was not taught by France –by Baudelaire, for example.* Baudelaire learned his lesson from America.

Cooper's novels fall into two classes:his white novels, such as *Homeward Bound, Eve Effingham, The Spy, The Pilot*, and then the *Leatherstocking Series*. Let us look at the white novels first.

The Effinghams are three extremely refined, genteel Americans who are 'Homeward Bound' from England to the States. Their party consists of father, daughter, and uncle, and faithful nurse. The daughter has just finished her education in Europe. She has, indeed, skimmed the cream off Europe. England, France, Italy, and Germany have nothing more to teach her. She is bright and charming, admirable creature; a real modern heroine; intrepid, calm, and self-collected, yet admirably

标准来衡量的话,这一时期的英国和法国文学倒显得笨拙、幼稚了。

不错,欧洲的颓废传到美国,这是意料之中的事。而美国的影响又传到了欧洲,受到那里的同化后又反馈到这纯洁的国土上,被当做某种现代而高雅的东西。事情就是这样怪。

库柏引用一位法国人的话说:"美国还未成熟就先烂了。"这话说得极是。美国并非受法国人指教——不是波德莱尔指教美国人而是他从美国人那儿学到东西[波德莱尔曾翻译过爱伦·坡的诗歌,很受其影响]。

库柏的小说可分为两类。一种是写白人生活的,如《归途》、《伊薇·埃芬厄姆》、《间谍》和《水手》。另一种是"皮袜子"系列故事。让我们先看一看他的白人小说。

埃芬厄姆家三人是十分有修养的美国人,他们正在从英国到美国的"归途"中。这三人分别是父亲、女儿和叔叔,还有一位忠实的保姆。女儿刚刚结束了在欧洲的学业,她可算得上是获得了欧洲的精华了。英国、法国、意大利和德国再也没什么可教她的了。她聪明、迷人、讨人喜欢,是个真正的现代女性。她勇敢、沉着、有自制力,就是冲动起来时也招人喜欢,

impulsive, always in perfectly good taste; clever and assured in her speech, like a man, but withal charmingly deferential and modest before the stronger sex. It is the perfection of the ideal female. We have learned to shudder at her, but Cooper still admired.

On board is the other type of American, the parvenu, the demagogue, who has 'done' Europe and put it in his breeches pocket, in a month. Oh, Septimus Dodge, if a European had drawn you, that European would never have been forgiven by America. But an American drew you, so Americans wisely ignore you.

Septimus is the American self-made man. God had no hand in his make-up. He made himself. He has been to Europe, no doubt seen everything, including the Venus de Milo. 'What, is that the Venus de Milo?' And he turns his back on the lady. He's seen her. He's got her. She's a fish he has hooked, and he's off to America with her, leaving the scum of a statue standing in the Louvre.

That is one American way of Vandalism.* The original Vandals would have given the complacent dame a knock with a battle-axe, and ended her. The insatiable American looks at her. 'Is that the Venus de Milo? -come on!' And the Venus de Milo stands there like a naked slave in a market-place, whom someone has spat on.

总是那么落落大方。她言谈机智而自信，像个男子汉，可在男人面前却又妩媚、恭顺。这可真是个理想的女性。她这副样子令我们不寒而栗，可库柏却喜欢她。

船上有一位另一类型的美国人，暴发户，煽动人心者。这人一月之内就跟欧洲绝交了。哦，塞普提莫斯·多吉[小说中人物的名字不是"塞普提莫斯"，而应该是"斯蒂德法斯特"，劳伦斯记忆有误]，如果哪个欧洲人吸引了你，他是永远得不到美国人原谅的。可吸引你的是美国，所以美国人明智地冷落你。

塞普提莫斯是个靠个人奋斗起家的美国人。上帝没帮他一把，他靠自己奋斗成材。他到过欧洲，毫无疑问见多识广，包括看到过米洛的维纳斯雕像。"米洛的维纳斯是什么？"他对这女人置之不理。他见到了她，知道她是怎么一回事了。她是他钓上来的一条鱼，他带着她回美国了，只把雕像的渣垢留在卢浮宫里。

这是美国人对艺术品破坏的一种方式，如同汪达尔人[the Vandals，日尔曼人的一个部落，在3—4世纪时摧毁了罗马帝国的一些省份，后征服了高卢、西班牙和北非，最终洗劫了罗马城。Vandal这个词及派生出的vandualism意指对文化的恣意毁灭]一样。而最早的汪达

Spat on!

I have often thought, hearing American tourists in Europein the Bargello in Florence,* for example, or in the Piazza di San Marco in Venice –exclaiming, 'Isn't that just too cunning! ' or else, 'Aren't you perfectly crazy about Saint Mark's! Don't you think those cupolas are like the loveliest turnips upside down, you know' –as if the beautiful things of Europe were just having their guts pulled out by these American admirers. They admire so wholesale. Sometimes they even seem to grovel. But the golden cupolas of St Mark's in Venice are turnips upside down in a stale stew, after enough American tourists have looked at them. Turnips upside down in a stale stew. Poor Europe!

And there you are. When a few German bombs fell upon Rheims Cathedral* up went a howl of execration. But there are more ways than one of vandalism. I should think the American admiration of five–minutes tourists has done more to kill the sacredness of old European beauty and aspiration than multitudes of bombs would have done.

But there you are. Europe has got to fall, and peace hath her victories.

Behold then Mr Septimus Dodge returning to Dodge –town victorious. Not

尔人则干脆会给这贵妇人像一斧头让她完蛋。美国人就是用这样贪婪的目光来看她的。“那就是米洛的维纳斯吗？来吧！”米洛的维纳斯站在那儿活像一个市场上的裸体奴隶，谁都可以唾骂她。唾骂吧！

我常听到在欧洲旅行的美国人感叹，在佛罗伦萨的巴杰罗宫[应该是波蒂斯塔宫，建于1254—1436年，现为意大利雕塑博物馆]或在威尼斯的圣马可广场[指圣马可大教堂前的广场]：“那真是太精致了！”或者：“看到圣·马可教堂真让人发疯！你不以为那些圆顶屋子正像倒栽的萝卜吗？”听这话，好像欧洲美好的东西的内脏都已被美国的崇拜者掏空了。他们对此毫无选择地崇拜，有时显出五体投地的样子。威尼斯的圣·马可教堂的金色圆顶受到过多的美国人观看后就成了腐水中的倒栽萝卜。腐水中的倒栽萝卜，可怜的欧洲。

你看，当德国的几颗炸弹落在雷姆斯大教堂[1914年德国轰炸了法国西北部的雷姆斯，炸毁了那里12世纪建起的大教堂]上时，立即引来一阵大声的咒骂。可是破坏的方法多的是呢。我以为美国那些短期旅游者的崇拜比众多的炸弹对古欧洲的美与抱负更有杀伤力。

可是你看，欧洲非衰落不可，和平胜利了。

crowned with laurel, it is true, but wreathed in lists of things he has seen and sucked dry. Seen and sucked dry, you know: Venus de Milo, the Rhine or the Coliseum: swallowed like so many clams, and left the shells.

Now the aristocratic Effinghams, Homeward Bound from Europe to America, are at the mercy of Mr Dodge:Septimus. He is their compatriot,so they may not disown him. Had they been English, of course, they would never once have let themselves become aware of his existence. But no. They are American democrats, and therefore, if Mr Dodge marches up and says: 'Mr Effingham? Pleased to meet you, Mr Effingham' –why, then Mr Effingham is *forced* to reply: 'Pleased to meet you, Mr Dodge.' If he didn't he would have the terrible hounds of democracy on his heels and at his throat, the moment he landed in the Land of the Free. An Englishman is free to continue unaware of the existence of a fellowcountryman, if the looks of that fellow–countryman are distasteful. But every American citizen is free to force his presence upon you, no matter how unwilling you may be.

Freedom!

The Effinghams detest Mr Dodge. They abhor him. They loathe and despise him. They have an unmitigated contempt for him. Everything he is, says, and does,

看吧，塞普提莫斯·多吉先生荣归故里。尽管他没有头戴桂冠，可他着实见过不少东西、吸收了不少知识，借此可炫耀一番：米洛的维纳斯像、莱茵河或大剧院。他像吃蛤一样，把肉吃下，把壳甩掉。

埃芬厄姆家的三个贵族人士正从欧洲返回美国，此时正听任多吉先生摆布。他是他们的同胞，所以他们不能不认他。如果他们是英国人，他们当然不会理会他的存在。可他们不是英国人，他们是美国的民主主义者。所以当多吉先生走上前来说："埃芬厄姆先生吗?很高兴认识您。"随后埃芬厄姆先生就得被迫回答："很高兴认识您，多吉先生。"如果不这样的话，一旦他踏上那块"自由之土"他就会被民主的猎狗追踪追杀。一个英国人，如果他对他的某个同胞看不上眼，他可以不理他。可是美国人却不管不顾，非要让你意识到他的存在不可。

自由!

埃芬厄姆厌恶多吉，怕他。他们恨他，鄙视他。他们实在看他不起。他的一切言行在他们看来都是粗鄙下作的。可他自我介绍时他们又被迫回答："见到你很高兴，多吉先生。"

seems to them too vulgar, too despicable. Yet they are forced to answer, when he presents himself: 'Pleased to meet you, Mr Dodge.'

Freedom!

Mr Dodge, of Dodge-town, alternately fawns and intrudes, cringes and bullies. And the Effinghams, terribly 'superior' in a land of equality, writhe helpless. They would fain snub Septimus out of existence. But Septimus is not to be snubbed. As a true democrat, he is unsnubbable. As a true democrat, he has right on his side. And right is might.

Right is might. It is the old struggle for power.

Septimus, as a true democrat, is the equal of any man. As a true democrat with a full pocket, he is, by the amount that fills his pocket, so much the superior of the democrats with empty pockets. Because though all men are born equal and die equal, you will not get anybody to admit that ten dollars equal ten thousand dollars. No, no, there's a difference there, however far you may push equality.

Septimus has the Effinghams on the hip. He has them fast, and they will not escape. What tortures await them at home, in the Land of the Free, at the hands of the hideously affable Dodge, we do not care to disclose. What was the persecution of

自由!

这位多吉先生不时地讨好、打搅、奉承,时而霸道。这令"优越"的埃芬厄姆们每每退缩,因为这是人人平等的国家。他们倒想冷落他。可塞普提莫斯可冷落不得。他是个民主主义者,不容忽视:作为真正的民主主义者,他有他的权利,而权利就是力量[此句借典于林肯1860年2月27日的讲演]。

权利就是力量。这是自古以来的权力之争。

作为真正的民主主义者,塞普提莫斯与任何人都一样。他是个有钱的民主主义者,与那些囊空如洗的民主主义者相比,他是优越之人。尽管说人生来平等、死后平等,可没人承认十美元与一万美元相等。不,不,无论你怎样强调平等,差别还是有的。

塞普提莫斯使埃芬厄姆们处于不利地位,他紧紧地控制着他们,从而他们无法逃脱。在号称"自由之土"的家乡和这位极和蔼的多吉手中他们将会受到怎样的折磨?对此我们就不表了。一位趾高气扬的君主、一位掠夺成性的勋爵或一位审判官似的修道院长对人施加的迫害与成千上万的多吉对人的迫害相比又算得了什么?骄傲的埃芬厄姆们就像被活埋

a haughty Lord or a marauding Baron or an inquisitorial Abbot compared to the persecution of a million Dodges? The proud Effinghams are like men buried naked to the chin in ant–heaps, to be bitten into extinction by a myriad ants. Stoically, as good democrats and idealists, they writhe and endure, without making too much moan.

They writhe and endure. There is no escape. Not from that time to this. No escape. They writhed on the horns of the Dodge dilemma.*

Since then Ford* has gone on worse.

Through these white novels of Cooper runs this acid of ant–bites, the formic acid of democratic poisoning. The Effinghams feel superior. Cooper felt superior. Mrs Cooper felt superior too. And bitten.

For they were democrats. They didn′t believe in kings, or lords, or masters, or real superiority of any sort. Before God, of course. In the sight of God, of course, all men were equal. This they believed. And therefore, though they felt terribly superior to Mr Dodge, yet, since they were his equals in the sight of God, they could not feel free to say to him: ‘Mr Dodge, please go to the devil.’ They had to say: ‘Pleased to meet you.’

于蚂蚁堆中,他们会让这成堆的蚂蚁吃个一干二净。而他们这几个民主主义者、理想主义者抽搐着,一声不吭地苦苦忍耐。

他们痉挛地忍耐着,别无出路。一直没有出路。没有。他们在多吉[约翰·多吉与霍拉斯·多吉于 1912 年创建了他们的汽车公司,但都于 1920 年死于流感]的进退维谷境地里痛苦地挣扎着。

那以后福特[福特公司的 T 型车在 1908—1927 年间最为流行,售出了 1500 万辆。但劳伦斯 1922 年在美国旅行时乘坐的朋友的福特汽车一路上经常抛锚]变得更差劲。

从库柏的这些白人小说中流出蚁虫的毒液，这是所谓民主的毒液。埃芬厄姆们感到自己是优越之人。库柏也自认为优越。库柏太太亦觉得自己优越。全都给咬了。

他们是民主主义者。他们不相信什么君主、主子或任何优越感。在上帝面前,人人平等,这一点他们相信。因此,尽管他们感到比多吉先生优越,可因为在上帝面前他们是平等的,这就无法自由地说:“多吉先生,见鬼去吧。”他们不得不说:“认识您很高兴。”

这真是个弥天大谎! 民主之谎。

What a lie to tell! Democratic lies.

What a dilemma! To feel so superior. To know you are superior. And yet to believe that, in the sight of God, you are equal. Can't help yourself.

Why couldn't they let the Lord Almighty look after the equality, since it seems to happen specifically in His sight, and stick themselves to their own superiority. Why couldn't they?

Somehow they daren't.

They were Americans, idealists. How dare they balance a mere intense feeling against an IDEA and an IDEAL?

Ideally–i.e.,in the sight of God, Mr Dodge was their equal.

What a low opinion they held of the Almighty's faculty for discrimination.

But it was so. The IDEAL of EQUALITY.

Pleased to meet you, Mr Dodge.

We are equal in the sight of God, of course. But er–

Very glad to meet you, Miss Effingham. Did you say–*er*? Well now, I think my bank balance will bear it.

Poor Eve Effingham.

真是两难啊! 感到优越,认识到自身的优越性,可又不得不相信在上帝面前人人平等。你对此一筹莫展。

既然平等特别展现在上帝的视野里,那为什么不能让全能的上帝关照平等之事,而他们照样自顾优越?为什么不?

他们不敢。

他们是美国人,是理想主义者。他们何以仅仅为了一种强烈的感受而敢于违反一种观念和一种理想?

理想地说——也就是说在上帝面前,多吉先生是与他们同等的人。

他们对上帝的分辨能力估价太低了。

可事实如此。平等的理想。

见到您很高兴,多吉先生。

在上帝面前我们当然是平等的。可是——

见到您很高兴,埃芬厄姆小姐。你这样说过吗?我想我的银行余额可以容忍这种平等。

可怜的伊薇·埃芬厄姆。

伊薇! 想想吧,伊薇! 天堂之鸟。智慧果[伊薇的名字与夏娃的名字拼写一样。这

Eve! Think of it. Eve! And birds of paradise. And apples.*

And Mr Dodge.

This is where apples of knowledge get you, Miss Eve. You should leave´em alone.

'Mr Dodge, you are a hopeless and insufferable inferior.'

Why couldn´t she say it? She felt it. And she was a heroine.

Alas, she was an American heroine. She was an EDUCATED WOMAN. She KNEW all about IDEALS. She swallowed the IDEAL of EQUALITY with her first mouthful of KNOWLEDGE. Alas for her and that apple of Sodom that looked so rosy. Alas for all her knowing.

Mr Dodge (in check knickerbockers): Well, feeling a little uncomfortable below the belt, are you, Miss Effingham?

Miss Effingham (With difficulty withdrawing her gaze from the INFINITE OCEAN): Good morning, Mr Dodge. I was admiring the dark blue distance.

Mr Dodge: Say, couldn´t you admire something a bit nearer?

Think how easy it would have been for her to say 'Go away! ' or 'Leave me, varlet! ' –or 'Hence, base–born knave! 'Or just to turn her back on him.

与天堂和智慧果一起均暗示伊甸园],还有多吉先生。

是智慧果令你这样的,伊薇小姐。你应该离开他们才是。

"多吉先生,你这下等人毫无希望,令人难以忍受。"

她为什么不能这样说呢?她有所感,她本是个女中豪杰呢。

哦,她却原来是个美国女豪杰,是个受过教育的女人。她懂得所有的理想。她吞下的第一口知识中就有所谓平等的理想。哀哉,她,还有那玫瑰色的所多玛苹果[也称死海之果,外表光鲜内里腐烂,一碰即化为灰烬]。哀哉,她所有的智识。

多吉先生(身着格子灯笼裤):哦,埃芬厄姆小姐,腰带下[below the belt,这个暗喻有性暗示。不过原作中多吉并无此意。该对话是劳伦斯的杜撰]有点不舒服吗?

埃芬厄姆小姐(勉强把目光从辽阔的海面上收回):早晨好,多吉先生。我真喜欢那深蓝色的远方。

多吉先生:你就不能喜欢近处么?

你想想,说一句"走开",对她来说该有多么容易。啊她还可以说:"别缠我,恶棍! "或:"下流坯! "或干脆背过身去不理他。

可他会转到那边去。

But then he would simply have marched round to the other side of her.

Was she his superior, or wasn't she?

Why surely, intrinsically, she was. Intrinsically Fenimore Cooper was the superior of the Dodges of his day. He felt it. But he felt he ought not to feel it. And he never had it out with himself.

That is why one rather gets impatient with him. He feels he is superior, and feels he ought not to feel so, and is therefore rather snobbish, and at the same time a little apologetic. Which is surely tiresome.

If a man feels superior, he should have it out with himself. 'Do I feel superior because I am superior? Or is it just the snobbishness of class, or education, or money?'

Class, education, money won't make a man superior. But if he's just *born* superior, in himself, there it is. Why deny it?

It is a nasty sight to see the Effinghams putting themselves at the mercy of a Dodge, just because of a mere idea or ideal. Fools. They ruin more than they know. Because at the same time they are snobbish.

Septimus at the Court of King Arthur.*

她到底是否比他优越?

当然了,从本质上说是这样的。从本质上说,库柏比他那个时代的多吉们要优越得多。他对此有所感,可他觉得不该有这种想法。所以他从未流露过这种情绪。

就是因为这一点,人们才无法忍受他。他明明有优越感,可他又觉得自己不该这样;他既势利又为此内疚。这可真叫人烦。

如果一个人感到优越,他就该表露出来。"我优越,我应该有优越感吗?或者说,这不过是阶级、教育或金钱带来的势利?"

阶级、教育和金钱并不能使一个人优越。优越是天生的。为何要否认呢?

看到埃芬厄姆们听任多吉的摆布,真不舒服。他们仅仅是为了一种观念和一种理想才这样的。愚蠢! 他们所毁灭的远远超出了他们所意识到的程度。因为他们仍是势利眼。

塞普提莫斯在亚瑟王的朝廷上[马克·吐温著有小说名为《一个北方佬在亚瑟王的朝廷上》]。

塞普提莫斯:哈,亚瑟! 见到您很高兴。顺便问一句,那把长剑是怎么

Septimus: Hello, Arthur! Pleased to meet you. By the way, what´s all that great long sword about?

Arthur: This is Excalibur, the sword of my knighthood and my kingship.*

Septimus: That so! We´re all equal in the sight of God, you know, Arthur.

Althur: Yes.

Septimus: Then I guess it´s about time I had that yerd-and-a-half of Excalibur to play with. Don´t you think so? We´re equal in the sight of God, and you´ve had it for quite a while.

Arthur: Yes, I agree. (Hands him Excalibur.)

Septimus (prodding Arthur with Excalibur): Say, Art, which is your fifth rib?*

Superiority is a sword. Hand it over to Septimus, and you´ll get it back between your ribs. -The whole moral of democracy.

But there you are. Eve Effingham had pinned herself down on the Contrat Social, and she was prouder of that pin through her body than of any mortal thing else. Her IDEAL. Her IDEAL of DEMOCRACY.

When America set out to destroy Kings and Lords and Masters, and the whole paraphernalia of European superiority, it pushed a pin right through its own body,

回事?

亚瑟:这是亚瑟王的神剑[亚瑟称王是因为他能把神剑从石头中拔出],它是骑士与王位之剑。

塞普提莫斯:是这样! 可我们在上帝面前人人平等,你知道的,亚瑟。

亚瑟:是的。

塞普提莫斯:那好。我想现在该我玩一玩那把一码半长的亚瑟王之剑了。你说是吗?在上帝面前我们是平等的。这把剑你保留了很久了。

亚瑟:好,我同意(说着交出了亚瑟王之剑)。

塞普提莫斯(用剑刺向亚瑟)道:说,亚瑟,你的第五根肋骨[第五根肋骨指人最易被刺致死的位置]在哪儿?

优越是一把剑。如果你把它交给塞普提莫斯,你就会被它刺死——这就是民主之德。

可是,伊薇·埃芬厄姆把自己钉在《社会契约论》上了,她为这钉在自己身上的钉子感到骄傲,把它看得比任何别的事都更重要。她的理想,民主之理想。

当美国开始毁灭王权、贵族等欧洲优越的道具时,他恰恰是把一根

and on that pin it still flaps and buzzes and twists in misery. The pin of democratic equality. Freedom.

There'll never be any life in America till you pull the pin out and admit natural inequality. Natural superiority, natural inferiority. Till such time, Americans just buzz round like various sorts of propellers, pinned down by their freedom and equality.

That's why these white novels of Fenimore Cooper are only historically and sardonically interesting. They people are all pinned down by some social pin, and buzzing away in social importance or friction, round and round on the pin. Never real human beings. Always things pinned down, choosing to be pinned down, transfixed by the idea or ideal of equality and democracy, on which they turn loudly and importantly, like propellers propelling. These States. Humanly, it is boring. As a historic phenomenon, it is amazing, ludicrous, and irritating.

If you don't pull the pin out in time, you'll never be able to pull it out. You must turn on it for ever, or bleed to death.

Naked to the waist was I
And deep within my breast did lie,

针插进了自己的体内,他现在仍然在这根针上痛苦地挣扎、呻吟着。这根针就是民主平等和自由。

如果不拔掉这根钉子并承认自然的不平等。美国就不会有什么生活。自然的优越,自然的卑下。达不到这个境界,美国人就只能像各式各样的螺旋桨一样拴在自由和平等上嗡嗡转。

就是在这个意义上说，菲尼莫·库柏的白人小说只具有历史意义和讽刺意义。人们,无论自以为有社会地位还是与社会格格不入,都被这样或那样的钉子钉着嗡嗡打转。这不是真正的人。他们被钉住,心甘情愿地被钉住,为平等和民主的理念和理想所钉住,像螺旋桨一样高声叫着趾高气扬地旋转。这些州。从人道的角度说,令人厌倦。作为一种历史现象,它令人吃惊、可笑、恼火。

如果你不及时拔出这根钉子,你就永远无法把它拔出来了。你只能永远在钉子上打转,流血至死。

我赤裸上身,
那剑戟深深

Though no man any blood could spy,

The truncheon of a spear-*

It is already too late?

Oh God, the democratic pin!

Freedom, Equality, Equal Opportunity, Education, Rights of Man.

The pin! The pin!

Well, there buzzes Eve Effingham, snobbishly impaled. She is a perfect American heroine, and I'm sure she wore the first smartly-tailored 'suit' that every woman wore. I'm sure she spoke several languages. I'm sure she was hopelessly competent. I'm sure she 'adored' her husband, and spent masses of his money, and divorced him because he didn't understand LOVE.

American women in their perfect 'suits'. American men in their perfect coats and skirts!

I feel I'm the superior of most men I meet. Not in birth, because I never had a great-grandfather.* Not in money, because I've got none. Not in education, because I'm merely scrappy.* And certainly not in beauty or in manly strength.

Well, what then?

刺进我的胸膛，

却没有一滴血流淌——

[见 William Morris(1834—1896):The Defence of Guenevere and Other Poems.]

是否太晚了？

哦，上帝，民主之针啊！

自由，平等，平等的机遇、教育、人权。

针！针！

可伊薇·埃芬厄姆为势利心所封住，嗡嗡叫着。她是个十足的美国女杰。我相信，她穿着女人最时髦精致的套服[这里的套服指的不是上装与长裤的搭配，而是上装与裙服的搭配]。我相信她可以说几国话。但我相信她一定没什么本事。我相信她"崇拜"她丈夫，大把大把地花他的钱。又因为他不懂什么叫爱而与他离异。

身着精美套服的美国女人，身着精美裙服的美国男人。

我相信我在我见到过的大多数男人里算得上优越。我优越，但并非生来优越，我连曾祖父都没有[劳伦斯曾说他父亲的祖父可能是法国大革命期间在滑铁卢

Just in myself.

When I´m challenged, I do feel myself superior to most of the men I meet. Just a natural superiority.

But not till there enters an element of challenge.

When I meet another man, and he is just himself –even if he is an ignorant Mexican pitted with small–pox –then there is no question between us of superiority or inferiority. He is a man and I am a man. We are ourselves. There is no question between us.

But let a question arise, let there be a challenge, and then I fell he should do reverence to the gods in me, because they are more than the gods in him. And he should give reverence to the very me, because it is more at one with the gods than is his very self.

If this is conceit, I am sorry. But it´s the gods in me that matter. And in other men.

As for me, I am so glad to salute the brave, reckless gods in another man. So glad to meet a man who will abide by his very self.

Ideas! Ideals! All this paper between us. What a weariness.

与拿破仑作战的法国人];我优越,但并非因为我有钱,我从未有过钱;我优越,并非我受过良好教育,我的学是断断续续上的[劳伦斯中学毕业后做过工,后一边当学徒教员一边进修,后考入诺丁汉大学学院读师范大专班]。我优越,也并非我漂亮或有男子汉的力气。

那,又是因为什么呢?

仅仅因为我自身。

当我受到挑战时,我的确感到我比我遇到的大多数人都优越。这仅仅是一种自然的优越。

当然,这只是在遇上挑战的情况下。

当我遇到另一个自在的人,即便他是一个长着天花的墨西哥人,我们之间也毫无优越与否可言。他是个人,我也是人。我们就是我们自己。我们之间没什么问题。

可是,让什么问题产生,令其有个什么挑战吧,这样,我会感到他应该尊敬我心中的神,因为这个神大于他的神。他应该对我尊敬,因为我比他更接近神,与神一体。

如果说这是自负的话,我只能表示歉意。可事关重要的是我身上的

If only people would meet in their very selves, without wanting to put some idea over one another, or some ideal.

Damn all ideas and all ideals. Damn all the false stress, and the pins.

I am I. Here am I. Where are you?

Ah, there you are ! Now, damn the consequences, we have met.

That's my idea of democracy, if you can call it an idea.

神，对别人来说亦是如此。

至于我，我十分乐于敬重别人身上那勇敢无忌的神。我十分乐意结识遵循自我行事的人。

观念！理想！我们之间有这一纸之隔。这真令人厌倦。

如果人们都以其自我相见，无需以观念或理想相加，那该多好。

让所有的观念和理想都见鬼去吧。让一切虚伪的压力和钉子都见鬼去吧。

我就是我。我在这里，你在哪里？

啊，你在那里！别去管什么后果吧，我们相识了。

如果你称之为观念的话，这就算是我的民主观吧。

CHAPTER 5
Fenimore Cooper's Leather stocking Novels

In his *Leatherstocking* books, Fenimore is off on another track. He is no longer concerned with social white Americans that buzz with pins through them, buzz loudly against every mortal thing except the pin itself. The pin of the Great Ideal.

One gets irritated with Cooper because he never for once snarls at the Great Ideal Pin which transfixes him. No, indeed. Rather he tries to push it through the very heart of the Continent.

But I have loved the Leatherstocking books so dearly. Wish-fulfilment!

Anyhow, one is not supposed to take LOVE seriously, in these books. Eve Effingham, impaled on the social pin, conscious all the time of her own ego and of nothing else, suddenly fluttering in throes of love: no, it makes me sick. LOVE is never LOVE until it has a pin pushed through it and becomes an IDEAL. The ego, turning on a pin, is wildly IN LOVE, always. Because that's the thing to be.

菲尼莫·库柏的"皮袜子"小说

菲尼莫的"皮袜子"系列小说走的是另一条路。他不再关心那些美国白人了——他们被"钉子"钉着，嗡嗡叫着，这钉子就是他们的远大理想。

你会为库柏从不抱怨那根钉住他的伟大理想之钉而愤怒。不，他不仅不抱怨，他还试图把这钉子钉入美洲大陆的心脏。

可我一直极喜爱那些"皮袜子"系列小说。那可真算得上是愿望的满足呢！

在这些书中，爱算不得是件郑重的事。伊薇·埃芬厄姆被社会的钉子紧紧钉住，除了她的"自我"对什么都不在意，可忽然间又为爱感到痛苦起来。这可真令我厌恶。爱，如果不被什么钉子钉住、变成一种理想就算

Cooper was a GENTLEMAN, in the worst sense of the word. In the Nineteenth Century sense of the word. A correct, clockwork man.

Not altogether, of course.

The great national Grouch was grinding inside him. Probably he called it COSMIC URGE. Americans usually do: in capital letters.

Best stick to National Grouch. The great American grouch.

Cooper had it, gentleman that he was. That is why he flitted round Europe so uneasily. Of course, in Europe he could be, and was, a gentleman to his heart′s content.

'In short,' he says in one of his letters, 'we were at table two counts, one monsignore, and English Lord, an Ambassador, and my humble self.'

Were we really!

How nice it must have been to know that one self, at least, was humble.

And he felt the democratic American tomahawk wheeling over his uncomfortable scalp all the time.

The great American grouch.

Two monsters loomed on Cooper′s horizon.

不得爱。那被钉住团团转的“自我”闹起爱情来总是意乱迷狂，因为那才是它要的东西。

从贬义上说，库柏是一位绅士。这是十九世纪的标准。他是个一丝不苟的人。

当然，也不尽然。

他很有点民族脾性。可能他称之为“宇宙冲动”。美国常把这两个词大写。

最好按照民族脾性做事。大美国的脾性。

库柏这个绅士就有这脾性。因此他在欧洲游历起来很是不安。当然了，在欧洲他尽可以心满意足地做他的绅士。

“一言以蔽之，”他在一封信中说，“我们是双重身份的人，既是显贵，是英国贵族，一个大使，又是贱民。”

这话说得极是!

知道自己卑贱，这是多么好啊。

他感到美国的民主战斧总在削着他的头皮，令他难受。

MRS COOPER　　MY WORK
MY WORK　　MY WIFE
MY WIFE　　MY WORK
THE DEAR CHILDREN
MY WORK!!!

There you have the essential keyboard of Cooper´s soul.

If there is one thing that annoys me more than a business man and his BUSINESS, it is an artist, a writer, painter, musician, and MY WORK. When an artist says MY WORK, the flesh goes tired on my bones. When he says MY WIFE, I want to hit him.

Cooper grizzled about his work. Oh, heaven, he cared so much whether it was good or bad, and what the French thought, and what Mr Snippy Knowall said, and how Mrs Cooper took it. The pin, the pin!

But he was truly an artist: then an American:then a gentleman.

And the grouch grouched inside him, throught all.

They seem to have been specially fertile in imagining themselves 'under the wigwam', do these Americans, just when their knees were comfortably under the

大美国人的脾性。

库柏的视野中出现了两个魔鬼。

库柏太太　　我的作品
我的作品　　我的太太
我的太太　　我的作品
亲爱的孩子们
我的作品!!!

你由此看到了库柏心中的键盘。

如果说有什么比商人及其商务更令我厌倦的话，那就是艺术家、作家、画家、音乐家和“我的作品”。当一位艺术家说“我的作品”时，会令我感到懒洋洋的。当他说“我的太太”时，我真想揍他。

库柏为他的作品感到焦虑。天啊，他太关心他的作品是好是坏、法国人怎么想、挑剔的万事通先生说什么以及库柏太太做何感想等等。钉子，钉子!

可他是个真正的艺术家，一个美国人，一位绅士。

mahogany, in Paris, along with the knees of

4 Counts

2 Cardinals

1 Milord

5 Cocottes

1 Humble self

You bet, though, that when the cocottes were being raffled off, Fenimore went home to his WIFE.

Wish Fulfilment		*Actuality*
THE WIGWAM	vs	MY HOTEL
CHINGACHGOOK*	vs	MY WIFE
NATTY BUMPPO*	vs	MY HUMBLE SELF

Fenimore, lying in his Louis Quatorze hotel in Paris, passionately musing about Natty Bumppo and the pathless forest, and mixing his imagination with the Cupids and Butterflies on the painted ceiling, while Mrs Cooper was struggling with her latest gown in the next room, and the dejeuner was with the Countess at eleven...

Men live by lies.

他的脾性贯穿于一切。

美国人在巴黎舒舒服服地与伯爵、主教、绅士、妓女(还有他卑下的自我)同桌进餐时,他们尤其会想自己是在“小木屋”里。

你敢打赌,那些妓女们一走,菲尼莫就会回家去找他老婆。

愿望的满足	(对比)	现实
小木屋		我的饭店
钦加哥[《最后一个莫希干人》中的部族酋长]		我的太太
纳蒂·班波[“皮袜子”系列小说中的主人公,他的绰号是“皮袜子”]		卑贱自我

菲尼莫躺在巴黎路易十四风格的饭店里,充满激情地缅怀着纳蒂·班波和浓密的森林,将他的幻想与天花板上绘着的丘比特和蝴蝶融为一体。而库柏太太此时正在另一间屋中试最时髦的衣服,十一时她将同伯爵夫人共进午餐……

人是靠撒谎活着的。

其实,菲尼莫爱的是那温文尔雅的欧洲大陆,他急切地等待着报界赞扬他的作品。

In actuality, Fenimore loved the genteel continent of Europe, and waited gasping for the newspapers to praise his WORK.

In another actuality he loved the tomahawking continent of America, and imagined himself Natty Bumppo.

His actual desire was to be: *Monsieur Fenimore Cooper, le grand écrivain américain.*

His innermost wish was to be: Natty Bumppo.

Now Natty and Fenimore, arm-in-arm, are an odd couple.

You can see Fenimore: blue coat, silver buttons, silver-and-diamond buckle shoes, ruffles.

You see Natty Bumppo:a grizzled, uncouth old renegade, with gaps in his old teeth and a drop on the end of his nose.

But Natty was Fenimore´s great wish: his wish-fulfilment.

'It was a matter of course,' says Mrs Cooper, 'that he should dwell on the better traits of the picture rather than on the coarser and more revolting, though more common points. Like West, he could see Apollo in the young Mohawk.'*

The coarser and more revolting, though more common points.

另一方面，他又爱那刀光剑影的美洲大陆，把自己想像成为纳蒂·班波。

他真正的愿望是成为“伟大的美国作家库柏先生”。

他从心里想成为纳蒂·班波。

纳蒂和菲尼莫手挽着手，是奇特的一对儿。

你可以看到菲尼莫的形象：蓝衣，银扣，鞋的搭扣上装饰着银和钻石，衣服打着皱边。

你可以看到纳蒂·班波的形象：头发灰白，粗野，牙齿间缝隙极大，鼻子尖上插着什么东西。

可是纳蒂是菲尼莫的希望——愿望的满足。

“当然了，”库柏太太说，“他应该描绘出那些优点来，而不是反映那粗野、反叛和普通的特征。像画家韦斯特一样，他在年轻的莫霍克族人身上看到了阿波罗的影子。”[美国画家 Benjamin West(1738—1820)在罗马看到阿波罗神像时感叹说："真像莫霍克族年轻的武士！"莫霍克族是北美印第安人的一族]

粗野、反叛但普通的特征。

You see now why he depended so absolutely on MY WIFE. She had to look things in the face for him. The coarser and more revolting, and certainly more common points, she had to see.

He himself did so love seeing pretty-pretty, with the thrill of a red scalp now and then.

Fenimore, in his imagination, wanted to be Natty Bumppo, who, I am sure, belched after he had eaten his dinner. At the same time Mr Cooper was nothing if not a gentleman. So he decided to stay in France and have it all his own way.

In France, Natty would not belch after eating, and Chingachgook could be all the Apollo he liked.

As if ever any Indian was like Apollo. The Indians, with their curious female quality, their archaic figures, with high shoulders and deep, archaic waists, like a sort of woman! And their natural devilishness, their natural insidiousness.

But men see what they want to see:especially if they look from a long distance, across the ocean, for example.

Yet the Leatherstocking books are lovely. Lovely half-lies.

They form a sort of American *Odyssey*, with Natty Bumppo for Odysseus.

现在你看明白了，他是多么绝对地依赖“我的太太”。她为他对事物做直接的观察。她得看到那些粗野、反叛，当然亦是更为普通的特征。

而他自己却那么喜欢看到印第安人的头颅，为此感到无比欣喜。

菲尼莫把自己想像成纳蒂·班波，此人一定是个吃了饭就打饱嗝的人。可库柏先生依旧是位绅士。因此他决定呆在法国，自行其是。

在法国，纳蒂就不会在饭后打饱嗝了，而钦加哥完全是他喜欢的阿波罗。

印第安人里要是有像阿波罗的就好了。印第安人那原始的躯体，高耸的肩和长腰，使他们看起来有一种奇特的女相。像女人！还有，他们生来就有一股子魔气和恶气。

可人总是要看自己想看到的东西，特别是从远距离处，横隔一个大洋时，更是如此。

当然，“皮袜子”系列小说是美的。是美妙的半掺谎言的作品。

这些作品构成了某种美国的《奥德赛》，纳蒂·班波则是其中的奥德修斯。

Only, in the original *Odyssey*, there is plenty of devil, Circes and swine and all. And Ithacus is devil enough to outwit the devils.* But Natty is a saint with a gun, and the Indians are gentlemen through and through, though they may take an occasional scalp.

There are five *Leatherstocking* novels: a decrescendo of reality, and a crescendo of beauty.

1. *Pioneers*: A raw frontier-village on Lake Champlain, at the end of the eighteenth century. Must be a picture of Cooper's home, as he knew it when a boy. A very lovely book. Natty Bumppo an old man, an old hunter half civilized.

2. *The last of the Mohicans*: A historical fight between the British and the French, with Indians on both sides, at a Fort by Lake Champlain. Romantic flight of the British general's two daughters, conducted by the scout, Natty, who is in the prime of life; romantic death of the last of the Delawares.

3. *The Prairie*: A wagon of some huge, sinister Kentuckians trekking west into the unbroken prairie. Prairie Indians, and Natty, an old, old man; he dies seated on a chair on the Rocky Mountains, looking east.

4. *The Pathfinder*: The Great Lakes. Natty, a man of about thirty-five, makes

只是在原来的《奥德赛》中才有不少魔鬼，如那位把人变成猪的女魔赛西等。伊萨科斯具有足够的魔力战胜这些魔鬼[伊萨卡是奥德修斯的故乡，伊萨科斯是劳伦斯的笔误，可能他要说的是奥德修斯]。可纳蒂是一位握枪的圣人，印第安人又是些彻头彻尾的绅士——当然他们偶尔也会砍个人头什么的。

“皮袜子”故事有五部，是现实的“渐弱”曲，却是美的“渐强”曲。

1.《开拓者》：十八世纪末詹普伦湖畔的一座荒蛮的边寨，极有可能是库柏家乡的一幅画，他从小就熟习那种氛围。这是一部很美的书。纳蒂·班波是一位半开化的老猎人。

2.《最后一个莫希干人》：詹普伦湖畔的一个要塞中英法争战，双方各有印第安人参战。英军司令的两个女儿在年富力强的侦察员纳蒂的操纵下浪漫地逃走了；德拉瓦尔家族的最后一个人浪漫地死了。

3.《草原》：一辆载着一群高大恶毒的肯塔基人的马车向西驶向完好的草原。草原上的印第安人和纳蒂这个老朽，他是在落基山上坐在椅子中面朝东部死去的。

4.《探路者》：在湖区，三十五岁左右的纳蒂向要塞守官那位健壮的

an aboritve proposal to a bouncing damsel, daughter of the Sergeant at the Fort.

5. *Deerslayer*: Natty and Hurry Harry, both quite young, are hunting in the virgin wild. They meet two white women. Lake Champlain again.

These are the five Leatherstocking books: Natty Bumppo being Leatherstocking, Pathfinder, Deerslayer, according to his ages.

Now let me put aside my impatience at the unreality of this vision, and accept it as a wish-fulfilment vision, a kind of yearning myth. Because it seems to me that the things in Cooper that make one so savage, when one compares them with actuality, are perhaps, when one considers them as presentations of a deep subjective desire, real in their way, and almost prophetic.

The passionate love for America, for the soil of America, for example. As I say, it is perhaps easier to love America passionately, when you look at it through the wrong end of the telescope,across all the Atlantic water, as Cooper did so often, than when you are right there. When you are actually in America, America hurts, because it has a powerful disintegrative influence upon the white psyche. It is full of grinning, unappeased aboriginal demons, too, ghosts, and it persecutes the white men, like some Eumenides, until the white men give up their absolute whiteness. America

女儿求婚失败。

5.《杀鹿人》:纳蒂和哈利·海利这两位年轻人在未开垦的土地上打猎时遇上了两个白人妇女。又是在詹普伦湖畔。

这就是“皮袜子”五部曲,纳蒂·班波分别出现在书中,扮演着“皮袜子”、“探路者”和“杀鹿人”的角色。

现在,请允许我容忍他书中的不真实,把它看做是愿望的满足和某种渴望的神话。这是因为,库柏所描写的那些让人变得如此野蛮的东西,与现实相比较及把它们看成是一种深刻的主观愿望的表述时,或许有它真实的一面。

比如,对美国激情的爱、对美国土地的爱,要我说,从望远镜的反面越过大西洋遥望美国(正像库柏所做的那样)时,你会很容易激情四射地爱上美国,可真让你亲临其境就不那么简单了。一旦你身处美国,你就会感到它让人痛苦,因为它对白人的心灵有一种撕裂的力量。它充满了龇牙咧嘴、心怀不满的土著魔王,就像复仇女神一样折磨着白人,直至白人放弃自身的种性。美国潜隐着暴力和抵抗的紧张。美国的白人觉得力不

is tense with latent violence and resistance. The very common sense of white Americans has a tinge of helplessness in it, and deep fear of what might be if they were not common-sensical.

Yet one day the demons of America must be placated, the ghosts must be appeased, the Spirit of Place atoned for. Then the true passionate love for American Soil will appear. As yet, there is too much menace in the landscape.

But probably, one day America will be as beautiful in actuality as it is in Cooper. Not yet, however. When the factories have fallen down again.

And again, this perpetual blood-brother theme of the *Leatherstocking* novels, Natty and Chingachgook, the Great Serpent. At present it is a sheer myth. The Red Man and the White Man are not blood-brothers: even when they are most friendly. When they are most friendly, it is as a rule the one betraying his race-spirit to the other. In the white man-rather high-brow-who 'loves' the Indian, one feels the white man betraying his own race. There is something unproud, underhand in it. Renegade. The same with the Americanized Indian who believes absolutely in the white mode. It is a betrayal. Renegade again.

In the actual flesh, it seems to me the white man and the red man cause a feel-

从心,深感恐惧。

但总有一天美国之魔会得到慰藉,鬼魂终会得到满足,地域之灵会回还。然后才会有真正的美国之爱。而目前,这块土地上有着太多的威胁。

不过,很可能,有朝一日美国会像库柏的书里写得那么美。当然现在还不是。那应该是工厂都倒塌以后的事。

让我们再次回到“皮袜子”故事的“血谊兄弟”主题上来:纳蒂和“大蛇”钦加哥。眼下这还是个神话。印第安人和白人并非亲兄弟,即便当他们最友好时他们也不是兄弟。当他们最友好时,那就是一个人出卖他的种族精神。一位高尚的白人“爱”印第安人,他让人感到是在背叛他的种族。这有那么点卑下和下作。叛徒。美国的印第安人也是一样,只要坚信白人的模式,就是背叛,是叛徒。

我以为,事实上白人和印第安人都让对方感到是一种压迫,不管他的心有多好。印第安人的生活与白人的生活截然两样。你无法让两条相异而流的河水平静相汇。

ing of oppression, the one to the other, no matter what the good will. The red life flows in a different direction from the white life. You can't make two streams that flow in opposite directions meet and mingle soothingly.

Certainly, if Cooper had had to spend his whole life in the backwoods, side by side with a Noble Red Brother, he would have screamed with the oppression of suffocation. He had to have Mrs Cooper, a straight strong pillar of society, to hang on to. And he had to have the culture of France to turn back to, or he would just have been stifled. The Noble Red Brother would have smothered him and driven him mad.

So that the Natty and Chingachgook myth must remain a myth. It is wish-fulfilment, an evasion of actuality. As we have said before, the folds of the Great Serpent would have been heavy, very heavy, too heavy, on any white man. Unless the white man were a true renegade, hating himself and his own race-spirit, as sometimes happens.

It seems there can be no fusion in the flesh. But the spirit can change. The white man's spirit can never become as the red man's spirit. It doesn't want to. But it can cease to be the opposite and the negative of the red man's spirit. It can open

当然,如果库柏在林中同一个高尚的印第安兄弟为邻生活一辈子的话,他会憋闷得大叫起来。他必须得依靠库柏太太这根坚实的社会支柱。另外,他必须得依靠法国的文化,否则他就会窒息——那些高尚的印第安人会令他窒息,令他发疯。

因此,纳蒂和钦加哥的神话就只能是一个神话。它是一种愿望的满足,是对现实的逃避。正像我们说过的,那条蜷曲的大蛇对任何白人来说都是太沉重了,除非那白人是一个叛徒,既恨自己又恨他本种族的精神。这样的人倒是偶尔也有。

似乎两种肉体是无法融合的。可精神是可以改变的。白人的精神永远也无法变得同印第安人的精神一样。它压根不想这样。但它可以不再成为印第安人精神的对立和否定力量。它可以开拓一片新的广阔精神领域,让印第安人的精神在那里有一块栖身之地。

开拓一片新的广阔精神领域意味着脱掉旧的意识。旧的意识像一座拥挤不堪的监牢,我们在里面日渐腐烂。

如果你不蜕掉紧绷绷的皮肤,你就不会生出新的、舒适的皮肤。

out a new great area of consciousness, in which there is room for the red spirit too.

To open out a new wide area of consciousness means to slough the old consciousness. The old consciousness has become a tight–fitting prison to us, in which we are going rotten.

You can't have a new, easy skin before you have sloughed the old, tight skin.

You can't.

And you just can't, so you may as well leave off pretending.

Now the essential history of the people of the United States seems to me just this: At the Renaissance the old consciousness was becoming a little tight. Europe sloughed her last skin, and started a new, final phase.

But some Europeans recoiled from the last final phase. They wouldn't enter the *cul de sac* of post–Renaissance, 'liberal' Europe. They came to America.

They came to America for two reasons:

(1) To slough the old European consciousness completely.

(2) To grow a new skin underneath, a new form. This second is a hidden process.

The two processes go on, of course, simultaneously. The slow forming of the

你不能。

既然不能,就别再装假。

美国的人民史在我看来大致上如此:在文艺复兴时期,旧的意识开始变得束缚人了。欧洲蜕了它最后一层皮,换了新的,进入了最后的发展阶段。

可有人退出了这最后的阶段,他们不愿进入文艺复兴后的死胡同即"自由"欧洲。于是他们来到美洲。

他们来美洲的原因有二:

①彻底摆脱旧欧洲意识。

②生长出一层新皮。这第二个进程是在暗中进行的。

这两个进程当然是同步的。新皮的缓慢生长过程正是旧皮的缓慢蜕变过程。这条不朽的蛇时而会感到幸福,感到一层闪着金光的奇特皮肤包住了自己;而有时它又会感到厌恶。似乎它的内脏被拽出来,他再一次强行挣扎着摆脱旧皮。

摆脱!摆脱!它用各种婉转的口气呼喊着。

new skin underneath is the slow sloughing of the old skin. And sometimes this immortal serpent feels very happy, feeling a new golden glow of a strangely-patterned skin envelop him: and sometimes he feels very sick, as if his very entrails were being torn out of him, as he wrenches once more at his old skin, to get out of it.

Out! Out! he cries, in all kinds of euphemisms.

He's got to have his new skin on him before ever he can get out.

And he's got to get out before his new skin can ever be his own skin.

So there he is, a torn divided monster.

The true American, who writhes and writhes like a snake that is long in sloughing.

Sometimes snakes can't slough. They can't burst their old skin. Then they go sick and die inside the old skin, and nobody ever sees the new pattern.

It needs a real desperate recklessness to burst your old skin at last. You simply don't care what happens to you, if you rip yourself in two, so long as you do get out.

It also needs a real belief in the new skin. Otherwise you are likely never to make the effort. Then you gradually sicken and go rotten and die in the old skin.

David Herbert Lawrence

它必得换上新皮才能挣脱旧皮。

它必得从旧皮里挣脱出来，新皮肤才能成为自己的。

它就是这样一个四分五裂的魔王。

真正的美国，扭曲着，像一条长期在蜕皮的蛇。

有时蛇并不能蜕皮。它们无法挣脱旧皮。于是它们就在旧皮下生病、死去，没有谁见到它新的样子。

冲破你的旧皮，需要一种决绝的勇猛。你压根儿不应该在意将发生什么，只要你能挣脱出来就行。

这还需要对新皮肤有真正的信仰。否则你就不会如此这般地努力，就会渐渐披着旧皮烂掉、死去了事。

菲尼莫在旧皮中活得很安全：一个绅士，跟欧洲人差不多一样十分得体。他安全地生活在旧皮中，却想像着一张新皮下美国的美艳状。

他恨民主。于是他躲避民主，幻想着有某种超越民主的东西。可他无时不属于民主。

躲避！可这并不能使梦想产生价值。

Now Fenimore stayed very safe inside the old skin: a gentleman, almost a European, as proper as proper can be. And, safe inside the old skin, he imagined the gorgeous American pattern of a new skin.

He hated democracy. So he evaded it, and had a nice dream of something beyond democracy. But he belonged to democracy all the while.

Evasion! –Yet even that doesn't make the dream worthless.

Democracy in America was never the same as Liberty in Europe. In Europe Liberty was a great life–throb. But in America Democracy was always something anti–life. The greatest democrats, like Abraham Lincoln, had always a sacrificial, self–murdering note in their voices. American Democracy was a form of self–murder, always. Or of murdering somebody else.

Necessarily. It was a *pis aller*. It was the *pis aller* to European Liberty. It was a cruel form of sloughing. Men murdered themselves into this democracy. Democracy is the utter hardening of the old skin, the old form, the old psyche. It hardens till it is tight and fixed and inorganic. Then it must burst, like a chrysalis shell. And out must come the soft grub, or the soft damp butterfly of the American–at–last.

America has gone the *pis aller* of her democracy. Now she must slough even

美国的民主与欧洲的自由向来不同。在欧洲,自由是生命的巨大搏动。可在美国,民主却历来是与生命为敌的。最伟大的民主主义者诸如亚伯拉罕·林肯之类,他们发出的声音里总有那么点牺牲和自戕音符。美国的民主历来是一种自戕的形式。不是自戕就是害人。

这是必要的,是最后的一个步骤,对欧洲的自由来说这是最后的一步,一种残酷的蜕变。人要进入这种民主状态就得自戕。民主是旧皮肤、旧形式和旧心理的紧紧束缚。它束缚着人,直至把人绷得死死的。然后它就会崩溃,就像蝶蛹一样挣破残壳,吐出柔软的蛴螬或柔软湿润的美国蝴蝶。

美国经历了民主的最后阶段。现在她甚至必须蜕掉这层皮了。

库柏梦幻中超越民主的是什么呢?他幻想钦加哥和纳蒂·班波的永恒友谊成为一个新社会的核心。他幻想的是一种新的人类关系。两个男人间赤诚的关系超越了性的深刻,超越财富,超越父子情,超越婚姻,超越爱。这情谊太深了,以至于超越了爱。两个男人赤诚相见,无爱,无言。这就是新社会的新核心,是通向新纪元的途径。它首先需要的是残酷的脱

that, chiefly that, indeed.

What did Cooper dream beyond democracy? Why, in his immortal friendship of Chingachgoodk and Natty Bumppo he dreamed the nucleus of a new society. That is, he dreamed a new human relationship. A stark, stripped human relationship of two men, deeper than the deeps of sex. Deeper than property, deeper than fatherhood, deeper than marriage, deeper than love. So deep that it is loveless. The stark, loveless wordless unison of two men who have come to the bottom of themselves. This is the new nucleus of a new society, the clue to a new world-epoch. It asks for a great and cruel sloughing first of all. Then it finds a great release into a new world, a new moral, a new landscape.

Natty and the Great Serpent are neither equals nor unequals. Each obeys the other when the moment arrives. And each is stark and dumb in the other's presence, starkly himself, without illusion created. Each is just the crude pillar of a man, the crude living column of his own manhood. And each knows the godhead of this crude column of manhood. A new relationship.

The Leatherstocking novels create the myth of this new relation. And they go backwards, from old age to golden youth. That is the true myth of America. She

胎换骨，然后才能轻松地进入一个新世界、新精神、新光景。

纳蒂和绰号“大蛇”的钦加哥既非势均力敌也非相差悬殊。时机一到，双方各自服从于对方。在对方面前，各自显得赤诚沉默，保持着自身的面目，没有任何幻想。各自都是一个顶天立地的男子汉，是粗砺、生机勃勃的男性支柱。他们都懂得生机勃勃、顶天立地的男子汉心中的神是怎样的。这是一种新的关系。

“皮袜子”系列故事创造了这种新关系的神话。而这神话是逆时针转动的，从老年到金色的童年。这是美国真正的神话。它从古老始，陈旧的皮肤打着皱褶，在着旧皮下挣扎。渐渐地，这层老皮蜕变了，年轻的皮肤生出来了。这就是美国的神话。

事实上，《开拓者》毫无疑问就是库柏城的事，那时库柏城才开始孕育：詹普伦湖畔的山林中一座小村寨，不过是一条荒凉的街道，道两旁是小木屋。这是住着野性边疆人的荒村，与文明形成鲜明对照。

冬天里，一个黑奴驾着雪橇穿过厚厚的雪地向这座边城驶来。雪橇中坐着一位漂亮的姑娘坦波小姐，还有她英俊的父亲——开拓者札吉·

starts old, old, wrinkled and writhing in an old skin. And there is a gradual sloughing of the old skin, towards a new youth. It is the myth of America.

You start with actuality. *Pioneers* is no doubt Cooperstown, when Cooperstown was in the stage of inception: a village of one wild street of log cabins under the forest hills by Lake Champlain: a village of crude, wild frontiersmen, reacting against civilization.

Towards this frontier–village in the winter time, a negro slave drives a sledge through the mountains, over deep snow. In the sledge sits a fair damsel, Miss Temple, with her handsome pioneer father, Judge Temple. They hear a shot in the trees. It is the old hunter and backwoodsman, Natty Bumppo, long and lean and uncouth, with a long rifle and gaps in his teeth.

Judge Temple, is 'squire' of the village, and he has a ridiculous, commodious 'hall'for his residence. It is still the old English form. Miss Temple is a pattern young lady, like Eve Effingham: in fact, she gets a young and very genteel but impoverished Effingham for a husband. The old world holding its own on the edge of the wild. A bit tiresomely too, with rather more prunes and prisms than one can digest. Too romantic.

坦波，他们听到林中枪声响了，这时老猎人纳蒂·班波出现了。他身材颀长，外表粗犷，手握一杆长长的猎枪。他的牙齿全露着缝隙。

札吉·坦波是村里的绅士，住在一座可笑的“大宅子”里。这仍然是旧英国的样子。坦波小姐是一位标致的女子，很像伊薇·埃芬厄姆，后者找了一位年轻的穷绅士做丈夫。旧的世界仍占据着这荒蛮世界的边缘，那装腔作势的样子令人生厌。这也太浪漫了点儿。

与这“大宅子”和乡绅形成对比的是那些真正的“边民”，是叛逆。这两类人相见在村里的酒馆、冰冷的教堂、圣诞游乐场、冰湖上和大型的射鸽会上。那是美好辉煌的生命图景。菲尼莫绘出的只是它的色彩罢了。

或许我的鉴赏力还太幼稚，可《开拓者》中的这些图景在我看来描绘得十分美妙。原始的村落街道，冬夜里窗口中闪亮着的火光。酒馆里粗犷的猎人和醉汉印第安醉汉约翰。教堂外，人们冒雪奔向火堆。还有圣诞欢宴上的丰富食物及雪地中射猎火鸡的比赛。春，绿了森林，人们从树木中分泌出槭糖来，鸽群从南方飞铺天盖地飞回来，被猎人成群地射下。人们在处女湖上热热闹闹地夜钓，还有的在猎鹿。

Against the 'hall' and the gentry, the real frontiers-folk, the rebels. The two groups meet at the village inn, and at the frozen church, and at the Christmas sports, and on the ice of the lake, and at the great pigeon shoot. It is a beautiful, resplendent picture of life. Fenimore puts in only the glamour.

Perhaps my taste is childish, but these scenes in Pioneers seem to me marvellously beautiful. The raw village street, with woodfires blinking through the unglazed window-chinks, on a winter's night. The inn, with the rough woodsman and the drunken Indian John; the church, with the snowy congregation crowding to the fire. Then the lavish abundance of Christmas cheer, and turkey-shooting in the snow. Spring coming, forests all green, maple sugar taken from the trees: and clouds of pigeons flying from the south, myriads of pigeons shot in heaps; and night-fishing on the teeming, virgin lake; and deer-hunting.

Pictures! Some of the loveliest, most glamorous pictures in all literature.

Alas, without the cruel iron of reality. It is all real enough. Except that one realizes that Fenimore was writing from a safe distance, where he would idealize and have his wishfulfilment.

Because, when one comes to America, one finds that there is always a certain

图卷！所有文学中最美好绚丽的图卷。

可这里却没有残酷的现实。真实是够真实的。可你意识到，菲尼莫是躲在遥远安全的地方写这些的，他尽可以把一切理想化并使他的愿望得到满足。

这是因为，你一到美国你就会发现这片国土上总有那么一种反抗的魔力。白人的心中有某种痛苦的反抗力。霍桑表达了这一点，而库柏则文过饰非。

美国的自然图景从未与白人融洽过，从没有过。白人从没有像身在美国这样痛苦过。他们身居的这块土地尽管是那样美丽，对我们来说却有点恶，磨牙吮血般地对立。

库柏掩饰了这种抵抗力，可事实上这是掩盖不了的。他意欲与这自然风景融为一体，为此他去了欧洲，从那边看到了这一切。其实那不过是一种幻象罢了。

当然，总有一天，这种浑然一体是会实现的。

这里所说的神话是纳蒂的故事。这位驼背的林中老猎人同他的印第

slightly devilish resistance in the American landscaps, and a certain slightly bitter resistance in the white man´s heart. Hawthorne gives this. But Cooper glosses it over.

The American landscape has never been at one with the white man. Never. And white men have probably never felt so bitter anywhere, as here in America, where the very landscape, in its very beauty, seems a bit devilish and grinning, opposed to us.

Cooper, however, glosses over this resistance, which in actuality can never quite be glossed over. He wants the landscape to be at one with him. So he goes away to Europe and sees it as such. It is a sort of vision.

And, nevertheless, the oneing will surely take place–some day.

The myth is the story of Natty. The old, lean hunter and backwoodsman lives with his friend, the grey–haired Indian John, and old Delaware chief, in a hut within reach of the village. The Delaware is christianized and bears the Christian name of John. He is tribeless an lost. He humiliates his grey hairs in drunkenness, and dies, thankful to be dead, in a forest fire, passing back to the fire whence he derived.

And this is Chingachgook, the splendid Great Serpent of the later novels.

安朋友约翰一起生活，后者头发花白，是旧德拉瓦尔家族的酋长，他就住在离村子不远的一间茅棚里。德拉瓦尔家族皈依了基督教，所以名字里才有了约翰这个字眼。他不属于任何家族，四海为家。他喝醉了以后嘲笑自己的白头发，最后死于一场林火，如愿以偿，正可谓从火中来再回火中去。

这就是后期小说中绰号“大蛇”的钦加哥。

毫无疑问，库柏从小就知道纳蒂和印第安人约翰。毫无疑问，就是从那时起这些人点燃了他的想像之火。等他长大成人以后，变成了社会上的显赫人物，有了库柏太太做靠山，这两个人对他倒成了神话。于是他寻找他们，从中寻回到了自己的童年。

至于故事本身：札吉·坦波不过是批准狩猎规则的工具。可纳蒂一辈子都在野林中持枪打猎，他是那样天真幼稚，根本不知道自己何以在松林中侵入了札吉的领土。他在禁猎期射死了一只鹿。法官极同情他，可又必须对他绳之以法。纳蒂这位古稀老人在万分惊恐中被套上枷锁投入了牢狱。尽管他们很快就释放了他，可他们的确曾把他投进了监狱。

No doubt Cooper, as a boy, knew both Natty and the Indian John. No doubt they fired his imagination even then. When he is a man, crystallized in society and sheltering behind the safe pillar of Mrs Cooper, these two old fellows become a myth to his soul. He traces himself to a new youth in them.

As for the story: Judge Temple has just been instrumental in passing the wise game laws. But Natty has lived by his gun all his life in the wild woods, and simply childishly cannot understand how he can be poaching on the Judge´s land among the pine trees. He shoots a deer in the close season. The Judge is all sympathy, but the law must be enforced. Bewildered Natty, an old man of seventy, is put in stocks and in prison. They release him as soon as possible. But the thing was done.

The letter killeth.*

Natty´s last connection with his own race is broken. John, the Indian, is dead. The old hunter disappears, lonely and severed, into the forest, away, away from his race.

In the new epoch that is coming, there will be no letter of the law.

Chronologically, *The Last of the Mohicans* follows *Pioneers*. But in the myth, *The Prairie* comes next.

字句可以杀人[见《新约·哥林多后书》3-6："字句叫人死，精意叫人活。"此句被哈代用作小说《无名的裘德》的题记]。

纳蒂与他那个种族的最后联系中断了。印第安人约翰死了。于是这位老猎人孤独地消失了，他逃进了森林，远远、远远地离开了他的种族。

在即将到来的新世纪中，不会再有什么法律条文。

从时间上算，《最后一个莫希干人》是紧随《开拓者》写出的。可在神话中，《草原》应排在《开拓者》后。

库柏当然了解他自己的美国。他曾到过西部旅行，见过大草原并在草原上和印第安人一同野营[此处劳伦斯记忆有误，库柏有过去西部的打算，但没有成行]。

《草原》如同《开拓者》一样带着不少现实的印记。这是一部奇特、美妙的著作，充满了末日感。书中有高大的肯塔基男人，有他们母夜叉似的女人。他们在大篷车中野营，他们的身影投射在草原上显得那样高大。这些开拓者与札吉·坦波不同。恐怖，野蛮，杀气腾腾，这些憔悴的白人向西进军，走向大陆的另一端，走向末日。末日复仇的巨大翅膀似乎在西部上空张开了，阴郁地冲着这些侵犯者张开。你会在弗兰克·诺瑞斯[1870—1902,

Cooper of course knew his own America. He travelled west and saw the prairies, and camped with the Indians of the prairie.

The Prairie, like *Pioneers*, bears a good deal the stamp of actuality. It is a strange, splendid book, full of sense of doom. The figures of the great Kentuckian men, with their wolfwomen, loom colossal on the vast prairie, as they camp with their wagons. These are different pioneers from Judge Temple. Lurid, brutal,tinged with the sinisterness of crime; these are the gaunt white men who push west, push on and on against the natural opposition of the continent. On towards a doom. Great wings of vengeful doom seem spread over the west, grim against the intruder. You feel them again in Frank Norris´s novel, *The Octopus*.* While in the West of Bret Harte* there is a very devil in the air, and beneath him are sentimental selfconscious people being wicked and goody by evasion.

In *The Prairie* there is a shadow of violence and dark cruelty flickering in the air. It is the aboriginal demon hovering over the core of the continent. It hovers still, and the dread is still there.

Into such a prairie enters the huge figure of Ishmael, ponderous, pariah-like Ishmael and his huge sone and his were-wolf wife. With their wagons they roll on

美国作家。《章鱼》描写农民与铁路托拉斯之间的战争]的小说《章鱼》中再次体验到这一点。布莱特·哈特[布莱特·哈特(1836—1902),美国著名短篇小说作家。他加入了19世纪的淘金潮,并以此为背景写作,其著名小说有《乱世福子》]笔下的西部,空气中有一个穷凶极恶的魔鬼,魔鬼下的人一个个多愁善感、自我意识极强,阴险而伪善。

《草原》为暴力和残酷的阴影所笼罩。那是盘旋在大陆中央上的土著之魔。现在它们仍在盘旋,那里仍然有恐怖。

就是在这样的草原上出现了伊斯梅尔沉重的身影。他几乎像一个贱民,还带着几个身强体壮的儿子和母夜叉一样的妻子。他们驾着大篷车从肯塔基边界像希腊神话中的独眼巨人一样滚滚驶向荒蛮的草原。日复一日,他们似乎是急匆匆走向天边,可他们的挺进的力度每况愈下,不得不停下来歇歇脚。他们受到谋杀的威胁,只好躲到草原上的一座小山中,在那里他们像半个神似的,坚持与大自然和狡猾的印第安人作战。

开拓者对西部野蛮的侵犯,有犯罪!

就在这时,老猎人纳蒂来了,他恰似一个和平使者,还带来了温和的印第安骑手们。不过他更像一个影子。

from the frontiers of Kentucky, like Cyclope into the savage wilderness. Day after day they seem to force their way into oblivion. But their force of penetration ebbs. They are brought to a stop. They recoil in the throes of murder and entrench themselves in isolation on a hillock in the midst of the prairie. There they hold out like demi-gods against the elements and the subtle Indian.

The pioneering brure invasion of the West, crime-tinged!

And into this setting, as a sort of minister of peace, enters the old hunter Natty, and his suave, horse-riding Sioux Indians. But he seems like a shadow.

The hills rise softly west, to the Rockies. There seems a new peace: or is it only suspense, abstraction, waiting?Is it only a sort of beyond?

Natty lives in these hills, in a village of the suave, horseriding Sioux. They revere him as an old wise father.

In these hills he dies, stitting in his chair and looking far east, to the forest and great sweet waters, whence he came. He dies gently, in physical peace with the land and the Indians. He is an old, old man.

Cooper could see no further than the foothills where Natty died, beyond the prairie.

这儿的山峦缓缓向西伸延，直至落基山脉。那儿似乎有一种新的宁静，或许这只是一种悬念、茫然或等待？无法超越吗？纳蒂就住在这山中的一座宁静的村子里。这里的西奥克斯印第安人都是骑手，他们把他尊为智慧的老父亲。

他就坐在椅子中遥望着东方死在山里，死时他仍望着那生于斯长于斯的森林和甘甜的大河流水。他静静地死去，终于求得与大地和印第安人融为一体。他太老、太老了。

库柏只能看到纳蒂死去的山脚一带，无法超越草原。

其他的小说又把我们带回东部。

《最后一个莫希干人》既是一种历史的叙述，又是一部真切的“浪漫”小说。我自己更喜欢里面的浪漫情调，它具有一种神话的意义，而叙述不过是一些记录罢了。

我们第一次看到了库柏笔下真正的女人：黑皮肤漂亮的科拉和她文弱的妹妹白百合[科拉的妹妹叫爱丽丝，不是白百合，劳伦斯记忆有误]。这是一个很好的对比：一个是黑皮肤性感的女人，另一个则是碧眼金发“纯洁”温顺可人

The other novels bring us back east.

The last of the Mohicans is divided between real historical narrative and true 'romance'. For myself, I prefer the romance. It has a myth meaning, whereas the narrative is chiefly record.

For the first time we get actual women: the dark, handsome Cora and her frail sister, the White Lily. The good old division, the dark sensual woman and the clinging, submissive little blonde, who is so 'pure'.

These sisters are fugitives through the forest, under the protection of a Major Heyward, a young American officer and Englishman. He is just a 'white' man, very good and brave and generous, etc., but limited, most definitely *borné*. He would probably love Cora, if he dared, but he finds it safer to adore the clinging White Lily of a younger sister.

This trio is escorted by Natty, now Leatherstocking, a hunter and scout in the prime of life, accompanied by his inseparable friend Chingachgook, and the Delaware's beautiful son –Adonis rather than Apollo –Uncas, The last of the Mohicans.

There is also a 'wicked' Indian, Magua, handsome and injured incarnation of

的白女人。

这两姐妹逃到森林中，受到年轻的美军少校(英国人)黑沃德的庇护。他是个白人，善良、勇敢、慷慨，可头脑不够灵活。如果有胆量，他很可能爱上科拉，可为了保险起见，他还是追求起那位白百合花似的温顺妹妹。

这三个人受到纳蒂的掩护。此时纳蒂正当年，绰号"皮袜子"，既是猎人，又是侦察员。与他同行的人有他的亲密朋友钦加哥和德拉瓦尔英俊的儿子恩卡斯，他不像阿波罗，倒像阿童尼斯，他就是"最后一个莫希干人"。

还有一个"恶毒"的印第安人叫马哇，相貌英俊，但人很刻毒。

科拉是大红的女性之花，刚烈、激情十足，是西印度群岛上一个英国军官和一个克瑞奥勒女人的后代。科拉爱恩卡斯，恩卡斯也爱她。可马哇也对科拉怀有欲望，欲望极强。这是一团迷人的肉欲之火。为此菲尼莫让科拉、恩卡斯和马哇全都死去，只剩下那白百合花传宗接代。她将给黑沃德生一堆后代。这就是我们"百合花腐烂"的今天[见莎士比亚十四行诗第94首："腐烂的百合，其臭胜过芜草。"]。

evil.

Cora is the scarlet flower of womanbood, fierce, passionate offspring of some mysterious union between the British officer and a Creole woman in the West Indies. Cora loves Uncas, Uncas loves Cora. But Magua also desires Cora, violently desires her. A lurid little circle of sensual fire. So Fenimore kills them all off, Cora, Uncas, and Magua, and leaves the White Lily to carry on the race. She will breed plenty of white children to Major Heyward. These tiresome 'lilies that fester',* of our day.

Evidently Cooper –or the artist in him –has decided that there can be no blood–mixing of the two races, white and red. He kills´em off.

Beyond all this heart–beating stand the figures of Natty and Chingachgook:two childless, womanless men, of opposite races. They are the abiding thing. Each of them is alone, and final in his race. And they stand side by side, stark, abstract, beyond emotion, yet eternally together. All the other loves seem frivolous. This is the new great thing, the clue, the inception of a new humanity.

And Natty, what sort of a white man is he? Why, he is a man with a gun. He is a killer, a slayer. Patient and gentle as he is, he is a slayer. Self–effacing, self–forgetting, still he is a killer.

很明显，是库柏或者说是作为艺术家的库柏决定，这两个种族之间不应混血。于是他让这些人全死了。

超越这一切的是纳蒂和钦加哥的形象。这两人都没有后嗣，没有女人，但属于两个对立的种族。他们构成了一种永恒。他们都独身，是两个完全不同的种族的人。可他们两人却能相互比肩、若即若离、超越情感地在一起永久不分。其他所有的爱都显得轻浮。这是一件伟大的新事物，是新人类的起点和孕育。

那么纳蒂是怎样的白人呢?哦，他是个扛枪打猎的人，是个杀生者。他有耐性，很有绅士气派，可他却是个杀生者。虽然不显山露水，不自以为是，可终归是个杀生者。

他曾有两次将敌人从高处摔下来。有一次摔下来的是英俊而恶毒的马哇，他一枪把他从高处射下来，他从空中掠过，可怕地掉落下来，摔死了。

这就是纳蒂，白人的先驱，一个杀生者。在《杀鹿人》中，他射下在空中高飞的鸟儿，鸟儿落下来死了，从看不见的地方落到了看得见的地方。

Twice, in the book, he brings and enemy down hurtling in death through the air, downwards. Once it is the beautiful, wicked Magua –shot from a height, and hurtling down ghastly through space, into death.

This is Natty, the white forerunner. A killer. As in *Deerslayer*, he shoots the bird that flies in the high, high sky so that the bird falls out of the invisible into the visible, dead, he symbolizes himself. He will bring the bird of the spirit out of the high air. He is the stoic American killer of the old great life. But he kills, as he says, only to live.

Pathfinder takes us to the Great Lakes, and the glamour and beauty of sailing the great sweet waters. Natty is now called Pathfinder. He is about thirty–five years old, and he falls in love. The damsel is Mabel Dunham, daughter of Sergeant Dunham of the Fort garrison. She is blonde and in all things admirable. No doubt Mrs Cooper was very much like Mabel.

And Pathfinder doesn′t marry her. She won′t have him. She wisely prefers a more comfortable Jasper. So Natty goes off to grouch, and to end by thanking his stars. When he had got right cleat, and sat by the campfire with Chingachgook, in the forest, didn′t he just thank his stars! A lucky escape!

通过这件事他完全成了一个自我象征:他要把被视作灵魂的鸟儿从高空中摘下来,他这个斯多葛式的美国人要杀死旧的生灵。据他自己说,他杀生只是为了生存。

《探路者》把我们带到美丽的大湖区,在这广淼的域上航行是多么迷人!在这本书中,纳蒂又成为“探路者”了,此时他正值三十五岁年华,他恋爱了。他爱上的姑娘是要塞守军上士邓海姆的女儿梅贝尔·邓海姆。她碧眼金发,一身的魅力。毫无疑问这梅贝尔就是库柏太太的化身。

可“探路者”并未娶她。是她不要他。她喜欢一个更讨人喜欢的人,名叫杰斯波。于是纳蒂开始发牢骚,但还是认命了。他弄明白了一切,和钦加哥坐在营火旁时,他岂止是感谢自己的星运,这简直是一件幸事!

对某个年龄段的男人来说,他们极容易陷入爱的纠缠中不能自拔。他们并非总是有幸被拒绝。

不管可怜的梅贝尔做了什么,她反正没成为班波夫人。

结婚不是纳蒂的事。他另有使命。

“皮袜子”系列小说中最吸引人的一部是《杀鹿人》。这里的纳蒂是一

Men of an uncertain age are liable to these infatuations. They aren't always lucky enough to be rejected.

Whatever would poor Mabel have done, had she been Mrs Bumppo?

Natty had no business marrying. His mission was elsewhere.

The most fascinating *Leatherstocking* book is the last, Deerslayer. Natty is now a fresh youth, called Deerslayer. But the kind of silent prim youth who is never quite young, but reserves himself for different things.

It is a gem of a book. Or a bit of perfect paste. And myself, I like a bit of perfect paste in a perfect setting, so long as I am not fooled by pretence of reality. And the setting of Deerslayer could not be more exquisite. Lake Champlain again.

Of course it never rains: it is never cold and muddy and dreary: no one has wet feet or toothache: no one ever feels filthy, when they can't wash for a week. God knows what the women would really have looked like, for they fled through the wilds without soap, comb, or towel. They breakfasted off a chunk of meat, or nothing, lunched the same and supped the same.

Yet at every moment they are elegant, perfect ladies, in correct toilet.

Which isn't quite fair. You need only go camping for a week, and you'll see.

个血气方刚的青年，绰号“杀鹿人”。他成熟沉寂，什么事都做得出。

这是一部书的宝石精华所在，或者说是人造宝石。我个人倒是喜欢完美背景下的人造宝石，只要不被假象所迷惑就行。《杀鹿人》的背景实在太美了。又是詹普伦湖。

对了，这里没有雨，没有阴冷潮湿的天气，没有人弄湿脚，没有人牙痛，一个星期不洗澡也不会感到肮脏。天晓得在这里生活的女人会是什么样子。她们整日在旷野中奔波，却不用肥皂、梳子或毛巾。早饭要么大块吃肉，要么什么都不吃，午饭和晚饭也是如此。

可她们总是梳妆打扮得高雅得体，时时显出贵妇人的样子。

其实并不尽然。你只需过上一周的野营生活，你就会看到真实情况。

可这本书不是一个真实故事而是一个神话。姑且把它当做一个可爱的神话来读吧。格利莫格拉斯湖。

那扛着长枪的年轻杀鹿人和一位高大英俊的猎人在一起，那后者叫哈利·海利，生着金色的络腮胡。那杀鹿人似乎出生在一株铁杉树下，出自松果，是年轻的林中之子。他沉默寡言、单纯，但爱寻思，道德感强，打

But it is a myth, not a realistic tale. Read it as a lovely myth. Lake Glimmerglass.

Deerslayer, the youth with the long rifle, is found in the woods with a big, handsome, blonde-bearded backwoodsman called Hurry Harry. Deerslayer seems to have been born under a hemlock tree out of a pine-cone: a young man of the woods. He is silent, simple, philosophic, moralistic, and an unerring shot. His simplicity is the simplicity of age rather than of youth. He is race-old. All his reactions and impulses are fixed, static. Almost he is sexless, so race-old. Yet intelligent, hardy, dauntless.

Hurry Harry is a big blusterer, just the opposite of Deerslayer. Deerslayer keeps the centre of his own consciousness steady and unperturbed. Hurry Harry is one of those floundering people who bluster from one emotion to another, very self-conscious, without any centre to them.

These two young men are making their way to a lovely, smallish lake, Lake Glimmerglass. Oh this water the Hutter family has established itself. Old Hutter, it is suggested, has a criminal, coarse, buccaneering past, and is a sort of fugitive from justice. But he is a good enough father to his two grown-up girls. The family lives in

枪百发百中。他之单纯是一种衰老的单纯而不是年轻的单纯。他的衰老是种族的衰老。他的全部反应和冲动都是循规蹈矩的、僵化的。他几乎无性,老得不成样子。可他聪明、勤劳、坚强。

同杀鹿人相反,哈利·海利则是个咆哮的家伙。杀鹿人我行我素,心地恬淡。可哈利·海利却爱胡言乱语,喜怒无常,感情用事,行无定准。

这两个年轻人一起向娇小美丽的格利莫格拉斯湖进发。这里住着哈特一家。据说老哈特过去当过海盗,犯过罪,是个逃犯。可对他的两个女儿来说,他却是个很好的父亲。他一家人住在水中的一座“城堡”似的木屋中,它建在水中的柱子上。这老头儿还建了一座“方舟”(船上之家),驾船带女儿们去捕河狸。

他的两个女儿也必然是黑暗和光明的象征。黑皮肤的朱迪丝充满激情,无所畏惧,有点为犯罪所诱惑。她是一朵红得发紫的花。海蒂妹妹碧眼金发,柔弱而单纯,又是一朵白百合花。可叹的是,这百合已开始腐烂。她有点蠢。

这两位猎人到达湖区的林子中时,战争开始了[这里指英法为争夺加拿大的

a log hut 'castle', built on piles in the water, and the old man has also constructed an 'ark', a sort of house-boat, in which he can take his daughters when he goes on his rounds to trap the beaver.

The two girls are the inevitable dark and light. Judith, dark, fearless, passionate, a little lurid with sin, is the scarlet-and-black blossom. Hetty, the younger, blonde, frail and innocent, is the white lily again. But alas, the lily has begun to fester. She is slightly imbecile.

The two hunters arrive at the lake among the woods just as war has been declared. The Hutters are unaware of the fact. And hostile Indians are on the lake already. So, the story of thrills and perils.

Thomas Hardy's inevitable division of women into dark and fair, sinful and innocent, sensual and pure, is Cooper's division too.* It is indicative of the desire in the man. He wants sensuality and sin, and he wants purity and 'innocence'. If the innocence goes a little rotten, slightly imbecile, bad luck!

Hurry Harry, of course, like a handsome impetuous meatfly, at once wants Judith, the lurid poppy-blossom. Judith rejects him with scorn.

Judith, the sensual woman, at once wants the quiet, reserved, unmastered Deer-

战争]。可哈特家的人们对此并不在意。充满敌意的印第安人早已聚在湖边。于是可怕的故事开始了。

托马斯·哈代曾把女人分为黑与白，罪恶与单纯，肉感与纯洁[这里指哈代《无名的裘德》里两个肤色不同的女人]。库柏也这样区分女人。这暗示出男人的欲望。男人要肉欲和罪恶，也要纯洁与"单纯"。如果这纯洁腐败了，再加点愚，就算是交了噩运！

哈利·海利这个英俊粗暴的人，像肉蝇一样渴望朱迪丝这朵迷人的毒花儿。可朱迪丝却看不起他，不要他。

朱迪丝这个性感女人一下子就爱上了文静洒脱的杀鹿人。她想控制他。杀鹿人有点被她迷住了，仅仅是有点儿。他是不会让她控制住的。他这样一位善思索的老精灵，是不会受到性勾引的。可能他至死还是个童男子。

他这样做是对的。他宁可独善其身，也不愿被这种虚假的性挑逗拉下水。他恪守孤独，他的魂是孤独的，永远孤独，因此他能保持自身的完整，肉体上也是独立的。这是一种诚实而无畏的苦行僧主义，杀鹿人一直

slayer. She wants to master him. And Deerslayer is half tempted, but never more than half. He is not going to be mastered. A philosophic old soul, he does not give much for the temptations of sex. Probably he dies virgin.

And he is right of it. Rather than be dragged into a false heat of deliberate sensuality, he will remain alone. His soul is alone, for ever alone. So he will preserve his integrity, and remain alone in the flesh. It is a stoicism which is honest and fearless, and from which Deerslayer never lapses, except when, approaching middle age, he proposes to the buxom Mabel.

He lets his consciousness penetrate in loneliness into the new continent. His contacts are not human. He wrestles with the spirits of the forest and the American wild, as a hermit wrestles with God and Satan. His one meeting is with Chingachgook, and this meeting is silent, reserved, across an unpassable distance.

Hetty, the White Lily, being imbecile, although full of vaporous religion and the dear, good God, 'Who governs all things by his providence', is hopelessly infatuated with Hurry Harry. Being innocence gone imbecile, like Dostoevsky's Idiot, she longs to give herself to the handsome meat-fly. Of course he doesn't want her.

And so nothing happens:in that direction. Deerslayer goes off to meet Chin-

这样苦行，只是到了中年时，才向丰腴的梅贝尔求婚。

在孤独中他的意识穿透了新大陆。他所接触的不是人类。他是在与森林和野性的美国之灵角斗着，就像一个隐士在同上帝和撒旦搏斗一样。他惟一接触的是钦加哥，这种沟通是在沉默中隔着难以超越的距离进行的。

海蒂这朵白百合花，尽管愚笨，尽管她深信宗教和亲爱善良的上帝(她认为上帝用神力统治一切)，却深深地爱上了哈利·海利。纯真但愚笨(就像陀思妥耶夫斯基的"白痴")，她渴望献身于这个英俊的血肉之躯。可他又不想要她。

于是在这方面没发生什么事。杀鹿人去和钦加哥相会并帮他追求一位印第安姑娘。替他人做嫁衣裳。

这痛苦的故事记录了白人心灵的幻灭。白人的心灵分为两半：纯洁和欲望，灵与肉。肉欲总被看成耻辱，正因此才更为人渴望。精神则让人觉得超俗、振奋、崇高，不可避免地与罪恶和耻辱作对。因此白人是在自我对立。他的一面与另一面势不两立，直到它成为一个痴人讲的故事，令

gachgook, and help him woo an Indian maid. Vicarious.

It is the miserable story of the collapse of the white psyche. The white man´s mind and soul are divided between these two things: innocence and lust, the Spirit and Sensuality. Sensuality always carries a stigma, and is therefore more deeply desired, or lusted after. But spirituality alone gives the sense of uplift, exaltation, and 'winged life', with the inevitable reaction into sin and spite. So the white man is divided against himself. He plays off one side of himself against the other side, till it is really a tale told by an idiot, and nauseating.

Against this, one is forced to admire the stark, enduring figure of Deerslayer. He is neither spiritual nor sensual. He is a moralizer, but he always tries to moralize from actual experience, not from theory. He says: 'Hurt nothing unless you´re forced to.' Yet he gets his deepest thrill of gratification, perhaps, when he puts a bullet through the heart of a beautiful buck, as it stoops to drink at the lake. Or when he brings the invisible bird fluttering down in death, out of the high blue. 'Hurt nothing unless you´re forced to.' And yet he lives by death, by killing the wild things of the air and earth.

It´s not good enough.

人厌烦的。

在此，人们不得不敬慕那位僵硬、忍耐性极强的杀鹿人。他既不是精神至上者也不是肉欲至上者。他是个道学家，可他总是从实际出发而不是空谈理论。他说："不到迫不得已时不要伤害任何东西。"可当一头漂亮的雄鹿低头饮水时，他的枪子儿却从鹿的心中穿过[劳伦斯记忆有误，枪杀饮水鹿的是哈特，而不是杀鹿人]。此时他感到了从未有过的快活。当他把鸟儿从空中射下来时，他也是这样感觉的。"不到迫不得已时不要伤害任何东西。"可他是靠杀生活着的，杀飞禽和走兽。

这并不太好。

可你读到的是美国白人的神话。别的，如爱啦，民主啦，陷入情欲啦，不过是些插曲罢了。美国人的心灵其实是残酷、孤独、苦行僧一般的，是杀手一样的心。它从未软化过。

当然这灵魂经常破碎。于是你见到了迷人的罪恶和朱迪丝，见到了海蒂的蠢笨、纯洁的欲望和海利身上的残暴、自大和自我意识力量。可也有崩溃。

But you have there the myth of the essential white America. All the other stuff, the love, the democracy, the floundering into lust, is a sort of by-play. The essential American soul is hard, isolate, stoic, and a killer. It has never yet melted.

Of course, the soul often breaks down into disintegration, and you have lurid sin and Judith, imbecile innocence lusting, in Hetty, and bluster, bragging, and self-conscious strength, in Harry. But there are the disintegration products.

What true myth concerns itself with is not the disintegration product. True myth concerns itself centrally with the onward adventure of the integral soul. And this, for America, is Deerslayer. A man who turns his back on white society. A man who keeps his moral integrity hard and intact. An isolate, almost selfless, stoic, enduring man, who lives by death, by killing, but who is pure white.

This is the very intrinsic -most American. He is at the core of all the other flux and fluff. And when this man breaks from his static isolation, and makes a new move, then look out, something will be happening.

真正的神话关心的不是崩溃，而是完整的灵魂向前行进的冒险。对美国来说，这就是杀鹿人。一个背弃了白人社会的人。一个独善其身的人。一个孤独、苦行几乎失去自我、顽强的人，他靠杀生活着，可他又是那么纯洁。

这是一个十分内在的美国人。他是其余一切的中心。一旦这个人脱离了静止的孤独并采取新的行动，看吧，会发生点什么事的。

CHAPTER 6
Edgar Allan Poe

Poe has no truck with Indians or Nature. He makes no bones about Red Brothers and Wigwams.

He is absolutely concerned with the disintegration-processes of his own psyche. As we have said, the rhythm of American art-activity is dual.

(1) A disintegrating and sloughing of the old consciousness.

(2) The forming of a new consciousness underneath.

Fenimore Cooper has the two vibrations going on together. Poe has only one, only the disintegrative vibration. This makes him almost more a scientist than an artist.

Moralists have always wondered helplessly why Poe's 'morbid' tales need have been written. They need to be written because old things need to die and disinte-

埃德加·爱伦·坡

坡与印第安人和大自然没什么联系。对红种印地安兄弟和他们的小木屋不屑一顾。

他只醉心于他心灵的崩溃过程。正如我们前面所说,美国的艺术活动有双重节奏。

①旧意识的崩溃与蜕变。

②在这之下新意识的形成。

菲尼莫·库柏身上同时有着两种震动并行不悖。而坡只有一种,只有崩溃的震动。这使他更像个科学家而非艺术家。

道学家们一直弄不明白坡的那些"可怕"故事何以写得出。这些故事

grate, because the old white psyche has to be gradually broken down before anything else can come to pass.

Man must be stripped even of himself. And it is a painful, sometimes a ghastly process.

Poe had a pretty bitter doom. Doomed to seethe down his soul in a great continuous convulsion of disintegration, and doomed to register the process. And then doomed to be abused for it, when he had performed some of the bitterest tasks of human experience, that can be asked of a man. Necessary tasks, too. For the human soul must suffer its own disintegration, consciously, if ever it is to survive.

But Poe is rather a scientist than an artist. He is reducing his own self as a scientist reduces a salt in a crucible. It is an almost chemical analysis of the soul and consciousness. Whereas in true art there is always the double rhythm of creating and destroying.

This is why Poe calls his things 'tales'. They are a concatenation of cause and effect.

His best pieces, however, are not tales. They are more. They are ghastly stories of the human soul in its disruptive throes.

之所以写得出，是因为旧的事物应该死去，应该崩溃；旧的白人心灵要渐渐崩溃，才会产生新的东西。

人甚至要把自己剥得精光才行。这是痛苦，有时甚至是可怕的过程。

坡的命运是悲惨的。他注定要在崩溃中剧烈抽搐而停止心灵的活动，同时他命中注定要记录下这一切。可一旦他经历了一个人所能够经历的痛苦，他注定要为此遭受屈辱。这些经历是必要的。人的灵魂必得清醒地遭受崩溃的痛苦，如果它想生存下来的话。

可是坡与其说是个艺术家倒不如说是位科学家。他像科学家在坩埚中溶解盐一样把自己化为灰烬。这几乎是在对灵魂和意识进行化学分析。在真正的艺术中总颤动着创造与毁灭的双重节奏。

为此，坡把他的作品称之为“故事”。这些故事组成了一连串的因果关系。

可他最优秀的作品并非故事。它们比故事的内涵要深远得多。这些是人类灵魂在分裂中痛苦挣扎着的可怕故事。

另外，这也是些“爱情”小说。

Moreover, they are 'love' stories.

Ligeia and *The Fall of the House of Usher* are really love stories.

Love is the mysterious vital attraction which draws things together, closer, closer together. For this reason sex is the actual crisis of love. For in sex the two blood-systems, in the male and female, concentrate and come into contact, the merest film intervening. Yet if the intervening film breaks down, it is death.

So there you are. There is a limit to everything. There is a limit to love.

The central law of all organic life is that each organism is intrinsically isolate and single in itself.

The moment its isolation breaks down, and there comes an actual mixing and confusion, death sets in.

This is true of every individual organism, from man to amoeba.

But the secondary law of all organic life is that each organism only lives through contact with other matter, assimilation, and contact with other life, which means assimilation of new vibrations, non-material. Each individual organism is vivified by intimate contact with fellow organisms: up to a certain point.

So man. He breathes the air into him, he swallows food and water. But more

《莉盖娅》和《厄舍古屋的倒塌》的确是爱情小说。

爱是神秘的生命吸引，它把一切连得愈来愈紧，直至连在一起。因此，性是爱的真正关键。在性中，男女的两套血液系统集中交汇，它们之间本来只有一层薄翳，一旦这层薄翳破裂，其结果就是死亡。

你看，什么东西都有个限度。爱也有个限度。

所有的有机生命都有一个主导规律，那就是每个有机体都是内在孤独、我行我素的。

其孤独一旦被破坏，混淆和混乱一旦产生，死亡即开始。

从人到变形虫，对每个个体的有机体来说情形都是如此。

可这些有机生命又有另一个规律，那就是每一个有机体只有与其他东西相接触、与其他生命兼容并蓄才能生存——这意味着吸收新的非物质的震颤。每个个体有机体通过与其他有机体亲密接触——达到某种程度——获得新生。

人亦如此。他呼吸空气，吞下食物和水。其实际意义要比这重大得多：他获得了别人的生命，他与他们发生了接触并且也把生命给予了别

than this. He takes into him the life of his fellow men, with whom he comes into contact, and he gives back life to them. This contact draws nearer and nearer, as the intimacy increases. When it is a whole contact, we call it love. Men live by food, but die if they eat too much. Men live by love, but die, or cause death, if they love too much.

There are two loves: sacred and profane, spiritual and sensual.

In sensual love, it is the two blood-systems, the man´s and the woman´s, which sweep up into pure contact, and almost fuse. Almost mingle. Never quite. There is always the finest imaginable wall between the two blood-waves, through which pass unknown vibrations, forces, but through which the blood itself must never break, or it means bleeding.

In spiritual love, the contact is purely nervous. The nerves in the lovers are set vibrating in unison like two instruments. The pitch can rise higher and higher. But carry this too far, and the nerves begin to berak, to bleed, as it were, and a form of death sets in.

The trouble about man is that he insists on being master of his own fate, and he insists on oneness. For instance, having discovered the ecstasy of spiritual love, he

人。这种接触随着亲密程度的增长而愈来愈频密。当这种接触成为全方位时，我们称之为爱。人本是靠食物活着的，可进食过多也会因此而死。人因为有爱才能活，可爱得过分也会因爱而死。

爱有两种：神圣的和世俗的，精神的和肉欲的。

在肉恋中，男人和女人的血液系统高涨起来相交汇，几乎混溶一起。几乎，但并非完全。他们的两股血浪之间总有那么一层可以想像的屏障，那种未知的颤动与力量可以透过它传导，但血液不可冲破它，那将意味着流血。

在精神恋中接触是纯神经方面的。相爱者双方的神经像并连一起似的共同颤动。振动频率可愈来愈高。可这样太过分的话，神经也会断裂，也会流血，从而造成某种死亡。

人的烦恼在于，他既坚持要掌握自己的命运又坚持融合。比如，发现了精神爱的狂喜后，他便坚持永远如此下去，除了这个什么旁的都不要，只有这才是生活。他称之为“强化”的生活。他要自己的神经与他人的神经在极度紧张和激动的融合中震颤。从而他发现了某种幻觉的兴奋，发

insists that he shall have this all the time, and nothing but this, for this is life. It is what he calls 'heightening' life. He wants his nerves to be set vibrating in the intense and exhilarating unison with the nerves of another being, and by this means he acquires an ecstasy of vision, he finds himself in glowing unison with all the universe.

But as a matter of fact this glowing unison is only a temporary thing, because the first law of life is that each organism is isolate in itself, it must return to its own isolation.

Yet man has tried the glow of unison, called love, and he *likes* it. It gives him his highest gratification. He wants it. He wants it all the time. He wants it and he will have it. He doesn't want to return to his own isolation. Or if he must, it is only as a prowling beast returns to its lair to rest and set out again.

This brings us to Edgar Allan Poe. The clue to him lies in the motto he chose for *Ligeia*, a quotation from the mystic Joseph Glanvill:*

And the will therein lieth, which dieth not. Who knoweth the mysteries of the will, with its vigour? For God is but a great will pervading all things by nature of its intentness. Man doth not yield himself to the angels, not unto death utterly, save on-

觉自己与整个宇宙都辉煌地融为一体了。

可事实上,这辉煌的融合只是暂时的。正如生命的首要规律所揭示的那样,每个有机体都是孤独的,它必须回归自身的孤独状态中。

可是,人经历了那称之为爱的光辉的融合,他喜欢这个,这东西给了他最大的快感。他需要这个,什么时候都要。他需要它,一定要得到它不可。他并不想回归到自身的孤独中。如果要回归,那也如同一头四处觅食的野兽,不过是回窝里来歇歇脚,还准备再出去。

说到这里,让我们来谈谈埃德加·爱伦·坡吧。他为《莉盖娅》所选择的箴言为我们提供了认识他的线索,这段话出自那位神秘的约瑟夫·格兰威尔[Joseph Glanville(1636—1680),哲学家。但这段箴言却是爱伦·坡的杜撰]。

"意志永不死。有谁知道意志的神秘和力量?上帝不过是决意渗透一切的一个巨大意志。人,只要他的薄弱意志不倒,他就既不会服从天使也不会全然服从死亡。"

这是一个意义深远的格言,也是致命的箴言。

因为,如果上帝是一个巨大的意志,那么宇宙不过是一个工具罢了。

ly throught the weakness of his feeble will.

It is a profound saying: and a deadly one.

Because if God is a great will, then the universe is but an instrument.

I don't know what God is. But He is not simply a will. That is too simple. Too anthropomorphic. Because a man wants his own will, and nothing but his will, he needn't say that God is the same will, magnified *ad infinitum.*

For me, there may be one God, but He is nameless and unknowable.

For me, there are also many gods, that come into me and leave me again. And they have very various wills, I must say.

But the point is Poe.

Poe had experienced the ecstasies of extreme spiritual love. And he wanted those ecstasies and nothing but those ecstasies. He wanted that great gratification, the sense of flowing, the sense of unison, the sense of heightening of life. He had experienced this gratification. He was told on every hand that this ecstasy of spiritual, nervous love was the greatest thing in life, was life itself. And he had tried it for himself, he knew that for him it was life itself. So he wanted it. And he would have it. He set up his will against the whole of the limitations of nature.

我不知道上帝是什么样的。可能他并非只是一个意志。这未免太简单、太有人类学的味道。人是需要意志的,只需要他的意志,但他没有必要说是上帝就是这同一个意志,是个无穷尽的意志。

在我看来,可能有一个上帝,但他既没有名字,也无法让人认知。

在我看来,也可以说有许多上帝在我体内进进出出。我必须说他们有许多个意志。

可现在要说的是坡的问题。

坡经历过极端精神恋的狂喜。他需要的不是别的什么,仅仅是这种狂喜。他要的是那种巨大的满足,那种流溢、交融之感和生命的强化。他经历了这种满足。他认为无论如何,这种精神和神经的爱所带来的狂喜是生活中最伟大的事,是生活本身。他曾亲身相试,深知这就是生活本身。所以他渴望这个,一定要得到它。为此他决心与自然界的一切局限性作斗争。

这是一个勇敢的人,他勇于按照自己的信仰和经验行动。可他同时又是一个自高自大的蠢人。

This is a brave man, acting on his own belief, and his own experience. But it is also an arrogant man, and a fool.

Poe was going to get the ecstasy and the heightening, cost what it might. He went on in a frenzy, as characteristic American women nowadays go on in a frenzy, after the very same thing: the heightening, the flow, the ecstasy. Poe tried alcohol, and any drug he could lay his hand on.* He also tried any human being he could lay his hands on.

His grand attempt and achievement was with his wife; his cousin, a girl with a singing voice. With her he went in for the intensest flow, the heightening, the prismatic shades of ecstasy. It was the intensest nervous vibration of unison, pressed higher and higher in pitch, till the blood-vessels of the girl broke, and the blood began to flow out loose. It was love. If you call it love.

Love can be terribly obscene.

It is love that causes the neuroticism of the day. It is love that is the prime cause of tuberculosis.

The nerves that vibrate most intensely in spiritual unisons are the sympathetic ganglia of the breast, of the throat, and the hind brain. Drive this vibration over-in-

坡一定要获得那种狂喜和兴奋，付出多大的代价都在所不惜。他像今日典型的美国妇女一样疯狂地追求着这一样东西：兴奋、流溢和狂喜。坡试图酗酒，而且弄得到的毒品都试过[劳伦斯可能读到过坡酗酒的描述。至于毒品和麻醉品，坡的很多短篇小说里的主人公和叙述者都酗酒或吸食吗啡和鸦片。所以劳伦斯推断坡也使用毒品]。他还“试”过他所能“试”的人。

他最大的企图和成功是在他妻子身上获得的。他妻子本是他的表妹，一个声如歌唱的女人[爱伦·坡在二十六岁上迎娶了自己的表妹 Virginia Clemm，曾描写过她歌唱的声音]。他与她一道经历了最汹涌的流溢、最强烈的兴奋和最炫目的狂喜。这是最紧张的神经交融，愈来愈紧张，终于导致姑娘血流如注。这就是爱，如果你称之为爱的话。

爱可以是极淫秽的东西。

是爱造成了今日的神经病。爱是肺结核的根源。

在精神的交融中振动最剧烈的是胸腔、喉部和后脑的交感神经结[劳伦斯可能在 1917 年读到了 Janes Pryse 所著的有关“七个主要神经结”的著作，将此与自己的“血液意识”理论结合发展出了自己的一套神秘物质主义世界观并以此对文学作品甚至社会和人性进行分

tensely, and you weaken the sympathetic tissues of the chest –the lungs –or of the throat, or of the lower brain, and the tubercles are given a ripe field.

But Poe drove the vibrations beyond any human pitch of endurance.

Being his cousin, she was more easily keyed to him.

Ligeia is the chief story. Ligeia! A mental–derived name. To him the woman, his wife, was not Lucy. She was Ligeia. No doubt she even preferred it thus.

Ligeia is Poe's love–story, and its very fantasy makes it more truly his own story.

it is a tale of love pushed over a verge. And love pushed to extremes in a battle of wills between the lovers.

Love is become a battle of wills.

Which shall first destroy the other, of the lovers? Which can hold out longest, against the other?

Ligeia is still the old–fashioned woman. Her will is still to submit. She wills to submit to the vampire of her husband's consciousness. Even death.

'In stature she was tall, somewhat slender, and, in her latter days, even emaciated. I would in vain attempt to portray the majesty, the quiet ease, of her de-

析。详见劳伦斯的两本哲学随笔《精神分析与无意识》和《无意识断想》，它们构成了劳伦斯后期思想的核心，是其性爱理论的基础，亦是其文学观的基础]。这种振荡如果太剧烈的话，胸腔的交感组织——肺、喉或小脑的交感组织就会变弱，从而给结核提供了成熟的病灶。

坡使这种振荡超过了人所能忍受的限度。

作为他的表妹，她更容易与他产生共鸣。

《莉盖娅》是他的主要作品。莉盖娅！一个苦心炮制的名字。对他来说，他的妻子不是露茜，她是莉盖娅。毫无疑问，她甚至喜欢这个名字。

《莉盖娅》是坡的爱情小说，而它愈是古怪愈能说明这个故事写的就是坡自己。

这是一个超越一切的爱的故事。两个恋人意志的争斗达到了极端。

爱是意志的战争。

两个恋人谁会首先毁掉另一个呢？哪个能坚持得持久？

莉盖娅还是个旧式女人。她的意志终究是要屈服对方。她要屈服丈夫那魔鬼般的思想，甚至要向死亡低头。

meanour or the incomprehensible lightness and elasticity of her footfall... I was never made aware of her entrance into my closed study, save by the dear music of her low sweet voivce, as she placed her marble hand upon my shoulder.'

Poe has been so praised for his style. But it seems to me a meretricious affair. 'Her marble hand' and 'the elasticity of her footfall' seem more like chair-springs and mantel-pieces than a human creature. She never was quite a human creature to him. She was an instrument from which he got his extremes of sensation. His *machine à plaisir,** as somebody says.

All Poe's style, moreover, has this mechanical quality, as his poetry has a mechanical rhythm. He never sees anything in terms of life, almost always in terms of matter, jewels, marble, etc.,* -or in terms of force, scientific. And his cadences are all managed mechanically. This is what is called 'having a style'.

What he wants to do with Ligeia is to analyse her, till he knows all her component parts, till he has got her all. in his consciousness. She is some strange chemical salt which he must analyse out in the test-tubes of his brain, and then-when he's finished the analysis-E *finita la commedia*!

But she won't be quite analysed out. There is something, something he can't

"她高高的个子，很苗条，后来甚至变得很憔悴了。我无法描述她举止的高雅与娴静，举手投足的轻盈与纤巧……她走进我关着门的书房时从来都不惊动我，除非她那如歌的甜美声音和放在我肩上的那双玉手才能让我意识到她的到来。"

人们一直在赞美坡的风格，可我觉得那是一种虚华。"她那双玉手"和"举手投足的轻盈与纤巧"听起来像椅子上的弹簧和壁炉台，而不是人。在他眼里她从来都不是个人。她只是一件工具，他从她那里获得极端的感觉。正如有人指出的那样，她是他的"快感工具"[此引语见 Mademoiselle de Maupin by Théophile Gautier]。

坡的风格具有某种机械呆板的特征，这正如他的诗的节奏比较呆板一样。他从不用生命的观点观察事物，他几乎总是用物质的观点看事物，眼里都是珠宝或大理石什么的[在《厄舍古屋的倒塌》和《利盖雅》中可见珍珠和红宝石流光溢彩的描述]。他还用力量和科学的观点看问题。他的节奏十分呆板。这就是他的"风格"。

他要对莉盖娅所做的就是分析她，直到他了解了她全部的组成部

get. Writing of her eyes, he says: 'They were, I must believe, far larger than the ordinary eyes of our own race' –as if anybody would want eyes 'far larger' than other folks'. 'They were even fuller than the fullest of the gazelle eyes of the tribe of the valley of Nourjahad' –which is blarney. 'The hue of the orbs was the most brilliant of black and, far over them, hung jetty lashes of great length' –suggests a whip-lash.* 'The brows, slightly irrgular in outline, had the same tint. The "strangeness", horever, which I found in the eyes, was of a nature distinct from the formation, or the colour or the brilliancy of the features, and must, after all, be referred to the expression.' –Sounds like an anatomist anatomizing a cat–

Ah, word of no meaning! behind whose vast latitude of mere sound we entrench our ignorance of so much of the spiritual. The expression of the eyes of Ligeia! How for long hours have I pondered upon it! How have I, through the whole of a midsummer night, struggled to fathom it! What was it–that something more profound than the well of Democritus* –which lay far within the pupils of my beloved! What was it?I was possessed with a passion to discover...

It is easy to see why each man kills the thing he loves. To know a living thing is to kill it. You have to kill a thing to know it satisfactorily. For this reason, the de-

分，直到他从理智上全部弄懂了她。她是某种奇特的化学盐，他必须用他头脑这根试管彻底地分析她，一旦分析完毕，这场喜剧就结束了！

可她是分析不透的。有什么东西他无法得到。描述她的眼睛时，他这样写道："它比我们一般人的眼睛要大得多。"似乎谁都愿意有一对比他人"大得多"的眼睛。"它们甚至比诺亚哈德峡谷中瞪羚的眼睛还要圆。"——这是一种奉承。"眼珠黑亮黑亮的，眼睫毛细长而黑。"让人想起鞭子[英语中"睫毛"与"鞭打"是一个词 lash]。"眉毛不够规则，但颜色也极黑。眼睛的这种独特是天生的，这容颜美艳夺目。"——这话听起来真像一位解剖家在解剖一只猫。

"啊，语言无用！我们的语言不过是声音，它掩盖了我们对于精神境界的无知。莉盖娅眼神！我是如何久久地为它凝神苦思！在整个仲夏夜，我一直苦苦地要解开它的谜！它是怎么回事?这深藏在我爱人眸子后面那比德谟克利特之井更为深远的东西！它是什么?我充满激情要去发现……"[Democritus(？460—？370B.C.)，希腊哲学家。此句可能与其深水之好坏论述有关。]

由此我们可以轻易地明白人是如何杀死他的爱物的。要弄懂一件活

sirous consciousness, the spirit, is a vampire.

One should be sufficiently intelligent and interested to know a good deal *about* any person one comes into close contact with. About her. Or about him.

But to try to know any living being is to try to suck the life out of that being.

Above all things, with the woman one loves. Every sacred instince teaches one that one must leave her unknown. You know your woman darkly, in the blood. To try to know her mentally is to try to kill her. Beware, oh woman, of the man who wants to find out wbat you are. And, oh men, beware a thousand times more of the woman who wants to know you or get you, what you are.

It is the temptation of a vampire fiend, is this knowledge.

Man does so horribly want to master the secret of life and of individuality with his mind. It is like the analysis of protoplasm. You can only analyse dead protoplasm, and know its constituents. It is a death–process.

Keep knowledge for the world of matter, force, and function. It has got nothing to do with being.

But Poe wanted to know –wanted to know what was the strangeness in the eyes of Ligeia. She might have told him it was horror at his probing, horror at being

生生的事物就等于杀死了它。要十分了解一件事你就得杀死它。为此，我们说那渴望着的意识——精神是一头吸血鬼。

一个人与另一个人打交道，非得十分了解对方不可。了解她或他。

可是，要了解任何一个活生生的生命，就等于从他(她)那里吸吮生命。

对于所爱的女人尤其如此。全部神圣的直觉告诉我们，应该让她保持陌生，你只应该在冥冥中通过血液感知你的女人。试图理智地了解她就是试图戕害她，啊，女人，请注意，那些男人要弄明白你到底是怎么回事。啊，男人，请注意，女人更要弄明白你到底是怎么回事。

这种了解是吸血魔王的诱惑。

男人的确十分渴望用理智控制生命与个性的秘密。这有点像分析细胞质，只有死的细胞质才会供你分析，分析它的成分。这是一个死亡的过程。

对物质、力量和功能世界的了解与生命是毫无关系的。

可坡想要了解——了解莉盖娅眼睛中的奇特现象。她很可能已告诉

vamped by his consciousness.

But she wanted to be vamped. She wanted to be probed by his consciousness, to be known. She paid for wanting it, too.

Nowadays it is usually the man who wants to be vamped, to be known.

Edgar Allan probed and probed. So often he seemed on the verge. But she went over the verge of death before he came over the verge of knowledge. And it is always so.

He dicided, therefore, that the clue to the strangeness lay in the mystery of will. 'And the will therein lieth, which dieth not...'

Ligeia had a 'gigantic volition' ....'An intensity in thought, action, or speech was possibly, in her, a result, or at least an index'(he really meant indication) 'of that gigantic volition which, during our long intercourse, failed to give other and more immediate evidence of its existence.'

I should have thought her long submission to him was chief and ample 'other evidence'.

'Of all the women whom I have ever known, she, the outwardly calm, the ever-placid Ligeia, was the most violently a prey to the tumultuous vultures of stern pas-

过他，让他如此探索、吸血鬼般地吸吮是多么可怕。

可她又想被吸吮。她愿意被他的意识吸吮、愿意被他了解。为此她也付出了代价。

如今愿意被吸吮、被了解的一般是男人。

埃德加·爱伦·坡苦苦地百般探索。他时常似乎达到了极限。可还未等他越过知识的极限她已越过了死亡的界限。事情总是这样。

于是他决意认为，了解那"奇特现象"的线索在于意志的神秘。"意志不死……"

莉盖娅有一个"坚强的意志"……"思维行为或语言呈现出紧凑感，这很可能是那坚强意志的结果或标志"。"在我们长久的交往中它并未显出其存在的明显迹象。"

我想，她那样久地服从于他，这本身足以算得上迹象了。

"我认识的女人中，表面上十分文静的莉盖娅其实最容易为激情所俘获。对于这种激情我只能通过那双神奇的大眼睛中进行估量，那双愉快的眼睛令我惊喜。她那十分低沉的声音透出几乎富有魔力的旋律，抑

sion. And of such passion I could form no estimate, save by the miraculous expansion of those eyes which at once so delighted and appalled me–by the almost magical melody, modulation, distinctness, and placidity of her very low voice–and by the fierce energy (rendered doubly effective by contrast with her manner of utterance)of the wild words which she habitually uttered.'

Poor Poe, he had caught a bird of the same feather as himself. One of those terrible cravers, who crave the further sensation. Crave to madness or death. 'Vultures of stern passion' indeed! Condors.

But having recognized that the clue was in her gigantic volition, he should have realized that the process of this loving, this craving, this knowing, was a struggle of wills. But Ligeia, true to the great tradition and mode of womanly love, by her will kept herself submissive, recipient. She is the passive body who is explored and analysed into death. And yet, at times, her great female will must have revolted. 'Vultures of stern passion! ' With a convulsion of desire she desired his further probing and exploring. To any lengths. But then, 'tumultuous vultures of stern passion'. She had to fight with herself.

But Ligeia wanted to go on and on with the craving, with the love, with the

扬顿挫清晰流畅；她习惯中口吐豪言，言谈中都透着一种狂放的力度(与她说话的姿态相比，这力度似乎是加倍的)。”

可怜的坡，他找的恋人与他原是一路人。她也在拼命追求更玄妙的感觉。追求到发疯以至于死亡的境地。真是“激情十足的秃鹫”！

既然他已意识到那线索就在她坚强的意志中，他就应该明白这种爱、追求和了解的进程是意志的斗争。莉盖娅的确依从伟大的传统和妇人之道，坚持服从与接受。她是一个被动体，任人分析与探索直至死亡。可她那巨大的女人意志也会时有反抗。“激情十足的秃鹫！”她仍渴望他进一步的探索，直至无穷。可是，她这“激情十足的秃鹫”还得与自己作斗争才行。

莉盖娅要继续这种追寻、爱、感觉，继续探索和了解直至走到尽头。

可是没有尽头。只有死亡，是一种终止。男人女人都得上这一当。男人为寻求最终的知识总会以被出卖而告结束。

“她爱我，对此我深信不移。我极容易地察觉到，以她那样的胸怀，爱绝不会是一般的激情所致。但只有在死亡中我才深深地感受到她的情有

sensation, with the probing, with the knowing, on and on to the end.

There is no end. There is only the rupture of death. That's where men, and women, are 'had'. Man is always sold, in his search for final knowledge.

That she loved me I should not have doubted; and I might have been easily aware that, in a bosom such as hers, love would have reigned no ordinary passion. But in death only was I fully impressed with the strength of her affection. For long hours, detaining my hand, would she pour out before me the overflowing of a heart whose more than passionate devotion amounted to idolatry.

(Oh, the indecency of all this endless intimate talk!)

How had I deserved to be so blessed by such confessions? (Another man would have felt himself cursed.) How had I deserved to be so cursed with the removal of my beloved in the hour of her making them? But upon this subject I cannot bear to dilate. Let me say only that in Ligeia's more than womanly abandonment to a love, alas! all unmerited, all unworthily bestowed, I at length recognized the principle of her longing, with so wildly earnest a desire, for the life which was now fleeing so rapidly away. It is this wild longing –it is this eager vehemence of desire for life – but for life, that I have no power to portray, no utterance capable of expressing.

多么重。她一连数小时抓紧我的手，向我倾诉衷肠，她那激情的献身精神使她把我当成偶像崇拜着。”

(啊，这没完没了的情话是多么不洁！)

“我何以配得上享有她的坦露胸怀?(换个人会感到是被诅咒。)我何以受得了我爱人的离去?那才是对我的诅咒，我不想夸大这一点。我只能说，莉盖娅对爱的献身是一般女性所不能企及的。尽管我是那么微不足道，但我还是终于意识到了她那狂热的渴求。可是，那生命却飞速地流逝了。那对生命的狂热渴求——仅仅是生命——是我无力描述、无法表达的。”

够了，这些无论如何也够了。

“无者有了也要被剥夺。”[详见《新约·马太福音》25:29:“凡有的，还要加给他，叫他余;没有的，连他所有的也要夺过来。”]

“占有生命的人仍被赐予生命，没有生命的人有了生命也会被剥夺。”

或许，她就是其中之一。

Well, that is ghastly enough, in all conscience.

'And from them that have not shall be taken away even that which they have.'*

'To him that hath life shall be given life, and from him that hath not life shall be taken away even that life which he hath.'

Or her either.

These terribly conscious brids, like Poe and his Ligeia, deny the very life that is in them; they want to turn it all into talk, into knowing. And so life, which will not be known, leaves them.

But poor Ligeia, how could she help it? It was her doom. All the centuries of the spirit, all the years of American rebellion against the Holy Ghost, had done it to her.

She dies, when she would rather do anything than die. And when she dies the clue, which he only lived to grasp, dies with her.

Foiled!

Foiled!

No wonder she shrieks with her last breath.

On the last day Ligeia dictates to her husband a poem. As poems go, it is

这些理智的鸟——如坡和他的莉盖娅，否认他们身上的生命本身；他们想把这生命全变成空谈，变成要了解的东西。于是，那不可知的生命离他们而去了。

可是可怜的莉盖娅又能怎样呢?这是她的命。一个世纪接一个世纪的精神，多年来美国对圣灵的反叛决定了她的命运。

她在她仍想做什么事的时候死了。她死了。他要掌握的线索也随她而去了。

泡影!

泡影!

难怪她死前用尽最后一口气仰天长啸。

在她弥留之际，她向丈夫口授了一首诗。这些诗句极端虚伪、夸张。不过如果你为莉盖娅设身处地想想，你就会觉得这诗十分真实可信。

熄灭了，全部的光芒，全熄灭了!

一块尸布暴风雨般

rather false, meretricious. But put yourself in Ligeia's place, and it is real enough, and ghastly beyond bearing.

Out-out are all the lights-out all!
And over each quivering form
The curtain, a funeral pall,
Comes down with the rush of a storm,
While the angels, all pallid and wan,
Uprising,unveiling, affirm
That the play is the tragedy,'Man',
And its hero, the Conqueror Worm.

Which is the American equivalent for a William Blake poem. For Blake, too, was one of these ghastly, obscene 'Knowers'.

'"O God! " half shrieked Ligeia, leaping to her feet and extending her arms aloft with a spasmodic movement, as I made an end of these lines -"O God! O Divine Father! shall these things be undeviatingly so? Shall this conqueror be not once conquered? Are we not part and parcel in Thee? Who-who knoweth the mysteries of the will with its vigour? Man doth not yield him to the angels, nor unto

落下，遮住
　　颤抖的躯体。
苍白憔悴的天使们撩开尸布
　　飞入云端，宣告
一场悲剧的完结，主人公
　　是胜利的可怜虫。

这是美国化的威廉·布莱克式的诗。布莱克也是这类魔鬼般下流的"了解者"。

"'啊，天啊！'当我写完这些诗行时，莉盖娅痉挛般地跳起，展开双臂大叫着。'啊，上帝！神明之父！难道事情就是这样不可改变吗？难道这位征服者一次也不被别人征服吗？难道我们不是你的一分子吗？谁，谁知道意志的神秘及其力量？人，只要他的薄弱意志不倒，他就既不会服从天使也不会全然服从死亡。'"

death utterly, save only through the weakness of his feeble will." '

So Ligeia dies. And yields to death at least partly. *Anche troppo.*

As for her cry to God–has not God said that those who sin against the Holy Ghost shall not be forgiven?*

And the Holy Ghost is within us. It is the thing that prompts us to be real, not to push our own cravings too far, not to submit to stunts and high–falutin, above all, not to be too egoistic and wilful in our conscious self, but to change as the spirit inside us bids us change, and leave off when it bids us leave off, and laugh when we must laugh, particularly at ourselves, for in deadly earnestness there is always something a bit ridiculous. The Holy Ghost bids us never be too deadly in our earnestness, always to laugh in time, at ourselves and everything. Particularly at our sublimities. Everything has its hour of ridicule –everything.

Now Poe and Ligeia, alas, couldn't laugh. They were frenziedly earnest. And frenziedly they pushed on this vibration of consciousness and unison in consciousness. They sinned against the Holy Ghost that bids us all laugh and forget, bids us know oue own limits. And they weren't forgiven.

Ligeia needn't blame God. She had only her own will, her 'gigantic volition' to

莉盖娅就这样死了,至少是部分地向死亡屈服了。这也有点过分了。

至于她对上帝发出的呼唤,上帝不是说过,那些与圣灵作对的人不会得到宽恕吗?[详见《新约·马太福音》12:31:"亵渎圣灵的人绝不可赦免。"]

那神灵就在我们心中。它激励我们变得真实,令欲望不要太盛,让我们不听信花招和夸夸其谈,特别是,它让我们严防过分自私利己,严防过分自以为是。它还告诉我们随内在的精神改变自己,它让我们该放手时就放手,该嘲弄自己就嘲弄,因为当我们死认真的时候我们总会显得有点可笑。圣灵告诫我们不必死认真,应随时嘲弄自己、嘲弄一切。尤其应该嘲弄自己的所谓崇高。任何事物都有其可笑之时——一切。

可是坡和莉盖娅却笑不出来。他们认真得发狂。他们发狂地推动意识的震颤和意识的交汇。他们这是在与圣灵作对,本来圣灵是告诫我们该笑就笑,该忘就忘,让我们知道自己的局限性。他们不这样,因此他们得不到宽恕。

莉盖娅用不着抱怨上帝。因为她的一切都归咎于她的意志、她的"巨

thank, lusting after more consciousness, more beastly knowing.

Ligeia dies. The husband goes to England, vulgarly buys or rents a gloomy, grand old abbey, puts it into some sort of repair, and furnishes it with exotic, mysterious, theatrical splendour. Never anything open and real. This theatrical 'volition' of his. The bad taste of sensationalism.

Then he marries the fair-haired, blue-eyed Lady Rowena Trevanion, of Tremaine. That is, she would be a sort of Saxon-Cornish blue-blood damsel. Poor Poe!

In halls such as these -in a bridal chamber such as this -I passed, with the Lady of Tremaine, the unhallowed hours of the first month of our marriage -passed them with but little disquietude. That my wife dreaded the fierce moodiness of my temper-that she shunned me and loved me but little -I could not help perceiving, but it gave me rather pleasure than otherwise. I loathed her with a hatred belonging more to demon than to man. My memory flew back(oh, with what intensity of regret!) to Ligeia, the beloved, the august, the beautiful, the entombed. I revelled in recollections of her purity... etc.

Now the vampire lust is consciously such.

大意志"，她拼命追求更多的意识，拼命要了解。

莉盖娅死后，她丈夫去了英国，很庸俗地买下或租下了一座阴郁巨大的旧教堂，修茸一番，修饰出一种神秘、戏剧性的异域情调来。一切都不公开、不真实。他的意志是"戏剧性"的。对感官刺激的追求趣味也不高雅。

然后他娶了特利门纳碧眼金发的罗文娜·特利温宁女士。她是一位萨克逊和康沃尔混血的大家闺秀。可怜的坡!

"就是在这样的大厦中，这样的新房中，我和这个特利门纳女人度过了我们俗世的蜜月，无忧无虑。我妻子对我的阴郁脾气很怕，于是她躲避我，不怎么亲近我，我情不自禁感到一种快意。我恨她，我所心怀的不是一个人的仇恨而是一个魔鬼的仇恨。我的记忆开始向回流淌(好悔啊)，流向莉盖娅，可爱的，那秋日，那美，那坟墓中的。我沉浸在对她纯洁的回忆中……"

这就是有意识的吸血鬼欲望。

In the second month of the marriage the Lady Rowena fell ill. It is the shadow of Ligeia hangs over her. It is the ghostly Ligeia who pours poison into Rowena's cup. It is the spirit of Ligeia, leagued with the spirit of the husband, that now lusts in the slow destruction of Rowena. The two vampires, dead wife and living husband.

For Ligeia has not yielded unto death utterly. Her fixed, frustrated will comes back in vindictiveness. She could not have her way in life. So she, too, will find victims in life. And the husband, all the time, only uses Rowena as a living body on which to wreak his vengeance for his being thwarted with Ligeia. Thwarted from the final knowing her.

And at last from the corpse of Rowena, Ligeia rises. Out of her death, through the door of a corpse they have destroyed between them, reappears Ligeia, still trying to have her will, to have more love and knowledge, the final gratification which is never final, with her husband.

For it is true, as William James and Conan Doyle* and the rest allow, that a spirit can persist in the after-death. Persist by its own volition. But usually,the evil persistence of a thwarted will, returning for vengeance on life. Lemures, vampires.

It is a ghastly story of the assertion of the human will, the will-to-love and the

婚后第二个月，罗文娜夫人病了。是莉盖娅的阴影在笼罩着她。是莉盖娅的鬼魂在罗文娜的杯子里下了毒。是莉盖娅的魂附着在丈夫的魂上，缓慢地毁灭着罗文娜。两个吸血鬼，一个亡妇，一个是未亡夫。

莉盖娅并未全然死去，她那顽固但受挫的意志回来报复。她无法在生活中自行其是，于是她要在生活中寻找替死鬼，丈夫因为在莉盖娅那里受挫，无法彻底了解她，于是他把罗文娜当作惟一的活靶子来施行报复。

最终莉盖娅借她和丈夫毁了的罗文娜的尸还了魂。她起死回生了。她依然念念不忘她的意志，她依旧要与丈夫一起拥有更多的爱、了解和最终的满足——事实上这满足她从未得到过。

的确，正如威廉·詹姆斯和柯南道尔等人所言[William James(1842-1910)，美国哲学家和心理学家，对唯灵论表示出某种暧昧态度。Sir Arthur Conan Doyle(1859-1930)，英国作家，创造了神探福尔摩斯的小说形象。于 1891 加入了通灵研究学会，坚信可以与死后的灵魂沟通。1918 年出版了《新启示录》，1926 年出版《惟灵论史》]，人死后灵魂依旧存留于世，它靠的是其自身的意志。一般来说，这受挫的意志恶毒地坚持着依旧对生活

will-to-consciousness, asserted against death itself. The pride of human conceit in Knowledge.

There are terrible spirits, ghosts, in the air of America.

Eleanora, the next story, is a fantasy revealing the sensational delights of the man in his early marriage with the young and tender bride. They dwelt, he, his cousin and her mother, in the sequestered Valley of Many-coloured Grass, the valley of prismatic sensation, where everything seems spectrum-coloured. They looked down at their own images in the River of Silence, and drew the god Eros from that wave: out of their own self-consciousness, that is. This is a description of the life of introspection and of the love which is begotten by the self in the self, the self-made love. The trees are like serpents worshipping the sun. That is, they represent the phallic passion in its poisonous or mental activity. Everything runs to consciousness: serpents worshipping the sun. The embrace of love, which should bring darkness and oblivion, would with these lovers be a daytime thing bringing more heightened consciousness, visions, spectrum-visions, prismatic. The evil thing that daytime love-making is, and all sex-palaver.

In *Berenice* the man must go down to the sepulchre of his beloved and pull out

施行报复。这即是所谓亡灵,吸血鬼。

这令人毛骨悚然的故事讲的是人的意志、爱的意志、理性的意志、与死亡相斗争的意志。它为人的知识而骄傲。

在美国的空中,游荡着太多可怕的精灵。

《伊琳诺拉》这篇怪诞的小说所展示的是一位男子娶了媳妇,和他温柔的新娘度过的销魂时光。他、表妹及表妹的母亲住在与世隔绝的“五彩芳草”峡谷中,这峡谷唤起人的各种感觉,每样东西都泛着一层神光。他们低头在“静谧”河中看着自己的倒影,从中发现了爱神——全是他们的臆想。这是对内省生活的描述,那爱是他们自以为是的爱。那里的树像在对太阳祈祷的蛇。这些树体现出某种费勒斯[即英文 phallus]的意淫激情。一切都进入主观意识中:蛇在崇拜太阳。本该带来黑暗与忘却的爱的拥抱对这些恋人来说却成了白日里的事,让他们更多思、多念,胡思乱想。白日里的做爱及谈情说爱是可恶的事。

《勃兰尼斯》中,那男人进到他爱人的墓穴中,把她的三十二颗白牙

her thirty–two small white teeth, which he carries in a box with him. It is repulsive and gloating. The teeth are the instruments of biting, of resistance, of antagonism. They often become symbols of opposition, little instruments or entities of crushing and destroying. Hence the dragon´s teeth in the myth. Hence the man in *Berenice* must take possession of the irreducible part of his mistress. '*Toutes ses dents étaient des idées,*' he says. Then they are little fixed ideas of mordant hate, of which he possesses himself.

The other great story linking up with this group is *The Fall of the House of Usher*. Here the love is between brother and sister. When the self is broken, and the mystery of the recognition of otherness fails, then the longing for identification with the beloved becomes a lust. And it is this longing for identification, utter merging, which is at the base of the incest problem. In psychoanalysis almost every trouble in the psyche is traced to an incest–desire. But it won´t do. Incest–desire is only one of the modes by which men strive to get their gratification of the intensest vibration of the spiritual nerves, without any resistance. In the family, the natural vibration is most nearly in unison. With a stranger, there is greater resistance. Incest is the getting of gratification and the avoiding of resistance.

拔出装在一个盒子中带了出来，这真令人恶心，让人看不起。牙是食咬和抵抗工具，时常是对立的象征，这小小的、粉碎与破坏的工具。从而这牙齿成为神秘的龙牙。为此这男人无论如何要获得情妇的这些必不可少的东西。“每颗牙都是个意念。”他说。这是他镂骨铭心的恨。

与这一组故事相关的另一篇了不起的小说是《厄舍古屋的倒塌》。这里的爱情发生在兄妹之间。一旦人的自我崩溃、认知他人的神秘消失，与爱人认同的愿望就变成了一种欲。正是这种认同和彻底融合的愿望成为乱伦的基础。在精神分析学中，几乎所有心理问题都可回溯到乱伦问题上。当然并不尽然。乱伦不过是人们借以获得最紧张的神经震颤所带来的快感的一种形式，它不受任何阻抗。在一家人之间，自然的精神震颤几乎是同步的。可是，与陌生人之间，它就会受到阻抗，乱伦就是快感的获得与对阻抗的逃避。

全部罪恶的根源在于我们都渴望这种精神快感、这种流溢、这种明显的生命的兴奋、这种认知和这个“五彩芳草谷”，甚至是五光十色的草

The root of all evil is that we all want this spiritual gratification, this flow, this apparent heightening of life, this knowledge, this valley of many-coloured grass, even grass and light prismatically decomposed, giving ecstasy. We want all this without resistance. We want it continually. And this is the root of all evil in us.

We ought to pray to be resisted, and resisted to the bitter end. We ought to decide to have done at last with craving.

The motto to *The Fall of the House of Usher* is a couple of lines from Béranger.

Son caur est un luth suspendu:
Sitôt qu'on le touche il résonne.

We have all the trappings of Poe's rather overdone, vulgar fantasy. 'I reined my horse to the precipitous brink of a black and lurid tarn that lay in unruffled lustre by the dwelling, and gazed down -but with a shudder even more thrilling than before -upon the remodelled and inverted images of the grey sedge, and the ghastly tree-stems, and the vacant and eye-like windows.' The House of Usher, both dwelling and family, was very old. Minute fungi overspread the exterior of the house, hanging in festoons from the eaves. Gothic archways, a valet of stealthy step, sombre tapestries, ebon black floors, a profusion of tattered and antique furniture, feeble

与光，从中获得狂喜。我们希望毫无阻抗地获得这些。我们要不断地得到，这就是我们心中全部的罪恶之根。

我们应该祈求阻抗，尝尝阻抗的苦头才行。我们应该决定最终放弃渴望。

《厄舍古屋的倒塌》的墓志铭是法国诗人贝朗瑞[Béranger(1780-1857)，法国诗人]的两行诗：

> 他的心似一把高悬的诗琴[诗琴是14—17世纪盛行于欧洲的一种拨弦乐器]，
> 触动它，淙淙的乐音流溢。

我们看到了坡所写下的过分俗气的畅想。

“我牵马来到悬崖边，崖下屋旁湖水清澈恬静。可我低头俯视水面时却不禁一阵惊恐，我看到了水中的倒影：灰沙草、鬼魂样的树干和空洞洞眼睛一样的屋窗。”厄舍古屋作为住房和家是太古旧了。屋外长满青苔，

gleams of encrimsoned light through latticed panes, and over all 'an air of stern, deep, and irredeemable gloom' –this makes up the interior.

The inmates of the house, Roderick and Madeline Usher, are the last remnants of their incomparably ancient and decayed race. Roderick has the same large, luminous eye, the same slightly arched nose of delicate Hebrew model, as characterized Ligeia. He is ill with the nervous malady of his family. It is he whose nerves are so strung that they vibrate to the unknown quiverings of the ether.* He, too, has lost his self, his living soul, and become a sensitized instrument of the external influences; his nerves are verily like an aeolian harp which must vibrate. He lives in 'some struggle with the grim phantasm, Fear,' for he is only the physical, post-mortem reality of a living being.

It is a question how much, once the true centrality of the self is broken, the instrumental consciousness of man can register. When man becomes selfless, wafting instrumental like a harp in an open window, how much can his elemental consciousness express? The blood as it runs has its own sympathies and responses to the material world, quite apart from seeing. And the nerves we know vibrate all the while to unseen presences, unseen forces. So Roderick Usher quivers on the edge of mate-

从房檐一直铺到墙根。哥特式的拱门，隐秘的台阶，阴郁的挂毯，乌木地板，奇形怪状的古式家具，暗红色的光线透过窗格照射进来。最主要的是，屋里有一种"严峻、深幽、无法改变的阴郁气氛"。

屋里的两位居民——罗德里克·厄舍和麦德琳娜·厄舍是一个古老、灭绝中的种族里最后两个人。罗德里克长着一双莉盖娅那样迷人的大眼睛和略微拱起的鼻子，这是典型的希伯莱相貌。他患上了这个家族的通病——神经质。他的神经太紧张了，剧烈的精神震动波及到冥冥的以太[以太曾被认为是传导无线电波和电磁放射的媒质。这一概念在19世纪被普遍接受。但随着相对论和场的发现，以太就成了陈旧的概念被抛弃。劳伦斯对当时最新的科学理论没有及时的把握，也说明了新理论的普及需要较长的过渡阶段]。他失去了自我和活生生的灵魂，变成了传导外界影响的工具。他的神经的确像风神的竖琴在颤动。他活着，"与某种阴郁的幻觉——恐惧斗争着"，因为他是一具还魂尸体。

问题是，一旦人的自我中心崩溃了，那变成工具的意识能有几许表达？当一个人失去了自我，像窗口的一只琴一样被人弹奏，他能够进行多

rial existence.

It is this mechanical consciousness which gives 'the fervid facility of his impromptus'. It is the same thing that gives Poe his extraordinary facility in versification. The absence of real central or impulsive being in himself leaves him inordinately, mechanically sensitive to sounds and effects, associations of sounds, associations of rhyme, for example-mechanical, facile, having no root in any passion. It is all a secondary, meretricious process. So we get Roderick Usher's poem. *The Haunted Palace*, with its swift yet mechanical subtleties of rhyme and rhythm, its vulgarity of epithet. It is all a sort of dream-process, where the association between parts is mech-anical, accidental as far as passional meaning goes.

Usher thought that all vegetable things had sentience. Surely all material things have a form of sentience, even the inorganic: surely they all exist in some subtle and complicated tension of vibration which makes them sensitive to external influence and causes them to have an influence on other external objects, irrespective of contact. It is of this vibration or inorganic consciousness that Poe is master: the sleep-consciousness. Thus Roderick Usher was convinced that his whole surroundings, the stones of the house, the fungi, the water in the tarn, the very reflected image of the

少自我表现?人的血液只要流动，它对身外的物质世界就自有其同情和反响，但这是看不见的。我们知道我们的神经总是冲着看不见的存在和力量传导自己的颤动。罗德里克·厄舍就是在物质存在边缘上颤抖着。

正是这种机械的思维给予了他“创作即兴曲的热情与熟练”。它赋予坡非凡的韵律才能。由于缺少真正的生命中心与生命冲动，他才对声音效果异常敏感，当然他对这种音乐之间的联系和韵律间的联系的敏感是机械性的，不是扎根于激情之中。因此，这是次要的、浮华的。于是我们有了罗德里克·厄舍的诗《鬼魂缠绕的地方》。这首诗节奏快但韵律枯燥，用词庸俗。这诗的进程是梦幻曲似的，阕与阕之间的连接显得呆滞、突兀、毫无情感可言。

厄舍以为，所有植物性的东西都有感知。不错，一切物质都会有这样或那样形式的感知，甚至无机物也莫不如此。它们微妙、复杂的紧张颤动使得它们对外界的影响很敏感，同时也对外界目标施其影响。坡所懂得的正是这种颤动或无机意识——这是一种沉睡意识。为此，小说中的罗

whole, was woven into a physical oneness with the family, condensed, as it were, into one atmosphere–the special atmosphere in which alone the Ushers could live. And it was this atmosphere which had moulded the destinies of his family.

But while ever the soul remains alive, it is the moulder and not the moulded. It is the souls of living men that subtly impregnate stones, houses, mountains, continents, and give these their subtlest form. People only become subject to stones after having lost their integral souls.

In the human realm, Roderick had one connection:his sister Madeline. She, too, was dying of a mysterious disorder, nervous, cataleptic. The brother and sister loved each other passionately and exclusively. They were twins, almost identical in looks. It was the same absorbing love between them, this process of unison in nerve–vibration, resulting in more and more extreme exaltation and a sort of consciousness, and a gradual break–down into death. The exquisitely sensitive Roger, vibrating without resistance with his sister Madeline, more and more exquisitely, and gradually devouring her, sucking her life like a vampire in his anguish of extreme love. And she asking to be sucked.

Madeline died and was carried down by her brother into the deep vaults of the

德里克·厄舍深信，整个环境，房子的石头，绿苔，湖中之水，水中的倒映景物与这个家交织成一体，浓缩为一种氛围——一种只有厄舍家人才能生存其中的氛围。正是这种氛围决定了这个家的命运。

可只要灵魂活着，它就是命运的主人而不是被人决定命运。活生生的人的灵魂微妙地孕育了石头、房屋、山峦和大陆，赋予它们以形状。可人一旦失去了自己完整的自我就会成为石头的奴仆。

在人世间，与罗德里克惟一有关的是他的妹妹麦德琳娜。她也患有某种神秘的紊乱症——倔强症。这兄妹二人热恋着。他们是双胞胎，看上去没什么两样。是同样专注的爱——神经的同步震颤造成了极度的兴奋与思虑，从而使他们双双缓缓崩溃死去。那位极其纤敏的罗德里克与妹妹麦德琳娜在精神上毫无阻抗地共振，一点点地缓缓蚕食她，如同一个吸血鬼一样怀着无上的爱吸食她的生命。而她又自愿让他吸吮。

麦德琳娜死后被哥哥运到深深的地窖中。可她并没有全然死去。哥哥感到一种难言的恐怖与悔恨，几乎是发疯地打着转儿。八天以后他们

house. But she was not dead. Her brother roamed about in incipient madness–a madness of unspeakable terror and guilt. After eight days they were suddenly startled by a clash of metal, then a distinct, hollow metallic, and clangorous, yet apparently muffled, reverberation. Then Roderick Usher, gibbering, began to express himself: 'We have put her living in the tomb! Said I not that my senses were acute? I now tell you that I heard her first feeble movements in the hollow coffin. I heard them–many, many days age –yet I dared not –I dared not speak.'

It is the same old theme of 'each man kills the thing he loves'. He knew his love had killed her. He knew she died at last, like Ligeia, unwilling and unappeased. So, she rose again upon him.

But then without those doors there did stand the lofty and enshrouded figure of the lady Madeling of Usher. There was blood upon her white robes, and the evidence of some bitter struggle upon every portion of her emaciated frame. For a moment she remained trembling and reeling to and fro upon the threshold, then, with a low moaning cry, fell heavily inward upon the person of her brother, and in her violent and now final death–agonies bore him to the floor a corpse, and a victim to the terrors he had anticipated.

被一种金属断裂的声音突然惊起，随后是一阵清晰、空旷的金属震颤，显然那声音是被压抑住了。罗德里克·厄舍开始谵妄般地表白自己：“我们把她活活地放进了坟墓中！我说过我太敏感。我告诉你吧，我听到了她在棺材中轻轻的动静，我听到这声音已有好多天了，可是我不敢——不敢说出来。”

这又是那个“人诛之所爱”的老主题。他了解他的爱人并因此杀了她。他知道她像莉盖娅一样不情愿地含冤而死。于是她又还魂来寻他。

“尽管有几道门，可厄舍家的麦德琳娜小姐还是出现了，她那高雅的身段裹在云雾中。她的白袍子上有血迹，由此可见她那羸弱的身躯是如何苦苦抗争的。她先是在门坎上颤栗不稳地晃动，随后一阵低吟，重重地倒在哥哥身上，竭尽死力把他摔死在地，他成了恐怖的牺牲品。他早就料到会是这样。”

这描写很吸引人，很有点戏剧性，真的。对恋人来说，在最后一刻其心理的确如此，他们不能分离，不能孤独地倾听圣灵的声音。我们全靠圣

It is lurid and melodramatic, but it is true. It is a ghastly psychological truth of what happens in the last stages of this beloved love, which cannot be separate, cannot be isolate, cannot listen in isolation to the isolate Holy Ghost. For it is the Holy Ghost we must live by. The next era is the era of the Holy Ghost. And the Holy Ghost speaks individually inside each individual: always, for ever a ghost. There is no manifestation to the general world. Each isolate individual listening in isolation to the Holy Ghost within him.

The Ushers, brother and sister, betrayed the Holy Ghost in themselves. They would love, love, without resistance. They would love, they would merge, they would be as one thing. So they dragged each other down into death. For the Holy Ghost says you must not be as one thing with another being. Each must abide by itself, and correspond only within certain limits.

The best tales all have the same burden. Hate is as inordinate as love, and as slowly consuming, as secret, as underground, as subtle. All this underground vault business in Poe only symbolizes that which takes place beneath the consciousness. On top, all is fair-spoken. Beneath, there is awful murderous extremity of burying alive. Fortunato, in *The Cask of Amontillado*, is buried alive out of perfect hatred, as

灵才能活。下个世纪是圣灵的时光。圣灵就在每个人心中说话:永远是个圣灵。对于大千世界来说并不见什么明示,但每个孤独的人却在倾听自己心中圣灵的声音。

厄舍家的兄妹背叛了自己心中的圣灵。他们要爱,爱,毫无节制地爱。他们要爱,要交融为一体。他们相互牵扯着,只能走向死亡,因为圣灵说你们不能成为一个生命体,每个人都应我行我素,有所节制。

优秀的故事都带有这同一个重负。恨与爱同样过度、煎熬人、秘不可宣、微妙难解。坡笔下的这些“地窖”之事是潜意识的象征。表面上,一切都简单易懂;可在深层中,竟是这种活埋人的极端行为。《阿芒蒂拉多的桶》中的弗吐纳托像厄舍家的麦德琳娜女士一样被活埋,不同的是前者是因为恨被埋,后者是因为爱被活埋。恨的欲望亦会消耗并控制被恨者的灵魂,正如同爱欲是控制被爱者或让被爱者控制一样。但在两种情况下,双方的灵魂都会消解,双方都会在越雷池的过程中失却自我。

蒙特利索要彻底吞噬弗吐纳托的灵魂。完整杀害他是没什么必要

the lady Madeline of Usher is buried alive out of love. The lust of hate is the inordinate desire to consume and unspeakably possess the soul of the hated one, just as the lust of love is the desire to possess, or to be possessed by, the beloved, utterly. But in either case the result is the dissolution of both souls, each losing itself in transgressing its own bounds.

The lust of Montresor is to devour utterly the soul of Fortunato. It would be no use killing him outright. If a man is killed outright his soul remains integral, free to return into the bosom of some beloved, where it can enact itself. In wallingup his enemy in the vault, Montresor seeks to bring about the indescribable capitulation of the man´s soul, so that he, the victor, can possess himself of the very being of the vanquished. Perhaps this can actually be done. Perhaps, in the attempt, the victor breaks the bonds of his own identity, and collapses into nothingness, or into the infinite. Becomes a monster.

What holds good for inordinate hate holds good for inordinate love. The motto, *Nemo me impune lacessit*, might just as well be *Nemo me impune amat*.

In *William Wilson* we are given a rather unsubtle account of the attempt of a man to kill his own soul. William Wilson the mechanical, lustful ego succeeds in

的。如果一个人完整地死了,他的灵魂仍是完好无损的,可以自由自在地重归某个所爱的人心中自行活动起来。蒙特利索把他的敌人活埋于地窖,为的是捕捉他的灵魂,从而就可以占有他的生命。或许这可以办得到。或许这位壮士因此而突破了自身的界限,化为虚无或变得永恒,成为一个魔王。

对过度恨适用的对于过度爱也适用。那句箴言所谓"侵害我者无不受罚"亦可说成是"爱我者无不受罚"。

在《威廉·威尔森》中,我们看到一个人试图杀害自己的灵魂,描写很细致。机械的威廉·威尔森成功地杀死了活生生的威廉·威尔森。那欲望的自我仍继续存在,渐渐没人广漠的永恒。

《陈尸所街上的谋杀案》和《金甲虫》是两个极呆板的故事,作者的兴趣在于从一系列细微的因果关系中寻出什么答案来。这兴趣是科学的而不是艺术的,旨在研究心理反应。

对凶杀题材的着迷本身就令人不解。凶杀不仅仅意味着杀人。凶杀

killing William Wilson the living self. The lustful ego lives on, gradually reducing itself towards the dust of the infinite.

In the *Murders in the Rue Morgue* and *The Gold Bug* we have those mechanical tales where the interest lies in the following out of a subtle chain of cause and effect. The interest is scientific rather than artistic, a study in psychologic reactions.

The fascination of murder itself is curious. Murder is not just killing. Murder is a lust to get at the very quick of life itself, and kill it–hence the stealth and the frequent morbid dismemberment of the corpse, the attempt to get at the very quick of the murdered being, to find the quick and to possess it. It is curious that the two men fascinated by the art of murder, though in different ways, should have been De Quincey* and Poe, men so different in way of life, yet perhaps not so widely different in nature. In each of them is traceable that strange lust for extreme love and extreme hate, possession by mystic violence of the other soul, or violent deathly surrender of the soul in the self:an absence of manly virtue, which stands alone and accepts limits.

Inquisition and torture are akin to murder:the same lust. It is a combat between inquisitor and victim as to whether the inquisitor shall get at the quick of life itself,

是一种欲望，它要夺取生命核心，杀死它。于是，有人经常偷偷地肢解尸体，为的是取得被害者的生命核心并拥有它。这两个人都为凶杀的艺术所着迷，尽管方式不同——就如同德·昆西 [此时劳伦斯可能想到了德·昆西的文章《谋杀被看做是一种艺术》]和坡，生活方式尽管截然不同，可本质上并无多大差别。在他们身上都可以寻出爱的极端与恨的极端，他们要么被对方灵魂中神秘的暴力所攫取，或者自我中的灵魂挣扎着屈服。这是缺少男子汉气质的表现，孤独而有限度。

审讯和刑罚与凶杀相似，是同样的欲望。这是一场审讯者和被审讯者之间的斗争，斗争的焦点是审讯者是否会得到生命的核心并刺破它，刺破灵魂的核心。人的罪恶意志试图这样做。人的勇敢灵魂拒绝自己的生命核心被刺破。这不免令人感到奇怪，可是的确如此。正如受挫的意志会在人死后以恶魔的形式坚持不死，勇敢的精灵也会保留生命的核心与真理，哪怕历尽折磨和死亡。如今的社会是恶魔。它会以某种微妙的方式毁灭人之生活的核心，什么方式都可能。但是，只要人倾听自己心中圣灵

and pierce it. Pierce the very quick of the soul. The evil will of man tries to do this. The brave soul of man refuses to have the lifequick pierced in him. It is strange:but just as the thwarted will can persist evilly, after death, so can the brave spirit preserve, even through torture and death, the quick of life and truth. Nowadays society is evil. It finds subtle ways of torture, to destroy the life-quick, to get at the life-quick in a man. Every possible form. And still a man can hold out, if he can laugh and listen to the Holy Ghost. -But society is evil, evil, and love is evil. And evil breeds evil, more and more.

So the mystery goes on. La Bruyère* says that all our human unhappiness *viennent de ne pouvoir être seuls*. As long as man lives he will be subject to the yearning of love or the burning of hate, which is only inverted love.

But he is subject to something more than this. If we do not live to eat, we do not live to love either.

We live to stand alone, and listen to the Holy Ghost. The Holy Ghost, who is inside us, and who is many gods. Many gods come and go, some say one thing and some say another, and we have to obey the God of the innermost hour.It is the multiplicity of gods within us make up the Holy Ghost.

的声音他仍能坚持不退却。可是社会是恶魔，恶魔，爱也是恶魔。恶滋生恶，愈来愈多。

神秘一直这样持续。拉·布吕耶尔[Jean de la Bruyère(1645—1696)法国作家、格言作家]说，我们人类所有的不幸都源自不能孤独。只要人活着，他就会注定屈从于爱的渴求或燃烧的仇恨，恨不过是爱的另一面。

可人注定要做的不仅如此。如果我们活着不是为了吃，那么我们也不是为爱才活着的。

我们活着是为了独善其身，为了倾听圣灵之声。他就在我们心中，他是诸多个神，他们来来去去，你说东他说西，而我们要服从的是最神圣时刻的圣灵，我们心中的诸多神汇成了圣灵。

可是坡只懂得爱，爱，爱，这是剧烈的神经震颤，是高度的思虑。毒品，女人，自我毁灭，五彩缤纷的狂喜统统来自高度的思虑和爱。他心中的人的灵魂早已靠边站了。但它没有迷失。他清清楚楚地告诉我们这灵魂如何如何，告诉我们，我们应该懂这一点。

But Poe knew only love, love, love, intense vibrations and heightened consciousness. Drugs, women, self-destruction, but anyhow the prismatic ecstasy of heightened consciousness and sense of love, of flow. The human soul in him was beside itself. But it was not lost. He told us plainly how it was, so that we should know.

He was an adventurer into vaults and cellars and horrible underground passages of the human soul. He sounded the horror and the warning of his own doom.

Doomed he was. He died wanting more love, and love killed him.* A ghastly disease, love. Poe telling us of his disease:trying even to make his disease fair and attractive. Even succeeding.

Which is the inevitable falseness, duplicity of art, American art in particular.

他是一个敢于闯入可怕的人类灵魂地狱的冒险家。他发出了灭亡的恐怖与警告之声。

他注定要灭亡。他为爱而死，是爱害死了他[劳伦斯推断坡死在妓院。坡的死因众说不一，但他最可能是酗酒而死]。爱，可怕的病。坡向我们讲他的病情，甚至想使这病变得美丽诱人。他甚至成功了。

这不可避免导致虚伪，是欺骗，美国的艺术尤其如此，是欺骗的艺术。

CHAPTER 7
Nathaniel Hawthorne and The Scarlet Letter

Nathaniel Hawthorne writes romance.

And what's romance? Usually, a nice little tale where you have everything As You Like It, where rain never wets your jacket and gnats never bite your nose and it's always daisytime. *As You Like It* and *Forest Lovers*, etc. *Morte D' Arthur*.

Hawthorne obviously isn't this kind of romanticist: though nobody has muddy boots in *The Scarlet Letter*, either.

But there is more to it. *The Scarlet Letter* isn't a pleasant, pretty romance. It is a sort of parable, an earthly story with a hellish meaning.

All the time there is this split in the American art and artconsciousness. On the top it is as nice as pie, goody-goody and lovey-dovey. Like Hawthorne being such a

纳撒尼尔·霍桑与《红字》

纳撒尼尔·霍桑创作的是罗曼司。

什么样的作品算罗曼司呢?一般来说,是一个美好的小故事,其中事事让你如意:雨水永远不会打湿你的衣衫,蚊虫永远不会叮咬你的鼻子,时光永远极美妙宜人。《如愿》[莎士比亚的戏剧,以森林为背景]、《森林爱侣》[Maurice Hewlett(1861—1923,英国小说家,诗人)的小说名]及《亚瑟之死》[Sir Thomas Malory(d.1471)所著传奇故事]等作品即是。

可是,霍桑并非此种浪漫小说家,尽管《红字》里也没谁的靴子溅上了泥水。

其意义远不止于此。《红字》并不是一部令人愉悦、娇美的罗曼司。它

blue-eyed darling, in life, and Longfellow and the rest such sucking-doves. Hawthorne's wife said she 'never saw him in time', which doesn't mean she saw him too late. But always in the 'frail effulgence of eternity'.

Serpents they were. Look at the inner meaning of their art and see what demons they were.

You must look through the surface of American art, and see the inner diabolism of the symbolic meaning. Otherwise it is all mere childishness.

That blue-eyed darling Nathaniel knew disagreeable things in his inner soul. He was careful to send them out in disguise.

Always the same. The deliberate consciousness of Americans so fair and smooth-spoken, and the under-consciousness so devilish. Destroy! destroy! destroy! hums the under-consciousness. Love and produce! Love and produce! cackles the upper consciousness. And the world hears only the Love-and-produce cackle. Refuses to hear the hum of destruction underneath. Until such time as it will have to hear.

The American has got to destroy. It is his destiny. It is his destiny to destroy the whole corpus of the white psyche, the white consciousness. And he's got to do it

是一个寓言，一个实实在在的人间故事，却内含地狱般的意义。

美国的艺术与艺术思维中一直存在这种分裂。表面上它漂亮、伪善、多情得不行，就像霍桑本人在生活中是个碧眼宝贝，还有朗费罗等鸽子似的人物也是这样。霍桑的妻子说她总也认不清他，他身上总笼罩着一层“永恒的微光”。

他们是蛇。请看看他们艺术的内在含义吧，看看他们都是些怎样的魔鬼。

你非得透过美国艺术的表面才能看到其象征意义之下的内在恶魔。否则它看上去与幼童毫无异样。

霍桑这位碧眼宝贝儿深知自己灵魂中的那些不愉快的东西。他会巧加掩饰后把它们泄露出来。

总是这样。美国人总是苦心经营，表面上公允、平淡，可他们的潜意识却是如此险恶。毁灭！毁灭！毁灭！他们的潜意识在这般吟鸣。爱，创造！爱，创造！他们的清醒意识又这样呼叫。而这个世界听到的只有“爱，创造”，拒绝倾听潜意识中毁灭的吟唱。总有一天这世界非得听听毁灭二字

secretly. As the growing of a dragon-fly inside a chrysalis or cocoon destroys the larva grub, secretly.

Though many a dragon-fly never gets out of the chrysalis case:dies inside. As America might.

So the secret chrysalis of *The Scarlet Letter*, diabolically destroying the old psyche inside.

Be good! Be good! warbles Nathaniel. Be good, and never sin! Be sure your sins will find you out.

So convincingly that his wife never saw him 'as in time'.

Then listen to the diabolic undertone of *The Scarlet Letter*.

Man ate of the tree of knowledge, and became ashamed of himself.

Do you imagine Adam had never lived with Eve before that apple episode? Yes, he had. As a wild animal with his mate.

It didn't become 'sin' till the knowledge-poison entered. That apple of Sodom.

We are divided in ourselves, against ourselves. And that is the meaning of the cross symbol.

In the first place, Adam knew Eve as a wild animal knows its mate, momenta-

不可。

美国人非得去毁灭不可。他命中注定要这样做。他命中注定要毁灭白人的心理主体——白人的意识。他得悄悄地这样做，正如一只蜻蜓悄悄毁灭蝶蛹和幼体脱颖而出一样。

但是不少蜻蜓并未冲破茧壳，而是死在壳里，美国或许也会这样。

《红字》这只秘密的蝶蛹凶恶地在内部毁灭着旧的心理。

"要善！善良！"纳撒尼尔在歌唱，"好好待着，别犯罪！做了坏事是会暴露的。"

他的话太令人信服了，连他妻子都无法看清他的真实面目。

那么让我们来听听《红字》的恶魔含义吧。

人吃了禁果，从而为自己感到羞耻。

你是否知道在吃禁果之前亚当和夏娃是否早就厮混在一起了?是的。他是个野兽，同他的伴儿生活在一起。

直到智慧的毒药泼进来，他们吃了那罪恶之果，这事儿方才成其为"罪恶"。

neously, but vitally, in blood-knowledge, Blood-knowledge, not mind-knowledge. Blood-knowledge, that seems utterly to forget, but doesn't. Blood-knowledge, instinct, intuition, all the vast vital flux of knowing that goes on in the dark, antecedent to the mind.

Then came that beastly apple, and the other sort of know-ledge started.

Adam began to look at himself. 'My hat! ' he said. 'What's this? My Lord! What the deuce! -And Eve! I wonder about Eve.'

Thus starts knowing. Which shortly runs to understanding, when the devil gets his own.

When Adam went and took Eve, after the apple, he didn't do any more than he had done many a time before, in act. But in consciousness he did something very different. So did Eve. Each of them kept an eye on what they were doing, they watched what was happening to them. They wanted to know. And that was the birth of sin. Not doing it, but knowing about it. Before the apple, they had shut their eyes and their minds had gone dark. Now, they peeped and pried and imagined. They watched themselves. And they felt uncomfortable after. They felt self-conscious. So they said, 'The act is sin. Let's hide. We've sinned.'

我们自身分裂为二,相互斗争。这就是那个“红字”的意义。

起先,亚当对夏娃就如同一头野兽对他的伴侣那样,靠偶然的感知认识她,当然这感知靠的是生命与血液。这是一种血液的认知而不是智慧的认知。血液的知识似乎会被全然忘却,其实不然。血液的知识即本能,直觉,即黑暗中知识的巨大洪波,先于头脑的知识而产生。

随后有了那可咒的苹果,另一种知识将至。

亚当开始审视自己。“啊呀!”他说,“这是什么?我的天!见鬼了!夏娃!我想知道夏娃是怎么回事。”

从此开始了了解,不久这了解就进入了理解。魔鬼得手了。

吃了苹果后,亚当再拥有夏娃时,从行为上说他跟以前做的没什么两样。可他这次想的可就完全是另一回事了。夏娃亦是如此。他们都开始注意自己的所作所为,看着在自身发生的一切。他们要了解。这就是罪恶的开端。不是行为,而是对行为的了解。吃禁果前,他们对此视而不见,头脑中一片混沌。现在他们窥视着,想像着。他们在观看自己。随后他们感到不舒服。他们有了自我意识,所以他们会说:“这行为就是罪恶。咱们

No wonder the Lord kicked them out of the Garden. Dirty hypocrites.

The sin was the self-watching, self-consciousness. The sin, and the doom. Dirty understanding.

Nowadays men do hate the idea of dualism. It´s no good, dual we are. The cross. If we accept the symbol, then, virtually, we accept the fact. We are divided against ourselves.

For instance, the blood hates being known. Hence the profound instinct of privacy.

And on the other hand, the mind and the spiritual consciousness of man simply hates the dark potency of blood-acts:hates the genuine dark sensual orgasms, which do, for the time being, actually obliterate the mind and the spiritual consciousness, plunge them in a suffocating flood of darkness.

You cant´ get away from this.

Blood-consciousness overwhelms, obliterates, and annuls mind-consciousness.

Mind-consciousness extinguishes blood-consciousness, and consumes the blood.

We are all of us conscious in both ways. And the two ways are antagonistic in

藏起来吧，咱们犯罪了。”

难怪上帝把他们驱逐出了伊甸园，肮脏的伪君子。

这种罪恶来自人的自窥与自我意识。罪恶与灭亡。肮脏的理解。

如今人们的确恨二元论。这可不好，我们是二重性的人。十字架。如果我们接受这种象征，那就等于接受了这事实了。我们自我分裂后自我作对。

比如我们的血液就仇恨被了解。所以我们才有巨大的隐私本能。

而在另一方面，人的头脑和精神又仇恨黑暗的血液力量：仇恨那全然黑暗的性高潮。的确，黑暗的性高潮会使头脑和精神变得一片混沌，把它们抛入令人窒息的暗流之中。

你无法逃避。

血液意识使理智意识黯然失色，使之销声匿迹。

理智意识使血液意识灭亡，它消耗血液。

我们都有这两种意识。这两方面在我们体内势不两立。

它们永远会这样。

us.

They will always remain so.

That is our cross.

The antagonism is so obvious, and so far-reaching, that it extends to the smallest thing. The cultured, highly-conscious person of today loathes any form of physical, 'menial' work: such as washing dishes or sweeping a floor or chopping wood. This menial work is an insult to the spirit. 'When I see men carrying heavy loads, doing brutal work, it always makes me want to cry,' said a beautiful, cultured woman to me.

'When you say that, it makes me want to beat you,' said I, in reply. 'When I see you with your beautiful head pondering heavy thoughts, I just want to hit you. It outrages me.'

My father hated books, hated the sight of anyone reading or writing.

My mother hated the thought that any of her sons should be condemned to manual labour. Her sons must have something higher than that.

She won. But she died first.

He laughs longest who laughs last.

这就是我们的十字架。

这种对立太明显，影响太大，它已波及到最微小的事情。今日有文化、意识极强的人都仇视任何形式的“卑下”的体力工作如洗盘子、扫地或伐木。这种卑下的工作是对精神的污辱。“我一看到有人背着重负、干粗活儿，我几乎要哭。”一位有文化的女人对我说。

“一听你说这个，我就想揍你，”我回答说，“当我看到你那漂亮的脑袋里思想如此沉重，我就要揍你。这让我恼火。”

我父亲仇恨书籍，看到谁读书写字他就恨。

而我母亲则讨厌让她的任何儿子做体力活儿。她的儿子应该比那高雅得多。

她胜利了。可她先于父亲死去了。

笑到最后的人笑得最久。

我们所有的人身上都存在着肉与灵、血液与精神之间的对立。人的头脑为自己的血液感到“羞耻”。血液被头脑所毁灭，从而出现了苍白的脸。

There is a basic hostility in all of us between the physical and the mental, the blood and the spirit. The mind is 'ashamed' of the blood. And the blood is destroyed by the mind, actually. Hence pale-faces.

At present the mind-consciousness and the so-called spirit triumphs. In America supremely. In America, nobody does anything from the blood. Always from the nerves, if not from the mind. The blood is chemically reduced by the nerves, in American activity.

When an Italian labourer labours, his mind and nerves sleep, his blood acts ponderously.

Americans, when they are doing things, never seem really to be doing them. They are 'busy about' it. They are always busy 'about' something. But truly immersed in doing something, with the deep blood-consciousness active, that they never are.

They admire the blood-conscious spontaneity. And they want to get it in their heads. 'Live from the body,' they shriek. It is their last mental shriek. Co-ordinate.

It is a further attempt still to rationalize the body and blood. 'Think about such and such a muscle,' they say, 'and relax there.'

眼下,理智和所谓精神占了上风。在美国尤其如此。在美国,没有人是依照自己的血性做事的。总是依照精神。在美国人的行动中,血液的化学成分被精神所减少。

当一个意大利劳工干活时,他的头脑和神经都进入休眠状态,只有他的血液在沉重地运行。

美国人做起事来从来不像在真正干什么事,他们在"忙"。他们总是在"忙"什么事。可他们从未真正沉浸其中,其血液意识并不活跃。

他们羡慕血液意识的自发冲动。他们想从头脑中获得这种自发冲动。"依照肉体的冲动生活。"他们叫着,可这叫声发自他们的头脑。乱了。

这仍旧是在试图进一步使肉体和血液理智化。"想想某块某块肌肉,"他们说,"让那儿松弛一下。"

每次你让头脑战胜你的肉体,你就会在某一处造成更为深刻、更为危险的情结或紧张。

可怕的美国人,他们的血已不再是血。一股病态的精神流。

堕落。

And every time you 'conquer' the body with the mind (you can say 'heal' it, if you like)you cause a deeper, more dangerous complex or tension somewhere else.

Ghastly Americans, with their blood no longer blood. A yellow spiritual fluid.

The Fall.

There have been lots of Falls.

We fell into knowledge when Eve bit the apple. Self-conscious knowledge. For the first time the mind put up a fight against the blood. Wanting to understand. That is to intellectualize the blood.

The blood must be shed, says Jesus.

Shed on the cross of our own divided psyche.

Shed the blood, and you become mind-conscious. Eat the body and drink the blood, self-cannibalizing,* and you become extremely conscious, like Americans and some Hindus. Devour yourself, and God knows what a lot you'll know,what a lot you'll be conscious of.

Mind you don't choke yourself.

For a long time men believed that they could be perfected through the mind, through the spirit. They believed, passionately. They had their ecstasy in pure con-

有太多的堕落。

夏娃吃了禁果，从此我们就落入了知识的陷阱。自我意识的知识。人的头脑从此第一次开始与血液作对。要理解，这等于把血液智识化。

这血非流不可。耶稣说。

流在我们分裂心灵的十字架上。

流了血，你就变得理智。吃肉、喝血，这是自食其身［详见《新约·马太福音》26:28:"这是我立约的血，为多人流出来，使罪得赦。"］，从而你就像一些美国人或印度教的信仰者一样变得十二分理智。即便吃掉你自己，天晓得你会获得多少知识，你会懂多少事情。

小心。别噎着。

很久以来，人已深信，他们可以通过理智和精神变得完美起来。他们极其相信这一点。他们在纯精神领域内可以获得无比的狂喜。他们相信纯洁、童贞和精神之翼。

美国人很快就拔掉了精神之鸟的羽毛。美国迅速杀死了对精神的信仰，但行动上依旧故我。他们在行动上仍有过之而无不及。美国人尽管内

sciousness. They believed in purity, chastity, and the wings of the spirit.

America soon plucked the bird of the spirit. America soon killed the belifef in the spirit. But not the practice. The practice continued with a sarcastic vehemence. America, with a perfect inner contempt for the spirit and the consciousness of man, practises the same spirituality and universal love and knowing all the time, incessantly, like a drug habit. And inwardly gives not a fig for it. Only for the sensation. The pretty-pretty sensation of love, loving all the world. And the nice fluttering aeroplane sensation of knowing, knowing, knowing. Then the prettiest of all sensations, the sensation of understanding. Oh, what a lot they understand, the darlings! So good at the trick, they are. Just a trick of self-conceit.

The Scarlet Letter gives the show ayaw.

You have your pure-pure young parson Dimmesdale.

You have the beautiful Puritan Hester at his feet.

And the first thing she does is to seduce him.

And the first thing he does is to be seduced.

And the second thing they do is to hug their sin in secret, and gloat over it, and try to understand.

心十分瞧不起人的精神和意识，可仍然像使用毒品一样一直习惯性地鼓吹精神、博爱和了解。其实他们内心并不在乎这些。他们这样只是为了求得感觉，那美妙绝伦的爱的感觉，爱全世界。他们要的是了解，了解，了解，了解的感觉对他们来说如同坐在忽悠忽悠的飞机里。所有感觉中最漂亮的要算理解了。哦，他们理解得太多了，宝贝们!他们太会玩这种把戏了。纯粹是自傲的把戏。

可是，一部《红字》却让这个把戏露了馅儿。

这里有一位纯而又纯的年轻牧师丁梅斯代尔。

美丽的清教徒海斯特就拜倒在他脚下。

她做的第一件事就是引诱他。

他做的第一件事就是上了她的钩。

他们做的第二件事就是隐瞒他们的罪恶。他们为此得意，试图相互理解。

这是新英格兰的神话。

杀鹿人拒绝受朱迪丝·哈特的引诱［见菲尼莫·库柏的小说《杀鹿人》］。至少撒

Which is the myth of New England.

Deerslayer refused to be seduced by Judith Hutter.* At least the Sodom apple of sin didn't fetch him.

But Dimmesdale was seduced gloatingly.* Oh, luscious Sin!

He was such a pure young man.

That he had to make a fool of purity.

The American psyche.

Of course, the best part of the game lay in keeping up pure appearances.

The greatest triumph a woman can have, especially an American woman, is the triumph of seducing a man:especially if he is pure.

And he gets the greatest thrill of all, in falling. –'Seduce me, Mrs Hercules.'*

And the pair of them share the subtlest delight in keeping up pure appearances, when everybody knows all the while. But the power of pure appearances is something to exult in. All America gives in to it. Look pure!

To seduce a man. To have everybody know. To keep up appearances of purity. Pure!

This is the great triumph of woman.

旦的苹果未能让他上钩。

可是丁梅斯代尔却洋洋自得地上钩[霍桑的原作中并无引诱的细节，所以这里的"洋洋自得地上钩"也就缺乏根据了]。哦，诱人的罪恶！

他是个多么纯洁的年轻人啊。

他要愚弄清教。

美国人的心灵。

当然，这场游戏的最精彩部分是如何保持纯洁的形象。

一个女人，特别是一个美国女人可以取得的胜利是成功地引诱一个男人，特别是一个纯洁的男人。

而他则获得了最大的快感——堕落——"勾引我吧，赫克利斯[赫克利斯是希腊神话中的大力神。此处可能指海斯特的诱惑力大如赫克利斯]太太。"

这两人分享着保持纯洁面目的快乐，其实别人早已知道他们是怎么回事。可是纯洁的面目值得他们欢悦。整个美国都这样。看上去纯洁！

引诱一个男人。要让人们都知道。可还要保持纯洁的面目。纯洁！

这是女人的巨大胜利。

A. The Scarlet Letter. Adulteress! The great Alpha. Alpha! Adulteress! The new Adam and Adama! American!

A. Adulteress! Stitched with gold thread, glittering upon the bosom. The proudest insignia.

Put her upon the scaffold and worship her there. Worship her there. The Woman, the Magna Mater. A. Adulteress! Abel!

Abel! Abel! Abel! Admirable!

It becomes a farce.

The fiery heart. A. Mary of the Bleeding Heart. Mater Adolerata! A. Capital A. Adulteress. Glittering with gold thread. Abel! Adultery. Admirable!

It is, perhaps, the most colossal satire ever penned. *The Scarlet Letter*. And by a blue-eyed darling of a Nathaniel.

Not Bumppo, however.

The human spirit, fixed in a lie, adhering to a lie, giving itself perpetually the lie.

All begins with A.

Adulteress. Alpha. Abel, Adam. A. America.*

A，红字。通奸妇！这了不起的第一个字母，第一个！通奸妇！新亚当和亚当娜！美国人！

A，通奸妇！这 A 字绣着金线边，在她胸上熠熠闪光，这令人骄傲的标志。

把她放在绞刑架上让人们崇拜她，这个女人，这个伟大的母亲。A，通奸妇！亚伯[Magna Mater 是古罗马人崇拜的伟大女性。亚伯是亚当和夏娃的次子，被其兄该隐所杀害。此处可能指海斯特被丁梅斯代尔所危害]！

亚伯！亚伯！亚伯！令人景慕！

它成了一个笑话。

愤怒的心。A，心在流血的圣母玛利亚。悲哀的圣母！A，大写的 A。通奸妇。绣着金线的红字。亚伯！通奸。可景慕的人！

或许这是有史以来写下的最大的讽刺。《红字》。由一位叫纳撒尼尔的碧眼宝贝儿写就。

当然不是班波 [见库柏的"皮袜子"系列小说]。

人的精神凝固于一个谎言中，胶固于一个谎言，永远给自身一个谎

The Scarlet Letter.

'Had there been a Papist among the crowd of Puritans, he might have seen in this beautiful woman, so picturesque in her attire and mien, and with the infant at her bosom, an object to remind him of the image of Divine Maternity, which so many illustrious painters have vied with one another to represent; something which should remind him, indeed, but only by contrast, of that sacred image of sinless Motherhood, whose infant was to redeem the world.'

Whose infant was to redeem the world indeed! It will be a startling redemption the world will get from the American infant.

Here was a taint of deepest sin in the most sacred quality of human life, working such effect that the world was only the darker for this woman's beauty, and more lost for the infant she had borne.

Just listen to the darling. Isn't he a master of apology?

Of symbols, too.

His pious blame is a chuckle of praise all the while.

Oh, Hester, you are a demon.* A man must be pure, just so that you can seduce him to a fall. Because the greatest thrill in life is to bring down the Sacred

言。

一切都始于一个 A 字。

通奸妇。字母表中的头一个字母。亚伯。亚当。A，美国 [这几个字的字头字母全是 A]。

《红字》。

“如果清教徒人群中有一位天主教徒，他就会发现这位如花似玉、风采非凡的美妇人，她怀中抱着一婴儿，其形态令人想起圣母，这幅形象可是许多著名画家竞相描绘的。她确实令人想起什么，当然是通过对比，想起那圣洁的母亲，她的婴孩将为这个世界赎罪。”

那婴孩将为这个世界赎罪，的的确确！世界的罪恶将会由这个美国婴孩赎回，一种令人吃惊的赎罪。

“人生最神圣的本质受到了最难以抹消的玷污。因为有了这妇人的美，这世界愈显得黑暗，因为她的孩子的出生，这世界愈显得迷惘。”

听听这宝贝儿在说什么。他不是可以算得上辩解大师了吗？

亦是象征大师。

Saint with a flop into the mud. Then when you´ve brought him down humbly wipe off the mud with your hair, another Magdalen.* And then go home and dance a witch´s jig of triumph, and stitch yourself a Scarlet Letter with gold thread, as duchesses used to stitch themselves coronets. And then stand meek on the scaffold and fool the world. Who will all be envying you your sin, and beating you because you´ve stolen an advantage over them.

Hester Prynne is the great nemesis of woman. She is the knowing Ligeia* risen diabolic from the grave. Having her own back. Understanding.

This time it is Mr Dimmesdale who dies. She lives on and is Abel.

His spiritual love was a lie. And prostituting the woman to his spiritual love, as popular clergymen do, in his preachings and loftiness, was a tall white lie. Which came flop.

We are so pure in spirit. Hi-tiddly-i-ty!

Till she tickled him in the right place, and he fell.

Flop.

Flop goes spiritual love.

But keep up the game. Keep up appearances. Pure are the pure. To the pure

他虔诚的谴责同时也是赞美的窃笑。

哦,海斯特,你是一个魔鬼。一个男人必须是纯洁的,仅仅是为了让你引诱他、让他堕落。一生中最大的快乐莫过于把圣人拉入泥坑。把他拉入泥坑,再谦卑地用你的头发擦干他身上的泥水,又一个末大拉 [见《约翰福音》7:3,玛利亚·末大拉用她的头发蹭去耶稣脚上的泥]。然后回家,跳一个女巫胜利舞,然后用金线绣上一个红字,就像公爵夫人绣自己的头饰一样。再往后就是怯生生地站在绞刑台上愚弄人世。人们都妒嫉你犯了罪,他们会揍你,因为你抢了先。

海斯特·白兰是女人中的一大复仇女神。她是又一个从坟墓中复活的魔女莉盖娅 [见爱伦·坡的小说《莉盖娅》],她要了解。她要找回属于她的东西。理解。

这一次该丁梅斯代尔先生死了。她继续活下来,成为亚伯。

他的精神恋是个谎言。他像一般的牧师一样,在高尚的布道中让女人成为他精神爱的妓女,可这是弥天大谎,终于会不打自招。

我们的精神太纯洁了。纯洁无瑕!

all things, etc.*

Look out, Mister, for the Female Devotee. Whatever you do, don't let her start tickling you. She knows your weak spot. Mind your Purity.

When Hester Prynne seduced Arthure Dimmesdale it was the beginning of the end. But from the beginning of the end to the end of the end is a hundred years or two.

Mr Dimmesdale also wasn't at the end of his resources. Previously, he had lived by governing his body, ruling it, in the interests of his spirit. Now he has a good time all by himself torturing his body, whipping it, piercing it with thorns,* macerating himself. It's a form of masturbation. He wants to get a menta! grip on his body. And since he can't quite manage it with the mind, witness his fall-he will give it what for, with whips. His will shall lash his body. And he enjoys his pains. Wallows in them. To the pure all things are pure.

It is the old self-mutilation process, gone rotten. The mind wanting to get its teeth in the blood and flesh. The ego exulting in the tortures of the mutinous flesh. I, the ego, I will triumph over my own flesh. Lash! Lash! I am a grand free spirit. Lash! I am the master of my soul! Lash! Lash! I am the captain of my soul. Lash! Hurray!

她搔中了他的要害部位，于是他倒下了。

失败。

精神恋失败了。

可这把戏还要耍下去，门面还要撑下去。纯洁的人本纯洁。纯洁者样样纯洁[见《新约·提多书》1:15:“在洁净的人，凡物都洁净。”]。

小心，先生，小心你的女信徒。不管做什么，别让她搔痒你。她知道你的弱点。小心保持你的纯洁。

海斯特·白兰引诱了亚瑟·丁梅斯代尔，从此末日就开始了。可是从末日开始到末日结束却经过了一二百年时间。

丁梅斯代尔先生并未日暮途穷。起先，他用精神统治自己的肉体。现在他的好时光来了：自己折磨自己的肉体，抽打、用荆棘刺自己的皮肉[霍桑的原文中没有荆棘刺肤的情节]、让自己消瘦。这是一种手淫。他是想用自己的头脑控制自己的肉体，既然他无法全然控制自己的身体，眼看着自己的肉体堕落，于是他就用鞭子抽打它，惩罚天。他的意志要抽打他的肉体，他从痛苦中获得欢愉。他沉浸在自虐中。对纯洁的人来说一切皆纯。

'In the fell clutch of circumstance,' etc. etc.

Good-bye Arthur. He depended on women for his Spiritual Devotees, spiritual brides. So, the woman just touched him in his weak spot, his Achilles Heel of the flesh. Look out for the spiritual bride. She's after the weak spot.

It is the battle of wills.

'For the will therein lieth, which dieth not-'

The Scarlet Woman becomes a Sister of Mercy. Didn't she just, in the late war. Oh, Prophet Nathaniel!

Hester urges Dimmesdale to go away with her, to a new country, to a new life. He isn't having any.

He knows there is no new country, no new life on the globe today. It is the same old thing, in different degrees, everywhere. *Plus ca change, plus c'est la même chose*.

Hester thinks, with Dimmesdale for her husband, and Pearl for her child, in Australia, maybe, she'd have been perfect.

But she wouldn't. Dimmesdale had already fallen from his integrity as a minister of the Gospel of the Spirit. He has lost his manliness. He didn't see the point of

这是自古就有的自我折磨术。人的理智要控制他的血肉。他的自我为着自身的肢离破碎而狂喜。“我”,这个自我,我要战胜我的肉体。抽!抽!我是个无比自由的精灵。抽!我是我灵魂的主人!抽!抽!我是我灵魂的船长。抽!快抽啊!“身陷残酷的际遇掌控中,”如此这般。

再见,亚瑟。他需要女人做他的精神信徒,精神新娘。于是,这女人正触到了他的弱点——他的“阿喀琉斯之踵”。注意你的精神新娘,她在寻找你的弱点。

这是一场意志间的斗争。

“意志不死——”

这佩带红字的女人成了慈悲的姐妹。她不是刚刚经历了那场战争吗?哦,预言家霍桑!

海斯特怂恿丁梅斯代尔随她走,去一个新的国家,奔向一种新生活。可他不。

他知道今日的世界上既没有新国家也没有新生活。这是一件古而又古的事,处处尽然,只是程度不同。事情越是改变,越是趋同!

just leaving himself between the hands of a woman and going away to a 'new country', to be her thing entirely. She'd only have despised him more, as every woman despises a man who has 'fallen' to her; despises him with her tenderest lust.

He stood for nothing any more. So let him stay where he was and dree out his weird.

She had dished him and his spirituality, so he hated her. As Angel Clare was dished, and hated Tess. As Jude in the end hated Sue: or should have done.* The women make fools of them, the spiritual men. And when, as men, they've gone flop in their spirituality, they can't pick themselves up whole any more. So they just crawl, and die detesting the female, or the females, who made them fall.

The saintly minister gets a bit of his own back, at the last minute, by making public confession from the very scaffold where he was exposed. Then he dodges into death. But he's had a bit of his own back, on everybody.

'Shall we not meet again?' whispered she, bending her face down close to him. 'Shall we not spend our immortal life together? Surely, surely, we have ransomed one another with all this woe! Thou lookest far into eternity with those bright dying eyes. Tell me what thou seest!'

海斯特以为有丁梅斯代尔做她的丈夫，有女儿珠儿，他们三人到了澳大利亚或许日子会极完美。

可这不可能。丁梅斯代尔这个传播福音书精神的牧师早已丧失了自己的道德。他失去了自己的丈夫气。他不愿意让一个女人掌握自己，逃向一个新国家，完全受她控制。她像所有蔑视"堕落"的男人那样蔑视他，可同时又对他怀有温情。

他不再捍卫什么，那就让他在原地忍受着吧。

她挫败了他和他的精神，为此他恨她。正像安吉尔·克莱尔被苔丝挫败了后仇恨苔丝那样。正像裘德终于恨上了苏一样——或者说他应该恨[这四人分别是哈代小说《苔丝》和《无名的裘德》中的两对恋人]。女人愚弄了精神化的男人。男人们一旦精神上被挫败了，他就再也爬不起来了。他们只能爬行，致死死都恨女人，是女人让他们堕落的。

这圣洁的牧师最终站在断头台上向公众忏悔，总算挽回了点什么。随后他死了。但他总算小小地报复了每个人。

"我们不再见面了吗?"她把头低向他说，"我们不白头到老吗?我们受

'Hush, Hester –hush,' said he, with tremulous solemnity. 'The law we broke! – the sin here so awfully revealed! Let these alone be in thy thoughts. I fear! I fear! '

So he dies, throwing the 'sin' in her teeth, and escaping into death.

The law we broke, indeed. You bet!

Whose law!

But it is truly a law, that man must either stick to the belief he has grounded himself on, and obey the laws of that belief, or he must admit the belief itself to be inadequate, and prepare himself for a new thing.

There was no change in belief, either in Hester or in Dimmesdale or in Hawthorne or in America. The same old treacherous belief, which was really cunning disbelief, in the Spirit, in Purity, in Selfless Love, and in Pure Consciousness. They would go on following this belief, for the sake of the sensation of it. But they would make a fool of it all the time. Like Woodrow Wilson,* and the rest of modern Believers. The rest of modern Saviours.

If you meet a Saviour, today, be sure he is trying to make an innermost fool of you. Especially if the saviour be an UNDERSTANDING WOMAN, offering her love.

Hester lives on, pious as pie, being a public nurse. She becomes at last an ac-

了苦，已经赎罪了！你那双明亮绝望的眼睛看到了永恒。告诉我，你看到什么了！"

"嘘，海斯特，嘘，"他阴郁、颤抖着说，"我们犯了法！我们的事发了！我想的就是这个。我怕！我怕！"

所以他死了，把"罪恶"甩给了她，他自己躲了。

我们确实犯了法。

是谁的法?!

可它的确是法，人必得严守自己赖以立足的信仰并服从这信仰之法，否则他就该承认这信仰的不足，从而准备接受新生事物。

信仰不可改变，无论是海斯特、丁梅斯代尔、霍桑还是美国皆是如此。这是一个陈旧危险的信仰——对精神、清教、无私的爱和纯洁思想，其实是不相信。他们是为了信仰而信仰。可他们一直是在愚弄这信仰，正如同伍德罗·威尔逊[美国第二十八任总统]等现代信徒一样，他们是现代的救世主。

记住，如果你遇到一位今日的救世主，他肯定会试图愚弄你，特别

knowledged saint, Abel of the Scarlet Letter.

She would, being a woman. She has had her triumph over the individual man, so she quite loves subscribing to the whole spiritual life of society. She will make herself as false as hell, for society´s sake, once she´s had her real triumph over Saint Arthur.

Blossoms out into a Sister-of-Mercy Saint.

But it´s a long time before she really takes anybody in. People kept on thinking her a witch. which she was.

As a matter of fact, unless a woman is held, by man, safe within the bounds of belief, she becomes inevitably a destructive force. She can´t help herself. A woman is almost always vulnerable to pity. She can´t bear to see anything physically hurt. But let a woman loose from the bounds and restraints of man´s fierce belief, in his gods and in himself, and she becomes a gentle devil. She becomes subtly diabolic. The colossal evil of the united spirit of Woman. WOMAN, German woman or American woman, or every other sort of woman, in the last war, was something frightening. As every man knows.

Woman becomes a helpless, would-be-loving demon. She is helpless. Her very

是，如果一位要“理解”的女人向你施以爱情的话更是如此。

海斯特活了下来，显得极虔诚，当了一位公共护士。最终她成了一位众人皆知的圣女，一位佩带红字的亚伯。

作为一个女人，她要这样的。她已战胜了一个男人，所以她乐意参与社会的全部精神生活。一旦她战胜了神圣的亚瑟，她就拼命作假，为这个社会的缘故。

她荣升为一个慈悲的圣女。

可要想让别人承认可不那么简单。人们一直以为她是个女巫，她的确是。

事实是，如果一个女人不被男人牢牢地用信仰约束着，她就会不可避免地变成一股破坏力量。她无法控制自己。一个女人几乎不可能没有怜悯心。她无法目睹任何人肉体上受损伤。可是如果一个女人挣脱了男人坚定的信仰约束，她不再信他的神和他自己，这女人就会变成一头温柔的魔鬼。她会带上微妙的鬼气。女人的精神会汇合成一头巨大的鬼，女人，德国女人、美国女人或任何别种女人在第一次世界大战中显得可怕

love is subtle poison.

Unless a man believes in himself and his gods, genuinely: unless he fiercely obeys his own Holy Ghost;his woman will destroy him. Woman is the nemesis of doubting man. She can't help it.

And with Hester, after Ligeia, woman becomes a nemesis to man. She bolsters him up from the outside, she destroys him from the inside. And he dies hating her, as Dimmesdale did.

Dimmesdale's spirituality had gone on too long, too far. It had become a false thing. He found his nemesis in woman. And he was done for.

Woman is a strange and rather terrible phenomenon, to man. When the subconscious soul of woman recoils from its creative union with man. it becomes a destructive force. It exerts, willy-nilly, an invisible destructive influence. The woman herself may be as nice as milk, to all appearance, like Ligeia. But she is sending out waves of silent destruction of the faltering spirit in men, all the same. She doesn't know it. She can't even help it. But she does it. The devil is in her.

The very women who are most busy saving the bodies of men, and saving the children: these women-doctors, these nurses, these educationalists, these public-

极了。哪个男人都知道这一点。

女人成了一个无法自制的、具有爱的潜能的魔鬼。她不能自制。她的爱是莫名的毒药。

一个男人如果不真心实意地相信自己和自己的神——服从自己的圣灵,他的女人就会毁灭他。对于持怀疑态度的男人来说,女人是复仇女神。她非得这样不可。

海斯特是莉盖娅之后男人的复仇女神。她表面上支撑着他,可她却毁了他的内心,丁梅斯代尔至死都恨她。

丁梅斯代尔的精神走得太远了,最终变得虚假起来。他发现女人是复仇女神。从此他完了。

对男人来说,女人陌生而有点可怕。一旦女人的潜意识脱离了与男人共同进行创造的联盟,这潜意识就会变成一种破坏力量。它对男人无形中施加毁灭的影响。女人可能会像莉盖娅一样表面上十分美好,可她其实会默默地鼓起毁灭的浪头冲击男人那抖动不稳的精神。她并未意识到这一点。她甚至无法禁止自己。她情不自禁要这样,她心中有个魔鬼。

spirited women, these female saviours:they are all, from the inside, sending out waves of destructive malevolence which eat out the inner life of a man, like a cancer. It is so, it will be so, till men realize it and react to save themselves.

God won't save us. The women are so devilish godly. Men must save themselves in this strait, and by no sugary means either.

A woman can use her sex in sheer malevolence and poison, while she is behaving as meek and good as gold. Dear darling, she is really snow-white in her blamelessness. And all the while she is using her sex as a she-devil, for the endless hurt of her man. She doesn't know it. She will never believe it if you tell her. And if you give her a slap in the face for her fiendishness, she will rush to the first magistrate, in indignation. She is so absolutely blameless, the she-devil, the dear, dutiful creature.

Give her the great slap, just the same, just when she is being most angelic. Just when she is bearing her cross most meekly.

Oh, woman out of bounds is a devil. But it is man's fault. Woman never asked, in the first place, to be cast out of her bit of an Eden of belief and trust. It is man's business to bear the responsibility of belief. If he becomes a spiritual fornicator and

那些最忙于拯救男人和儿童的肉体的女人们：女医生、护士、教育家，富有公共精神的女救世主之类，她们都会鼓起毁灭的恶浪来吞食男人的内心，就如同癌症一样。情况仍会这样，直至男人意识到这一点并反过来自救了。

上帝并不能拯救我们。女人是过于凶恶的神。男人必须把自己救出困境，但没有什么轻松的办法。

女人可以利用自己的性来搞阴谋、使毒计，而表面上却装得极懦弱、极善良。亲爱的宝贝儿，她真是洁白无瑕。可她却像个魔鬼不断地用性来伤害她的男人。她并未意识到这一点。如果你告诉她，她也绝不会相信。如果因为她的恶毒你给她一个耳光，她会气愤地跑去找国家总统。她绝没有错，这个魔鬼，宝贝儿，有责任感的女人。

给她一大耳光，就在她最像天使的时候，给她一大耳光。当她羞涩地佩戴十字架时，给她一耳光。

哦，一个不受拘束的女人就是一个魔鬼。可这是男人的过错。女人从未要求男人把她逐出信仰与信任的伊甸园。男人负有信仰的责任。如果

liar, like Ligeia's husband and Arthur Dimmesdale, how can a woman believe in him? Belief doesn't go by choice. And if a woman doesn't believe in a man, she believes, essentially, in nothing. She becomes, willy-nilly, a devil.

A devil she is, and a devil she will be. And most men will succumb to her devilishness.

Hester Prynne was a devil. Even when she was so meekly going round as a sick-nurse. Poor Hester. Part of her wanted to be saved from her own devilishness. And another part wanted to go on and on in devilishness, for revenge. Revenge! REVENGE! It is this that fills the unconscious spirit of woman today. Revenge against man, and against the spirit of man which has betrayed her into unbelief. Even when she is most sweet and a salvationist, she is her most devilish, is woman. She gives her man the sugar-plum of her own submissive sweetness. And when he's taken this sugar-plum in his mouth, a scorpion comes out of it. After he's taken this Eve to his bosom, oh, so loving, she destroys him inch by inch. Woman and her revenge! She will have it, and go on having it, for decades and decades, unless she's stopped. And to stop her you've got to believe in yourself and your gods, your own Holy Ghost, Sir Man; and then you've got to fight her, and never give in. She's a devil. But in the

他变成了精神上的私通者和撒谎者如同莉盖娅的丈夫及亚瑟·丁梅斯代尔，女人怎么能相信他呢?信仰是由不得选择的。如果一个女人连男人都不相信，那她压根儿就不会相信什么了。她身不由已地变成了一个魔鬼。

她是个魔鬼，将来也还会是的。大多数男人都会败在她的魔力下。

海斯特·白兰就是个魔鬼，即便她温顺地尽一个护士之职时她仍是一个魔鬼。可怜的海斯特。她的一半想着摆脱自己的魔鬼。可另一半却想继续做鬼，为的是报复。报复！复仇！就是这东西充满了今日女人的精神。报复男人，报复男人的精神，是它让她丧失信仰的。女人最最甜美、最像个救世主时也还是魔鬼。她把自己的柔顺与甜美都献给她的男人。可一旦男人吞下她这颗甜果，甜果中就会钻出毒蝎来。他把这个无比可爱的夏娃拥在怀中后她就会一点点地毁灭他。女人，女人的复仇！她会一直这样下去而不会停止复仇的。要想制止她，你就得相信自己和你自己心中的神，你的圣灵。然后你就要跟她斗，永不退却。她是个魔鬼，可她总归会被战胜的。她只有一点点愿意被征服的本能，因此你要战胜她的大部分本能，进行殊死搏斗，最终博取她那一丁点解脱的欲望，从而制止她复

long run she is conquerable. And just a tiny bit of her wants to be conquered. You´ve got to fight three-quarters of her, in absolute hell, to get at the final quarter of her that wants a release, at last, from the hell of her own revenge. But it´s a long last. And not yet.

'She had in her nature a rich, voluptuous, oriental characteristic-a taste for the gorgeously beautiful.' This is Hester. This is American. But she repressed her nature in the above direction. She would not even allow herself the luxury of labouring at fine, delicate stitching. Only she dressed her little sin-child Pearl vividly, and the scarlet letter was gorge-ously embroidered. Her Hecate and Astarte insignia.

'A voluptuous, oriental characteristic-' That lies waiting in American women. It is probable that the Mormons* are the forerunners of the comming real America. It is probable that men will have more than one wife, in the coming America. That you will have again a half-oriental womanhood, and a polygamy.

The grey nurse, Hester. The Hecate, the hell-cat. The slowly-evolving voluptuous female of the new era, with a whole new submissiveness to the dark, phallic principle.

But it takes time. Generation after generation of nurses and political women

仇。不过现在还离那远着呢。

"她天生性欲旺盛,有一种东方性格,美感极强。"这是海斯特。这是美国。可她却用前面所说过的方式压抑自己的天性。她甚至不为自己绣制精细奢侈的服饰。她只是把那罪恶之女珠儿打扮得漂漂亮亮,把那红字绣得极华美。那是冥界女神和性爱女神的标记。

"性感,东方性格"在等待美国的女人。很可能摩门教徒[1830 年创立于美国的一个基督教教派,初期提倡一夫多妻制,但 1890 年后很少实践]是未来真正美国人的先驱。很可能未来的美国男人可以有一个以上的妻子。又会出现半东方式的女性存在形式和一夫多妻制。

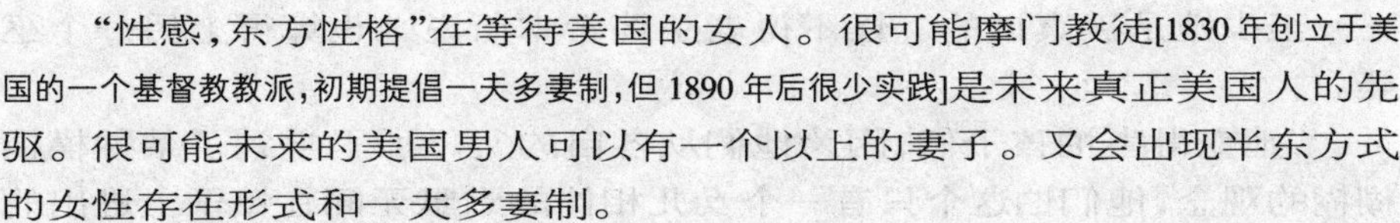

这桌灰衣的女护士,海斯特,这冥界女神,地狱中的猫。这新世纪缓慢进化中淫荡的女性,她对黑暗的费勒斯原则抱一种新的屈从态度。

可是这需要时间,需要一代接一代的护士、女政客和救世者们。最终结果是性崇拜图像在黑暗中再次树立起来,出现新式的温顺女性。要达到这种深度。女人在这方面变得深刻起来。我们最终要打破理智——精神意识的疯狂,女人会选择再次体验那了不起的屈从。

and salvationists. And in the end, the dark erection of the images of sex-worship once more, and the newly submissive women. That kind of depth. Deep women in that respect. When we have at last broken this insanity of mental-spiritual consciousness. And the women choose to experience again the great submission.

'The poor, whom she sought out to be the objects of her bounty, often reviled the hand that was stretched to succour them.'

Naturally. The poor hate a salvationist. They smell the devil underneath.

'She was patient -a martyr indeed -but she forebore to pray for her enemies, lest, in spite of her forgiving aspirations, the words of the blessing should stubbornly twist themselves into a curse.'

So much honesty, at least. No wonder the old witch-lady Mistress Hibbins claimed her for another witch.

'She grew to have a dread of children;for they had imbibed from their parents a vague idea of something horrible in this dreary woman gliding silently throught the twon, with never any companion but only one child.'

'A vague idea! ' Can't you see her 'gliding silently'? It's not a question of a vague idea imbibed, but a definite feeling directly received.

“她要施恩的那些可怜人时常辱没她的这只拯救他们的手。”

很自然，那些可怜的人仇恨一位救世主式的人物。他们可以嗅出救世主身上隐藏的魔气。

“她很有耐心，像个烈女，但她克制不为她的敌人祈祷，生怕她宽容忍让，那些祝福的话自身会变成咒语。”

至少她是极真诚的。怪不得老巫婆希本斯说她也算得上另一个巫婆。

“她变得害怕孩子们，因为他们从各自的父母那里学到了某种模模糊糊的观念，他们怕这个只有一个女儿相伴的默默无闻在镇子上进出的女人。”

“模模糊糊的观念”，你是否发现她“默默无闻进出”?这不是学到模模糊糊的观念的问题，而是孩子们直接的感觉。

“有时，多少天里或几个月中有那么一会，她会感到有一双人的眼睛在盯着那块耻辱的标记，于是她感到些儿轻松，似乎有人分享了一半痛苦。可不一会儿，那更为难耐的痛苦又回到了她身上，因为就在她感到放

But sometimes, once in many days, or perchance in many months, she felt an eye –a human eye –upon the ignominious brand, that seemed to give a momentary relief, as if half her agony were shared. The next instant, back it all rushed again, with a still deeper throb of pain; for in that brief interval she had sinned again. Had Hester sinned alone?

Of course not. As for sinning again, she would go on all her life silently, changelessly 'sinning'. She never repented. Not she. Why should she? She had brought down Arthure Dimmesdale, that too–too snow–white bird, and that was her life–work.

As for sinning again when she met two dark eyes in a crowd, why, of course. Somebody who understood as she understood.

I always remember meeting the eyes of a gipsy woman, for one moment, in a crowd, in England. She knew,and I knew. What did we know! I was not able to make out. But we knew.

Probably the same fathomless hate of this spiritual conscious society in which the outcast woman and I both roamed like meek–looking wolves. Tame wolves waiting to shake off their tameness. Never able to.

松的那一刻她又犯了罪。海斯特是独自犯罪的吗?"

当然不是。说到重新犯罪,她倒愿意一辈子这样默默、毫无悔改地犯罪下去。她从不悔悟,她才不呢。她为什么要悔悟呢?她已经毁了亚瑟·丁梅斯代尔那个过于洁白无瑕的人,这是她毕生的工作。

一当她在人群中与两只黑眼睛相遇,她就又一次犯罪。有人像她一样理解这一切。

我一直记得在英国时我的目光曾与人群中的一位吉卜赛女郎的目光相遇。她明白,我也明白。我们明白什么!我弄不清,可我们都明白。

或许这皆出于这个精神化的社会中孕育着同样深刻的仇恨,这个流浪女人和我在这个世界中像两头温顺的狼。两头温顺的狼等待甩掉自己温顺的外衣,可总也甩不掉。

还有那"性欲的旺盛、东方性格"深知费勒斯神的神秘。她绝不背叛费勒斯神而投降于这个尽是"情人"的白人社会。只要我能坚持,我也不会这样。这些诱惑力强、精神化的白人妇女"了解"得太多了。人们时常被引诱,被"了解"。"我可以像读一本书一样读懂他。"我的第一个情人曾这

And again, that 'voluptuous, oriental' characteristic that knows the mystery of the ithyphallic gods. She would not betray the ithyphallic gods to this white, leprous-white society of 'lovers'. Neither will I, if I can help it. These leprous-white, seducing, spiritual women, who 'understand' so much. One has been too often seduced,and 'understood'. 'I can read him like a book,' said my first lover of me. The book is in several volumes, dear. And more and more comes back to me the gulf of dark hate and other understanding, in the eyes of the gipsy woman. So different from the hateful white light of understanding which floats like scum on the eyes of white, oh, so white English and American women, with their understanding voices and their deep, sad words, and their profound, good spirits. Pfui!

Hester was scared only of one result of her sin: Pearl. Pearl, the scarlet letter incarnate. The little girl. When women bear children, they produce either devils or sons with gods in them. And it is an evolutionary process. The devil in Hester produced a purer devil in Pearl. And the devil in Pearl will produceshe married an Italian Count -a piece of purer devilishness still.*

And so from hour to hour we ripe and ripe.

And then from hour to hour we rot and rot.

样说，亲爱的，这部书可有好几集呢。我越来越觉得那吉卜赛女人的眼睛里闪耀出黑暗的仇恨与别样的理解，那目光与白人妇女的目光太不一样了，白人的目光就像浮着一层污垢。哦，英国和美国的女人就是这样，她们凭借自己的理解力发出发自肺腑的哀声，唱出深刻的精神之歌来。呸!

海斯特惟一害怕的恶果是珠儿这孩子。珠儿是红字的化身。这小女孩儿。女人分娩，生出的或者是魔鬼或者是心怀圣灵的儿子。这是个进化的过程。海斯特这魔鬼却生出珠儿这么一个纯洁的魔鬼来。珠儿嫁给了一位意大利伯爵[原作中珠儿的丈夫国籍并不明确，这是劳伦斯的推断]，她会生出更为纯洁的魔鬼来。

于是，我们愈来愈成熟。

于是，我们愈来愈腐朽。

这孩子的这种气质"时常令她母亲不无痛苦地扪心自问这孩子是为什么而生，善还是恶"。

为了恶而生，海斯特。不过别急，恶与善同样重要。恶行与善行都是必须的，既然你生下了一个小恶种，请一定让这恶种去同世上猖獗的虚

There was that in the chile 'which often impelled Hester to ask in bitterness of heart, whether it were for good or ill that the poor little creature had been born at all'.

For ill, Hester. But don't worry. Ill is as necessary as good. Malevolence is as necessary as benevolence. If you have brought forth, spawned, a young malevolence, be sure there is a rampant falseness in the world against which this malevolence must be turned. Falseness has to be bitten and bitten, till it is bitten to death. Hence Pearl.

Pearl. Her own mother compares her to the demon of plague, or scarlet fever, in her red dress.* But then, plague is necessary to destroy a rotten false humanity.

Pearl, the devilish girl-child, who can be so tender and loving and understanding, and then, when she has understood, will give you a hit across the mouth, and turn on you with a grin of sheer diabolic jeering.*

Serves you right, you shouldn't be understood. That is your vice. You shouldn't want to be loved, and then you'd not get hit across the mouth. Pearl will love you: marvellously. And she'll hit you across the mouth: oh, so neatly. And serves you right.

伪作斗争。虚伪应该咬死。于是有了珠儿。

珠儿，她的母亲给她穿上红装，把她比作瘟疫鬼或猩红热病[这个比喻并非白兰所为，是出自原著中的叙述文字]，来一场瘟疫是必要的，它可以毁灭腐朽、虚伪的人类。

珠儿，这恶魔般的女孩儿，她是那么温顺、可人而通情达理，可一旦她明白了什么，她就会给你一个耳光[原作中珠儿并未打过白兰，只是把花扔在她胸上]，随后极恶毒地嘲笑你。

这可是你活该，你不该让人理解。让人理解是你的罪过。你不该想让人爱，那样你就不会挨耳光。珠儿会很爱你的，也会给你一大耳光。你活该。

或许珠儿是所有文学中顶有现代味的孩子。

旧派文人霍桑，有着孩童样的魅力，他会告诉你一切，当然他会矫饰一番。

可以说海斯特一方面仇恨她的孩子，可另一方面却视珠儿为她的宝贝，因为珠儿是女性对生活报复的继续。不过女性的报复是两方面的。首

Pearl is perhaps the most modern child in all literature.

Old-fashoned Nathaniel, with his little-boy charm, he'll tell you what's what. But he'll cover it with smarm.

Hester simply hates her child, from one part of herself. And from another, she cherishes her child as her one precious treasure. For Pearl is the continuing of her female revenge on life. But female revenge hits both ways. Hits back at its own mother. The female revenge in Pearl hits back at Hester, the mother, and Hester is simply livid with fury and 'sadness', which is rather amusing.

The child could not be made amenable to rules. In giving her existence a great law had been broken; and the result was a being whose elements were perhaps beautiful and brilliant, but all in disorder, or with an order peculiar to themselves, amidst which the point of variety and arrangement was difficult or impossible to discover.

Of course, the order is peculiar to themselves. But the point of variety is this: 'Draw out the loving, sweet soul, draw it out with marvellous understanding;and then spit in its eye.'

Hester, of course, didn't at all like it when her sweet child drew out her moth-

先是报复她的母亲。珠儿报复了母亲海斯特,海斯特为此气得脸色铁青,很“忧伤”,这事很有意思。

“这孩子无拘无束的。要想管住她是不可能的。其结果是造就了她美好动人的性情,可一切都乱了套,她只按她自己的那一套行事,她那套花样简直让人找不到头绪。”

当然了,她那一套只属于她自己。她的花招是,“把那可爱、甜美的灵魂拽出来,用绝妙的理解把它拽出,然后对它蔑然视之。”

当她可爱的孩子以其热望和深刻的理解拽出海斯特的灵魂加以嘲弄和蔑视时,海斯特并不高兴。可做母亲的必须经历这样的一个过程才行。

珠儿的目光很独特。“聪颖但难解,极其古怪,时而显得很刻毒,但总的来说是透着灵气。这目光令海斯特常常情不自禁地发问:珠儿是否是人类的孩子?”

一个小魔鬼!可她却是她母亲和圣人丁梅斯代尔所生的孩子呀。珠儿尽管大胆地表示自己的古怪,但她比她的父母更直爽。她发现人世间的

erly soul, with yearning and deep understanding: and then spit in the motherly eye, with a grin. But it was a process the mother had started.

Pearl had a peculiar look in her eyes: 'a look so intelligent yet so inexplicable, so perverse, sometimes so malicious, but generally accompanied by a wild flow of spirits, that Hester could not help questioning at such moments whether Pearl was a human child.'

A little demon! But her mother, and the saintly Dimmesdale, had borne her. And Pearl, by the very openness of her perversity, was more straightforward than her parents. She flatly refuses any Heavenly Father, seeing the earthly one such a fraud. And she has the pietistic Dimmesdale on toast, spits right in his eye: in both his eyes.

Poor, brave, tormented little soul, always in a state of recoil, she'll be a devil to men when she grows up. But the men deserve it. If they'll let themselves be 'drawn', by her loving understanding, they deserve that she shall slap them across the mouth the moment they are drawn. The chickens! Drawn and trussed.

Poor little phenomenon of a modern child, she'll grow up into the devil of a modern woman. The nemesis of weak-kneed modern men, craving to be love-drawn.

父亲不过是一个大骗子，因此她公然否认有什么神圣之父。她任意耍弄虚假虔诚的丁梅斯代尔，无情地蔑视他。

可怜、美丽、忍受着折磨的小人儿，她总是畏缩着，一旦她长大，她会成为男人的魔鬼的。不过男人们也活该，如果他们愿意被她那可爱的理解所“引诱”，那他们就活该挨她的耳光。一群活该挨宰的小鸡!

现代儿童中的一个小可怜儿，她会成长为一个魔鬼似的现代妇女。对那些经不住引诱的现代男士来说，她正是一个复仇女神。

这可恶的三角关系中的第三人是海斯特的丈夫罗格·齐林乌斯。他是个伊丽莎白时代的老医生，花白胡子，身着长毛大衣，缩着肩。又一个用宗教方法治病的人，有点像个炼丹术士，一个魔术师。他像弗兰西斯·培根一样，是一位处在现代科学边缘上的魔术师[培根本是哲学家和散文家，但时常亦被看做科学家，因为他在《学问的进步》中对科学作了分类]。

罗格·齐林乌斯属于老派知识分子，与中世纪的炼丹术士如罗格·培根[Roger Bacon(1214—1292)，芳济会僧侣，学者和科学家]是一脉相承的。他对炼丹术这样的黑暗科学和秘术深信不移。他远非一个基督教徒，远非一个无私有

The third person in the diabolic trinity, or triangle, of the *Scarlet Letter*, is Hester's first husband, Roger Chillingworth. He is an old Elizabethan physician, with a grey beard and a long-furred coat and a twisted shoulder. Another healer. But something of an alchemist, a magician. He is a magician on the verge of modern science, like Francis Bacon.*

Roger Chilling worth is of the old order of intellect, in direct line from the medieval Roger Bacon* alchemists. He has an old, intellectual belief in the dark sciences, the Hermetic philosophies. He is no Christian, no selfless aspirer. He is not an aspirer. He is the old authoritarian in man. The old male authority. But without passional belief. Only intellectual belief in himself and his male authority.

Shakespeare's whole tragic wail is because of the downfall of the true male authority, the ithyphallic authority and masterhood. It fell with Elizabeth. It was trodden underfoot with Victoria.

But Chillingworth keeps on the intellectual tradition. He hates the new spiritual aspirers, like Dimmesdale, with a black, crippled hate. He is the old male authority, in intellectual tradition.

You can't keep a wife by force of an intellectual tradition. So Hester took to

追求的人。他不是一个有追求的人。他是个独裁主义者,男性独裁主义者。但他毫无激情的信仰。他只有理智的信仰,相信自身和男权。

莎士比亚之所以发出悲剧的哀嚎,是因为真正的男性独裁垮了——费勒斯的权威与霸权倒了,它随着伊丽莎白女王一起倒了,在维多利亚时期则被踏在脚下。

可齐林乌斯却保持着知识的传统。他对丁梅斯代尔这种新的精神追求者恨之入骨。他是精神传统中的旧男性霸主。

你无法靠精神传统的力量守住你的老婆。于是海斯特才勾引丁梅斯代尔。

可她嫁的是罗格,她是同老罗格一起海誓山盟的夫妻。他们是毁灭精神圣人丁梅斯代尔的同谋。

"你干吗这样冲我笑?"她问她那复仇的老丈夫,"你是不是像那些黑人在我们周围的森林中搜寻什么?难道毁了我的灵魂的不正是你吗?是你在怂恿我。"

"不是你的灵魂!"他又笑道,"不是你的灵魂!"

seducing Dimmesdale.

Yet her only marriage, and her last oath, is with the old Roger. He and she are accomplices in pulling down the spiritual saint.

'Why dost thou smile so at me-' she says to her old, vengeful husband, 'Art thou not like the Black Man that haunts the forest around us? Hast thou not enticed me into a bond which will prove the ruin of my soul?'

'Not thy soul! ' he answered with another smile.'No, not thy soul! '

It is the soul of the pure preacher, that false thing, which they are after. And the crippled physician -this other healer-blackly vengeful in his old, distorted male authority, and the 'loving' woman, they bring down the saint between them.

A black and complementary hatred, akin to love, is what Chillingworth feels for the young, saintly parson. And Dimmesdale responds, in a hideous kind of love. Slowly the saint´s life is poisoned. But the black old physician smiles, and tries to keep him alive. Dimmesdale goes in for selftorture, self-lashing his own white, thin, spiritual saviour´s body. The dark Chillingworth listens outside the door and laughs, and prepares another medicine, so that the game can go on longer. And the saint´s very soul goes rotten. Which is the supreme triumph. Yet he keeps up appearances

他们追捕的是那纯洁的牧师的灵魂，这虚伪的人。而这位瘸子医生——另一个用宗教方法治病的人，满怀邪恶的复仇欲和变态的男性权威，是他和这位“可爱”的女人一起把圣人丁梅斯代尔给毁了。

那邪恶的仇恨近乎于爱，这就是齐林乌斯对这位年轻圣洁的牧师所怀的感情。而丁梅斯代尔亦报之以一种恨也似的爱。渐渐地，这圣人的生命被毒化了。但那邪恶的老医生却笑了，他还试图让他恢复活力。但丁梅斯代尔却选择了自我折磨，他自己抽打着这具洁白、瘦弱的精神救世主的肉体。那邪恶的齐林乌斯在门外倾听着笑了，并为丁梅斯代尔准备好了另一服药剂，从而让这场戏演得再久一些。圣人的灵魂却早已烂了，那是他最大的胜利，可他仍保持着表面上的平静。

这瘸子，这个满腹邪恶复仇的男性霸主和那个脸色苍白的堕落圣人！男性的两半相互毁灭着。

丁梅斯代尔最终来了一手“绝招儿”。他终于站在绞刑架上公开忏悔，然后遁入死亡之门，他击败了海斯特并让齐林乌斯第二次戴上了绿帽子。这报复干净利索。

still.

The black, vengeful soul of the crippled, masterful male, still dark in his authority:and the white ghastliness of the fallen saint! The two halves of manhood mutually destroying one another.

Dimmesdale has a 'coup' in the very end. He gives the whole show away by confessing publicly on the scaffold, and dodging into death, leaving Hester dished, and Roger as it were, doubly cuckolded. It is a neat last revenge.

Down comes the curtain, as in Ligeia's poem.

But the child Pearl will be on in the next act, with her Italian Count and a new brood of vipers. And Hester greyly Abelling, in the shadows, after her rebelling.

It is a marvellous allegory. It is to me one of the greatest allegories in all literature. *The Scarlet Letter*. Its marvellous under-meaning! And its perfect duplicity.

The absolute duplicity of that blue-eyed *Wunderkind* of a Nathaniel. The American wonder-child, with his magical allegorical insight.

But even wonder-children have to grow up in a generation or two.

And even SIN becomes stale.

像莉盖娅的诗所说的那样，大幕落下了。

可是珠儿会同她的意大利伯爵一起出现在下一场戏中，变成一条新的毒蛇。而海斯特就隐没在附近，反抗之后，依旧是个阴郁的受害者模样。

这是一篇精彩的寓言。我认为这是所有文学中最伟大的寓言之一。《红字》。了不起的内涵！完美的双重意义。

蓝眼睛的神童纳撒尼尔赋予本书绝对的双重意义。他是美国的神童，具备了魔幻般、寓言般的洞察力。

但是，即使是神童也会长大。

甚至罪恶也会变得乏味。

CHAPTER 8
Hawthorne´s Blithedale Romance

No other book of Nathaniel Hawthorne is so deep, so dual, and so complete as The Scarlet Letter: this great allegory of the triumph of sin.

Sin is a queer thing. It isn´t the breaking of divine commandments.It is the breaking of one´s own integrity.

For instance, the sin in Hester and Arthur Dimmesdale´s case was a sin because they did what they tbougbt it wrong to do. If they had really wanted to be lovers, and if they had had the honest courage of their own passion, there would have been no sin, even had the desire been only momentary.

But if there had been no sin, they would have lost half the fun, or more, of the game.

David Herbert Lawrence

霍桑的《福谷传奇》

纳撒尼尔·霍桑的著作中，数《红字》最为深刻、最有两重性并且最为完美，这是一个罪恶得胜的伟大寓言。

罪恶是个奇怪的东西，它并非是破坏神旨，而是破坏自身的完整。

比如，海斯特和亚瑟·丁梅斯代尔之所以犯了罪是因为他们做了自认为是错的事，如果他们真的相爱，如果他们诚实、勇敢地对待自己的激情，何罪有之，甚至有过那样的欲念也不为过。

可是如果不犯点罪，这游戏就少了一半的乐趣，甚至更多。

正是因为他们做了自认为错的事，这行为才有害。人发明了罪恶是为了欣赏猥亵感，同时也是为了推卸行为的责任。圣父告诉人们如何行

It was this very doing of the thing that they themselves believed to be wrong, that constituted the chief harm of the act.Man invents sin,in order to enjoy the feeling of being naughty. Also, in order to shift the responsibility for his own acts. A Divine Father ttells him what to do.And man is naughty and doesn´t obey. And then shiveringly, ignoble man lets down his pants for a flogging.

If the Divine Father doesn´t bring on the flogging, in this life, then sinful Man shiveringly awaits his whipping in the afterlife.

Bah, the Divine Father, like so many other Crowned Heads, has abdicated his authority.* Man can sin as much as he likes.

There is only one penalty: the loss of his owm integrity.Man should never do the thing he believes to be wrong. Because if he does, he loses his own singleness, wholeness, natural honour.

If you want to do a thing,you´ve either got to believe, sincerely, that its your true nature to do this thing-or else you´ve got to let it alone.

Believe in your own Holy Ghost. Or else, if you doubt, abstain.

A thing that you sincerely believe in cannot be wrong, because belief does not come at will. It Comes only from the Holy Ghost within. Therefore a thing you truly

动,可人却淘气,不从。于是不光彩的人只好脱下裤子挨鞭子了。

如果圣父不在今生惩罚他,那么犯罪人就得颤抖着等到来世去挨鞭子了。

哈,圣父像许多加冕的帝王一样逊了位[1917—1922年间,帝王退位或被处死导致四个欧洲王室灭亡:在俄国,俄皇被处死;在德国,德皇退位;在奥匈帝国,皇帝退位;在土耳其,苏丹统治结束]。因此人尽可以任意犯罪。

惩罚只有一个,那就是让人自身分裂。人永远不要做自以为错的事,如果他做了,他就失却了自己的独立、自己的完整与天然荣誉。

如果你要做什么事, 你就得真正相信是你的自然本性要你这样做的,否则就别做。

相信你自己的圣灵。如果有疑问,就弃之。

你真正相信的东西是不会错的,因为信仰并非随意产生。它只来自你心中的圣灵。所以说,你诚挚相信的东西是不会错的。

可是也有信仰是假的。也有罪恶的信仰,即:一个人不会做错事。还有的信仰是半真半假的,这是最要不得的东西。魔鬼就潜伏在十字架后

believe in, cannot be wrong.

But there is such a thing as spurious belief. There is such a thing as evil belief: a belief that one cannot do wrong. There is also such a thing as a half-spurious belief. And this is rottenest of all. The devil lurking behind the cross.

So there you are. Between genuine belief, and spurious belief, and half-genuine belief, you´re as likely as not to be in a pickle. And the half-genuine belief is much the dirtiest, and most deceptive thing in life.

Hester and Dimmesdale believed in the Divine Father, and almost gloatingly sinned against Him. The Allegory of Sin.

Pearl no longer believes in the Divine Father. She says so. She has no Divine Father. Disowns Papa both big and little.

So she can´t sin against him.

What will she do, then, if she´s got no god to sin against? Why, of course, she´ll not be able to sin at all. She´ll go her own way gaily, and do as she likes, and she´ll say, afterwards, when she´s made a mess: 'Yes, I did it.But I acted for the best, and therefore I am blameless. It´s the other person´s fault. Or else it´s Its fault.'

She will be blameless, will Pearl, come what may.

面。

我们就夹在真信仰、假信仰和半真半假的信仰之间,很可能就陷入这种尴尬境地中。半真半假的信仰是生活中顶肮脏、顶骗人的东西。

海斯特和丁梅斯代尔相信圣父,可又公然犯罪。这是个犯罪的寓言。

珠儿已不再相信圣父,她自己如是说。她心中没有圣父。她否认与圣父有任何关系。

所以她就不会犯罪。

如果不以犯罪来抗神,那她做什么?当然,她无罪可犯。她高高兴兴走她自己的路,做她爱做的事,干糟了一件事后她会说:"是的,是我做的。不过我尽了最大的努力,所以对我无可指责。那是别人的错。或者说这是这事情自己的错。"

不管发生什么,珠儿是无可指责的。

今日的世界不过是一连串的"珠儿"。而美国则是一根穿着洁白无瑕"珠儿"的绳子。美国人不会犯罪,什么都做得出,因为他们心中没有要与之作对的神。他们只是一些个人。没有神的人。

And the world is simply a string of Pearls today. And America is a whole rope of these absolutely immaculate Pearls, who can't sin, let them do what they may, because they've no god to sin against. Mere men, one after another. Men with no ghost to their name.

Pearls!

Oh, the irony, the bitter,bitter irony of the name! Oh, Nathaniel, you great man! Oh,America, you Pearl, you Pearl without a blemish!

How can Pearl have a blemish, when there's no one but herself to judge Herself? Of course she'll be immaculate, even if, like Cleopatra, she drowns a lover a noght in her dirty Nile. The Nilus Flux of her love.

Candida!

By Hawthorne's day it was already Pearl. Before swine, of course. There never yet was a Pearl that wasn't cast before swine.

It's Part of her game, part of her pearldom.

Because when Circe lies with a man, he's a swine after it, if he wasn't one before.* Not she. Circe is the great white impeccable Pearl.

And yet, oh, Pearl, there's a Nemesis even for you.

珠儿!

哦,讽刺,尖刻而又尖刻的讽刺,这个名字!哦,纳撒尼尔,你这了不起的人!哦,美国,你这颗珠儿,洁白无瑕的珠儿!

珠儿怎么会有瑕疵呢?没有别人评判她的行为,只有她自己评判她自己。是的。即便她像那位克莉奥帕特拉一样每晚在肮脏的尼罗河中淹死一位情人,她依旧是洁白无瑕的人。尼罗河洪流般的爱[据说克莉奥帕特拉在尼罗河中淹死情人是一种有性象征的行为。尼罗河洪流暗示女人的性欲,亦象征不稳定]。

肯迪达[见萧伯纳 1895 年的同名话剧]!

在霍桑时期,她就是珠儿。当然是在猪面前[见《马太福音》7:6:"不要把你们的珍珠丢在猪面前,恐怕它践踏了珍珠,再转过来咬你们。"]。还没有哪颗珍珠不曾被抛在猪面前的呢。

这是她的把戏的一部分,是她本身的一部分。

赛西一旦和某个男人性交,性交后这男人就会变成猪[荷马史诗中的女妖赛西能把男人变成猪,但并没有她引诱男人的情节]。而她却不会变成猪。赛西是一颗了不起的无瑕珍珠。

There´s a Doom, Pearl.

Doom! What a beautiful northern word. Doom.*

The doom of the Pearl.

Who will write that Allegory?*

Here´s what the Doom is, anyhow.

When you don´t have a Divine Father to sin against;and when you don´t sin against the Son; which the Pearls don´t, because they all are very strong on LOVE, stronger on LOVE than on anything: then there´s nothing left for you to sin against except the Holy Ghost.

Now, Pearl, come, let´s drop you in the vinegar.

And it´s a ticklish thing sinning against the Holy Ghost. 'It shall not be forgiven him.'*

Didn´t I tell you there was Doom?

It shall not be forgiven her.

The Father forgives: the Son forgives:* but the Holy Ghost does not forgive. So take that.

The Holy Ghost doesn´t for give because the Holy Ghost is within you. The

可是，哦，珠儿，甚至对你来说也有一位复仇女神。

末日在等待你，珠儿。

末日！这是一个多么美的北方词[Doom这个词源自古英语与古挪威语]。末日。珠儿们的末日。

谁会书写这个寓言呢[这里指中世纪英语里的寓言《珍珠》]?

无论如何，末日就在这里。

当你不以犯罪来对抗圣父和圣子时就是末日。珠儿们就不这样做，因为她们在爱情上都很强大，比在其他方面更为强大。然后就只有对抗圣灵了。

珠儿来，把你扔到醋里吧[意思是"让生活变酸，令人生厌"]。

与圣灵作对是件棘手的事。"它不会原谅他的。"[详见《新约·马太福音》12:31:"亵渎圣灵的人绝不可赦免。"]

我是否对你说过有末日这东西?

它不会原谅她的。

圣父会原谅，圣子会原谅[见《圣经》教堂传教书(Ecclesiasctius)2:2:"主心充满同情

Holy Ghost is you: your very You. So if, in your conceit of your ego, you make a break in your own you, in your own integrity, how can you be forgiven? You might as well make a rip in your own bowels, You know if you rip your own bowels they will go rotten and you will go rotten. And there's an end of you, in the body.

The same if you make a breach with your own Holy Ghost. You go soul-rotten. Like the Pearls.

These dear Pearls, they do anything they like, and remain pure. Oh, purity!

But they Can't stop themselves from going rotten inside. Rotten Pearls, fair outside. Their souls smell, because their souls are putrefying inside them.

The sin against the Holy Ghost.

And gradually, from within outwards, they rot. Some form of dementia. A thing disintegrating. A decomposing psyche. Dementia.

Quos vult perdere Deus, dementat prius.

Watch these Pearls, these Pearls of modern women. Particularly American women. Battening on love. And fluttering in the first batlike throes of dementia.

Yor can have your cake and eat it. But my God, it will go rotten inside you.

Hawthorne's other books are nothing compared to *The Scarlet Letter.*

与怜悯，久经磨难，施怜恕罪"；《新约·以弗所书》1:3-7："我们藉这爱子的血得蒙救赎，过犯得以赦免，乃是照他丰厚的恩典。"]，但圣灵不会原谅。接受这现实吧。

圣灵不会原谅，这是因为圣灵在你心中[见《哥林多前书》6:19"你的身体就是圣灵的殿……"]。圣灵就是你，就是你自己。所以，如果你的自我与你对立，要打破你的完整性，你怎么能求得原谅呢?你还不如在自己的腹部切一刀。你知道如果你在腹部切一刀，你的五脏六腑就会腐烂，你也会腐烂。于是你的肉体末日就到了。

同样，如果你与你的圣灵决裂，你的灵魂就会腐烂，不少珠儿们就是这样的。

这些可爱的珠儿们，她们为所欲为，可还显得纯洁。哦，纯洁!

可她们无法防止自己内心腐烂。腐败的珠儿们，金玉其表。她们的灵魂散发着恶臭，因为灵魂在她们体内腐烂了。

与圣灵作对的罪恶。

渐渐地，他们从内到外都腐烂了。这是一种衰败症。分裂。分裂的心灵。衰败症。

But there are good parables, and wonderful dark glimpses of early Puritan America, in *Twice Told Tales.*

The House of the Seven Ganbles has 'atmosphere'. The passing of the old order of the proud, bearded, black-browed Father:an order which is slowly ousted from life, and lingeringly haunts the old dark places. But comes a new generation to sweep out enen the ghosts, with these new vacuum cleaners.* No ghost could stand up against a vacuum cleaner.

The new generation is having no ghosts or cobwebs.It is setting up in the photography line, and is just going to make a sound financial thing out of it. For this purpose all old hates and old glooms, that belong to the antique order of Haughty Fathers, all these are swept up in the vacuum cleaner, and the vendetta-born young couple effect a perfect understanding under the black cloth of a camera and prosperity. *Vivat Indus. ia*!

Oh, Nathaniel, you savage ironist! Ugh, how you'd have hated it if you'd had nothing but the prosperous 'dear'young couple to write about! If you'd lived to the day when America was nothing but a Main Street.*

The Dark Old Fathers.

上帝欲毁灭谁，就先让他发疯。

看看这些珠儿，这些现代妇女吧，特别是美国妇女。她们靠爱活着，在衰败的痛苦中挣扎着。

糕饼是你的，想吃就吃，想占有就占有[英文成语 You cannot eat your cake and have it 的反意，表示两者兼得]。可是，天啊，它会在你心中腐烂。

霍桑别的书是无法与《红字》相媲美的。

不过还是有些不错的寓言使人借以管窥早期清教的美国，这些寓言收在《重讲一遍的故事》中。

《七个尖角顶的屋子》就很有"氛围"。那骄傲、留着胡须和黑眉毛的父亲的指令代代传下来，尽管它渐渐远离生活，但仍旧阴魂不散，在老地方徘徊，可是新的一代甚至可以用吸尘器[1903 年出现了真空吸尘器，1920 年代吸尘器已经在欧美很普遍]把鬼魂驱赶走。在真空吸尘器面前没有什么鬼魂挺得住。

新的一代人摒弃了魔鬼和陈腐的东西。他们拥护照相术，而且要靠它发大财。为此，所有属于傲慢的父辈的旧仇和宿怨都被吸尘器一扫而光，那对伴随族间仇杀而生的爱人在照相机镜头的黑罩布下达成了完美

The Beloved Wishy-Washy Sons.

The Photography Business.

???

Hawthorne came nearest to actuality in the *Blitbedale Romance*. This novel is a sort of picture of the notorious Brook Farm experiment. There the famous idealists and transcen dentalists of America met to till the soil and hew the timber in the sweat of their own brows, thinking high thoughts the while, and breathing an atmosphere of communal love, and tingling in tune with the Oversoul, like so many strings of a super-celestial harp. An old twang of the Crèvecœur instrument.

Of course they fell out like cats and dogs. Couldn´t stand one another. And all the music they made was the music of their quarrelling.

You can´t idealize hard work. Which is why America invents so many machines and contrivances of all sort: so that they need do no physical work.

And that´s why the idealists left off brookfarming, and took to bookfarming.

You can´t idealize the essential brute blood-activity, the brute blood desires, the basic, sardonic blood-knowledge.

That you can´t idealize.

的谅解。工业万岁！

哦，纳撒尼尔，你这野蛮的讽刺家！如果你没别的可写而只能写“可爱”的年轻爱侣，你会悔恨的！或许你会活到那一天，美国已一无是处，只剩一条《大街》[美国作家 Sinclair Lewis(1885—1951)的成名作，劳伦斯读后感到恐怖]。

阴郁的老父辈。

可爱的软弱儿子们。

照相术之类的东西。

???

在《福谷传奇》中，霍桑最接近现实。小说写的是有名的布鲁克农场实验的事[见前注：霍桑等人于 1841—1847 年间在麻省的布鲁克农场进行绿色城郊的试验]。那些著名的美国理想主义者和超验主义者一起来耕地、伐木，他们辛勤劳作，理想远大，在这里呼吸着集体之爱的气息，像无数根超灵的琴弦一样与上帝产生共鸣，这是一曲克里夫库尔[见有关克里夫库尔的一章]的老调。

当然，他们吵得很凶，因为他们无法相互容忍。他们弹奏的惟一音乐就是争吵声。

And you can't eliminate it.

So there's the end of ideal man.

Man is made up of a dual consciousness, of which the two halves are most of the time in opposition to one another-and will be so as long as time lasts.

You've got to learn to change from one consciousness to the other, turn and about. Not to try to make either absolute, or dominant. The Holy Ghost tells you the how and when.

Never did Nathaniel feel himself more spectral-of course he went brookfarming-than when he was winding the horn in the morning to summon the transcendental labourers to their tasks, or than when marching off with a hoe ideally to hoe the turnips, 'Never did I feel more spectral,' says Nathaniel.

Never did I feel such a fool, would have been more to the point.

Farcical fools,trying to idealize labour. You'll never succeed in idealizing hard work. Before you can dig mother earth you've got to take off your ideal jacket.The harder a man works, at brute labour, the thinner becomes his idealism, the darker his mind. And the harder a man works, at mental labour, at idealism, at transcendental occupations, the thinner becomes his blood, and the more brittle his nerves.

你不能把艰苦的工作理想化。为此,美国发明了各式各样的机器,从而他们就不用再干体力活儿。

于是,理想主义者们离开了布鲁克农场去著书立说了。

你无法把最根本的、粗野的血液行为理想化。粗野的血液欲望,根本的、具有讽刺意味的血性知识。

你无法把这一切理想化。

你也无法消除这一切。

理想化的人是没有出路的。

人生来具有双重意识,他的两半几乎总是处在对立之中——只要时间存在,永远如此。

你必须学会从一种意识向另一种意识转变,将两者交替,这并非是要你把其中任何一种绝对化、主导化。圣灵会告诉你什么时候、如何转化。

纳撒尼尔去过布鲁克农场,早晨他吹起号角招呼那些超验主义劳动者集合干活儿或者很理想地荷锄去挖萝卜。时而感到自己身上有股从未

Oh, the brittle-nerved brookfarmers!

You´ve got to be able to do both: the mental work,and the brute work. But be prepared to step from one pair of shoes into another. Don´t try and make it all one pair of shoes.

The attempt to idealize the blood!

Nathaniel knew he was a fool.attempting it.

He went home to his amiable spouse and his sanctum sanctorum of a study.

Nathaniel!

But the *Blithedale Romance*. It has a beautiful, wintry-evening farm-kitchen sort of opening.

Dramatis Personae:

1. *I.* The narrator: whom we will call Nathaniel.* A wisp of a sensitive, withal deep, literary young man no longer so very young.

2. *Zenobia:* a dark, proudly voluptuous clever woman with a tropical flower in her hair. Said to be sketched from Margaret Fuller, in whom Hawthorne saw some 'evil nature'. Nathaniel was more aware of Zenobia´s voluptuousness than of her 'mind'.

有过的灵鬼气。"我从未感到我身上这么有灵鬼气。"纳撒尼尔说。

最好说"我从未感到自己有多么傻",这才更中肯些。

可笑的傻瓜们试图把劳动理想化。你永远也不会成功的。在耕耘大地母亲之前,你应先脱去你理想的外衣。人干粗活儿干得愈苦,他的理想主义就愈淡漠,他的意识就愈黯淡。反之,人愈是为理想主义和超验的东西殚精竭虑,他的血液就愈淡泊,他的神经就愈脆弱。

哦,这些神经脆弱的布鲁克农场上的农夫们!

你应该学会体脑并用。不过也该准备好跳槽,不必在一棵树上吊死。

试图使血液理想化!

纳撒尼尔知道他的企图有多么傻。

于是他回家去找他温顺的妻子,躲进他那最最神圣的书斋里去了。

纳撒尼尔!

不过,《福谷传奇》有一个极美的开篇,像是冬夜里农家的厨房。

剧中人

1. "我":叙述者,我们姑且称他为纳撒尼尔吧[原小说中的叙述人名为 Miles

3. *Hollingsworth:* a black-bearded blacksmith with a deepvoiced lust for saving criminals. Wants to build a great Home for these unfortunates.

4. *Priscilla:* a sort of White Lily, a clinging little mediumistic sempstress who has been made use of in public seances. Asort of prostitute soul.

5. *Zenobia's Husband:* an unpleasant decayed person with magnetic powers and teeth full of gold-or set in gold. It is he who has given public spiritualist demonstrations, with Priscilla for the medium. He is of the dark, sensual, decayed handsome sort, and comes in unexpectedly by the back door.

PLOT Ⅰ.-I, Nathaniel, at once catch cold, and have to be put to bed. Am nursed with inordinate tenderness by the blacksmith, whose great hands are gentler than a woman's, etc.

The two men love one another with a love surpassing the love of women, so long as the healing-and-salvation business lasts.* When Nathaniel wants to get well and have a soul of his own, he turns with hate to the black-bearded, booming salvationist, Hephaestos of the underworld.Hates him for tyrannous monomania.

PLOT Ⅱ. -Zenobia, that clever lustrous woman, is fascinated by the criminal saving blacksmith, and would have him at any price. Meanwhile she has the subtlest

Coverdale]。一位羸弱敏感但又深沉的文人,年龄已不算太年轻。

2. 赞诺比亚:黑皮肤,聪明、骄傲而性感的女人,头发上插着一朵热带花儿。据说是玛格利特·福尔勒[Sara Margaret Fuller(1810–1850),美国作家、记者、女性主义先锋,与霍桑、爱默森和梭罗是朋友,编辑超验主义刊物《日晷》,霍桑在此发表重要作品《十九世纪妇女》]的化身,霍桑在她身上看到了某种"恶的天性"。纳撒尼尔更关心的不是赞诺比亚的头脑而是她的"性感"。

3. 霍林渥斯:一个长着黑胡须的铁匠,他一个心眼儿要拯救犯人。为此他打算为这些不幸的人建一个大家。

4. 普里西拉:一种白百合花样的人。她是个依赖性很强的女裁缝,在降神会上常被人利用当招魂工具,有点像个妓女。

5. 赞诺比亚的丈夫:一个不招人喜欢、堕落的人。他镶着一口金牙或镀金牙,能量很大。是他拿普里西拉当工具在大庭广众下招魂。他是那种阴郁、性欲强烈、堕落的美男子,他会很突兀地从后门出现。

情节之一:我(霍桑)感冒了,得卧床休息。那铁匠对我十分温柔,照顾得很周到,他那双大手比女人的还温柔,等等。

current of under standing with the frail but deep Nathaniel. And she takes the White Lily half-pityingly, half contemptuously under a rich and glossy dark wing.

PLOT Ⅲ. –The blacksmith is after Zenobia, to get her money for his criminal asylum:of which, of course, he will be the first inmate.

PLOT Ⅳ. –Nathaniel also feels his mouth watering for the dark–luscious Zenobia.

PLOT Ⅴ. –The White Lily, Priscilla, vaporously festering,turns out to be the famous Veiled Lady of public spiritualist shows: she whom the undesirable Husband, called the Professor, has used as a medium. Also she is Zenobia´s halfsister.

Débâcle

Nobody wants Zenobia in the end.She goes off without her flower.The blacksmith marries Priscilla. Nathaniel dribblingly confesses that he,too,has loved Prissy all the while. Boo–hoo!

Conclusion

A few years after, Nathaniel meets the blacksmith in a country lane near a humble cottage, leaning totteringly on the arm of the frail but fervent Priscilla. Gone are all dreams of asylums, and the saviour of criminals can´t even save himself from

这两个男人相爱了，这爱胜过了女人的爱情[见《撒姆尔记 2》大卫哀悼约拿单的话“你对我的爱奇妙非常，胜过女人。”]。有人要安抚，有人要救世，就会有这样的事。当纳撒尼尔要有自己的灵魂时，终于仇恨起这位黑胡子救世主、阴间的铁匠来。他恨的是他那霸道的偏执狂症。

情节之二：赞诺比亚这位聪明、光彩照人的女子迷上了那位热心于拯救犯人的铁匠，她无论如何也要得到他。与此同时她同这位柔弱但思想深沉的纳撒尼尔达成了某种暧昧的默契。她还对那位白百合花女子施以怜悯与保护，但又不失其蔑视。

情节之三：铁匠向赞诺比亚要钱以建立他的罪犯收容院。当然他自己会第一个住进去的。

情节之四：纳撒尼尔也对那黑皮肤性感强烈的赞诺比亚垂涎欲滴。

情节之五：白百合花普里西拉成为公共招魂表演会上著名的“蒙面女郎”。赞诺比亚的那位不招人喜欢的丈夫自诩教授，把普里西拉当成了招魂工具。其实她是赞诺比亚同父异母的妹妹。

his own Veiled Lady.

There you have a nice little bunch of idealists, transcentalists, brookfarmers, and disintegrated gentry. All going slightly rotten.

Two Pearls: a white Pearl and a black Pearl: the latter more expensive, lurid with money.

The white Pearl, the little medium, Priscilla, the imitation pearl, has truly some 'supernormal' Powers. She could drain the blacksmith of his blackness and his smith-strength.

Priscilla, the little Psychic Prostitute.The degenerate descendant of Ligeia. The absolutely yielding, 'loving' woman, who abandons herself utterly to her lover. Or even to a gold-toothed 'professor' of spiritualism.

Is it all bunkum, this spiritualism? Is it just rot, this Veiled Lady?

Not quite. Apart even from telepathy, the apparatus of human consciousness is the most wonderful message-receiver in existence. Beats a wireless station to nothing.

Put Prissy under the tablecloth then.Miaow!

What happens? Prissy under the tablecloth, like a canary when you cover his

解体

最终没有人要赞诺比亚。她花都没戴就默默地走了。铁匠娶了普里西拉。纳撒尼尔无耻地坦白他也一直爱着这女子！呸!

尾声

几年后纳撒尼尔在一座破烂的农房附近遇上了那位铁匠,他正倚着那柔弱但热情的普里西拉蹒跚而行。收容所的梦想早已化为泡沫,这位拯救犯人的救世主甚至不能把自己从“蒙面女郎”的手中拯救出来。

好了,你看到了这样一批理想主义者、超验主义者汇集于布鲁克农场。这是一群崩溃的绅士阶层。全都有点腐败的味道。

共有两个珠儿:一个白,一个黑,后者更为富有,腰缠万贯。

那白珍珠普里西拉是一个小小的工具,是一个仿制品,但她的确有一些“超常”的力量。她能够吸干那铁匠的怒火和他的力量。

普里西拉是一个精神上的娼妓。是堕落的莉盖娅的后代。她绝对顺

cage, goes into a 'sleep', a trance.

A trance, not a sleep. Atrance means that all her individual, personal intelligence goes to sleep, like a hen with her head under her wing. But the apparatus of consciousness remains working. Without a soul in it.

And what can this apparatus of consciousness do,when it works? Why, surely something. A wireless apparatus goes tick-tick-tick, taking down messages. So does your human apparatus. All kinds of messages. Only the soul, or the under consciousness, deals with these mcssages in the dark, in the under-conscious. Which is the natural course of events.

But what sorts of messages? All sorts. Vibrations from the stars, vibrations from unknown magnetos, vibrations from unknown people, unknown passions. The human apparatus receives them all and they are all dealt with in the under conscious.

There are also vibrations of thought, many, many. Necessary to get the two human instruments in key.

There may even be vibrations of ghosts in the air. Ghosts being dead wills, mind you, not dead souls. The soul has nothing to do with these dodges.

But some unit of force may persist for a time, after the death of an individual-

从于她的情人,是个"可爱的"女人。她甚至委身于一个镶了金牙的招魂术"教授"。

什么招魂术,全是骗人。这个蒙面女郎,纯粹是腐化。是这样吗?

也不尽然。即便没有心灵感应这一说,人的意识也可以说是美妙的信号接收器,可以绝对战胜无线电台。

给普里西拉蒙上一块布。她会叫!

会怎么样?布罩下的普里西拉会像一只金丝雀被笼子蒙上一样,她会"睡"过去,阴魂附体了。

是阴魂附体的迷糊,不是"睡"。这意味着她全部的智慧都已休眠,就像一头母鸡把头窝在翅膀下。但是她的意识仍在活动,只是没了灵魂。

当这意识仍旧在活动时,它都做些什么呢?肯定有事可做。就像无线电在不停地记录信号,人体器官也是一样,记录下各种信号来。灵魂或潜意识在冥冥中处理这些信号。这才是自然的做法。

是什么信号呢?各种信号,发自各种物体的震颤,从行星、未知的磁电机、未知的人到未知的激情。人的器官接收到所有这一切并在潜意识中

some associations of vibrations may linger like little clouds in the etheric atmosphere after the death of a human being,or an animal. And these little clots of vibration may transfer themselves to the conscious-apparatus of the medium. So that the dead son of a disconsolate widow may send a message to his mourning mother to tell her that he owes Bill Jackson seven dollars: or that Uncle Sam´s will is in the back of the bureau: and cheer up, Mother, I´m all right.

There is never much worth in these 'messages', because they are never more than fragmentary items of dead, disintegrated consciousness. And the medium has, and always will have, a hopeless job, trying to disentangle the muddle of messages.

Again, coming events may cast their shadow before. The oracle may receive on her conscious-apparatus material vibrations to say that the next great war will break out in 1925. And in so far as the realm of cause-and-effect is master of the living soul, in so far as events are mechanically maturing, the forecast may be true.

But the living souls of men may upset the mechanical march of events at any moment.

Rien de certain.

Vibrations of subtlest matter. Concatenations of vibrations and shocks! Spiritu-

处理这些信号。

还有许多许多思想的震颤。因此有必要让这两种人类的乐器音调和谐。

甚至空中会有发自鬼魂的震颤。鬼魂是死亡的意志，请记住，而不是死亡的灵魂。灵魂与这些诡计无关。

不过，人死后他有些力量仍会坚持留在人间——在某些情况下人或动物死后有些震颤就像云一样弥留在空中不肯散去。这些震颤力会自行转移到某些媒介的意识器官中。于是，一位忧郁的寡妇的儿子死后，他会把信号传达给哀痛的母亲，告诉她他欠比尔·杰克逊七块钱，或者说山姆大叔的遗嘱藏在镜子后面，妈妈，我是对的。

这些信号是没有什么价值的，因为它们永远不过是些死亡、崩溃意识的碎片而已，而媒介则徒劳地想解析这些混乱的信号。

即将发生的事可以预先投下阴影。大预言家的意识器官可以获得某种震颤，从而预言下次大战将在 **1925** 年爆发。目前，在因果之说仍统治着活生生的灵魂、事物都在呆板地成熟的情况下，这种预言或许是对的。

alism.

And what then?It is all just materialistic, and a good deal is, and always will be, charlatanry.

Because the real human soul, the Holy Ghost, has its own deep prescience, which will not be put into figures, but flows on dark, a stream of prescience.

And the real human soul is too proud, and too sincere in its belief in the Holy Ghost that is within, to stoop to the practices of these spiritualist and other psychic tricks of material vibrations.

Because the first part of reverence is the acceptance of the fact that the Holy Ghost will never materialize: will never be anything but a ghost.

And the secong part of reverence is the watchful observance of the motions, the comings and goings within us, of the Holy Ghost, and of the many gods that make up the Holy Ghost.

The Father had his day, and fell.

The Son has had his bay, and fell.

It is the day of the Holy Ghost.

Bust when souls fall corrupt, into disintegration, they have no more day. They

但是活生生的人的灵魂会随时搅乱事件的呆板进程的。

世事无常。

微小事物的震颤。一连串的震颤与冲击! 招魂术。

还有什么?这都太物质化, 不仅现在, 将来还是骗人的。

因为真正的人的灵魂——圣灵会有深刻的预见。这预见无法用形象表现而是在黑暗中流动, 那是一股股预见之流。

而真正的人类灵魂是高傲的, 它无比诚挚地相信自己内里的圣灵, 绝不会屈尊去招什么魂, 不会干那些物质震颤之类的心灵把戏。

因为首先要敬畏的是, 圣灵不会物质化, 它永远只会是鬼魂。

第二要敬畏的是, 密切关注我们心中圣灵的运动, 注意到筑成圣灵的许多个神。

圣父曾如日中天, 但堕落了。

圣子也曾如日中天, 但现在其肉体发出了恶臭[见《约翰福音》11:39, 拉撒路死后四天尸体发臭, 仍在耶稣手中复活]。

现在轮到圣灵了。

have sinned against the Holy Ghost.

These people in Blithedale Romance have sinned against the Holy Ghost, and corruption has set in.

All, perhaps, except the I, Nathaniel, He is still a sad, integral consciousness.

But not excepting Zenobia. The Black Pearl is rotting down. Fast. The cleverer she is, the faster she rots.

And they are all disintegrating, so they take to psychic tricks. It is a certain sign of the disintegration of the psyche in a man, and much more so in a woman, when she takes to spiritualism, and table-rapping, and occult messages, or witch-craft and supernatural powers of that sort. When men want to be supernatural, be sure that something has gone wrong in their natural stuff. More so, even, with a woman.

And yet the soul has its own profound subtleties of knowing. And the blood has its strange omniscience.

But this isn't impudent and materialistic, like spiritualism and magic and all that range of pretentious supernaturalism.

可是，灵魂堕落，分裂后就没有什么好日子可言了。这些灵魂已对圣灵犯下了罪。

《福谷传奇》中的这些人对圣灵犯下了罪，因此他们堕落了。

除了“我”纳撒尼尔以外别人都这样。他仍旧有一个忧郁但完整的意识。

赞诺比亚可不是。这颗黑珍珠腐烂得极快。她愈是聪明，腐烂得愈快。

他们都崩溃了，所以他们玩起灵魂的把戏来。这是男人心灵崩溃的象征，对女人来说更是如此——她求助于招魂术、降神、念咒、巫术等一切超自然的办法。当男人想变得超越自然，这证明他的自然本质出了毛病。女人如果这样，毛病就更大了。

可是，灵魂有其感知的最微妙形式。血液中有其奇特的全知全能的上帝。

但这并不像招魂术、魔法等虚假的超自然主义一样轻率和物质化。

CHAPTER 9
Dana´s Two Years Before The Mast

You can´t idealize brute labour. That is to say, you can´t idealize brute labour, without coming undone, as an idealist.

The soil! The great ideal of the soil. Novels like Thomas Hardy´s and pictures like the Frenchman Millet´s.* The soil. What happens when you idealize the soil, the mother-earth, and really go back to it?Then with overwhelming conviction it is borne in upon you, as it was upon Thomas Hardy, that the whole scheme of things is against you. The whole massive rolling of natural fate is coming down on you like a slow glacier, to crush you to extinction. As an idealist.

Thomas Hardy´s Pessimism is an absolutely true finding. It is the absolutely true statement of the idealist´s last realization, as he wrestles with the bitter soil of beloved mother-earth. He loves her, loves her, loves her. And she just entangles and crushes him like a slow *Laocoön* snake. The idealist must perish, says mother-earth.

达纳的《两年水手生涯》

[Richard Henry Dana(1815—1882),在文学史上并没有地位,但作为早期美国文学开拓者,其作品在19世纪和20世纪初颇具特色和影响,1910年代其小说被当做古典美国作品介绍到了英国,与其他大家作品齐名。]

你不能把体力劳动理想化。这就是说,你要把体力劳动理想化,你就是一个失败的理想主义者。

土地!对土地寄予的伟大理想。托马斯·哈代的小说及法国画家米莱的绘画[见《还乡》和《苔丝》中的自然景物描写和米莱的著名乡村风景画《拾麦穗》]。土地。可如果你把大地母亲理想化然后再回到其怀抱中,又会怎样呢?它让你确信正如它让托马斯·哈代确信一样,一切事物都与你作对。滚滚而至的自然命运像一座冰山一样向你缓缓压下来,要把你砸成齑粉。让你理想主义。

托马斯·哈代的悲观主义是一个绝对真实的发现。这是他同他热爱

Then let him perish.

The great imaginative love of the soil itself! Tolstoy had it,* and Thomas Hardy. And both are driven to a kind of fanatic denial of life, as a result.

You can't idealize mother-earth. You can try. You can even succeed. But succeeding, you succumb. She will have no pure idealist sons. None.

If you are a child of mother-earth, you must learn to discard your ideal self, in season, as you discard your clothes at night.

Americans have never loved the soil of A merica as Europeans have loved the soil of Europe. America has never been a blood-home-land. Only an ideal home-land. The home-land of the idea, of the spirit. And of the pocket. Not of the blood.

That has yet to come, when the idea and the spirit have collapsed from their false tyranny.

Europe has been loved with a blood love. That has made it beautiful.

In America, you have Fenimore Cooper's beautiful land scape: but that is wish-fulfilment, done from a distance. And you have Thoreau in Concord. But Thoreau sort of isolated his own bit of locality and put it under a lens, to examine it. He almost anatomized it, with his admiration.

着的大地母亲艰苦角斗时发出的一个理想主义者最后绝对真实的宣言。他爱她，爱她，爱她。可她却像《拉奥孔》中的蛇一样缠住他，慢慢地毁了他。大地母亲说，理想主义者必死。那就让他死去吧。

对土地富有想像的爱，了不起！托尔斯泰有这种爱[见《安娜·卡列宁娜》里庆祝春天的描写。托尔斯泰自己则为农家子弟建设过学堂]，托马斯·哈代亦然。其结果，他们双双走向对生活疯狂的否定。

你不能把大地母亲理想化。你尽可以试试。你甚至可以成功。可一旦成功，你也就等于完了。她不容任何纯粹的理想主义之子。一个也不要。

如果你是大地母亲的儿子，你必须学会及时甩掉你理想的自我，就像夜里脱掉衣服一样。

美国人从未像欧洲人爱欧洲的土地那样热爱美国的土地。美国从来也不是一块血性的祖国之土，只是一个理想的祖国，观念化、精神化的祖国。还是金钱的祖国，但不是血性的祖国。

这一天会到来的，当观念与精神因虚伪的暴政而崩溃的时候。

America isn't a blood-home-land. For every American, the blood-home-land is Europe. The spirit-home-land is America.

Transcendentalism. Transcend this home-land business, exalt the idea of These States till you have made it a universal idea, says the true American. The oversoul is a world-soul, not a local thing.

So, in the next great move of imaginative conquest, Americans turned to the sea. Not to the land. Earth is too specific, too particular. Besides the blood of white men is wine of no American soil. No, no.

But the blood of all men is ocean-born. We have our material universality, our blood-oneness, in the sea. The salt water.

You can't idealize the soil. But you've got to try. And trying, you reap a great imaginative reward. And the greatest reward is failure. To know you have failed, that you must fail. That is the greatest comfort of all, at last.

Tolstoi failed with the soil: Thomas Hardy too: and Giovanni Verga; the three greatest.

The further extreme, the greatest mother, is the sea. Love the great mother of the sea, the Magna Mater. And see how bitter it is. And see how you must fail to

欧洲一直受着血性的爱，这种爱使它变得极美丽。

在美国，你看到了菲尼莫·库柏所描绘出的美丽风光——可这是一种愿望的自我满足，是在远离美国的他乡描绘出来的。你还看到康考德的梭罗对美国有所描述。但是梭罗有点把他的地区性孤立起来并将其置于凹透镜下进行观察。他几乎是怀着仰慕的心剖析这景物的。

美国可不是一个血性的祖国。对每个美国人来说，他血性的祖国是欧洲。而美国则是他精神化了的祖国。

超验主义。超越祖国的概念，升华这些州的观念，直至让它成为一个全球概念，美国人如是说。超灵是世界的超灵，绝非一个地区的事。

所以，在下一个富有想像的征服的伟大举动中，美国人转向了海洋。不再是土地。土地过于具象了。再说，白人的血绝不是美国的土地上所酿出的酒。不，不是。

但是所有人的血液都生自海洋。我们物质的宇宙性、我们血液的同一性都在海洋中。盐水。

你不能把土地理想化。不过你可以试试，只要试试，你就可以获得巨

win her to your ideal: forever fail. Absolutely fail.

Swinburne tried in England. But the Americans made the greatest trial. The most vivid failure.

At a certain point, human life becomes uninteresting to men. What then?They turn to some universal.

The greatest material mother of us all is the sea.

Dana's eyes failed him when he was studying at Harvard. And suddenly, he turned to the sea, the naked Mother. He went to sea as a common sailor before the mast.

You can't idealize brute labour. Yet you can. You can go through with brute labour, and know what it means. You can even meet and match the sea, and KNOW her.

This is what Dana wanted: a naked fighting experience with the sea.

KNOW THYSELF. That means, know the earth that is in your blood. Know the sea that is in your blood. The great elementals.

But we must repeat: KNOWING and BEING are opposite, antagonistic states. The more you know, exactly, the less you are. The more you are, in being, the less

大想像力的奖励。最大的奖励莫过于失败。要知道你输了，你非输不可。这即是最大的安慰。

托尔斯泰在与土地的较量中失败了，还有托马斯·哈代和乔万尼·维尔迦[劳伦斯崇尚的意大利古典作家，劳伦斯将他的很多作品翻译成了英文出版]也失败了。这三个伟大人物全败了。

再进一步的极端，最伟大的母亲，就是大海。爱大海母亲吧，她是伟大的母亲。试试看，这样该有多痛苦。你若想把她理想化，你非失败不可。绝对要失败。

史文朋[英国19世纪诗人]试图在英国这样。而美国人则做了最大的尝试。但它一败涂地。

在某种程度上说，生活对人来说已失去意义。然后呢?他们转向更广远的东西。

我们最伟大的物质之母就是大海。

达纳在哈佛读书时视力衰退了。随后他突然闯大海去了，那赤裸的母亲。他来到海上，当上了一名普通水手。

you know.

This is the great cross of man, his dualism. The blood-self, and the nerve-brain self.

Knowing, then, is the slow death of being. Man has his epochs of being, his epochs of knowing. It will always be a great oscillation. The goal is to know how not-to-know.

Dana took another great step in knowing: knowing the mother sea. But it was a step also in his own undoing. It was a new phase of dissolution of his own being. Afterwards, he would be a less human thing. He would be a knower: but more near to mechanism tham before. That is our cross, our doom.

And so he writes, in his first days at sea, in winter, on the Atlantic:

Nothing will compare with the early breaking of the day upon the wide ocean. There is something in the first grey streaks stretching along the eastern horizon, and throwing an indistinct light upon the face of the deep, which creates…a feeling of loneliness, of dread, and of melancholy foreboding, which nothing else in nature can give.

So he ventures wakeful and alone into the great naked watery universe of the

你不能把体力劳动理想化。不过你可以试试。你彻底干一下就知道它意味着什么了。你甚至可以与大海相识，跟它较量较量，然后你就了解她了。

了解你自己[在古希腊城市特尔斐的阿波罗神殿里书有希腊文“上帝说‘了解你自己’”]。这就是说，要了解你血液中的土地。了解你血液中的大海。了解这些伟大的自然要素。

可我们必须重复：了解与生命是两相对立的。你了解得越多，你的生命就越少。你愈是有生气，你了解的就愈少。

这是人背负的巨大十字架——双重性。血液的自我与精神的自我。

了解是生命缓慢的死亡。人有其生命的时代，亦有了解的时代。这一直是一个具大的摇摆。其目标是懂得“如何不懂”。

达纳迈出了了解的另一大步伐：了解大海母亲。不过这也是走向他毁灭的一步，这是毁灭他生命的一个新阶段。从此后，他少了几分人气。他是个“了解者”，比从前更呆板了。那就是我们的十字架，我们的末日。

他在刚来到大西洋海上不久的那个冬天写道：

end of life, the twilight place where integral being lapses, and warm life begins to give out. It is man moving on into the face of death, the great adventure, the great undoing, the strange extension of the consciousness. The same in his vision of the albatross. 'But one of the finest sights that I have ever seen was an albatross asleep upon the water, during a calm off Cape Horn, when a heavy sea was running. There being no breeze, the surface of the water was unbroken, but a long, heavy swell was rolling, and we saw the fellow, all white, directly ahead of us, asleep upon the waves, with his head under his wing; now rising on the top of a huge billow, and then falling slowly until he was lost in the hollow between. He was undisturbed for some time, until the noise of our bows, gradually approaching, roused him, when, lifting his head, he stared upon us for a moment, and then spread his wide wings, and took his flight.'

We must give Dana credit for a profound mystic vision. The best Americans are mystics by instinct. Simple and bare as his narrative is, it is deep with profound emotion and stark comprehension. He sees the last light-loving incarnation of life exposed upon the eternal waters: a speck, soltary upon the verge of the two naked principles, aerial and watery. And his own soul is as the soul of the albatross.

什么也比不上辽阔大海上的日出美。第一片灰白色在东方地平线上伸延，在海面上洒下朦胧的光影，它令人……感到孤独、恐惧，产生一种忧郁的预感，大自然中没什么别的会让人产生如此感受。

他就是这样清醒但孤独地冒险进入生命末日的水域，这里正是夕阳西下之地，完整的生命在此沉没，热烈的生活开始结束。人正走向死亡，这是一大冒险，伟大的毁灭，是意识奇特的伸延。他对信天翁的看法也是一样。“我看到的最大奇景是一只在水上熟睡的信天翁，那是在水深流急的海面上离开牛角岬后来到一片风平浪静的水域时看到的。没有一丝风，水面一平如镜，可有一道大浪正滚过来，我们看到了那家伙，浑身雪白，就在我们面前，睡在浪头上，头扎在翅膀中。它忽而升到浪尖上时而缓缓没入浪峰下。直到我们的船头驶近，声音惊醒了它，它才扬起头，凝视我们片刻，随后展开双翅飞去。”

对达纳这神秘的洞察力，我们定要加以赞赏。最优秀的美国人是些

It is a storm-bird. And so is Dana. He has gone down to fight with the sea. It is a metaphysical, actual struggle of an integral soul with the vast, non-living, yet potent element. Dana never forgets, never ceases to watch. If Hawthorne was a spectre on the land, how much more is Dana a spectre at sea. But he must watch, he must know, he must conquer the sea in his consciousness. This is the poignant difference between him and the common sailor. The common sailor lapses from consciousness, becomes elemental like a seal, a creature. Tiny and alone, Dana watches the great seas mount round his own small body. If he is swept away, some other man will have to take up what he has begun. For the sea must be mastered by the human consciousness, in the great fight of the human soul for mastery over life and death, in KNOWLEDGE. It is the last bitter necessity of the Tree. The Cross. Impartial, Dana beholds himself among the elements, calm and fatal. His style is great and hopeless, the style of a perfect tragic recorder.

Between five and six the cry of 'All starbowlines ahoy! 'summoned our watch on deck, and immediately all hands were called. A great cloud of a dark slate-colour was driving on us from the south-west; and we did our best to take in sail before we were in the midst of it. We had got the light-sails furled, the courses

本能的神秘主义者。他的叙述简洁明快，可它充满了感情和黑暗的悟性。他看到了热爱光的生命化身正置身于永恒的海上：一个白点，孤独地身处水天交接处。从而他的灵魂也变得如同信天翁的一样。

那是一只风暴中的鸟儿，达纳也是这样一只鸟儿。他就是去同大海搏斗的。这是一场完整的灵魂与宏大、非生命但强有力的自然之间展开的形而上但又实际的斗争。达纳从未忘却，也从未停止观察。如果说霍桑是陆地上的精灵，达纳就是海上更大的精灵。可他必须观察、必须了解、必须在思想上战胜大海，这就是他与普通水手之间明显的区别。普通的水手没有什么思想，变得如同海豹和动物一样。可达纳这孤独的小个子却在凝视着自身周围大海的奔涌。如果他被海浪卷走，自有别人继续他所开创的事业。人的思想一定要在了解中、在为争取统治生与死的搏斗中制服大海。这是智慧之树所做的最后一件必须做的事。十字架。达纳毫无偏见地观察着身处大自然中的自己，冷静而悲观。他的风格伟大而绝望，完全是一个悲剧的记录者。

hauled up, and the top-sail reef-tackles hauled out, and were just mounting the foreriggi ng when the storm struck us. In an instant the sea, which had been comparatively quiet, was running higher and higher; and it became almost as dark as night. The hail and sleet were harder than I had yet felt them, seeming almost to pin us down to the rigging.

It is in the dispassionate statement of plain material facts that Dana achieves his greatness. Dana writes from the remoter, non-emotional centres of being-not from the passional emotional self.

So the ship battles on, round Cape Horn, then into quieter seas. The island of Juan Fernandez, Crusoe's island, rises like a dream from the sea, like a green cloud, and like a ghost Dana watches it, feeling only a faint, ghostly pang of regret for the life that was.

But the strain of the long sea-voyage begins to tell. The sea is a great disintegrative force. Its tonic quality is its disintegrative quality. It burns down the tissue, liberates energy. And after a long time, this burning-down is destructive. The psyche becomes destroyed, irritable, frayed, almost dehumanized.

So there is trouble on board the ship, irritating discontent, friction unbearable,

五六点钟时，一声“喂，全上右舷板”把我们全召上甲板来。只见西南方向有一块铅灰色的云压了过来。我们赶忙尽快收帆减速，免得遇上大浪。我们收起了轻帆，船开始迎风行驶。顶帆缆绳断了，我们刚要上去装新的，暴风雨就扑面而来。一瞬间，平静的大海狂涛翻卷，顿时一片昏天黑地。冰雹和雨夹雪极其坚硬，似乎要把我们砸倒在缆绳上动弹不得。

正是通过对物质世界不动声色的叙述，达纳显示出其了不起的境界。达纳凭着遥远而毫无感情色彩的生命核心在写作，而不是凭借激情的自我写作。

这条船就是这样在牛角岬附近搏斗着驶入较平静的海面。随之，朱安·费尔南迪兹岛梦一般地从海中升起。这是鲁滨孙之岛。它像一片绿云浮在海上，达纳像个幽灵般地凝视着它，只是对生活的遗憾，为此痛不欲生。

但是长途的海上旅行开始显出其严峻性来。大海是一股巨大的分裂性力量。它令人振奋之处是它的分裂性格。它烧掉你的肌体，解放你的能

and at last a flogging. This flogging rouses Dana for the first and last time to human and ideal passion.

Sam by this time was seized up –that is, placed against the shrouds, with his wrists made fast to the shrouds, his jacket off, and his back exposed. The captain stood on the break of the deck, a few feet from him, and a little raised, so as to have a good swing at him, and held in his hand the bight of a thick, strong rope. The officers stood round, and the crew grouped together in the waist. All these preparations made me feel sick and almost faint, angry and excited as I was. A man–a human being made in God's likeness –fastened up and flogged like a beast! The first and almost uncontrollable impulse was resistance. But what was to be done? –The time for it had gone by–

So Mr Dana couldn't act. He could only lean over the side of the ship and spew.

Whatever made him vomit?

Why shall man not be whipped?

As long as man has a bottom, he must surely be whipped. It is as if the Lord intended it so.

量。很久以后，它开始毁灭你。你的心灵被它毁灭，变得愤怒、紧张、几乎失去人性。

于是船上出了麻烦，愤怒、不满、令人难以忍受的摩擦，最后出现了鞭打惩罚。皮鞭令达纳第一次也是最后一次心中升起人的理想激情。

这时山姆被绑了起来。他的双手捆在锁链上，上衣被剥掉，光着膀子。船长站在船楼上，离他不远，但位置稍高一些，以便能狠抽他一顿；他手里握着一截粗绳。船上的官儿们站在四周，船员们聚集在船中部。这些准备工作令我感到恶心，几乎昏过去。我太气愤、太激动了。——一个人，一个照上帝的模子创造出来的人竟被这么五花大绑，像一头牲口一样被抽打！让人控制不住的第一冲动就是反抗。可有什么办法呢？就这样了。

达纳先生无法有所举动。他只能斜依船舷呕吐。

是什么令他呕吐呢？

Why?For lots of reasons.

Man doth not live by bread alone, to absorb it and to evacuate it.

What is the breath of life?My dear, it is the strange current of interchange that flows between men and men, and men and women, and men and things. A constant current of interflow, a constant vibrating interchange. That is the breath of life.

And this interflow, this electric vibration is polarized. There is a positive and a negative polarity. This is a law of life, of vitalism.

Only ideas are final, finite, static, and single.

All life-interchange is a polarized communication. A circuit.

There are lots of circuits. Male and female, for example, and master and servant. The idea, the IDEA, that fixed gorgon, monster, and the IDEAL, that great stationary engine, these two gods-of-the-machine have been busy destroying all natural reciprocity and natural circuits, for centuries, I DEAS have played the very old Harry with sex relationship, that is, with the great circuit of man and woman. Turned the thing into a wheel on which the human being in both is broken. And the IDEALhas mangled the blood-reciprocity of master and servant into an abstract horror.

Master and servant-or master and man relationship is, essentially, a polarized

人怎样才能不受鞭打呢?

只要人长着屁股，他注定是要被抽打的。这似乎是天意。

为什么?原因很多。

人并非只靠面包活着，吃喝拉撒。

生活的本质是什么?亲爱的，它是男人与男人、男人与女人、人和万物之间相互交流的一股奇特电流。不停的交流，不停的震颤交流。这就是生活的本质。

而这种交流、这种电流的震颤是相互极化的。有正极也有负极。这是生命的规律，是活力论的规律。

只有观念是终极的、有限的、停滞的、孤单的。

所有的生命交流都是极化的交流。是一个回路。

有不少回路。男人和女人，比如，主人和仆人就是。观念这可怕的魔鬼和理想这台固定式发动机是两个机器上帝，它们几个世纪以来一直在毁灭一切自然的交流和自然回路。观念一直在毁灭性关系，也就是说毁灭男女关系的两极回路。而理想则破坏了主人与仆人间的血液流程，使

flow, like love. It is a circuit of vitalism which flows between master and man and forms a very precious nourishment to each, and keeps both in a state of subtle, quivering, vital equilibrium. Deny it as you like, it is so. But once you abstract both master and man, and make them both serve an idea: production, wage, efficiency, and so on: so that each looks on himself, as an instrument performing a certain repeated evolution, then you have changed the vital, quivering circuit of master and man into a mechanical machine unison. Just another way of life: or anti-life.

You could never quite do this on a sailing ship. A master had to be master, or it was hell. That is, there had to be this strange interflow of master-and-man, the strange reciprocity of comand and obedience.

The reciprocity of command and obedience is a state of unstable vital equilibrium. Everything vital, or natural, is unstable, thank God.

The ship had been at sea many weeks. A great strain on master and men. An increasing callous indifference in the men, an increasing irritability in the master.

And then what?

A storm.

Don't expect me to say why storms must be. They just are. Storms in the air,

其变成一件恐怖的事。

主人与仆人或者说主人与普通人的关系从根本上说像爱一样是一种极化的回流。它是生命的回路，在主人与仆人间回流，对双方来说都有好处，使双方保持一种微妙、震颤的生命平衡。尽管你要否认它，可事实如此。可一旦你将他们抽象化，令他们为一种观念服务：生产、工资、效率等等，他们各自把自己看做是一件进行重复进化的工具，那就等于改变了他们之间活生生、震颤着的回路，把他们变成了一个机械的统一体。这是另一种生活方式，或者说是反生活。

在一艘行驶的船上你不应这样做。主人就是主人，否则就糟了。这就是说，船上应该有这种奇特的主仆交流，这种奇特的命令与服从的交流。

命令与服从的交流是一种不稳定的生命平衡。感谢上帝，任何有生命或自然的东西都是不稳定的。

这艘船在海上已有好几个星期了。这对主人和仆人来说都是个考验。仆人们变得愈来愈冷漠，主人变得愈来愈暴怒。

那会怎么样?

storms in the water, storms of thunder, storms of anger. Storms just are.

Storms are a sort of violent readjustment in some polarized flow. You have a polarized circuit, a circuit of unstable equilibrium. The instability increases till there is a crash. Everything seems to break down. Thunder roars, lightning flashes. The master roars, the whip whizzes. The sky sends down sweet rain. The ship knows a new strange stillness, a readjustment, a refinding of equilibrium.

Ask the Lord Almighty why it is so. I don´t know. I know it is so.

But flogging? Why flogging? Why not use reason or take away jam for tea?

Why mot? Why not ask the thunder please to abstain from this physical violence of crashing and thumping, please to swale away like thawing snow.

Sometimes the thunder does swale away like thawing snow, and then you hate it. Muggy, sluggish, inert, dreary sky.

Flogging.

You have a Sam, a fat slow fellow, who has got slower and more slovenly as the weeks wear on. You have a master who has grown more irritable in his authority. Till Sam becomes simply wallowing in his slackness, makes your gorge rise. And the master is on red hot iron.

一场暴风雨。

别指望我告诉你为什么非得有这暴风雨不可。有就是有。暴风雨在空中，在水上，雷雨，愤怒的暴风雨。暴风雨就是暴风雨。

暴风雨在某些极化的流程中是一种剧烈的调整。你有一个极化的回路，它不稳定、不平衡。这不稳定加剧着直至爆发。一切似乎都崩溃了。雷吼，电闪，主人吼，皮鞭刷刷作响。天空下起甘甜的雨。船在体验一种新的、奇特的宁静，这是一种新的调整，从而寻找到新的平衡。

至于说为何如此，那就去问上帝吧。我不知道。我只知道它就是这样。

可为什么用鞭打呢?为什么不讲理?或者用茶点时不给他果酱来惩罚他?

为什么不? 为什么不请天雷免除这种剧烈的粉碎与打击，像化雪一样悄然退去。

有时雷电的确会像雪花一样消融，可你又恨它。湿热，死水一潭，慵懒的天。

Now these two men, Captain and Sam, are there in a very unsteady equilibrium of command and obedience. A polarized flow. Definitely polarized.

The poles of will are the great ganglia of the voluntary nerve system, located beside the spinal column, in the back. From the poles of will in the backbone of the Captain, to the ganglia of will in the back of the sloucher Sam, runs a frazzled, jagged current, a staggering circuit of vital electricity. This circuit gets one jolt too many, and there is an explosion.

'Tie up that lousy swine! ' roars the enraged Captain.

And whack! whack! down on the bare back of that sloucher Sam comes the cat.

What does it do?By Jove, it goes like ice-cold water into his spine. Down those lashes runs the current of the Captain's rage, right into the blood and into the toneless ganglia of Sam's voluntary system. Crash! Crash! runs the lightning flame, right into the cores of the living nerves.

And the living nerves respond. They start to vibrate. They brace up. The blood begins to go quicker. The nerves begin to recover their vividness. It is their tonic. The man Sam has a new clear day of intelligence, and a smarty back. The Captain has a new relief, a new ease in his authority, and a sore heart.

鞭打。

你看到了山姆这个胖家伙，他行动缓慢，随着时光的流逝他变得愈来愈懒散。你看到那位主人变得愈来愈暴怒、霸道。最终山姆笨重地打着滚，令你恶心。那位主人则暴跳如雷。

船长和山姆这两个人正处在命令与服从的不稳定平衡中。极化的流程。绝对极化。

意志的两极构成意志神经结系统，它位于脊背的脊椎旁。从船长的意志两极到萎靡不振的山姆的意志神经结，流着一股疲惫、颤动的生命电流，形成一个回路。这电流让人震荡太剧烈，于是就会爆发。

“把这头脏猪给我绑起来。”愤怒的船长叫着。

拼命抽打！抽打着慵懒的山姆赤裸的脊背。

这是干什么?天啊，鞭子像冰冷的水注入他的脊椎。随着鞭子流出的是船长的怒气，那股怒气正涌入山姆的血液中，涌入他那无言的意志神经结中。打！打！闪光般的怒火正烧入那些活生生的神经核心。

那活生生的神经核心开始反应了，开始震颤，紧张起来。血液开始流

There is a new equilibrium, and a fresh start. The physical intelligence of Sam is restored, the turgidity is relieved from the veins of the Captain.

It is a natural form of human coition, interchange.

It is good for Sam to be flogged, It is good, on this occasion, for the Captain to have Sam flogged. I say so. Because they were both in that physical condition.

Spare the rod and spoil the physical child.

Use the rod and spoil the ideal child.

There you are.

Dana, as an idealist, refusing the blood-contact of life, leaned over the side of the ship powerless, and vomited: or wanted to. His solar plexus was getting a bit of its own back. To him, Sam was an 'ideal' being, who should have been approached through the mind, the reason, and the spirit. That lump of a Sam!

But there was another idealist on board, the seaman John, a Swede. He wasn't named John for nothing, this Jack-tar of the Logos. John felt himself called upon to play Mediator, Interceder, Saviour, on this occasion. The popular Paraclete.

'Why are you whipping this man, sir?'

But the Captain had got his dander up. He wasn't going to have his natural

得更快。神经开始重又变得活跃。鞭打对他的神经是一种激励。山姆从此变得清爽、聪颖了。船长也松了一口气，人轻松多了，疼痛的心也释然。

从此取得了新的平衡，有了新的起点。山姆的肉体聪明度恢复了，船长的血管也消肿了。

这是人与人交媾的自然形式。

对山姆来说，挨一顿抽打是件好事。在这种情况下，船长抽打山姆一顿也是件好事。我这么说是有道理的。因为他们的身体状况决定了他们必须这样做。

肉体这东西不打不成器。

理想这东西也得打一顿才行。

你说呢?

达纳这个理想主义者拒绝承认生命的血液接触，只会倚靠在船舷上无力地呕吐。他的太阳神经丛受到了一点报复。在他看来，对山姆这种"理想"化的人物，应该以"理"相待，通过精神上的接触改变他。这个笨山姆!

passion judged and interfered with by these long-nosed salvationists Johannuses. So he had nosy John hauled up and whipped as well.

For which I am very glad.

Alas, however, the Captain got the worst of it in the end. He smirks longest who smirks last. The Captain wasn't wary enough. Natural anger, natural passion has its unremitting enemy in the idealist. And the ship was already tainted with idealism. A good deal more so, apparently, than Herman Melville's ships were.

Which reminds us that Melville was once going to be flogged. In White Jacket. And he, too, would have taken it as the last insult.

In my opinion there are worse insults than floggings. I would rather be flogged than have most people 'like' me.

Melville too had an Interceder: a quiet, self-respecting man, not a saviour. The man spoke in the name of Justice. Melville was to be unjustly whipped. The man spoke honestly and quietly. Not in any salvationist spirit. And the whipping did not take place.

Justice is a great and manly thing. Saviourism is a despicable thing.

Sam was justly whipped. It was a passional justice.

船上还有另一个理想主义者，他就是瑞典海员约翰。他叫约翰并不是没有理由的，他是懂“道”的海员。此时他觉得自己应充当斡旋者、调解者、救世者的角色了[斡旋者和调解者暗指耶稣基督，他是上帝和人之间的斡旋者]。他成了一个下凡的圣灵了。

“长官，你凭什么抽这个人？”

此时的船长已是怒发冲冠。他绝不要长鼻子的救世主约翰评价、搅乱他的自然激情。于是他把爱管闲事的约翰捆起来也抽了一顿。

对此我感到高兴。

可惜，船长最终结局不妙。笑到最后的人才笑得最久。船长警惕性不够高。自然的愤怒和激情是理想主义者的死敌。而这艘船却早已被理想主义腐蚀了。它比赫尔曼·麦尔维尔笔下的船在这方面有过之而无不及。

这令我们想起，在《白外套》中，“麦尔维尔”几乎受到鞭挞。他亦认为这是人间最难以容忍的屈辱。

我倒认为世上还有比受鞭挞更让人难以容忍的污辱，我宁受鞭挞也不愿让人们“喜欢”。

But Melville's whipping would have been a cold, disciplinary injustice. A foul thing. Mechanical justice even is a foul thing. For true justice makes the heart's fibres quiver. You can't be cold in a matter of real justice.

Already in those days it was no fun to be a captain. You had to learn already to abstract yourself into a machine-part, exerting machine-control. And it is a good deal bitterer to exert machine-control, selfless, ideal control, than it is to have to obey, mechanically. Because the idealists who mechanically obey almost always hate the man who must give the orders. Their idealism rarely allows them to exonerate the man for the office.

Dana's captain was one of the real old-fashioned sort. He gave himself away terribly. He should have been more wary, knowing he confronted a shipful of enemies and at least two cold and deadly idealists, who hated all 'masters' on principle.

As he went on, his passion increased, and he danced about the deck, calling out as he swung the rope, 'If you want to know what I flog you for, I'll tell you. It's because I like to do it!-Because I like to do it!-It suits me. That's what I do it for!'

The man writhed under the pain. My blood ran cold, I could look on no longer. Disgusted, sick and horror-stricken, I turned away and leaned over the rail and

麦尔维尔也有人替他调解，那是一个文静自尊的人，不是个救世主。这人以正义的名义说话。麦尔维尔就要被人无理地鞭打了，那人诚恳、平静地替他讲理，而不是像个救世主那样发话。于是这顿鞭打没有变成现实。

正义是一件伟大而富有男子气的东西。而救世主义则是可鄙的。

鞭挞山姆是正义之举。是激情的正义。

而麦尔维尔的被鞭打则是一种冷酷、惩罚性的非正义，肮脏的事。机械的正义甚至也是肮脏的。真正的正义会使心震颤的。面对真正的正义你是无法冷酷起来的。

在那些日子里，当船长并非好玩的事。你得学会变成一副机器零件，施行机械性的统治。施行机械性的、失去自我的理性统治比机械地服从更让人痛苦。因为机械地服从着的理想主义者总是仇恨发布命令的人。他们的理想主义使他们很难原谅他。

达纳的船长的确是那种老派人物。这人几乎忘却了自我，这真可怕。他应该更有点警惕性，意识到他这一船人都是他的敌人，至少有两个冷

looked down in the water. A few rapid thoughts of my own situation, and of the prospect of future revenge, crossed my mind; but the falling of the blows, and the cries of the man called me back at once. At length they ceased, and, turning round, I found that the Mate, at a signal from the captain, had cut him down.

After all, it was not so terrible. The captain evidently did not exceed the ordinary measure. Sam got no more than he asked for. It was a natural event. All would have been well, save for the moral verdict. And this came from theoretic idealists like Dana and the seaman John, rather than from the sailors themselves. The sailors understood spontaneous Passional morality, not the artificial ethical. They respected the violent readjustments of the naked force, in man as in nature.

The flogging was seldom, if ever, alluded to by us in the forecastle. If any one was inclined to talk about it, the others, with a delicacy which I hardly expected to find among them, always stopped him, or turned the subject.

Two men had been flogged: the second and the elder, John, for interfering and asking the captain why he flogged Sam. It is while flogging John that the captain shouts, 'If you want to know what I flog you for, I'll tell you–'

'But the behaviour of the two men who were flogged,' Dana continues,

漠的理想主义者是仇视“主人”的。

“他的激情愈来愈强烈，一边舞着手中的绳一边在甲板上跺着脚叫唤：‘要是你想知道我为什么抽你的话，那我就告诉你——因为我愿意这样做！我喜欢这样！我干这事顶合适了。就为这个！’

“那人疼得直扭动。我的血变冷了，我再也看不下去了。我感到恶心、恐怖，转过身倚着栏杆看着下面的海水。我开始思考我的处境和未来复仇的事。可是下落的皮鞭声和受刑人的喊叫声又打断了我的思路。他们终于停止了这场鞭打，我转过身发现船长向大副打个手势，大副砍断了捆绑山姆的绳子。”

总的说来这还不算太可怕。船长做得并不过分。山姆不过是受到了应有的惩罚罢了。这是寻常小事一桩。除了道德上的判断，一切都不错。这结论出自理论上的理想主义者达纳和约翰这样的人，而不是出自海员们自己。海员们理解的是自然冲动的激情道德而不是虚伪的伦理。他们

toward one another, showed a delicacy and a sense of honour which would have been worthy of admiration in the highest walks of life. Sam knew that the other had suffered solely on his account, and in all his complaints he said that if he alone had been flogged it would have been nothing, but that he never could see that man without thinking what had been the means of bringing that disgrace upon him; and John never, by word or deed, let anything escape him to remind the other that it was by interfering to save his shipmate that he had suffered.

As a matter of fact, it was John who ought to have been ashamed for bringing confusion and false feeling into a clear issue. Conventional morality apart, John is the reprehensible party, not Sam or the captain. The case was one of passional readjustment, nothing abnormal. And who was the sententious Johannus, that he should interfere in this?And if Mr Dana had a weak stomach as well as weak eyes, let him have it. But let this pair of idealists abstain from making all the other men feel uncomfortable and fuzzy about a thing they would have left to its natural course, if they had been allowed. No, your Johannuses and your Danas have to be creating 'public opinion', and mugging up the life-issues with their sententious-ness. O idealism!

The vessel arrives at the Pacific coast, and the swell of the rollers falls in our

遵从人和自然心中赤裸裸力量的剧烈调整。

“在前甲板上我们极少谈到鞭挞人的事，如果有谁要谈这个话题，别人就会很小心地打断他的话并换个话题。”

共有两个人遭到鞭打。第二个年纪稍大点的是约翰，因为他阻止船长抽打山姆，他还质问船长为何鞭挞人。船长在抽打约翰时叫道：“如果你想知道我为什么抽你，我就告诉你——”

达纳继续写道：

“这两个被鞭挞的人的相互关系表现出一种微妙的义气，很令人敬慕。山姆知道另一个人是为他受苦的，他抱怨道，他自己受鞭挞倒没什么，可一看到约翰他就会想到自己受到的污辱。而约翰总是在言行上流露出他是为了拯救船友才受苦的。”

blood –the weary coast stretches wonderful, on the brink of the unknown.

Not a human being but ourselves for miles –the steep hill rising like a wall, and cutting us off from all the world–but the 'world of waters'. I separated myself from the rest, and sat down on a rock, just where the sea ran in and formed a fine spouting–horn. Compared with the dull, plain sand–beach of the rest of the coast, this grandeur was as refreshing as a great rock in a weary land. It was almost the first time I had been positively alone... My better nature returned strong upon me. I experienced a glow of pleasure at finding that what of poetry and romance I had ever had in me had not been entirely deadened in the laborious life I had been lately leading. Nearly an hour did I sit, almost lost in the luxury of this entire new scene of the play in which I was acting, when I was aroused by the distant shouts of my companions.

So Dana sits and Hamletizes by the Pacific –chiefactor in the play of his own existence. But in him, self–consciousness is almost nearing the mark of scientific indifference to self.

He gives us a pretty picture of the then wild, unknown bay of San Francisco. – 'The tide leaving us, we came to anchor near the mouth of the bay, under a high

事实上，约翰应对他的行为感到羞耻。是他把一件简单的事搞乱了并掺入了虚假的感情。如果不考虑传统的道德，约翰应受指责，受指责的不应是山姆或船长。这件事是激情的调整，没什么不正常的。那爱说教的约翰算什么？如果达纳先生的胃太脆弱、视力也太脆弱的话，就随他去吧。可是不能让这两个理想主义者再如此下去了，他们的行为令其他人不舒服，令人们会对一件很自然的事感到茫然无解。约翰们、达纳们，你们应该制造“公众舆论”，用他们尖刻的话来专心研究生命问题。哦，理想主义！

船到达了太平洋海岸，我们血液中的巨浪也随之平息了。冗长的海岸线在未知世界的边缘延伸，十分美好。

除了我们不再有别人，陡峭的山峦像高墙般耸起，绵延数英里，把我们与世隔绝，只有“水世界”。我离开大家，独自一人坐在海湾的一块石头上。与海岸边平庸的沙滩相比，这儿的壮丽景色就如同令人厌倦的原野上耸起的石头令人赏心悦目，这是我第一次感到独处一方的好处……

and beautifully sloping hill, upon which herds of hundreds of red deer and the stag with his high-branching antlers were bounding about, looking at us for a moment, and then starting off affrighted at the noises we made for the purpose of seeing the variety of their beautiful attitudes and motions-'

Think of it now, and the Presidio! The idiotic guns.

Two moments of strong human emotion Dana experiences: one moment of strong but impotent hate for the captain, one strong impulse of pitying love for the Kanaka boy, Hope-a beautiful South Sea Islander sick of a white man's disease, phthisis or syphilis. Of him Dana writes-

but the other, who was my friend, and Aikane -Hope -was the most dreadful object I had ever seen in my life; his hands looking like claws; a dreadful cough, which seemed to rack his whole shattered system; a hollow, whispering voice, and an entire inability to move himself. There he lay, upon a mat on the ground, which was the only floor of the oven, with no medicine, no comforts, and no one to care for or help him but a few Kanakas, who were willing enough, but could do nothing. The sight of him made me sick and faint. Poor fellow! During the four months that I lived upon the beach we were continually together, both in work and in our excursions in the

善良的天性又回到我身上。我十分惊喜地发现我心中的诗意与浪漫情调并未在最近沉重的生活中泯灭。我一直在这儿坐了近一个钟头，浑然忘我，陶醉于这良辰美景中，直到远处伙伴们的叫声把我唤醒。

达纳就这样坐在太平洋岸边像哈姆雷特一样沉思——扮演他自我存在这场戏中的主角。可是此时他的自我意识几乎达到了对自我全然漠视的地步。

达纳为我们绘出的是当年荒蛮的旧金山海湾：

"海潮退去了，我们来到美丽山坡下的湾边抛锚。山坡上几百头赤鹿和牡鹿顶着高高的鹿角在奔跑，看看我们，随后又害怕地离去。是我们弄出来的声音把它们吓跑了，我们本来是想凑近看一看它们多彩多姿的表情和形态的。"

想想吧，想想那要塞！白痴样的猎枪。

*woods and upon the water. I really felt a strong affection for him, and preferred him to any of my own countrymen there. When I came into the oven he looked at me, held out his hand and said in a low voice, but with a delightful smile, 'Aloha, Aikane! Aloha nui! *' I comforted him as well as I could, and promised to ask the captain to help him from the medicine chest.*

We have felt the pulse of hate for the captain–now the pulse of Saviour–like love for the bright–eyed man of the Pacific, a real child of the ovean, full of the mystery–being of that great sea. Hope is for a moment to Dana what Chingach–gook is to Cooper –the heart's brother, the answerer. But only for an ephemeral moment. And even then his love was largely pity, tinged with philanthropy. The inevitable saviourism. The ideal being.

Dana was mad to leave the California coast, to be back in the civilzed east. Yet he feels the poignancy of departure when at last the ship draws off. The Pacific is his glamour–world: the eastern States his world of actuality, scientific, materially real. He is a servant of civilization, an idealist, a democrat, a hater of masters, a KNOWER. Conscious and self–conscious, without ever forgetting.

When all sail had been set and the decks cleared up, the California *was a*

达纳经历了两次人类情感的冲动：一次是对船长强烈但无力的仇恨，另一次是对肯纳卡的小男孩儿霍普所表露出的怜爱。霍普是一个漂亮的南海岛民，染上了白人的病——肺结核或梅毒。关于他，达纳这样写道：

但我另一个朋友霍普则是我一生中遇到的最可怕的人。他的手看上去像爪子。他可怕地咳嗽着，几乎身体架子都会被这咳嗽震散了。他的声音空旷细弱，他几乎不能动弹。他躺在一张席子上，没有药品，没有人看护照顾他，只有几个肯纳卡人倒是很好心，可他们什么事也做不成。看到他，我感到恶心，差点昏过去。可怜的人！在海滩上住的那四个月中，我们常在一起工作或到林中水边出游。我的确十分喜欢他，觉得他比我船上的乡亲们都好。当我到他屋里去看他时，他伸出手声音低沉但却是微笑着对我说："阿洛哈，兄弟！阿洛哈，没事儿！"[夏威夷话，问候或送别的意思]我尽量安慰他，并许诺说我会请求船长给他点药。

我们曾有过对船长的恨，现在则爱起这位太平洋上长着明亮眼睛的

speck in the horizon, and the coast lay like a low cloud along the north-east. At sunset they were both out of sight, and we were once more upon the ocean, where sky and water meet.

The description of the voyage home is wonderful. It is as if the sea rose up to prevent the escape of this subtle explorer. Dana seems to pass into another world, another life, not of this earth. There is first the sense of apprehension, then the passing right into the black deeps. Then the waters almost swallow him up, with his triumphant consciousness.

The days became shorter and shorter, the sun running lower in its course each day, and giving less and less heat, and the nights so cold as to prevent our sleeping on deck; the Magellan Clouds in sight of a clear night; the skies looking cold and angry; and at times a long, heavy, ugly sea, setting in from the Southward, told us what we were coming to.

They were approaching Cape Horn, in the southern winter, passing into the strange, dread regions of the violent waters.

And there lay, floating in the ocean, several miles off, an immense irrcgular mass, its top and points covered with snow, its centre a deep indigo. This was an

人来——这爱是一种救世主的爱。霍普是真正的大海之子，充满了大海的神秘。一时间，霍普对达纳来说就如同钦加哥[库柏《最后的莫希干人》里的人物]之于库柏，是贴心兄弟，是知音。但这时间并不长。甚至在此时，他的爱也主要是怜悯，还带点慈善味道。归根结底还是一种救世主义。理想主义者。

达纳注定要离开加利福尼亚海岸回到文明的东部去。可当船终于启航时他感到了离别的痛苦。太平洋是令他眩惑的世界，而东部才是真实、精确、实实在在的地方。他是一个文明的仆人，一个理想主义者，民主主义者，他仇恨主人，是个"了解者"。他的意识和自我意识极强，从不会忘却。

风帆涨起，甲板清理完毕，加利福尼亚号已变成地平线上的一个小点，海岸线就像东北方的一块低云。夕阳斜下时分，一切景物均已在视线中消逝，我们又来到了水天交接的大海上。

iceberg, and of the largest size. As far as the eye could reach, the sea in every direction was of a deep blue colour, the waves running high and fresh, and sparkling in the light; and in the midst lay this immense mountain-island, its cavities and valleys thrown into deep shade, and its points and pinnacles glittering in the sun. But no description can give any idea of the strangeness, splendour, and, really, the sublimity of the sight. Its great size–for it must have been two or three miles in circumference, and several hundred feet in height; its slow motion, as its base rose and sank in the water and its points nodded against the clouds; the high dashing of the waves upon it, which, breaking high with foam, lined its base with a white crust; and the thundering sound of the cracking of the mass, and the breaking and tumbling down of hugh pieces; together with its nearness and approach, down of hugh pieces; together with its nearness and approach, which added a slight element of fear–all combined to give it the character of true sublimity–

But as the ship ran further and further into trouble, Dana became ill. First it is a slight toothache. Ice and exposure cause the pains to take hold of all his head and face. And then the face so swelled, that he could not open his mouth to eat, and was in danger of lock-jaw. In this state he was forced to keep his bunk for three or four

归航的这一段描写很精彩。似乎那大海翻腾着在阻挡这位探险家逃跑。达纳似乎进入了另一个世界、另一种生活中，已不再是我们这个地球。先是一种恐惧感，然后是没入黑暗的海洋。后来，海水几乎吞没他，连同他那志得意满的思想。

“白天越来越短，太阳一日懒似一日，放射出愈来愈弱的热量，夜晚太冷了，我们已无法在甲板上过夜。明朗的夜空中可见到麦哲伦星云[位于赤道以南，离银河最近的星云]。天空看上去冷酷而恼怒。时而从南部滚过一道丑陋的狭长海浪，它告诉我们所处的位置。”

他们这是接近牛角岬了。在南半球的冬季，他们进入了一片奇妙、可怕、恶浪翻滚的水域。

“几英里外漂着一大块形状怪异的东西，它的顶上和边边角角处覆盖着白雪，正中露出深深的靛蓝。这是一座冰山，是最大号的冰山。目光

days.

At the end of the third day, the ice was very thick; a complete fog-bank covered the ship. It blew a tremendous gale from the east-ward, with sleet and snow, and there was every promise of a dangerous and fatiguing night. At dark, the captain called the hands aft, and told them that not a man was to leave the deck that night; that the ship was in the greatest danger; any cake of ice might knock a hole in her, or she might run on an island and go to pieces. The look-outs were then set, and every man was put in his station. When I heard what was the state of things, I began to put on my things, to stand it out with the rest of them, when the mate came below, and looking at my face ordered me back to my berth, saying if we went down we should all go down together, but if I went on deck I might lay myself up for life. In obedience to the mate's orders, I went back to my berth; but a more miserable night I never wish to spend.

It is the story of a man pitted in conflict against the sea, the vast, almost omnipotent element. In contest with this cosmic enemy, man finds his further ratification, his further ideal vindication. He comes out victorious, but not till the sea has tortured his living, integral body, and made him pay something for his triumph in

所及之处，但见海水呈现出清亮的靛蓝海浪翻涌，浪花飞溅。海浪之中浮着这座巨大的冰山岛。'岛'上深凹着洞穴和峡谷，棱角和顶端在阳光下熠熠生辉。其奇妙、辉煌和雄伟是难以用语言来形容的。这座冰山简直太大了。它的周长足有两三英里，高有几百码。它缓缓地沉浮着，它的顶端几乎与天上的云相触。海浪扑打着它，在冰山的高处粉碎开来。泡沫飞舞着，在冰山底座处结成厚厚的白花花的硬壳。冰山嘎嘎作响，时而散落下大块大块的冰。它快要漂到我们面前了，那气势不禁令人产生一丝恐惧，这一切都使得大冰山更加崇高庄严。"

可是当船一步步陷入困境时，达纳却病了。先是轻微牙痛。可是冰冷的环境和户外工作使得他整个头和脸部都疼痛起来。后来他面部全肿了以致无法张开嘴巴吃东西，他面临着患牙关紧闭症的危险。在这种情况下他被迫卧床三四天。

"到第三天时，冰层变厚了。海上的浓雾锁住了我们的船。一股强风

consciousness.

The horrific struggle round Cape Horn, homewards, is the crisis of the Dana history. It is an entry into chaos, a heaven of sleet and black ice-rain, a sea of ice and iron-like water. Man fights the element in all its roused, mystic hostility to conscious life. This fight is the inward crisis and triumph of Dana's soul. He goes through it all consciously, enduring, knowing. It is not a mere overcoming of obstacles. It is a pitting of the deliberate consciousness against all the roused, hostile, anti-life water of the Pole.

After this fight, Dana has achieved his success. He knows. He knows what the sea is. He knows what the Cape Horn is. He knows what work is, work before the mast. He knows, he knows a great deal. He has carried his consciousness open-eyed through it all. He has won through. The ideal being.

And from his book, we know too. He has lived this great experience for us; we owe him homage.

The ship passes through the strait, strikes the polar death-mystery, and turns northward, home. She seems to fly with new strong plumage, free. 'Every rope-yarn seemed stretched to the utmost, and every thread of the canvas; and with this sail

从东部席卷而来，夹带着冻雨和大雪，一切迹象表明一个可怕的夜晚将降临。黄昏时分船长唤来船员们，告诉人们是夜不许离开甲板。他说船遇上了最大的危险，任何一块冰都会在船上打出一个洞来，或许船会撞上一座岛而落个粉身碎骨的下场。船上派了观察哨，别人也各就各位。当我听说了我们船的处境时，我开始穿上衣服，准备和其他人一起战斗。这时大副走到下面看看我的脸命令我回去卧床休息。他说，如果我们要下沉就一块儿淹死，与其让我上甲板倒不如让我卧床休息。我服从了他的命令回床上休息去了。可这个夜晚更令人痛苦。”

这是一个与大海这广袤、几乎是无所不能的自然物作对的人的故事。在与这位宇宙敌手作斗争的过程中，人发现了自身的价值，也得到了理性的报应，他最终胜利了，可是大海摧残了他活生生的囫囵肉体，让他为自己精神上的胜利付出了代价。

归乡路上在牛角岬附近发生的这场可怕的斗争是达纳历史上的一场危机。他投身于混乱之中——铺天盖地的雨夹雪和冰雨，一片冰封水

added to her the ship sprang through the water like a thing possessed. The sail being nearly all forward, it lifted her out of the water, and she seemed actually to jump from sea to sea. '

Beautifully the sailing-ship nodalizes the forces of sea and wind, converting them to her purpose. There is no violation, as in a steam-ship, only a winged centrality. It is this perfect adjusting of ourselves to the elements, the perfect equipoise between them and us, which gives us a great part of our life-joy. The more we intervene machinery between us and the naked forces the more we numb and atrophy our own senses. Every time we turn on a tap to have water, every time we turn a handle to have a fire or light, we deny ourselves and annul our being. The great elements, the earth, air, fire, water, are there like some great mistress whom we woo and struggle are there like some great mistress whom we woo and struggle with, whom we heave and wrestle with. And all our appliances do but deny us these fine embraces, take the miracle of life away from us. The machine is the great neuter. It is the eunuch of eunuchs. In the end it emasculates us all. When we balance the sticks and kindle a fire, we partake of the mysteries. But when we turn on an electric tap there is, as it were, a wad between us and the dynamic universe, We do not know what we

域。人以某种神秘的力量敌视理性生活并为此去与大自然作斗争。这场斗争是达纳灵魂内部的危机与胜利，他明明白白地经历了这一切，忍受了下来。这并非只是在战胜阻障，它其实是与南极地带敌视生命的大海作斗争。

通过斗争，达纳取得了胜利。他知道了，知道了大海为何物，知道牛角岬为何物，知道了劳动为何物——作为一个水手是什么滋味。他懂了，懂得了许多。在这个过程中他的意识始终是清醒的。他胜利了。他这个理想的人。

通过他的书，我们也有所获，他代我们经历了一场伟大的经验，我们应向他致敬。

这条船穿过了海峡，冲破了极地的死亡神话，向北回乡了。它似乎浑身生出了坚实的新羽毛，自由地飞翔着。

每一根绳都绷得紧紧的，每一面风帆都高高扬起。这条船像着了魔似的在水面上飞腾。风帆几乎倾倒，把船从水面上拔起，它几乎是在海面

lose by all our labour-saving appliances. Of the two evils it would be much the lesser to lose all machinery, every bit, rather than to have, as we have, hopelessly too much.

When we study the pagan gods, we find they have now one meaning, now another. Now they belong to the creative essence, and now to the material-dynamic world. First they have one aspect, then another. The greatest god has both aspects. First he is the source of life. Then he is mystic dynamic lord of the elemental physical forces. So Zeus is Father, and Thunderer. *

Nations that worship the material-dynamic world, as all nations do in their decadence, seem to come inevitably to worship the Thunderer. He is Ammon, Zeus, Wotan and Thor, Shango of the West Africans.* As the creator of man himself, the Father is greatest in the creative world, the Thunderer is greatest in the material world. He is the god of force and of earthly blessing, the god of the bolt and of sweet rain.

So that electricity seems to be the first intrinsic principle among the Forces. It has a mystic power of readjustment. It seems to be the overlord of the two naked elements, fire and water, capable of mysteriously enchaining them, and of my steriously

上奔腾跳跃着前行。

帆船乘风破浪，驾驭着自然力为自己服务。蒸汽船丝毫没有损害什么，它只是在高速中保持着平衡。就是这种使我们适应自然的调整和平衡使我们获得了极大的生活乐趣。我们愈是让机器介入我们与自然力之间，我们的感官就愈是迟钝和萎缩。每次我们拧水龙头，每次我们扭动旋钮点火或开电灯我们都是在否定自身、埋没自己的生命。自然中的要素，土壤、空气、火和水就如同一些了不起的情妇，我们追求她们，同她们较量。可所有的工具只能褫夺我们与这些“情妇”的美妙拥抱，褫夺我们生活中的奇迹。机器是最大的无性人，是阉人中的阉人，到头来它会阉割我们大家的。当我们摆弄树枝点火时，我们是在分享着神秘。可当我们去按一个电钮时，它就把我们与充满活力的自然界分开了。我们不知道我们那些省力的工具让我们都失去了些什么。机器这魔鬼，失去得越多越好，可事实上是我们拥有的太多了。

当我们研究异教的神时，我们发现，其意义时有不同。一忽儿这神属

sundering them from their connections. When the two great elements become hopelessly clogged, entangled, the sword of the lightning can separate them. The crash of thunder is really not the clapping together of waves of air. Thunder is the noise of the explosion which takes place when the waters are loosed from the elemental fire, when old vapours are suddenly decomposed in the upper air by the electric force. Then fire flies fluid, and the waters roll off in purity. It is the liberation of the elements from hopeless conjunction. Thunder, the electric force, is the counterpart in the material-dynamic world of the life-force, the creative mystery, itself, in the creative world.

Dana gives a wonderful description of a tropical thunder-storm.

When our watch came on deck at twelve o'clock it was as black as Erebus; not a breath stirring; the sails hung heavy and motionless from the yards; and the perfect stillness, and the darkness, which was almost palpable, were truly appalling. Not a word was spoken, but everyone stood as though waiting for something to happen. In a few minutes the mate came forward, and in a low tone which was almost a whisper, gave the command to haul down the jib. When we got down we found all hands looking aloft, and then, directly over where we had been standing, upon the main

于创造的本质，一忽儿又属于物质世界。一会儿这样，一会儿那样。最至高无上的神具有两种特性。其一，他是生命的源泉；其二，他是大自然物质力量神秘而强大的主人。所以宙斯既是上帝又是主神朱庇特[宙斯是希腊神话里的主神；朱庇特则是罗马神话里的主神]。

崇拜物质力量世界的民族是颓废的民族，他们注定要崇尚朱庇特。他是阿蒙，宙斯，沃坦，托尔和尚过神[他们分别是埃及、希腊、日耳曼、北欧和加勒比地区的的主神]。而作为造物主的上帝是创世的主人。朱庇特是物质世界的主人——他是力量之神、大地之神、电和雨之神。

所以，电似乎成了自然力中的主要因素。电有着神秘的调整功能。它似乎是火和水这两大要素的主子，它神秘地控制它们并神秘地把它们分开。当这两大要素无望地纠缠一团时，电之剑可以把它们斩开。雷鸣可以说并非气浪相击所致，它是水从火中分离出来时的爆炸声，是电在高空中突然把水蒸气击开的。随后火变成流质飞舞，流出清纯的水来。这是自然成分无法团结时分崩离析的声音，雷这种电力正是物质世界中的生命力的对应物，雷是创世领域内的创世神秘物。

topgallant mast-head, was a ball of light, which the sailors name a corposant (corpus sancti). They were all watching it carefully, for sailors have a notion that if the corposant rises in the rigging, it is a sign of fair weather; but if it comes lower down, there will be a storm. Unfortunately, as an omen, it came down and showed itself on the top-gallant yard-arm.

In a few minutes it disappeared and showed itself again on the fore top-gallant yard, and, after playing about for some time, disappeared again, when the man on the fore-castle pointed to it upon the flying-jib-boom-end. But our attention was drawn from watching this by the falling of some drops of rain. In a few minutes low growling thunder was heard, and some random flashes of lightning came from the south-west. Every sail was taken in but the top-sail. A few puffs lifted the top-sails, but they fell again to the mast, and all was as still as ever. A minute more, and a terrific flash and peal broke simultaneously upon us, and a cloud appeared to open directly over our heads and let down the water in one body like a falling ocean. We stood motionless and almost stupefied, yet nothing had been struck. Peal after peal rattled over our heads with a sound which actually seemed to stop the breath in the body. The violent fall of the rain lasted but a few minutes, and was succeeded by

达纳对赤道地区的雷雨有绝妙的描述：

瞭望哨子来到甲板上时，天黑得伸手不见五指，四下里阒寂无声，船帆纹丝不动，静谧，黑魆，令人胆寒。没人说话，但人人都默立着等着什么事情发生。不一会儿，大副走过来，压低嗓门命令降帆。我们发现大家都仰望着顶桅杆上端的灯笼，船员们称之为"火球"。大家一丝不苟地凝视着它，船员们都知道，如果这火球上升，就意味着天气会好；如果光球下滑，就会有一场暴风雨。不幸得很，它下滑了。

片刻以后，它又消失了，随后又出现在帆桁上，晃动一阵后消失了。前甲板上的人指着船首的斜帆桁尾部，它有滑到那里了。此时我们已无法再盯着它了，因为雨点已开始啪啪掉落。几分钟后沉闷的雷声传来，接着西南部闪电交错。除了中桅帆以外，所有的帆都收了起来。中桅帆鼓起了一会儿就也收贴在桅杆上了，一切又都回复了原先的静寂。可没一会儿，突然一个可怕的闪电伴随着一个炸雷在我们头上同时出现，一团乌云似乎在我们的头顶上裂开，倾下翻江倒海般的大水。我们纹丝不动地

occasional drops and showers; but the lightning continued incessant for several hours, breaking the midnight darkness with irregular and blinding flashes.

During all this time hardly a word was spoken, no bell was struck, and the wheel was silently relieved. The rain fell at intervals in heavy showers, and we stood drenched through, and blinded by the flashes, which broke the Egyptian darkness with a brightness which seemed almost malignant, while the thunder rolled in peals, the concussion of which appeared to shake the very ocean. A ship is not often injured by lightning, for the electricity is separated by the great number of points she presents, and the quality of iron which she has scattered in various parts. The electric fluid ran over our anchors, topsail-sheets and ties; yet no harm was done to us. We went below at four o'clock, leaving things in the same state.

Dana is wonderful at relating these mechanical, or dynamic-physical events. He could not tell about the being of men: only about the forces. He gives another curious instance of the process of recreation, as it takes place within the very corpuscles of the blood. It is salt this time which arrests the life-activity, causing a static arrest in Matter, after a certain sundering of water from the fire of the warm-substantial body.

站着，呆若木鸡。还好，没什么东西被雷电击坏。一个炸雷又一个炸雷在我们头上轰鸣着，几乎令人窒息。猛烈的雷雨只折腾了几分钟就收敛了，只剩下小雨点和毛毛雨。可闪电却永无休止地一个接一个打着。以其炫目的光焰划破子夜的黑暗。

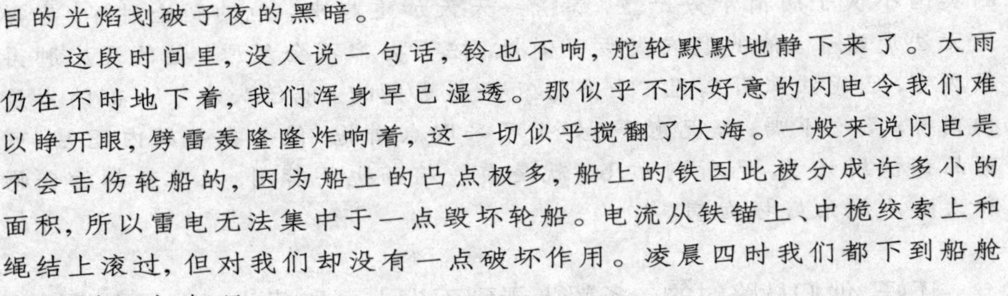

这段时间里，没人说一句话，铃也不响，舵轮默默地静下来了。大雨仍在不时地下着，我们浑身早已湿透。那似乎不怀好意的闪电令我们难以睁开眼，劈雷轰隆隆炸响着，这一切似乎搅翻了大海。一般来说闪电是不会击伤轮船的，因为船上的凸点极多，船上的铁因此被分成许多小的面积，所以雷电无法集中于一点毁坏轮船。电流从铁锚上、中桅绞索上和绳结上滚过，但对我们却没有一点破坏作用。凌晨四时我们都下到船舱中，船上一切如旧。

达纳在叙述这些机械的或剧烈的物理运动时显得很了不起。但是他无法讲述人的生命，他只会描述力量。不过他倒是记下了一种奇特创造现象——它发生在血球中。这次是“盐”阻止了生命的活动。火热坚实的

The scurvy had begun to show itself on board. One man had it so badly as to be disabled and off duty; and the English lad, Ben, was in a dreadful state, and was gradually growing worse. His legs swelled and pained him so that he could not walk; his flesh lost its elasticity, so that if it were pressed in, it would not return to its shape; and his gums swelled until he could not open his mouth. His breath, too, became very offensive; he lost all strength and spirit; could eat nothing; grew worse every day; and, in fact, unless something was done for him, would be a dead man in a week at the rate at which he was sinking. The medicines were all gone, or nearly all gone; and if we had had a chest-full, they would have been of no use; for nothing but fresh provisions and terra firma has any effect upon the scurvy.

However, a boat-load of potatoes and onions was obtained from a passing ship. These the men ate raw.

The freshness and crispness of the raw onion, with the earthy state, give it a great relish to one who has been a long time on salt provisions. We were perfectly ravenous after them. We ate them at every meal, by the dozen; and filled our pockets with them, to eat on the watch on deck. The chief use, however, of the fresh provi sions was for the men with the scurvy. One was able to eat, and he soon brought himself to by gnawing upon raw potatoes; but the other, by this time, was

肉体中水与火分开了，出现了生命的停滞。

坏血病开始在船上出现。一个人病情太重，已无法工作了。那个叫本的英国小伙子病情十分严重，病情一天天加重起来。他的腿全肿了，疼得他无法走路了。他的肌肉失去了弹性，按下去都不会复原。他的牙床肿得很厉害，已无法张开嘴巴。呼出的气都是恶臭的。他已失去了全部的力量和精神，不吃不喝，每况愈下。如果不采取点措施，他会在一周内死去。可药品都快用光了，已所剩无几。就是有一箱药也不管用，只有新鲜的食物和大陆才能治好坏血病。

还好，他们从路过的一条船上弄到不少土豆和葱头。人们干脆把这些东西生吃下去。

清新、鲜嫩的葱头带着泥土味儿让我们这些长久以来在盐水中生活的人大开胃口，我们太馋这些东西了。我们每顿都吃，一吃就是十几个。

hardly able to open his mouth; and the cook took the potatoes raw, pounded them in a mortar, and gave him the juice to suck. The strong earthy taste and smell of this extract of the raw potatoes at first produced a shuddering through his whole frame, and after drinking it, an acute pain, which ran through all parts of his body; but knowing by this that it was taking strong hold, he persevered, drinking a spoonful every hour or so, until, by the effect of this drink, and of his own restored hope, he became so well as to be able to move about, and open his mouth enough to eat the raw potatoes and onions pounded into a soft pulp. This course soon restored his appetite and strength; and ten days after we spoke the Solon, *so rapid was his recovery that, from lying helpless and almost hopeless in his berth, he was at the mast-head, furling a royal.*

This is the strange result of the disintegrating effect of the sea, and of salt food. We are all sea born, science tells us. The moon, and the sea, and salt, and phosphorus, and us: it is a long chain of connection. And then the earth: mother-earth. Dana talks of the relish which the earthy taste of the onion gives. The taste of created juice, the living milk of Gea. And limes, which taste of the sun.

How much stranger is the interplay of life among the elements, than any chemical interplay among the elements themselves. Life-and salt-and phosphorus-and the

吃完口袋里还装上些，带到甲板的瞭望哨位上去吃，新鲜食品对治坏血病最管用。还能吃的就开始大嚼土豆，身体就恢复了。可有一个连嘴巴都张不开了，于是厨师就把生土豆放在研钵中捣烂，捣出汁来给他吸吮。浓郁的陆地气息令他浑身为之一颤，吸了一口土豆汁后，他禁不住周身疼痛难忍。他知道这很起作用，于是坚持每小时喝一勺儿。靠着土豆汁他有了希望，他好了，可以动了，嘴巴可以张开吃一些捣成泥的生土豆和葱头了。这种良方很快使他恢复了胃口和力量。十天以后他迅速康复，一个绝望的卧床病人走上了船头，升起了主帆旁的轻帆。

这是大海和腌制食物造成的奇怪后果。科学告诉我们，我们都是海洋生物。月亮、大海、盐、磷和我们，组成了一条长长的链子。还有地球，大地母亲。达纳谈到了葱头的陆地气息。谈到了地母吉雅新鲜的乳汁。还有石灰，那是太阳的气息。

自然元素中生命的相互影响比元素之间的化学性相互影响要奇特得多。生命——盐、磷、大海和月亮。生命——硫、碳、火山和太阳。上升与

sea-and the moon. Life-and sulphur-and carbon-and vol-canoes-and the sun. The way up, and the way down. The strange ways of life.

But Dana went home, to be a lawyer, and a rather dull and distinguished citizen. He was once almost an ambassador. And Pre-eminently respectable. *

He had been. He KNEW. He had even told us. It is a great achievement.

And then what?-Why, nothing. The old vulgar humdrum. That´s the worst of knowledge.It leaves one only the more lifeless.Dana lived his bit in two years, and knew, and drummed out the rest. Dreary lawyer´s years, afterwards.

We know enough. We know too much. We know nothing.

Let us smash something. Ourselves included.But the machine above all.

Dana´s small book is a very great book: contains a great extreme of knowledge, knowledge of the great element.

And after all, we have to know all before we can know that knowing is nothing.

Imaginatively, we have to know all: even the elemental waters.And know and know on, until knowledge suddenly shrivels and we know that forever we don´t know.

Then there is a sort of peace, and we can start afresh, knowing we don´t know.

下降，生命奇特的方式[劳伦斯曾读到赫拉克利特的名言："上升与下降的途径全然相同。"]。

可是达纳回去当律师，成了一个无聊、但出色的公民。有一次他几乎差点当上大使，是个极受人尊重的人哩[1840 达纳成为麻省律师。1876 年曾被提名为驻英国公使，但未获参议院批准]。

他有经历。他"懂"。他甚至对我们讲了这些。这是一大成功。

那，还怎么样?没什么。陈词滥调罢了。这是顶没用的知识了。它只能让人更无生气。达纳过了两年像样的日子，有了阅历，然后开始打发日子。律师的日子很乏味。

我们了解得够多了，太多了。我们什么都不知道。

让我们打碎什么吧，包括我们自己，首要的是机器。

达纳的这本小书了不起，它包容了极端化的知识，那是自然的知识。

无论如何，我们得先要弄懂一切才能懂得知识一文不值这个道理。

从想像的角度说，我们应该了解一切，甚至自然界的水。了解，不断地了解，直至知识突然萎缩，我们意识到我们什么也不了解。

随之而来的是某种宁静，我们又可重新开始。因为我们知道我们一无所知。

CHAPTER 10
Herman Melville´s Typee and Omoo

The greatest seer and poet of the sea for me is Melville. His vision is more real than Swinburne´s,* because he doesn´t personify the sea, and far sounder than Joseph Conrad´s,* because Melville doesn´t sentimentalize the ocean and the sea´s unfortunates. Snivel in a wet hanky like Lord Jim.

Melville has the strange, uncanny magic of sea-creatures, and some of their repulsiveness. He isn´t quite a land animal. There is something slithery about him. Something always half-seas-over. In his life they said he was mad-or crazy. He was neither mad nor crazy. But he was over the border. He was half a water animal, like those terrible yellow-bearded Vikings* who broke out of the waves in beaked ships.

He was a modern Viking. There is something curious about real blue-eyed Peo-

赫尔曼·麦尔维尔的《泰比》和《奥穆》

我认为麦尔维尔是最伟大的海洋预言家和海洋诗人，他的洞察比史文朋 [1837—1909，拉斐尔前派诗人，批评家] 来得更真切，因为他从不把大海拟人化；比约瑟夫·康拉德 [1857—1924，英国作家。劳伦斯不喜欢其作品《基姆爷》的感伤和妥协] 来得更准确，因为麦尔维尔从不把大海及其不幸伤感化(康拉德笔下的吉姆爷是个能哭湿手帕的人)。

麦尔维尔身上具有海生物的奇异和魔力，也有海生物令人生厌的特点。他算不上是个陆地动物。他有那么点滑溜溜的样子，像是被大海镇住了。他活着时人们都说他疯了。其实他既不疯也不癫，只是两栖而已。他是一只半海洋性动物，就像那些长着可怕的黄胡子[北欧海盗并非都生着黄胡子，

ple. They are never quite human, in the good classic sense, human as brown-eyed people are human: the human of the living *humus*. About a real blue-eyed person there is usually something abstract, elemental. Brown-eyed People are, as it were, like the earth, which is tissue of bygone life, organic, compound. In blue eyes there is sun and rain and abstract, uncreate element, water, ice, air, space, but not humanity. Brown-eyed people are people of the old, old world: Allzu menschlich. Blue-eyed people tend to be too keen and abstract.

Melville is like a Viking going home to the sea, encumbered with age and memories, and a sort of accomplished despair, almost madness. For he cannot accept humanity. He can't belong to humanity. Cannot.

The great Northern cycle of which he is the returning unit has almost completed its round, accomplished itself. Balder the beautiful is mystically dead, and by this time he stinketh. Forget-me-nots and sea-poppies fall into water, The man who came from the sea to live among men can stand it no longer. He hears the horror of the cracked church bell, and goes back down the shore, back into the ocean again, home, into the salt water. Human life won't do. He turns back to the elements. And all the vast sun-and-wheat consciousness of his day he plunges back into the deeps,

但19世纪的绘画中都这样描绘他们]、敢于乘着鸟嘴形船头的船劈波斩浪的北欧海盗。

他是个现代的北欧海盗。那些生着真正蓝眼睛的人总有那么点让人捉摸不透。用旧的观点看，他们有点不大像人，人应该生着棕色的眼睛。蓝眼睛的人一般来说显得莫测难解，自然属性较强。而棕眼睛的人则像土地，是远古年代生命的产物，是有机物、化合物。在蓝眼睛人身上，有着太阳、雨水和自然界未经人化的要素：水，冰，空气和空间，但没有人气。棕眼睛的人是古而又古的世界中的人，太过为人了。蓝眼睛的人似乎过于敏锐、莫测。

麦尔维尔就像一个海盗，奔向海洋对他来说如同回家乡一样。他受着岁月、记忆及其绝望感的重负，几乎要疯了，因为他无法接受人类。他无法归属于人类，不能。

他几乎完成了一个海盗周游的循环路线。漂亮的波德死得很神秘，现在他已经发臭了[这个人物出自英国诗人和随笔作家马修·阿诺德（1822—1888）的诗《死去的波德》。在北欧神话中，年轻英俊的神波德被另一个失明的神霍德杀死，后者是受了恶人洛基的误

burying the flame in the deep, self-conscious and deliberate. As blue flax and sea-poppies fall into the waters and give back their created sun-stuff to the dissolution of the flood.

The sea-born people, who can meet and mingle no longer: who turn away from life, to the abstract, to the elements: the sea receives her own.

Let life come asunder, they say. Let water conceive no more with fire. Let mating finish. Let the elements leave off kissing, and turn their backs on one another. Let the merman turn away from his human wife and children, let the seal-woman forget the world of men, remembering only the waters.

So they go down to the sea, the sea-born people. The Vikings are wandering again. Homes are broken up. Cross the seas, cross the seas, urges the heart. Leave love and home. Leave love and home. love and home are a deadly illusion. Woman, what have I to do with thee? It is finished. *Consummatum est*. The crucifixion into humanity is over. Let us go back to the fierce, uncanny elements: the corrosive vast sea. Or Fire.

Basta! It is enough. It is enough of life. Let us have the vast elements. Let us get out of this loathsome complication of living humanly with humans. Let the sea

导。劳伦斯在自己的小说《恋爱中的女人》里仿照这个神话，让北欧型美男子主人公杰拉德因受了恶人洛克(发音与洛基相似)的影响而自戕]。勿忘我和海罂粟落水了。那位从大海里上来住在人间的人无法忍受了。他听到教堂钟声可怕地鸣响起来，就回到大海咸水里的家中。他无法容忍人类的生活，于是又投入自然的怀抱。他全部的陆地意识被投入海中，把火焰深深埋入海底，明明白白有意为之，把自我意识和思考全埋入海底，就像蓝色的亚麻和黄色海罂粟，落水后把它们吸收的阳光给予洪水，随之一起消融。

原本生于大海的人们却无法相处，他们背离了生活，走向神秘，走向自然，大海接受了属于它自己的。

他们说，让生活分裂吧。让水不再与火相容。让交配终止吧。让自然中的各种要素不再接吻，让它们各自相背吧。让鱼人离开他的人间妻子和孩子[见阿诺德的诗《被遗弃的鱼人》中鱼人恳求其人间伴侣回到他和孩子身边，劳伦斯记忆有误]，让海豹女忘记人的世界，只记住大海吧 [劳伦斯在 1917 年通过音乐家格雷学到了《赫布里底人的歌》，其中有海豹女的歌]。

就这样，那些生于海洋的人下到大海中去了。北欧海盗又开始漫游，

wash us clean of the leprosy of our humanity and humanness.

Melville was a northerner, sea-born. So the sea claimed him. We are most of us, who use the English language, water-people, sea-derived.

Melville went back to the oldest of all the oceans, to the Pacific. *Der Grosse oder Stille Ozean.*

Without doubt the Pacific Ocean is aeons older than the Atlantic or the Indian Oceans. When we say older, we mean it has not come to any modern consciousness. Strange convulsions have convulsed the Atlantic and Mediterranean Peoples into phase after phase of consciousness, while the Pacific and the Pacific peoples have slept. To sleep is to dream: you can't stay unconscious. And, oh heaven, for how many thousands of years has the true Pacific been dreaming, turning over in its sleep and dreaming again: idylls: nightmares.

The Maoris, the Tongans, the Marquesans, the Fijians, the Polynesians: holy God, how long have they been turning over in the same sleep, with varying dreams? Perhaps, to a sensitive imagination, those islands in the middle of the Pacific are the most unbearable places on earth. It simply stops the heart, to be translated there, unknown ages back, back into that life, that pulse, that rhythm. The scientists

没有家了。横渡大海，横渡大海，他们的心这样激励着他们。离开爱和家。离开爱和家吧。爱和家是一种无望的幻象。女人，我和你有什么关系[见《约翰福音》2: 4]?一切都结束了。束缚人的十字架完了。让我们回到野性、神秘莫测的自然怀抱中去，到毁灭性的大海中或火中去吧。

够了。够了。活够了，让我们投身于大自然。让我们离开这可咒的人世。让大海洗净我们身上的人世和人情的麻风病。

麦尔维尔是个生于海洋的北方人。所以大海接受他。我们大多数讲英语的人都是水中的人，都来自海的世界。

麦尔维尔回到了最古老的海域太平洋。广渺而安宁的水域。

毫无疑问，太平洋比大西洋和印度洋要古老得多。我们所说的古老，是指它还未被现代意识所浸染。奇特的震动把大西洋和地中海人震人一种又一种新的意识中，而太平洋和太平洋水域的人则一直在沉睡。沉睡即是做梦：你无法毫无意识地醒着。天啊，太平洋沉睡了几千年了，它在睡梦中翻个身，随后又接着做梦。这既是牧歌又是梦魇。

毛利人、汤加岛人、马库斯岛人、斐济岛人和波利尼西亚人[波利尼西亚

say the South Sea Islanders belong to the Stone Age. It seems absurd to class people according to their implements. And yet there is something in it, The heart of the Pacific is still the Stone Age; in spite of steamers. The heart of the Pacific seems like a vast vacuum, in which, mirage-like, continues the life of myriads of ages back. It is a phantom-persistence of human beings who should have died, by our chronology, in the Stone Age. It is a phantom, illusion-like trick of reality: the glamorous South Seas.

Even Japan and China have been turning over in their sleep for countless centuries. Their blood is the old blood, their tissue the old soft tissue. Their busy day was myriads of years ago, when the world was a softer place, more moisture in the air, more warm mud on the face of the earth, and the lotus was always in flower. The great bygone world, before Egypt.* And Japan and China have been turning over in their sleep, while we have 'advanced'. And now they are starting up into nightmare.

The world isn't what it seems.

The Pacific Ocean holds the dream of immemorial centuries. It is the great blue twilight of the vastest of all evenings: perhaps of the most wonderful of all dawns.

人包括了汤加人、马库斯人和毛利人。而斐济则属于密克罗尼西亚]，天啊，他们在同样的沉睡中翻了多少次身，又做了多少不同的梦？或许，对一个富有敏感想像力的人来说，太平洋中心水域的这些岛屿是世上最难以令人忍受的地方了。到那儿去，回到不知多么古远的年月，返回到那种生命、那种脉搏、那种节奏，这简直是在令心脏停止跳动。科学家们说太平洋南部的岛民属于石器时代。似乎按照人使用的工具划分人的类别有点荒谬，可这也并非毫无道理。尽管有了蒸汽船，可太平洋的中心部分仍属于石器时代。这恰似一片巨大的真空，古远年代的生命像蜃景一样延续着。这是石器时代的人幽灵一般地坚守着，按照我们的年代学，这些人是早该死了的。这是一种幽灵的顽固存在，是现实玩弄的一种幻象。南太平洋，这迷人的海域。

甚至日本和中国也在无数个世纪的沉睡中翻来覆去。他们的血是古老的，他们的肌体是古老而柔软的。他们忙碌的日子则是几千年前的日子，那时的世界比现在柔和得多，空气湿润得多，地球表面温暖得多，荷花成年成月地盛开着。那是在埃及之前伟大的世界[劳伦斯把日本错排在了埃及

Who knows?

It must once have been a vast basin of soft, lotus-warm civilization, the Pacific. Never was such a huge man-day swung down into slow disintegration as here. And now the waters are blue and ghostly with the end of immemorial peoples. And phantom-like the islands rise out of it, illusions of the glamorous Stone Age.

To this phantom Melville returned. Back, back, away from life. Never man instinctively hated human life, our human life, as we have it, more than Melville did. And never was a man so passionately filled with the sense of vastness and mystery of life which is non-human. He was mad to look over our horizons. Anywhere, anywhere out of our world. To get away. To get away, out!

To get away, out of our life. To cross a horizon into another life. No matter what life, so long as it is another life.

Away, away from humanity. To the sea. The naked salt, elemental sea. To go to sea, to escape humanity.

The human heart gets into a frenzy at last, in its desire to dehumanize itself.

So he finds himself in the middle of the Pacific. Truly over a horizon. In another world. In another epoch. Back, far back, in the days of palm trees and lizards

文明之前。日本最早的起源大约在公元前660年]。而当日本和中国在睡梦中翻身时，我们已经变“先进”了。现在他们开始做噩梦了。

这世界并非它表面上的样子。

这太平洋盛有无数世纪的梦幻。它是一切夜晚中蓝色的薄暮，或许亦是最美好的黎明。谁个知晓。

这太平洋肯定曾经是一个温暖文明的盆地。这里人类缓慢地崩溃了，在这方面别的地方是无法与之比拟的。现如今，这里的水碧蓝而闪着灵光，因为这里葬着无数个人。无数个岛屿魔影般地从中耸起，这是石器时代辉煌的幻象。

麦尔维尔就是返归到这种幻象中来的，从而远离了生活。没有哪个人像麦尔维尔那样本能地仇视生活，那是我们人类的生活。没有哪个人像麦尔维尔那样充满激情，对非人类的生活深感其广渺和神秘。他天生来就是要超越我们的视野的人。不管是哪儿吧，反正是超越我们的世界。为的是逃走，逃出去!

逃走，逃离我们的生活。越过一道地平线进入另一种生命。不管它是

and stone implements. The sunny Stone Age.

Samoa, Tahiti, Raratonga, Nukuheva: the very names are a sleep and a forgetting. The sleep-forgotten past magnificence of human history. 'Trailing clouds of glory. '*

Melville hated the world: was born hating it. But he was looking for heaven. That is, choosingly. Choosingly, he was looking for paradise. Unchoosingly, he was mad with hatred of the world.

Well, the world is hateful. It is as hateful as Melville found it. He was not wrong in hating the world. *Delenda est Chicago.* He hated it to a pitch of madness, and not without reason.

But it's no good persisting in looking for paradise 'regained'.

Melville at his best invariably wrote from a sort of dream-self, so that events which he relates as actual fact have indeed a far deeper refefence to his own soul, his own inner life.

So in *Typee* when he tells of his entry into the valley of the dread cannibals of Nukuheva. Down this narrow, steep, horrible dark gorge he slides and struggles as we struggle in a dream, or in the act of birth, to emerge in the green Eden of the

什么生命，只要是另一种生命即可。

逃，逃离人类，逃向大海这赤裸的盐的世界。到海上去，逃离人类。

人的心灵最终因为人要变得非人而发疯。

于是他发现他来到了太平洋的腹地。的确是跨越了一道地平线，来到了另一个世界，另一个纪元，退回到椰树、蜥蜴和石器的年代。阳光灿烂的石器时代。

萨摩亚、塔希提、汤加岛、努库西瓦岛，这些名称本身就意味着沉睡与忘却。人类历史上沉睡与忘却的迷人之处。“光荣的流云”[沉睡、忘却、流云等详见华兹华斯诗《童年记忆》中的诗句]。

麦尔维尔仇恨这世界，他天生就恨这世界。他在寻找天堂。他在寻觅，刻意地寻觅天堂。可对这个世界他却别无选择，为此他恨得发疯。

是的，这世界的确可恨。麦尔维尔恨它，这一点不错。它必须毁灭。他恨透了它，这并非没有理由。

但是坚持寻找“复乐园”并无裨益。

麦尔维尔总是在梦幻般地写他的作品。因此，我们可以说，他叙述的

Golden Age, the valley of the cannibal savages. This is a bit of birth-myth, or re-birth myth, on Melville's part-unconscious, no doubt, because his running under-consciousness was always mystical and symbolical. He wasn't aware that he was being mystical.

There he is then, in Typee, among the dreaded cannibal savages. And they are gentle and generous with him, and he is truly in a sort of Eden.

Here at last is Rousseau's Child of Nature and Château-briand's Noble Savage* called upon and found at home. Yes, Melville loves his savage hosts. He finds them gentle, laughing lambs compared to the ravening wolves of his white brothers, left behind in America and on an American whaleship.

The ugliest beast on earth is the white man, says Melville.

In short, Herman found in Typee the paradise he was looking for. It is true, the Marquesans were'immoral', but he rather liked that. Morality was too white a trick to take him in. Then again, they were cannibals. And it filled him with horror even to think of this. But the savages were very private and even fiercely reserved in their cannibalism, and he might have spared himself his shudder. No doubt he had partaken of the Christian Sacraments many a time. 'This is my body, take and eat. This

所谓真实其实都与他的灵魂和内心生活有关。

所以，在《泰比》中，他讲了他来到努库西瓦那可怕的食人肉的峡谷中的故事。他下到这狭窄、深邃、可怕的黑谷中，梦一般地挣扎着，如同在挣扎出母腹进入黄金时代的绿色伊甸园。可怕的食人肉的野蛮人群。这对于麦尔维尔来说是一个出生或再生的神话，当然他对此并无意识，因为他那流动着的潜意识总是神秘、富有象征意味的。他从未意识到自己身上的神秘气质。

在《泰比》中，他来到了可怕的、食人肉的野人之中。不过这些人对他很好，很大方，他倒似真真儿地来到了一座伊甸园中。

他终于在此发现了卢梭的“自然之子”和夏多布里昂的“高贵野蛮人”[“自然之子”一词源自法国思想家爱尔维修的小说。“高贵的野蛮人”一词则源自约翰·德莱顿的诗]。是的，麦尔维尔爱他的野蛮地主。与美国及美国捕鲸船上恶狼般掠夺成性的白人兄弟相比，这是些个温顺、微笑着的羊。

世上顶顶丑恶的兽就是白人，麦尔维尔如是说。

一言以蔽之，赫尔曼发现泰比族人这儿是他久已企盼的天堂。的确，

is my blood. Drink it in remembrance of me'. And if the savages liked to partake of their sacrament without raising the transubstantiation quibble, and if they liked to say, directly: 'This is thy body, which I take from thee and eat. This is thy blood, which I sip in annihilation of thee', why surely their sacred ceremony was as awe-inspiring as the one Jesus substituted. But Herman chose to be horrified. I confess, I am not horrified; though, of course, I am not on the spot. But the savage sacrament seems to me more valid than the Christian: less side-tracking about it. Thirdly, he was shocked by their wild methods of warfare. He died before the great European war, so his shock was comfortable.

Three little quibbles: morality, cannibal sacrament, and stone axes. You must have a fly even in Paradisal ointment. And the first was a ladybird.

But paradise. He insists on it. Paradise. He could even go stark naked, as before the Apple episode. And his Fayaway, a laughing little Eve, naked with him, and hankering after no apple of knowledge, so long as he would just love her when he felt like it. Plenty to eat, needing no clothes to wear, sunny, happy people, sweet water to swim in: everything a man can want. Then why wasn't he happy along with the savages?

马库斯岛上的居民是不讲什么道德的。但他对此很欣赏。道德这苍白的东西很难令他就范。再者，这些人还是些吃人肉者，这令他一想起就毛骨悚然。不过，在这方面，野蛮人做得很隐秘，赫尔曼大可不必胆寒。毫无疑问，他不止一次分享过圣餐。“这是我的身体，拿去吃了吧。这是我的血，喝了它就能记住我。”[见英国国教的《大众祈祷书》]如果野蛮人在吃圣餐时毫无矫饰地直言：“这是你的身体，我拿去吃了。这是你的血，我喝了它，从此就没了你。”这和耶稣的仪式一样可怕。赫尔曼自愿受惊吓。但是说真的，我不怕——或许这是因为我不是当事人的原因吧。但是，野蛮人的圣餐在我看来比基督教圣餐来得实在，少了许多旁枝末节。还有，他也为这些人野蛮的战事方法所震惊[《泰比》中记载岛国人杀了敌人后将其头颅挂在家里]。他在欧洲大战前就去世了，从这个意义上说，他所经受的震惊可算轻多了。

这里有三个遁词：道德、人肉筵席和石斧。但是要知道，即使在天堂的药膏中也会有一只苍蝇。这头一只就是瓢虫[此句源自《传道书》10: 1，意为美味中一只苍蝇]。

他坚持要天堂。天堂。他甚至可以像食禁果之前那样赤身裸体。他

Because he wasn't.

He grizzled in secret, and wanted to escape.

He even pined for Home and Mother, the two things he had run away from as far as ships would carry him. HOME and MOTHER. The two things that were his damnation.

There on the island, where the golden-green great palm-trees chinked in the sun, and the elegant reed houses let the sea-breeze through, and people went naked and laughed a great deal, and Fayaway put flowers in his hair for him-great red hibiscus flowers, and frangipani-O God, why wasn't he happy? Why wasn't he?

Because he wasn't.

Well, it's hard to make a man happy.

But I should not have been happy either. One's soul seems under a vacuum, in the South Seas.

The truth of the matter is, one cannot go back. Some men can: renegade. But Melville couldn't go back: and Gauguin couldn't really go back: and I know now that I could never go back. Back towards the past, savage life. One cannot go back. It is one's destiny inside one.

的费尔维斯是一个微笑着的小夏娃，同他一样赤身裸体。他们并不追求什么知识之果，只要他想爱她就爱她，这就够了。有吃有喝，不需要穿衣服，阳光明媚，人人幸福，在甘洌的水中畅游——一个人想什么就有什么。既然如此，他为何不能与野蛮人幸福相处呢？

因为他不能。

他偷偷地抱怨，想逃走。

他甚至渴望着家和母亲，轮船把他愈载愈远，离家和母亲太遥远了。家和母亲，是这两样东西毁了他。

岛上，金绿色的大棕榈树在阳光下摇曳，形状高雅的苇子房四面透进海风，人们赤身裸体欢笑不止，费尔维斯把鲜花戴在他头上——那是大红的木槿花儿和鸡蛋花。天啊，他为什么还是不高兴呢？为什么？

因为他不能。

哦，让人高兴起来并非易事。

我也不会高兴的。因为在南太平洋，人的灵魂似处在真空中一般。

实际原因是，人不能倒退。有的人可以，那是些叛徒。可是麦尔维尔

There are these peoples, these 'savages'. One does not despise them. One does not feel superior. But there is a gulf. There is a gulf in time and being. I cannot commingle my being with theirs.

There they are, these South Sea Islanders, beautiful big men with their golden limbs and their laughing, graceful laziness. And they will call you brother, choose you as a brother. But why cannot one truly be brother?

There is an invisible hand grasps my heart and prevents it opening too much to these strangers. They are beautiful, they are like children, they are generous: but they are more than this. They are far off, and in their eyes is an easy darkness of the soft, uncreate past. In a way, they are uncreate. Far be it from me to assume any 'white' superiority. But they are savages. They are gentle and laughing and physically very handsome. But it seems to me, that in living so far, through all our bitter centuries of civilization, we have still been living onwards, forwards. God knows it looks like a *cul de sac* now. But turn to the first negro, and then listen to your own soul. And your own soul will tell you that however false and foul our forms and systems are now, still, through the many centuries since Egypt, we have been living and struggling forwards along some road that is no road, and yet is a great life-develop-

不能倒退。高更[高更曾下决心住在塔西提岛，中途回了巴黎又返回塔西提，最终死在马库斯岛]也实在不能倒退。我知道我一辈子也不能倒退，不能倒退到过去野蛮的生活。一个人不能倒退，这是命。

对于那些“野蛮人”，我们并不蔑视他们，并不对他们显示自己的优越。但是有一道鸿沟，时间和生命上的鸿沟。我无法把我的生命与他们的融会。

这些南海岛国人，高大漂亮，有着金色的四肢，笑容可掬，生性懒惰。他们称你为兄弟。你为什么不能做他们的兄弟？

有一只无形的手抓着我的心，令它别对这些陌生人太敞开。他们漂亮，像孩子一样，他们慷慨大方。但远不止这些。他们遥远得很，在他们目光中可现出不开化的悠闲。某种意义上说，他们不开化。我自然不够摆白人优势的架子，但我认为他们野蛮。是的，他们人很不错，乐呵呵的，体态健美得很。但我觉得，历经几世纪痛苦的文明，我们仍在向前走着。天晓得为什么现在有点如入绝境了。不过你看看黑人，听听你心灵的呼唤试试，你的心会告诉你，不管我们现今的形式和体制有多么虚伪肮脏，自古

ment. We have struggled on, and on we must still go. We may have to smash things. Then let us smash. And our road may have to take a great swerve, that seems a retrogression.

But we can't go back. Whatever else the South Sea Islander is, he is centuries and centuries behind us in the life-struggle, the consciousness-struggle, the struggle of the soul into fullness. There is his woman, with her knotted hair and her dark, inchoate, slightly sardonic eyes. I like her, she is nice. But I would never want to touch her. I could not go back on myself so far. Back to their uncreate condition.

She has soft warm flesh, like warm mud. Nearer the reptile, the Saurian age. *Noli me tangere.**

We can't go back. We can't to back to the savages: not a stride. We can be in sympathy with them. We can take a great curve in their direction, onwards. But we cannot turn the current of our life backwards, back towards their soft warm twilight and uncreate mud. Not for a moment. If we do it for a moment, it makes us sick.

We can only do it when we are renegade. The renegade hates life itself. He wants the death of life. So these many 'reformers' and 'idealists' who glorify the savages in America. They are death-birds, life-haters. Renegades.

埃及以来的这些年月中我们的确在沿着一条不成其为路的路向前行着，挣扎着，这仍算得上可观的生命进步。我们挣扎向前，过去这样，将来还必须这样。或许我们不得不毁灭点什么，那就毁灭好了。或许我们的路会来个大急转弯，那似乎是倒退也未可知。

但我们不能往后退。不管南海的岛民如何，他们在生命搏斗、灵魂搏斗和为心灵的完善而斗争方面比我们落后了几百年哩。他的女人，盘着头发，目光漆黑，迷茫而有点讽刺味儿。我喜欢她，她不错。可我一辈子也不想抚摸她。因为我不想倒退，不想倒退到不开化的境地中去。

她有着柔软温暖的肉体，就像热乎乎的泥。这有点近似爬虫，仍处在蜥蜴阶段那样。"别碰我"[耶稣基督复活后对末大拉的玛利亚说的第一句话]。

我们无法倒退，无法倒退到野蛮人阶段，一步也不能退。我们倒是可以同情他们。可以顺他们的方向绕一个大圈，但是还要朝前行才是。我们就是不能把我们的生活之流向后逆转，转向他们那柔和温暖的黄昏和不开化的泥土。一刻也不行。如果我们这样做了，哪怕只一会儿工夫，我们都会因此恶心。

We can't go back, and Melville couldn't. Much as he hated the civilized humanity he knew. He couldn't go back to the savages; he wanted to, he tried to, and he could't.

Because, in the first place, it made him sick; it made him physically ill. He had something wrong with his leg, and this would not heal. It got worse and worse, during his four months on the island. When he escaped, he was in a deplorable condition-sick and miserable, ill, very ill.

Paradise!

But there you are. Try to go back to the savages, and you feel as if your very soul was decomposing inside you. That is what you feel in the South Seas, anyhow: as if your soul was decomposing inside you. And with any savages the same, if you try to go their way, take their current of sympathy.

Yet, as I say, we must make a great swerve in our onward-going life-course now, to gather up again the savage mysteries. But this does not mean going back on ourselves.

Going back to the savages made Melville sicker than anything. It made him feel as if he were decomposing. Worse even than Home and Mother.

只有我们成了叛徒我们才会这样做。叛徒仇恨生活本身，他要的是让生活死去。于是这些为数不少的“改良者”和“理想主义者”就盛赞美国的野蛮人。这些叛徒，死东西，仇恨生活的人。

我们不能倒退。麦尔维尔也不能。尽管他恨文明了的人类，但他不能回到野蛮人中去。他想这样，他试过，可他不能。

因为，这样做的第一个结果就是肉体上生病。他的腿出了毛病，伤口总也不能愈合。情况越来越糟，到岛上的头四个月中一天坏似一天。逃离之后，他的状态很可悲，仍然病得很厉害。

天堂!

试试倒退到野蛮人阶段吧。你会感到你的灵魂在粉碎。在南太平洋你就会有如是感觉。跟任何野蛮人在一起你都会这样的。与任何野蛮人在一起都是如此。如果你要倒退到他们的路上，与他们共苦，就会如此。

但是，我又要说的是，在我们前进的过程中我们又该来个急转弯，去收集野蛮人的秘密。当然这并不意味着让我们倒退。

倒退使得麦尔维尔大病难愈。他只感到几乎破碎了。

And that is what really happens. If you prostitute your psyche by returning to the savages, you gradually go to pieces. Before you can go back, you have to decompose. And a white man decomposing is a ghastly sight. Even Melville in Typee.

We have to go on, on,on, even if we must smash a way ahead.

So Melville escaped, and threw a boat-hook full in the throat of one of his dearest savage friends, and sank him, because that savage was swimming in pursuit. That's how he felt about the savages when they wanted to detain him. He'd have murdered them one and all, vividly, rather than be kept from escaping. Away from them-he must get away from them-at any price.

And once he has escaped, immediately he begins to sigh and pine for the 'Paradise'-Home and Mother being at the other end even of a whaling voyage.

When he really was Home with Mother, he found it Purgatory. But Typee must have been even worse than Purgatory, a soft hell, judging from the murderous frenzy which possessed him to escape.

But once aboard the whaler that carried him off from Nukuheva, he looked back and sighed for the Paradise he had just escaped from in such a fever.

Poor Melville! He was determined Paradise existed. So he was always in Purga-

这是真的。如果你出卖你的灵魂，向野蛮倒退，你就会渐渐支离破碎。倒退之前你得先破碎才行。一个白人的毁灭是可怕的。甚至麦尔维尔身处泰比族人中也是可怕的。

我们得向前，向前，向前，即使不得不粉碎什么，也得向前。

于是麦尔维尔逃了。他把一只船钩子打进一位亲爱的野蛮人朋友的喉咙中，把他淹死了，因为那个人游水来追他，野蛮人要强留他时他就会这样对待他们，全杀了他们，绝不留下。他必须不惜任何代价离他们而去。

他一经逃离，就开始叹气，就渴求起"天堂"来——家和母亲就在彼岸，即使要乘捕鲸船回去。

当他真的回到了家，见到了妈，但又发现家如同炼狱。可泰比族人那儿却比炼狱还坏，那是地狱，他必须逃离那儿不可。

可一经登上归乡的捕鲸船离开努库西瓦，他又回首遥望那座他疯狂中逃离的天堂，为此叹息不止。

可怜的麦尔维尔！他认准了，世上有天堂。为此他不得不总受炼狱的

tory.

He was born for Purgatory. Some souls are purgatorial by destiny.

The very freedom of his Typee was a torture to him. Its ease was slowly horrible to him. This time he was the fly in the odorous tropical ointment.

He needed to fight. It was no good to him, the relaxation of the non-moral tropics. He didn´t really want Eden. He wanted to fight. Like every American. To fight. But with weapons of the spirit, not the flesh.

That was the top and bottom of it. His soul was in revolt, writhing for ever in revolt. When he had something definite to rebel against-like the bad conditions on a whaling ship-then he was much happier in his miseries. The mills of God were grinding inside him, and they needed something to grind on.

When they could grind on the injustice and folly of missionaries, or of brutal sea-captains, or of govenments, he was easier. The mills of God were grinding inside him.

They are grinding inside every American. And they grind exceeding small.

Why? Heaven knows. But we´ve got to grind down our old forms, our old selves, grind them very very small, to nothingness. Whether a new somethingness

折磨。

他生就是炼狱的人。有人命中注定是受炼狱折磨的人。

泰比族人的自由之于他是一种折磨。泰比人的懒散令他渐渐怕起来。这下他们成了热带臭油中的苍蝇了。

他需要斗争。不道德的赤道地区的松弛对他没有好处。他并非真想要伊甸园。他要的是斗争，如同每个美国人一样。斗争，用精神来斗，而不是靠肉体。

这就是事情的原本。他的灵魂在抗争，一直在抗争。一旦他有了斗争的目标——如捕鲸船上恶劣的条件，他就会苦中作乐地斗下去。上帝的磨盘[见 Friedrich von Logau(1604—1655)的《报应》:"上帝之磨磨得缓慢，但磨得细微。"]在他体内运转，这磨盘需要磨点什么。

当这磨盘磨着邪恶、传教士的愚蠢不义、野蛮的船长和政府时，他感到很松快。上帝的磨盘在他心中运转。

这磨盘在每个美国人体内运转。它磨得极细。

为什么?天知道。我们是得磨掉我们的旧形式和我们旧的自我，把它

will ever start, who knows? Meanwhile the mills of God grind on, in American Melville, and it was himself he ground small: himself and his wife, when he was married. For the present, the South Seas.

He escapes on to the craziest, most impossible of whaling ships. Lucky for us Melville makes it fantastic. It must have been pretty sordid.

And anyhow, on the crazy *Julia*, his leg, that would never heal in the paradise of Typee, began quickly to get well. His life was falling into its normal pulse. The drain back into past centuries was over.

Yet, oh, as he sails away from Nukuheva, on the voyage that will ultimately take him to America, oh, the acute and intolerable nostalgia he feels for the island he has left.

The past, the Golden Age of the past–what a nostalgia we all feel for it. Yet we don't want it when we get it. Try the South Seas.

Melville had to fight, fight against the existing world, against his own very self. Only he would never quite put the knife in the heart of his paradisal ideal. Somehow, somewhere, somewhen, love should be a fulfilment, and life should be a thing of bliss. That was his fixed ideal. *Fata Morgana.*

That was the pin he tortured himself on, like a pinned–down butterfly.

们磨得细细的直至磨得无影无踪。或许会有什么新东西出现，谁知道呢。与此同时上帝的磨盘在美国人麦尔维尔心中继续磨着，把他自身越磨越细小，还搭上他的妻子。现在被磨着的还有南太平洋。

他最终逃上了最疯狂，也是最没出路的捕鲸船。所幸麦尔维尔让这船变得很精彩，在这之前它一定很肮脏。

无论怎样，在船上他那在泰比族天堂里无法愈合的腿伤迅速好转了。他的生活也转入正轨。向过去的倒退完结了。

可是，瞧啊，当他乘船离开努库西瓦，注定要回美国时，啊，他对那离他而去的海岛产生了一股多么不可遏制的思恋啊。

过去，过去那金子般的日子，我们都留恋它。可得到它时我们却又都不需要它。不信你就到南太平洋去试试。

麦尔维尔必须与现存世界斗，与他自身斗。只是，他不能把刀子捅向他的天堂般的理想之心。不知何原因、何地、何时，爱将成为一种满足，生活将成为一种福音。这就是他执着的理想。骗局。

他就被钉在这根钉子上受着折磨，如同一只被钉着的蝴蝶。

Love is never a fulfilment. Life is never a thing of continuous bliss. There is no paradise. Fight and laugh and feel bitter and feel bliss: and fight again. Fight, fight. That is life.

Why pin ourselves down on a paradisal ideal? It is only ourselves we torture.

Melville did have one great experience, getting away from humanity: the experience of the sea.

The South Sea Islands were not his great experience. They were a glamorous world outside New England. Outside. But it was the sea that was both outside and inside: the universal experience.

The book that follows on from *Typee* is *Omoo.*

Omoo is a fascinating book; picaresque, rascally, roving. Melville, as a bit of a beachcomber. The crazy ship *Julia* sails to Tahiti, and the mutinous crew are put ashore. Put in the Tahitian prison. It is good reading.

Perhaps Melville is at his best, his happiest, in *Omoo*. For once he is really reckless. For once he takes life as it comes. For once he is the gallant rascally epicurean, eating the world like a snipe, dire and all baked into one *bonne boucbe*.

For once he is really careless, roving with that scamp, Doctor Long Ghost. For once he is careless of his actions, careless of his morals, careless of his ideals: iron-

爱从来都不会十全十美。生活绝不会一成不变地幸福下去。压根儿就没有天堂。斗争、欢笑、痛苦、欢乐，斗争再斗争，这才是生活。

为什么要把我们自己钉在天堂的理想这根钉子上?这是自找折磨。

麦尔维尔的确获得了远离人世的伟大经验，这就是出海的经验。

南太平洋岛国的经历算不上多了不起，那不过是新英格兰以外的一个炫目的世界。倒是那里的大海，既是外部世界亦是他的内心世界：一种普遍的经验。

《泰比》下面的一部著作是《奥穆》。

《奥穆》是一本迷人的书，满篇的传奇与流浪故事。麦尔维尔就有点流浪汉气质。那发疯的“朱丽亚”号驶到塔西提岛，叛乱的船员们被押解上岸，关在岛上的狱中。这书读起来很有趣。

或许在写《奥穆》时麦尔维尔的境况最佳，人也最快活。一时间他毫无顾忌，顺其自然地生活，恰似一个勇敢的享乐主义流浪汉，欲一口吞下这世界，像吞下沙锥鸟一样，连泥沙一起囫囵吞下，如同吃美味小吃。

一时间他的确是毫无顾忌地同那个流氓朗·葛斯特医生一起流浪，

ic,as the epicurean must be. The deep irony of your real scamp: your real epicurean of the moment.

But it was under the influence of the Long Doctor. This long and bony Scotsman was not a mere ne´er–do–well. He was a man of humorous desperation, throwing his life ironically away. Not a mere loose–kneed loafer, such as the South Seas seem to attract.

That is good about Melville: he never repents, Whatever he did, in Typee or in Doctor Long Ghost´s wicked society, he never repented. If he ate his snipe, dirt and all, and enjoyed it at the time, he didn´t have bilious bouts afterwards, which is good.

But it wasn´t enough. The Long Doctor was really knocking about in a sort of despair. He let dis ship drift rudderless.

Melville couldn´t do this. For a time, yes. For a time, in this Long Doctor´s company, he was rudderless and reckless. Good as an experience. But a man who will not abandon himself to despair or indifference cannot keep it up.

Melville would never abandon himself either to despair or indifference. He always cared. He always cared enough to hate Missionaries, and to be touched by a real act of kindness. He always cared.

对自己的行为、精神和理想都采取放任态度，这就很有点反讽的意味了，伊壁鸠鲁式的人必然会这样。做一个真正的坏蛋，多么深刻的反讽，一时间你真成了一个伊壁鸠鲁式的人了。

朗医生是有影响的。这个长身瘦骨的苏格兰人并非一个一事无成者。他是个绝望但又有幽默感的人，自嘲般地对待生活。他也不是个软骨头二流子。而南太平洋就很吸引这样的人。

麦尔维尔从不忏悔，这很好。无论他有何作为(在泰比族人中或在朗医生那可怕的圈子中)，他都不忏悔。如果他吃下他的沙锥鸟，连泥沙一起囫囵吞下，一时间很享受，过后也没得胆病，那就很好。

可这并不够。朗医生的确绝望了，他四处流浪，对他的船放任自流了。

麦尔维尔不能这样。当他随朗医生而行时他可以这样没主心骨，毫无顾忌。作为一种经验这也不算坏。可作为一个不甘绝望的人却不能这样下去。

麦尔维尔无论如何也不会绝望或漠然。他心里总有牵挂。他总是仇

When he saw a white man really 'gone savage', a white man with a blue shark tattooed over his brow, gone over to the savages, then Herman's whole being revolted. He couldn't bear it. He could not bear a renegade.

He enlisted at last on an American man-of-war. You have the record in *White Jacket*. He was back in civilization, but still at sea. He was in America, yet loose in the seas. Good regular days, after Doctor Long Ghost and the *Julia*.

As a matter of fact, a long thin chain was round Melville's ankle at the time, binding him to America, to civilization, to democracy, to the ideal world. It was a long chain, and it never broke. It pulled him back.

By the time he was twenty-five his wild oats were sown; his reckless wanderings were over. At the age of twenty-five he came back to Home and Mother, to fight it out at close quarters. For you can't fight it out by running away. When you have run a long way from Home and Mother, then you realize that the earth is round, and if you keep on running you'll be back on the same old doorstep-like a fatality.

Melville came home to face out the long rest of his life. He married and had an ecstasy of a courtship and fifty years of disillusion.

He had just furnished his home with disillusions. No more Typees. No more

恨传教士，厌恶为一切善行所感动。他总是很留意。

一当他看到一个白人真的“变野”(额头上刺上一条蓝鲨鱼文身)，他就会打心里反感。他对此无法忍受。他无法容忍一个叛徒。

他最终注册到一条美国战舰上服役。你可以在《白外套》中看到他上船后的记录。他又回到了文明世界，不过仍留在大海上。他回了美国，但是仍然在海上自有地生活，在朗医生和“朱丽亚”号之后过起颇有规律的日子了。

其实，有一条细长的链子拴着他的脚，要把他拉回美国、文明、民主和理念的世界。这链子极长，永不会断，终于把他拉了回来。

25 岁上，他已放荡够了，不再流浪。他回到了家和母亲身边，近距离作战。你无法靠逃跑取胜。当你远远地离开家和母亲，你会发现这地球是圆的，如果你再跑下去，你又会返回原先的位置，这是命。

麦尔维尔回家来面对余生悠长的时间。他成了家。有过狂热的求婚和五十年的失望。

他是用绝望来装饰自己的家的。再也没有泰比族人，再也没了天堂，

paradises. No more Fayaways. A mother: a gorgon. A home: a torture box. A wife: a thing with clay feet. Life: a sort of disgrace. Fame: another disgrace, being patronized by common snobs who just know how to read.

The whole shameful business just making a man writhe.

Melville writhed for eighty years.

In his soul he was proud and savage.

But in his mind and will he wanted the perfect fulfilment of love; he wanted the lovey-doveyness of perfect mutual understanding.

A proud savage-souled man doesn't really want any perfect lovey-dovey fulfilment in love: no such nonsense. A mountain lion doesn't mate with a Persian cat; and when a grizzly bear roars after a mate, it is a she-grizzly he roars after-not after a silky sheep.

But Melville stuck to his ideal. He wrote *Pierre* to show that the more you try to be good the more you make a mess of things: that following righteousness is just disastrous. The better you are, the worse things turn out with you. The better you try to be, the bigger mess you make. Your very striving after righteousness only causes your own slow degeneration.

Well, it is true. No men are so evil today as the idealists, and no women half so

再也没了费尔维斯。一个母亲：怪而丑的妇人。一个家：折磨人的盒子。一个妻子：平凡的女子。生活：一种屈辱。名望：又一种屈辱——他受着一帮势利小人的庇护，这些人大字不识几个。

这整桩屈辱的事会让一个人枯竭。

麦尔维尔枯竭了八十年。

他的灵魂是骄傲、野性的。

可他理智上却追求爱的完美，他要的是那种多情的相互理解。

一个有着骄傲、野性灵魂的人并不要完美的多情和理解的爱，那简直是一派胡言。一头山上的狮子是不会和一头波斯猫配对的。一头大灰熊如果冲着它的配偶嚎叫、追逐，那头配偶一定是一头母熊而不是一头皮毛光滑的羊。

可是麦尔维尔仍死抱着他的理想不放。他写了《皮埃尔》，试图表明你越是想好你越会把事情弄得一团糟——按照正义办事的结果是灾难。你越是好，你的情况就越是不妙。你越是想好，事情就越糟。你追逐正义只能使你渐渐堕落。

evil as your earnest woman, who feels herself a power for good. It is inevitable. After a certain point, the ideal goes dead and rotten. The old pure ideal becomes in itself an impure thing of evil. Charity becomes pernicious, the spirit itself becomes foul. The meek are evil. The pure in heart have base, subtle revulsions: like Dostoevsky´s *Idiot*. The whole Sermon on the Mount becomes a litany of white vice. *

What then?

It´s our own fault. It was we who set up the ideals. And if we are such fools, that we aren´t able to kick over our ideals in time, the worse for us.

Look at Melville´s eighty long years of writhing. And to the end he writhed on the ideal pin.

From the 'perfect woman lover' he passed on to the 'perfect friend'. He looked and looked for the perfect man friend.

Couldn´t find him.

Marriage was a ghastly disillusion to him, because he looked for perfect marriage.

Friendship never even made a real start in him–save perhaps his half–sentimental love for Jack Chase, in White Jacket.

Yet to the end he pined for this: a perfect relationship; perfect mating; perfect

是的，这是真的。今日世上没有比理想主义者更恶的了。没有比你那认真的女人更恶的了，因为她自以为是善的力量。这是不可避免的。超过一定的度，理想就会死亡、腐烂。古老纯洁的理想本身会成为邪恶污秽的东西。慈善变成恶毒，精神本身变成了肮脏。懦弱就是恶。心中的纯洁有其卑鄙渺小的反感，就如同陀斯妥耶夫斯基的《白痴》一样。山上的布道也变成了对白人之罪恶冗长历数[见《马太福音》5—7章，耶稣登山训众论道]。

怎么回事?

这是我们自己的错。是我们自己树立起那些个理想来的。如果我们是一群不能及时甩掉我们的理想的傻瓜，景况只能更坏。

看看麦尔维尔那长达八十年的痛苦挣扎吧。最终他仍在理想的钉子上扭动。

从追求“完美的女情人”到追求“完美的朋友”。他一直在寻觅完美的男性朋友。

知音难觅。

他的婚姻太令他失望，因为他要的是十全十美的婚姻。

mutual understanding. A perfect friend.

Right to the end he could never accept the fact that perfect relationships cannot be. Each soul is alone, and the aloneness of each soul is a double barrier to perfect relationship between two beings.

Each soul sbould be alone. And in the end the desire for a 'perfect relationship' is just a vicious, unmanly craving.

'*Tous nos malbeurs viennent de ne pouvoir être seuls.*'

Melville, however, refused to draw his conclusion. Life was wrong, he said. He refused Life. But he stuck to his ideal of perfect relationship, possible perfect love. The world ought to be a harmonious loving place. And it can't be. So life itself is wrong.

It is silly arguing. Because, after all, only temporary man sets up the 'oughts'.

The world ought not to be a harmonious loving place. It ought to be a place offierce discord and intermittent harmonies: which it is.

Love ought not to be perfect. It ought to have perfect moments, and wildernesses of thorn bushes–which it has.

A 'perfect' relationship ought not to be possible. Every relationship should have its absolute limits, its absolute reserves, essential to the singleness of the soul

可能他并未有过真正的友谊，只是在《白外套》中他对杰克·契斯有过一种半感伤的爱。

直到临终他都死抱住“完美的关系”不放。完美的结合，完美的相互理解，完美的朋友。

直到死，他都不肯承认世上压根儿就没有完美的关系。每个灵魂都是孤独的，这孤独对两个生命结成完美的关系不啻是双重的阻障。

每个灵魂都应该孤独。说到底，寻求“完美关系”的欲望不过是一种有害的、非人的渴求。

还好，麦尔维尔总算是拒绝下结论的。生活是个错误，他说。他拒绝了生活。可他仍坚守他那完美关系和完美的爱的理想。这世界应该是个和谐与爱的地方。可这是不可能的事。所以说生活本身是个错误。

争论这个显得傻气，因为只有一时冲动的人才会给自己定下什么“应该”。

这世界就不应该是一个和谐与爱的地方。它应该是个乱世，乱中有和谐，这才是这世界的本来样子。

in each person. A truly perfect relationship is one in which each party leaves great tracts unknown in the other party.

No two persons can meet at more than a few points, consciously. If two people can just be together fairly often, so that the presence of each is a sort of balance to the other, that is the basis of perfect relationship. There must be true separatenesses as well.

Melville was, at the core, a mystic and an idealist.

Perhaps, so am I.

And he stuck to his ideal guns.

I abandon mine.

He was a mystic who raved because the old ideal guns shot havoc. The guns of the 'noble spirit'. Of 'ideal love'.

I say, let the old guns rot.

Get new ones, and shoot straight.

爱就不应该完美。它应该既有完美之时也有满是荆棘的荒野，这才是爱的本来面目。

“完美”的关系是不可能的。任何一种关系都该有其绝对限度和绝对的保留，这对每个人灵魂的孤独是必须的。真正完美的关系意味着一方对另一方有大大的保留。

没有哪两个人能够在许多问题上一致。如果两个人能时常一致，以至于一个人的存在成为另一个人的平衡力量，这是完美关系的基础。当然真正的独立也是必须的。

从本质上说，麦尔维尔是个神秘者和理想主义者。

或许，我也是。

但他坚守自己的理想。

而我则放弃了它。

他胡言乱语地狂叫是因为旧的理想之枪把一切都打乱了。“高尚”精神之枪。“理想的爱”之枪。

我说，让那些旧的枪烂掉吧。

拿起新的枪，照直射吧。

CHAPTER 11
Herman Melville´s Moby Dick

Moby Dick, or the White Whale.

A hunt. The last great hunt.

For what?

For Moby Dick, the huge white sperm whale: who is old, hoary, monstrous, and swims alone; who is unspeakably terrible in his wrath, having so often been attacked; and snow-white.

Of course he is a symbol.

Of what?

I doubt if even Melville knew exactly. That´s the best of it.

He is warm-blooded, he is lovable. He is lonely Leviathan, not a Hobbes sort.

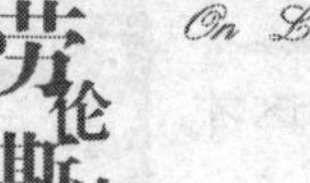

赫尔曼·麦尔维尔的《莫比·迪克》

莫比·迪克是一条白鲸。

一次追捕。最后的大追捕。

追捕什么？

追捕莫比·迪克这头巨大的雄鲸，他老了，像个魔鬼，独自游弋着，他时常遭到攻击，因此发起疯来十分可怕。他白得像雪。

当然，他是一个象征。

象征什么？

我怀疑，可能连麦尔维尔都不懂得很确切。这一点最好。

他是个热血动物，很可爱。他是个孤独的海怪，不是吗？

Or is he?

But he is warm-blooded and lovable. The South Sea Islanders, and Polynesians, and Malays, who worship shark, or crocodile, or weave endless frigate-bird distortions, why did they never worship the whale? So big!

Because the whale is not wicked. He doesn´t bite. And their gods had to bite.

He´s not a dragon. He is Leviathan. He never coils like the Chinese dragon of the sun. He´s not s serpent of the waters. He is warm-blooded, a mammal. And hunted, hunted down.

It is a great book.

At first you are put off by the style. It reads like journalism. It seems spurious. You feel Melville is trying to put something over you. It won´t do.

And Melville really is a bit sententious: aware of himself, self-conscious, putting something over even himself. But then it´s not easy to get into the swing of a piece of deep mysticism when you just set out with a story.

Nobody can be more clownish, more clumsy and sententiously in bad taste, than Herman Melville, even in a great book like *Moby Dick*. He preaches and holds forth because he´s not sure of himself. And he holds forth, often, so amateur-

他是个热血动物，很可爱。南太平洋上的岛国人，波利尼西亚人，马来人，他们崇拜鲨鱼或鳄鱼，也不断地编织形形色色的军舰鸟。可他们为什么不崇拜鲸鱼呢?他多大呀!

鲸鱼并不恶。它不咬人。可它们的神却不得不咬。

它不是一条龙。他是《圣经》中的怪兽。他从不像中国的太阳龙那样蜷曲。他也不是水中的蛇。他是一只热血哺乳动物。可他被追捕着。

这是一部大书。

首先你反感它的文体。它读起来像新闻稿，看上去有点假。你感觉到麦尔维尔试图把什么强加给你，可这不行。

麦尔维尔的确有点装腔作势，他自负，甚至要把什么东西强加给自己。如果你仅把它当做一个故事的话，就很难深得神秘主义的真谛。

没有谁像麦尔维尔一样滑稽、笨拙而出言无趣，这个麦尔维尔甚至在《莫比·迪克》这样一本伟大著作中也是如此。他布道，说教，因为他不自信。他时常在说教时显得很幼稚。

作为艺术家的他比作为一个人的他要伟大得多。作为一个人，他不

ishly.

The artist was so much greater than the man. The man is rather a tiresome New Englander of the ethical mystical -transcendentalist sort: Emerson, Longfellow, Hawthorne, etc. So unrelieved, the solemn ass even in humour. So hopelessly *au grand sérieux*, you feel like saying: Good God, what does it matter? If life is a tragedy, or a farce, or a disaster, or anything else, what do I care! Let life be what it likes. Give me a drink, that´s what I want just now.

For my part, life is so many things I don´t care what it is. It´s not my affair to sum it up. Just now it´s a cup of tea. This morning it was wormwood and gall. Hand me the sugar.

One wearies of the *grand sérieux*. There´s something false about it. And that´s Melville. Oh dear, when the solemn ass brays! brays! brays!

But he was a deep, great artist, even if he was rather a sententious man. He was a real American in that he always felt his audience in front of him. But when he ceases to be American, when he forgets all audience, and gives us his sheer apprehension of the world, then he is wonderful, his book commands a stillness in the soul, an awe.

过是个令人厌倦的新英格兰人，一个像爱默森、朗费罗和霍桑那样的道德家和神秘超验者。这人太单调，是头阴郁的驴子，甚至幽默时也如此。他过于严肃，他会令你发问：老天啊，这是怎么了？至于生活是悲剧、闹剧、灾难还是别的什么，这与我何干？生活该是什么样就是什么样。给我来点酒，我这会儿只需要这个。

对我来说，生活就是我不在乎为何物的东西。总结生活不是我的事。刚才它还是一杯茶。而今早它则是苦艾和苦胆了[见《旧约·耶利米哀歌》："记住我的苦难吧，它如同苦艾和苦胆。"]。把糖给我递过来。

人们对严肃者已厌了。那副样子有点虚假，麦尔维尔就是这样的人。亲爱的，他这阴郁的驴子也会咆哮！咆哮！咆哮！

可他是一位深刻的伟大艺术家，尽管他是个很装腔作势的人。说他是个真正的美国人，那是因为他总感觉到他的听众就在他面前。当他不再是美国人，当他忘了他的听众并放弃他对这世界的恐怖感，他就是个很了不起的人，他的书令人灵魂肃然起敬、生畏。

作为人，麦尔维尔几乎是死人。这就是说他难以对人的接触有什么

In his 'human' self, Melville is almost dead. That is, he hardly reacts to human contacts any more; or only ideally: or just for a moment. His human-emotional self is almost played out. He is abstract, self-analytical and abstracted. And he is more spell-bound by the strange slidings and collidings of Matter than by the things men do. In this he is like Dana. It is the material elements he really has to do with. His drama is with them. He was a futurist long before futurism found paint. The sheer naked slidings of the elements. And the human soul experiencing it all. So often, it is almost over the border: psychiatry. Almost spurious. Yet so great.

It is the same old thing as in all Americans. They keep their old-fashioned ideal frock-coat on, and an old-fashioned silk hat, while they do the most impossible things. There you are: you see Melville hugged in bed by a huge tattooed South Sea Islander, and solemnly offering burnt offering to this savage's little idol, and his ideal frock-coat just hides his shirt-tails and prevents us from seeing his bare posterior as he salaams, while his ethical silk hat sits correctly over his brow the while. That is so typically American: doing the most impossible things without taking off their spiritual get-up. Their ideals are like armour which has rusted in, and will never more come off. And meanwhile in Melville his bodily knowledge moves naked, a

反应。有的话也是理想化的或一时半时的事。他心中人——情感的自我几乎丧失殆尽。他深奥莫测、有自我解剖精神、心不在焉。他所迷恋的是物质那奇特的滑动与碰撞，而绝非人的所作所为。在这方面他很像达纳。他要对付的是物质，他的戏是与物质同在的。他是未来派发现绘画之前的未来派。纯粹自然因素的滑动。而人的灵魂经历了这一切。有时它几乎越界进入了精神病学领域。这几乎有点荒谬，可这是伟大的。

所有的美国人都有这老毛病。他们舍不得丢弃老式的理想燕尾服，戴着旧式的缎子帽，却做了最多出格的事。你瞧，麦尔维尔被一位刺着文身的大块头南太平洋人拥抱着，阴郁地向这个野蛮人的小小偶像奉献烤制的礼品。此时他那理想的外衣遮住了他的尾巴，阻止我们在他鞠躬时看到他的臀部，同时他那道德的缎帽仍不偏不倚地正压在眉毛上方。这就是典型的美国人：做最见不得人的事时也不脱掉他们的精神外衣。他们的理想就像盔甲锈在身上再也脱不掉了。与此同时，麦尔维尔的肉体在活生生赤裸的自然中全然赤裸地感知着。他以纯粹肉体的敏感颤动如同优质的无线电台一样记录下外部世界的影响。他同样以超越痛苦与欢

living quick among the stark elements. For with sheer physical vibrational sensitiveness, like a marvellous wireless-station, he registers the effects of the outer world. And he records also, almost beyond pain or pleasure, the extreme transitions of the isolated, far-driven soul, the soul which is now alone, without any real human contact.

The first days in New Bedford introduce the only human being who really enters into the book, namely, Ishmael, the 'I' of the book. And then the moment's heart's-brother, Queequeg, the tattooed, powerful South Sea harpooner, whom Melville loves as Dana loves 'Hope'. The advent of Ishmael's bedmate is amusing and unforgettable. But later the two swear 'marriage', in the language of the savages. For Queequeg has opened again the flood-gates of love and human connection in Ishmael.

'As I sat there in that now lonely room, the fire burning low, in that mild stage when, after its first intensity has warmed the air, it then only glows to be looked at; the evening shades and phantoms gathering round the casements, and peering in upon us silent, solitary twain: I began to be sensible of strange feelings. I felt a melting in me. No more my splintered heart and maddened hand were turned against

欣的能力记录下孤独灵魂的极端变化——这是从没有真正接触过他人的孤魂。

新贝德福德的头几天讲到了书中惟一一个真正的人，名叫以实玛利，即书中的“我”[据《旧约·创世纪》记载，名为以实玛利的人是亚伯拉罕与其妻子的女仆所生的儿子，后成为弃儿，在荒野中长大，成为弓箭手，所以才有后面的以实玛利猎杀与被猎杀之说]。随后是奎奎格这位南海叉鱼手、贴心兄弟。麦尔维尔爱这位文身壮汉正如达纳爱“霍普”一样。以实玛利的同屋的到来是件难忘的趣事。后来这两人竟用野人的语言宣誓“结婚”。奎奎格再一次打开了以实玛利心中的爱与人类联系的血肉之门。

“我坐在那孤零零的房里，炉火猛烈燃烧了一阵以后现在火势渐弱了，只有一点点火星儿了。夜色与魔影聚集在窗扉，悄悄窥视我们这沉静的一对：我开始产生某种奇特的感觉。我感到我体内什么在溶化着。我那破碎的心与发疯的手已不再与这狼一样的世界作对，这温柔的野人已把它赎回了。他坐在那儿，他那漠然相儿流露出毫无文明化的虚伪与温情的欺骗的本性。他是野人，很耐看，我开始感到被他神秘地吸引着。”

the wolfish world. This soothing savage had redeemed it. There he sat, his very indifference speaking a nature in which there lurked no civilized hypocrisies and bland deceits. Wild he was; a very sight of sights to see; yet I began to feel myself mysteriously drawn towards him.'

So they smoke together, and are clasped in each other's arms. The friendship is finally sealed when Ishmael offers sacrifice to Queequeg's little idol, Gogo.

'I was a good Christian, born and bred in the bosom of the infallible Presbyterian Church. How then could I unite with the idelater in worshipping his piece of wood? But what is worship? –to do the will of God–that is worship. And what is the will of God? –to do to my fellow man what I would have my fellow man do to me–that is the will of God.'

–Which sounds like Benjamin Franklin, and is hopelessly bad theology. But it is real American logic.

'Now Queequeg is my fellow man. And what do I wish that this Queequeg would do to me? Why, unite with me in my particular Presbyterian form of worship. Consequently, I must unite with him; ergo I must turn idolater. So I kindled the shavings;helped prop up the innocent little idol; offered him burnt biscuit with Quee-

他们一起吸着烟，相拥着。后来当以实玛利为奎奎格的小偶像果果献祭品时，他们的友谊结束了。

“我是一个基督教的圣徒，在一贯正确的长老会教堂里长大的。我怎能与这偶像崇拜者一起崇拜他的木偶像呢?那什么是信仰呢?——实现上帝的意志就是信仰。那什么是上帝的意志呢?——对待我的伙伴就如同我的伙伴对待我一样，这就是上帝的意志。”

这话听起来像本杰明·富兰克林的语言，但却是很坏的神学。不过这是真正的美国逻辑。

“既然奎奎格是我的伙伴了，我希望他对我怎样呢?对了，与我一同遵从长老会的教规和信仰，我定要同他团结一心，为此，我也得变成一个偶像崇拜者。于是我点燃了刨花，竖起单纯的小偶像并供上烤饼干，行了两三次额手礼，吻了他的鼻子。做完这一切，我们就脱衣上床，心安理得了。不过不聊一会儿我们是不会睡的。我不知道这是为什么，但是确实没有比在床上更合适的地方能让朋友之间敞开心扉了。丈夫和妻子就是在床上相互掏心窝子坦诚相见；有些老夫妻常常躺在床上叙旧一直叙到东

queg; salaamed before him twice or thrice; kissed his nose; and that done, we undressed and went to bed, at peace with our own consciences and all the world. But we did not go to sleep without some little chat. How it is I know not; but there is no place like bed for confidential disclosures between friends. Man and wife, they say, open the very bottom of their souls to each other; and some old couples often lie and chat over old times till nearly morning. Thus, then, lay I and Queequeg–a cosy, loving pair–'

You would think this relation with Queequeg meant something to Ishmael. But no. Queequeg is forgotten like yesterday´s newspaper. Human things are only momentary excitements of amusements to the American Ishmael. Ishmael, the hunted, But much more Ishmael the hunter. What´s a Queequeg? What´s a wife? The white whale must be hunted down. Queequeg must be just 'KNOWN', then dropped into oblivion.

And what in the name of fortune is the white whale?

Elsewhere Ishmael says he loved Queequeg´s eyes: 'large, deep eyes, fiery black and bold'. No doubt like Poe, he wanted to get the 'clue' to them. That was all.

方破晓。我和奎奎格也是这样躺着，很相爱的一对儿……"

你可能会以为同奎奎格的这种关系对以实玛利来说很重要吧？不，才不呢。他忘掉了奎奎格就像忘掉了一张昨日的旧报纸。对于美国人以实玛利来说，人间的事不过是一时兴起借此取乐罢了。以实玛利，你这被猎杀的人，不，以实玛利更是猎杀别人的人。奎奎格算怎么回事?妻子算什么?他要去追捕白鲸。至于奎奎格，了解了他就把他忘在脑后了。

那么白鲸到底象征着什么?

以实玛利曾说过他爱奎奎格的眼睛："大而深邃的眼睛，黑亮亮的透着野气与大胆。"毫无疑问，他像爱伦·坡一样要获得了解这目光的"线索"。就这目的。

这两个人从贝德福德来到南图克特，受雇到教友派捕鲸船"佩阔德"号上干活。这太奇特、太神妙、太像幻觉了。这是灵魂的航行，也是一次真正的捕鲸航行，于是我们随着这条奇特的船和这些神奇的船员们来到了大海上。与他们比，阿耳戈英雄 [希腊神话中随依阿宋远航觅取金羊毛的英雄们]只能算老实的羔羊了。尤利西斯曾战胜了赛西女魔和岛上的妖妇们[荷马史诗中

The two men go over from New Bedford to Nantucket, and there sign on to the Quaker whaling ship, the *Pequod*. It is all strangely fantastic, phantasmagoric. The voyage of the soul. Yet curiously a real whaling voyage, too. We pass on into the midst of the sea with this strange ship and its incredible crew. The Argonauts were mild lambs in comparison. And Ulysses went defeating the Cirdes and overcoming the wicked hussies of the isles. But the *Pequod´s* crew is a collection of maniacs fanatically hunting down a lonely, harmless white whale.

As a soul history, it makes one angry. As a sea yarn, it is marvellous: there is always something a bit over the mark, in sea yarns. Should be. Then again the masking up of actual seaman´s experience with sonorous mysticism sometimes gets on one´s nerves. And again, as a revelation of destiny the book is too deep even for sorrow. Profound beyond feeling.

You are some time before you are allowed to see the captain, Ahab: the mysterious Quaker. Oh, it is a God-fearing Quaker ship.

Ahab, the captain. The captain of the soul.

I am the master of my fate,
I am the captain of my soul!

把人变成猪的女魔和仙女或公主]。可“佩阔德”上的船员们却是一个疯狂的群体，他们要捕杀一只孤独、无害的白鲸。

作为一部灵魂的历史，它令人气愤。作为一部海上奇谈，它是神妙的：海上传奇总有那么点子夸张。这也应该。但是给真实的海员经历蒙上一层夸张的神秘感却令人受不了。另外，作为命运的启示录，这本书是太深刻了，绝不只是揭示悲伤。它超越了感觉。

过了好一阵子你才见到船长艾哈伯这个神秘人物。啊，这是一只上帝都怕的船。

艾哈伯船长，灵魂的船长。

“我是我命运的主宰，
我是我灵魂的船长！”

艾哈伯！

“啊/船长/我的船长/我们可怕的航行已走完。”[见惠特曼悼念林肯总统的

Ahab!

'Oh, captain, my captain, our fearful trip is done. '

The gaunt Ahab, Quaker, mysterious person, only shows himself after some days at sea. There's a secret about him! what?

Oh, he's a portentous person. He stumps about on an ivory stump, made from sea-ivory. Mody Dick, the great white whale, tore off Ahab's leg at the knee, when Ahab was attacking him.

Quite right, too. Should have torn off both his legs, and a bit more besides.

But Ahab doesn't think so. Ahab is now a monomaniac. Moby Dick is his monomania. Moby Dick must DIE, or Ahab can't live any longer. Ahab is atheist by this.

All right.

This *Pequod*, ship of the American soul, has three mates.

1. Starbuck: Quaker, Nantucketer, a good responsible man of reason, forethought, intrepidity, what is called a dependable man. At the bottom, afraid.

2. Stubb: 'Fearless as fire, and as mechanical.' Insists on being reckless and jolly on every occasion. Must be afraid too, really.

诗:《啊, 船长, 我的船长! 》]

憔悴的艾哈伯, 这神秘的人, 等船到海上几天后才露面。他这人有个秘密! 是什么?

哦, 他是个不祥的人。他踩在一截海象象牙上。莫比·迪克这条大白鲸在艾哈伯攻击它时把他的腿咬掉了半截。

它做得也对。应该咬掉他的两条腿或更多才是。

可艾哈伯不这样想。此时他已经成了一个偏执狂, 死活要杀莫比·迪克。莫比·迪克必死, 否则艾哈伯就再也活不下去了。

在这一点上他是个无神论者。

很对。

"佩阔德"这艘美国灵魂之舟上有三个大副。

1. 斯塔巴克: 教友派教徒, 南塔克特岛人。他理性强, 责任心强, 思考周密, 坚忍不拔, 是那种靠得住的人。可他内心深处是恐惧。

2. 斯达伯: "无所畏惧的人, 机器般的人。"他鲁莽, 时时处处都嘻嘻哈哈的。他一定也是个怕事的人。

3. Flask: Stubborn, obstinate, without imagination. To him 'the wondrous whale was but a species of magnified mouse or water-rat-'

There you have them: a maniac captain and his three mates, three splendid seamen, admirable whalemen, first-class men at their job.

America!

It is rather like Mr Wilson and his admirable, 'efficient' crew, at the Peace Conference.* Except that none of the Pequodders took their wives along.

A maniac captain of the soul, and three eminently practical mates.

America!

Then such a crew. Renegades, castaways, cannibals: Ishmael, Quakers.

America!

Three giant harpooners to spear the great white whale.

1. Queequeg, the South Sea Islander, all tattooed, big and powerful.

2. Tashtego, the Red Indian of the sea-coast, where the Indian meets the sea.

3. Daggoo, the huge black negro.

There you have them, three savage races, under the American flag, the maniac captain, with their great keen harpoons, ready to spear the white whale.

3. 弗拉斯克：呆板，僵死，毫无想像力。在他眼中，“这条神奇的鲸鱼不过是一只大老鼠或者说是一只水鼠罢了”。

这几个人：一个疯船长和他的三个副手。这是三个优秀的海员，可敬的捕鲸手，第一流的干将。

美国！

这极像威尔逊先生巴黎和会上他那班可敬的、有“效率”的人马[威尔逊总统(1856—1924)曾率团参加1919年的巴黎和会，其夫人随同前往]。所不同的是，“佩阔德”号上的人没有带老婆的。

一个疯狂的船长和三个讲求实际的副手。

美国！

这样的船员：叛徒，流放者，食人肉者。以实玛利，教友派教徒。

美国！

三个身高力强的叉手来叉这条大白鲸。

1. 奎奎格，南太平洋岛民，浑身刺满了文身，高大而强壮。

2. 塔什泰果，生长于海边的红种印第安人。

And only after many days at sea does Ahab's own boat-crew appear on deck. Strange, silent, secret, black-garbed Malays, fire worshipping Parsees. These are to man Ahab's boat, when it leaps in pursuit of that whale.

What do you think of the ship *Pequod*, the ship of the soul of an American?

Many races, many peoples, many nations, under the Stars and Stripes. Beaten with many stripes.

Seeing stars sometimes.

And in a mad ship, under a mad captain, in a mad, fanatic's hunt.

For what?

For Moby Dick, the great white whale.

But splendidly handled. Three splendid mates. The whole thing practical, eminently practical in its working. American industry!

And all this practicality in the service of a mad, mad chase.

Melville manages to keep it a real whaling ship, on a real cruise, in spite of all fanatics. A wonderful, wonderful voyage. And a beauty that is so surpassing only because of the author's awful flounderings in mystical waters. He wanted to get metaphysically deep. And he got deeper than metaphysics. It is a surpassingly beau-

3. 塔果，大块头黑人。

你看到三个野人站在美国国旗下，投身于疯狂的船长麾下，手持锋利的钢叉随时准备叉白鲸。

只是到了海上几天后，艾哈伯自己的船员才出现在甲板上。奇特、神秘、黑皮肤的马来人和崇拜火的帕西人，就是这些人当船员去捕杀鲸鱼。

你是怎么看待“佩阔德”这艘美国灵魂之舟的？

各色种族的人，各个民族的人聚集在星条旗下［美国国旗的蓝底上的星星代表现有州的数目，而红白条则代表建国初期的十三个州］，被抽打得浑身是鞭痕［劳伦斯在此把玩辞藻：鞭痕与星条旗的“条”在英文中都是stripes。原句典出《路加福音》12: 47］。

时不时眩惑，眼冒金星儿。

一条发疯的船，由一个发疯的船长指挥，进行一场疯狂的追捕。

追捕什么？

捕杀莫比·迪克这条大白鲸。

安排得很漂亮。三个优秀的副手。全部工作都很实际。美国的工业！

tiful book, with an awful meaning, and bad jolts.

It is interesting to compare Melville with Dana, about the albatross–Melville a bit sententious.

'I remember the first albatross I ever saw. It was during a prolonged gale in waters hard upon the Antarctic seas. From my forenoon watch below I ascended to the overcrowded deck, and there, lashed upon the main hatches, I saw a regal feathered thing of unspotted whiteness, and with a booked Roman bill sublime. At intervals it arched forth its vast, archangel wings–wondrous throbbings and flutterings shook it. Though bodily unharmed, it uttered cries, as some King's ghost in supernatural distress. Through its inexpressible strange eyes I thought I peeped to secrets not below the heavens–the white thing was so white, its wings so wide, and in those for ever exiled waters, I had lost the miserable warping memories of traditions and of towns. I assert then, that in the wondrous bodily whiteness of the bird chiefly lurks the secret of the spell–'

Melville's albatross is a prisoner, caught by a bait on a hook.

Well, I have seen an albatross, too: following us in waters hard upon the Antarctic, too, south of Australia. And in the Southern winter. And the ship, a P. and

这一切实际性的东西都为这疯狂又疯狂的追捕服务。

麦尔维尔总算能让这艘船看上去像一条真的捕鲸船，走的是一条真正的航道，尽管一切都显得有点疯狂。美妙，极美妙的航行。它显示出超常的美，只是因了这作者在神秘的海水中拼命的挣扎，他试图达到超验的深奥，于是他变得比玄学派更深邃。这是一本美不胜收的书，寓意不凡。

把麦尔维尔与达纳做一比较是很有趣的，比较一下他们对信天翁的描述，可见麦尔维尔有点说教味儿。

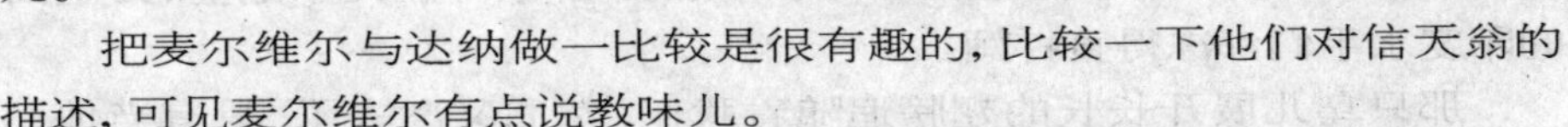

“我还记得我见到的第一只信天翁。那是在南极附近的海面上狂风大作经久不息的时候。我从午前的瞭望哨上到挤满人群的甲板上，看到一只洁白无瑕、长着高贵羽毛的鸟儿在扑打着主舱，这鸟儿的鹰钩鼻子很有罗马气度。它不时地振动一下那两扇宽大的翅膀——奇妙地抽动、颤抖着。尽管没人伤害它的躯体，可它仍旧发出某种超自然的悲鸣。透过它那奇特莫测的眼睛，我觉得我窥视到了不属于人世的秘密——它太洁

O. boat, nearly empty. And the lascar crew shivering.

The bird with its long, long wings following, then leaving us. No one knows till they have tried, how lost, how lonely those Southern waters are. And glimpses of the Australian coast.

It makes one feel that our day is only a day. That in the dark of the night ahead other days stir fecund, when we have lapsed from existence.

Who knows how utterly we shall lapse.

But Melville keeps up his disquisition about 'whiteness'. The great abstract fascinated him. The abstract where we end, and cease to be. White or black. Our white, abstract end!

Then again it is lovely to be at sea on the *Pequod*, with never a grain of earth to us.

It was a cloudy, sulfry afternoon; the seamen were lazily lounging about the decks, or vacantly gazing over into the lead-coloured waters. Queequeg and I were mildly employed weaving what is called a sword-mat, for an additional lashing to our boat. So still and subdued, and yet somehow preluding was all the scene, and such an incantation of reverie lurked in the air that each silent sailor seemed re-

白了，它的翅膀太宽大了，它永远流放在水域上。看着它，我几乎把传统和城市忘却。我敢说，从这鸟儿神奇的白色躯体内勃发出的是神咒的秘密——"

麦尔维尔笔下的信天翁是一个被带诱饵的钩子钩住的囚犯。

我也见过一只信天翁。那也是在靠近南极的澳大利亚南部水面上，它就尾随着我们的船。那还是南半球的冬季，那条邮船几乎是空的。上面的印度水手们都冻得直打颤。

那只鸟儿展开长长的翅膀追随着我们，然后又离去了，只有当他们有了经历，他们才知道那南极水域是多么令人茫然、是多么孤独。只需扫一眼澳大利亚海岸就会知道这一点。

它令人感到我们的一天只是一天。接下来的黑夜里，当我们的存在消失后将有更多天躁动。

天晓得我们是否会彻底消失。

可麦尔维尔试图继续他对"白"的探究。某种抽象奥妙的东西令他着

solved into his own invisible self–

In the midst of this preluding silence came the first cry: 'There she blows! there! there! there! She blows! ' And then comes the first chase, a marvellous piece of true sea–writing, the sea, and sheer sea–beings on the chase, sea–creatures chased. There is scarcely a taint of earth–pure sea–motion.

'Give way, men, 'whispered Starbuck, drawing still further aft the sheet of his sail; 'there is time to kill a fish yet before the squall comes. There´s white water again! –Close to! –Spring! ' Soon after, two cries in quick succession on each side of us denoted that the other boats had got fast; but hardly were they overheard, when with a lightning–like hurtling whisper Starbuck said: 'Stand up! ' and Qucequeg, harpoon in hand, sprang to his feet. –Though not one of the oarsmen was then facing the life and death peril so close to them ahead, yet, their eyes on the intense countenance of the mate in the stern of the boat, they knew that the imminent instant had come; they heard, too, an enormous wallowing sound, as of fifty elephants stirring in their litter. Meanwhile the boat was still booming through the mist, the waves curbing and hissing around us like the erected crests of enraged serpents.

'That´s his hump. There! –There, give it to him! 'whispered Starbuck. –A short

迷。这就是我们的末日，我们的生命终止于斯。或白或黑。我们白人会莫名其妙地终止！

乘“佩阔德”号出海是太美了，上面没有一点泥土。

“这是一个阴云密布、燠热难耐的下午，海员们懒洋洋地在甲板上踱步，茫然地看着铅灰色的水面。奎奎格和我慢慢编着甲板上的席子，用来防备大风的再次袭击。整个场面显得憋闷，似有什么事要发生，空气中弥散着一种梦的咒语，每个海员似乎都溶解隐没了——”

就在这战前的宁静中，突然传来一声大叫：“它在那儿！在那儿！在那儿！在那儿！它窜出来了！”随后开始了第一次捕杀，这是一篇绝妙的真正的海上诗篇。大海，追杀中的海生物，被捕杀的海生物。没有大陆的气息，全然是大海的涌动。

“让开，兄弟，”斯塔巴克喃喃着把船头的风帆拉得更紧绷。“暴风到来之前还有时间杀这条大鱼。翻白沫了！近点！叉！”紧接着，两边传来的迅速叫喊声说明别的船也加快了速度，不过听不到它们的声响。突然斯

rushing sound leapt out of the boat; it was the darted iron of Queequeg. Then all in one welded motion came a push from astern, while forward the boat seemed striking on a ledge; the sail collapsed and exploded; a gush of scalding vapour shot up near by; something rolled and tumbled like an earthquake beneath us. The whole crew were half suffocated as they were tossed helter-skelter into the white curling cream of the squall. Squall, whale, and harpoon had all blended together; and the whale, merely grazed by the iron, escaped-

Melville is a master of violent, chaotic physical motion; he can keep up a whole wild chase without a flaw. He is as perfect at creating stillness. The ship is cruising on the Carrol Ground, south of St Helena. -

'It was while gliding through these latter waters that one serene and moonlight night, when all the waves rolled by like scrolls of silver; and by their soft, suffusing seethings, made what seemed a silvery silence, not a solitude; on such a silent night a silvery jet was seen far in advance of the white bubbles at the bow-'

Then there is the description of brit.

'Steering north-eastward from the Crozetts we fell in with vast meadows of brit, the minute, yellow substance upon which the Right Whale largely feeds. For leagues

塔巴克哑着嗓门儿叫道:“起来!”奎奎格手持钢叉一跃而起。尽管水手们并未面临生死攸关的时刻,可他们从船尾上大副那紧张的神情中可知,紧要关头到了。他们还听到一声惊天动地的巨响,似乎有五十头大象在怒吼。同时这艘船也在吼叫,巨浪刷刷滚滚翻涌着,就像无数毒蛇发怒后钻出水面的蛇头。”

“那是它的背。在那儿,在那儿,叉它!”斯塔巴克低声叫着。随之鱼叉飞出船舷,这是奎奎格掷出的,一瞬间,从船尾冲过一股推力,船向前冲去似乎要撞到暗礁上去。篷帆落下来破了。附近升腾起一团蒸汽,只觉得船下有什么东西翻滚、震荡着如同发生了地震。全部船员几乎被暴风卷起的浪涛所窒息,忙乱成一团。暴风雨,鲸鱼和钢叉都搅在一起。而那条几乎被叉住的鲸鱼则乘机逃跑了——”

麦尔维尔在描述剧烈混乱的场景方面是一位大师,他可以毫无缺憾地一口气把这场疯狂的追捕写下来。在写静方面他同样出色。捕鲸船这时正在圣·赫勒拿岛南面的凯罗·格兰德附近航行。

and leagues it undulated round us, so that we seemed to be sailing through boundless fields of ripe and golden wheat. On the second day, numbers of Right Whales were seen, who, secure from the attack of a Sperm Whaler like the *Pequod*, with open jaws sluggishly swam through the brit, which, adhering to the fringing fibres of that wondrous Venetian blind in their mouths, was in that manner separated from the water that escaped at the lip. As moving mowers who, side by side, slowly and seethingly advance their scythes through the long wet grass of the marshy meads; even so these monsters swam, making a strange grassy, cutting sound; and leaving behind them endless swaths of blue on the yellow sea. But it was only the sound they made as they parted the brit which at all reminded one of mowers. Seen from the mast-heads, especially when they paused and were stationary for a while, their vast black forms looked more like lifeless masses of rock than anything else- '

This beautiful passage brings us to the apparition of the squid.

'Slowly wading through the meadows of brit, the *Pequod* still held her way northeastward towards the island of Java; a gentle air impelling her keel, so that in the surrounding serenity her three tall, tapering masts mildly waved to that languid breeze, as three mild palms on a plain. And still, at wide intervals, in the silvery

“在一个月光皎洁的静夜，银色的海浪荡漾着。柔和的海面一片银白、寂静，倒不显孤独。在这样一个静夜里，可看到白浪包围的船头前有一块银色的东西——”

还有一段有关小鲱鱼的描写：

“从克罗塞兹向东北方向驶去，我们遇上了一大群小鲱鱼，这种小黄鱼是鲸鱼的食物。一群又一群的小鲱鱼翻涌着包围我们，我们似乎是在一望无垠的成熟的金黄麦田中航行。第二天就出现了无数大鲸鱼。它们没有受到过‘佩阔德’这种捕鲸船的捕杀，此时正张着大嘴缓缓地穿过鲱鱼群游过来。这群小鲱鱼就聚在鲸鱼那一张张百叶帘式的大口边沿，就那么离开了水面。鲸鱼像一台台割草机一样并排缓行，携着浪头劈开这些小鱼群。这些魔鬼边游边咬着发出奇特的轧草声，在它们身后的黄色水面上扫出一条长长的蓝色。只是它们劈开鲱鱼群的声音令人想起割草机。从桅杆顶上向下看，当它们停下不动的那一刻，它们真像一片黑压压毫无生气的大石头——”

night, that lonely alluring jet would be seen.

'But one transparent-blue morning, when a stillness almost preter-natural spread over the sea, however unattended with any stagnant calm; when the long burnished sunglade on the waters seemed a golden finger laid across them, enjoining secrecy; when all the slippered waves whispered together as they softly ran on; in this profound hush of the visible sphere a strange spectre was seen by Daggoo from the main-mast head.

'In the distance, a great white mass lazily rose, and rising higher and higher, and disentangling itself from the azure, at last gleamed before our prow like a snow-slide, new slid from the hills. Thus glistening for a moment, as slowly it subsided, and sank. Then once more arose, and silently gleamed. It seemed not a whale; and yet, is this Moby Dick? thought Daggoo-'

The boats were lowered and pulled to the scene.

'In the same spot where it sank, once more it slowly rose. Almost forgetting for the moment all thoughts of Moby Dick, we now gazed at the most wondrous phenomenon which the secret seas have hitherto revealed to manking. A vast pulpy mass, furlongs in length and breadth, of a glancing cream-colour, lay floating on the

从这段优美的描写进而转向对幻象般的鱿鱼的描述。

"'佩阔德'在草甸子般的鲱鱼群中穿行着向东北方的扎瓦岛驶去。轻风徐徐地抚着船身，在一片寂静中，船上的三顶大桅杆随微风摇曳正如同三只温厚的手掌抚在平原上。但是在银色的月夜里，还时而见得到那块迷人孤独的黑东西。

"清晨，天空呈现出透明的蓝色，某种不可思议的寂静笼罩着海面，海水一片平静。狭长亮闪闪的阳光似一根金色的手指头抚着水面，把玩着海的神秘。光洁的海浪齐声呢喃轻轻翻滚。这一望无垠的静寂海面上竟出现了一个奇特的鬼影，这是塔果在主桅杆上见到的。

"在远方，有一大块白东西懒洋洋地耸起来，越耸越高，脱离了蓝色的水面，最终像雪崩一样在我们的船头崩裂。它的光芒瞬间即逝，随之陷入海里，然后又耸起，静静地闪光。这看上去并不像一条鲸鱼。也没准是莫比·迪克吧?塔果想——"

一艘艘小船降下到海面上。

water, innumerable long arms radiating from its centre, and curling and twisting like a nest of anacondas, as if blindly to clutch at any hapless object within reach. No perceptible face or front did it have; no conceivable token of either sensation or instinct; but undulated there on the billows, an unearthly, formless, chance-like apparition of life. And with a low sucking it slowly disappeared again.

The following chapters, with their account of whale hunts, the killing, the stripping, the cutting up, are magnificent records of actual happening. Then comes the queer tale of the meeting of the *Jeroboam*, a whaler met at sea, all of whose men were under the domination of a religious maniac, one of the ship's hands. There are detailed descriptions of the actual taking of the sperm oil from a whale's head. Dilating on the smallness of the brain of a sperm whale, Melville significantly remarks–'for I believe that much of man's character will be found betokened in his backbone. I would rather feel your spine than your skull, whoever you are–'And of the whale, he adds:

'For, viewed in this light, the wonderful comparative smallness of his brain proper is more than compensated by the wonderful comparative magnitude of his spinal cord. '

"就在它陷下去的地方它重又缓缓耸起来。一时间我们都不去想什么莫比·迪克了，只顾凝视神秘的大海此时此地向人类展示的神奇景观。一团二米见方的奶黄色肉体漂在水上，长着无数长长的臂膀，如同一群蟒蛇一样扭动着似乎盲目地扑向什么目标。它没有一张清楚的面孔和正面，没有迹象表明它有感觉和本能。可它在浪尖上随波起伏，似一个奇幻、无形的偶然生命。接着，它又被大海缓缓吸进去。"

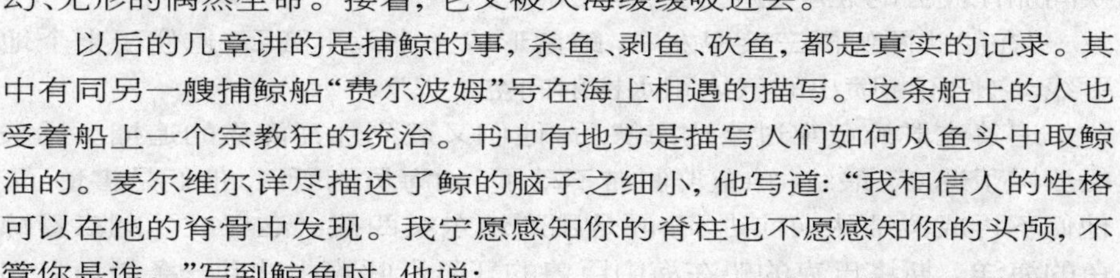

以后的几章讲的是捕鲸的事，杀鱼、剥鱼、砍鱼，都是真实的记录。其中有同另一艘捕鲸船"费尔波姆"号在海上相遇的描写。这条船上的人也受着船上一个宗教狂的统治。书中有地方是描写人们如何从鱼头中取鲸油的。麦尔维尔详尽描述了鲸的脑子之细小，他写道："我相信人的性格可以在他的脊骨中发现。我宁愿感知你的脊柱也不愿感知你的头颅，不管你是谁。"写到鲸鱼时，他说：

"从这一点看，那奇妙的脑袋虽小，可是它的脊髓却容量极大，补充了脑的容量。"

In among the rush of terrible awful hunts, come touches of pure beauty.

'As the three boats lay there on that gently rolling sea, gazing down into its eternal blue noon; and as not a single groan or cry of any sort, nay not so much as a ripple or a thought, came up from its depths; what landsman would have thought that beneath all that silence and placidity the utmost monster of the seas was writhing and wrenching in agony! '

Perhaps the most stupendous chapter is the one called The Grand Armada, at the beginning of Volume Ⅲ. The *Pequod* was drawing through the Sunda Straits towards Java when she came upon a vast host of sperm whales.

'Broad on both bows, at a distance of two or three miles, and forming a great semicircle embracing one-half of the level horizon, a continuous chain of whale-jets were up-playing and sparkling in the noonday air. '

Chasing this great herd, past the Straits of Sunda, themselves chased by Javan pirates, the whalers race on. Then the boats are lowered. At last that curious state of inert irresolution came over the whales, when they were, as the seamen say, gallied. Instead of forging ahead in huge martial array they swam violently hither and thither, a surging sea of whales, no longer moving on. Starbuck's boat, made fast to a

在可怕的捕杀过程中也有些纯美的景象。

"这三条船伏在微波荡漾的海面上，凝视着这里永久的蓝色正午。没有人呻吟或叫喊，没有，一点没有。陆地上的人无论如何也想像不出，就在这静谧与安宁之下，海中最凶的魔王正在痛苦地挣扎、扭动着！"

或许最惊人的章节是第三卷始初的"大船"。"佩阔德"号穿过桑达海峡向加瓦驶去的途中遇上了一群大鲸鱼。

"在船头两侧两三英里左右，鲸鱼形成一个大半圆圈，遮住了半个地平线，它们不断喷出的气体和水柱射向空中。"

追着这群鲸鱼穿过桑达海峡后，他们又遭到加瓦海盗的追捕。后来船放慢了速度。最终，鲸鱼群僵滞不动了，如海员们所说，他们是害怕了。他们不再成群结队向前进发，而是剧烈地东突西撞。这里成了翻滚着鲸鱼的海洋。斯塔巴克的船在海中巨兽的狂吼乱呼声中冲向一条鲸鱼。它疯狂地穿过沸沸扬扬的怪兽群落，直驶到一个清澈的环礁湖。四周是发疯的鲸鱼群，而这里则是一派宁静。母鲸们正安详地游弋，小鲸则嗅着捕

whale, is towed in amongst this howling Leviathan chaos. In mad career it cockles through the boiling surge of monsters, till it is brought into a clear lagoon in the very centre of the vast, mad, terrified herd. There a sleek, pure calm reigns. There the females swam in peace, and the young whales came snuffing tamely at the boat, like dogs, And there the astonished seamen watched the love-making of these amazing monsters, mammals, now in rut far down in the sea-

'But far beneath this wondrous world upon the surface, another and still stranger world met our eyes, as we gazed over the side. For, suspended in these watery vaults, floated the forms of the nursing mothers of the whales, and those that by their cnormous girth seemed shortly to become mothers. The lake, as I have hinted, was to a considerable depth exceedingly transparent; and as human infants while sucking will calmly and fixedly gaze away from the breast, as if leading two different lives at a time; and while yet drawing moral nourishment, be still spiritually feasting upon some unearthly reminiscence, even so did the young of these whales seem looking up towards us, but not at us, as if we were but a bit of gulf-weed in their newborn sight. Floating on their sides, the mothers also seemed quietly eyeing us. - Some of the subtlest sccrets of the seas seemed divulged to us in this enchanted

鲸船，像一条条小狗。海员们吃惊地看着这些鬼怪们做爱，它们正在发情期，在海上——

“在这奇妙幻景下面你会发现另一个更为陌生的世界。鲸妈妈在海面上为小鲸哺奶，还有一些膨胀着鱼腹的鲸，一眼看上去就知道它们要做妈妈了。如前所说，这环礁湖很深，很清澈。那些小鲸婴正在咂乳。婴儿在吃奶时常常要把目光移开母乳沉静凝视别处，似乎在同一时刻做两件事。一边吃奶一边追忆什么不可思量的东西过一种精神生活。这些鲸孩也是这样，它们抬头看着我们(其实并没真看)，似乎在它们幼小眼里我们不过是一些芦草。妈妈们在孩子周围游着，目光同样安详地落在我们身上。这迷人的环礁湖似乎向我们展示了大海自身最微妙的秘密。我们在海中看到海中巨兽们的爱侣。尽管受着这样那样的种种恐吓，这些不可思议的动物仍旧自由自在、无所畏惧，是的，它们自由自在地过着放浪欢愉的生活——”

捕鲸的过程中着实有些惊心动魄之处，几乎是超人和非人的场面，

pond. We saw young Leviathan amours in the deep. And thus, though surrounded by circle upon circle of consternation and affrights, did these inscrutable creatures at the centre freely and fearlessly indulge in all peaceful concernments; yea, serenely revelled in dalliance and delight–'

There is something really overwhelming in these whale–hunts, almost superhuman or inhuman, bigger than life, more terrific than human activity. The same with the chapter on ambergris: it is so curious, so real, yet so unearthly. And again in the chapter called *The Cassock* –surely the oldest piece of phallicism in all the world's literature.

After this comes the amazing account of the Try–works, when the ship is turned into the sooty, oily factory in mid–ocean, and the oil is extracted from the blubber. In the night of the red furnace burning on deck, at sea, Melville has his startling experience of reversion. He is at the helm, but has turned to watch the fire: when suddenly he feels the ship rushing backward from him, in mystic reversion–

'Uppermost was the impression, that whatever swift, rushing thing I stood on was not so much bound to any haven ahead, as rushing from all havens astern. A stark bewildering feeling, as of death, came over me. Convulsively my hands grasped

大于生活，比人的活动更有趣。写龙涎香的那一章即是如此，极其奇特，但真实而神妙。《教士的黑长袍》这一章是世界文学中最早的阳物描述。

这以后是对炼鲸油炉子的描述。这艘船在大海上变成了一座灰尘飞扬、油乎乎的炼油厂。这些油是从鲸脂中提炼出的。就在炼油炉高燃的那一夜，麦尔维尔惊异地产生了一种倒退感。他在舵轮里盯着炉子中的火，此时他突然感到船神秘地离开他向后滑去——

"我深深感到，我无论站在什么飞快行驶的东西上，我都不觉得它在驶向任何港湾，倒像是从港湾向后倒冲。我感到某种死样的东西攫住了我。于是我的双手抽动着握住舵柄，可我感到这舵柄有些在迷狂中向相反方向转。天啊，我这是怎么了！"

这种梦样的经历是一种实在的心灵经验。他命令所有的人别去看那炉火，那红色的火焰映得一切东西都现出鬼色。似乎是他盯着火的目光引起了倒退毁灭的恐惧。

或许是吧。他是个海生动物。

the tiller, but with the crazy conceit that the tiller was, somehow, in some enchanted way,inverted. My God! What is the matter with me, I thought! '

This dream-experience is a real soul-experience. He ends with an injunction to all men, not to gaze on the red fire when its redness makes all things look ghastly. It seems to him that his gazing on fire has evoked this horror of reversion, undoing.

Perhaps it had. He was water-born.

After some unhealthy work on the ship, Queequeg caught a fever and was like to die.

'How he wasted and wasted in those few, long-lingering days, till there seemed but little left of him but his frame and tattooing. But as all else in him thinned, and his cheek-bones grew sharper, his eyes, nevertheless, seemed growing fuller and fuller; they took on a strangeness of lustre; and mildly but deeply looked out at you there from his sickness, a wondrous testimony to that immortal health in him which could not die, or be weakened. And like circles on the water, which as they grow fainter, expand; so his eyes seemed rounding and rounding, like the circles of Eternity. An awe that cannot be named would steal over you as you sat by the side of

奎奎格因为做了些有损于健康的工作生病了，快要死去了。

“那漫长的几日里，他消耗着，最终形销骨立，只剩下一把骨头和文身，他瘦干了，颧骨凸出，可他的眼睛却愈来愈大。这双眼睛带上了某种奇特的欲望。他的目光柔和而深邃，看着你，在证实他永恒的健康，他不会死，不会虚弱下去。如同水上的涟漪，圈子越宽，漪纹愈浅淡，他的眼睛圆睁着，像是永恒的光圈，你坐在这个衰弱下去的野人身旁，会感到一种难以言状的恐惧袭上心头——”

可是奎奎格没有死。“佩阔德”也出了东海峡来到广渺的太平洋上。“对于沉思中的流浪占星师，这宁静的太平洋永远是他的选择。这里奔涌着的是世界中心的水。”

战斗仍在太平洋继续。

“已是夕阳西下之时，叉鱼的血战已结束，船在夕阳辉映下美丽的大海上航行，太阳和鲸鱼都死了。空中弥漫着喜气与悲哀——祈祷的花圈在玫瑰色的天空中卷起，似乎从遥远的马尼拉群岛上绿色的修道院里吹

this waning savage-'

But Queequeg did not die-and the *Pequod* emerges from the Eastern Straits, into the full Pacific. 'To any meditative Magian rover, this serene Pacific once beheld, must ever after be the sea of his adoption. It rolls the midmost waters of the world-'

In this Pacific the fights go on:

'It was far down the afternoon, and when all the spearings of the crimson fight were done, and floating in the lovely sunset sea and sky, sun and whale both stilly died together; then such a sweetness and such a plaintiveness, such inwreathing orisons curled up in that rosy air, that it almost seemed as if far over from the deep green convent valleys of the Manila isles, the Spanish land-breeze had gone to sea, freighted with these vesper hymns. Soothed again, but only soothed to deeper gloom, Ahab, who had sterned off from the whale, sat intently watching his final wanings from the now tranquil boat. For that strange spectacle, observable in all sperm whales dying-the turning of the head sunwards, and so expiring-that strange spectacle, beheld of such a placid evening, somehow to Ahab conveyed wondrousness unknown before. "He turns and turns him to it; how slowly, but how steadfastly, his homage-rendering and invoking brow, with his last dying motions. He too worships

来的风，和着晚钟的鸣声吹向大海。艾哈伯感到欣慰，但愈感忧虑。他坐着，全神贯注盯着鲸鱼离开这条平静的船。这是一场奇景，鲸鱼临死之前，头朝向太阳，然后死去，这宁静夜色中的奇观似对艾哈伯展示出他以前不曾懂得的奇妙。'它一次次转向太阳，缓慢但坚定，它在拜神，临死前它的眉毛在祈祷。它也崇拜火……'"

艾哈伯喃喃自语着。热血动物鲸鱼最后一次转向太阳，是太阳把它生育在水中的。

可在下一章中我们发现，艾哈伯崇拜的其实是雷电。他从头到脚都烙下了雷电的痕迹。那是暴风雨和雷电袭击"佩阔德"号时，雷电给桅杆顶上带来巨大的火球，指南针也改变了方向。后来一切都完了，生命自身神秘地改变了。这些捕杀莫比·迪克的杀手们只有疯狂与占有欲。船长艾哈伯同低能的黑人孩子此普手拉手一起前行。他曾被残酷地甩下，一个人在海上游着水。现在是这太阳的低能儿同这个北方的偏执狂、船长和主人同行。

fire…"'

So Ahab soliloquizes: and so the warm-blooded whale turns for the last time to the sun, which begot him in the waters.

But as we see in the next chapter, it is the Thunder-fire which Ahab really worships: that living sundering fire of which he bears the brand, from head to foot; it is storm, the electric storm of the *Pequod*, when the corposants burn in high, tapering flames of supernatural pallor upon the masthead, and when the compass is reversed. After this all is fatality. Life itself seems mystically reversed. In these hunters of Moby Dick there is nothing but madness and possession. The captain, Ahab, moves hand in hand with the poor imbecile negro boy, Pip, who has been so cruelly demented, left swimming alone in the vast sea. It is the imbecile child of the sun hand in hand with the northern monomaniac, captain and master.

The voyage surges on. They meet one ship, then another. It is all ordinary day-routine, and yet all is a tension of pure madness and horror, the approaching horror of the last fight.

'Hither and thither, on high, glided the snow-white wings of small unspecked birds; these were the gentle thoughts of the feminine air; but to and fro in the

船仍在继续行进，他们遇到了另一些船。全都是日常琐事，却充满了紧张、疯狂和恐惧，直到最后一场拼杀。

"洁白无瑕的鸟儿展着雪白的翅膀在空中飞翔，空气是温柔女性化的。可在海中，在蓝色的深渊处却滚动着巨大的水中怪兽鲸鱼、箭鱼和鲨鱼。这才是雄性的海，充满了力度和杀机——"

这一天，艾哈伯承认他太疲倦了，承受不住压力了。"斯塔巴克，我看上去很老吗?非常非常老吗?我感到头晕，腰酸，背痛，好像我是乐园之后蹒跚了无数个世纪的亚当。"这里是艾哈伯决战前的喀西玛尼园[耶路撒冷附近的花园，耶稣基督上十字架前在这里度过了最后一夜]，这是人类的灵魂寻找自我征服的喀西玛尼园，是无限的意识取得的最后成就。

最终他们发现了那条鲸。艾哈伯上到桅杆上看到了它。"从这儿看过去，鲸鱼离我们有个几英里样子，在浪涛中耸起它光闪闪的脊背，一口又一口地向空中喷着气。"

小船都降下来，向白鲸靠拢。

deeps, far down in the bottomless blue, rushed mighty leviathans, sword-fish and sharks; and these were the strong, troubled, murderous thinkings of the masculine sea-'

On this day Ahab confesses his weariness, the weariness of his burden. 'But do I look very old, so very, very old, Starbuck? I feel deadly faint, and bowed, and humped, as though I were Adam staggering beneath the piled centuries since Paradise-' It is the Gethsemane of Ahab, before the last fight: the Gethsemane of the human soul seeking the last self-conquest, the last attainment of extended consciousness-infinite consciousness.

At last they sight the whale. Ahab sees him from his hoisted perch at the masthead- 'From this height the whale was now seen some mile or so ahead, at every roll of the sea revealing his high, sparkling hump, and regularly jetting his silent spout into the air. '

The boats are lowered, to draw near the white whale.

'At length the breathless hunter came so nigh his seemingly unsuspectful prcy that his entire dazzling hump was distinctly visible, sliding along the sea as if an isolated thing, and continually set in a revolving ring of finest, fleecy, greenish foam.

“最终捕鲸手屏住呼吸靠近他那似乎没有什么警觉的猎物，但见白鲸的脊背露出水面，像一个孤独的东西在水中畅游，不停地搅起一圈漂亮、毛茸茸的蓝色泡沫。他看到了远处微微露出的头在水面上搅起的大片涟漪。在它前面的远方，柔和如土耳其地毯的水面上它白色的宽额头闪着光芒，一圈圈波纹伴着它的影子。它的后面，蓝色的海水不停地涌满它身后留下的水涡。它的两侧明亮的水泡在欢舞，忽而飞来一群欢快的水鸟，它们那成百双轻足划破了水面。船上破损的桅杆在鲸鱼身后耸立着，看似叉在鱼背上。时而有一群水鸟飞来飞去遮住这条鲸，小鸟儿悄然站在桅杆上，杆顶上的羽毛像一面面小旗子在飞扬。

“轻松愉快——在激流中歇息，鲸鱼在这里游荡。”

与鲸鱼的搏斗太精彩、太可怕了，无法引用其中一节来概括它。这场搏斗连续了三天整。帕西叉鲸手的尸体前日被撕碎，现在又被鱼叉掀到白鲸身边，这幅可怕的图景令人产生神秘、梦一样的恐惧。那可怕、被激怒的白鲸与捕鲸船厮打起来，这船是我们这个文明世界的象征。它猛烈

He saw the vast involved wrinkles of the slightly projecting head, beyond. Before it, far out on the soft, Turkish rugged waters, went the glistening white shadow from his broad milky forehead, a musical rippling playfully accompanying the shade; and behind, the blue waters interchangeably flowed over the moving valley of his steady make; and on either side bright bubbles arose and danced by his side. But these were broken again by the light toes of hundreds of gay fowl softly feathering the sea, alternate with their fitful flight; and like to some flagstaff rising from the pointed hull of an argosy, the tall but shattered pole of a recent lance projected from the white whale´s back; and at intervals one of the clouds of soft-toed fowls hovering, and to and fro shimmering like a canopy over the fish, silently perched and rocked on this pole, the long tail-feathers streaming like pennons. '

A gentle joyousness-a mighty mildness of repose in swiftness, invested the gliding whale-

The fight with the whale is too wonderful and too awful, to be quoted apart from the book. It lasted three days. The fearful sight, on the third day, of the torn body of the Parsee harpooner, lost on the previous day, now seen lashed on to the flanks of the white whale by the tangle of harpoon lines, has a mystic dream-horror. The aw-

地冲撞着捕鲸船，不一会儿，最后一条捕鲸小船上传来一声叫喊：

"'船！天啊，大船哪儿去了？'很快，人们透过昏暗的光线惊讶地发现正在倾斜的船影，它真像一个蒸发气体的海市蜃楼。只有桅杆顶还露出水面来。那些异教徒叉鱼手似忠诚，似昏头涨脑，仍旧坚守着岗位，在沉船上还忘不了盯住海面。现在这孤独的船陷入了绝境，它上面的全体船员、漂荡的桨橹和叉鱼枪，不管是生的还是死的都在漩涡中沉浮打旋，漩涡终于把'佩阔德'的最后一点痕迹吞没了——"

天鸟，雄鹰，圣约翰之鸟，印第安之鸟，美国，都随这条船下沉了。精神的雄鹰。下沉！

"现在，小小的飞鸟们在懒散的海湾上鸣叫着飞翔。阴郁的白浪拍击着悬崖般的海岸。随后一切都下沉了，大海铺天盖地而来，像尸布一样，如同五千年前一样翻腾。"

一部世界上最奇特、最美妙的小说就这样结束了，它的神秘及其痛苦的象征之页合上了。这是一部海的史诗，没有第二个人写得出。它又是

ful and infuriated whale turns upon the ship, symbol of this civilized world of ours. He smites her with a fearful shock. And a few minutes later, from the last of the fighting whale-boats comes the cry:

'The ship! Great God, where is the ship?'Soon they, through dim bewildering mediums, saw her sidelong fading phantom, as in the gaseous *Fata Morgana*; only the uppermost masts out of the water; while fixed by infatuation, or fidelity, or fate, to their once lofty perches, the pagan harpooners still maintained their sinking look-outs on the sea. And now concentric circles seized the lone boat itself, and all its crew, and each floating oar, and every lance-pole, and spinning, animate and inanimate, all round and round in one vortex, carried the smallest chip of the *Pequod* out of sight-

The bird of heaven, the eagle, St John's bird, the Red Indian bird, the American, goes down with the ship, nailed by Tashtego's hammer, the hammer of the American Indian. The eagle of the spirit. Sunk!

'Now small fowls flew screaming over the yet yawning gulf; a sullen white surf beat againgst its steep sides; then all collapsed; and the great shroud of the sea rolled on as it rolled five thousand years ago.'

So ends one of the strangest and most wonderful books in the world, closing up

一部奇异象征、寓意深远而又令人疲惫的书。

它是一本了不起的书，很了不起的书，是迄今最伟大的写海的书。它令人灵魂生畏。

厄运。

末日。

末日！末日！末日！有什么东西似乎在极黑暗的美国之树里呢喃着末日。末日！

什么的末日呢？

是我们白人之日的末日。我们要完了，要完了。美国体内孕育着末日。我们白人的日子寿数已尽。

哦，如果我寿数已尽了，我的末日比决定了我末日的我更伟大。所以，我接受我的末日，它是伟大的象征，比我更伟大。

麦尔维尔懂这一点。他知道他的种族末日到了。他的白人灵魂的末日到了。他那伟大的白人时代末日到了。他自己的末日到了。理想主义

its mystery and its tortured symbolism. It is an epic of the sea such as no man has equalled; and it is a book of esoteric symbolism of profound significance, and of considerable tiresomeness.

But it is a great book, a very great book, the greatest book of the sea ever written. It moves awe in the soul.

The terrible fatality.

Fatality.

Doom.

Doom! Doom! Doom! Something seems to whisper it in the very dark trees of America. Doom!

Doom of what?

Doom of our white day. We are doomed, doomed. And the doom is in America. The doom of our white day.

Ah, well, if my day is doomed, and I am doomed with my day, it is something greater than I which dooms me, so I accept my doom as a sign of the greatness which is more than I am.

Melville knew. He knew his race was doomed. His white soul, doomed. His great white epoch, doomed. Himself, doomed. The idealist, doomed. The spirit,

者的末日到了。精神要完了。

倒退。“不是驶向任何港湾，而是远离所有的港湾。”

我们的巨大恐惧，是我们文明的倒退，远离港湾。

最后一次可怖的追捕。白鲸。

莫比·迪克到底是个什么物件？它是白种人最深层的血性生命，是我们深层中的血性。

可它却受着我们白人意识中疯狂偏执的捕杀。我们要把它追个走投无路，令它屈从于我们的意志。在这场自我捕杀中我们请了黑种人与浅肤色种人来帮忙，有红种人、黄种人和黑种人，有东方的也有西方的，有教友派的也有敬火派的，我们让他们全卷入了这场疯狂的捕杀，这其实是我们的末日，是自戕。

白种人最后一个阳具。被逼入理智和理想意志的绝境。我们的血性屈从了我们的意志。我们的血性意识被寄生其上的大脑或理想意识削弱了活力。

doomed.

The reversion. 'Not so much bound to any haven ahead, as rushing from all havens astern. '

That great horror of ours! It is our civilization rushing from all havens astern.

The last ghastly hunt. The White Whale.

What then is Moby Dick? He is the deepest blood-being of the white race; he is our deepest blood-nature.

And he is hunted, hunted, hunted by the maniacal fanaticism of our white mental consciousness. We want to hunt him down. To subject him to our will. And in this maniacal conscious hunt of ourselves we get dark races and pale to help us, red, yellow, and black, east and west, Quaker and fire-worshipper, we get them all to help us in this ghastly maniacal hunt which is our doom and our suicide.

The last phallic being of the white man. Hunted into the death of upper consciousness and the ideal will. Our blood-self subjected to our will. Our blood-consciousness sapped by a parasitic mental or ideal consciousness.

Hot blooded sea-born Moby Dick. Hunted by monomaniacs of the idea.

Oh God, oh God, what next, when the *Pequod* has sunk?

She sank in the war, and we are all flotsam.

火热的、血性的海生物莫比·迪克，被理智偏执狂所追捕。

“哦，上帝。哦，上帝。‘佩阔德’沉了，接下来将是什么呢?”

它在这次大战[此处指第一次世界大战]中沉了，我们都是水上漂浮的残骸。

接下来是什么?

谁知道?谁晓得?

无论西班牙人还是撒克逊美国人都无法回答。

“佩阔德”沉了，它是美国白人的灵魂之舟。它沉了，带走了船上的黑人、印第安人、波利尼西亚人、澳洲人、教友派教徒和好心的、公事公办的美国佬和以实玛利，他们全淹死了。

“轰隆！”维切尔·林赛[1879—1931，美国诗人]会说。

用基督的话说就是：完了。

结束了!

《莫比·迪克》初版发表于 1851 年。如果那大白鲸在 1851 年撞沉了大白人的灵魂之舟，那后来至今的这些年又如何了呢?

或许是阴魂不散吧。

Now what next?

Who knows? *Quien sabe? Quien sabe, senor?*

Neither Spanish nor Saxon America has any answer.

The *Pequod* went down. And the Pequod was the ship of the white American soul. She sank, taking with her negro and Indian and Polynesian, Asiatic and Quaker and good, business-like Yankees and Ishmael: she sank all the lot of them.

Boom! as Vachel Lindsay* would say.

To use the wordw of Jesus, IT IS FINISHED.

Consummatum est!

But *Moby Dick* was first published in 1851. If the Great White Whale sank the ship of the Great White Soul in 1851, what's been happening ever since?

Post-mortem effects, presumably.

Because, in the first centuries, Jesus was Cetus, the Whale. And the Christians were the little fishes. Jesus, the Redeemer, was Cetus, Leviathan. And all the Christians all his little fishes.

因为，在纪元初那几个世纪，基督是鲸鱼座，即是鲸鱼。而基督徒们则就是些个小鱼罢了。基督这个救世主就是鲸鱼座，大海兽。因此全体基督徒都是他的小鱼。

CHAPTER 12
Whitman

Post–Mortem effects?

But what of Walt Whitman?

The 'good grey poet'.

Was he a ghost, with all his physicality?

The good grey poet.

Post–mortem effects. Ghosts.

A certain ghoulish insistency. A certain horrible pottage of human parts. A certain striency and portentousness. A luridness about his beatitudes. *

DEMOCRACY! THESE STATES! EIDOLONS! LOVERS, ENDLESS LOVERS!

ONE IDENTITY!

ONE IDENTITY!

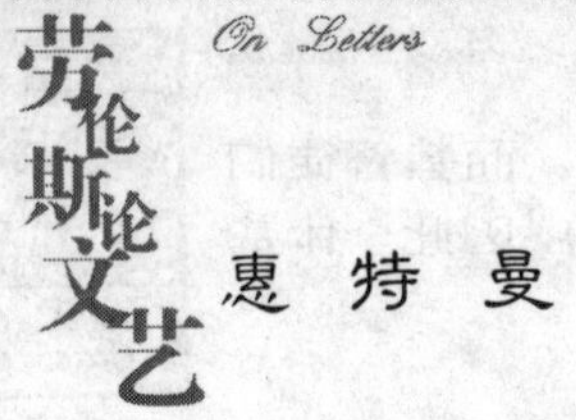

惠 特 曼

是阴魂不散吗?

瓦特·惠特曼是怎样的一个人?

这个"优秀的忧郁诗人"。

他那么迷恋肉体,他是个幽灵吗?

这个优秀的忧郁诗人。

死后依然缠人的幽灵。

某种尸鬼仍然阴魂不散。这是人的器官之汤,可怕的浓汤。听起来刺耳而又奇特,他的福音[这里指耶稣登山训众论福所讲的福音,见《马太福音》5: 3–11]很恐怖。

民主! 这些州! 鬼影! 情人,没完没了的情人!

I AM HE THAT ACHES WITH AMOROUS LOVE. *

Do you believe me, when I say post-mortem effects?

When the *Pequod* went down, she left many a rank and dirty steamboat still fussing in the seas. The *Pequod* sinks with all her souls, but their bodies rise again to man innumerable tramp steamers, and ocean-crossing liners. Corpses.

What we mean is that people may go on, keep on, and rush on, without souls. They have their ego and their will; that is enough to keep them going.

So that you see, the sinking of the *Pequod* was only a metaphysical tragedy after all. The world goes on just the same. The ship of the soul is sunk. But the machine-manipulating body works just the same: digests, chews gum, admires Botticelli and aches with amorous love.

I AM HE THAT ACHES WITH AMOROUS LOVE.

What do you make of that? I AM HE THAT ACHES. First generalization. First uncomfortable universalization. WITH AMOROUS LOVE! Oh, God! Better a bellyache. A bellyache is at least specific. But the ACHE OF AMOROUS LOVE!

Think of having that under your skin. All that!

I AM HE THAT ACHES WITH AMOROUS LOVE.

同一种身分!

同一种身分!

我就是那个因为情爱而痛苦的人[这些都是惠特曼《草叶集》中的诗名和诗句]。

当我说这是阴魂不散时,你相信我吗?

当"佩阔德"号沉没后,仍有不少尸首和肮脏的小船在海上漂流。"佩阔德"号的灵魂沉没了,可人们的躯体又浮起来去充斥流浪的小船和远洋轮。尸体。

我的意思是,人可以毫无灵魂地活着,东奔西忙。他们有自己的自我和意志,光这些就足够让他们活下去了。

所以你瞧,"佩阔德"号的沉没只是一种形而上的悲剧罢了。这世界依然日复一日地运转。灵魂之舟沉了,可机器操纵着的肉体仍旧依然:消化、嚼着胶姆糖、艳羡波提切利[1842 年开始出现美国人嚼胶姆糖的记录。19 世纪末—20 世纪初很多美国人蜂拥到弗罗伦萨在尤菲季博物馆观看波提切利(1444? —1510,意大利画家)的画,主要是看他画的维纳斯]因情爱而痛苦。

我就是那个因情爱而痛苦的人[惠特曼诗集《亚当的孩子们》中一首诗的标题和第一行]。

Walter, leave off. You are not HE. You are just a limited Walter. And your ache doesn´t include all Amorous Love, by any means. If you ache you only ache with a small bit of amorous love, and there´s so much more stays outside the cover of your ache, that you might be a bit milder about it.

I AM HE THAT ACHES WITH AMOROUS LOVE.

CHUFF! CHUFF! CHUFF!

CHU-CHU-CHU-CHU-CHUFF! *

Reminds one of a steam-engine. A locomotive. They´re the only things that seem to me to ache with amorous love. All that steam inside them. Forty million foot-pounds pressure.* The ache of AMOROUS LOVE. Steam-pressure. CHUFF!

An ordinary man aches with love for Belinda,* or his Native Land, or the Ocean, or the Stars, or the Oversoul: if he feels that an ache is in the fashion.

It takes a steam-engine to ache with AMOROUS LOVE. All of it.

Walt was really too superhuman. The danger of the superman is that he is mechanical.

They talk of his 'splendid animality'. Well, he´d got it on the brain, if that´s the place for animality.

你怎么理解这句话——我是那个痛苦的人?这是最概括性的话,是最令人不舒服的广义。因为情爱!哦,上帝!还不如肚子痛的好。肚子痛好歹还具体点。可这个痛是因为情爱!

想想吧,你的皮肤下什么地方因为情爱痛!

我就是那个因为情爱而痛苦的人。

瓦特,去你的吧。你不是那个人。你只是一个有限的瓦特罢了。你的痛苦绝不全是为了情爱。如果你痛苦,那只是因为有一点点情爱的缘故,更多的是痛苦以外的东西,所以你不如把这痛苦看得轻点的好。

> 我就是那个因情爱而痛苦的人。
> 乡下人!乡下人!乡下人!
> 乡——下——人!
> [原文是 CHUFF! CHUFF! CHUFF! /CHU-CHU-CHU-CHU-CHUFF! 很像蒸汽机车开动的声音]

这个词听起来很像一台蒸汽机和机车。我觉得只有这东西才会因为

I am he that aches with amorous love:

Does the earth gravitate, does not all matter, aching, attract all matter?

So the body of me to all I meet or know.

What can be more mechanical? The difference between life and matter is that life, living things, living creatures, have the instinct of turning right away from some matter, and of bliss–fully ignoring the bulk of most matter, and of turning towards only some certain bits of specially selected matter. As for living creatures all helplessly hurtling totether into one great snowball, why, most very living creatures spend the greater part of their time getting out of the sight, smell or sound of the rest of living creatures. Even bees only cluster on their own queen. And that is sickening enough. Fancy all white humanity clustering on one another like a lump of bees.

No, Walt, you give yourself away. Matter does gravitate, helplessly. But men are tricky–tricksy, and they shy all sorts of ways.

Matter gravitates because it is helpless and mechanical.

And if you gravitate the same, if the body of you gravitates to all you meet or know, why, something must have gone seriously wrong with you. You must have bro-

情爱而痛苦。因为它肚子里满是蒸气，压力有四千万呎磅[呎磅是一种旧的功率单位。四千万呎磅相当于72,000马力]。情爱的痛苦。蒸气压力。乡下人。

一个普通人会因为爱个贝琳达 [见爱尔兰流行作家Maria Edgeworth的同名小说]而痛苦，或为他的祖国、大洋或星球，或为上帝，只要他感到那痛苦很时髦。

要因着情爱痛苦，那需要有一台蒸汽机的马力方可。其他莫不如此。

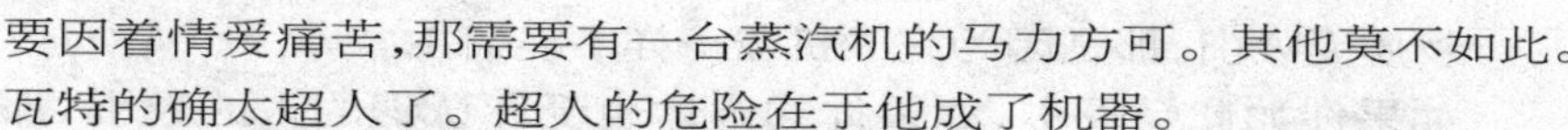

瓦特的确太超人了。超人的危险在于他成了机器。

人们大谈他那“出色的动物性”。不错，可他的动物性在他的头脑中，或许那是藏动物性的地方。

“我是那个因为情爱而痛苦的人:

地球是否有引力，是否一切物质吸引一切?

我的肉体受所有我熟识的人的吸引。”

还有比这更像机器的吗?生命与物质的区别在于: 生命、活生生的东西或动物本能地离开某些物质，快活地忽视大部分物质并归属于某些优选的物质。至于说活生生的动物都情不自禁地碰碰撞撞到一起成为一个大雪团，那是因为多数活生生的动物大多数时间里都远离其他类活生生

ken your main-spring.

You must have fallen also into mechanization.

Your Moby Dick must be really dead. That lonely phallic monster of the individual you. Dead mentalized.

I only know that my body doesn't by any means gravitate to all I meet or know, I find I can shake hands with a few people. But most I wouldn't touch with a long prop.

Your mainspring is broken, Walt Whitman. The mainspring of your own individuality. And so you run down with a great whirr, merging with everything.

You have killed your isolate Moby Dick. You have mentalized your deep sensual body, and that's the death of it.

I am everything and everything is me and so we're all One in One Identity, like the Mundane Egg,* which has been addled quite a while.

'Whoever you are, to endless announcements-'

'And of these one and all I weave the song of myself.'

Do you? Well then, it just shows you haven't *got* any self. It's a mush, not a woven thing. A hotch-potch, not a tissue. Your self.

的动物,不视、不闻。甚至蜜蜂也只围着自己的蜂王转[劳伦斯这个论断不符合事实。蜜蜂并不对一个蜂王从一而终]。这真够让人恶心的。你可以想像所有的白人像一群蜜蜂一样拥挤成一团是什么滋味。

哦,瓦特,你露馅了。物质的确会情不自禁地受吸引,可人却是诡计多端的,他会尝试各种办法。

物质受吸引,那是因为它像机器一样不能自主。

如果你如此受吸引,如果你的肉体也受你认识的人的吸引,那说明你身上哪儿出了毛病。你的"主发条"一定断了。

你一定是受制于机器的。

你体内的莫比·迪克肯定是死了——那个孤独的阳具魔鬼是个性的你,它由于精神化而死去。

我惟一知道的是我的肉体并非受到我熟知的人的吸引。我发觉我可以跟不少人握握手,可大多数人我只能跟他们保持距离。

你的"主发条"断了,瓦特·惠特曼,你的个性的主发条断了。所以你像机器一样顷刻间停止了转动,与一切融合在一起。

你杀死了你孤独的莫比·迪克。你使你深不可测的性感肉体精神化

Oh, Walter, Walter, what have you done with it? What have you done with yourself? With your own individual self? For it sounds as if it had all leaked out of you, leaked into the universe.

Post-mortem effects. The individuality had leaked out of him.

No, no, don´t lay this down to poetry. These are post mortem effects. And Walt´s great poems are really huge fat tomb-plants, great rank graveyard growths.

All that false exuberance. All those lists of things boiled in one pudding-cloth! No, no!

I don´t want all those things inside me, thank you.

'I reject nothing, 'says Walt.

If that is so, one might be a pipe open at both ends, so everything runs through.

Post-mortem effects.

'I embrace ALL, 'says Whitman. 'I weave all things into myself. '*

Do you really! There can´t be much left of you when you´ve done. When you´ve cooked the awful pudding of One Identity.

'And whoever walks a furlong without sympathy walks to his own funeral dressed in his own shroud. '*

了，这就意味着死亡。

我是一切，一切都是我，我们千人一面如同世俗的鸡蛋一样 [许多古老的民族都相信地球是鸡蛋状是因为它是造物主生的一个蛋]，这是臭蛋。

“无论你是何人，听我无休止的谈话——”

“我编织着我自己的歌——”

是吗？好吧，这正说明你根本没有任何自我。你的自我只是一团烂泥，绝不是一件织品；是一锅杂烩，决不是织锦。

哦，瓦特，瓦特，你对此都做了些什么？你对你自己采取了什么措施——对你的自我?似乎一切都已从你体内漏出，漏到宇宙中去了。

阴魂不散。个性从他身上漏尽了。

不，不，不要把这个归咎于诗。这是死尸的影响。瓦特的伟大诗行实在是高大的坟墓之树，是墓地上成片的林木。

全都是虚伪的激情洋溢。一堆东西都裹在一块布丁布里煮[用面包屑做布丁时需要把各种原料先装在布里煮，用板油时则不用。惠特曼的很多组诗内容混杂，与组诗的标

Take off your hat then, my funeral procession of one is passing.

This awful Whitman. This post-mortem poet. This poet with the private soul leaking out of him all the time. All his privacy leaking out in a sort of dribble, oozing into the universe.

Walt becomes in his own person the whole world, the whole universe, the whole eternity of time, as far as his rather sketchy knowledge of history will carry him, that is. Because to be a thing he had to know it. In order to assume the identity of a thing he had to know that thing. He was not able to assume one identity with Charlie Chaplin, for example, because Walt didn't know Charlie. What a pity! He'd have done poems, paens and what not, Chants, Songs of Cinematernity.

'Oh, Charlie, my Charlie, another film is done-'

As soon as Walt knew a thing, he assumed a One Identity with it. If he knew that an Eskimo sat in a kyak, immediately there was Walt being little and yellow and greasy, sitting in a kyak.

Now will you tell me exactly what a kyak is?

Who is he that demands petty definition? Let him behold me sitting in a kyak.

I behold no such thing. I behold a rather fat old man full of a rather senile,

题不符，因此被劳伦斯认为是杂烩]！不，不！

我不要让这些东西藏在我体内，谢谢你了。

“我什么都不拒绝，”[这个句子不完全是惠特曼的原句]瓦特说。

如果是这样，一个人就成了一支两头通气的管子，一切都可以从中穿过。

死尸的影响。

“我拥抱一切，”惠特曼说，“我把一切织成我自己。”[这个句子不完全是惠特曼的原句]

是真的吗？当你完了以后什么也剩不下。当你弄出那首可怕的诗《同一种身份》，你自己就没什么东西剩下了。

“毫无同情心行走的人会身着自己的尸布走向自己的葬礼。”[惠特曼《我自己的歌》中的诗句]

摘掉你的帽子吧，我的葬礼队伍正在走过来。

这可怕的惠特曼。这个还阴魂不散的诗人。这个漏尽了灵魂的人。他的私生活全滴滴答答渗漏到世上来。

瓦特自己变成了整个世界，整个宇宙，整个永恒的时间，只要他摆脱

self-conscious sensuosity.

DEMOCRACY. *EN MASSE*. ONE IDENTITY.

The universe is short, adds up to ONE.

ONE.

I.

Which is Walt.

His poems, *Democracy*, *En Masse*, *One Identity*, they are long sums in addition and multiplication, of which the answer is invariably MYSELF.

He reaches the state of ALLNESS.

And what then? It´s all empty. Just an empty Allness. An addled egg.

Walt wasn´t an Eskimo. A little, yellow, sly, cunning, greasy little Eskimo. And when Walt blandly assumed Allness, including Eskimoness, unto himself, he was just sucking the wind out of a blown egg-shell, no more. Eskimos are not minor little Walts. They are something that I am not, I know that. Outside the egg of my Allness chuckles the greasy little Eskimo. Outside the egg of Whitman´s Allness too.

But Walt would´t have it. He was everything and everything was in him. He drove an automobile with a very fierce headlight, along the track of a fixed idea,

不了他对历史肤浅的认识，就会这样。要想成为什么你必得先认识这东西不可。为了认同什么，他得先认识那东西。他无法与查理·卓别林共有同一种身分，因为他压根儿不认识卓别林。好不可惜！否则他就会做诗或赞美诗，写教堂圣歌，和《电影之歌》了。

“哦，查理，我的查理，又一部新电影成了——”

一旦瓦特认识了什么东西，他就要与之认同。一旦他知道爱斯基摩人是坐在皮褡子中的，立即他也就坐在马鞍子两侧的皮褡中了。这个瓦特在皮褡子中显得矮小、面目焦黄、浑身油腻腻的。

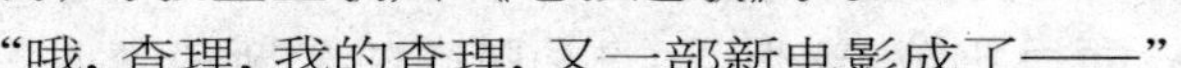

好了，你能确切告诉我皮褡子是个什么样吗？

谁这么苛刻地要求定义？让他来看看我坐在皮褡子中是什么样吧。

我没见到过这样的玩意儿。我只见到了一位胖胖的老者，感官颇为迟钝了。

民主、全体、同一种身分。

宇宙是短暂的，加起来成了个一。

一。

《民主》、《全体》和《同一种身份》是一些极长的作品[这些并非惠特曼诗的题

through the darkness of this world. And he saw everything that way. Just as a motorist does in the night.

I, who happen to be asleep under the bushes in the dark, hoping a snake won't crawl into my neck; I, seeing Walt go by in his great fierce poetic machine, think to myself: What a funny world that fellow sees!

ONE DIRECTION! toots Walt in the car, whizzing along it.

Whereas there are myriads of ways in the dark, not to mention trackless wildernesses, as anyone will know who cares to come off the road-even the Open Road.

ONE DIRECTION! whoops America, and sets off also in an automobile.

ALLNESS! shrieks Walt at a cross-road, going whizz over an unwary Red Indian.

ONE IDENTITY! chants democratic *En Masse*, pelting behind in motor-cars, oblivious of the corpses under the wheels.

God save me, I feel like creeping down a rabbit-hole, to get away from all these automobiles rushing down the ONE IDENTITY track to the goal of ALLNESS.

A woman waits for me-*

He might as well have said: 'The femaleness waits for my maleness.' Oh,

目，而是惠特曼诗歌中的一些重要理念。“同一个方向”亦非直接引语]，其答案绝对是“我自己”。

他达到了“全体”的境界。

那又怎么样呢？全是空的，空的“全体”，一只臭蛋。

瓦特不是个矮小、面目焦黄、狡猾、浑身油腻腻的爱斯基摩人。可当他盲目地与“全体”认同（包括爱斯基摩人）时，他正是从一只破碎的鸡蛋中呼吸其气味。爱斯基摩人可不是矮小的瓦特。他们是一些与我不同的人，我知道这一点。油腻腻的爱斯基摩人正在我这只“全体”的蛋外面讥声笑着，当然也是惠特曼的“全体”之蛋。

可瓦特拒不承认这一点。他是一切，一切都寓于他身上，他驾着灯光刺眼的汽车，沿着他既定理想的轨迹横穿这黑暗的世界。沿途他看到了一切，就像一个在夜色中开着摩托车的驾驶员看到的一切一样。

我碰巧在黑夜里睡在灌木丛中，希望蛇不要爬进我的领口。这时我看到了瓦特，他正驾着他那发狂的诗之车。我暗自思忖：那家伙看到的是怎样好笑的一个世界啊！

“一个方向！”瓦特的车呜呜呜叫着朝这方向飞驰。

beautiful generalization and abstraction! Oh, biological function.

'Athletic mothers of these States-' Muscles and wombs. They needn't have had faces at all.

As I see myself reflected in Nature,

As I see through a mist, One with inexpressible completeness, sanity, beauty,

See the bent head, and arms folded over the breast, the Female I see.

Everything was female to him: even himself. Nature just one great function.

This is the nucleus-after the child is born of woman, man is born of woman,

This is the bath of birth, the merge of small and large, and the outlet again-

'The Female I see-'

If I'd been one of his women, I'd have given him Female, with a flea in his ear.

Always wanting to merge himself into the womb of something or other.

'The Female I see-'

Anything, so long as he could merge himself.

Just a horror. A sort of white flux.

Post-mortem effects.

He found, as all men find, that you can't really merge in a woman, though you

可是黑暗中有无数条路，更不用说那无路可走的荒野了。任何在意迷路的人都懂，甚至会在大路上迷失呢。

"同一个方向！"美国叫喊着也驾车驶去。

全体！瓦特驶到一个十字路口，撞上一个粗心大意的印第安人时大叫着。

同一种身分！民主的《全体》在摩托车后唱着，全然不顾车轮下的一具具尸体。

老天救救我，我感到像从兔子洞里爬过，逃离这些沿着《同一种身分》的轨道奔向《全体》目标的汽车。

"一个女人在等我——"[《亚当的孩子们》中的一首诗名和第一行]

他倒不如说："女性在等待我的男性。"哦，多美的概括与抽象总结！哦，生物的作用。

"体格健壮的美国母亲们——"肌肉与子宫，她们根本不需有面孔。

"我看到自然中的我，

透过迷雾，一个难以言表的

完整之人，心智健全而美丽，

may go a long way. You can't manage the last bit. So you have to give it up, and try elsewhere if you insist on merging.

In *Calamus** he changes his tune. He doesn't shout and thump and exult any more. He begins to hesitate, reluctant, wistful.

The strange calamus has its pink-tinged root by the pond, and it sends up its leaves of comradeship, comrades from one root, without the intervention of woman, the female.

So he sings of the mystery of manly love, the love of comrades. Over and over he says the same thing: the new world will be built on the love of comrades, the new great dynamic of life will be manly love. Out of this manly love will come the inspiration for the future.

Will it though? Will it?

Comradeship! Comrades! This is to be the new Democracy of Comrades. This is the new cohering principle in the world: Comradeship.

Is it? Are you sure?

It is the cohering principle of true soldiery, we are told in *Drum Taps*. It is the cohering principle in the new unison for creative activity. And it is extreme and

看到低着的头，护着乳的双臂，
　　我看到的是女性。”
在他眼里什么都是女性的，甚至他自己也是。大自然只有一种官能。
“这是核心——儿童由女人所生，然后男人
　　也由女人所生，
这是分娩的沐浴——小的与大的在
　　这里交融，随后又是发泄——”
“我看到的是女性——”
如果我是他的女人之一，我会把女性与跳蚤一起给他。
总要把自己融入某个东西的子宫。
“我看到的女性——”
只要他能与之相融，什么都行。
简直太可怕了。某种白色流。
阴魂的影响。

他像所有的男人一样发现，你无法真正地融于一个女人，无论你跨越多么漫长的路程来寻她都不成。你无法坚持到底。所以你不得不放弃

alone, touching the confines of death. Something terrible to bear, terrible to be responsible for. Even Walt Whitman felt it. The soul´s last and most poignant responsibility, the responsibility of comradeship, of manly love.

Yet you are beautiful to me, you faint-tinged roots, you make me think of death.

Death is beautiful from you (what indeed is finally beautiful except death and love?)

I think it is not for life I am chanting here my chant of lovers, I think it must be for death,

For how calm, how solemn it grows to ascend to the atmosphere of lovers,

Death or life, I am then indifferent, my soul declines to prefer(I am not sure but the high soul of lovers welcomes death most)Indeed, O death, I think now these leaves mean precisely the same as you mean-

This is strange, from the exultant Walt.

Death!

Death is now his chant! Death!

Merging! And Death! Which is the final merge.

这种尝试转而去别处。

在《白菖》中[《白菖》是《草叶集》中的一组，主题是男性爱]，他变换了语调，他不再呼喊、擂打、激动。他开始犹豫、勉强、渴望。

那奇特的白菖长着粉红色的根，生长在湖畔，它伸出同志情谊的叶子，这是同根的同志，没有女人、女性的插足。

他就是这样歌唱着男性爱——同志爱的神秘。他一遍又一遍地重复着一个东西：新的世界建立在同志爱之上，新的、伟大的、蓬勃的生命将是男性爱。由这男性爱将生发出对未来的向往。

会这样吗?会吗?

同志情!同志!这将是新的同志的民主。这是世上最有内聚力的原则：同志情。

是吗?你相信吗?

《桴鼓集》告诉我们这是真正的军人的凝聚。这是为了创造而齐心协力的内聚原则。当然这原则是极端而孤立的，它触动了死亡的戒规。这是令人难以承受的可怕东西，太可怕了，令人无法担负这种责任，连瓦特·惠特曼自己都感到了这一点。人类灵魂中最终也是最强烈的责任感即是

The great merge into the womb. Woman.

And after that, the merge of comrades: man–for–man love.

And almost immediately with this, death, the final merge of death.

There you have the progression of merging. For the great mergers, woman at last becomes inadequate. For those who love to extremes. Woman is inadequate for the last merging. So the next step is the merging of man–for–man love. And this is on the brink of death. It slides over into death.

David and Jonathan. And the death of Jonathan.

It always slides into death.

The love of comrades.

Merging.

So that if the new Democracy is to be based on the love of comrades, it will be based on death too. It will slip so soon into death.

The last merging. The last Democracy. The last love. The love of comrades.

Fatality. And fatality.

Whitman would not have been the great poet he is if he had not taken the last steps and looked over into death. Death, the last merging, that was the goal of his

同志情——男性爱的责任。

你是我眼中的美人，你这气味清淡的根，
　　你令我想到死。
你的死是美的(除了死与爱还有什么终
　　归是美?)
我不是为生唱着恋人的颂歌，而是为了死，
多么宁馨，多么庄重，上升到爱的境界，
死与生我都不在乎，我的灵魂喜爱
(我不知道是否恋人的崇高灵魂最爱死)
死，真的，这些草叶与你意蕴相同——

热情奔放的瓦特写出这样的诗行，令人奇怪。

死!

他在为死唱颂歌！死!

交融！还有死！死是最终的交融。

manhood.

To the mergers, there remains the brief love of comrades, and then Death.

Whereto answering, the sea

Delaying not, hurrying not

Whispered me through the night, very plainly before daybreak. Lisp´d to me the low and delicious word death.

And again death, death, death, death.

Hissing melodions, neither like the bird nor like my arous´d child´s heart,

But edging neat as privately for me rustling at my feet,

Creeping thence steadily up to my ears and laving me softly all over,

Death, death, death, death, death–

Whitman is a very great poet, of the end of life. A very great post-mortem poet, of the transitions of the soul as it loses its integrity. The poet of the soul´s last shout and shriek, on the confines of death. *Après moi le déluge*.

But we have all got to die, and disintegrate.

We have got to die in life, too, and disintegrate while we live.

But even then the goal is not death.

融入子宫。女人。

随后是同志间的交融：男性之间的爱。

几乎尾随而来的是死亡，终归与死亡交融。

你看到了交融的嬗递进程。对于那些伟大的交融者们来说，只有女人是不够的。对于那些爱到极端的人，最终的交融中女人是不够的。所以下一步出现的就是男性之间的爱。而这种爱是濒临死亡边缘的。终归会滑向死亡。

历史上有大卫和约拿旦。约拿旦死了。

这种爱终归会死。

这种同志爱。

交融。

所以，如果这新的民主将是建立在同志爱之上的话，这就意味着它也是建立在死亡之上。它会很快滑向死亡的。

最终的交融，最终的民主。最终的爱。这同志爱。

厄运，除了厄运还是厄运。

惠特曼如果没有走最后这几步去遥望到死亡的话，他就不会是个伟

Something else will come.

Out of the cradle endlessly rocking.

We've got to die first, anyhow. And disintegrate while we still live.

Only we know this much: Death is not the goal. And Love, and merging, are now only part of the death process. Comrade-ship-part of the death-process. Democracy-part of the death-process. The new Democracy-the brink of death. One Identity-death itself.

We have died, and we are still disintegrating.

But IT IS FINISHED.

Consummatum est.

Whitman, the great poet, has meant so much to me. Whitman, the one man breaking a way ahead. Whitman, the one pioneer. And only Whitman. No English pioneers, no French. No European pioneer-poets. In Europe the would-be pioneers are mere innovators. The same in America. Ahead of Whitman, nothing. Ahead of all poets, pioneering into the wilderness of unopened life, Whitman. Beyond him, none. His wide, strange camp at the end of the great high-road. And lots of new little poets camping on Whitman's camping ground now. But none going really beyond.

大的诗人了。死，这最终的交融，这才是他男性的目标。

对这些交融者来说，同志爱稍纵即逝，然后就是死。

大海，向哪个方向作答？
莫停留，莫慌张，
透过夜幕向我悲切呢喃着死亡，
声音低沉而美好。
又是死，死，死，死。
啁啾着的风琴声，不像鸟也不像我
　　渴望着的童心，
偎依着我在我脚下瑟瑟，
渐渐爬上我的耳朵温存地摩挲我
死，死，死，死，死——

惠特曼是一位写生命终结的伟大诗人。是一位很伟大的阴魂诗人，他写的是灵魂失却完整向别处的转化，他是灵魂在死亡线上的最终呼吼

Because Whitman's camp is at the end of the road, and on the edge of a great precipice. Over the precipice, blue distances, and the blue hollow of the future. But there is no way down. It is a dead end.

Pisagh. Pisgah sights. And Death. Whitman like a strange, modern, American Moses. Fearfully mistaken. And yet the great leader.

The essential function of art is moral. Not aesthetic, not decorative, not pastime and recreation. But moral. The essential function of art is moral.

But a passionate, implicit morality, not didactic. A morality which changes the blood, rather than the mind. Changes the blood first. The mind follows later, in the wake.

Now Whitman was a great moralist. He was a great leader. He was a great changer of the blood in the veins of men.

Surely it is especially true of American art, that it is all essentially moral. Hawthorne, Poe, Longfellow, Emerson, Melville: it is the moral issue which engages them. They all feel uneasy about the old morality. Sensuously, passionally, they all attack the old morality. But they know nothing better, mentally. Therefore they give tight mental allegiance to a morality which all their passion goes to destroy. Hence

的诗人。我死了，爱谁谁吧。

当然，我们都要死，都要溃烂。

可我们活着就得死，活着时就得溃烂。

可尽管如此，我们的目标也不是死。

将有什么东西到来。

“爬出摇个不停的摇篮。”

可是，我们要先死才是，活着时就得崩溃。

我们所知道的只有这一点：死亡不是目标。而爱和交融现在不过是死亡过程的一部分。同志情——死亡过程的一部分。民主——死亡过程的一部分。新民主——死亡的边缘。同一种身分——死亡本身。

我们尽管已经死了，可我们仍在溃烂。

彻底完了。

惠特曼这位大诗人对我来说是太重要了。惠特曼一个人向前冲锋，他是一个先锋，只有惠特曼一人，前无古人，后无来者，英国没有，法国也没有这样的先锋，欧洲的所谓先锋只是革新者。在美国也是一样，在他们之前什么也没有，没有哪个诗人像惠特曼一样闯入原始生命的荒漠中。

the duplicity which is the fatal flaw in them, most fatal in the most perfect American work of art, *The Scarlet Letter*. Tight mental allegiance given to a morality which the passional self repudiates.

Whitman was the first to break the mental allegiance. He was the first to smash the old moral conception that the soul of man is something 'superior' and 'above' the flesh. Even Emerson still maintained this tiresome 'superiority' of the soul. Even Melville could not get over it. Whitman was the first heroic seer to seize the soul by the scruff of her neck and plant her down among the potsherds.

'There!' he said to the soul. 'Stay there!'

Stay there. Stay in the flesh. Stay in the limbs and lips and in the belly. Stay in the breast and womb. Stay there. Oh, Soul, where you belong.

Stay in the dark limbs of negroes. Stay in the body of the prostitute. Stay in the sick flesh of the syphilitic. Stay in the marsh where the calamus grows. Stay there, Soul, where you belong.

The Open Road. The great home of the Soul is the open road. Not heaven, not paradise. Not 'above'. Not even 'within'. The soul is neither 'above' nor 'within'. It

惠特曼。 没人能超过他。他那宽大奇特的营帐设在大道的尽头。现如今，已有不少小诗人在惠特曼的营地宿营了。可他们没有一个超过惠特曼的，因为惠特曼的营帐是在大道尽头，在一个陡峭的悬崖之畔。悬崖的那边是一片碧蓝，是空邈的未来。但绝无出路，这已是死路一条。

比斯开，比斯开山顶上看到的景物[《圣经》中摩西眺望上帝赐给亚伯拉罕迦南的地方。一般指对得不到的东西遥远的一瞥]。死。惠特曼就如同一个奇异的现代美国摩西。尽管错误很严重，但他不失为一个伟大的领袖。

艺术的根本作用是载道，而非审美、博彩、消闲与怡情。是载道。艺术的根本作用是载道。

但这“道”是充满激情、含蓄的，绝非说教。一种道要改变的是你的血性而非你的理性。先改变你的血性，而后才是理性。

惠特曼即是一个伟大的道学家。他是一个伟大的领袖。他要给人血管里的血液施行大变革。

不错，美国文学尤其如此载道。霍桑、坡、朗费罗、爱默生和麦尔维尔所迷恋的均是道德主题。他们都不满旧的道德。他们本能地激情地抨击旧道德，可他们的理智上并不那么清楚什么是比旧道德更好的新道德。

is a wayfarer down the open road.

Not by meditating. Not by fasting. Not by exploring heaven after heaven, inwardly, in the manner of the great mystics. Not by exaltation. Not by ecstasy. Not by any of these ways does the soul come into her own.

Only by taking the open road.

Not through charity. Not through sacrifice. Not even through love. Not through good works. Not through these does the soul accomplish herself.

Only through the journey down the open road.

The journey itself, down the open road. Exposed to full contact. On two slow feet. Meeting whatever comes down the open road. In company with those that drift in the same measure along the same way. Towards no goal. Always the open road.

Having no known direction even. Only the soul remaining true to herself in her going.

Meeting all the other wayfarers along the road. And how? How meet them, and how pass? With sympathy, says Whitman. Sympathy. He does not say love. He says sympathy. Feeling with. Feel with them as they feel with themselves. Catching the

他们理智上所忠孝的道德其实是他们的非理性所要毁灭的。于是有了他们最致命的缺陷——双重性，在最完美的美国艺术作品《红字》中，这种缺陷就最为致命。激情的自我欲毁灭一种道德，可理智却还死死地依恋着它。

惠特曼是头一个打破这种理智上的依恋的。他是第一个抨击所谓人的灵魂高于优于人的肉体的旧道德观念的人。要知道，甚至爱默生还坚持这种讨厌的“优越”论呢。甚至麦尔维尔也不能放弃这观念。而惠特曼则头一个揪住灵魂的脖子，把它摔得粉碎，他不愧是个英雄。

“呆在那儿！”他对灵魂说，“呆在那儿！”

呆在那儿，呆在肉体中。呆在四肢、双唇和腹中。呆在乳房中，呆在子宫中。呆在那儿，哦，灵魂，呆在你所附属的地方。

呆在黑人那黝黑的四肢中。呆在娼妓的肉体中。呆在梅毒患者的肉体中。呆在长满白菖的湿地上。呆在那儿，灵魂，呆在你所附属的地方。

《宽阔的大路》。灵魂之家即是宽阔的大路。不是天，不是天堂。不是“上方”。甚至不是“内里”。灵魂既非“上方”也非“内里”。它是在大路上的徒步旅行。

vibration of their soul and flesh as we pass.

It is a new great doctrine. A doctrine of life. A new great morality. A morality of actual living, not of salvation. Europe has never got beyond the morality of salvation. America to this day is deathly sick with saviourism. But Whitman, the grwatest and the first and the only American teacher, was no Saviour. His morality was no morality of salvation. His was a morality of the soul living her life, not saving herself. Accepting the contact with other souls along the open way, as they lived their lives. Never trying to save them. As life try to arrest them and throw them in gaol. The soul living her life along the incarnate mystery of the open road.

This was Whitman. And the true rhythm of the American continent speaking out in him. He is the first white aboriginal.

'In my Father's house are many mansions. '*

'No,' said Whitman. 'Keep out of mansions. A mansion may be heaven on earth, but you might as well be dead. Strictly avoid mansions. The soul is herself when she is going on foot down the open road. '

It is the American heroic message. The soul is not to pile up defences round

不是靠沉思。不是靠斋戒。不是靠从一个天堂向另一个天堂的探索——像那些神秘大师那样在内心中做如此探讨。也不是靠兴奋和激情。靠这些办法灵魂是无法复归其自身的。

惟一的办法就是走上宽敞的大路。

不是通过行善，不是通过牺牲，甚至不是通过爱。不是通过好好工作。绝不是借此灵魂就可以自我完善。

惟一的办法就是走上宽敞的大路。

这样的旅行——走上宽敞的大路。彻底的接触，靠一双缓缓移动的脚行走，与一切出现在大路上的东西相遇，与同路上同步游荡的人为伴，漫无目标，只沿着大路走下去。

甚至连方向都没有。灵魂只管忠实自身即可。

与别的徒步旅行者在路上相识。如何相识?又如何别离?惠特曼说的是同情心。是同情心，他说的不是爱。同情，与他们共同感受，就如同他们自己感受自己一样。在与他们擦身而过的时候就摸准他们灵魂与肉体的颤动旋律。

这是一条伟大的新教义，生命的教义。这是一种伟大的道德，一种实

herself. She is not to withdraw and seek her heavens inwardly, in mystical ecstasies. She is not to cry to some God beyond, for salvation. She is to go down the open road, as the road opens, into the unknown, keeping company with those whose soul draws them near to her, accomplishing nothing save the journey, and the works incident to the journey, in the long life-travel into the unknown, the soul in her subtle sympathies accomplishing herself by the way.

This is Whitman´s essential message. The heroic message of the American future. It is the inspiration of thousands of Americans today, the best souls of today, men and women. And it is a message that only in America can be fully understood, finally accepted.

Then Whitman´s mistake. The mistake of his interpretation of his watchword: Sym pathy. The mystery of SYMPATHY. He still confounded it with Jesus, LOVE, and with Paul´s CHARITY. Whitman, like all the rest of us, was at the end of the great emotional highway of Love. And because he couldn´t help himself, he carried on his Open Road as a prolongation of the emotional highway of Love, beyond Calvary. The highway of Love ends at the foot of the Cross. There is no beyond. It was

实在在生命的道德而不是救世的道德。欧洲从未摆脱过救世的道德观。今日的美国也患上了救世主义病，可是惠特曼这个美国第一位也是惟一一位最伟大的导师却不是一位大救星。他的道德绝不是救世道德。他的道德就是让灵魂生存而不是拯救灵魂。让自己的灵魂在大道上与其他灵魂相接触，千万不要试图去拯救别的灵魂。干脆抓住它们把它们扔进地狱中去。灵魂沿着大路上的神秘方向行走生活着。

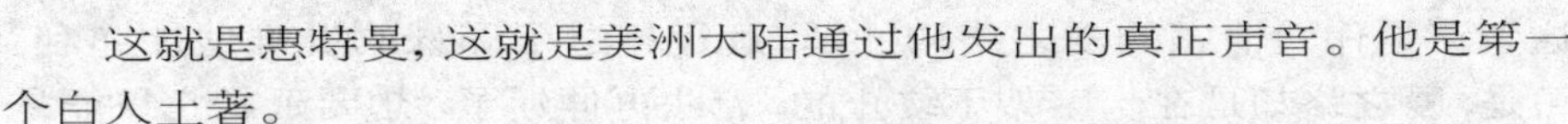

这就是惠特曼，这就是美洲大陆通过他发出的真正声音。他是第一个白人土著。

在我父亲的家里有许多住处[出自《圣经》，《约翰福音》第十四章，第二节]。

“不，”惠特曼说，“呆在外面吧。一座屋子可能是地球上的天堂，可你也许会是死人。一定要躲开屋子。灵魂一经踏上大路才是它自己。”

这是美国的英雄启示。灵魂不会为自己竖起一堵防护墙的。它不会退回内心去在神秘的狂喜中寻觅自己的天堂。它不会向远方的上帝呼救。反之它要踏上宽敞的大道走向未知世界，与那些靠近它的灵魂结伴，只完成这段旅程，在通向未知世界的漫长旅途上做完与旅程有关的工作并随之完善自我。

a hopeless attempt to prolong the highway of love.

He didn't follow his Sympathy. Try as he might, he kept on automatically interpreting it as Love, as Charity. Merging!

This merging, *en masse*, One Identity, Myself monomania was a carry-over from the old Love idea. It was carrying the idea of Love to its logical physical conclusion. Like Flaubert and the leper. The decree of unqualified Charity, as the soul's one means of salvation, still in force.

Now Whitman wanted his soul to save itself; he didn't want to save it. Therefore he did not need the great Christian receipt for saving the soul. He needed to supersede the Christian Charity, the Christian Love, within himself, in order to give his Soul her last freedom. The high-road of Love is no Open Road. It is a narrow, tight way, where the soul walks hemmed in between compulsions.

Whitman wanted to take his Soul down the open road. And he failed in so far as he failed to get out of the old rut of Salvation. He forced his Soul to the edge of a cliff, and he looked down into death. And there he camped, powerless. He had carried out his Sympathy as an extension of Love and Charity. And it had brought

这就是惠特曼根本的启示，是美国未来的启示。它激励了今日美国成千上万的人，这些都是今日美利坚最优秀的男女们。这个启示只能在美国才能全然为人理解并最终得到接受。

惠特曼有错误。他错就错在对“同情”这个格言的解释上。“同情”是神秘的。他仍然把“同情”与耶稣的“爱”和保罗的“博爱”混为一谈。惠特曼同咱们一样走到了爱之大道的尽头。他无法自持，所以他走上了大路，这条路是伟大情感的爱之路的伸延，远远超过了耶稣的受难地加弗利。可是，爱之路却是在十字架下终止的，无法再伸延了。想要延长它只能是妄想。

他并没有按照自己的《同情》去做，尽管他很努力依此去做，可他还是一个劲儿不由自主地把同情解释为爱和兄弟博爱。混淆！

这种混淆(交融)，全体，同一种身分，自我偏执狂全来自旧的爱之观。这等于是把爱的观念变为合乎逻辑的肉体行为。这真像福楼拜和麻风病患者[见福楼拜 1877 年作品《圣朱利安与病人传奇》，朱利安裸身温暖麻风病人]。把不合格的博爱当做一种拯救灵魂的手段，这种做法还很有效呢。

现在惠特曼想让他的灵魂自救，他自己是不会救自己的灵魂的。所

him almost to madness and soul-death. It gave him his forced, unhealthy, post-mortem quality.

His message was really the opposite of Henley's rant:

I am the master of my fate,
I am the captain of my soul,

Whitman's essential message was the Open Road. The leaving of the soul free unto herself, the leaving of his fate to her and to the loom of the open road. Which is the bravest doctrine man has ever proposed to himself.

Alas, he didn't quite carry it out. He couldn't quite break the old maddening bond of the love-compulsion; he couldn't quite get out of the rut of the charity habit-for Love and Charity have degenerated now into habit: a bad habit.

Whitman said Sympathy. If only he had stuck to it! Because Sympathy, means feeling with, not feeling for. He kept on having a passionate feeling for the negro slave, or the prostitute, or the syphiliytic-which is merging. A sinking of Walt

以他才不需要基督教的教义去拯救灵魂呢。他要的是超越基督教的善和爱，从而让灵魂最后获得自由。爱之路绝不是宽敞大道。它是一条狭窄的羊肠小径，灵魂在这条路上受着挤迫。

惠特曼要把他的灵魂带到大道上。可是他失败了，他没能够摆脱"救世"的旧套子。他把自己的灵魂逼到悬崖边上，然后又盯着下面的死亡。他就在岸畔安营扎寨，他已失去了力气。他把同情当做爱与善的伸延，可这下却几乎把他拖向疯狂与灵魂的死亡。就是这一点赋予了他一种做作，不健康的阴魂之气。

他的启示的确是在与诗人汉利[英国诗人]唱反调。

我是我命运的主宰，
我是我灵魂的船长。

惠特曼启示的基调是《宽阔的大路》。让灵魂解脱，复归其自身，把他的命运交给大道。这才是人之最美好的教义。

可是呀，他并没有很好地这样去做。他不能彻底地摆脱那旧的令人

Whitman´s soul in the souls of these others.

He wasn´t keeping to his open road. He was forcing his soul down an old rut. He wasn´t leaving her free. He was forcing her into other people´s circumstances.

Supposing he had felt true sympathy with the negro slave? He would have felt with the negro slave. Sympathy–com–passion–which is partaking of the passion which was in the soul of the negro slave.

What was the feeling in the negro´s soul? ,

'Ah, I am a slave! Ah, it is bad to be a slave! I must free myself. My soul will die unless she frees herself. My soul says I must free myself. '

Whitman came along, and saw the slave, and said to himself: 'That negro slave is a man like myself. We share the same identity. And he is bleeding with wounds. Oh, oh, is it not myself who am also bleeding with wounds?'

This was not sympathy. It was merging and self–sacrifice. 'Bear ye one another´s burdens'; 'Love thy neighbour as thyself'; 'Whatsoever ye do unto him, ye do unto me. '*

If Whitman had truly sympathized, he would have said: 'That negro slave suf-

发疯的做作的爱之枷锁。他不能彻底摆脱"善"的陋习——爱和善现如今已堕落为一种陋习。

惠特曼讲同情。如果他真的照此办事就好了！因为同情意味着"与人分享感受"而非"怜悯"。可他却一直怀着激情怜悯黑人奴隶、妓女或梅毒病患者——这意味着某种交融。瓦特·惠特曼的灵魂陷没在别人的灵魂中了。

他并没有坚持沿他的大道走下去。他不过是强迫自己的灵魂走入了死套子中。他并没有让自己的灵魂自由，反之，他把自己的灵魂逼迫进别人的情境中。

或许他真的是同情黑奴？他也许会与黑奴同感。同情——同病相怜——意味着分享黑奴灵魂中的激情。

黑人灵魂中的感觉是什么呢?

"哦，我是一个奴隶！啊，做一个奴隶太不好了！我要让自己自由。我的灵魂不自由毋宁死。我的灵魂对我说我一定要让自己自由。"

惠特曼看到了奴隶，自言自语道："那个黑奴是与我一样的人。我们的身分是相同的。可他却受伤流着血。哦，哦，这难道不是我自己的伤口

fers from slavery. He wants to free himself. His soul wants to free him. He has wounds, but they are the price of freedom. The soul has a long journey from slavery to freedom. If I can help him I will: I will not take over his wounds and his slavery to myself. But I will help him fight the power that enslaves him when he wants to be free,if he wants my help,since I see in his face that he needs to be free. But even when he is free,his soul has many journeys down the open road,before it is a free soul. '

And of the prostitute Whitman would have said:

'Look at that prostitute! Her nature has turned evil under her mental lust for prostitution. She has lost her soul. She knows it herself. She likes to make men lose their souls. If she tried to make me lose my soul, I would kill her. I wish she may die. '

But of another prostitute he would have said:

'Look! She is fascinated by the Priapic mysteries.* Look,she will soon be worn to death by the Priapic usage. It is the way of her soul. She wishes it so. '

Of the syphilitic he would say:

同样在流血吗?"

这绝不是同情,它只是交融与自我牺牲。"分担对方的重负","爱你的邻居如同爱你自己","怎样待别人也怎样待我。"[这些引语均出自《圣经》]

如果惠特曼真的是同情,他就应该说:"那黑奴深受奴隶制之苦。他要自由。他的灵魂要他获得自由。灵魂从奴隶到自由得走过一段长长的道路。如果我能帮他我会帮助他的。当然我不会把他的伤口变成自己的伤口,不会替他当奴隶。但是如果他要自由,如果他需要我的帮助,我肯定会帮他同奴役他的力量作斗争的。即使是他人身获得了自由,他的灵魂离自由还远得很,他的灵魂还要在大道下行很长的路程才能获得自由。"

关于妓女,惠特曼会这样说:

"看那个娼妇!她一脑子的男盗女娼,本性变坏了。她没了灵魂,她明白。她也喜欢让男人失去灵魂。要是她试图使我也丢魂儿,我就杀了她。我巴不得她快死。"

可对另一个娼妇,他又会这样说:

"看!她让普里阿普斯的阳具迷住了[Priapus,希腊神话中园林之神,其神像上的

'Look! She wants to infect all men with syphilis. We ought to kill her.'

And of still another syphilitic:

'Look! She has a horror of her syphilis. If she looks my way I will help her to get cured.'

This is sympathy. The soul judging for herself, and preserving her own integrity.

But when, in Flaubert, the man takes the leper to his naked body; when Bubi de Montparnasse* takes the girl because he knows she's got syphilis; when Whitman embraces an evil prostitute: that is not sympathy. The evil prostitute has no desire to be embraced with love; so if you sympathize with her, you won't try to embrace her with love. The leper loathes his leprosy, so if you sympathize with him, you'll loathe it too. The evil woman who wishes to infect all men with her syphilis hates you if you haven't got syphilis. If you sympathize you'll feel her hatred, and you'll hate too, you'll hate her. Her feeling is hate, and you'll share it. Only your soul will choose the direction of its own hatred.

The soul is a very perfect judge of her own motions, if your mind doesn't dictate to her. Because the mind says Charity! Charity! you don't have to force your

阳具坚挺，是阳物崇拜的对象]。等着瞧吧，她会让这东西折磨死的，这就是她的灵魂之路。她愿意这样。”

关于梅毒者，他会说：

“瞧啊！她要把梅毒染上所有的男人。我们得杀了她才行。”

可对另一个梅毒患者他又会说：

“你瞧！她让梅毒吓坏了。如果她朝我看一眼，我就帮她治好。”

这就是同情。灵魂自己判断自己并能保持自身的完整。

可在福楼拜笔下，男人却光着身子去染麻风病。波比·德·蒙特帕纳斯[见 Charles-Louis Philippe(1874—1909)的小说 Bubu of Montparnasse]与一个女子做爱是因为他知道这女子患了梅毒。当惠特曼拥抱一个恶娼时，他给她的绝不是同情。那恶娼绝无要他拥抱的欲望，不要他的爱。所以，如果你同情她，就不要怀着爱心去拥抱她。麻风病人是讨厌自己的麻风病的，所以，如果你同情他，你也该与他一起恨才对。如果你还没染上梅毒，那想把梅毒传染给所有男人的恶娼会恨透你的，如果你同情她，你就会感受到她的仇恨，因此你也会恨起来，会恨她。她的感情就只是一个恨字，你也得跟她分享这份恨才是。只有你的灵魂才会选择恨的方向。

soul into kissing lepers or embracing syphilitics. Your lips are the lips of your soul, your body is the body of your soul; your own single, indivdual soul. That is Whitman's message. And your soul hates syphilis and leprosy. Because it is a soul, it hates these things, which are against the soul. And therefore to force the body of your soul into contact with uncleanness is a great violation of your soul. The soul wishes to keep clean and whole. The soul's deepest will is to preserve its own integrity, against the mind and the whole mass of disintegrating forces.

Soul sympathizes with soul. And that which tries to kill my soul, my soul hates. My soul and my body are one. Soul and body wish to keep clean and whole. Only the mind is capable of great perversion. Only the mind tries to drive my soul and body into uncleaness and unwholesomeness.

What my soul loves, I love.

What my soul hates, I hate.

When my soul is stirred with compassion, I am compassionate.

What my soul turns away from, I turn away from.

That is the true interpretation of Whitman's creed: the true revelation of his

只要你的头脑不指挥你的灵魂，灵魂本身是可以绝好地判断自己的行为的，你的头脑大叫“博爱、博爱”，可你没必要强迫你的灵魂去亲吻麻风病或拥抱梅毒。你的双唇是属于你的灵魂的，你的肉体也是属于你的灵魂的，属于你独有的、个性的灵魂。这就是惠特曼的启示。你的灵魂仇恨梅毒和麻风。正因为这是灵魂，它才仇恨与灵魂为敌的这些玩意儿。正因此，强迫从属灵魂的肉体与肮脏龌龊相触是对你灵魂最大的不恭。灵魂是要清洁和完整的。灵魂之至深的意志是要保持自身的完整性，与理智和破坏完整性的力量作斗争。

灵魂与灵魂相怜。什么要试图杀死我的灵魂，我的灵魂将恨之入骨。我的灵魂和肉体是一体。灵魂和肉体希望保持贞洁与完整，只有理智才会产生大变态。只有理智才想把我的灵与肉驱赶向龌龊之地和分裂之状。

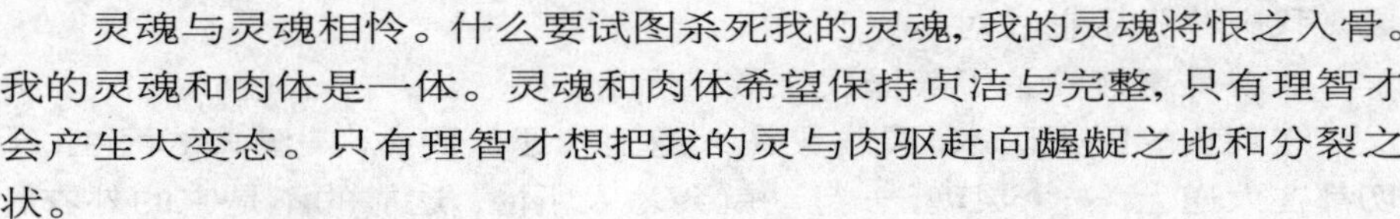

吾爱吾灵所爱。

吾恨吾灵所恨。

当我的灵魂中激起同情心时，我就变得极有同情心。

吾避吾灵所避。

Sympathy.

And my soul takes the open road. She meets the souls that are passing, she goes along with the souls that are going her way. And for one and all, she has sympathy.The sympathy of love, the sympathy of hate, the sympathy of simple proximity; all the subtle sympathizings of the incalculable soul, from the bitterest hate to passionate love.

It is not I who guide my soul to heaven. It is I who am guided by my own soul along the open road, were all men tread. Therefore, I must accept her deep motions of love, or hate, or compassion, or dislike, or indifference. And I must go where she takes me, for my feet and my lips and my body are my soul. It is I who must submit to her.

This is Whitman´s message of American democracy.

The true democracy, where soul meets soul, in the open road. Democracy. American democracy where all journey down the open road, and where a soul is known at once in its going. Not by its clothes or appearance. Whitman did away with that. Not by its family name. Not even by its reputation. Whitman and Melville both discounted that. Not by a progression of piety, or by works of Charity. Not by works

这些才是对惠特曼之教义的真正解释：这就是他的《同情》的真正启示。

我的灵魂走上了大道，它与其他灵魂相遇，与那些志同道合者同行。它对它们全都拥有同情之心。爱的同情，恨的同情，或者干脆是亲和的同情。从最恨到最爱，没完没了的说不清道不明的灵魂上的同情。

指引我的灵魂升天的不是我。倒是我的灵魂把我引上众生之道。所以，我必须按照我灵魂深处的行动而行动，或爱，或恨，或同情，或厌，或淡然。我必须接受，必须听从它的指引，我的脚我的唇和我的肉都是我的灵。我应该服从它才对。

这就是惠特曼关于美国民主的启示。

在真正的民主国家，灵与灵在大道上相遇。民主，美国式的民主，一切都在大道上，一个灵魂，一行动就会为人所懂。这靠的不是它的外衣和外貌，惠特曼不需要这些，靠的不是其家族的姓名，更不是它的名望。惠特曼和麦尔维尔都不把这些当一回事。也不是靠虔诚和行善。绝不是靠做什么。什么都不靠，只靠它自身。灵魂不靠什么来推动，它只靠两只脚自个儿行走。它全靠自己受人赏识。如果它是个伟大的灵魂，它就会在路

at all. Not by anything, but just itself. The soul passing unenhanced, passing on foot and being no more than itself. And recognized, and passed by or greeted according to the soul's dictate. If it be a great soul, it will be worshipped in the road.

The love of man and woman: a recognition of souls, and a communion of worship. The love of comrades: a recognition of souls, and a communion of worship. Democracy: a recognition of souls, all down the open road, and a great soul seen in its greatness, as it travels on foot among the rest, down the common way of the living. A glad recognition of souls, and a gladder worship of great and greater souls, because they are the only riches.

Love, and Merging, brought Whitman to the Edge of Death! Death! Death!

But the exultance of his message still remains. Purified of MERGING, purified of MYSELF, the exultant message of American Democracy, of souls in the *Open Road*, full of glad recognition, full of fierce readiness, full of the joy of worship, when one soul sees a greater soul.

The only riches, the great souls.

上被人崇拜。

男女之爱即是灵魂之交，是崇拜的交流。同志之情亦是灵魂之交和崇拜的交流。民主即是灵魂之交。在大道上，一个灵魂在芸芸众生路的徒步旅行中见其伟大。灵与灵的交往是令人欢喜的，对伟大灵魂的崇拜更令人欢喜，只有它们才是世上最宝贵的财富。

爱与交融把惠特曼推向死亡的边缘！死亡！死亡！

但他的启示仍令人激动。被交融所净化，被自我所净化，当一个灵魂见到了另一个更伟大的灵魂时，它对之表示认可，对之欣然崇拜，这就是美国式民主的启示，这就是《宽阔的大路》上灵魂的启示。

伟大的灵魂是惟一的财富。